London
for Children

timeout.com

KidsOut

Edited and designed by
Time Out Guides Limited
Universal House
251 Tottenham Court Road
London W1T 7AB
Tel + 44 (0)20 7813 3000
Fax + 44 (0)20 7813 6001
Email guides@timeout.com
www.timeout.com

Editorial

Editor Ronnie Haydon
Deputy Editor Simon Cropper
Listings Editor Cathy Limb
Researchers Shane Armstrong, Eli Dryden,
Holly Furneaux, Rebecca Wootten
Proofreader Nick Rider
Indexer Mike Harrison

Editorial/Managing Director Peter Fiennes
Series Editor Sarah Guy
Deputy Series Editor Cath Phillips
Guides Co-ordinator Anna Norman

Design

Group Art Director John Oakey
Art Director Mandy Martin
Art Editor Scott Moore
Senior Designer Tracey Ridgewell
Designers Astrid Kogler, Sam Lands
Digital Imaging Dan Conway
Ad make-up Charlotte Blythe
Picture Editor Kerri Littlefield
Acting Picture Editor Kit Burnet
Acting Deputy Picture Editor Martha Houghton
Picture Desk Trainee Bella Wood

Advertising

Group Commercial Director Lesley Gill
Sales Director/Sponsorship Mark Phillips
Sales Manager Alison Gray
Advertisement Sales Matthew Salandy, Jason Trotman, Terina Rickit
Copy Controller Oliver Guy
Advertising Assistant Sabrina Ancilleri

Administration

Chairman Tony Elliott
Managing Director Mike Hardwick
Group Financial Director Richard Waterlow
Group General Manager Nichola Coulthard
Group Circulation Director Jim Heinemann
Group Production Director Mark Lamond
Production Controller Samantha Furniss
Group Marketing Director Christine Cort
Marketing Manager Mandy Martinez
Marketing Executives Sandie Tozer, Sammie Squire
Marketing Assistant Claire Hojem
Accountant Sarah Bostock

Features in this guide were written and researched by:
Introduction Ronnie Haydon. **Story of London** David Littlefield, Ronnie Haydon. **New London** David Littlefield. **Festivals & Events** Cathy Limb.
Around Town Introduction Ronnie Haydon. Southwark & Bankside David Littlefield. The City Sue Webster. Kensington & Chelsea Ronnie
Haydon. West End Hugh Graham. Bloomsbury & Holborn Hugh Graham. Westminster David Littlefield. Marylebone Sue Webster. North London
Natalia Marshall. East London Simon Coppock. South-east London Hugh Graham. South west London Rick Jones, Lisa Osborne. West London
Simon Cropper, Daniel Holmes. **Eating** Ronnie Haydon. **Shopping** Nana Ocran, Sue Webster. **Arts & Entertainment** Cyrus Shahrad. **Parties**
Cyrus Shahrad. **Sport & Leisure** Andrew Shields. **Days Out** Simon Cropper, Fiona Cumberpatch, Ronnie Haydon, Cyrus Shahrad. **Directory**
Ronnie Haydon.

The editor would like to thank the following:
Lisa Baughn; Lloyd Bolton; Christi Daugherty; Will Fulford-Jones; Ruth Jarvis; Rick, John, Bruce and Jane Jones; Tim, Robert and Richard Jones;
Ria and Anaya Makwana; Alice, Daisy, Joseph and Karen Malivoire; Sophia and Georgia Marshall Evangelou; Jack, Carey and Perry Miller;
Sara O'Reilly and Katy; James Perks; Mary and Teresa Trafford; Julie Wells.

Maps by john@jsgraphics.co.uk
Illustrations The Story of London by Matt Pattinson.
Cover photography by Tricia de Courcy Ling
Photography pages 10, 12, 15 AKG Photo; 19 Associated Press; 273 Paul Avis; 57 Sarah Blee; 7, 9, 140, 144, 146, 148, 152, 154, 155,
157, 271, 269, 279, 281 Heloise Bergman; 252 Andrew Brackenbury; 35, 44, 55, 59, 63, 65, 71, 81, 83, 87, 90, 91, 96, 97, 99, 107 (top),
111, 113, 124, 130, 138, 139, 161, 163, 168, 179, 181, 186, 189, 193, 196, 197, 202, 204, 218, 219, 231, 258, 260, 265, 293 Tricia
de Courcy Ling; 122, 159, 164, 171, 234, 244 Matt Carr; 133, 153 Dominic Dibbs; 151 Suzy Del Campo; 38, 52, 100 Amanda Edwards;
250 Tony Gibson; 126 Sara Hannant; 30, 31 Robert Hind; 49, 51, 60, 62, 70, 78, 86, 93, 107(bottom), 115, 143, 247, 254 Hadley Kincade;
252 Mark Leach; 95, 207, 224, 225, 236, 240, 257 Jon Perugia; 40, 41, 116, 117 Natalie Pecht; 20 Rex Features; 174, 184, 262
Alys Tomlinson.
The following images were supplied by the featured establishments/artist: pages 21, 23, 25, 28, 33, 34, 57, 72, 75, 89, 103, 108, 109,
134, 209, 210, 215, 219, 226, 245, 277, 283, 286, 290.

Repro by Icon Reproduction, Crowne House, 56-58 Southwark Street, London SE1 1UN
Printed and bound by Southernprint, Factory Road, Upton Industrial Estate, Poole, Dorset BH16 5SN

Distribution by Seymour Ltd (020 7396 8000)

Tate Britain for Families 2003

Innovative, challenging ways to introduce children to art. These expertly-planned activities promote fun exploration by children and adults together.

Art Trolley year-round sessions at weekends and every Thursday in school holidays. Interactive games, puzzles and practical art activities to help you see artworks afresh. Free.

Artspace Hands-on sculpture, jigsaws, dressing up and other creative games and books in a comfortable family area off the main gallery. Weekends all year and Mondays – Sundays in school holidays. Free.

Monthly **Tate Tales** story telling sessions involve you in dramatic stories where anything might happen! Free **Holiday Workshops** Practical and fun art workshops linked to the gallery's exhibitions programme. Small fee.

plus children's audiotours, activity bags and explorer trails available daily; easy access for pushchairs; baby change facilities; family picnic area at weekends and holidays; a riverside walk close by to let off steam.

Tate Tales and holiday activities supported by John Lyon's Charity. Art Trolley sponsored by Tate & Lyle PLC. Artspace supported by Tate Members.

Illustrations: Sara Fanelli

BRITAIN

For more information, visit www.tate.org.uk/britain/eventseducation/family or call 020 7887 3959

Contents

Introduction

A city of many faces, London presented a rather stern one to its young visitors for many decades. Children tripped politely around the zoo and crept like snails around hushed galleries and musems. The last few years, however, have seen the old city come over all playful. Child-friendliness pops up in unexpected quarters. The Tower of London, built to intimidate rebels, is a veritable fun factory. Not a school holiday goes by without activities to delight the kids, and the Beefeaters are positively avuncular. Art galleries have children turning out artworks with scissors and sticky tape, the Science Museum invites them for sleepovers, even the G F Handel Museum runs half-term high jinks with costumes, trails and the amusing Handel Bag.

Getting the children involved is a rewarding strategy for all of the city's tourist venues. It's also a wise one. If the hearts of children are won today, future visitors are guaranteed. And it's not just the visitor attractions addressing themselves to the family market. All over this great, ever-expanding city of ours, acts are being cleaned up.

Accessibility to all is the watchword. As well as the abolition of admission charges to some of the best museums in the world, the ease of travelling between them is being given plenty of attention. On this score, Londoners have a friend in Ken. Mayor Livingstone's transport strategy, including the contentious Congestion Charge, has reduced traffic chaos in central London. Buses travel faster along their lanes, and a new fleet has been brought into service with disabled passengers and laden parents in mind. The new layout north of Trafalgar Square has given priority to the pedestrian in the epicentre of town – the point from which all distances from London are measured.

Exploring the length and breadth of London with our children for this guide, we're always enchanted by the city's diversity, its proud cultural heritage and its wicked sense of humour. Most of all, we love its ever-changing moods, and the increasingly benevolent face it shows our young. This is a city that knows how to have fun, and the *Time Out London for Children Guide* can show you how.

THE TIME OUT LONDON FOR CHILDREN GUIDE

This is the third edition of the *Time Out London for Children Guide*, produced by the people behind the successful listings magazines, and travel guide series. It is written by resident experts to provide you with all the information you'll need to explore the city, whether you're a local or a first-time visitor.

THE LOWDOWN ON THE LISTINGS

Addresses, phone numbers, websites, transport information, opening times, admission prices and credit card details are included in the listings.

Details of facilities, services and events were all checked and correct as we went to press. Before you go out of your way, however, we'd advise you to phone and check opening times, ticket prices and other particulars. While every effort has been made to ensure the accuracy of the information contained in this guide, the publishers cannot accept any responsibility for any errors it may contain.

FAMILY-FRIENDLY INFORMATION

Having visited all the places with our children, we've added essential information for families. Where we think it's important, we've stated whether a building can accommodate pushchairs ('buggy access'), or if there's a place to change a nappy ('nappy-changing facilities'). We've also listed a spot nearby where you can eat your packed lunch ('nearest picnic place').

Attractions are required to provide reasonable facilities for disabled visitors, although it's always best to check accessibility before setting out.

Disabled visitors requiring information about getting around can call GLAD (Greater London Action on Disability) on 7346 5808 (7326 4554 minicom) or check the website www.glad.org.uk.

PRICES AND PAYMENT

We have noted where venues accept the following credit cards: American Express (AmEx), Diners Club (DC), MasterCard (MC) and Visa (V).

THE LIE OF THE LAND

Map references are included for each venue that falls on our street maps (starting on p312) but we recommend that you follow the example of the locals and invest in a standard A-Z map of the city.

PHONE NUMBERS

The area code for London is 020. All phone numbers given in this guide take this code unless otherwise stated, so add 020 if calling from outside London; otherwise, simply dial the number as written. The international dialling code for the UK is 44.

Sponsors & advertisers

We would like to thank our sponsor Nickelodeon for its involvement in this guide. However, we would like to stress that no establishment has been included because it has advertised in any of our publications and no payment of any kind has influenced any review. The opinions given in this book are those of *Time Out* writers and editors and are entirely independent.

In Context

Guy Fawkes and fellow plotters meet their maker. See p14.

The Story of London

Two millennia of pain and progress, triumph and tragedy.

ROMAN LONDON

London's recorded history begins in AD 43 when Roman emperor Claudius and his legions invaded. But it is unlikely that the Romans were the first to establish themselves on the banks of the Tamesis (what the Romans called the Thames). The Latin name Londinium could well derive from any number of ancient origins. As historian Peter Ackroyd points out, raiding the old Celtic and Gaelic languages throws up any number of possibilities: Llyn-don, for example, means town (don) by the stream (llyn); 'lunnd' means marsh; 'Laindon', long hill; while the adjective 'londos' translates as fierce. Whatever caused the Romans to coin the name, we certainly have them to thank for our ancient city wall (built in AD 200), remnants of which survive in the City of London today. The first bridge across the Thames, which crossed at roughly the point of the present day London Bridge, was also a Roman achievement. The wall was erected after the British outpost of the Empire was sacked by warlike Boudicca. She led her armies against the soldiers who had seized her lands and raped her daughters. The settlement was almost

destroyed, but the Romans rebuilt and surrounded their town with a two-mile-long, 18-foot-high defensive wall in an attempt to keep out native rebellions. That worked for about 200 years, but continued invasions and internal strife forced the Roman Empire into decline. In 410 the last troops were withdrawn and London was left to decay, to be picked over by Angles and Saxons.

SAXON & VIKING LONDON

It is uncertain just how much attention was paid to the scattered ruins of Roman London by the Saxon settlers, who crossed the North Sea to set up homes and farms in eastern and southern England during the fifth and sixth centuries. But they certainly established an important trading centre nearby. 'Lundenwic', wic meaning marketplace, stood west of the Roman city, about where where Covent Garden is today. The name Aldwych comes from the Saxon words 'the old wic'. What is now Trafalgar Square was the site of farm buildings. The Strand is so called because it used to be just that, a strand, or beach for grounding ships.

London's first bishop, Mellitus, was a missionary sent by the Pope who eventually converted the East Saxon King Sebert to Christianity. In 604 Mellitus founded a wooden cathedral, dedicated to St Paul, inside the old city walls. Although his people turned back to paganism after Sebert's death, later generations of Christians rebuilt St Paul's. In the ninth century another wave of invaders arrived: the Vikings. They crossed the North Sea to ransack London, forcing the king of the time, Alfred of Wessex, to reoccupy the old Roman town. The stone walls were still standing and could be defended by his soldiers. While Alfred reigned, churches were built and markets thrived in London, although Winchester was still the capital of England. As the Saxon city prospered, harassment from the Vikings continued until the 11th century when the English were forced to bow to Danish king. King Cnut (Canute), who reigned from 1016 to 1040. During this time London took over from Winchester as the capital. Edward the Confessor, an English king, gained the throne in 1042 and devoted considerable time and expense to building Westminster Abbey, which replaced an old wooden church called St Peter's. Edward, who had moved into the new Palace of Westminster, died one week after his abbey was consecrated in December 1065. At least it was ready in time for his burial. His death was a pivotal moment in history. Edward's cousin William, Duke of Normandy, swore that his kinsman had promised him the crown. But Edward's brother-in-law Harold was a solid favourite with the English people, with the result that their armies began slugging it out at Hastings. On 14 October 1066 William defeated Harold and marched to London. He was crowned in the Abbey on Christmas Day.

Tsk! The youth of yesterday

Some things never change. In 1385 churchman Robert Braybroke complained that children exercised their minds through mischief and idleness: 'They play ball inside and outside the church and engage in other destructive games there, breaking and greatly damaging the glass windows and the stone images of the church.'

Game-playing was as important then as it is now. Kids played 'cobnutte', now called conkers, and would slide on ice, using animals' shin bones as primitive skates. In his complaint Braybroke was overlooking one vital fact of mitigation – life for kids was tough. When they weren't dying in droves, children suffered hardship, poverty, hunger and abuse. What's more, they weren't considered deserving of special care; they were merely small versions of adults and had to pull their weight very early on. They were even stolen. One Alice de Salesbury was forced to stand in the pillory for stealing the daughter of a grocer and, by forcing her to beg, making an income from the poor girl.

Kids were even thrown in jail and faced the death penalty just like their elders. In 1816 a report shows nine- and ten-year-olds locked in Newgate prison, while a traveller described seeing in the jail a group of 12-year-olds 'all under the sentence of death, smoking and playing very merrily together'. There were even cases of six-year-olds appearing in court. Kids also began working life early on, often from the age of six or seven, and their masters or parish workhouses could easily get away with serious maltreatment. Dickens, in his *Oliver Twist*, wasn't exaggerating too much. Those who hadn't turned to crime found work where they could get it, as errand boys, holding horses, hailing cabs or as beer carriers. Some, dressed in red uniforms, cleaned the streets of horse manure. There is little romance about this kind of life. Far from the jovial cockney sparrows immortalised in *Mary Poppins*, chimney sweeps, for example, were an unfortunate bunch. Known as 'climbing boys', unscrupulous parents would sometimes sell their children as apprentices from as young as four years old. They were forced up London's narrow and crooked chimneys under threat of punishment – reluctant climbers were pricked with pins or scorched with fire. On a visit to London in 1860, Tolstoy was horrified by what he saw: 'When I see these dirty tattered children, with their bright eyes and angels' faces, I am filled with apprehension as if I were seeing drowning people. How to save them? Which to save first?'

Some could not be saved. In 1839 almost half the funerals in London were for children aged under ten. This is typical for an age with no health or welfare services. A century before, there were 23,500 deaths in London, half of which were under-tens, the vast majority of which were under two. If kids weren't being worked to death, they lived in conditions which made catching whooping cough, TB, pneumonia and measles easy.

Philanthropists helped. Captain Thomas Coram, for example, set up his foundling hospital in 1742. It was quickly over-subscribed and children often turned away. Those who were admitted led fairly predictable lives – boys tended to join the army, while girls trained as maids. It wasn't until the founding of the welfare state, compulsory education and the relatively prosperous years of the 1950s that the lives of children began to change. The concept of the teenager arrived, and youths forged their own identities. Lads from south London took their cue from Savile Row and Jermyn Street tailors who were trying to resurrect Edwardian respectability among their customers – and the Teddy Boy was born. The rest is history.

Zeppelins stalk the city in **World War I**. *See p17.*

MEDIEVAL LONDON

William, who knew he had to keep the prosperous merchants in the City of London sweet, gave them independent trading rights in return for taxes. The charter drawn up to state this is kept at the Guildhall. But he was still worried about the large, possibly rebellious, population of the city and ordered strongholds to be built along its wall. One of these is the White Tower, the tallest building in the Tower of London. London became a hotbed of political struggle. Fighting for supremacy were three powerful bodies: the king and aristocracy; the Church; and the lord mayor and city guilds.

In the early Middle Ages, the king made all the laws in the country, aided by lords and bishops. During the 14th and 15th centuries, the Palace of Westminster became the seat of law and government, and the king's meetings with the noblemen and clergy – called Parliaments – became increasingly important. As the number of advisors to the king grew, Parliament divided into two groups, the House of Lords (populated by nobles and members of the clergy chosen by the king) and the House of Commons (powerful people elected by rich merchants and landowners). Trade with Europe

grew. Imports of spices, cloth, furs, precious metals and wine crowded the wharves by London Bridge and people travelled from miles around to the city's markets, or 'cheaps' around Westcheap (now Cheapside). Foreign traders and craftsmen settled around the port of London. The population grew from about 18,000 in 1100 to more than 50,000 in the 1340s. Of course, with crowds come hygiene problems: London was incredibly dirty and smelly. In the east, Houndsditch gained its name because people threw dead dogs into the boundary ditch. At Smithfield, the meat market, butchers dumped animal guts wherever they wanted. Filthy conditions let the Black Death spread. Around 30 per cent of England's population died during the plague's blackest moments (1348-9). The epidemic reoccurred on several occasions over the next three centuries.

With plague killing many of the workers, London was left with a labour shortage, and the working populace found itself greatly overstretched. When the poll tax – a charge of a shilling a head – was introduced, the poor peasants revolted. In 1381 thousands of them, led by Wat Tyler and Jack Straw, marched on London and rioted. A 14-year-old King Richard II rode out to face and bargain with the angry mob at Smithfield, but the treacherous Lord Mayor William Walworth became angered by Tyler's belligerence and disrespect – so he fatally stabbed him. This put a stop to the rioting, and the ringleaders were rounded up and hanged.

TUDOR & STUART LONDON

In Tudor times, new lands were discovered and new trade brought to London. The city became one of the largest in Europe. Henry VII, who brought an end to the Wars of the Roses by defeating Richard III at the Battle of Bosworth and marrying Elizabeth of York, left his mark on London by commissioning the building of the wonderful Henry VII Chapel in Westminster Abbey, where he and his queen are buried. His successor was wife collector (and dispatcher) Henry VIII. His first marriage to Catherine of Aragon failed to produce an heir, so the King, in 1527, determined that the union should be annulled. As the Pope refused to co-operate, Henry defied the Catholic Church, demanding that he himself be recognised as Supreme Head of the Church of England and ordering the execution of anyone who refused to go along (including his chancellor Sir Thomas More). Thus England began the transition to Protestantism. The subsequent dissolution of its monasteries changed the face of medieval London: the land sold off as a result was given over to streets and houses. On a more positive note, Henry also founded the Royal Dockyards at Woolwich. The land he kept for hunting purposes became the Royal Parks (Hyde, Regent's, Greenwich

WHERE WILL THE NICKTOONS TAKE YOU TODAY?

ALL TOONS! ALL DAY!

Watch favourite shows like The Wild Thornberrys, Rugrats, The Adventures of Jimmy Neutron: Boy Genius, SpongeBob SquarePants and As Told By Ginger everyday from 6.00am to 7.00pm on Nicktoons TV.

nick.co.uk  ntl:home

and Richmond). His daughter Queen Mary's five-year reign saw a brief Catholic revival. She was nicknamed 'Bloody Mary' following her order that 300 Protestants be burned at the stake in Smithfield. Mary's half-sister Elizabeth I oversaw a huge upsurge in commerce: the Royal Exchange was founded by Sir Thomas Gresham in 1566 and London became Europe's leading commercial centre. With Drake, Raleigh and Hawkins sailing to America and beyond, new trading enterprises were developing all the time. By 1600 there were 200,000 people living in London, 12,000 of whom were beggars. Conditions were overcrowded and rat-infested. Plague was a constant threat. During the Elizabethan era London became an important cultural centre, particularly for drama. Two famous theatres, the Rose (1587) and the Globe (1599), were built on the south bank of the Thames, and the plays of William Shakespeare and Christopher Marlowe first performed. More earthy drama often took place on the street. Bankside was considered a 'naughty place' where people visited taverns and engaged in popular pursuits of bear-baiting, cockfighting and brothel-visiting. Elizabeth's successor, the Stuart James I, narrowly escaped being blown up. The Gunpowder Plot was instigated by a group of Catholics led by Guy Fawkes, who planned to protest at their persecution by dynamiting the Palace of Westminster from the cellar. Unfortunately for Fawkes, one of his co-conspirators warned his brother-in-law not to attend Parliament on 5 November – this prompted a thorough search and the scheme was foiled. Four of the plotters were killed while resisting arrest, while the remainder of the gang were dragged through the streets and executed, their heads were displayed on spikes. Although James I escaped death, his son Charles I was less lucky. When Charles threatened the City of London's tax-free status he stirred up trouble for himself. Eventually civil war broke out, in which

Transport through the ages

The history of London's transport is, in many ways, a history of scientific and social progress. Although the horse was, from Roman to Victorian times, a fundamental piece of the transport infrastructure, horse ownership was not widespread – only the motor car has put private transport within the reach of (almost) everyone.

Public transport was introduced in the 16th century when the hackney coach (from the French for a nag – 'haquenée' – made an appearance: a two-seat carriage pulled by two horses, one of which was ridden by the driver. But the most comfortable, luxurious and expensive mode of transport was the sedan chair, introduced in 1711. The sedan was a one-seater, essentially a padded box with front and back shafts enabling it to be carried by a pair of strong men. One advantage was that it was slim enough to be carried through your average front door, enabling well-to-do occupants to embark and alight in the privacy of their home, without the inconvenience of being rained on or setting expensively shod feet on dirty streets. Before the advent of adequate street lighting, boys would accompany hackney coaches and sedans with torches on dark nights. Sedan chairs survived well into the 19th century – the last reported sighting was in Mayfair in 1841.

The omnibus arrived in 1829, an elongated carriage drawn by three horses that could accommodate up to 18 passengers. Named after its alleged French inventor Monsieur Omnes (who adopted the Latin phrase Omnes Omnibus – 'All for Everyone') the first London route linked Paddington to Bank. By the 1850s, 3,000 omnibuses were pounding the London streets, each one carryng around 300 people a day. It was around this time that the vehicles began to be refered to as 'buses', although the abbreviation wasn't made official until the 1920s. Motorised buses were introduced in 1897, although horse-drawn versions didn't disappear until 1916.

The advent of the railway had a profound effect on the fabric of the capital. Estimates show that up to 100,000 people were displaced by the laying of the tracks through heavily populated districts and even cemeteries. The construction of grand rail termini, situated on the boundaries of London, was greeted with adulation. Paddington, at that time, was hardly part of London, though – its distance from the centre was a factor behind the introduction of underground lines.

The Metropolitan line, driven between Paddington and Farringdon, opened in 1863 after three years of mayhem and mishap. The project very nearly turned into a fiasco. In May 1860 a train driver crashed through King's Cross mainline station and finished up in the construction site; the following November a shunting train blew up, killing three people; in May 1861 the northern retaining wall of the project caved in; and in April 1862 the Fleet sewer broke through, flooding the line and bringing down the scaffolding. But when opened to the public on 10 January 1863, the Metropolitan line was an outstanding success – so successful, in fact, that contemporary reports have a quite striking familiarity: 'It soon became apparent that the locomotive power and rolling stock at the disposal of the company was by no means in proportion to the requirements of the opening day,' said the Daily Telegraph, 'Every station became crowded with intending travellers...The crowding at King's Cross was immense.'

This London bus was one of the casualties during the **General Strike** in 1926. *See p18.*

Charles and his Royalists were the losers. Charles was tried for treason and beheaded outside the Banqueting House in Whitehall in 1649. Once the Puritans, led by Oliver Cromwell, had declared Britain a Commonwealth, London became a dull place. Theatres were closed down and the drinking and gambling dens of Bankside went with them.

When the exiled Charles II was restored to the throne in 1660, the English in general (and Londoners in particular) were relieved. But the 1660s turned out to be a difficult time for the population of London, to say the least. In 1664-5 bubonic plague killed nearly 100,000 Londoners before cold weather brought an end to its spread. The plague represents a tragedy of unimaginable proportions: at its height, 10,000 people were dying each week. Businesses collapsed, leaving people unemployed, penniless and driven to crime; when plague was diagnosed in a house, the occupants were locked inside in appalling conditions for 40 days, while watchmen outside ensured no one escaped. London reeked of death. And then, the following year, an oven in Farriner's bakery in Pudding Lane started a fire that lasted three days and destroyed four-fifths of the City. More than 13,000 houses were destroyed, along with 87 churches and 44 livery company halls. Rumours of a Popish plot abounded, and Frenchman Robert Hubert was forced to confess to starting the fire. He

was later hanged. Today, Christopher Wren's Monument (*see p51*) marks a spot near where the fire broke out (incidentally, the 202-foot-high tower later became a popular spot for committing suicide; after the sixth death in 1842, the open gallery was enclosed by a cage). London was rebuilt in brick and stone. One of the busiest people at this time was Christopher Wren, who as well as completing his greatest work, the new St Paul's Cathedral, also oversaw the rebuilding of 51 city churches. The Royal Exchange was also rebuilt in the City, but by this time many merchants preferred to conduct their business in coffee houses – one of which was later to become insurance giant Lloyds of London.

GEORGIAN LONDON

When the throne passed to George, the great-grandson of James I, the country had to settle for a Hanoverian, German-speaking king. In Parliament, the Whig party, led by Sir Robert Walpole, was in power. Walpole was the first prime minister and was given 10 Downing Street as an official home. This address has been occupied by the serving prime minister ever since. Streets and squares of attractive Georgian houses around central London are testament to how the city boomed during the Georgian period. It was at this time, too, that crossings over the river were built to increase accessibility. Westminster Bridge (built 1750) and

Key events

66 BC? Ludgate built by King Lud (legendary).

AD 43 The Roman invasion. Londinium is founded.

61 Boudicca sacks the city.

122 Emperor Hadrian visits Londinium.

200 A rebuilt Londinium is protected by a city wall.

410 The last Roman troops leave Britain.

c600 Saxon London is built to the west.

604 The first St Paul's cathedral is built.

841 First Viking raid.

c871 The Danes occupy London.

886 King Alfred retakes London.

1013 The Danes take London; King Cnut reigns.

1042 King Edward builds Westminster Abbey.

1066 William, Duke of Normandy, defeats Harold.

1067 Work begins on the Tower of London.

1099 First recorded flood in London.

1123 St Bartholomew's Hospital founded.

1197 Henry Fitzailwyn becomes the city's first mayor.

1240 First Parliament sits at Westminster.

1294 First recorded mention of Hammersmith.

1348-9 The Black Death ravages London.

1357 The first Sanitary Act passed in London.

1381 Wat Tyler leads the Peasants' Revolt.

1388 Tyburn, near Marble Arch, becomes the principal place of execution.

1397 Richard (Dick) Whittington becomes Lord Mayor.

1497 The first image of London published in a 'Chronycle of Englonde'.

1513 Henry VIII founds Woolwich Royal Dockyard

1534 Henry VIII breaks away from the Catholic Church.

1554 200 Protestant martyrs burned at Smithfield.

1571 The first permanent gallows set up at Tyburn.

1572 First known map of London printed.

1599 The Globe Theatre is built on Bankside.

1605 Guy Fawkes' Gunpowder Plot is discovered.

1635 London's first public postal service established.

1642 The Puritans defeat the Royalists at Turnham Green.

1649 Charles I is tried for treason and beheaded.

1664-5 The Great plague kills thousands.

1666 The Great Fire destroys London.

1675 Building starts on a new St Paul's Cathedral.

1680 Downing Street built.

1683 The first Sadler's Wells 'musick house' built.

1686 The first May Fair takes place at Mayfair.

1694 The Bank of England opens at Cheapside.

1711 St Paul's is completed.

1742 Thomas Coram founds his orphanage.

1750 Westminster Bridge is built.

1769 Blackfriars Bridge opens.

1784 The first balloon flight over London

1803 The first railway (horse drawn) opens.

1820 Regent's Canal opens.

1824 National Gallery founded.

1827 Regent's Park Zoo opens.

1829 Robert Peel founds the Metropolitan Police.

Blackfriars Bridge (1763) joined London Bridge, which until then had been the only bridge to span the river. While the well-to-do enjoyed their Georgian homes, life for the poor was squalid. Living in slum conditions and grinding poverty, ruined by the cheap and plentiful gin that they drank to escape ghastly reality, it's little wonder people turned to street crime. Gangs emerged, many numbering 20-30 members, who enjoyed near immunity from arrest. Thieves even set up their own market on Tower Hill to sell their ill-gotten gains. The notorious Gregory Gang, one of many which struck at people leaving and entering the capital, included notorious highwayman Dick Turpin. The writer Henry Fielding and his brother John established a volunteer force of 'thief takers' in 1751 to help the parish constables and watchmen catch these criminals. This force, originally known as the Bow Street Runners, eventually became the Metropolitan Police (established 1829).

1888

1833 The London Fire Brigade is established.

1835 Madame Tussaud's opens.

1843 Trafalgar Square is laid out.

1851 The Great Exhibition takes place in Hyde Park.

1858 The Great Stink permeates London.

1863 World's first underground railway opens.

1866 The Sanitation Act is passed.

1868 Last public execution in Newgate Prison.

1869 The first J Sainsbury grocery opens in Drury Lane.

1883 World's first power station built at Holborn Viaduct.

1884 Greenwich Mean Time is established.

1888 Jack the Ripper preys on East End women.

1890 The first electric underground railway opens.

1897 Motorised buses introduced.

1898 The first escalator installed in London, in Harrods.

1915-18 Zeppelins bomb London.

1916 Horse-drawn buses disappear.

1940-4 The Blitz devastates much of London.

1948 Olympic Games held in London.

1951 The Festival of Britain takes place.

1952 The last of the city's 'pea-soupers'.

1953 Queen Elizabeth II is crowned.

1966 England win the World Cup at Wembley.

1975 Work begins on the Thames barrier (completed 1982).

1982 The last of London's docks close.

1990 Poll Tax protestors riot.

1992 Canary Wharf opens.

1997 Britain mourns Princess Diana.

2000 Londoners celebrate a new millennium.

2002 Queen Mother dies aged 101.

If it hadn't been for the work of enlightened people like Fielding and other philanthropists, life for the poor in London would have been far worse. Attempts to alleviate their suffering included the founding of five major new hospitals. St Bartholomew's and St Thomas's had been established by monks many years before but they were joined by Westminster, Guy's, St George's, London and the Middlesex Hospitals from 1720 to 1745, all of which went on to become world-famous teaching hospitals. Big-hearted sea captain Thomas Coram built his Foundling Hospital for abandoned children during this time (the entrance arcades of this hospital, which was demolished in 1926, still remain at the top of Lamb's Conduit Street, in front of Coram's Fields park; *see p60*).

VICTORIAN LONDON

By the time Victoria came to the throne in 1837, five more bridges spanned the Thames and the city's first railway line (London Bridge to Greenwich) had been laid. London, the administrative and financial capital of the British Empire, was a huge, grimy industrial town. Fine buildings, posh shops and grand houses made rich living easy, but a few streets away, slums continued to breed misery.

Down by the river, life became increasingly malodorous. A less-than-modern sewerage system meant that city dwellers' waste products flowed into the Thames. As there were now millions of Londoners, this resulted in filthy, disease-ridden water. Smallpox, typhus and cholera were everyday concerns. The year 1858 was famous for its smell: the 'Great Stink' meant that politicians in the Houses of Parliament could not work with their windows open during the hot summer. Bad smells continued until 1860, when Joseph Bazalgette's drainage system was completed.

Novelist Charles Dickens wrote prolifically about London's social problems, as did Frederick Engels, who complained that the children he saw in Long Acre were 'sickly' and 'half starved'. In 1872 an observer recalled 'the lanes which open off Oxford Street, stifling alleys thick with human effluvia, troops of pale children crouching on filthy staircases; the street benches at London Bridge where all night whole families huddle close, heads hanging, shaking with cold... abject, miserable poverty. But as the years rolled by, improvements were made to ease the lot of Londoners. The new sewage system made a great difference, and some slum housing was replaced by social housing funded by philanthropists, such as George Peabody.

20TH-CENTURY LONDON

The last few years of Victoria's reign had been somewhat gloomy, so when Edward VII came to the throne in 1901, a new, fun-filled era began. The luxurious Ritz Hotel on Piccadilly was opened and the Café Royal on Regent Street was the favourite haunt of fashionable people. Department stores, an American idea, made it across to England – the first to open was stately Selfridges, in 1909, followed two years later by Whiteley's in Bayswater. World War I saw the first bomb to be dropped on London. It came from a Zeppelin and landed near Guildhall. Terrifying nightly raids continued throughout the Great War, killing 650 people.

When it was finally over, and those soldiers who had survived were promised 'homes for heroes' on their return, political change was set in motion. Few homes materialised and the mood of the nation was black. In 1924 David Lloyd George's Liberal Party was deposed in favour of a promised fresh start with the Labour Party, under Ramsay MacDonald. While the upper classes partied their way through the 'Roaring Twenties', the working classes were in the grip of mass unemployment caused by the post-war slump. Dissatisfaction was expressed when all the workers downed tools to support the striking miners. The General Strike of 1926 lasted for nine days: the army was called in to help distribute food and students drove the buses. After the strike, unemployment continued to rise. The New York Stock Exchange crash of 1929 had a devastating knock-on effect; the British economic situation was grim.

Nevertheless, the London County Council worked to improve conditions for its people. As the city's population grew (8.7 million in 1939), so did its sprawl. Suburbia expanded, and with it the tube lines. The main entertainment for people was the radio, until 1936 at least, when the first television broadcast went out live from the British Broadcasting Corporation (BBC) at Alexandra Palace studios. On 3 September 1939 Britain declared war on Germany and Londoners began digging air raid shelters and sending children and pregnant women to the countryside. In fact, the air raids did not begin until almost a year later. In September 1940 600 German bombers devastated east London and the docks. The raids continued for 57 nights in a row. The Strand was hit, and so were the House of Commons, St Thomas's Hospital, Buckingham and Lambeth palaces and St Paul's Cathedral. Nearly 30,000 bombs were dropped on London alone; around 15,000 people were killed and 3,500,000 houses destroyed or damaged. People took refuge in the tube stations – 79 stations became official shelters, and 177,000 people regularly used them. They were safe unless the stations themselves were hit. This happened at Marble Arch, Bank and Balham.

Londoners during the Blitz became known for their resilience. In 1944 a new type of bomb began flattening Londoners' homes – the V1 flying bomb, or doodlebug. These caused widespread destruction, as did their successor, the more powerful V2 rocket,

Time Out arrives in 1968. *See p19.*

500 of which were dropped on east London. By the end of the war about a third of the great city and the East End was in ruins. Even when the war ended the country was suffering.

In the General Election that took place soon after VE Day, Churchill was defeated by the Labour Party under Clement Attlee. Swift changes went ahead to try to improve the life of the nation. The National Health Service was founded in 1948; public transport and communications services were overhauled. But for all these initiatives, life in the city seemed drab and austere. For Londoners facing a terrible housing shortage there were ambitious initiatives to put a roof over their heads. Some of the buildings whisked up for them – prefabricated bungalows – were supposed to be temporary, but many are still inhabited more than 50 years later. High-rise estates, a new concept, often put up in a hurry, were consequently rather shoddy. Many tower blocks have since been pulled down, while others have been refurbished and reclad beyond recognition.

It was not all doom for Londoners, though. The city hosted the Olympic Games in 1948 and, in 1951, the Festival of Britain, which celebrated all that was great about British technology and design. It took place on derelict land on the south bank of the river, and when it ended, the land became the site of the South Bank Centre arts complex. During the 1950s Britain enjoyed a gradual return to relative prosperity. Families were inspired to buy into the suburban dream, in gleaming new towns away from the filthy city. They had a point: air pollution was a problem. Clean Air Acts, the first in 1956 introduced as a result of the Great Smog four years earlier, finally ensured the reduction of noxious gas emissions. With people moving out of town, London was facing a labour shortage. Workers from the country's former colonies, particularly the West Indies, were recruited for London Transport and in the hospitals. Many of these immigrants faced an unfriendly reception from indigenous Londoners: matters came to a head in the Notting Hill race riots of 1958. Some parts of London were more tolerant, though, Soho, with its jazz joints and clubs, for one. The 1960s belonged to swinging London. It became the fashion capital of the world, and Carnaby Street the hippest street. To find out where the gigs were, young people bought a fold-out

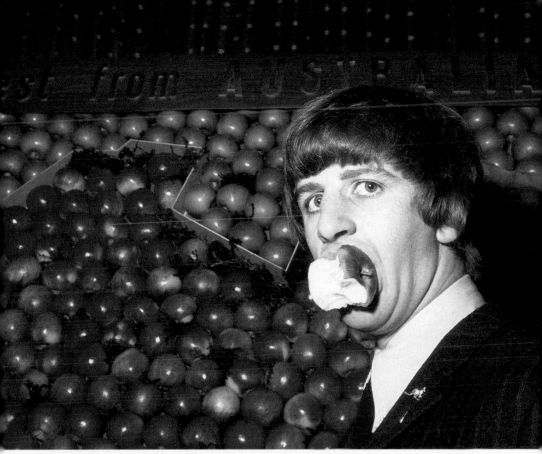

A rare **Beatle** called Ringo devastates the apple crops in 1964.

weekly guide to London called *Time Out*; the first issue came out in August 1968. People from around the world started flocking to Abbey Road, NW8, because it adorned the cover of the Beatles album of the same name. Hyde Park was the hottest place to be in the summer of '69: the Rolling Stones played a free gig there for half a million fans.

During the 1970s, the lights went out, often literally, on London's glamour. Inflation, unemployment, strikes, IRA bombs and an increasingly fractured Labour government all contributed to an air of gloom. The punk explosion made a few sparks fly, but that fire was shortlived. Margaret Thatcher came to power in 1979, and the 1980s are generally regarded as her decade. Her Conservative government made sweeping changes, and stood up for 'market forces'. This was the era of the yuppie (Young Urban Professionals), who benefited from the Conservatives' monetarist policies and the arrival of the global economy. Meanwhile, the gap between these yuppies and less fortunate people on low pay was only too apparent.

It did not take long for the underdogs to start snarling, giving rise to the inner city riots, first in Brixton in 1981, and four years later in Tottenham. One of the lasting legacies of the Thatcher era is the Docklands redevelopment. This scheme, set up in 1981 to create a new business centre in the docks to the east of the City, was slow to take shape, but is now considered an unqualified success. Businesses and residents are continuing to move into smart office buildings and apartment blocks around the Isle of Dogs and the whole area exudes prosperity. But this is one prominent area of London that's becoming divided into two halves; little of the wealth from the banks and businesses is filtering through to the community. In 1986 the Greater London Council, with its anti-Thatcher outlook (despite being Conservative back in the 1960s), was abolished and County Hall was sold to a Japanese corporation. But history has a way of turning back on you – the GLC's former leader, 'Red' Ken Livingstone, bided his time and, in 2000, was voted mayor with authority over all the city. When a city's economy

Mayor Ken Livingstone has a remedy for tackling inner city congestion.

booms, however, a bust is often just around the corner, and that is what happened to London in the early 1990s. There was a slump in house prices and the reign of the yuppies came to an end. The last straw for beleaguered Londoners was the introduction of a poll tax. Demonstrations against it led to riots in Trafalgar Square. It marked the loosening of Mrs Thatcher's grip on the nation, leading to her replacement by John Major in 1990. The recession continued and its effects were only too evident in London. The numbers of rough sleepers rose as people lost their homes through unemployment and mortgage rate rises. The IRA stepped up their campaign against the mainland, bombing the City in 1992 (destroying the medieval church of St Ethelburga-the-Virgin) and Docklands in 1996. Most of the capital cheered up when Tony Blair's New Labour ousted the Tories in May 1997, but went into shock when, later that year, Princess Diana was killed. The gates of Kensington Palace were the focus for the nation's tears and bouquets.

THE 21ST CENTURY

New Labour continued with Conservative plans to celebrate the new millennium with the Millennium Dome. But the spectacular tent on the once-derelict Greenwich pensinsula signally failed to capture the spirit of the nation and voices were raised about massive sums of money swallowed up by the enterprise. In 2003 the Dome stands sad and empty and, although plans are afoot to rescue this white elephant, it is likely to remain so for some time.

London does have problems. Housing is both cripplingly expensive and in short supply, leading some to campaign for a reintroduction of tower blocks. Transport is taking an achingly long time to improve and, indeed, often seems to be getting much worse. The closure of the Central Line in early 2003 tested the patience of commuters to the limit. Many campaigners against Ken Livingstone's £5 daily congestion charge hoped that the scheme would be delayed until the tube system was running properly, to no avail. But most seem to be paying the charge with few complaints, and only time will tell whether it has been the success that was promised. Uncertainty over the situation in the Middle East continues to dampen tourist and economic indicators, leaving the financial heart of the capital beating weakly. But if history shows anything, it is that London (and Londoners) can weather any storm. If you need convincing, just look upwards — the skyline is being filled with some of the most ambitious and imaginative structures on Earth.

Laban Dance Centre

New London

Bold designs are sprouting in London like mushrooms after autumn rain – and some are more digestible than others.

Seen from the train heading east towards Greenwich, the new **Laban Dance Centre** rises from a sea of semi-industrial dereliction like an iridescent mirage. Described by one architecture critic as 'one of the best new buildings in London', the Laban is the spearhead of a regenerative drive through Deptford. Both Lewisham and Greenwich councils are backing the plan, which sees the building as a magnet for other arts-related projects. They hope that incoming artists, designers and creative industries will gentrify the area (as previously happened in Hoxton and Bankside), and make it attractive to commercial developers. The new Laban centre is such a fine building that the plan stands every chance of success; watch prices around Deptford Creek start rising soon.

For £22 million you'd expect something decent, but the Laban goes further. This professional dance school, which caters for dancers of all ages and abilities, represents the first new building in the UK for Swiss architects Herzog and de Meuron – the people who transformed Bankside power station into the fabulously successful **Tate Modern**. The difference with the Laban, though, is that it's all brand new. Its form is loosely influenced by the

tough, shed-like aesthetic of the warehouses crowding this part of the riverbank, and many of its materials have an industrial feel. The large block is clad in polycarbonate panels, much like those stocked by DIY outlets for roofing greenhouses, and the central stairway and ramp inside are cast in rough concrete.

But don't be fooled – this is a beautiful and well crafted building. Colours inside that cladding make the Laban's bulk shimmer against a blue sky like oil on water, and that concrete has a wonderful tactile presence that will make children want to run their fingers over its entire length. Inside, broad ramps channel you around spaces brightened by Michael Craig-Martin's giant murals; you're offered glimpses of dancers rehearsing behind glass screens; suddenly you turn a corner and the building stretches out further than you were expecting; and then the roof opens up, bringing daylight into the depths of the labyrinth. It's almost worth enrolling in a dance class just to explore the place.

In fact, the Laban doesn't offer just dance classes (although that is its main role – even up to MA standard). The centre also contains a fabulous 300-seat theatre, a well-stocked library on dance, a pilates venue and the obligatory café and bar.

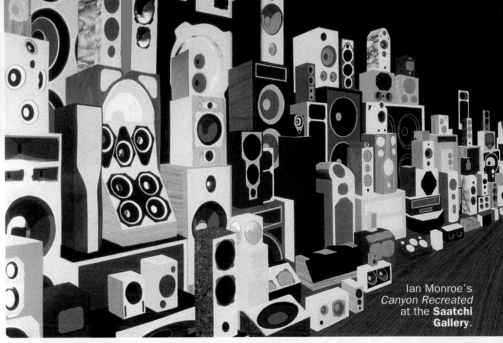

Ian Monroe's
Canyon Recreated
at the **Saatchi
Gallery**.

Landscaping outside, barely begun as this guide
went to press, is also to include an earth
amphitheatre for outside rehearsals and dance
displays, which will be provided free. If your child
is even vaguely interested in dance, this place is sure
to inspire him or her further – ask about Dancability
classes every Wednesday (8691 8600, Creekside,
SE8. Nearest rail, Greenwich and Deptford, or
DLR to Greenwich, Cutty Sark or Deptford Bridge).

MOVERS AND SHAKE-UPS

Further west, along Tooley Street near Tower Bridge,
the **Unicorn Theatre** is busy building a dedicated
venue of its own. Designed by Keith Williams, a small
award-winning practice based in Covent Garden,
this £11.25 million building will be large and
impressive enough to put the Unicorn firmly on the
theatrical map. Designed as a series of interlocking
blocks of concrete, glass and copper, the building
aims to treat children as adults and eschew overtly
child-like images and gimmicks. Williams has even
toured local schools asking kids for their views, and
his plans have had junior thumbs up. The building
will house two theatres, and seating will be basic:
a semi-circular series of steps along which children
will sit – a straightforward, cost-effective solution
that is a far cry from the practice's remodelling of
the Birmingham Rep auditorium four years ago.
The new Unicorn will be completed by summer 2004.

Further west again, Charles Saatchi has relocated
his infamous collection of contemporary art from its
original home in St John's Wood to **County Hall**.

This cultural import represents yet another notch in
the gradual redevelopment of this splendid building,
which was inaugurated in 1922 and was the seat of
the Greater London Council until Margaret Thatcher
abolished it in the mid 1980s. The neo-classical
edifice is also home to the **London Aquarium** and
a hotel, among other things, but a third of it remains
to be redeveloped – including the debating chamber
itself. Rumour has it that pop impresario Pete
Waterman is considering buying a chunk of the
space and turning it into recording facilities for the
use of local kids. In any event, it can't be denied that
RHWL, the architects responsible for the new and
already famous **Saatchi Gallery** have done a
sensitive alteration job. Why do anything else?
Damien Hirst's shark in formaldehyde surely
provides all the brutality any building needs.

Up north in Swiss Cottage, further arts projects
are leading the regeneration crusade. A handsome
yet funky, beautifully-lit £15.7 million building
has become the home of the 300-seat **Hampstead
Theatre**, while refurbishment work on Sir Basil
Spence's 1960s library is very nearly complete, and
new landscaping is under way.

HIP T-SQUARE

The **National Gallery** has also launched a
rebuilding programme of its own. Prompted by the
arrival of Charles Saumarez Smith, formerly of the
National Portrait Gallery next door, the National
has begun work to punch a whole new entrance into
the gallery's **Trafalgar Square** elevation by 2005.

The £21 million East Wing scheme promises to open up some spectacular light shafts. The designs, by the Dixon Jones practice (which masterminded the successful extension to the NPG) will create a new shop and café and at the same time greatly improve circulation spaces around the gallery. It will also mean being able to enter the building without having to climb up all those steps.

This scheme is closely linked to the paving of the north side of Trafalgar Square. Work is still in progress, but soon to be completed. When the messy building site is at last cleared up visitors will be able to walk undisturbed between the National and **Nelson's Column**. The work also involves digging into the wall on the square's north side, to create a café on one side and a much-needed public loo on the other. This is part of the GLA 'World Squares for All' initiative, and mayor Ken Livingstone has said that he wants T-Square to continue to function as 'a forum for free speech' – though strangely, **Parliament Square** garden, managed by the GLA since February 2002, will not get the same status. 'Parliament Square should be a symbolic and dignified place at the heart of government. Rallies and demonstrations on the square are not therefore considered appropriate,' says a GLA report. Incidentally, the fourth plinth on T-Square is to be occupied by a rotating sequence of contemporary sculpture – models of submissions were due to be exhibited during the summer of 2003, with the first piece due to be in place during 2004.

QUICK QUICK FLOW

Moving around London is definitely getting easier (and not before time). The congestion charge appears to have succeeded in reducing the number of cars on the road, thankfully, while cross-river transit has improved immeasurably with the addition of new pedestrian footbridges. The **Millennium Bridge** linking the attractions of St Paul's and Tate Modern is proving a tremendous success, and the pair of new structures that cling to the **Hungerford rail bridge** have made walking between the Embankment and the South Bank a real pleasure.

Redevelopment plans are not advancing quite so fast at the **South Bank Centre**, the untidy and increasingly decrepit collection of arts venues between Hungerford and Waterloo bridges. The good news is that Lambeth council has agreed to a £50 million refurbishment plan for the the **Royal Festival Hall**. The future of this building is very bright – architectural practice Allies and Morrison (designers of the new landscaping around the remodelled **Tate Britain**) is planning to strip away much of the clutter that has accumulated in the hall since the 1960s, and improve the accoustics in the main concert auditorium. A new building nearby will provide much-needed staff accommodation, freeing up precious space in the RFH for public use.

But the future of the rest of the South Bank Centre remains uncertain. The SBC has long been the subject of radical modernisation plans, all of which have come to nothing. Although *Evening Standard* art critic Brian Sewell went a tad over the top when he called the centre an 'ugly, charmless, inefficient and indefensible relic of cheapjack post-war shoddiness', it is a fact that this complex of brutalist buildings has never been loved by the public (except skateboarders, the neglected concrete ramparts being their mecca). Managers, meanwhile, appear to be at a loss. The most recent plan for the area, by architect Rick Mather, involves constructing a new set of concert halls and a base for the **British Film Institute** underneath a sloping park on what is currently **Jubilee Gardens**. But Lambeth planners don't like the idea, and neither does Ken Livingstone. Whatever the solution turns out to be, it's not going to materialise for a few years yet.

ANIMAL MAGIC

In south London, another long-term ambition is nearing completion – the refurbishment of **Crystal Palace Park**. Building work was mysteriously suspended early in 2003 but Bromley council is confident that the park (or the 40 per cent of it that is being remodelled) will open during the autumn. The 19th-century dinosaurs have been repaired and repainted, redundant buildings have been demolished, crumbling features restored and a huge planting programme undertaken, including 600 trees, 10,000 waterside plants and 25,000 shrubs. Crystal Palace Park now comes near to doing what its Victorian designers had in mind – that is, functioning as a grand civic space. Thankfully, its enormous concert platform, made from cor-ten steel (a material designed to go rusty evenly) and shortlisted for an architectural award when completed in 1998, remains an unsullied monumental sculpture – unspoiled by vandals and actually improved by the weather.

Crystal Palace's carnivorous horrors are merely models, but you can get the real thing at the new Darwin Centre at the **Natural History Museum**. Completed in late 2001, the present building is just the first chunk of a £65 million construction programme which will culminate in 2007. The centre represents a valiant effort on the part of the NHM to open up its vast storeroom to the public gaze, and even allow visitors a glimpse of what its naturalists get up to behind the scenes. But be warned, it's not for the squeamish. Some of the stuff on display in countless ranks of jars is positively stomach-churning: there's even the head of an unborn elephant. Kids with a taste for gore and the macabre will love it; others will need to be guided around the displays with care (call 7942 6128 to book tickets for tours).

HALL OVER THE COALS

Creepy-crawlies of the political variety can now be viewed at the egg-shaped **City Hall** building near **Tower Bridge**. This peculiar object, photogenic though it is, ain't all it's cracked up to be. Many in the architectural world speak of it in unfavourable terms, but worst of all is its lack of openness – for a public building it's disappointingly impenetrable. The much-publicised roof gallery (dubbed 'London's Living Room') is open to the public on just two weekends every month, while the walk up its spiral ramp can be taken only when the council is in session (call 7983 4100 for details). There are two reasons behind the building's shape: firstly, its form offers a relatively low surface area to the sun, reducing the need for expensive cooling systems; and secondly, its tilt away from the river prevents its shadow falling on the riverside walkway. These are laudable aims, but the building looks frankly awkward, and the overall aspect of its patch is not enhanced by the cluster of glass and steel office buildings nearing completion nearby. One wonders if this whole 'More London' complex will one day meet the same fate as the recently demolished **Paternoster Square** development, the 1960s scheme that did little to celebrate the presence of St Paul's. Incidentally, the replacement Paternoster development is on the cusp of completion, bringing a decade of debate and building work to an end. Let's hope this scheme lasts longer than its forebear.

TOWERING AMBITIONS

Norman Foster, architect of City Hall, has also been applying his penchant for complex geometry across the river, where his **Swiss Re** 'gherkin' building will soon be ready for occupation by insurance brokers. Even under construction, the 600ft tower had an extraordinary impact on the skyline of the capital, but no less extraordinary is the power of the software packages that went into its design. This is a building that could not have been built a decade ago. Like the GLA building, it has an environmental agenda: its circular form will direct the prevailing winds in much the same way as an aircraft wing, employing varying pressures to suck air into the building for ventilation. This distinctive tower is not to everybody's taste, but nobody can fail to be awed by its ingenuity when stood at its base, looking up.

The Swiss Re tower is possibly (or indeed probably) the first of a rash of new towers to sprout in the City. Last year English Heritage lost an important battle with the architects of the proposed Heron Tower, who will soon add another building of similar height to London's skyline. And at least another two towers are on the drawing board, as is the monster 1,033ft 'Shard of Glass' being designed to stand on a site hard by London Bridge. If built, it would be the 18th tallest building in the world and the tallest in Europe; it would dominate the city and become an instant icon for London. But, unsurprisingly, English Heritage is on the warpath…

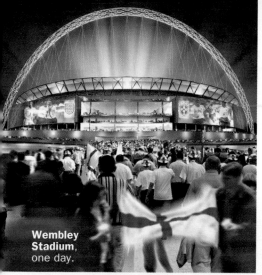

Wembley Stadium, one day.

Tower builders have an ally, however, in Ken Livingstone, who is keen to see 'clusters' of tall buildings around London, functioning as beacons and advertising its economic strength. In all, he reckons the capital could find space in the City, Elephant and Castle, Docklands and Croydon for around 20 new towers in the coming decade.

PERPETUAL MOTION?

The capital's building drive remains healthy, in spite of the economic slowdown. The corporate construction programme at Paddington Basin is coming along at a truly impressive rate, and will soon culminate in newly rescued paths along the canal, faced by gleaming office blocks. **Canary Wharf** continues to generate new steel and glass structures (few showing much architectural merit), while **Kings Cross** and **St Pancras** are set to remain construction sites for the next five years. This enormous transport programme will provide Londoners with a new tube station and a link to the Channel Tunnel, as well as a new area of housing and workplaces to the north. Detailed plans are still on the drawing board, but this year should see the result of a competition to decide the fate of the disused gasometers. Ambitious plans to completely regenerate **Elephant and Castle** by 2013 seem, however, to have hit the buffers.

ARCHITECTURAL ARCHIVES

If your interest in architecture runs to more than visiting buildings, the **Victoria & Albert Museum** aims to please by summer 2004, with the opening of its new architecture gallery. In an attempt to bring this difficult subject to life, the museum intends to combine architectural drawings and models with interactive exhibits showing how buildings are conceived and constructed. Plans are at still in the early stages, but one idea is to build small walk-in

towers which will bombard visitors with sounds and images from different building types – an airport, a monastery and a Japanese temple, for example. To tie in with the project, the Royal Institute of British Architects plans to move its entire collection of 600,000 historical drawings over to the V&A, where it will be combined with the museum's own drawing collection. At present the RIBA's archive offers only limited access, but the move – branded 'Architecture for All' – will let members of the public get their hands on any drawing, free of charge, on demand. In fact, the V&A's archive already operates by these rules – according to curators, if you've got clean hands you can see any drawing or print you like. And – perhaps surprisingly – that goes for kids, too.

The museum's most ambitious scheme is truly extraordinary. Designed by architect Daniel Libeskind (the man behind the new Jewish Museum in Berlin, which is so intriguing that it attracted thousands of visitors even before the exhibits were put in place), the £75 million **Spiral** building will provide a new entrance and giant exhibition spaces for the museum. But fundraising for the extension, an asymmetrical structure which looks like a card house frozen in mid-collapse, is going slowly. Trustees are still in the process of raising funds, so the finished building can't be expected until at least 2006.

GOALS

New sporting venues are also the subject of long-term plans, whether London pitches for the 2012 Olympic Games or not. The development of new venues and stadia has transpired to be a catalogue of administrative fudge and incompetence. Plans for a snazzy athletics stadium at Picketts Lock have been scrapped, while the future of the **Millennium Dome** and **Wembley Stadium** emerges from the mist only slowly. Norman Foster finally prevailed with his design for Wembley, beating off a rival bid from Birmingham. Demolition work is now almost complete, but it will be more than two years before the giant arch is raised over the new ground – a new icon to replace the two towers.

The Dome is now lined up as an indoor sporting arena, hosting events like ice-skating and boxing matches, but designs, dates and financing have yet to emerge. (Incidentally, the closure of the London Arena has been a disappointment for many, not least ice hockey fans. It is to be replaced, most likely, by boring offices and swanky apartments.) **Arsenal** has a more definitive future: the club has received the go-ahead for a massive redevelopment which will see a new world-class stadium built near Finsbury Park; the existing ground will be converted into flats, leaving the pitch as open space and a memorial garden to the fans who have had their ashes scattered on the hallowed turf.

U2 in the front.

The new Meriva.
Two Worlds. One Car

The New Meriva with Twin Audio.®

The new Meriva isn't just another family car, it's like two different worlds. Yours. And the kids. It comes with a revolutionary **Twin Audio**® system which, thanks to headphones in the back, allows the kids to listen to their favourite CD, while you listen to the radio. Or vice versa. It means you'll never hear phrases like 'Turn it up, we like this one' and 'Dad, do we have

Cheeky girls in the back.

to listen to this?' ever again. And if you think that sounds good there's also a **FlexSpace®** seating system which gives you the flexibility to transform the Meriva from a five seater car to a four, three, two or one seater car without breaking into a sweat. Cheeky eh? **The new Meriva. From £10,995. www.vauxhall.co.uk/meriva or call 0845 600 1500.**

VAUXHALL
A Century in Motion

City of London Festival.
See p29.

Festivals & Events

This city celebrates in style.

There's more to London's calendar than fusty ceremonies and archaic rituals. Though royal and governmental occasions do play a part, this is also a city that heartily enjoys fun and frivolity. Here we've listed the best of London's annual events; from summer riverside festivals to winter sporting spectacles. Many more are advertised in *Time Out* magazine and in the national press. Advance booking may be required and some events charge admission; others are free. Dates (where confirmed) are correct at time of going to press, but always double check nearer the time.

Summer

Wildlife Week
London Wildlife Trust reserves & centres throughout London (7261 0447/www.wildlondon.org.uk). **Date** 31 May-8 June 2003.
Every year, the first week in June is the time to celebrate London's greenness. Events in parks, woods and nature reserves across the city include open days, workshops and children's activities such as 'mini beast hunts' and pond-

dipping for slimy, slithery specimens. Ring the LWT or check the website to find out what's going on near you.

Derby Day
Epsom Downs Racecourse, Epsom Downs, Surrey (01372 470047/www.epsomderby.co.uk). Epsom Town Centre or Tattenham Corner rail then shuttle bus. **Date** 6, 7 June 2003.
Oaks Day – the fillies version of the Derby and a classic in its own right – is on 6 June; 7 June is the famous Derby Day. Stands and spectator enclosures at this prestigious flat race are open to all, from toffs in toppers in the grandstand, to families picnicking on the hill in the middle of the course. The race is the day's highlight, but a market, entertainers, jugglers and funfair all add to the day's carnival atmosphere. This year's entertainment culminates in a celebration concert on the hill after racing. Check the website for updates.

Young Pavement Artists Competition
Colonnade Walk, 123 Buckingham Palace Road, SW1 (7732 1651). Victoria tube/rail. **Map** p318 H10. **Date** 7 June 2003.
Part of a national event, this day out for lowdown scribblers (just turn up and pay £1 for a pitch and chalk) also includes entertainment, in the form of music, magicians and face painting. Judging categories are for children aged four to 18, and

parents can also join in with the 19-plus group. Celebrity guests in the past have included Rolf Harris. The fun starts at noon, with judging at 4pm.

Coin Street Festival

Gabriel's Wharf, 56 Upper Ground, SE1 (7401 3610/ www.coinstreetfestival.org). Southwark tube/Blackfriars or Waterloo tube/rail. **Map** 320 8N. **Date** 15 June-Sept 2003.

These colourful South Bank events celebrate London's diverse cultures through international music, arts, crafts, performance, and food and drink. Free events confirmed include Sanctuary on 15 June (2-7pm), highlighting the refugee communities in London, and Community Celebration Day on 13 July: a giant village fete organised for and by local residents (but everyone's welcome), with story-telling, talent and fashion shows, face-painting and workshops for children to make and wear items to wear in an afternoon procession.

Trooping the Colour

Horseguards Parade, Whitehall, SW1 (7930 4466). Westminster tube/Charing Cross tube/rail. **Map** p319 K8. **Date** 14 June 2003.

The Queen's official birthday is marked each year by this colourful military parade that dates back to the early 18th century. The ceremony is watched by members of the Royal Family and invited guests; members of the public may observe from vantage points at either side of the Mall, beginning at 11am on Horseguards Parade. After the ceremony, the Queen rides in a carriage back to Buckingham Palace at the head of her Guards, before taking the salute at the palace from the balcony, when the Royal Air Force flies past overhead and a 41-gun Royal Salute is fired in Green Park. At 1pm there's a 62-gun Royal Salute at the Tower of London.

Wimbledon Lawn Tennis Championships

All England Lawn Tennis Club, PO Box 98, Church Road, Wimbledon, SW19 5AE (8944 1066/information 8946 2244/www.wimbledon.org.uk). Southfields tube/ Wimbledon tube/rail. **Date** 24 June-6 July 2003.

Enjoy smashing tennis, dazzling whites and strawberries and cream – assuming you manage to net tickets. For Centre and Number One court seats, apply to the All England Lawn Tennis Club for an application form to enter the public ticket ballot between August and November the year before. If picked, you will be notified in late January. The only way to secure a ticket otherwise is to queue on the day of the match. Once in, you can wander the outside courts. In the afternoon, returned show-court tickets are available from the resale booth opposite Court One.

City of London Festival

various venues in the City (7377 0540/www.colf.org). **Date** 23 June-10 July 2003.

This theme for 2003's programme, Trading Places, explores the cultural exhange between London, New York and Shanghai. Music, theatre, literature and dance performances are held in some of the City's most beautiful and historical buildings; there are also walks and art tours. Events include Silkroad Journeys, a Spitalfields Market Family Day celebrating Bengali and Chinese arts and culture, which takes place on Friday 4 July, 2003 (12.30-6pm). There are also Bach and Haydn concertos in Mansion House, choral music in Clothworkers' Hall, the Julian Joseph Jazz Quartet in Guildhall Great Hall, and the BBC Philharmonic in the grand surroundings of St Paul's cathedral. Check the website for a full programme and timetable.

Henley Royal Regatta

Henley Reach, Henley-on-Thames, Oxon (01491 572153/ www.hrr.co.uk). Henley-on-Thames rail. **Date** 2-6 July 2003; 30 June-4 July 2004.

This world-famous event is a well-heeled affair, where fancy hats and blazers are given an outing, though there is in fact no dress code, and any scruffy little herbert may attend. Nearly 300 races are held over the five days, with participating rowing crews from all over the world. A fireworks display is usually held on one of the evenings – call to check – and while picnics are not allowed, catering facilities and a bar are available.

Greenwich & Docklands International Festival

various venues near the Thames (8305 1818/ www.festival.org). **Date** 4-26 July 2003.

The programme for this year's Greenwich & Docklands Festival focuses on free outdoor spectacles and performances with a family-friendly appeal. The range of international activities and projects includes 'Encounters' (2-5 July), which marks the 400th anniversary of the death of Elizabeth I with a sculptural banquet, community choirs, pyrotechnics and multi-media effects. 'Dancing City' (12 July) features contemporary dance at Canary Wharf, 'Fanfire!' combines percussion and pyrotechnics at the Docklands campus of the University of East London, 'Heroines' (25, 26 July) celebrates the achievements of British South Asian women with performances, projections and music at Three Mills Green, and 'Tattoo' (26 July) has street theatre performances at Royal Arsenal Woolwich. Check the website for further details and updates.

London Heathrow Youth Games

Crystal Palace National Sports Centre, Ledrington Road, SE20 (8778 0131). Crystal Palace rail. **Date** 10-13 July 2003.

This mini Olympics event, now in its 26th year, sees 10,000 sporting hopefuls aged under 19 represent 33 London boroughs in sports competitions. The teams are selected through schools and development teams locally, and activities include archery, fencing, canoeing, football, tennis, athletics and show jumping. Call for a programme of events; over 400 spectators are admitted each day.

Soho Festival

St Anne's Gardens & part of Wardour Street, W1 (7439 4303/www.thesohosociety.org.uk). Tottenham Court Road tube. **Map** p317 K6. **Date** 13 July 2003.

Lots of family fun in the heart of the West End in aid of the Soho Society: attractions include a spaghetti-eating competition, live bands and Chinese lion dancers. Food, crafts, book and face-painting stalls are added draws, and spectators can cheer along a tug-of-war between Soho firemen and members of the Soho Society. The highlight of the day is the waiters' and bartenders' race at 4pm: watch the trail of fallen items grow as the racers negotiate a course around Soho with laden trays.

Rotherhithe Festival

various locations, Rotherhithe SE16 (7231 7845/ www.timeandtalents.org.uk). **Date** 13 July 2003.

A tribute to this enchanting part of the city, with roadshow, stalls, music recitals, street performers, sea-shanties, bouncy castles and a whole raft of family activities. Free buses run throughout the day to local attractions and venues on the peninsula, including the Surrey Docks Farm, Watersports Centre and the Brunel Engine House. Admission is free.

Swan Upping on the Thames

various points along the Thames. **Date** 14-18 July 2003.
Today, the Crown still owns all unmarked mute swans in open water, although in practice this means only certain parts of the Thames. Once a year the Queen's Swan Marker and the Swan Uppers of the Vinters' and Dyers' livery companies count, ring and check the health of the swans. Officials wear scarlet uniforms and each traditional Thames rowing skiff flies appropriate flags and pennants. When a brood of cygnets is sighted, a signalling cry of 'All up!' is given and the boats move into position. On passing Windsor Castle, the rowers stand to attention with oars raised and salute 'Her Majesty the Queen, Seigneur of the Swans'. This quaintly archaic ceremony can be seen from the towpaths along the Thames, starting at Sunbury Lock on 14 July.

Lambeth Country Show

Brockwell Park, SE24 (7926 6200). Brixton tube/rail then 2, 3, 37, 196 bus/Herne Hill rail. **Date** 26, 27 July 2003 (call to confirm dates).
This annual urban country show fills Brockwell Park with a mix of farmyard and domestic animal attractions (horse show, dog show, farm animals). Aside from meeting and greeting critters, kids can have fun on the bouncy castles and fairground rides, and there are also food and craft stalls, music and dancing.

Royal Horticultural Society Garden, Wisley

Woking, Surrey (01483 224234/www.rhs.org.uk/wisley). West Byfleet or Woking rail then taxi. **Date** 26 July- 10 Aug 2003.
One of Britain's best loved gardens, Wisley's 240 acres of richly planted borders, luscious rose gardens and exotica arrayed in glasshouses have long delighted horticulturists. Family Fortnight offers children aged between three and 12 a chance to get as green-fingered and grubby as their parents with fun introductory workshops (for a fee of £8). Children can learn about the culinary uses of herbs and choose a couple to plant up and take home in terracotta pots they've decorated themselves with aboriginal designs. There are also colouring competitions, puppet shows, garden trails and (conservation-oriented) storytelling, as well as percussion groups to make music using natural materials such as shells, gourds and seeds.

Marine Week

various locations throughout the South-East (7261 0447/ www.wildlondon.org.uk). **Date** 2-10 Aug 2003.
Marine Week comprises 50 free events in various places – all with the aim of introducing people to marine life. In 2002 events included a beach party at Hammersmith foreshore, Born to be Tidal arts events in front of Tate Modern and pirate boat trips in Camden. Call or check the website for information on what's happening in your area.

Notting Hill Carnival

Notting Hill, W10, W11 (8964 0544). Ladbroke Grove, Notting Hill or Westbourne Park tube. **Date** 24, 25 Aug 2003.
People who continue to associate the carnival with oppressive or intimidating crowds clearly aren't going on family parade day, held on 24 August (noon-9pm). The colourfully costumed dancers and performers from the many steel bands, Soca sound systems and floats, and infectious carnival spirit make even the most inhibited adults dance in the street, which works wonders on their kids.

Even better, why not buy a costume (from around £25) and enrol them with your nearest Masquerade or 'Mas' band through the carnival office (8964 0544). Clubs cater for various age groups, from babies to 16-year-olds, with the option of practising at meet-ups throughout the summer holidays or just turning up on the afternoon and falling into line with the

Mayor's Thames Festival

others (smaller children will be given places on the floats). It's not compulsory, completely unchoreographed and quite possibly the most fun you'll have all year. Check the website (www.nhct.org.uk) for regular updates.

Autumn

Great River Race
on the Thames, from Richmond, Surrey, to Island Gardens, E14 (8398 9057). **Date** 6 Sept 2003.
More than 250 boats compete in this 22-mile river marathon, aiming to scoop the UK Traditional Boat Championship. The race sets off from Ham House in Richmond at 11.20am and passes many historic landmarks until the finish at Island Gardens near Greenwich. This race attracts many fascinating entries from all over the world, and uniquely, also from crews of under-14s, who pit themselves against adults. Would-be competitors should contact the organisers for further information. Look out for replica Viking longships, stone age log boats, Chinese dragon-boats and the royal barge constructed for last year's Jubilee, the 'Jubilant'. Parents will inevitably hum along to a certain 1970s TV show theme tune as the Hawaiian outrigger canoes speed past.

Regent Street Festival
Regent Street, W1 (info 7491 4429). Oxford Circus tube. **Map** p318 J6. **Date** 7 Sept 2003.
Now in its fourth year, this free festival attracts over 120,000 visitors, so grab a programme in time for the noon kick-off. A celebrity opening from a stage situated at the junction of Regent Street and New Burlington Street is followed by live music (rock, pop, jazz, classical) which continues until 8pm. Regent Street is closed to traffic and packed with activities; highlights being a funfair, rides in a kids' train, toy demos, and a police exhibition area with dogs and horses. There are

also entertainers, storytelling, face painters and magicians. Many stores and restaurants will be offering special promotions, competitions and al fresco dining at food courts.

Mayor's Thames Festival
on the Thames, between Waterloo Bridge & Blackfriars Bridge (7928 8998/www.thamesfestival.org). **Map** p320 M7-O7. **Date** 13, 14 Sept 2003.
A celebration of the river, featuring a wealth of activities over the weekend. On Saturday, there are funfairs, food and craft markets, a picnic party and creative installations on the river and foreshore. Workshops and foreshore activities will appeal to environmentally-minded kids, and Improbable Theatre's *Sticky* outdoor show promises an innovative and fun spectacle for all. Don't miss the charity Thames Duck Race – tens of thousands of plastic yellow ducks bobbing on the tide from Waterloo Bridge – and the first duck past the London Eye wins a mystery 'massive prize'. On Sunday, the bazaars, workshops and mass choir concert remain; there are also street dance, costume parades, an Indian carnival and children's activities. The highlight is the 'Midnight Menagerie' night procession, featuring an enormous inflatable dragon, a parade of mythical and magical creatures, bands, illuminated boats, lantern processions, and a spectacular fireworks finale. Unmissable – and all free!

CBBC Prom in the Park
Hyde Park (booking/info line 0870 899 8001/www.bbc. co.uk/proms). Hyde Park Corner tube. **Map** p313 F7. **Date** 14 Sept 2003.
Hosted this year by presenters Angellica Bell and Matt Baker, this musical party is a light-hearted family afternoon out, featuring top acts from the charts and favourite stars from CBBC programmes as well as accessible classical music from the BBC Philharmonic. Gates open at 1pm and the on-stage entertainment starts at 2.30pm. Entry is free for under-threes.

City Harvest Festival
Capel Manor Gardens, Bullsmoor Lane, Enfield, Middx (8366 4442/www.capel.ac.uk). Turkey Street rail. **Date** 20 Sept 2003.
The urban farms we all love have a pleasant day out in the leafy acres of Enfield for this agricultural extravaganza. Events include a farm animal show and arena events, milking and shearing demonstrations, vegetable and plant sales, craft displays and stalls and children's activities.

London Open House
various venues throughout London (www.londonopen house.org). **Date** 20, 21 Sept 2003.
Now in its 11th year, this event is held to promote awareness and to celebrate the wealth of magnificent architecture across London. It's a wonderful chance to gain access to more than 500 buildings free of charge, many of which are usually closed to the public, from private homes to civic and industrial institutions, grand historical buildings to pumping stations. Some local boroughs also run architecture-related workshops and activities for children. Check the website for a full list of participating buildings in your area.

Horseman's Sunday
Church of St John & St Michael, Hyde Park Crescent, W2 (7262 1732). Edgware Road tube/Paddington tube/rail. **Map** p313 E6. **Date** 21 Sept 2003.
This ceremony dates back to 1969, when local riding stables fearing closure held an open-air service to protest. Starting at noon, a vicar on horseback rides out to bless and present rosettes to a procession of horses and riders, and delivers a short service with hymns and occasional guest speakers.

While there's little interaction between onlookers and the horses, it's nonetheless enjoyable to escape the suburbs to watch this equine pageant in the lovely setting of Hyde Park.

Punch & Judy Festival

Covent Garden Piazza, WC2 (7836 9136). Covent Garden tube. **Map** p319 L7. **Date** 5 Oct 2003.
With roots deep in folk drama and storytelling, Punch & Judy's brand of knockout nonsense has delighted children for centuries. This festival celebrates the enduring appeal of Old Red Nose and his long-suffering wife, engaging in mischief and slapstick and providing shout-along fun for kids of all ages. There will be performances dotted around the market building, with performances at set times, and this year the organisers are looking for young performers to have a go at staging a show (call in advance for details) and to join the Punch & Judy Fellowship. There are prizes awarded, and for non-entrants, puppetry goodies and memorabilia will be on sale at stands.

Pearly Kings & Queens Harvest Festival

St Martin-in-the-Fields, Trafalgar Square, WC2 (7766 1100/www.pearlies.co.uk). Charing Cross tube/rail. **Map** p319 L7. **Date** 5 Oct 2003.
Arrive early for the 3pm harvest thanksgiving service to watch the arrival of London's pearly kings and queens, splendidly dressed in their pearl button-covered suits. The vicar also wears a pearly stole during attendance, and St Martin's is decorated with fruit and harvest baskets. The crypt downstairs houses a brass-rubbing centre and café, and there's a market in the church grounds, should you wish to only observe the arrivals but not attend the hour-long service.

Trafalgar Day Parade

Trafalgar Square, WC2 (7928 8978/www.sea-cadets.org). Charing Cross tube/rail. **Map** p319 K7. **Date** 26 Oct 2003.
This grand parade of uniformed sea cadets and marching bands commemorates the 197th anniversary of the Battle of Trafalgar and the death of Admiral Lord Nelson, ending with the laying of a wreath at the foot of Nelson's Column in Trafalgar Square. Kids can board the Sea Cadets mobile display unit – a 1960s Routemaster bus – converted into the control room of a Royal Navy submarine, where they can raise the periscope, stalk enemy ships with sonar contacts, and try out their skills on dive-dive-dive action stations.

State Opening of Parliament

House of Lords, Palace of Westminster, SW1 (7219 4272/www.parliament.uk). Westminster tube. **Map** p319 L9. **Date** early/mid Nov 2003.
The state opening of Parliament by the Queen is a colourful ceremony that has changed little since the 16th century. Large crowds gather to watch her arrival and departure from the Palace of Westminster in the spectacular State Coach, attended by the Household Cavalry. As she enters the House of Lords, a gun salute is fired.The Queen's Speech, in the House of Lords, may only be observed via television.

London to Brighton Veteran Car Run

starting at Serpentine Road, Hyde Park, W2 (01753 681736). Hyde Park Corner tube. **Map** p313 E8. **Date** 2 Nov 2003.
This annual commemoration of the Emancipation Run of 1896 is now more of a motoring spectacle of 400 vintage cars than a race, although bronze medals are awarded to all who reach Brighton before 4.30pm. The first group of cars are the older ones, leaving Hyde Park Corner at 7.30am, so set your

alarm clock early to catch some real classics. If you can't get there, join the crowds lining the rest of the procession route, via Parliament Square and Westminster Bridge, then on through the streets of south London.

Bonfire Night

Date 5 Nov 2003.
Every year Britain celebrates the failure of the Gunpowder Plot of 1605, when Guy Fawkes attempted to blow up James I and his Parliament. A 'guy' is burnt on a giant bonfire and fireworks are let off. Most public displays are held on the weekend nearest to 5 November; among the best in London are those at Primrose Hill, Alexandra Palace and Crystal Palace. It's best to phone your council or check the local press nearer the time for specific details of individual firework displays (often free), as events have been known to be cancelled (usually due to bad weather) at the 11th hour.

Lord Mayor's Show

various streets in the City (7606 3030/www.lordmayors show.org). **Date** 8 Nov 2003.
One of London's most colourful and ancient traditions, this spectacle dates back to 1215 and the charter King John granted the City to elect its own mayor. The charter required the Lord Mayor to present himself at the Law Courts for approval and to swear loyalty to the Crown. The parade has thousands of participants: military personnel, horses, floats, figures in silly costumes, marching bands and the spectacular State Coach. Starting at 11am and marked by an aircraft flypast over the Royal Exchange, Mansion House and St Paul's Cathedral, the parade proceeds to the Royal Courts of Justice on the Strand, pausing as the Lord Mayor takes his oath, then sets off on the return journey from Victoria Embankment to Mansion House. The exact order of the procession is a closely guarded secret, but check the website nearer the time, or pick up a programme on the day.

Remembrance Sunday Ceremony

Cenotaph, Whitehall, SW1. Westminster tube/Charing Cross tube/rail. **Map** p319 L8. **Date** 9 Nov 2003.
An annual ceremony during which the Queen, the Prime Minister and other dignitaries lay poppy wreaths at the Cenotaph, Britain's national memorial to fallen heroes from both world wars, and observe two minutes' silence at 11am in their honour. Attended by hundreds of ex-servicemen, a short remembrance service is led by the Bishop of London, followed by a march down Whitehall afterwards.

Discover Dogs

Earl's Court 2 (entrance on Lillie Road), SW6 (7518 1012/www.the-kennel-club.org.uk). West Brompton tube. **Map** p314 A11. **Date** 22, 23 Nov 2003.
A canine extravaganza on a far less formal scale than Crufts, where you can meet more than 180 dogs, discuss pedigrees with breeders, and gather info on all matters of the mutt. The Good Citizen Dog Scheme offers discipline and agility courses, and children can join the Young Kennel Club, which encourages interest in care and training, and organises competitions, classes and camps. You can also meet husky teams, watch police dog agility demonstrations and witness silly (yet very watchable) doggy dances in Heelwork to Music displays.

Christmas Lights & Tree

Covent Garden, WC2 (7836 9136). Covent Garden tube. **Map** p317 L6.
Oxford Street, W1 (7629 2738). Oxford Circus tube. **Map** p316 G6.
Regent Street, W1 (7491 4429). Oxford Circus tube. **Map** p316 J6.

Giddy up! **London Harness Horse Parade**. *See p34.*

Bond Street, W1 (7821 5230). Oxford Circus tube.
Map p316 H6.
Trafalgar Square, SW1 (7983 4234). Leicester Square tube. **Map** p319 K7.
Date *all* mid Nov-early Dec 2003.
Each year since 1947, a giant fir tree given by Norway has taken up residence in Trafalgar Square. Decorative lights are switched on at a ceremony featuring carol singing and choirs. The main shopping streets boast impressive festive displays, particularly in the large department store windows, with the lights on Regent Street and Oxford Street invariably being switched on by some B-list celebrity. The lights on display at St Christopher's Place, Bond Street and Kensington High Street are often more charming and imaginative than those on the main thoroughfares.

Winter

International Showjumping Championships
Olympia, Hammersmith Road, W14 (7370 8202/ www.olympiashowjumping.com). Kensington (Olympia) tube/rail. **Date** 18-22 Dec 2003.
Top-class international showjumping action is interspersed with dog displays at the Agility Stakes, and the Shetland Pony Grand National. Trade stands located around the arena sell equestrian equipment and Christmas gifts, and a shopping village, located in the National Hall, will feature even more buys alongside riding accessories and essentials.

London International Boat Show
Excel, London Docklands, E16 (info 7069 5000/ www.londonboatshow.com). Customs House DLR. **Date** 8-18 Jan 2004.

One of London's most popular shows featuring all the latest in boating, watersports and holidays. All types of seagoing craft, from jetskis to windsurfers, are buffed up for display indoors and out, and there's also a stage for daily entertainment programmes. Sailing fans can seek out expert advice and peruse equipment for sale. Too cash-strapped for a new yacht? This is still an enjoyable day out to watch demonstrations, marine fashion shows and impressive vessels.

London International Mime Festival
various venues throughout London (7637 5661/ www.mimefest.co.uk). **Date** 10-25 Jan 2004.
This festival includes children's shows suitable for all ages, plus shows that are geared for people with hearing difficulties (they listen to the accompanying music through a loop system). It's colourful and accessible, with atmospheric lighting and design, so expect a wealth of dance-theatre, circus skills, puppetry, animation and mechanical theatre; full performance details are listed on the website.

Chinese New Year Festival
around Gerrard Street, Chinatown, W1 (7439 3822/ www.chinatown-online.co.uk). Leicester Square or Piccadilly Circus tube. **Map** p319 K6/7. **Date** 22 Jan 2004 (phone to confirm date).
The most important date in the Chinese calendar sees Chinatown colourfully decorated with red lanterns and paper dragons, crowded (sometimes uncomfortably so) with onlookers and street stallholders selling crafts and delicacies, and restaurants preparing delicious banquets. Formalities begin around noon, with musicians and drummers accompanying lion dancers through the streets. In 2003 the festivities also spread to Leicester Square, with Chinese acrobats and conjurer performances and martial arts and fireworks displays. Check the press for details of 2004's celebrations.

Spring

Great Spitalfields Pancake Day Race

Spitalfields Market (entrance on Commercial Street or Brushfield Street), E1 (7375 0441). Liverpool Street tube/rail. **Map** p321 R5. **Date** 24 Feb 2004.
Yes, those really *are* people dressed as penguins racing up and down the market with frying pans. A great giggle for both participants and spectators, these Spitalfields shenanigans are held each Shrove Tuesday in aid of Save the Children. Prizes are awarded to the best dressed team, and a shiny engraved frying pan awaits the race winner – this alone is reason enough for entry. Tossing starts at 12.30pm (pancakes are provided; bring your own pan); would-be competitors should phone the organisers a few days in advance.

London Marathon

Greenwich to Westminster Bridge via the Isle of Dogs, Victoria Embankment & St James's Park (7620 4117/ www.londonmarathon.co.uk). **Date** 18 Apr 2004 (phone to check).
Spectators can choose a vantage point from Greenwich to the Mall to cheer on the 35,000 elite and novice competitors, many of whom run the gruelling 26.2 miles in weird and wonderful fancy dress for charities. There's also a wheelchair race and a mini London Marathon for youngsters, and street entertainers and bands. Runners' applications must be in by the October before the race.

London Harness Horse Parade

Battersea Park, Albert Bridge Road, SW11 (01733 234451). Battersea Park or Queenstown Road rail/ 97, 137 bus. **Date** 12 Apr 2004.
An enjoyable Easter Monday park outing for animal lovers and families, with a fun-fair, fast-food stands and stalls as extra draws. First held in 1886, this parade sees splendidly groomed Shire horses through to dinky Shetland ponies. Judging starts from 9.30am, with a grand parade of the winners around noon. Look out for the 'young whips' – carts driven by seven- to eight-year-olds. Spangly-dressed London pearly kings and queens chat to visitors.

Museums & Galleries Month 2004

various venues (7233 9796/www.may 2004.org.uk). **Date** May-June 2004.
An annual, national event organised by museums and galleries across the country. Across London, over 250 venues will be running creative events and activities (classroom projects, open days) for all ages.

Canalway Cavalcade

Little Venice, W9 (British Waterways London (7286 6101). Warwick Avenue tube. **Date** May 2004.
Organised by the Inland Waterways, this bank holiday boat rally and trade show sees the pool of Little Venice transformed with the assembly of over 100 colourful narrowboats. The weekend's events include craft, trade and food stalls, kids' activities (canal art painting and badge-making), boat trips, beer tents and music. The charming lantern-light boat procession on is a must-see. Phone to confirm dates.

May Fayre & Puppet Festival

Garden of St Paul's Covent Garden, Bedford Street, WC2 (7375 0441). Covent Garden tube. **Map** p319 L7. **Date** 9 May 2004.
Commemorating the first sighting of Mr Punch in England by Samuel Pepys in 1662, this free day-long celebration of the art of puppetry makes for an unusual family outing. A grand procession (complete with brass band) around Covent Garden is followed by a service held in St Paul's church, with Mr Punch in the pulpit. And of course, there are Punch & Judy (and other puppet) shows, booths and stalls, as well as workshops where children can make and take home their own puppets, and dress up in hats and costumes. Bring a picnic to enjoy in the church gardens – joining in with the maypole dancing and juggling is hungry work.

Victoria Embankment Gardens Summer Events

Victoria Embankment Gardens, Villiers Street, WC2 (7375 0441/www. alternativearts.co.uk). Embankment tube. **Map** p319 L7. **Date** May-Aug 2004.
These free outdoor events across the summer include global music, dance, poetry and mime by the riverside. Activities in the 2003 festival included a Latin American cultural fiesta with music and dance, dance from diverse UK groups, midsummer performances of contemporary poetry and lunchtime contemporary jazz. There was also a cavalcade at the end of June at Paddington Recreation Ground, where clowns, jugglers, unicyclists, trapeze artists and stilt-walkers celebrated the circus and performance arts. Zeugma Opera also presented 'Lust for Life', a contemporary opera set in the city, and there was music, dance and drama from Africa, the Caribbean, America, Malaysia and Korea. Expect similar events and activities in 2004; check the website or phone nearer the time for further details.

Beating Retreat

Horseguards Parade, Whitehall, SW1 (7930 4466). Westminster tube/Charing Cross tube/rail. **Map** p319 K8. **Date** late May/early June 2004.
A colourful musical ceremony with the Mounted Bands of the Household Cavalry and the Massed Bands of the Guards Division, who beat a spectacular 'Retreat' on drums and pipes. Phone for tickets (for reserved tiered seating) to watch the hour-long march, which starts at 7pm.

Go bananas at the **Lord Mayor's Show**. *See p32.*

Around Town

Introduction

Dive in: London's lovely for all ages.

With so much to see and do, a family sightseeing trip around town needs planning. We've got every angle covered in these Around Town pages. We list the picture-postcard sights but have also travelled way out of central London to investigate the best parks, museums, city farms and galleries off the beaten tourist track. In every area, there's information on the best green spaces (**Parklife**), famous local faces and places (**London legends**) and nearby refreshment stops (**Lunch break**). And the best museums in town are free, so you can have a fab day out for the price of a family Travelcard. Pack up the coolbox and wake up the kids – London's calling.

USEFUL INFORMATION

Some of these restaurants and cafés we list in Lunch break features have their own review in the Eating chapter (*pp162-182*), but note that the review may refer to a different branch. In any case, it's always a good idea to ring to check that a listed place, whether it is a museum, gallery, restaurant or shop, is open before you visit, as some close at short notice.

If you plan to see loads of sights, it may be worth investing in a **London Pass**. The card, which lets you in free to more than 60 attractions (those that aren't free already), can be bought with or without a Travelcard thrown in. It also gives discounts in certain restaurants and theatres. For information about prices, call 0870 242 9988 or log on to www.londonpass.com. If we have included the initials '**LP**' in brackets before the admission price of a certain place, it means your London Pass will give you either free admission, tours or free entry to exhibitions. The initials '**EH**' mean that the sight is an English Heritage property, so members of the organisation can get in free to the special events taking place there. '**NT**' means that National Trust members can expect free admission.

Take a trip

By bike

London Bicycle Tour Company
1A Gabriel's Wharf, 56 Upper Ground, South Bank, SE1 (7928 6838/www.londonbicycle.com). Southwark tube/Blackfriars or Waterloo tube/rail. **Open** *Easter-Oct* 10am-6pm daily. *Nov-Easter* by appointment. **Fares** *(rickshaw) from £12 self drive.*
The bike hire company has rickshaws, which parents can pedal while the children relax on the seat behind. If you want a driver to take you to a specific place, the price is from £40 for an hour.

By bus

For a DIY tour, board a bus. London's new fleet includes the smart riverside bus, RV1, which takes a fine tour of north Southwark, crossing the river to reach Tower Gateway (east) and Covent Garden (west). The bus is stocked with information leaflets and information screens. With all bus tickets costing just £1 (40p for kids), this is thrifty sightseeing; guided bus tours, below, cost more:

Big Bus Company
7233 9533/www.bigbus.co.uk. **Departures** every 10-30mins from Green Park, Marble Arch & Victoria. *Summer* 8.30am-7pm daily. *Winter* 8.30am-4.30pm daily. **Fares** £17; £8 5s-15s; free under-5s. **Credit** AmEx, DC, MC, V.
Tickets for these informative bus rides, which include walking tours and a free river cruise, are interchangeable between routes, which cover 50 locations. Tour commentaries in 12 languages.

Original London Sightseeing Tour
8877 1722/www.theorginaltour.com. **Departures** from Baker Street, Covent Garden, Trafalgar Square, Victoria. *Summer* 9am-6pm daily. *Winter* 9.30am-5pm daily. **Fares** £15; £7.50 5s-15s; free under-5s. **Credit** MC, V.
This tour bus company's five routes allow access at over 90 stops. English-speaking or multilingual tours are available. A river cruise is included.

By duck

London Duck Tours *7928 3132/ www.londonducktours.com.* **Tours** *Feb-Nov* daily; ring for departure times. **Fares** £16.50; £11 under 12s; family ticket £49.
City of Westminster tours in a DUKW (an amphibious vehicle developed during World War II), comprise a 75-minute road and river adventure starting at the London Eye and ducking into the river at Vauxhall.

By taxi

Black Taxi Tours of London
7935 9363/www.blacktaxitours.co.uk. **Fares** *Day* £75. *Night* £85.
A tailored two-hour tour by taxi for up to five people; some of the tour guide/drivers are particularly good with children.

Southwark & Bankside

Take them to the river.

The south bank of the Thames has been slowly regenerating itself for the best part of a century. **County Hall**, now emerging as a mixed-use family entertainment centre, was begun in the 1920s, while the Festival of Britain in 1951 led to the clearance of riverside warehouses and the construction of the excellent **Royal Festival Hall**. The 1960s saw the emergence of the controversial **South Bank** complex, while the **National Theatre** followed in the '70s. Later additions, such as **Tate Modern**, the **Design Museum** and the **London Eye** continue to make the south bank what it was in Shakespeare's day – an entertainment centre.

Half a millennium ago, Southwark was famed for its inns, theatres, bear-baiting and general seediness. In fact, during the reign of Henry VIII, prostitutes lined the pockets of the Bishops of Winchester through the levy of constant fines – during this time, before the King closed the brothels down, women of easy virtue were known as Winchester Geese.

Now, of course, Southwark and the stretch of river that runs into Lambeth is a highly respectable piece of property. It is also home to some of the most charming museums in London – the **Museum of Garden History** and the **Old Operating Theatre**, for example, which provide a healthy balance to the gigantic arts institutions that are dotted liberally along the riverbank. Best of all is the generous promenade which links these attractions, a walk which hugs the river and passes conveniently and comfortably beneath busy bridges.

But the problem with fringing the river with tourist attractions is that the wealth doesn't yet appear to have penetrated far into the hinterland. Stick to the river and you'll be OK, but turn south and you will quickly discover busy roads and urban blight that is in danger of swallowing up brave little outposts like the **Bramah Museum of Tea & Coffee** or the **London Fire Brigade Museum**.

Ambitious building plans might do something to put this matter right, but most schemes are still located close to the Thames. The scheme to rebuild the South Bank Centre has ground to a halt, but something will emerge eventually (it has to). In the meantime, thankfully, the **Hayward Gallery** is getting a brand new entrance and the RFH is in the throes of a makeover. And as we went to press, pop impresario Pete Waterman was building a suite of recording studios in County Hall, specifically for local kids to book and cut a record.

Behind all this, the slab of monolithic offices on York Way adjacent to Waterloo station has been earmarked for demolition and replacement. But be warned, regeneration does have a downside: if a proposal to build Europe's tallest tower over London Bridge gets the go-ahead, it will turn this already confusing and busy district into a nightmarish building site for the next five years.

Since the useful tourist information centre under the giant stone spike near London Bridge has closed, visitors have had to find their own way around, but that's easily achieved. The new RV1 bus route links most of the area's attractions, but as usual, the best way to see the sights is on a walk. Once you're on the wonderful **Thameside Path**, the only decision to make is – which way to go? Treasures abound, whichever direction you take.

BFI London IMAX Cinema

1 Charlie Chaplin Walk, SE1 (7902 1234/www.bfi. org.uk/imax). Waterloo tube/rail. **Open** 12.30-8pm Mon-Fri; 10.45am-9.15pm Sat, Sun. **Admission** £7.50; £4.95 4s-15s; £6.20 concessions; add-on film £4.20 extra per adult or child; free under-4s. **Credit** AmEx, MC, V. **Map** p320 M8.

This drum-shaped 'image maximum' (IMAX) cinema, located within the roundabout at the southern end of Waterloo Bridge, contains the largest screen in the UK. The sheer size of the mechanics that make this system work is as impressive as the images you see on the screen: the projector is the size of a small house, while the visual and sound effects are enough to convince you that you're actually part of the action. The 450 seats are very steeply banked, so no one, not even a tot, has to look over anyone's head to see.

Most of the two- and three-dimensional films shown here are aimed at children: dinosaurs, haunted castles and undersea adventures are typical. *The Lion King* (£9.50 adults; £6 4-16 year-olds) is immensely popular, IMAX is also pinning hopes on a film from *Titanic* director James Cameron, *Ghosts of the Abyss*. This 3-D film, made especially for the IMAX format, brings you up close to the wreck of the actual Titanic. *Café. Nappy-changing facilities. Nearest picnic place: Jubilee Gardens.*

Bramah Museum of Tea & Coffee

40 Southwark Street, SE1 (7403 5650/www.bramah museum.co.uk). London Bridge tube/rail/381 bus. **Open** 10am-6pm daily. Closed 25, 26 Dec. **Admission** £4; £3.50 concessions; £3 under-14s; £10 family (2+4). **Credit** AmEx, MC, V. **Map** p310 P8.

This small but hugely informative museum was driven from its site near the river by rising rents, and has found itself a new home on busy Southwark Street. Its café, open to all (you don't have to visit the museum), is decorated in the quaint style of a traditional tea shop and serves a fabulous range of hot beverages. The museum's displays are basic, but offer up a wealth of information if you have the time to study the info

The **Dalí Universe** meets the **London Eye**. *See p40.*

GREAT FUN FOR ALL THE FAMILY

From sharks stingrays and piranhas to moray eels, lionfish and sideways walking crabs, London Aquarium is full of surprises with 350 different species to discover

Located in County Hall, right next to the London Eye, the London Aquarium is just over Westminster Bridge from Big Ben and the Houses of Parliament, and a short walk from Waterloo station

So, don't plan a day out in London with out visiting London's only Aquarium

Check out our special group, family and school rates

LONDON
AQUARIUM

FLOOD YOUR SENSES

Tel 020 7967 8000 www.londonaquarium.co.uk

sheets. For example, when a fleet of ships left England for the Far East in the 18th-century, it was a full two years before they returned with their cargo of tea; in fact, so much was the demand for tea, that the country began to have trouble paying for it. The solution was to sell Indian opium to China, in spite of official Chinese objections. That's just one of hundreds of forgotten tales this museum brings to light.
Buggy access. Café. Shop.

British Airways London Eye
Riverside Building, next to County Hall, Westminster Bridge Road, SE1 (booking line 0870 500 0600/customer services 0870 990 8883/www.ba-londoneye.com). Westminster tube/Waterloo tube/rail. **Open** *End of Jan-Apr, Oct-Dec* 9.30am-8pm daily. *May, Sept* 9.30am-8pm Mon-Thur; 9.30am-9pm Fri-Sun. *June* 9.30am-9pm Mon-Thur; 9.30am-10pm Fri-Sun. *July, Aug* 9.30am-10pm daily. Closed 25 Dec, most of Jan. **Admission** *Jan-31 Mar* £10.50; £8.50 concessions; £5 5s-15s; free under-5s. *Apr-31 Dec* £11; £10 concessions; £5.50 5-15s; free under-5s. **Credit** AmEx, MC, V. **Map** p319 M8.
Since the London Eye was constructed by British Airways to mark the year 2000, it has become one of the most familiar silhouettes on the skyline. It affords stunning views in most weather conditions. A 'flight' on the Eye is one revolution and lasts half an hour. Its stately pace, and the holiday atmosphere inside the all-window pod, makes it a suitably comfortable and literally uplifting experience for nippers.
When you're on the Eye, you can see right into the Queen's back garden at Buckingham Palace and, if the weather is good, all the way to Windsor. A £2 guide identifies the landmarks in four directions. The capsules accommodate 25 people, although the central seat is big enough for only a dozen elbow-to-elbow. Passengers are photographed before the ride and tempted with a picture at the end – £6 each, or £10 for two. Advance booking is advised; those who turn up on a whim will find long queues – especially on clear days. The ticket office, found in the adjacent corner of County Hall, is handsome and well-organised, and includes a shop and Costa Coffee outlet. Note that you can take a buggy on board, but there is a left luggage facility which rents out baby carriers.
Buggy access. Café. Nappy-changing facilities. Nearest picnic place: Jubilee Gardens.

Clink Prison Museum
1 Clink Street, SE1 (7378 1558/www.clink.co.uk). London Bridge tube/rail. **Open** 10am-6pm daily. Closed 25 Dec. **Tours** hourly when available. **Admission** £4; £3 5-15s; concessions; £9 family (2+2); free under-5s. *Tours* £2. **Credit** AmEx, DC, MC, V. **Map** p320 P8.
Located on the site of London's infamous Clink prison, this peculiar little place provides a fairly basic history of grime and punishment from the 12th to 18th centuries. Recreations show filthy miscreants making do in the squalor of what were obviously hellish conditions, while fearsome ironwear decorates the walls – shackles, chains, all the usual stuff of man's inhumanity to man. The pillory (a wooden T where the offender remains standing with his head and arms locked into place) is particularly interesting; for really heinous crimes like selling rotten meat, the victim's ears were often nailed to the contraption. Horrible. The museum is noisy with sound effects, voice-overs and overbearing monkish plainchant, which can be heard on the street outside.
Nearest picnic place: Southwark Cathedral Gardens. Shop.

Dalí Universe
County Hall, Riverside Building, Queen's Walk, SE1 (7620 2720/www.daliuniverse.com). Waterloo tube/rail. **Open** 10am-5.30pm daily. Closed 25 Dec. **Tours** phone for details. **Admission** (LP) £8.50; £7.50 concessions; £4.95 10-16s; £1 under-10s. **Credit** AmEx, DC, MC, V. **Map** p319 M8.
One of the world's largest permanent exhibitions of the works of surrealist artist Salvador Dalí lets you indulge in what often seems like artistic comedy: melting clocks, long-legged elephants, crutches, lobsters, ants and stretched buttocks casting long shadows over dreamlike sunny plains. Curated by long-time Dalí friend and collector Benjamin Levi, the exhibition covers Dalí's life and shows more than 500 pieces (not always originals) of the Spaniard's art, including the Mae West Lips sofa and artwork incorporated in the dream sequence in Hitchcock's film *Spellbound*.
Buggy access. Lift. Nearest picnic place: Jubilee Gardens. Shop.

Design Museum
28 Shad Thames, SE1 (7403 6933/www.designmuseum. org). Tower Hill tube/London Bridge tube/rail/15, 78, 100 bus. **Open** 10am-5.45pm (last entry 5.15pm) daily.

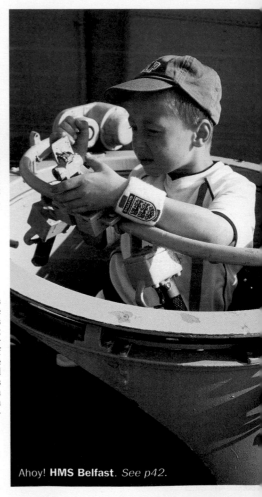

Ahoy! **HMS Belfast**. *See p42.*

Ahoy! **HMS Belfast**. *See p42.*

Admission £6; £4 5-15s, concessions; £16 family (2+2); free under-5s. **Credit** AmEx, MC, V. **Map** p321 S9.

This excellent and ever-improving Thameside museum just beyond Tower Bridge comes in three parts. A ground floor contains a café and a well-stocked shop selling both nifty little gadgets and heavyweight design tomes; an exhibition gallery for temporary shows is found upstairs, and a well-lit space for the permanent collection is on the top floor. Although the museum has a well-developed education and schools programme, most temporary exhibitions are worthy but probably have little to interest under-14s. The main collection, though, is different – this contains a variety of chairs in which you are invited to sit, as well as cabinets reminding you of what we once had to put up with (elderly vacuum cleaners, washing machines, telephones). Adults will glow with a sentimental pride, while kids will view these primitive domestic artefacts with amusement.

Buggy access. Café. Nappy-changing facilities. Nearest picnic place: Butler's Wharf riverside benches. Restaurant. Shop.

Fashion & Textile Museum

83 Bermondsey Street, SE1 (7403 0222/www.ftmlondon. org) London Bridge tube/rail. **Open** 11am-5.45pm Tue-Sun. **Admission** £6; £4 concessions, 5-16s; £16 family (2+2); free under-5s. **Credit** MC, V. **Map** p321 Q8.

Due to open as this guide went to press, this new museum represents the lifelong ambition of fashion designer Zandra Rhodes. The striking pink and yellow building, which incorporates elements from Rhodes' own textile designs, will host rotating exhibitions of fashion and textile designers – as well as paying homage to landmark boutiques. Shows on Mary Quant, Ossie Clark, John Galliano, Vidal Sassoon and Biba are promised. Museum staff also plan a range of exciting education programmes aimed at visitors of all ages.

Buggy access. Lift. Nearest picnic space: Bermondsey Playground, Leathermarket Gardens. Shop.

Florence Nightingale Museum

2 Lambeth Palace Road, SE1 (7620 0374/www.florence-nightingale.co.uk). Westminster tube/Waterloo tube/rail. **Open** 10am-5pm Mon-Fri; 11.30am-4.30pm Sat, Sun (last entry 1hr before closing). **Admission** (LP) £4.80; £3.80 5-18s, concessions; £12 family (2+2); free under-5s. **Credit** AmEx, MC, V. **Map** p319 M9.

This museum, tucked underneath the bulk of St Thomas's hospital, once had a lively education programme, but the education officer has since departed without replacement. It's not all bad news, though – a major expansion, and perhaps a new location, is planned. Focusing on the life and considerable achievements of this remarkable woman, curators are planning a major exhibition in 2004 to celebrate the 150th anniversary of Florence Nightingale's arrival in Scutari (Turkey), where she tended victims of the Crimean War. The museum also commemorates FN's birthday every 12 May. The shop sells Florence Nightingale shopping bags, tea towels, teddy bears and stacks of books about nursing.

Buggy access. Café (in hospital). Nappy-changing facilities (in hospital). Nearest picnic place: benches by entrance of St Thomas's hospital/Archbishop's Park. Restaurant (in hospital). Shop.

Golden Hinde

St Mary Overie Dock, Cathedral Street, SE1 (0870 011 8700/shop 7403 0123/www.goldenhinde.co.uk). Monument tube/London Bridge tube/rail. **Open** daily, times vary; phone for details. Closed 25 Dec. **Admission** £2.75; £2.35 concessions; £2 5-16s; £8 family (2+3); free under-4s. **Credit** MC, V. **Map** p321 P8.

This reconstruction of Sir Francis Drake's 16th-century flagship was built in 1973 to commemorate the admiral-pirate's 400th birthday, after which it sailed to San Francisco. The ship is open to the public only when no groups are visiting, so call first to check. Tickets are sold in the gift shop nearby. This beautifully made replica is surprisingly small, and one can only wonder at the conditions experienced by 16th-century sailors on their circumnavigation of the globe. The main gun deck can't be more than 3ft high (apparently the average height of the crew in Drake's day was 5ft 4in). The present 'crew' are students and actors who dress up and shout a lot. Children's activities include overnight living history experiences for sixes to 12s, pirate parties and workshops where kids learn Tudor songs and how to load a cannon.

Nearest picnic place: Southwark Cathedral Gardens/riverside benches. Shop.

Hayward Gallery

Belvedere Road, SE1 (box office 7960 4242/ www.hayward.org.uk). Embankment tube/Waterloo tube/rail. **Open** *During exhibitions* 10am-6pm Mon,

Thur-Sun; 10am-8pm Tue, Wed (phone to check). **Admission** varies; phone for details. **Credit** AmEx, DC, MC, V. **Map** p320 M8.

The Hayward Gallery is one of the most versatile exhibition spaces in Britain, but a rebuilding programme means it is closed until autumn 2003 (it reopens on 23 October). Visitors are promised a new entrance, an extended foyer and a new café. The architects behind the scheme were responsible for the highly successful remodelling of the Royal Court Theatre in Chelsea a couple of years back, and this time they are collaborating with American light artist Dan Graham. The neon tower on the roof was commissioned by the Arts Council in 1970. Its yellow, red, green and blue tubes are controlled by changes in the direction and strength of the wind.
Buggy access. Café. Lifts. Nappy-changing facilities. Nearest picnic place: Jubilee Gardens/riverside benches. Shop.

HMS Belfast

Morgan's Lane, Tooley Street, SE1 (7940 6323/6336/ www.iwm.org.uk). London Bridge tube/rail. **Open** *Mar-Oct* 10am-6pm daily. *Nov-Feb* 10am-5pm daily. Last entry 45mins before closing. **Admission** (LP) £8; £4.40 concessions; free under-16s (must be accompanied by an adult). **Credit** MC, V. **Map** p321 R8.

A sense of high adventure beckons children to this 11,500-ton World War II battlecruiser, now floating peacefully on the Thames between Tower and London bridges. Guided tours take in all nine decks, from the bridge to the boiler room, visiting the galley, sick bay, dentist, NAAFI canteen, mess deck and the permanent exhibition entitled HMS *Belfast* in War and Peace. Films, photos, documents and quiz sheets enhance the experience. But what kids really want to see are the three sets of guns that destroyed the German battleship *Scharnhorst* in 1943 and supported the D-Day landing a year later. There's usually a queue to climb into the port deck Bofors gun, which young enthusiasts can swivel, elevate and aim. The 'kip in a ship' experience is for groups of up to 50 children who sleep in the original sailors' bunks for up to three days. Accompanying adults take the officers' cabins.

The school holidays bring free daily study programmes aimed at seven- to-14-year-olds; term-time school events involve tailor-made workshops and talks.
Café. Nappy-changing facilities. Nearest picnic place: William Curtis Park. Shop.

London Aquarium

County Hall, Riverside Building, Westminster Bridge Road, SE1 (7967 8000/www.londonaquarium.co.uk). Westminster tube/Waterloo tube/rail. **Open** 10am-6pm (last entry 5pm) daily. Phone for later opening times during holidays. Closed 25 Dec. **Tours** (groups of 10 or more) phone for details. **Admission** (LP) £8.75; £6.50 concessions; £5.25 3-14s; £3.50 disabled; £25 family (2+2); free under-3s. **Credit** MC, V. **Map** p319 M9.

More than 350 species of fish are on view here in the bowels of County Hall. But it's the fish feeding frenzy which drives the kids wild. The sharks, named after characters on the 1970s children's show *Rainbow*, are fed on Tuesdays, Thursdays and Saturdays at 2.30pm; piranhas get their fill on Mondays, Wednesdays, Fridays and Sundays at 1pm. Divers descend into the Atlantic tank daily at noon to feed the rays, skates, dogfish and conger eels that dwell at the bottom. Children love the two touch-pools where they can stroke the skates and rays as they rise to the surface, or pat the crabs if they're careful. Talks takes place on the hour from 1-4pm, on subjects including sharks and coral reefs. An adoption scheme raises money to finance the upkeep of the fish. For £30-£80 adopters receive pictures, information and

regular bulletins on their ward's progress, while a £75 annual family card gets you in as often as you like. There's no cloak-room, so arrive as unencumbered as possible.
Buggy access. Café. Lifts. Nappy-changing facilities. Nearest picnic place: Jubilee Gardens. Shop.

London Dungeon

28-34 Tooley Street, SE1 (7403 7221/www.thedungeons. com). London Bridge tube/rail. **Open** *Late Mar-mid July* 10am-5.30pm daily. *Mid July-early Sept* 10am-7.30pm daily. *Early Sept-late Oct* 10am-5.30pm daily. *Early Nov-late Mar* 10.30am-5pm daily. Closed 25 Dec. **Admission** £12.50; £10 students; £7.50 5-14s, concessions; £2 reduction for wheelchair users, carers free; free under-5s. **Credit** AmEx, MC, V. **Map** p321 Q8.

Set under the Victorian railway arches of London Bridge, this museum is not recommended for young children or for those who object to fibreglass stonework and gravestones. Queues are often long during the summer months, in spite of the hefty admission prices. Once inside, the different exhibits attempt to recreate the horror of crime and punishment throughout the ages. The dark, grimy air, the haunting sounds and the disorientation evoked by weaving your way around different areas all add to the general atmosphere of ghastliness.

From spring 2003 white-faced visitors have been queuing up to catch the Great Plague: an actor-led attraction groaning with boils, chamber pots, piles of corpses, scuttling rats and a huge skull with wriggling worms. The Plague joins other London attractions, such as The Great Fire and the Judgement Day Barge, in their mission to deliver the grisliest history of London. Do not inflict this on anyone of a nervous or highly sensitive disposition. The shop is a delight for lovers of fake blood, stick-on warts and edible eyeballs.
Café. Nappy-changing facilities. Nearest picnic place: Hay's Galleria. Shop.

London Fire Brigade Museum

94A Southwark Bridge Road, SE1 (7587 2894/ www.london-fire.gov.uk). Borough tube/344 bus. **Tours** 10.30am, 2pm Mon-Fri by appointment only. Closed bank hols, 25 Dec. **Admission** £3; £2 7s-14s, concessions; free under-7s. **Credit** MC, V. **Map** p320 O9.

Visitors must book in advance for this museum of firefighting in London. Tours last roughly an hour and take in the appliance bay, where pumps dating back to 1708 stand in tribute to blazes of the past. Small children are given colouring pencils and encouraged to draw any of the 20 fire engines, ranging from a hand-pumped 1750s model to shiny red and brass vehicles from the early 20th century and today's stream-lined marvels. Older kids can try on uniforms. Exhibits in the eight small rooms detail the history of firefighting since the Great Fire in 1666 and include uniforms, equipment and paintings, including those executed by firemen-artists recording their Blitz experiences. The museum also displays one of only three George Crosses to be awarded to firefighters. Plastic fireman's helmets are on sale in the shop.
Nearest picnic place: Mint Street Park. Shop.

Museum of Garden History

Church of St Mary-at-Lambeth, Lambeth Palace Road, SE1 (7401 8865/www.museumgardenhistory.org). Lambeth North or Westminster tube/C10, 3, 344, 77, 507 bus. **Open** *Feb-mid Dec* 10.30am-5pm daily. **Admission** free; suggested donation £3; £2.50 concessions. **Credit** *Shop* (over £10) AmEx, MC, V. **Map** p310 L10.

This is a little green gem. Nestled against Lambeth Palace on a busy road junction, this former church transports you to a quieter, simpler time. Deconsecrated in 1972, St Mary's became the world's first museum dedicated to gardening – a

PARKLIFE Bankside's greensward

This slice of Thameside is not reknowned for its parks – you have to go west to Battersea or east to Greenwich for really grand open spaces. But Southwark and Bankside do, instead, have a wonderful promenade peppered with unexpected chunks of grass and landscaping.

In fact, it is one of these chunks that is inordinately holding up the redevelopment of the South Bank Centre. **Jubilee Gardens** – that large, flat and fairly bland slab of lawn fronting the London Eye – is Metropolitan Open Land, a designation that forbids building work. It was unfortunate, then, that architect Rick Mather suggested raising this tract of grassland and creating a rejuvenated South Bank Centre underneath. Local campaigners have been vociferous in their condemnation of the plan, which seems dead in the water, while Jubilee Gardens remains nothing very special. There is a tidy and well-equipped children's playground at its southern edge, though, with swings, ropewalks, a climbing frame and a slide.

William Curtis Park is much the same – another rather bland expanse, this time separating Tower Bridge from Ken Livingstone's egg-shaped GLA building (which has a useful stopping point in its granite amphitheatre outside). But as with Jubilee Gardens, the principal attraction of William Curtis Park is its location. The views from here are unparalleled, with unimpeded sightlines straight over to the Tower of London, while the muscular bulk of the Victorian gothic bridge soars above you. Fair weather makes this an ideal picnic spot and a place to relax after traipsing around the London Dungeon, HMS Belfast or the Design Museum.

Tate Modern has its own gardens. But, like much of its art, the grounds are rather uncompromising, with rubber-coated steel benches, which dissuade you from staying for too long. Littered with gangs of students and school parties in the summer, this north-facing garden has one significant drawback – the shadow of the Tate itself can obliterate much of the sun. But on hot days, this is a blessed relief.

Jubilee Gardens
Belvedere Road, SE1. Waterloo tube/rail.

William Curtis Park
Tooley Street, SE1. London Bridge tube/rail.

suitable function for a building which encompasses the tomb of the Tradescants, the pioneering family of gardeners and botanists. It was they who brought the first pineapple to Britain, much to the astonishment of the Stuart kings (explaining the motif in the stonework on nearby Lambeth Bridge). Captain William Bligh, of *Bounty* fame, is also buried here, along with half a dozen Archbishops of Canterbury. The exhibits are fascinating; they include giant seeds and gardening gear dating back centuries. Look out for the Pedlar's Window, a stained glass window illustrating a man and his dog. History has it that an early 16th-century pedlar came into an acre of land (now the site of County Hall) and donated it to the church on condition that an image of him be preserved in glass. The current window is the fourth, made in 1956 after its predecessor was destroyed in 1941. A plaque on the perimeter wall of St Thomas's, around the corner, records that Lieutenant Colonel John By, founder of Canada's capital Ottawa, was christened at St Mary's in 1779.
Buggy access. Café. Nearest picnic place: Archbishop's Park. Shop.

Namco Station
County Hall (riverfront entrance), Westminster Bridge Road, SE1 (7967 1066/www.namcostation.co.uk). Westminster tube/Waterloo tube/rail. **Open** 10am-midnight daily. Closed 25 Dec. **Admission** (LP) free. Games prices vary. **Map** p319 M9.
This is one of those dark, noisy hideaways beloved of children with pocket-money to waste. Three floors of slot machines and interactive games with names like House of the Dead and Beach Head 2000 line the walls, while bumper cars (£2 per car) and a bowling alley lurk downstairs (as do over-18s, who inhabit a bar tuned to the sports channel). McDonald's and an Oriental Buffet are next door.
Bar. Buggy access. Lifts. Nearest picnic place: Jubilee Gardens.

Old Operating Theatre, Museum & Herb Garret
9A St Thomas's Street, SE1 (7955 4791/www.thegarret. org.uk). London Bridge tube/rail. **Open** 10.30am-5pm (last entry 4.45pm) daily. Closed 15 Dec-5 Jan. **Admission** (LP) £4; £3 concessions; £2.50 6-16s; £10 family (2+4); free under-6s. **No credit cards. Map** p321 Q8.
A genuine Victorian operating theatre is the centrepiece of this wonderful museum whose education staff run talks and demonstrations to pre-booked groups of youngsters. Be sure to check in advance if talks are suitable for young ones – the subject matter can be fairly gruesome. Pills and Potions, aimed at seven- to 11-year-olds, shows the manufacture of medicines from herbs into tablets, infusions and creams. Victorian Surgery, suitable for less squeamish older students, includes the re-enactment of an amputation using a volunteer from the audience and real antique surgical equipment. Students, then as now, watch in nauseated wonder from the tiered observation gallery as the patient is laid on a wooden operating table resembling an old ironing board. Exhibits in the herb garret illustrate the history of medicine and nursing at Guy's and St Thomas's hospitals. Jars filled with formaldehyde preserve fascinating specimens. Note: a very narrow spiral staircase of 32 steps leads up to the museum and there are no lifts. Small children will have to be guided carefully.
Nearest picnic place: Southwark Cathedral Gardens. Shop.

Royal National Theatre
South Bank, SE1 (info 7452 3400/box office 7452 3000/www.nationaltheatre.org.uk). Waterloo tube/rail. **Open** 10am-11pm Mon-Sat. *Box office* 10am-8pm Mon-Sat. Closed 24, 25 Dec, Good Friday. **Tickets** *Olivier & Lyttelton* £10-£38. *Cottesloe* £10-£25. *Standby* £8, £16. *Backstage tours* £5; £4.25 concessions. **Credit** AmEx, DC, MC, V. **Map** p320 M8.

Burning to be a fireman? See if the cap fits at **London Fire Brigade Museum**. *See p42*.

Sir Denys Lasdun's landmark concrete theatre complex was remodelled a couple of years ago, and is now a far more accessible and friendly place than it was. Its ground floor terrace provides a decent, if little used, setting for refreshments while free exhibitions and music are commonly found inside. The NT runs a wide range of education and activity programmes, from half-term events to school-based initiatives. Activities take place throughout the year (call 7452 3388 for details).

Backstage tours (not suitable for under-sevens) occur three times a day throughout the year, last an hour and may be booked at the information desk (£5). Tours take in the rehearsal rooms, workshops where costumes and props are made, dressing rooms and the stage, where the guide demonstrates some of the more exciting items of stage machinery like the flying harnesses.

Buggy access. Cafés. Lifts. Nappy-changing facilities. Nearest picnic place: Bernie Spain Gardens. Restaurants. Shop.

Saatchi Gallery

County Hall, riverfront & Belvedere Road entrances, SE1 (7823 2363/advance tickets 0870 1160 278/ www.saatchi-gallery.co.uk). Westminster tube/Waterloo tube/rail. **Open** 10am-6pm Mon-Thur, Sun; 10am-10pm Fri, Sat (group bookings by appointment). **Admission** £8.50; £6.50 concessions; £5 pre-booked groups (over 10 people). **Credit** MC, V. **Map** p319 M9.

Charles Saatchi's collection of preserved sharks, sheep, cow parts, unmade beds and frozen blood moved from St John's Wood into County Hall in April 2003. The spaces are superb, occupying a suite of oak panelled rooms that were once the preserve of London's elected representatives. Thankfully, the designers have tried hard to do the bare minimum to the original building, and the artworks contrast magnificently with the institutional architecture. The main exhibition space, the circular conference hall, contains the most infamous works by *enfants terribles* Damien Hirst (who kicked off the exhibition programme with a six-month retrospective), Tracey Emin, Sarah Lucas et al – while smaller spaces provide more intimate settings for individual pieces. Aside from what one might think of the artwork, the Saatchi collection provides a much-needed element of respectability to County Hall. This is a serious art gallery, which will go a long way to balance a general drift towards cheap and tacky venues which have gained a worrying foothold in this glorious building.
Buggy access. Nearest picnic: Jubilee Gardens. Shop.

Shakespeare's Globe Exhibition

21 New Globe Walk, Bankside, SE1 (7902 1500/ www.shakespeares-globe.org). Mansion House or Southwark tube/London Bridge tube/rail. **Open** Oct-Apr 10am-5pm daily. *May-Sept Exhibition & theatre tour 9am-noon daily. Exhibition & virtual tour 12.30-4pm daily.* **Admission** *Late Sept-mid May* £8; £6.50 concessions; £5.50 5-15s; £24 family (2+3); free under-5s. *Mid May-late Sept (exhibition only)* £5; £4 concessions; £3.50 5-16s; free under-5s. **Credit** MC, V. **Map** p320 O7.

This is an authentic reconstruction of the Bard's own theatre, the 'wooden O' referred to in *Henry V*, built only 100 yards from where the original stood. The project was masterminded and paid for by American actor Sam Wanamaker, although he didn't live to see it through to completion. The construction is entirely as the original looked: oak beams, wattle and daub walls, thatched roof and wooden pegs holding it all together. Actor-led tours and workshops take place throughout the year and include attendance at stage performances from May to September. The theatre lies behind iron gates and beyond the Elizabethan-esque administration buildings. Exhibits include few period artefacts but plenty of costumes, props, touch-screen information displays and models of the theatres in Southwark at the end of the 16th century.

The remains of the Rose Theatre, discovered in 1989 during building work, lie around the corner in the basement of an office block. The Rose was where many of Shakespeare's early works were performed (he probably even acted in them).
Buggy access. Café. Nappy-changing facilities. Nearest picnic place: Southwark Cathedral Gardens. Restaurant. Shop.

South Bank Centre

Belvedere Road, SE1 (box office 7960 4203/poetry library 7921 0943/www.rfh.org.uk). Waterloo tube/rail. **Open** 10am-10pm daily. Closed 25 Dec. **Admission** *Foyers* free. **Map** p319 M8.

LONDON LEGEND Tradescant's Ark

John Tradescant, the professional gardener and servant of James I, is buried in the church of St Mary-at-Lambeth – now the home of the marvellous **Museum of Garden History** (*see p42*). Tradescant was also an avid collector. His treasure included, if the records are to be believed, two inch-long dragons, feathers from a phoenix, a piece of stone from the tomb of John the Baptist and a white blackbird.

Tradescant, who was widely travelled even by today's standards, displayed his collection in a (since demolished) building called Turret House. Most of the collection was legitimate – birds, fish, fossils, shells and fruits – which would have been curiosities of considerable interest four centuries ago, but it was the more dubious artefacts (such as Easter eggs from the Patriarchs of Jerusalem) that made what was nicknamed 'Tradescant's Ark' one of the regular sights of the borough.

The history of this collection is as bizarre as the claims made for its content. After the death of Tradescant, the items passed to his son – also called John, also a well-travelled and highly respected gardener, and also buried in St Mary-at-Lambeth. Tradescant junior added to the collection and passed it to his wife upon his death in 1662. But antiquary Alias Ashmole, a friend of the family, contested the will and complained that Mrs Tradescant was selling off some of the more valuable items to private collectors. Ashmole, who argued that the collection had been promised to him, then built a house next door to the 'ark' and harassed Mrs T until he drove her to distraction. She drowned herself in a pond.

Ashmole then acquired the collection, minus dragons and phoenix feathers, which he handed over to Oxford University – forming the core of what is now the world-famous Ashmolean Museum.

LUNCH BREAK

Various cafés and ice-cream shops are dotted around the **Tate Modern** grounds, where clusters of people lounge about and enjoy their picnics on the benches and grassy areas.

Butler's Wharf Chop House (Butler's Wharf Building, 36E Shad Thames SE1, 7403 3403), a smart Conran restaurant with excellent brunches at weekends.

Café 2 (Second floor, Tate Modern, Bankside, SE1 (7401 5014), a lovely place for a light lunch, drinks and cakes – if you can bag a table.

Cantina del Ponte (Butlers Wharf Building, 36C Shad Thames, SE1, 7403 5403), for a children's menu that includes soup, pizza and grilled chicken.

fish! (Cathedral Street, Borough Market, SE1, 7407 3803 & County Hall, Belvedere Road, SE1, 7401 6734; see p162), for fish in many varieties, or there's chicken on the children's menu if they prefer.

The People's Palace (Level 3, Royal Festival Hall, South Bank Centre, SE1, 7928 9999; see p162), smart though not snooty, with a kids' menu and fab views.

Pizza Express (4 Borough High Street, SE1, 7407 2995 & The Cardamon Building, 31 Shad Thames, SE1, 7403 8484; see p175), just the place if it's pizzas you fancy.

Southwark Cathedral Refectory (Southwark Cathedral, Monague Close, SE1 7407 5740; see p162), a lovely café that serves hot dishes and great cakes.

Starbucks (Winchester Wharf, Clink Street, SE1, 7403 0951), a deliciously cosy place to come to after a wintry visit to the Golden Hinde.

The South Bank Centre is made up of the Royal Festival Hall, the Purcell Room and the Queen Elizabeth Hall. The RFH is the most accessible of the three, a beautiful 'people's palace' that frequently runs free lunchtime musical events and public art shows. A smart new café opened in spring 2003, which makes a visit even more enjoyable. Gamelan, an Indonesian percussion ensemble, is a popular pursuit for over-sevens. Taster days are run at regular intervals, while a whole term's worth of banging and crashing can be booked for £26 by joining the Gong Club. Half-Term Heaven events tend to be fun, even barmy affairs (see p208).
Buggy access. Cafés. Lifts. Nappy-changing facilities. Restaurant.

Southwark Cathedral

Montague Close, SE1 (7367 6700/tours 7367 6734/tours 7367 6734/www.dswark.org). London Bridge tube/rail. **Open** *from 8am daily (closing times vary). Exhibition* 10am-6pm Mon-Sat; 11am-5pm Sun (last admission 30mins before closing). *Services* 8am, 8.15am, 12.30pm, 12.45pm, 5.30pm Mon-Fri; 9am, 9.15am, 4pm Sat; 8.45am, 9am, 11am, 3pm, 6.30pm Sun. **Admission** (LP) *Exhibition* £3; £2.50 concessions; £1.50 5-15s; £12.50 family (2+2); free under-5s. *Audio tour* £2.50; £2 OAPs; £1.25 under-16s, students. **Credit** AmEx, MC, V. **Map** p321 8P.

This beautiful and partly ancient building (a cathedral only since 1905) now boasts a new suite of facilities added in 2000, offering an interactive museum (the Long View of London), a well-stocked shop and a refectory (see p162). The architects worked hard to make the recent additions sympathetic to the medieval and Victorian structure, and it's a blend that works.

The church, which dates back to the 13th century, is a historian's treasure trove. As well as recent memorials – including one for the 51 victims of the *Marchioness* riverboat tragedy – there are memorials to Shakespeare (whose brother Edmund is buried here), John Gower (supposedly the first English poet) and John Harvard, benefactor of Harvard University. There's also a picturesque tomb topped by a stone carving of an emaciated body wrapped in a shroud. The windows contain images of Chaucer, who set off on pilgrimage to Canterbury from a pub in Borough High Street, and John Bunyan, who preached locally.
Buggy access. Lifts. Nappy-changing facilities. Nearest picnic place: churchyard. Restaurant. Shop.

Tate Modern

Bankside, SE1 (7887 8000/www.tate.org.uk). Southwark tube. **Open** *Galleries* 10.15am-6pm Mon-Thur, Sun; 10.15am-10pm Fri, Sat. Last admission 45mins before closing. Closed 25, 26 Dec. **Admission** free (charge for special exhibitions). **Map** p320 O7.

Tate Modern has everything going for it: a fabulous Thameside location; a wonderful collection; and scale. Visiting this former power station is an event in itself, and kids will be awed by the almost unimaginable volumes of space inside. Thankfully, the architects left behind some of the relics from the building's industrial days, and the original gantries and lifting gear are fully on view (incidentally, the original architect, Sir Giles Gilbert Scott, was the designer of the traditional phone box and the grandson of Sir George Gilbert Scott, architect of the building fronting St Pancras station). This place is almost too big – sculptor Anish Kapoor had to work hard to fill the central turbine room with 2003's extraordinary *Marsyas* piece.

The Tate's collection is vast, but highlights which might appeal to kids include: Cornelia Parker's *Cold Dark Matter* (pieces, and contents, of a shed that has been exploded); Monet's *Water Lilies*; Matisse's *The Snail*; and the shimmering, blurred edges of the Rothko room. Free collapsible chairs are available for those who want to sit and ponder their favourite painting (for education and activities, see p210).
Buggy access. Lifts. Nappy-changing facilities. Nearest picnic place: Tate Modern grounds. Restaurant. Shops.

Winston Churchill's Britain at War Experience

64-66 Tooley Street, SE1 (7403 3171/www.britainatwar. co.uk). London Bridge tube/rail. **Open** *Apr-Sept* 10am-5.30pm daily. *Oct-Mar* 10am-4.30pm daily. Last entry 30mins before closing. Closed 24-26 Dec. **Admission** £7.50; £5 concessions; £4 5-16s; £16 family (2+2); free under-5s. **Credit** AmEx, MC, V. **Map** p321 Q8.

In spite of (or maybe because of) its dated exhibition techniques and predictable content, this 'experience' actually manages to conjure up the austerity and horror of the Blitz rather well. An ancient, room-sized lift takes you down to the action, where you're greeted by mannequins lying in bunks, while a video relates stories of shocking wartime behaviour. A series of set pieces follow, taking in a BBC broadcasting room, a shabby pub and even a burning street that is staged to make you feel the action happened just moments before.
Buggy access. Nearest picnic place: Southwark Cathedral Gardens/William Curtis Park. Shop.

The City

Not just in it for the money.

Has the City changed much since the days of bowler hats and tightly furled brollies? From a child's perspective, there's probably little difference between that pre-war image and the now ubiquitous black suits worn by bustling bankers toting self-important briefcases. But this otherworldliness is as much a reason to visit as any other. Midweek, there's something fascinating about the hustle and bustle of London's financial district, just as its ghost-town quality at weekends has a certain peaceful appeal.

Underlying both these moods is the City's place in our Roman and medieval history – after all, this was once the whole of London. Around Tower Hill and at London Wall, the remains of Londinium's defences – impressively thick walls built by the Romans in AD 200 to keep barbarians out – can still be seen. The **Tower of London**, royal palace as well as fortress, vies with **St Paul's Cathedral** for prime example of man-made magnificence. On a smaller scale, the tiny, winding alleyways often lead to hidden surprises: a bomb site made into a garden, an ancient church lit by candles, or a row of higgledy-piggledy Tudor houses worthy of a chocolate box. In bad weather, the **Museum of London** is arguably the best free day out for families in the whole of London. In sunshine, outside trading hours it's possible to cycle with quite young children around the City from one historic site to another, so sparse is the traffic. Total distance covered? Never more than one Square Mile.

Bank of England Museum

Entrance on Bartholomew Lane, EC2 (7601 5545/cinema bookings 7601 3985/www.bankofengland.co.uk). Bank tube/DLR. **Open** 10am-5pm Mon-Fri. Closed bank hols. **Tours** by arrangement. **Admission** free; £1 audio guide. *Tours* free. **Map** p321 Q6.

The Bank of England is an awesome architectural monument, and towers above pedestrians like the temple of Mammon it is. The banking hall brings to life the personal nature of banking in times gone by, with its bewigged mannequins in period costume and thick wooden counters. Part of this room is a gift shop, where fun souvenirs such as chocolate coins, mugs announcing 'I Love Money' and feather inkpens can be picked up. In the Rotunda, you can sit and watch a film about the bank's origins in 1694 – a predictable tale of monarchs in debt and modest burghers roped in to finance a war with France. But the story of the way paper money eventually replaced gold is fascinating, and there are enough interactive exhibits to keep children happy. Dummies move and speak as you pass; a hand-engraved printing plate for £50 notes can be examined with a magnifying glass for discrepancies; a touch-screen explains the origin of different features of British banknotes, and the replica dealing desk is fun for those who understand what it's all about. Staff make a big effort to entertain school parties; children who come with

their families can fill out age-specific activity sheets (for fives to 16s). Most popular of all is a glass case with a hole into which visitors insert a hand and try to lift the gold bar enclosed therein. Its value fluctuates daily (roughly £96,000), but its weight – 28lbs – constantly surprises young and old. *Buggy access. Disabled: lift, toilet. Nappy-changing facilities. Nearest picnic place: St Paul's Cathedral garden. Shop.*

Barbican Centre

Silk Street, EC2 (7638 4141/box office 7638 8891/ www.barbican.org.uk). Barbican tube/Moorgate tube/rail. **Open** 10am-6pm Mon, Tue, Thur-Sat; 10am-8pm Wed; noon-6pm Sun. **Admission** free; phone for details of ticket prices for events. **Credit** AmEx, MC, V. **Map** p320 P5.

It's a pity the Barbican Centre's architecture – labyrinthine walkways, blank tower blocks and an unappetising façade of discoloured concrete – should be so off-putting, for its cultural offering is vast. Familiarity may breed content. There are pockets of calm, even beauty: the inner courtyard with its summer fountains and view of St Giles Church; the conservatory with its exotic plants (open to the public on Sunday afternoons); the library, with its extensive children's section.

DON'T MISS Museum of London

Our favourite galleries in the MoL and ten of the treasures they hold. *See p52.*

World City Gallery

Walk through an orderly Victorian shopping arcade. Take a break from the shops to listen to studio recordings of pre-war East End immigrants.

Lord Mayor's Coach Gallery

The Lord Mayor of London's state coach, of course, as well as the interactive, computerised photo and film archive next door.

Early Stewart Gallery

The Great Fire Experience and the glittering Cheapside Hoard of 16th- and 17th-century gems.

Roman Gallery

The star of this gallery is undoubtedly the Princess of the City – a skeleton of a 20-year-old Roman woman. She might have enjoyed a living room as laid out here, complete with mosaics and authentic decor. Look out, too, for the replica of the horned helmet from 150BC that was found under Waterloo Bridge.

London Before London

Artefacts from Heathrow Camp, a prehistoric settlement discovered on the modern airport site, and morphing effects to bridge the gap between the flints and the passenger jets.

History – a thing of the present, at the **Guildhall**. *See p50.*

And you can still see parts of the Roman walls on which the Barbican (originally a fortified watch tower) was built.

The best kid-related reasons to visit are the Saturday morning Cinema Club (*see p208*), the Family Concerts given by the resident London Symphony Orchestra and the holiday activities. The most exciting development in recent times has been the opening in spring 2003 of the lottery-funded LSO St Luke's Music Education Centre, in the former church on Old Street, EC1. This lovely building is now a venue for open rehearsals, performances, workshops and public events, with an emphasis on education. To join the Family News mailing list and find out more about LSO and Barbican projects for children, call 7382 2333 or email kcox@barbican.org.uk.
Bars. Buggy access. Cafés. Disabled access: lift, toilet. Nappy-changing facilities. Nearest picnic place: Barbican Lakeside Terrace. Restaurants. Shops.

Broadgate Arena

Broadgate Circle, EC2 (7505 4068/www.broadgateestates. co.uk). Liverpool Street tube/rail. **Open** *Mid Oct-mid Apr* noon-2.30pm, 3.30-6pm Mon-Thur; noon-2.30pm, 3.30-6pm, 7-10pm Fri; 11am-1pm, 2-4pm, 5-8.30pm Sat; 11am-1pm, 2-4pm, 5-7pm Sun. *From Apr* ring for details. **Admission** £7; £4 under-16s. **No credit cards. Map** p321 Q5.
The smallest and least expensive of London's three outdoor winter skating rinks (the other two are at Marble Arch and Somerset House, *see p256*) has a circular form, surrounded by a sort of amphitheatre of offices and shops in Broadgate Circle. Skates range from child's size six, if you are prepared to support them in their first, clinging experience of the ice. From April to September the rink is dismantled to make space for various corporate events, outdoor drama and music – call for details or email ljones@broadgateestates.co.uk to be sent the free Broadgate Live brochure every two months.
Buggy access. Disabled access; lift, ramp, toilet. Nearest picnic place: Finsbury Circus.

College of Arms

Queen Victoria Street, EC4 (7248 2762/www.college-of-arms.gov.uk). Blackfriars tube/rail. **Open** 10am-4pm Mon-Fri. Closed bank hols. **Tours** by arrangement 6.30pm Mon-Fri; prices vary. **Admission** free. **Map** p320 O7.
Don't miss this beautiful 17th-century house with heraldic gates in red, black and gold – you see it as you wander across the Millennium footbridge over the Thames connecting Tate Modern and the South Bank to St Paul's. A quasi-permanent (by popular demand) Golden Jubilee exhibition of carved and painted heraldic crests and crowns in the entrance hall has transformed this once subdued, if ancient institution. The collection makes for a gaudy thicket of richly symbolic beasts and byzants: lions, eagles, unicorns, lighthouses and, er, shovels (for Sir Harold Wilson) – pure Harry Potter for many. The more serious business carried on here is the granting of arms by royal heralds to modern knights and the tracing of family lineages. You can get help with your own family tree by making an appointment, to which you should bring along as much genealogical information as possible; a fee is charged for the work according to how long it is expected to take.
Nearest picnic place: St Paul's Cathedral garden. Shop.

Dr Johnson's House

17 Gough Square, off Fleet Street, EC4 (7353 3745/ www.drjohnsonshouse.org). Chancery Lane or Temple tube/Blackfriars tube/rail. **Open** *May-Sept* 11am-5.30pm Mon-Sat. *Oct-Apr* 11am-5pm Mon-Sat. Closed 24-26 Dec, 1 Jan, bank hols. **Tours** by arrangement; groups of 10 or more only. **Admission** £4; £3 concessions; £1 under-18s; free under-10s; £9 family (2+unlimited children). *Tours* £3. *Evening tours* by appointment only. **No credit cards. Map** p320 N6.
Few tourists are aware of this immaculately restored Georgian house, once home to Samuel Johnson, the lexicographer famous for his love of the capital ('When a man is

tired of London, he is tired of life') – it can be found via a maze of alleyways off Fleet Street. Gough Square itself is an pedestrianised backwater and has a statue of the good doctor's cat. His house will appeal to young students of literature and lovers of old buildings; make sure you read the information sheets quoting Johnson's gossipy views, and peruse the pictures of his friends – a motley lot of Christians, tarts and 'decayed tradesmen'. Highlights include a video, an 18th-century gout stool and a model of a toy workshop.

Nearest picnic place: Lincoln's Inn Fields/The Temple. Shop.

Guildhall

Corporation of London, PO Box 270, EC2 (7606 3030/ tours ext1463/www.corpoflondon.gov.uk). Bank tube/DLR. **Open** *May-Sept* 10am-5pm daily. *Oct-Apr* 10am-5pm Mon-Sat. Last entry 4.30pm. Closed 25, 26 Dec, 1 Jan. **Tours** by arrangement; groups of 10 or more people only. **Admission** free. **Map** p320 P6.

Gleaming old black Bentleys often sit in the square by the entrance to the Guildhall – testimony to the importance of the business going on within, for this ancient building (albeit with modern adjuncts) is the seat of local Government (*see below*). In this capacity it is at its most interesting at 1pm on various Thursdays each month, when the Court of Common Council meets in the 15th-century Great Hall (visitors are welcome; phone for dates).

On other days you can visit the Hall, a big, empty space with vaulted ceiling and marble monuments, but little to inspire children other than two wooden statues of Gog and Magog on the West Gallery. These giants represent the mythical conflict between the Britons and Trojan invaders; the result of this struggle was the founding of Albion's capital city, New Troy, on whose site London is said to stand. Visits to the Guildhall's enormous medieval crypt are allowed only in the context of group tours. Of more immediate appeal is a little room beyond the library devoted to a collection of watches, clocks and marine chronometers belonging to the Worshipful Company of Clockmakers. Arrive just before the hour for an enchanting sequence of chimes, tunes and strikes, or simply gaze in awe at the beautiful gold cases – often set with precious stones or enamelled – of watches whose innards are proudly exposed. The 700 exhibits include the silver skull watch said to have belonged to Mary Queen of Scots, the wristwatch worn by Edmund Hillary during his ascent of Mount Everest and quirky, tiny watch keys.

Buggy access. Disabled access: toilet.

How money makes the world go round

Walk around for a while in the inner precincts of the City and you may start to feel you've stepped across an invisible border into another country – Switzerland, perhaps. The prime disorienting factor may take a while to dawn on you: the streets are (for London) amazingly, breathtakingly clean. Around the Guildhall, it would be a challenge to find so much as a sweet wrapper. The realisation that you could practically picnic on the pavements here is wonderfully relaxing if you're in charge of a small person with a penchant for horizontal tantrums.

But does the outstanding cleanliness of Britain's best-known business district owe to the fact that its denizens are, for the main part, sober, hard-working adults whose minds are set only on worship at the Temple of Mammon? Nothing so simple nor so cynical. The City's rigorous street cleaning programme is just one of the most visible benefits of rule by the Corporation of London.

At 800 years old, the Corporation is the oldest local authority in England. Even the Parliament at Westminster is based on the Corporation's Court of Common Council, sometimes referred to as the 'Grandmother of Parliaments'. The ancient civic offices of the Lord Mayor and Sheriffs are still an integral part of the modern Corporation, and best appreciated by the public in annual events such as The Lord Mayor's Show. The Corporation's responsibilities are vast. It not only has the City streets swept 'at least once a day' (and hires a falconer to take out the pigeons); it's also the third largest sponsor of the arts in the UK (the Barbican, for example, was built in 1982 by the Corporation of London as a 'gift to the nation' and is still funded by it). It owns historic buildings such as Tower Bridge and the Monument, and comprises the largest Port Health Authority in the UK, responsible for a district which extends for nearly 100 miles along the Thames from Teddington to the outer Estuary. And as if that weren't enough, four famous markets – Billingsgate, Leadenhall, Smithfield and Spitalfields – fall within its domain.

Naturally, the Corporation also undertakes all the usual duties of a local authority – social housing, education, policing and so on. But its influence is felt far beyond the City of London, since it manages (brilliantly well, many users would say) more than 10,000 acres of open space in and around the capital: the list of green spaces in its care includes Bunhill Fields, Highgate Woods, Queen's Park, West Ham Park, Hampstead Heath, Epping Forest, Burnham Beeches, Ashtead Common, and West Wickham and Coulsdon Commons.

But where does the money for all this come from? Not, as you might expect, from the business rates of a very rich area, because the Corporation retains only a small proportion of the business rate collected within the City. The remainder is paid to the national non-domestic rates pool and gets redistributed among local authorities across the country. In fact, the bulk of money required for the Corporation's philanthropic activities comes from two historic funds. The first, City's Cash, is a private fund derived mainly from property, which has its origins in the 13th century. The second, a trust fund called Bridge House Estates, has its origins in medieval times and derives from the finance needed to build and maintain London Bridge.

The wonder of the City, then, is not that it produces so much wealth today, but that its past inhabitants were so careful about storing wealth for the future: you could call it the foresight saga.

Under then over at **Tower Bridge**. See p54.

Guildhall Art Gallery

Guildhall Yard, off Gresham Street, EC2 (7332 3700/ www.guildhall-art-gallery.org.uk). Mansion House or St Paul's tube/Bank tube/DLR/Moorgate tube/rail. **Open** 10am-5pm Mon-Sat (last entry 4.30pm); noon-4pm Sun (last entry 3.45pm). Closed 24-26 Dec, 1 Jan. **Admission** £2.50; £1 concessions; free under-16s. Free to all after 3.30pm daily, all day Fri. **Credit** *over £5* MC, V. **Map** p320 P6.
For a quick preview of paintings held in this attractive modern building opposite the Guildhall, you can check out the collection on the Corporation of London's computerised search facility, the Collage System. It would be a pity not to visit in person, however, for this is a relatively under-frequented gallery, which allows families ample crowd-free opportunities to see famous artworks as glowing originals.

The collection – like its owners – now seems largely conservative, yet when the gallery opened in the 19th century its daring exhibitions of work by the Pre-Raphaelites earned it a certain glam notoriety. Start in the basement and you'll see works by Dante Gabriel Rossetti, Holman Hunt, Tissot and others, their lush photographic detail a feast for the eyes of any visitor easily enthralled by frocks, furs and fab complexions. A diptych by Millais (*First and Second Sermon*) is just one of the paintings of children – this one illustrating the soporific effects of church attendance. Amen to that.

On the floors above, highlights include John Singleton Copley's vast 18th-century oil painting known as the *Siege of Gibraltar*. It's just one of many narrative pictures from that century and the next which are eminently accessible to children. Their tone is one of unadulterated melodrama, but they also afford sociological lessons (see the Egyptian princess holding up her little son so he can practise lashing the Israelite slaves with a miniature whip in Sir Edward Poynter's *Israel in Egypt*) – as do the paintings of London, dating from the

17th century to the present, on the ground floor: pubs in Peckham, Chelsea pensioners and pre-war coppers all get a showing. Margaret Thatcher is represented by a blue box containing what's left of her vandalised statue; apparently this will have to be rebuilt from scratch.

If the art leaves you cold, don't leave without popping down to the Roman amphitheatre, now open to the public after six years of painstaking work. Sections of stone wall are all that remain, but these have been given an atmospheric makeover with eerie lighting, glowing mesh figures and a soundtrack evoking the thrills and spills of gladiatorial combat.

School groups visit free and teachers receive a pack in advance, detailing themes which accord with the National Curriculum. A small shop at the entrance has a selection of remarkably inexpensive prints and stationery.
Buggy access. Disabled access: lift, toilet. Nearest picnic area: grassy area by London Wall. Shop.

The Monument

Monument Street, EC3 (7626 2717). Monument tube. **Open** 9.30am-5pm daily. Closed 24-26 Dec, 1 Jan. **Admission** £2; £1 5-15s; free under-5s. **No credit cards. Map** p321 Q7.
Though they generally have not the faintest idea what this, the world's tallest free-standing Doric column, is a monument to, most children are only too eager to climb it. Its spiral staircase numbers 311 steps, so you have plenty of time to explain its history on the way up: at 202ft, the column marks the exact distance to the bakery in Pudding Lane where the Great Fire of London broke out in 1666. It was built by Sir Christopher Wren and, despite the many skyscrapers being built nearby (the construction work and attendant cranes are best appreciated from the caged viewing platform at the top), still stands out thanks to its golden urn of flames. Children as young as

For weddings, christenings, eternal repose and directory enquiries: **St Paul's Cathedral**. *See p54.*

two make it to the top independently, and two treats await on the way down: the chance to peer down the centre of the spiral and imagine you are inside a Martin Escher painting; and the award of a certificate commemorating each visitor's climbing feat at the bottom.
Nearest picnic place: riverside by London Bridge.

Museum of London

150 London Wall, EC2 (7600 3699/24hr info 7600 0807/ www.museumoflondon.org.uk). Barbican or St Paul's tube/Moorgate tube/rail. **Open** 10am-5.50pm Mon-Sat; noon-5.50pm Sun. Closed 24-26 Dec, 1 Jan. **Admission** free. **Credit** *Shop* AmEx, MC, V. **Map** p320 P5.
Often missed by visitors all gallery-ed out by the museum cluster of South Kensington, the Museum of London is one of the capital's best free indoor entertainments for children.

Making so much history – from prehistoric times to the present – dynamic and appealing to visitors of all ages is no mean feat. Flintheads and fragments of pottery usually rates high on the yawn scale, yet this museum's London Before London gallery launches with an evocative soundtrack, lyrical text and clever mirror projections. Heathrow was once Caesar's Camp; look into the box and see the roundhouses morph into Jumbo jets! More recent times are covered in the World City Gallery, where black and white photographs of royalty and commoners are enlivened by audio accounts of their lives. Push a button to hear a Victorian housemaid describe her gruelling daily routine; hear how pre-war Jewish immigrants lived in East End tenement blocks, surviving on 'a ha'porth of chips' nightly. Antique model aeroplanes hang from the ceiling in this gallery; the Lord Mayor's red and gold state coach (still used annually in his Show) is parked by the

[handwritten notes: 0870 444 3852 New 2007 Have left luggage 50p/item]

computer terminals. The latter are wildly popular with young visitors. You can call up films of bourgeois bicyclists in Hampstead or a keeper taunting tiger cubs at the Zoo. Don't leave without walking through the reconstruction of Victorian street life, with its barber shop, pub and post office.

There are several new exhibitions for 2003: they include one on famous diarist Samuel Pepys (until 3 November), one on the 1920s (October 2003 to July 2004) and one on environmental issues. School holidays bring lots of family events, such as workshops in which to replicate Roman coins, shoes and so on, plus storytelling by costumed figures; at other times there are fun (and free) activity sheets to fill out. In good weather, the Barber Surgeon's Garden (partly enclosed by the ruined walls of the old Roman fort) is a lovely spot for a picnic, but if it's cold families are welcome to use the schools' room near the entrance to eat their own food.
Buggy access. Nearest picnic place: benches outside museum/grassy area by London Wall. Shop.

Museum of Methodism & John Wesley's House
Wesley's Chapel, 49 City Road, EC1 (7253 2262/ www.wesleyschapel.org.uk). Old Street or Moorgate tube/rail. **Open** 10am-4pm Mon-Sat, 12.30-1.45pm Sun. Closed 25 Dec-1 Jan, bank hols. **Tours** ad hoc arrangements on arrival. **Admission** free. *Tours* free. **Credit** MC, V. **Map** p321 Q4.
This lovely chapel, with its deep, gated courtyard ringed by Georgian buildings, is a haven from the thunderous traffic of City Road and known to the Methodist religion's adherents worldwide as 'the Cathedral of World Methodism'. It was built by John Wesley in 1778 and his description of it – 'perfectly neat but not fine' – sums up its homely architecture.

Museum displays in the crypt allude to Methodism's beginnings. Hogarthian prints depict the iniquitous effects of poverty, alcoholism and moral degradation in 18th-century England. John Wesley experienced a moment of grace which persuaded him to devote his life to serving God and helping the poor. It was during his days as an Oxford undergraduate that his rigorous and methodical programme of prayer, fasting and so on led to him being dubbed a 'Methodist'.

More evidence of this puritanical lifestyle is on show in the preacher's house, which may be visited as part of the ad hoc tours given by elderly stewards. This is naturally more lively than the museum and its missionary memorabilia; the house has been sympathetically restored and shows a kitchen with an open range and no running water, a bedroom with a tiny, curtained four-poster and a study with a 'chamber horse'. As if Wesley's foreign preaching tours did not offer sufficient equestrian exercise, this curious bouncing chair was supposed to simulate a good gallop.

Through the windows you can see Bunhill Fields, the dissenters' graveyard. Cross the road to wander through this secret garden, with its mossy graves tilted at odd angles and its memorials to non-conformists such as William Blake, Daniel Defoe (author of *Robinson Crusoe*), members of Oliver Cromwell's family, and Susanna Wesley (mother of John and Charles). There's a large grassy area just perfect for picnics. *Disabled access: toilet, lift. Nappy-changing facilities. Nearest picnic place: enclosed courtyard at entrance. Shop.*

St Bartholomew's Hospital Museum
West Smithfield, EC1 (7601 8152/tours 7837 0546). Barbican or St Paul's tube. **Open** 10am-4pm Tue-Fri. Closed over Christmas & Easter periods & bank hols. **Tours** 2pm Fri. **Admission** free. *Tours* £5; £4 concessions; accompanied children free. **No credit cards**. **Map** p320 O6.
One of London's medieval hospitals, St Bartholomew's reminds modern students of medicine that theirs is a relatively modern science. St Bart's was built in 1123 by Rahere, a courtier of Henry VIII, and its museum recalls its origins as

PARKLIFE How green was my City

Named for its proximity to a large sorting office (long since demolished), Postman's Park is the City's most charming green space. Hidden away between office buildings on King Edward Street and Aldersgate Street, it's prettily laid out with an old goldfish pond, lots of exotic shrubs and flagged paths. Its most famous feature is the Heroes Wall, a canopy-covered expanse of ceramic plaques inscribed in florid Victorian style. 'Frederick Alfred Croft, Inspector, aged 31,' begins one typical thumbnail drama. 'Saved a Lunatic Woman from Suicide at Woolwich Arsenal Station, But was Himself Run Over by the Train, Jan 11, 1878.' Many of the dead heroes were children who tried to rescue drowning companions, and so on; their fates draw gruesome morals for their modern peers.

The bombed-out churchyard of St Dunstan's-in-the-East, between Great Tower and Lower Thames Streets, is another delightful garden, concealed, like Postman's Park, from most passers-by and full of sweetly-scented climbing roses in season.

Less appealing but larger – in fact the largest green space in the City proper – is Finsbury Circus Gardens off City Road (not to be confused with Finsbury Square). It has a bowling green and a bandstand, but it's hard to get a square foot of grass to yourself in a summer lunch hour.

Fortune Street Gardens, close to the Barbican and Safeway, has the merit of play equipment for babies and older kids but is somewhat run down; still, a new partnership between Islington Council and the Corporation of London should see its refurbishment and replanting in 2003 or 2004. Aldermanbury Square (disabled access via the west entrance) close to the Guildhall is the site of the ruined St Mary Aldermanbury, which was destroyed by bombs in 1940. The remaining fabric has been taken to Missouri and reconstructed as a monument to Sir Winston Churchill, leaving grassy foundations and a nice, quiet place to sit. If summer temperatures really soar, a short walk away on Basinghall Street you'll find a series of low fountains in a shallow, rimless pool on the pavement – ideal for small hot feet!

Postman's Park
Between King Edward Street & Aldersgate Street, EC2 (7247 8548/www.cityoflondon.gov.uk). St Paul's tube. **Open** 8am-7pm Mon-Fri. **Map** p310 O6.

LUNCH BREAK

The City presents parents with a bit of a challenge when it comes to nourishing their offspring – awash with child-friendly eating places it ain't. In most circumstances your best bets are the branches of chain restaurants, as listed below. At weekends you need to be resourceful, for the very quietness which makes the area pleasant to stroll in means there's no trade for caterers: most are closed. If you're making for Tower Hill and environs, a neat trick is to take advantage of free parking on Saturday and Sunday on Safeway's on Thomas More Street (E1, 7702 2866) and make use of their hot buffets. They even provide a conservatory in which to consume the take-away food. Fast food outlets in Liverpool Street Station are another good bet. If you get tired of the arsey attitudes towards profit-hindering rugrats in the City, cross the river to the South Bank, where eating opportunities are more tourist-focused and hence more plentiful.

Carluccio's Caffè (12 West Smithfield, EC1, 7329 5904; see p162), for gorgeous Italian grub – just off the Square Mile, admittedly.
Just the Bridge (1 Paul's Walk, EC4, 7236 0000), just the thing for nursery faves like fishcakes, Welsh rarebit and, er, crispy duck spring rolls.
Lightship Ten (5A St Katherine's Docks Way, E1, 7481 3123), enlightening waterborne dining in swanky dock setting – for well-behaved children.
Pizza Express (125 London Wall, EC2, 7600 8880; see p175), one of many Pizza Expresses, this one's good for the Museum of London.
The Place Below (St Mary le Bow Church, Cheapside, EC2, 7329 0789; see p163), an atmospheric setting for veggie family meals.
Smith's of Smithfield (67-77 Charterhouse Street, EC1, 7251 7950; see p162) trendy, but friendly and great for burgers and organic breakfasts.
Best place for a picnic: Postman's Park (see p53).

a popular refuge for the chronically sick. Many sought miraculous cures, but more reliable (and easier to procure) remedies were rest, good diet and spiritual comfort. Teenagers can watch an instructive video on the history of the institution and are urged to make careful note of the old operating instruments. But to the casual visitor, leather 'lunatic restraints', a wooden head used by young would-be doctors to practise their head-drilling techniques (but also, apparently, as a football) and photographs documenting the slow progress of nurses from subordinate drudges to careerwomen make mildly edifying exhibits. A leaflet detailing other medical museums (including the Wellcome Trust, Florence Nightingale Museum and the Old Operating Theatre on the South Bank) offers further study potential for school groups.

Meanwhile don't miss the huge painting in grand historical style by William Hogarth, through the museum and up the stairs. Hogarth was born in Bartholomew's Close and offered his services free when he heard the hospital governors were about to commission a Venetian artist. His paintings of the Good Samaritan *et al* illustrate a fascinating range of skin and venereal diseases; quite a talking point for teenagers. *Buggy access. Nearest picnic place: hospital grounds. Shop.*

St Paul's Cathedral

Ludgate Hill, EC4 (7236 4128/www.stpauls.co.uk). St Paul's tube. **Open** 8.30am-4.30pm (last entry 4pm) Mon-Sat; services only Sun, 25 Dec. *Galleries, crypt & ambulatory* 9.30am-4pm Mon-Sat. Closed for special services, sometimes at short notice. *Tours* 11am, 11.30am, 1.30pm, 2pm Mon-Sat. **Admission** (LP) *Cathedral, crypt & gallery* £6; £3 6-16s; £5 concessions; free under-6s. *Tours* £2.50; £1 6-16s; £2 concessions; free under-6s. *Audio guide* £3.50; £3 concessions. **Credit** MC, V. **Map** p320 O6.
This towering landmark on Ludgate Hill is bound to impress youngsters with its sheer size and majesty; its architectural details may leave them underwhelmed. As one writer notes, St Paul's is best on 'splendid occasions of national thanksgiving – it needs trumpets and a great congregation.' To avoid the glazed-over look, try to book yourself in to a tour, when the practised arts of enthusiastic old retainers bring the place alive. Learn, for example, that the massive front doors only open for the likes of the Lord Mayor of London, and that

the last bride to pass through them was that tragic icon, Diana. Titter at the mental picture of the Queen Mother catching her heel in the gratings over the Crypt before they were tactfully sealed over; enjoy being let into the secret of the font, whose firmly stuck lid means a stone has to be removed from the side for christenings.

Most people know St Paul's architect was Sir Christopher Wren, and he is buried in the Crypt along with Nelson, Wellington and – even more popular with children – George Frampton, whose statue holds out a hand on which stands a miniature Peter Pan, a scaled-down replica of Frampton's sculpture in Kensington Gardens. Holman Hunt's inspiring painting, *The Light of the World* is a highlight of the Middlesex Regiment Chapel; climbing up to the Whispering Gallery in the Dome and testing the acoustics is probably the most thrilling part of any visit.

Children too young to benefit from paying the entrance fee can always take advantage of the cathedral's spacious café in the Crypt. The shop here is full of tasteful London souvenirs and there are some excellent children's versions of Biblical stories. To experience St Paul's as a place of worship, try Choral Evensong at 5pm daily, when the emphasis is on heavenly singing (the boys' choir sings on Mondays). *Café. Lifts. Nearest picnic space: Cathedral garden. Restaurant. Shop.*

St Swithin's Garden

Oxford Court, off Cannon Street, EC4 (no phone). Bank tube/DLR. **Open** 24hrs daily. **Admission** free. **Map** p321 Q7.
This small but carefully tended walled garden (at the back of Costa Coffee) is the burial place of Catrin Glendwr and two of her children. Catrin was the daughter of Owain Glendwr, the Welsh hero whose uprising ended bloodily in 1413. A memorial sculpture is dedicated not only to her, but to the suffering of all women and children in war. Benches and a beautiful magnolia tree make this a pleasant place to sit in.

Tower Bridge Experience

Tower Bridge SE1 (7403 3761/www.towerbridge.org.uk). Tower Hill tube/London Bridge tube/rail. **Open** 9.30am-6pm (last entry 5pm) daily. Closed 24-26 Dec, 1 Jan.

Just don't ask him for a sirloin. **The Tower of London**.

Admission £4.50; £3 5-15s, concessions; £16.50 family (2+3); free under-5s. **Credit** AmEx, MC, V. **Map** p321 R8. Many children are fascinated by London's most famous bridge, largely because it opens and closes like a Meccano set and has the added bonus of two picture-book Gothic towers. Seeing the inside of the bridge adds a little or a lot to the fantasy, depending on visitors' ages and enthusiasm for engineering. A lift takes you up to the walkways over the river, but the view is partially obscured by the glass inserted into the original ironwork. A video acts out Victorian opposition to the bridge's construction, and period photographs reveal fascinating things – like workmen in primitive diving suits gouging the clay to build the foundations, or a 'beach' made of imported sand below the bridge in 1934 for the entertainment of Londoners. Once at ground level again, the tour continues in the south tower where the smartly liveried engines slowly turn. Here, there are talking animatronic coalmen and buttons to press – some of which start audio commentary on pumps and gaskets in eight different languages. More amusing is a wind-up seat demonstrating hydraulic power and a model which allows you to 'make the bridge go up'. This, after all, is what every visitor would like to see for real: it happens most often in summer (sometimes several times a day). To find out when the next opening will happen, call 7940 3984. *Buggy access. Disabled access: lift, toilet. Nearest picnic place: William Curtis Park/Tower of London gardens. Shop.*

The Tower of London

Tower Hill, EC3 (7709 0765/www.hrp.org.uk). Tower Hill tube/Fenchurch Street rail. **Open** *Mar-Oct* 9am-5pm Mon-Sat; 10am-5pm Sun. *Nov-Feb* 10am-4pm Mon, Sun; 9am-4pm Tue-Sat. Closed 24-26 Dec, 1 Jan. **Tours** *Beefeater tours* (outside only, weather permitting) free; half-hourly 9.25am-2.50pm daily. *Short talks* given by yeoman warder (40mins)

free; advance tickets from kiosk outside Lanthorn Tower 3 times a day. **Admission** (LP) £11.50; £8.75 concessions; £7.50 5s-15s; family £34 (2+3); free under-5s. *Audio guide* £3. **Credit** AmEx, MC, V. **Map** p321 R7. Entrance fees at this picture-book castle may seem steep, but a day here for families turns out to be excellent value. This is because 'The Tower' is actually a veritable thicket of towers, each with its own history and points of interest, and children are treated like royalty by well-informed and kindly staff. Glance up under the first gate to see the spikes of the mighty portcullis hanging above you; shiver at the stories of traitors' heads chopped off and displayed on spikes around the Tower walls! Most young visitors, if asked what impresses them most, will hesitate between the dazzling riches of the Crown Jewels and the tales of royal executions. A permanent exhibition of torture instruments – 'Torture at the Tower' – aims to nourish the natural interest in violence and punishment (while keeping within the boundaries of good taste).

In the Armouries another temporary display, 'The Knight is Young', focuses on diminutive suits of armour, and there are plenty of opportunities to try on replica pieces. School holidays see lots of free activities for children. Family Trail booklets and pencils are handed out at the sentry box inside the main gate (completion merits a souvenir badge and rubber). Costumed actors give sterling performances, singing and dancing to medieval instruments and trading Blackadder-ish banter with onlookers. In fact, the only unfriendly 'staff' here are the famous ravens who guard the Tower; plenty of warning is given about their territorial nature and tendency to nip fingers, but this just makes them more fascinating. It was their ancestors, after all, who breakfasted on the eyes and flesh of the traitors' heads in days of yore. *Buggy access. Café. Nappy-changing facilities. Nearest picnic place: Trinity Square Memorial Gardens. Shop.*

Bloomsbury & Holborn

From high-minded past to playful present.

Synonymous with Virginia Woolf, publishing and academia, Bloomsbury might not seem like an obvious destination for a day out with the kids. But this elegant Georgian neighbourhood has plenty of childish appeal. **Coram's Fields**, London's famous park for children, is reason alone to visit, and in **Russell Square**, another famous green space, kids can splash around in the fountain in summer. Then there's the **British Museum**. Its amazing hoard of antiquities has always been intriguing, but the addition of the spectacular Great Court, London's only covered public square, is an extra draw. The new **British Library** is the repository of Britain's literary treasures. As well as being a research centre extraordinaire, it also houses a fascinating museum with a dizzying range of topics. **Pollock's Toy Museum** is a delightful slice of nostalgia evoking a pre-Game Boy era when wooden train sets and Snakes & Ladders were as fun as fun got. And a visit to the **Charles Dickens Museum**, in the house where the great author once lived, is entirely appropriate given the neighbourhood's literary past.

Although it will be closed until spring 2004, do visit the nearby **Foundling Museum** (40 Brunswick Square, WC1, 841 3600) when its doors open on what promises to be a fascinating collection recalling the social history of the hospital, an art gallery with works by Hogarth, Rysbrack, Gainsborough and Reynolds, and memorabilia relating to Handel, who helped to found the hospital.

British Library
96 Euston Road, NW1 (7412 7332/education 7412 7797/ www.bl.uk). Euston or King's Cross tube/rail. **Open** 9.30am-6pm Mon, Wed-Fri; 9.30am-8pm Tue; 9.30am-5pm Sat; 11am-5pm Sun, bank hols. Closed 22-26 Dec, 1 Jan. **Admission** free; donations appreciated. **Map** p317 K3.

DON'T MISS
Pollock's Toy Museum

As well as the old-fashioned board games and puzzles, certain characters lurking among the nostalgic displays at Pollock's Toy Museum are sure to whisk you down toyland's memory lane. Look out for the following star turns:
Pebbles Flintstone paper dolls
Enid Blyton's **Noddy** Theatre
Star Trek pop-up books
American **Action Man** and **GI Joe**
Toys from the **Stingray** series

One of the great libraries of the world, the British Library has a staggering collection of 150 million items – and growing – spread over 625km of shelves and 112,000 square metres. Each year, the library receives a copy of every publication produced in the UK and Ireland, including maps, newspapers, magazines, prints and drawings. At the heart of the building is the stunning King's Library, the library of George III, housed in a six-storey glass-walled tower. For the casual visitor, however, the John Ritblat Gallery displays the library's real treasures: the Magna Carta or Great Charter of 1215, Leonardo da Vinci's notebook, and Shakespeare's First Folio – the first collected edition of the Bard's plays. Children might prefer first editions of *The Jungle Book* by Kipling, *Alice's Adventures Underground* by Lewis Carroll, or some of the Beatles' handwritten lyrics. You can also listen to sound recordings of James Joyce and Bob Geldof. Other items of interest include an astounding philatelic collection – the library has some 80,000 stamps from around the world.

The major exhibition of 2003 will be The Painted Labyrinth: The World of the Lindisfarne Gospels (16 May-28 September), which celebrates the exquisite Anglo-Saxon painted manuscript – one of Britain's great artistic treasures. Other temporary exhibitions include Hamlet (June-August), the Suffragettes (September) and Ted Hughes (20 October–late November). For children, there are regular free demonstrations of bookbinding, printing and calligraphy. During holidays, the Education Office organises workshops, activities and storytelling sessions for children aged five to 11 and their families. To join the Education Department's free mailing list, write to the Education Service at the library itself, call 7412 7797 or see the website.
Buggy access. Café. Nappy-changing facilities. Lift. Nearest picnic place: St James' Gardens. Restaurant. Shop.

British Museum
Great Russell Street, WC1 (7636 1555/textphone 7323 8920/www.thebritishmuseum.ac.uk). Holborn, Russell Square or Tottenham Court Road tube. **Open** *Galleries* 10am-5.30pm Mon-Wed, Sat, Sun; 10am-8.30pm Thur, Fri. *Great Court* 9am-6pm Mon; 9am-9pm Tue, Wed, Sun; 9am-11pm Thur-Sat. Closed 24-26 Dec, 1 Jan. *Highlights tours* 10.30am, 1pm, 3pm daily; phone to check. *EyeOpeners tours* frequently; phone to check. **Admission** (LP) free; donations appreciated. Temporary exhibitions prices vary; phone for details. *Highlights tours* £8; £5 concessions, 11-16s; free under-10s. *EyeOpeners tours* free. **Credit** MC, V. **Map** p317 K5.
Trying to see all the exhibits at the British Museum is a bit like trying to speed-read the Encyclopedia Britannica: don't even try it. The British Museum, which embodies the Enlightenment concept that all arts and sciences are connected, is best appreciated in bite-size chunks.

The museum is known for its Ancient Egyptian artefacts – the Rosetta Stone, monumental statues of the pharaohs and mummies in glass cases – and Ancient Greek treasure, including the Elgin Marbles. The Celts gallery contains the Lindow Man, killed in 300 BC and preserved in peat ever since.

The year 2003 marks the British Museum's 250th anniversary. Exhibitions include: London, 1753, which takes a look at different London neighbourhoods in, you guessed it, 1753, through the use of prints, drawings and watercolours (until 23 November 2003); Well-being in World Cultures, a new anthropology gallery; and Treasure: Finding Our Past, an exhibition devoted to the discoveries of ancient treasures by ordinary people (7 November 2003-29 February 2004). The biggest highlight of 2003, however, will be the opening of the restored King's Library in November. Built in the 1820s, the library has a Grade I-listed interior, widely considered to be the finest neoclassical space in London. It will house a splendid new permanent exhibition, Enlightenment: Rethinking the World in the 18th Century, a 5,000-strong collection which will examine the formative period of the Museum's history.

If it all gets a little too overwhelming, the museum offers sampler tours of its top treasures, which start from the information desk (£8 for a 90-minute tour; £3.50 for an audio guide), or EyeOpener tours (free, 50 mins), which concentrate on specific aspects of the collection. There are also family backpacks, which contain puzzles and games. Lasting childhood memories are sure to result from a museum sleepover, in which children can doss down in the mummy galleries. Sleepovers are available only to Young Friends of the British Museum (membership costs £17.50). Finally, if visiting a museum with your children sounds like a living hell, the treasures of the museum are available for perusal from a souvenir guide (£6) and the website. *Buggy access. Cafés. Lifts. Nappy-changing facilities. Nearest picnic place: Russell Square. Restaurant. Shops.*

The **British Museum.**
See p56.

Courtauld Institute Gallery
Somerset House, Strand, WC2 (7848 2526/ education 7848 2922/www.courtauld.ac.uk). Covent Garden or Temple tube (closed Sun)/ Charing Cross tube/rail. **Open** 10am-6pm (last entry 5.15pm) daily; 31 Dec 10am-4pm; 1 Jan noon-6pm. Closed 24-26 Dec. Tours phone for details. **Admission** £5; £4 concessions; free under-18s, students, registered unwaged. Free to all 10am-2pm Mon (not bank hols). Annual ticket £10. **Credit** MC, V. **Map** p319 M7.
Housed in the glorious 18th-century Somerset House, the Courtauld has one of the finest art collections in London – or indeed in the country. The bulk of the collection comprises Impressionist and Post-Impressionist works, and the masses of masterpieces include a version of Manet's *Le Déjeuner sur l'herbe*, Cézanne's *The Card Players* and Gauguin's *Nevermore*. But the gallery also houses lovely Renaissance paintings including the work of Botticelli and Parmigianino, and there are rooms devoted to Rubens, Van Dyck and 17th- and 18th-century British Portraiture. A 20th-century gallery displays works by Matisse, Kandinsky, Hepworth and Moore.
The gallery encourages visits from schools and families. Art packs are free for children from the ticket desk. There are several educational programmes for children: topics range from Weather Watching, an examination of weather in paintings, to Gods and Goddesses, in which students try their hand at classical sculpture. Programmes for A-Level students provide more sophisticated lectures. Holiday and half-term sculpting and painting workshops are also a popular fixture: call 7848 2922 to book.

Buggy access. Cafés. Lift. Nappy-changing facilities (in Somerset House, near Gilbert Collection entrance). Nearest picnic place: Somerset House courtyard/Embankment Gardens. Restaurant. Shop.

Gilbert Collection
Somerset House, Strand, WC2 (7240 4080/www.gilbert-collection.org.uk). Covent Garden or Temple tube (closed Sun)/Charing Cross tube/rail. **Open** 10am-6pm (last entry 5.30pm) daily; 31 Dec 10am-4pm; 1 Jan noon-6pm. Closed 24-26 Dec. **Tours** phone for details. **Admission** £5; £4 concessions; free under-18s, students, registered unwaged. Free to all after 4.30pm daily. *Annual ticket* £10. **Credit** AmEx, MC, V. **Map** p319 M7.
Situated in the south building of Somerset House, the Gilbert Collection is London's newest museum of decorative arts. Consisting of the private collection of British businessman Sir Arthur Gilbert, the collection is a treasure trove of all things glittering: bejewelled snuff boxes, shiny silverware and golden trinkets once owned by Louix XV and Napoleon. The most famous piece is a magnificent silver swan, but the most glamorous items are surely the gem-encrusted boxes made for Frederick the Great of Prussia. The collection holds family workshops every Saturday morning and afternoon, and daily during the school holidays. Typical events include Shields and Chivalry (in which you create your own fabric shield), jewellery making,

make-your-own-mask sessions, and Exploring Precious Stones (in which you examine crystals under a microscope). For more information about children's workshops, contact the Education Department on 7420 9406.
Buggy access. Cafés. Lift. Nappy-changing facilities. Nearest picnic place: Somerset House courtyard/ Embankment Gardens. Restaurant. Shop.

Hermitage Rooms
Somerset House, Strand, WC2 (info 7845 4630/ www.hermitagerooms.co.uk). Covent Garden or Temple tube (closed Sun)/Charing Cross tube/rail. **Open** 10am-6pm (last entry 5pm) daily; 31 Dec 10am-4pm; 1 Jan noon-6pm. Closed 24-26 Dec. **Admission** £6; £4 concessions; free under-16s. **Credit** MC, V. **Map** p319 M7.
The third art collection in Somerset House is home to a rotating series of exhibitions from the State Hermitage Museum in St Petersburg. The rooms are decorated in grand style, and new exhibitions from Russia are unveiled once or twice a year. Recent highlights include Caspar David Friedrich and Masterpieces from Sir Robert Walpole's collection. Workshops for schools coincide with each exhibition: Call 7420 9406 for details, or join the Somerset House mailing list.
Buggy access. Cafés. Lift. Nappy-changing facilities. Nearest picnic place: Somerset House courtyard/ Embankment Gardens. Restaurant. Shop.

Museum & Library of the Order of St John
St John's Gate, St John's Lane, EC1 (7324 4074/ www.sja.org.uk/history). Farringdon tube/rail. **Open** 10am-5pm Mon-Fri; 10am-4pm Sat. Closed 24 Dec-2 Jan, bank hol weekends; phone to check. **Tours** 11am, 2.30pm Tue, Fri, Sat. **Admission** free; suggested donations for tours £5; £3.50 concessions. **Map** p320 O4.
Who knew that the St John's Ambulance people had such a fascinating history? This unsung little museum traces the history of the Order of the Hospital of St John of Jerusalem, set up during the Crusades to protect sick pilgrims from warring Muslims. The museum delivers a broad historical education, covering topics such as medieval medicine and warfare, caring for workers during the Industrial Revolution, and the rise of modern warfare, culminating in the Order's work during the Gulf War of 1991. Exhibits include traditional museum stuff – old silver, furniture, weaponry – and multimedia exhibits about the St John Ambulance brigade. Kids can also bone up on architecture here. Take a tour of the magnificent Priory of the Knights Hospitallers, with its Tudor Gate House, 16th- century church and 12th-century Crypt.
To get children into the spirit of things, the museum has activity packs, books and videos, and the Education Office organises school visits. You can also find out about getting

---

LONDON LEGEND Dickens in Bloomsbury

Charles Dickens had a miserable childhood: his family was sent to Marshalsea Prison for debt, and Charles was forced to leave school and work in a blacking (shoe polish) factory when he was 12. The poverty of his youth left deep scars. So when Dickens' career took off after the publication of *The Pickwick Papers* in 1836, he decided to move to the poshest house he could afford: 48 Doughty St, in Bloomsbury. In 1837, Dickens and his young family settled in what the author referred to as 'a frightfully first class mansion'. The family, which comprised his wife Catherine Hogarth, their baby son Charles, Dickens' brother Fred and young sister-in-law Mary, was very content here at first. At the time, Doughty Street was a gated enclave with its own uniformed guards. The good life agreed with Dickens: here he wrote *Oliver Twist* and *Nicholas Nickleby*, and entertained literary friends such as Wilkie Collins and William Thackeray. A chronic insomniac, Dickens would often roam the streets of Bloomsbury and the City at night, harvesting ideas for his stories.
But his three years at Doughty St were marred by tragedy: the death of his 17-year-old sister-in-law, Mary Hogarth, who collapsed suddenly in the house after a night at the theatre. She died in Dickens' arms and friends said he never recovered from the shock; Little Nell's heartrending death scene in *The Old Curiosity Shop* is thought to have been inspired by Mary's demise. Soon after this awful event, Dickens moved out of the house in Doughty Street and its evidently painful memories. His new home was in Devonshire Terrace near the pleasant green spaces of Regent's Park.

The house that provided the author with so much joy – and heartache – is now open to the public. The Charles Dickens Museum, the author's only surviving London residence, is full of memorabilia and artefacts: it's a must-see for the literary-minded and Dickens fans. Its passageways are decorated with paintings of famous Dickens characters, such as Little Nell, Uriah Heep and Little Dorrit. The rooms, meanwhile, are full of Dickens' personal effects: his lemon squeezer, walking stick, snuff box and more. Other displays include an array of his personal letters, the original manuscript of *Nicholas Nickleby*, and the desk on which Dickens wrote *Oliver Twist*. In the basement, there's a short film covering Dickens' life in London, and a Children's Handling Room, in which kids can write with the same type of quill pen used by the author, leaf through a first edition of *Nicholas Nickleby*, and handle other original artefacts. Special events for 2003 include Gore of Yore, a child-friendly historical exhibition based on the author's *A Child's History of England* (29 April-31 October); Christmas for Dickens, (December) and Peake's Bleak House, displaying never-before-seen illustrations by Mervyn Peake (of *Gormenghast* fame) which were intended for *Bleak House* (1 June-28 September 2004).

The Charles Dickens Museum
48 Doughty Street, WC1 (7405 2127/www.dickens museum.com). Chancery Lane or Russell Square tube/Kings Cross tube/rail. **Open** 10am-5pm Mon-Sat; 11am-5pm Sun. **Admission** £4; £2 5s-15s. **Credit** AmEX, MC, V. **Map** p317 M4.

Playtime past and present at **Pollock's Toy Museum**.

your children involved with St John's Ambulance work. Child recruits, known as Little Badgers and Cadets, are taught the rudiments of first aid and take exams in basic medicine. Membership is free, although you have to buy the uniform. *Buggy access. Shop.*

Petrie Museum of Egyptian Archaeology

University College London, Malet Place, WC1 (7679 2884/www.petrie.ucl.ac.uk). Goodge Street tube. **Open** 1-5pm Tue-Fri; 10am-1pm Sat. Closed 24 Dec-2 Jan, Easter hols. **Admission** free; donations appreciated. **Map** p317 K4.

If the British Museum has all the big showstopping pieces from Ancient Egypt, the Petrie Museum of Archaeology contains all the minutiae of Egyptian life: makeup pots, grooming accessories, jewellery and, most famously, the world's oldest piece of clothing (a dress that was worn by a teenager in 2800 BC). Some of it might be rather heavy going for young children, but there are items that might just take their fancy: a collection of ancient toys, for instance, a rat trap and the coiffured head of a mummy, with eyelashes and brows still intact. The dim surroundings give the place a wonderfully spooky, tomb-like atmosphere. In the summer holidays there are family backpacks with themed trails through the museum, and writing workshops and play schemes, all based around the collections. Special events, such as the museum's archeology weekend, held 19 and 20 July 2003, crop up regularly; check the website to see what's on.
Buggy access. Café. Lifts. Nearest picnic place: Gordon Square.

Pollock's Toy Museum

1 Scala Street (entrance on Whitfield Street), W1 (7636 3452/www.pollocksweb.co.uk). Goodge Street tube. **Open** 10am-5pm (last entry 4.30pm) Mon-Sat. Closed bank hols. **Admission** (LP) £3; £1.50 3-18s, students; free under-3s. **Credit** *Shop* MC, V. **Map** p316 J5.

The Pollock's Toy museum and traditional toyshop is a trip down memory lane, for parents at least. Housed in a four-storey Georgian townhouse, it's crammed with thousands of toys of yore. They don't make toys like they used to, say the grown ups, while children think the stuff is delightfully quaint. There's the oldest teddy bear in the world (dating from 1905), dolls the size of children, and vintage Action Men, not to mention dolls' houses, Snakes & Ladders, Victorian puppets and a huge range of tin toys. The creaky old house they all reside in adds to the Curiosity Shoppe feel. Speaking of which, the shop offers just about the best selection of vintage toys anywhere: handpainted Jack-in-the-boxes, Wooden toy theatres, ventriloquist puppets and dollhouse miniatures, yo-yos, marionettes, all delightful throwbacks to the era before PlayStation. The toy theatre can be booked for parties (minimum ten children; admission charges as above) and school groups are welcome (call first).
Nearest picnic place: Colville Place Gardens. Shop.

Prince Henry's Room

17 Fleet Street, EC4 (7936 4004). Temple tube (closed Sun). **Open** 11am-2pm Mon-Sat. Closed bank hol weekends. **Admission** free; donations appreciated. **Map** p320 N6.

Prince Henry's Room is one of the few survivors of the 1666 Great Fire of London still standing today. It's a beautiful oak-panelled space with one of the best Jacobean plaster ceilings in the city, and a good spot to take children interested in architecture and history. Formerly used by the lawyers of Prince Henry, eldest son of King James I of England, the room was built in 1610, the same year the 14-year-old Henry became the Prince of Wales. He did not last long, dying of typhoid at 18. His brother succeeded to the throne as Charles I. The rest of the building – now an office – was once a tavern called the Prince's Arms, a favourite haunt of Samuel Pepys, the chronicler of 17th century London life. A collection of Pepys memorabilia is on display.
Nearest picnic place: Temple Gardens.

PARKLIFE Coram's Fields

What does it have? What doesn't it have, more like. There are lawns, sandpits, a paddling pool, an astroturf football pitch, a basketball court, a toddler's gym, a wooden climbing tower, swings, a helter-skelter chute, an assault-course pulley and, most famously, a city farm: sheep, goats, geese, ducks, rabbits, guinea pigs and an aviary. During the summer, bands and circus performers entertain picnicking families. And staff are busy developing a wildlife garden, for which the help of young green thumbs would be welcome.

A visit to the neighbourhood would be incomplete without a stroll through London's famous children's park. Established in 1936, these seven acres have become a city institution. Mention it to a Bloomsbury resident and they'll tell you how the roosters wake them up in the morning; mention it to a night owl and they'll tell you a story about the surreal experience of walking home drunk in Bloomsbury and meeting sheep in the small hours. The site was famous long before it became a park, however: its origins date to 1747, the year retired sea captain Thomas Coram established the Foundling Hospital for abandoned children. After the orphanage was demolished in 1920s, developers were poised to swoop: happily, a campaign to turn the site into a children's park was successful, and today, it's a kids' oasis.

Parents love the park because it's safe. It's permanently staffed, and no adults are allowed in the park unaccompanied by children. What's more, no bullying, swearing, disobedience or racism is permitted. The park offers a range of sporting activities, all free (call the office for a list). Then there's t'ai chi, dancing, drama and other activities, some free, some not. A youth centre has free IT courses for 16-19 year olds. To make life easier for parents, there's a cafe in summer, toilets and shower rooms with disabled facilities, a nursery, a drop-in playgroup, and after-school and holiday play centres.

Coram's Fields

93 Guilford Street, WC1 (7837 6138). Russell Square tube. **Open** *May-Aug 9am-7pm daily. Sept-Apr 9am-dusk daily. Closed 25, 26 December.* **Admission** *free.*

Roman Bath

Strand Lane, WC2 (no phone). Temple tube (closed Sun). **Open** *10am-12.30pm Mon-Fri.* **Admission** *free.* **Map** *p319 M7.*

The Roman Bath was the site of many a cold plunge by David Copperfield, Charles Dickens's semi-autobiographical hero. It's not actually Roman at all – experts think it was built in the 1700s – and although its water comes from the Holy Well of St Clement, once believed to have spa qualities, it looks pretty grotty today. Opening times are limited, but this quirky site can always be viewed through a window and lit up from a switch on the adjacent wall.

St Clement Danes Church

Strand, WC2 (7242 8282). Temple tube (closed Sun). **Open** *9am-4pm daily. Closed bank hols.* **Admission** *free.* **Map** *p320 M6.*

Does the S Club 7 generation even learn nursery rhymes? If your children are familiar with the little ditty 'Oranges and lemons say the bells of St Clements', this church might be of some interest to them. The catchy little tune might not have originated here (experts reckon that honour goes to St Clements, St Clement's Court, EC4, 7626 0220), but the church has embraced the song with gusto: its bells ring out the tune three times a day (9am, noon and 3pm) and an annual

Oranges & Lemons service is held in April for the children of St Clement Danes Primary School, who perform a short play in return for free oranges and lemons. The church's curious name dates back to the time of Alfred the Great. Back then it was used by the Danes who, after ravaging England, married English women and settled here. Bombed by the Germans in 1941, the church was rebuilt in 1958 and dedicated to the RAF – daily prayers and memorial services for members of the air force are held here. Outside stands a statue of Arthur 'Bomber' Harris, one of the more controversial figures in RAF history – he ordered the raids on Dresden. *Buggy access. Nearest picnic place: Embankment Gardens.*

St Dunstan in the West

186A Fleet Street, EC4 (7242 6027). Chancery Lane tube. **Open** *10am-2pm Tue; 5-8pm Fri; 2-6pm Sat; 9am-2pm Sun. Closed bank hols.* **Admission** *free; donations appreciated.* **Map** *p320 N6.*

The best feature of this church can be seen without setting foot inside: the ancient clock (the first in London to acquire a minute hand), which dates from 1670. The rest of the church was rebuilt in 1833 in a Gothic style, but the clock still marks quarter past the hour with two giant clockwork statues emerging with enormous cudgels. Metaphysical poet and priest John Donne was rector here (1624-31). Inside, there's a

bust to Donne, who went on to become the Dean of St Paul's. He was just one of many literary greats, including Milton, Samuel Pepys and Izaak Walton (who wrote the *Compleat Angler*), who worshipped here.
Buggy access.

St Etheldreda
14 Ely Place, EC1 (7405 1061). Chancery Lane or Farringdon tube. **Open** 8am-7pm daily; phone to check. Closed 26 Dec. **Admission** free; donations appreciated. **Map** p320 N5.
St Etheldreda Church is London's only surviving example of Gothic architecture from the 13th century and the capital's oldest Catholic church. But kids might find it interesting for more curious reasons. Bizarrely, Ely Place, the atmospheric little enclave on which the church is situated, is not technically part of London. Owned by the Crown and ruled by its own commission, Ely Place is London's equivalent of the Vatican, subject to its own laws. Through a quirk of legal history, it's actually part of Cambridgeshire. Ely Place was also the street in which David Copperfield met Agnes Wakefield, and the strawberries grown in St Etheldreda's gardens received a mention for juiciness in Shakespeare's *Richard III*. The annual Strawberrie Fayre takes place in June.
Café (noon-2.30pm Mon-Fri).

Sir John Soane's Museum
13 Lincoln's Inn Fields, WC2 (7405 2107/education officer 7440 4247/www.soane.org). Holborn tube. **Open** 10am-5pm Tue-Sat; 6-9pm 1st Tue of mth. Closed bank hol weekends. **Tours** 2.30pm Sat. **Admission** free;

LUNCH BREAK

Bank Aldwych (1 Kingsway, WC2, 7379 9797; *see p163*), besuited giant with children's menu.
Café in the Park (Russell Square, WC2, no phone), a simple but functional caff in a new pavilion, purveyor of all-day breakfasts.
Court Café (British Museum, Great Russell Street, WC1, 7636 1555), for lavish hot chocolate and yummy pastries in the grand Great Court.
Navarro's (67 Charlotte Street, W1, 7637 7713; *see p163*), for filling Spanish tapas.
North Sea Fish Restaurant (8 Leigh Street, WC1, 7387 5892), a convenient stop-off for a great British plate of fish 'n' chips.
Pizza Express (30 Coptic Street, WC1, 7636 3232; *see p175*), for scrummy pizzas in close proximity to the British Museum.
Spaghetti House (20 Sicilian Avenue, WC1, 7405 5215; *see also p182*), the local link in a chain that does good junior-sized pasta platefuls.
Table Café (Habitat, 196 Tottenham Court Road, WC1, 7636 8330; *see also p163*), for colourful Italian food in a relaxed setting.
Wagamama (4A Streatham Street, WC1, 7323 9223 & 14A Irving Street, WC1, 7839 2323; *see p180*), for oodles of noodles, healthy juices in a smoke-free atmosphere.
Yo! Sushi (myhotel, 11-13 Bayley Street, Bedford Square, WC1, 7636 0076; *see p170*), for tasty morsels on colour-coded plates.
Best place for picnics: Coram's Fields (*see p60*).

donations appreciated. *Tours* £3; free concessions, under-16s. **Credit** *Shop* MC, V. **Map** p317 M5.
This museum is a London treasure. Highly cultured children will get the most out of their visit, but most kids enjoy the idiosyncratic collection of sculpture, painting, furniture, architectural models, antiquities, jewellery and other odds and sods that cram the rooms. The place is crawling with young sketchers – artists should bring their pad and pencil.
Sir John Soane (1753-1837) was one of the leading architects, and most obsessive collectors, of his day. Like Frederick Horniman after him (*see p132*), Soane's collection of curios grew so enormous he had to turn his house into a museum. Highlights include Hogarth's *Rake's Progress* and the 3,300-year-old sarcophagus of an Egyptian pharaoh. Then there are hundreds of plaster casts of ancient Greek statues, animals, cherubs and nymphs, ornate furniture and many of Soane's own architectural designs. For an extra magical atmosphere, visit on the first Tuesday evening of each month when the house is lit by candles.
Temporary exhibitions for 2003 – the museum's 250th anniversary – include John Flaxman: 1755-1826, devoted to the works of the great British sculptor (25 April-14 June 2003), Bob the Roman: the Heroic Antiquity and the Architecture of Robert Adam (27 June-27 September 2003) and George Dance the Younger 1741-1825, a survey of the architectural master who taught John Soane (10 October 2003-3 January 2004). The year 2004 has a more child-friendly exhibition planned: William West and the Rise of the Toy Theatre (January-March) while modernists will rush to see the Maggie Centres: Masterpieces of design by Frank Gehry, Daniel Libeskind, Zaha Hadid, Richard Rogers and others (March-June 2004).
Soane's mission was to educate people about art and architecture. To that end, the museum offers special lectures, tours and workshops for schoolchildren (call 7440 4247). Family trail leaflets are available from the reception area. Holiday drawing and architecture workshops for children are also held regularly. Bear in mind that under-12s are not allowed into the museum unless they're with an adult.
Nearest picnic place: Lincoln's Inn Fields. Shop.

Somerset House
Strand, WC2 (7845 4600/www.somerset-house.org.uk) Covent Garden or Temple tube (closed Sun)/Charing Cross tube/rail. **Open** 10am-6pm daily; extended opening hours for Courtyard & River Terrace. Closed 25 Dec. **Tours** phone for details. **Admission** *Parts of South Building, Courtyard & River Terrace* free; charge for exhibitions. **Credit** *Shop* MC, V. **Map** p319 M7.
Closed to the public for almost a century, Somerset House is now one of London's loveliest attractions. It was commissioned by King George III and is a splendid example of neoclassical architecture. It houses three fine art galleries: the Courtauld Institute Gallery (*see p57*), the Gilbert Collection (*see p57*) and the Hermitage Rooms (*see p58*). In winter it's also home to a new London institution: a lovely outdoor skating rink, situated in the fountain courtyard (book early: it sells out months in advance). During summer, the famous ice rink is replaced by a series of fountains – perfect for children to splash around in. And as if that weren't enough, the courtyard is the venue for free family events: puppet shows, storytelling, and art workshops. Other attractions include tours led by staff in period costume, talks on life in a Tudor palace and river history. Set on the north bank of the Thames, it's also a good spot for just enjoying a day by the river.
Buggy access. Cafés. Lift. Nappy-changing facilities. Nearest picnic place: Somerset House courtyard/River Terrace/Embankment Gardens. Restaurant. Shop.

Around Town

Kensington & Chelsea

Royal memories, palatial museums, posh parks and gardens – London doesn't get much grander than this.

Art in the park at the **Serpentine Gallery**

Designated a 'Royal' borough just after Queen Vic died, Kensington and Chelsea takes in some of London's grandest addresses. Victoria, who was born in **Kensington Palace** in 1819, had been a happy princess here. She passed on her fondness of the area to her beloved husband, Albert, who is remembered with a golden memorial opposite another, somewhat larger souvenir, the Royal Albert Hall. Prince Albert is always credited with the huge, ambitious and successful Great Exhibition in 1851, profits from which went to build famous museums. The **Science Museum** houses some of the world's greatest inventions, the **Natural History Museum** celebrates life in all its diversity, while the **Victoria & Albert Museum** is a repository of all beauty.

The other princess linked to fashionable Kensington and Chelsea is Princess Diana. Kensington Palace was her home, and many people think of her when they watch children play in the enchanting **Diana, Princess of Wales Memorial Playground** in Kensington Gardens – appropriately enough, since Diana, whose death in a Paris car crash shocked the nation in 1997, was famous for her love of children.

The southern gates of Hyde Park, London's poshest park, lead to the streets of Knightsbridge, London's poshest shopping area and home to that most opulent of department stores, **Harrods**. From here, Sloane Street runs toward Chelsea, and the world-renowned Royal Court Theatre on Sloane Square. The King's Road was the height of trendiness and home of punk a few decades ago, but is now a much cosier prospect – beloved of mummies and daddies thanks to its excellent batch of children's shops . From the King's Road it's a short walk south to Chelsea Royal Hospital, site of the hugely popular flower show every summer and the **National Army Museum**.

The rich and famous have super apartments near the waterfront and the Chelsea Embankment. From the Embankment you can admire a work of great beauty, the Albert Bridge, built in 1873, yet another monument to the love of Queen Victoria's long life.

Baden-Powell House
65-7 Queen's Gate, SW7 (7584 7031/www.scoutbase. org.uk). South Kensington tube. **Open** 7am-10pm daily. Closed 22 Dec-3 Jan. **Admission** free. **Map** p315 D10.

PARKLIFE Hyde Park & Kensington Gardens

Hyde Park is the largest of London's royal parks (one and a half miles long and about a mile wide), and was the first to be opened to the public. In the early 17th century all the best people came here to strut, take the air and hold duels with sworn foes.

Duelling is now conspicuous by its absence, but instead there's an awful lot of in-line skating and horsey antics. Every morning the soldiers of the Household Cavalry emerge smartly from their barracks and ride across the park to Horse Guards Road, prior to the Changing of the Guard (11.15am) at Buckingham Palace. Meanwhile, civilians keen to saddle up can trot over to the riding schools near posh Rotten Row, part of the wide riding track around Hyde Park.

Speakers' Corner, near Marble Arch, is where members of the public exercise their right of free speech every Sunday (it's the world's oldest platform for public speaking). More interesting than the oratory, at least as far as children are concerned, is the playground on South Carriage Drive, just beyond the Serpentine (a lake formed by the damming of the River Westbourne in the 18th century). Like all royal park playgrounds, it's clean and well kept, but its slides, swings and climbing frames aren't a patch on the earthly paradise (if you're six) that is the **Diana, Princess of Wales Memorial Playground**, in Kensington Gardens. The Park merges into the Gardens just beyond the **Serpentine Gallery**. If rowing floats your boat, the Serpentine is London's oldest and most famous boating lake. Boats are available for hire on the north bank and the season runs from March to October. You can row your boat to any part of the quarter-mile lake as long as you think you can get back within the time you have booked for. Kid under 12 must wear life jackets (provided).

Hyde Park

7298 2100/www.royalparks.gov.uk. High Street Kensington, Hyde Park Corner, Knightsbridge, Lancaster Gate or Marble Arch tube. **Open** 5am-midnight daily. **Map** p313 7E.

Around Town

This is a memorial hostel to Lord Baden-Powell (1857-1941), founder of scouting. Opened in 1961, it provides accommodation for about 300,000 people from 30 different countries each year, with family rooms for visitors with kids. There's an exhibition about the Chief Scout's life on the ground floor. *Buggy access. Café. Disabled access: toilet. Nappy-changing facilities. Nearest picnic place: Natural History Museum gardens. Shop.*

Chelsea Physic Garden

66 Royal Hospital Road (entrance at Swan Walk), SW3 (7352 5646/www.chelseaphysicgarden.co.uk). Sloane Square tube/11, 19, 22, 239, 319 bus. **Open** *Apr-Oct* noon-5pm Wed; 2-6pm Sun. *Tours* 1.30pm, 3.30pm (check blackboard to confirm); phone for group tours. **Admission** £5; £3 5-16s, students. *Tours* free. **Credit** *Shop* MC, V. **Map** p315 F12.

Beautiful it may be, but the Physic Garden is more a research and education centre than tourist attraction, which explains the rather sparse opening times. It opens all week, however, during the Chelsea Flower Show (19-23 May 2003; ring for 2004 dates) and the Chelsea Festival (16-20 June 2003). The high-walled garden was set up in 1673 and developed by Sir Hans Sloane in the early 18th century. Its 3.5 acres contain healing herbs and rare trees, dye plants and medicinal vegetables; you can even buy some to take home for your own physic garden. Children are encouraged to visit the garden in school groups or to take part in various regular activity days during the summer holidays. The education department organises craft, wildlife and microscopy workshops, and storytelling or music sessions. The tea shop serves lovely cakes. *Buggy access. Café. Disabled access: ramp, toilet. Nappy-changing facilities. Shop.*

Diana, Princess of Wales Memorial Playground

Near Black Lion Gate, Broad Walk, Kensington Gardens, W8 (7298 2117/recorded info 7298 2141). Bayswater or Queensway tube. **Open** 10am-8pm or 1hr before dusk if earlier, daily. Closed 25 Dec. **Admission** free. All adults must be accompanied by a child. (Adults may view the gardens 9.30-10am daily.) **Map** p312 C7.

This fenced-off Never-Never Land is an enchanting place for children. Building the playground alone cost £1.7 million, and upkeep is of prime importance: watchful rangers ensure it stays pristine and stop unaccompanied adults coming in.

The focal point is a pirate ship in a sea of fine white sand. Older children enjoy scaling the rigging to the crow's nest, little ones bring buckets and spades for the sand, and kids of all ages adore the ship's wheel, cabins, pulleys and ropes. When the weather's hot the mermaids' fountain and rocky outcrops are fab for water play (but remember to bring a change of clothes). Beyond these shipshape glories lies the teepee camp: a trio of wigwams, each large enough to hold a sizeable tribe. The tree house encampment has walkways, ladders, slides and 'tree phones'. By way of tribute to the area's connection with Peter Pan's creator JM Barrie, there are images from the 1930s version of the classic etched into the glass in the Home Under the Ground (which also houses the toilets and playground office).

Many of the playground's attractions have been designed to appeal to the senses: sensitive planting of scented shrubs, whispering willows and bamboo, metal dance chimes (tap your foot and hear the note) and touchy-feely sculpture are all carefully designed to engage young visitors to the full. What's more, much of the equipment has been designed for use by children with special needs.
Buggy access. Café. Disabled access: toilet. Nappy-changing facilities. Nearest picnic place: Kensington Gardens.

Kensington Palace

W8 (7937 9561/0870 751 7070/www.hrp.org.uk). Bayswater, High Street Kensington or Queensway tube. **Open** *1 Mar-31 Oct* 10am-6pm daily. *1 Nov-28 Feb* 10am-5pm daily. Last entry 1hr before closing. Closed 24-26 Dec. **Admission** (LP) incl audio guide £10.20; £6.60 5-15s; £7.70 concessions; £31 family (2+3). **Credit** AmEx, MC, V. **Map** p312 B8.

William III and his wife Mary came to live in this Jacobean mansion in 1689, when it was known as Nottingham House. Since then many royals have called it home. The future Queen Victoria was born in the palace in 1819; it has latterly been known as the last home of Princesses Diana and Margaret; and the Duke and Duchess of Kent both have apartments here. The palace is open for tours of the State Apartments, including the ground-floor room where Queen Victoria was baptised, the long King's Gallery, with its Tintoretto nudes and Van Dyck portrait of Charles I and, most popular, the Royal Ceremonial Dress Collection, including 14 lavish dresses worn by Diana, Princess of Wales. This year's special exhibition (until April 2004) is called Hats and Handbags: Accessories from the Royal Wardrobe. It consists of more than 70 items of headwear and a selection of bags as sported by Queen Elizabeth II since her youth. Just don't expect to find out what Her Majesty keeps in her handbag.
Buggy access. Café. Disabled toilet. Nappy-changing facilities. Nearest picnic place: palace grounds. Restaurant. Shop.

National Army Museum

Royal Hospital Road, SW3 (7730 0717/www.national-army-museum.ac.uk). Sloane Square tube/11, 19, 239 bus. **Open** 10am-5.30pm daily. Closed 24-26 Dec, Good Friday, 1st bank hol May. **Admission** free. **Map** p315 F12.

Hard by the Royal Hospital Chelsea (home to retired soldiers known as the Chelsea Pensioners and a small museum of its own), this extensive museum charts 1,000 years of British Army history. There are life-size figures and model battlefields, reconstructions and relics dating back centuries. Prime exhibits include the Road to Waterloo, which features a huge model of the battle starring 75,000 toy soldiers, and the skeleton of Napoleon's mount, Marengo. Redcoats is a permanent gallery that tells the story of the British soldier, starting with the archers of Agincourt in 1415 and following all the way

LUNCH BREAK

Around South Kensington

The restaurants in all three major museums (Science, Natural History and V&A) are, for families, a rather pricey option. You're better off in the cafés, such as the one in the Science Museum basement, where they serve popcorn and hot dogs, or the Globe Café in the Natural History, for children's lunch boxes and snacks. In fact, you're even better off bringing a packed lunch. At the Natural History and V&A Museums you can picnic on the front lawns (or the Pirelli Garden in the V&A). All three have indoor picnic areas, where there's plenty of space to spread out and eat your sandwiches. Outside the museums, try the following.
Café Crêperie (2 Exhibition Road, SW7, 7589 8947), for pancakes with flavourful fillings – sweet or savoury – from around £3.
Daquise (20 Thurloe Street, W7, 7589 6117), for borscht and potato pancakes, Polish style.
Oriental Canteen (2A Exhibition Road, SW7, 7581 8831), for cheap chicken, veggie or beef noodles.

Around Chelsea

Benihana (77 King's Road, SW3, 7376 7799; *see p165*), home of stir-crazy chefs and frying fun.
The Big Easy (332-4 King's Road, SW3, 7352 4071; *see p163*), for children's Tex-Mex menus.
Chelsea Physic Garden (66 Royal Hospital Road, SW3, 7352 5646, Wed & Sun only), a lovely setting for eminently civilised tea and cakes.
Ed's Easy Diner (362 King's Road, SW3, 7352 1956; *see p167*), for brilliant burgers and shakes.
Pizza Express (352A King's Road, SW3, 7352 9790; *see p175*), for pizzas and doughballs.

Around Kensington

Kensington Kiosk (Diana, Princess of Wales Memorial Playground), for burgers and other hot food.
Sticky Fingers (1A Phillimore Gardens, W8, 7938 5338; *see p164*), for a rock 'n' roll theme, a kids' menu – and a magician on Sundays.
Best place for picnics: Hyde Park and Kensington Gardens.

Free time in Albertopolis

Now that the big three are free (although donations are politely requested and gratefully accepted), you can, if you so wish, flit from one gigantic museum to the next, staying in each only long enough to look at the best bits. After all, we all know what they say about the attention spans of children.

On Sunday mornings, families in their hundreds beat a path to the calm, cool spaces of the **V&A** (*see p68*), steering for the information desk to find the whereabouts of the Cart. The Cart, since you ask, is a moveable arts and crafts feast for children aged three and over. The activities they're given relate to the gallery in which the Cart is parked – on a recent visit we learned about the treasures of the India gallery and made an elephant mask.

As you emerge from the elegantly arranged galleries of the V&A, you'll spot the Earth Galleries of the **Natural History Museum** (*see p67*) over the road, where you can ascend the fabulous elevator to the video screens of Restless Planet and its

disturbingly popular mock-up of the Kobe earthquake. An entire Japanese supermarket has been created to provide that authentic Far Eastern 'quake frisson: brace yourself for a shaking. Thrills of a different kind can be had at the dinosaur galleries – few families visit the Natural History without saying hi to the prehistoric lizards. And those who still have some energy left can follow one of the family trails, or take part in weekend or half-term activities.

The biggest noise on a typical weekend in Albertopolis seems to be the **Science Museum** (*see p67*), whose exhibits encourage exploration and investigation by their very nature. Under-fives are most at home in the basement Garden, where water play, construction games, dressing up and being thoroughly noisy are all encouraged. For older children, the IMAX cinema, flight simulators, Virtual Voyages and the hi-tech bits and pieces in the new Wellcome wing are the highlights of this vast, exhausting, inspiring national treasure.

up to the redcoats of the American Revolution; and the Nation in Arms covers the history of the army in two world wars and includes reconstructions of a trench in Flanders, a landing craft off the Normandy coast. The Modern Army gallery gives young visitors the chance to test a Challenger tank simulator, and a splendid art gallery displays, among others, works by Reynolds and Gainsborough.

School and family groups are given gallery trails to guide them round the various eras of the museum. There are also regular special events days throughout the year, and special events weekends every month. Subject matter for these weekends is well chosen and the activities based around them are

fascinating. Notable examples include the Horse in War (6 and 7 September), the Crimean War (4 and 5 October), Remembrance (8 and 9 November) and A Victorian Soldier's Christmas (6 and 7 December). This last one sounds intriguing: participating children discover how a Victorian soldier might have spent his Christmas if he were lucky enough to return home to Britain, then they'll take part in gift-making workshops, see a traditional pantomime, watch a Punch and Judy show and meet Queen Victoria. Ring for more details. *Buggy access. Café. Disabled access: lift, toilet. Nappy-changing facilities. Nearest picnic place: benches outside museum/Chelsea Hospital grounds. Shop.*

DON'T MISS Albertopolis

Natural History Museum
Maggoty provisions in the Creepy Crawlies gallery; the Kobe shake-up in Restless Planet; the T-Rex roaring in the Dinosaur Galleries. *See p67.*

Science Museum
Sussing out the Cessna in the Flight Galleries; flushing the plastic poo in the Secret Life of the Home; perusing the Pattern Pod in the Wellcome Wing; playing in the basement Garden. *See p67.*

Victoria & Albert Museum
A view of the mutability of life in the Time and Death wax tableau in Gallery 2/a; the true beauty of Canova's *The Three Graces* in the British Galleries; fashion artefacts – Biba platform shoes – in the Dress Gallery. *See p68.*

Natural History Museum
Cromwell Road, SW7 (7942 5000/www.nhm.ac.uk). South Kensington tube. **Open** 10am-5.50pm Mon-Sat; 11am-5.50pm Sun. Closed 24-25 Dec. *Tours* hourly, 11am-4pm daily; depending on guide availability. **Admission** free; charges apply for special exhibitions. *Tours* free. **Credit** *Shop* AmEx, MC, V. **Map** p315 D10.
The front door off the Cromwell Road leads you into the Life galleries, from where a left turn takes you to the Dinosaur bit – first stop for many children visiting this glorious storehouse of nature's wonders. Visitors to the Dinosaurs gallery skedaddle directly to see Tyrannosaurus rex. On the way, you pass animatronic Deinonychus, geological and botanical exhibits and other treasures from the Jurassic era: excellent stuff. Then there's Creepy Crawlies (gallery 33), which has an ant colony and some diverting displays revealing insects' domestic habits. The famous life-size blue whale (three buses long) still hangs in Discovering Mammals (Galleries 23 and 24), as it has done for more than half a century.
The Earth Galleries are approached via Exhibition Road. You travel up an escalator that takes you up through a suspended, revolving globe and leads to a series of impressive galleries designed to better acquaint visitors with the mysteries of their planet. Earth's Treasury presents its component minerals and rocks; Restless Surface examines how natural elements change the planet. Volcanoes and earthquakes are presented in all their fury.
Phase one of the spanking new Darwin Centre lets visitors go behind the scenes and see some unique collections for the first time. It houses 22 million specimens, of which 450,000 are stored in jars of alcohol. There are twice-daily tours to meet the scientists who work among the collections and learn about their research. Check the website for more information. Phase two is scheduled to open in 2007.
There are also activity trails (available from the box office), half-term and school holiday events programmes and weekend workshops for families. The themes of these change frequently, so it's best to check the website or ring the booking line (7942 5555) to find out what's on.
Outside in the grounds, until autumn 2003, there's a large exhibition entitled Earth from the Air: A Photographic Portrait of Our Planet, by French aerial photographer Yann Arthus-Bertrand. The selection of 150 images from his astonishing project creates a visual record of the state of our planet

today. The exhibition, which includes a giant walk-on map of the world, has been specially designed for all weather conditions. The Museum's Wildlife Garden is generally open during the summer, but mainly for tours. Staff run investigative sessions there to help people learn about British wildlife. Check the website for availability.
Buggy access. Cafés. Disabled toilet, lift. Nappy-changing facilities. Nearest picnic place: indoor eating area/museum grounds. Restaurant. Shops.

Oratory Catholic Church
Thurloe Place, Brompton Road, SW7 (7808 0900). South Kensington tube. **Open** 6.30am-8pm daily; phone to check. **Admission** free; donations appreciated. **Map** p315 E10.
Also known as the Brompton Oratory, this is the second largest Catholic church in the city (Westminster Cathedral occupies the top slot), and is full of extravagant marbles and mosaics designed to strike awe into mortal hearts. Many of the internal decorations are much older than the building itself. Mazzuoli's late 17th-century statues of the apostles, for example, once stood in Siena Cathedral. During the Cold War, the church was used by Russian spies as a dead letter box.
The Oratory's Junior Choir sings Mass at 10am on Sundays. Schola, the boys' choir of the London Oratory School, performs Mass on Saturday evenings during term time.
Buggy access. Disabled access: ramp. Nearest picnic place: Holy Trinity Brompton churchyard. Shop.

Science Museum
Exhibition Road, SW7 (7942 4454/recorded info 0870 870 4868/www.sciencemuseum.org.uk). South Kensington tube. **Open** 10am-6pm daily. Closed 24-26 Dec. **Admission** free; charges apply for special exhibitions. **Credit** *IMAX cinema, shops* AmEx, MC, V. **Map** p315 D9.
The English Tourism Council's Visitor Attraction of the Year for 2002 is huge, and on rainy Sundays it seems the world, his wife and his kids are here. They all have their favourite bit (parents of a certain age are strangely drawn to the Secret Life of the Home, in the basement). Landmark inventions in the vast collection include Stephenson's Rocket, one of the first steam engines; Arkwright's spinning machine; Bell's telephone; Whittle's turbojet aero engine; the Vickers Vimy aircraft in which Alcock and Brown crossed the Atlantic in 1919; and the Apollo 10 command module.
The Wellcome Wing, named after the medical charity that contributed to the project, contains much of specific interest to children. The Launch Pad is a technological adventure playground where children of all ages can mix science with fun. In the basement, the Garden, for three- to six-year-olds, involves learning through water play, soft play, construction and dressing up. Many people accompanied by under-fives spend their entire visit in the basement.
The Wellcome Wing's Virtual Voyages is an exciting 15-minute simulated ride to Mars, which involves plenty of motion and costs £3.50 for adults and £2.50 for children. Tickets for the five-storey IMAX® cinema cost £6.95 for adults, £5.95 for under-16s and £19.95 for families. The venue screens eye-popping 40-minute 3-D shows: *Space Station 3D*, filmed by astronauts and narrated by Tom Cruise, is the first 3D IMAX® film shot in space; the self-explanatory *Human Body* is narrated by Professor Robert Winston.
Science Night sleepovers (held once a month, except for August, for eight- to 11-year-olds) consist of an evening of activities followed by a sleepover among the exhibits. Not surprisingly, they're extremely popular, so book one to two months ahead. There are children's educational events and workshops every half-term and school holidays. These can't be booked in advance, so turn up early on the day. For details of events for children, sign up for the mailing list.

LONDON LEGEND Prince Albert's big party

Queen Victoria's love for her husband Albert knew no bounds, but her German consort enjoyed little in the way of affection from her subjects – until 1851, that is, the year of the Great Exhibition.

The brains behind the planning of a huge international event to celebrate achievements in manufacturing, science and the arts belonged in fact to a chap called Henry Cole. He approached Prince Albert for patronage, and encouraged statesman Sir Robert Peel to get involved. Once the project was under way and public excitement began to rise, Cole selflessly encouraged the nation to believe it had been Prince Albert's baby all along. Just as well then, that the Exhibition turned out to be an enormous success, enjoyed by six million people in six months. Queen Victoria herself visited several times, and wrote glowingly of the marvels she saw there.

The Crystal Palace, a colossal greenhouse which hosted the Great Exhibition in Hyde Park, was desiged by Joseph Paxton. It was 1,851 feet long, 100 feet high and covered 26 acres. When the Exhibition ended it was taken down and rebuilt in Sydenham (in the area now known as Crystal Palace park). The structure burned down in 1936, and London's next 'great' exhibition was held in the Millennium Dome (which its many detractors would gladly set fire to even today). Comparisons between the Victorian success and the year-long Dome exhibition of 2000-1 are, clearly, invidious.

The profits of the Great Exhibition, which came to £356,000 (a huge amount of money at the time), paid to put up the South Kensington Arts Centre, also affectionately known as Albertopolis.

The golden statue of Prince Albert in Hyde Park – a memorial to an enlightened patron of the arts and sciences – shows him holding a Great Exhibition catalogue. But, just like Henry Cole, Prince Albert was a modest man – 'I would rather not be made the prominent feature of such a monument'. There he stands, though, all gilded and especially gorgeous since restoration in 1998. Guided tours of the Albert Memorial can be booked on 7495 0916/www.tourguides.co.uk.

New exhibitions this year include Titanic: The Artefact Exhibition (until 28 September 2003). Currently the world's only collection of authentic artefacts recovered from the wreck of the Titanic eight decades after she sank, it takes you on a chronological journey of the Titanic, from its design and construction through its fateful maiden voyage. Attractions include full-sized room recreations of some of Titanic's luxurious interior spaces, including a first-class cabin. The other big show, planned for the end of 2003, is Lord of the Rings. Check the website for details and prices.
Buggy access. Cafés. Disabled access: lift, toilet. Lifts. Nappy-changing facilities. Nearest picnic place: basement of museum/Hyde Park. Restaurant. Shops.

Serpentine Gallery
Kensington Gardens (near Albert Memorial), W2 (7402 6075/www.serpentinegallery.org). Lancaster Gate or South Kensington tube. **Open** 10am-6pm daily. Closed 25 Dec. *Tours* free; 3pm Sat. **Admission** free. **Map** p313 D8.
It may be housed in a 1930s tearoom, but this gallery for contemporary art is coolly cutting edge: Damien Hirst won the Turner Prize here in 1994. It's a lovely, light space – even more so since it was refurbished a few years ago. Upcoming exhibitions include a collection from New York-based painter John Currin and the photographer Cindy Sherman. On Saturday mornings (10am-noon during term time), the very popular Children's Art Club offers tours of the artworks on display, plus discussions of the techniques and practical workshops for participants' own creativity and expression. Call 7298 1516 for an application form to join the waiting list.
Buggy access. Nappy-changing facilities. Nearest picnic place: Hyde Park/Kensington Gardens. Shop.

Victoria & Albert Museum
Cromwell Road, SW7 (7942 2000/www.vam.ac.uk). South Kensington tube. **Open** 10am-5.45pm Mon, Tue, Thur-Sun; 10am-10pm Wed. Closed 24-26 Dec. *Tours* daily; phone for details. **Admission** free; charges apply for special exhibitions. **Credit** AmEx, MC, V. **Map** p315 E10.

The V&A is truly a museum full of beautiful things – about four million of them, if you're counting. Named after its royal founders, this is Britain's national repository for the study of design and the arts. There are collections of costume, jewellery, tetiles, metalwork, glass, furniture, photographs, drawings, paintings and sculpture from cultures worldwide.

Home-grown treasures are housed in the British Galleries, which opened in 2001 and whose attractions include a range of interactive exhibits for children. In the Victorian Discovery Area, there are corsets and crinolines to try on and a crystal palace to build. The 18th century discovery area has children making domestic objects, and there's tapestry weaving or armour sampling in the Tudor and Stuart Discovery area. Then there are the World Galleries on the ground floor: look out for the Chinese Imperial robes and huge Persian carpets.

Facilities for children include activity backpacks, which children can carry on their adventures across the great spaces of the museum. These backpacks contain the wherewithal for activities linked to the collections. On Sundays (10.30am-5.30pm) children aged from three to 12 can look for the Activity Cart. Family trails are available daily; they provide an activity sheet for children and information sheet for adults.

From the central Pirelli Garden you can admire the handsome red-brick building, which, in 2007 (it is estimated) will be augmented by Daniel Libeskind's ambitious 'Spiral': for now, there's a model of it in the foyer. New this year is the Photography Gallery, which presents work from the V&A's famous photo collection. In October 2003 the major new exhibition Gothic: Art for England 1400-1547 (until January 2004) maps out Gothic culture and provides the focus for a range of children's and family events (making Gothic greeting cards and stained glass windows, Gothic story-telling).

A useful guide, called *What to See at the V&A*, costs £1.25 and is sold on the admission desks and in the shop. *See also* Museum of Childhood at Bethnal Green.
Buggy access. Café. Disabled access: lift, toilets. Nappy-changing facilities. Nearest picnic place: Pirelli Garden (outdoors) or basement picnic room (indoors). Restaurant. Shop.

West End

Jolly good show.

If Petula Clark had been singing about London, Downtown would have been called West End. That's because, for bright lights and big city vibe, the West End is the spiritual heart of London. It's all here: showy department store windows, theatreland glitter, buzzing nightlife and enough tourist attractions to merit a whole guidebook. The West End frontier is fuzzy – *EastEnders* characters talk about going 'up west', but for residents of Ealing, a trip to the West End is actually a long way east. For the purposes of this chapter, the West End includes Soho, Mayfair and Covent Garden.

To get a feel for the area's hustle and bustle, start at **Oxford Circus**. If you're looking for a flagship store – Nike, Top Shop et al – chances are it's here. Walk down **Regent Street**, which is especially pretty around Christmas, with its elaborate shop windows and twinkly lights. Here you'll find the celebrated **Hamleys** – for many kids, London's top attraction. West of Regent Street is Mayfair, London's most exclusive address. **Savile Row** is famous for its tailors, **Grosvenor Square** is home to the American Embassy, and **Berkeley Square** has its Rolls Royce showroom. Fantasy window shopping is also the order of the day on **Old Bond Street** and **New Bond Street**, where the filthy rich go to shop. The artistically minded might be interested in the many commercial galleries on **Cork Street** and **Dering Street**. At the southern end of Regent Street, the hurly burly of **Piccadilly Circus** teems with neon signs and hordes of teenagers. For young people, the main events in Piccadilly Circus are the massive Tower Records or the Trocadero, a funfair-cum-shopping arcade. *Eros* is at the Circus's centre. The winged statue of the boy Cupid was designed by Sir Alfred Gilbert in 1893, in memory of Victorian philanthropist Lord Shaftesbury (1801-85), a prominent figure in the Ragged Schools movement, which provided free education and clothing for deprived children.

Walk north-east up **Shaftesbury Avenue**, dominated by famous theatres along its northern side. Soho is to the north. With its peep shows and XXX bookshops, it's not exactly London's most child friendly corner. Still, it's not half as sleazy as it once was: villagey **Carnaby Street** is always buzzing, and **Berwick Street Market** is another lively spot – just watch your purse. To the south lies **Chinatown**, brimming with atmosphere and wonderful restaurants. Keep going east until you hit **Leicester Square**, home of London's biggest cinemas and frequently the venue for star-studded movie premières. Here you can pick up cheap same-day tickets for West End shows at the **Half-price Ticket Booth** on the south side of the square (www.tkts.co.uk, open 10am-7pm Mon-Sat, noon-3.30pm Sun) – expect to queue. Alternatively, try cut-price ticket shops on the north-east side of the square. Other things to look out for on Leicester Square include busking entertainers and the Charlie Chaplin statue. Just off the square on Leicester Place lies the **Prince Charles Cinema** (7 Leicester Place, WC2, 7734 9127), which quite often screens Sing-a-long-a Sound of Music (www.singalonga.co.uk).

Apsley House: The Wellington Museum

Hyde Park Corner, W1 (7499 5676/www.apsleyhouse. org.uk). Hyde Park Corner tube. **Open** 11am-5pm Tue-Sun, most bank hol Mons. Closed 1 Jan, 24-26 Dec, Good Friday, 1st bank hol May. **Admission** £4.50 (includes audio guide); £3 concessions; free under-18s, over-60s. **Credit** AmEx, DC, MC, V. **Map** p318 G8.

Apsley House, home of the first Duke of Wellington, is one of London's most splendid residences. Although it was built in 1778, the Duke – Arthur Wellesley – didn't settle here until after his victory over Napoleon at Waterloo in 1815. As soon as he moved in he set about enlarging the place: the result is the magnificent 90ft-long Waterloo Gallery, where the Duke housed his impressive art collection. The Duke's descendants still live here, but ten rooms were recently restored to their original splendour and are now open to the public.

Highlights of the collection include Goya's portrait of Wellington, Canova's colossal nude marble statue of Napoleon and ornately-framed paintings by Caravaggio, Rubens, Velázquez and Van Dyck. Outside, a majestic statue of Wellington stands on Hyde Park Corner. The Duke is depicted sitting on his horse, Copenhagen, which lived to the age of 28 and was buried with full military honours. The statue is surrounded by representatives of the Duke's regiments, one from each part of the United Kingdom: the Guards, Royal Highlanders, Inniskilling Dragoons and Welsh Fusiliers.

Special recorded audioguides make the whole experience more palatable for children, and the House offers a schools service, which includes kid-friendly tours by Victorian housekeepers. Every June the museum holds a Waterloo Week celebration, which involves a bit of dressing-up, painting and crafts. For more info about tours, events and workshops, call 7495 8525 and ask to be put on the free mailing list.
Buggy access. Lift. Nearest picnic place: Hyde Park. Shop.

Faraday Museum

Royal Institution, 21 Albemarle Street, W1 (7409 2992/ www.rigb.org). Green Park tube. **Open** 9am-5pm Mon-Fri. Closed 24-26 Dec, 1 Jan, bank holidays. **Tours** by arrangement. **Admission** £1; 50p concessions. *Tours* £5. **Map** p318 J7.

Get a handle on the baroque master at the **Handel House Museum**.

Michael Faraday was quite a chap. Born in 1791, the son of a London blacksmith, Faraday grew up in poverty and yet became one of the most important scientists in history. As a 14-year-old, he took a job as a bookbinder and pored over scientific books. He would eventually be known as 'the father of electricity': he invented the electric motor, discovered electromagnetic induction and developed electric lights for lighthouses. Although he advised the military on a range of issues, he was a strong moralist and refused to produce poison gases for use in the Crimean War. Faraday also shunned fame: he refused a knighthood, and preferred to work quietly at the Royal Institution. Here he launched a series of science lectures for children, called the Royal Institution Christmas Lectures, which continue to this day.

The museum is really only appropriate for scholarly children with a passion for science and maths. Exhibits include a re-creation of Faraday's lab and documents relating to his work. There's an extensive – and very serious – programme of school visits and lectures, and the Institution runs a maths masterclass for gifted students aged 11 and over. For details of these classes and programmes, ring or check the website. *Buggy access. Lift. Nearest picnic place: Berkeley Square or Green Park.*

Handel House Museum
25 Brook Street (entrance at rear), W1 (7495 1685/ www.handelhouse.org). Bond Street tube. **Open** 10am-6pm Tue, Wed, Fri, Sat; 10am-8pm Thur; noon-6pm Sun; bank hol Mons. Closed 24-26 Dec, 1 Jan. **Admission** £4.50; £3.50 concessions; £2 5-16s; free under-5s. **Credit** MC, V. **Map** p318 H6.
Once the home of George Frederic Handel, this handsome Mayfair house has been restored to its period glory and recently opened as a museum devoted to the composer. Fans of Jimi Hendrix also flock here, as the rock star lived next

door at no. 23 during the 1960s; his house is part of the museum. The introductory video about Handel's music and life is engaging, and the house is atmospheric and full of handsome oil paintings of Handel and friends.

The House has a strong education programme, with curriculum-based music, art and drama projects related to Handel's music and art collection. For lighter entertainment, there are regular baroque recitals; the Handel Bag, meanwhile, is a treasure trove of games and activities for kids, available upon request, and the family interactive trail is a child-friendly way of seeing the museum. At Christmas, the House is decked out in festive style and there are carol concerts. Children's activities also take place during school holidays: families might be led through the museum by costumed characters, while other sessions introduce young people to various musical instruments.
Buggy access. Lifts. Nappy-changing facilities. Nearest picnic place: Hanover Square. Shop.

Royal Academy of Arts
Burlington House, Piccadilly, W1 (7300 8000/ www.royalacademy.org.uk). Green Park or Piccadilly Circus tube. **Open** 10am-6pm Mon-Thur, Sat, Sun; 10am-10pm Fri. **Tours** times vary. **Admission** varies depending on exhibition, under-8s free. *Tours* free. **Credit** AmEx, MC, V. **Map** p318 J7.
The Royal Academy was Britain's first art school (it opened in 1768) and held the country's first annual open exhibition for artists. The tradition continues as the Summer Exhibition (June-August), which consistently pulls in large crowds with its thousands of paintings, sculptures and architectural designs. Anyone can submit an entry, regardless of age or nationality, and about ten per cent of works submitted are chosen for display (application forms are available each February). Although the Royal Academy has a permanent

PARKLIFE Phoenix Garden

Phoenix Garden reverses the Joni Mitchell line about paving paradise and putting up a parking lot: here they knocked down a parking lot and created a small oasis. Situated at the north end of Neal Street – just north of Shaftesbury Avenue – this shady little Shangri-La is a lovely spot in which to introduce kids to the wonders of nature in the heart of the city.

The brainchild of the Covent Garden Open Spaces Association (a private charity which campaigned ceaselessly for a bit of green space in the early 1980s), the garden is tranquillity personified in a sea of urban grit. It's a ragged, charming, overgrown little place, with a wealth of diverse plants, including willow, fig, cherry, and walnut trees. Crooked little pathways, wooden trellises, quirky flower pots and dainty little benches – one was donated by Michael Palin – add to the whimsical, Secret Garden feel.

And it's not just pretty: word of this little sanctuary has spread like wildfire in the animal kingdom, and the garden attracts thrushes, blackbirds, frogs, ladybirds and lacewings, all of which provide a natural pest control service (no pesticides are used). To complete the organic picture, all green waste is turned into compost. Paradise doesn't come cheap: the garden relies on volunteers and donors to keep it going, so greenfingered enthusiasts should go along, buy a plant grown in the garden or even get involved. If you'd rather just enjoy the garden with a cup of coffee, a small donation will get you a cuppa from the permanently-staffed, rustic garden shed. The higgledy-piggledy, eccentric atmosphere is usually rich fodder for a child's imagination – if not, there are a couple of big slides to play on in one corner. It's also a lovely spot for an impromptu, urban picnic. Grab a soup and sandwich and sneak off to Covent Garden's best-kept secret.

Phoenix Garden
21 Stacey Street (entrance on St Giles Passage), WC2 (7379 3187). Tottenham Court Road tube. **Open** dawn-dusk daily. **Admission** free. **Map** p317 K6. *Buggy access. Kiosk.*

Learn the tricks of the theatrical trade at the **Theatre Museum**. *See p77.*

collection, it is most famous for its temporary exhibitions – 1999's Monet in the Twentieth Century was widely considered to be the most popular show ever held in Britain. Future exhibitions look at 19th-century French painter Vuillard (January-April 2004) and 18th-century portraiture (autumn 2004). The gallery holds regular family workshops and lectures to coincide with each exhibition. For information on educational activities, call 7300 5995.
Buggy access. Café. Lift. Nappy-changing facilities. Nearest picnic place: Green Park/St James's Square. Restaurant. Shop.

St James's Church Piccadilly
197 Piccadilly, W1 (7734 4511/www.st-james-piccadilly. org). Piccadilly Circus tube. **Open** 8am-7pm daily (phone for details of evening events). Closed 24-26 Dec, some bank hols (phone to check). **Map** p318 J7.
A peaceful respite from the mayhem that is Piccadilly, St James's Church is a Wren creation (1676-84) and said to be one of the architect's favourite works. The church has a rich history: William Blake was baptised here, and Haydn, Handel and Mendelssohn were all organists at St James. It was badly bombed in World War II, but the interior has been painstakingly restored and is noteworthy for its elaborately carved woodwork and white marble font; it's a tranquil setting for lunchtime recitals and evening concerts.
St James's is known for its community spirit – one of its missions is to combat poverty – and welcomes people of all races, creeds and sexualities. It's also famous for its church-yard market (antiques on Tuesdays, arts and crafts from Wednesdays to Saturdays) and lovely garden, which is filled with biblical plants, herbs and flowers. An on-site Caffè Nero provides the coffee and cakes.
Buggy access. Café. Nearest picnic place: St James's Square or church gardens.

Trocadero
1 Piccadilly Circus, W1 (7439 1791/www.troc.co.uk). Piccadilly Circus tube. **Open** 10am-midnight daily. **Admission** free; individual attractions vary. **Credit** varies. **Map** p319 K7.
Let's face it: you can overload on cultural stuff. Sometimes mindless fun is the only way to entertain the kids and, if you're honest, yourself. That's where the Trocadero comes in handy. For kids, Funland is the main attraction. Sadly, all the hair-raising rides of yore have been removed, but this indoor funfair has still got central London's only ten-pin bowling alley, plus dodgems, kiddie rides and 250 up-to-date video games (virtual reality and all). There's also a pool hall (for over-18s) and a sports bar in which to catch the match of the day. A shopping concourse with HMV, the Gadget Shop, First Sport and Athena provides retail therapy, and there are a couple of cinemas – UGC Cinema, The Other Cinema – on hand should all else fail to keep everyone amused.
Cafés. Lift. Nappy-changing facilities. Nearest picnic place: Leicester Square/Trafalgar Square. Restaurants. Shops.

Covent Garden & St Giles

The heart of theatrical London, Covent Garden is also the city's most touristy area. It's easy to see why: as well as the glamorous old theatres, the area is all modish shops and restaurants set on picturesque, winding little streets. It wasn't always this pretty. It started out as Westminster Abbey's convent garden (hence the neighbourhood's name), but by the 18th century the area had fallen into lawlessness. The Bow Street Runners, London's first

police force, were formed here to combat the rampant crime and prostitution. In time, Covent Garden turned into London's main flower and veg market, which in 1973 moved south of the river to Vauxhall. When that happened, the piazza was taken over by bars, cafés, shops, craft stalls and licensed street performers. The latter are a great form of free entertainment for kids, but that economy is offset by the tourist prices on ice-creams and pizzas. For a less commercial experience, seek out the charming enclave of Neal's Yard – through an archway off Short's Gardens – with its pretty courtyard and wholefoods.

The neighbourhood's *raison d'être*, however, is the theatre. London's original theatre district was in Southwark, where playhouses sprang up during the Middle Ages beside gambling dens and brothels. In Cromwell's time, the puritans shut them all down; theatrical types moved across the river to Covent Garden, and the rest is history. **Theatre Royal Drury Lane**, the area's first playhouse, was built in 1663. Covent Garden's largest theatre is the Coliseum, home to the English National Opera (7632 8300; the venue will close for seven months in 2003). But the district's real jewel is the **Royal Opera House**, which is now open to the public for tours. The **Theatre Museum** is another top attraction.

London's Transport Museum

Covent Garden Piazza, WC2 (7379 6344/www.ltmuseum. co.uk). Covent Garden tube. **Open** 10am-6pm Mon-Thur, Sat, Sun; 11am-6pm Fri. Last entry 5.15pm. **Tours** 11am-4pm Sat, Sun. Check at cloakroom for times. **Admission** (LP) £5.95; £4.50 concessions; free under-16s when accompanied by an adult. *Tours* free. **Credit** MC, V. **Map** p319 L7.

This nostalgic museum – the most comprehensive urban transport museum in the world – recalls an era when public transport in Britain was the best on the planet (think on that long-departed time and weep). Kids are free to clamber aboard the old steam trains, double-decker buses and cabriolets in the display area. Adults can wax lyrical about old station signs, posters, uniforms and tickets. The old public transport signs – 'spitting strictly prohibited' – are delightful, as are adverts which graced the sides of buses: 'St Ivel Lactic Cheese Aids Digestion'. A costumed actress provides entertainment with tales of life as a bus conductor during the Blitz. There are exhibits on Frank Pick's distinctive roundel symbol for London Underground, and the collection of old London Transport posters. An entire gallery is devoted to Harry Beck's famous underground map. The museum also celebrates current transport successes – yes, there are a few – such as the DLR and Croydon's tram system.

Kidzones learning stations are scattered around, and simulators let children drive a train themselves. Family Packs are available (£2.50) with quizzes designed to improve children's literacy and number skills. A new Learning Centre has hands-on exhibits, computer games and crafts activities, plus an impressive multimedia research facility: here you can view old film footage of London's first trolleybus in action. Children under ten are admitted at the discretion of staff.

One of the biggest treats is the museum shop, filled with Corgi buses and trains, Mind The Gap T-shirts and underwear, and fascinating books on topics such as London's Disused Underground Stations.

Buggy access. Café. Lift. Nappy-changing facilities. Nearest picnic place: picnic area in ground-floor museum gallery/St Paul's churchyard. Shop.

LUNCH BREAK

Around Soho

Ed's Easy Diner (12 Old Compton Street, W1, 7434 4439; see *p167*), for high stools, great burgers, shakes and chips.
Fortnum & Mason (181 Piccadilly, W1, 7734 8040; see *p168*), for sundaes in the Fountain Restaurant and picnic fare in the food hall.
Häagen Dazs (14 Leicester Square, W1, 7287 9577), for fab ice-cream.
The Hard Rock Café (150 Old Park Lane, W1, 7629 0382; see *p168*), for burgers and rock'n'roll memorabilia.
Maison Bertaux (28 Greek Street, W1, 7437 6007), for the best croissants in London.
Patisserie Valerie (44 Old Compton Street, W1, 7437 3466), for wonderful French cakes.
Planet Hollywood (13 Coventry Street, W1, 7287 1000; see *p169*), for burgers and movie paraphernalia.
Rainforest Café (Trocadero, W1, 7434 3111; see *p169*), for burgers in a tropical setting.
Yo Sushi (Trocadero, W1, 7434 2724), for sushi on a conveyor belt.
Best place for picnics: Green Park.

Around Covent Garden

Belgo Centraal (50 Earlham Street, WC2, 7813 2233; see *p164*), where children eat free if a paying adult eats with them.
Food for Thought (31 Neal Street, WC2, 7836 9072/0239; see *p167*), for chunky veggie fuel.
The Great American Bagel Factory (18 Endell Street, WC2, 7497 1115), for ring-shaped lunch.
Neal's Yard Bakery & Tearoom (6 Neal's Yard, WC2, 7836 5199; see *p169*), for healthy wholemeal grub.
Pizza Express (9-12 Bow Street, WC2, 7240 3443; see *p175*), famed for its well-dressed pizzas.
Pizza Paradiso (31 Catherine Street, WC2, 7836 3609), for a great margherita pizza.
Rock & Sole Plaice (47 Endell Street, WC2, 7836 3785; see *p169*), for great fish and chips.
Spaghetti House (24 Cranbourn St, WC2, 7836 8168; see *p182*), which offers a special pasta meal deal for kids.
World Food Café (first floor, 14 Neal's Yard, WC2, 7379 0298; see *p170*), for global vegetarian food.
Best place for picnics: Phoenix Garden or St Paul's churchyard.

All the fun of the fare at **London's Transport Museum**. *See p74.*

Royal Opera House

Bow Street, WC2 (7304 4000/www.royaloperahouse.org).
Covent Garden tube. **Open** *Box office* 10am-8pm Mon-Sat.
Tours 10.30am, 12.30pm, 2.30pm Mon-Sat. **Tickets** £8;
£7 under-18s, concessions. **Credit** AmEx, DC, MC, V.
Map p319 L6.

Young opera buffs may be thin on the ground, but the spectacular ROH is open to the public and impressive to wander about in. The first building on the site was built in 1732 but, after two big fires, this stunning structure was built in 1858. Inside, temporary exhibitions on dancers such as Nureyev and Fonteyn appear periodically in the foyer, and there are free choral and classical music recitals every Monday lunchtime. Guided tours start in the pit lobby and include the dramatic Villar Floral Hall, with its bars, restaurants, mirrors, escalators and rooftop garden. The most interesting bit for children is the chance to peek backstage and into the dress-ing rooms: you may get to see performers in costume, or ballet dancers in rehearsals. Booking is strongly recommended.

Should you decide to brave an opera with your young one, introductory talks to help educate the public about opera are often held before productions. The Opera House is also trying to provide productions which are of interest to younger people; 2002's *Wind in the Willows* was a triumph. The Royal Ballet School's Young British Dancer of the Year show is also held every May (call 7836 8899 for dates). Finally, the Opera House also offers an unpaid work experience scheme to let over-16s get adminstrative and stage experience in ballet or opera. For all of the above events, and for the ROH2 brochure, which lists events of interest for young people, call the education office on 7212 9410.

Buggy access. Café. Lift. Nappy-changing facilities.
Nearest picnic place: Covent Garden piazza/St Paul's
churchyard. Restaurant. Shop.

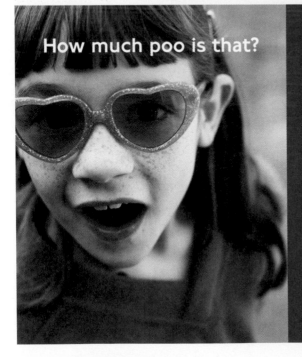
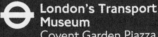

LONDON LEGEND The Ghost of Drury Lane

The West End's oldest theatre is also its spookiest. The **Theatre Royal Drury Lane** on Catherine Street, originally built in 1663, is reputed to be the most haunted theatre in the world. It's home to several thespian ghosts, the most famous being 'the Man in Grey', who dozens of actors have seen walking the back row of the upper circle – but only during the day. Dressed in tricorn hat, powdered wig and cloak, and carrying a sword, the ghost is thought to be that of an 18th-century actor who was killed during a stage fight. Despite the gory end, the ghost is generally considered to be a figure of good luck. Most actors spot the ghost during rehearsals: this is a good omen, since when such sightings occur the play in question usually goes on to become a smash hit. Perhaps for this reason, the theatre refuses to have his spirit exorcised.

But the Man in Grey is not the theatre's only ghost. Another spirit which has been spotted with some frequency is the ghost of comedian Dan Leno, who performed panto here until he died in 1904; actors who use his dressing room report looking in the mirror and seeing Leno's face staring back at them. The clown Grimaldi is another ghostly presence, identified by the aroma of lavender. Not quite so sweet is the spirit of Charles Macklin, who murdered fellow actor Thomas Halam in 1735 following an argument (over a wig, of all things).

For more spooky stories of Drury Lane's past, one-hour tours are available (adults £8.50; children £6.50; family £21 2+2); book on 7494 5000. You could always combine at tour with a performance of *My Fair Lady*, which runs at least until December 2003.

St Giles-in-the-Fields

60 St Giles High Street, WC2 (7240 2532). Tottenham Court Road tube. **Open** 9am-4pm Mon-Fri. Open for services Sun; phone for details. **Admission** free. **Map** p317 K6.

St Giles-in-the-Fields might be a lovely example of Palladian architecture, but the church's simple beauty belies a grim history. The church was named after the patron saint of outcasts, because the original church – built in 1101 – stood in the midst of a leper colony; 400 years later, the church could still not shake off its sickly history – the plague of 1665 is thought to have started in the parish, and large numbers of victims of that epidemic are buried in the shady churchyard. As if that weren't macabre enough, condemned prisoners on the way to the Tyburn gallows at Marble Arch were given a drugged drink known as the St Giles Bowl here; their corpses were brought back for burial. The present church was built in 1711, and this one seems to have been luckier: its grounds are a family-friendly bit of greenery in the heart of an urban jungle. The cool interior is perfect for the Friday lunchtime classical music concerts: these usually start at 1.10pm and last 40 minutes, but don't always run through the summer. *Buggy access. Nearest picnic place: Phoenix Garden.*

St Paul's Covent Garden

Bedford Street, WC2 (7836 5221/www.spcg.org). Covent Garden tube. **Open** 9am-4.30pm Mon-Fri; 9am-12.30pm Sun. Sunday service 11am. Closed 1 Jan, bank hols. **Admission** free; donations appreciated. **Map** p319 L7.

The parish chuch of Covent Garden is best known for its theatrical history: the vicar is chaplain to several West End Theatres, George Bernard Shaw set the opening scene of *Pygmalion* under the portico, and there are memorial stones to Charlie Chaplin, Noel Coward and Vivien Leigh inside. Office workers like it for its lovely enclosed garden, accessible via the gates in Bedford Street or alleys off King Street and Henrietta Street. But the part of the church kids will appreciate most is actually outside the building. The church's back wall has become a performance space for musicians, jugglers, acrobats, fire-eaters and magicians who entertain the passing crowds. Don't forget to put money in the hat. *Buggy access. Nearest picnic place: churchyard.*

Theatre Museum

Tavistock Street (entrance Russell Street), WC2 (7943 4700/group bookings 7943 4806/www.theatremuseum. org). Covent Garden tube. **Open** 10am-6pm (last entry 5.30pm) Tue-Sun. Closed 24-26 Dec, 1 Jan, bank hol Mons. **Tours** 11am, 2pm, 4pm Tue-Sun. **Admission** free. *Tours* £3.50 pre-booked groups; £2 concessions per person. **Credit** AmEx, MC, V. **Map** p319 L6.

There's no better place for a comprehensive theatre museum than right next to the Theatre Royal Drury Lane – the West End's oldest theatre. The permanent collection comprises costumes, playbills, posters, manuscripts, video recordings, set designs and other theatrical ephemera – the skull Victor Hugo gave Sarah Bernhardt, for instance, or costumes worn by Fonteyn; but much of its charm lies in the main exhibitions, many of which are family-oriented. The Sharmanka Kinetic Theatre display (until 7 September 2003) brings enormous mechanical sculptures to life beside images and folklore familiar to kids of all ages, and from July an exhibition focuses on the Redgrave dynasty, which spans five generations from Michael Redgrave to Joely Richardson.

The staff devise a praiseworthy range of original activity workshops. Stage Truck (noon-5pm every Saturday, also Thursdays in school holidays) gives four- to 16-year-olds the chance to create props from masks to finger puppets, or even design a model set of their own. Costume Workshops (daily, 12.30pm, 3pm daily) let kids dress up and act the part; Make Up Demonstrations (11.30am, 1pm, 2.30pm, 3.30pm, 4.30pm daily) select a specific characteristic to cosmetically create: old age, for example, or a nasty suppurating wound. There are also regular storytelling sessions for dramatic interpretations of the exhibits (first Saturday and Sunday of each month, also Wednesday and Friday in schools holidays; 2-2.30pm), and a Saturday Kids Club (10am-noon) runs drama classes based on West End shows for eight- to 12-year-olds.

The Education Department runs programmes that complement the National Curriculum: introduction to Victorian theatre, for instance, workshops on current productions such as *The Woman in Black*, seminars devoted to individual playwrights or niche studies on topics such as the History of Black Theatre in Britain. Call 7943 4806 for more info. *Buggy access. Nappy-changing facilities. Nearest picnic place: Covent Garden piazza or St Paul's churchyard.*

Westminster

The beating heart of the UK.

Real-life guards strut their stuff at **Buckingham Palace**. See p79.

This thriving slice of the capital can both awe visitors with grandeur and provide them with refuges for peace and respite. For 1,000 years Westminster has rivalled the City – it is literally the minster to the west of St Paul's – and the history of London is, in large part, the history of these two centres. Their tussle has even entered the language. During the dissolution of the monasteries under Henry VIII, money earmarked for Westminster Abbey, which started life as St Peter's, was redirected to St Paul's, leading to the expression 'Robbing Peter to pay Paul'.

Thankfully, in spite of its Royal and political connections, Westminster retained most of its historical allure. Under the careful stewardship of English Heritage and a rather reactionary council, the borough boasts few architectural eyesores and its rich streetscape has largely been preserved. It's still very easy to leave busy roads behind and wend your way from Buckingham Palace to Tate Britain via quiet and uncrowded streets. Stunning modern design is hardly absent, though. Channel 4's graceful hi-tech headquarters sits quietly and comfortably on Horseferry Road, while other fabulous examples of contemporary design are hidden behind classical facades – the Millennial extensions to the National Gallery and National Portrait Gallery are good examples.

In many ways, Westminster is a weird place. Royal gates, soldiers' barracks, armed policemen and wide boulevards nestle happily with quiet parks, busy cafés and the many homeless who seek refuge in the church of St Martin-in-the-Fields. The pedestrianisation of one side of Trafalgar Square, which has tucked a cafe and toilets into the north wall, has further made Westminster an accessible and easily negotiated place. Here, you can comfortably do everything on foot – it may well tire out the children, but there's never a shortage of something (or someone) to look at.

Banqueting House

Whitehall, SW1 (7930 4179/www.hrp.org.uk).
Westminster tube/Charing Cross tube/rail. **Open** 10am-
5pm (last entry 4.30pm) Mon-Sat. Sometimes closes
at short notice; phone to check. Closed bank hols.
Admission (LP) £4; £3 concessions; £2.60 5-15s; free
under-5s. **Credit** MC, V. **Map** p319 L8.
Built by architect Inigo Jones between 1619 and 1622,
Whitehall's Banqueting House is the first Renaissance building in London. The building was started by King James I as
an extension to Whitehall Palace, then decorated by James's
son Charles I who, in 1635, commissioned Rubens to paint a
baroque vision of the triumph of wisdom over falsehood.
Fourteen years later, Charles walked across St James's Park,
into Banqueting House and out through one of the tall windows on to a specially erected scaffold, where his head was
removed. More than 350 years later, historians now argue
over which window it was (as if it matters), but the confusion
does not stop the Sealed Knot Civil War re-enactment society
playing out the event one Sunday every January.
When fire destroyed Whitehall Palace in 1698 the hall was
all that was left. From 1700 the hall was used first as a chapel,
then as a museum. Nowadays it is primarily a tourist attraction, but classical concerts are performed at lunchtime on the
second Monday of every month (details on 0870 751 5187).
Nearest picnic place: St James's Park. Shop.

Buckingham Palace & Royal Mews

SW1 (7321 2233/www.royal.gov.uk). Green Park or
St James's Park tube/Victoria tube or rail. **Open** *State*
Rooms early Aug-late Sept 9.30am-4.15pm daily. *Royal*
Mews 1 Mar-31 July, 29 Sept-31 Oct 11am-4pm daily;
1 Aug-28 Sept 10am-5pm daily. Closed during Ascot,
state occasions, 25, 26 Dec. **Admission** (LP) £12; £10
concessions; £6 5-17s; £30 family (2+2); free under-5s.
Royal Mews £5; £4 concessions; £2.50 5-17s; £12.50
family (2+2); free under-5s. *Queen's Gallery* £6.50; £5
OAPs, students; £3 children; £16 family; free under-5s.
Credit AmEx, MC, V. **Map** p318 H9.

Buck House was originally bought from the Buckingham family by George III, but it was his son George IV who commissioned the extension that is now the public face of the building.
In its day, the building was hugely controversial; designed by
John Nash and started in 1819, it was still scarcely habitable
when Victoria came to the throne in 1837 – and even then it
had gone massively over-budget (Nash was sacked from the
project in 1830). Nonetheless, it is largely these spaces that
the public is permitted to see during the summer, when the
Royal family retires to the country.

Visitors queue from 9am onwards at the box office on
Constitution Hill for tickets to view 18 lavishly furnished
State Apartments, including the Music Room, and the
Ballroom. The artwork is good: Rembrandt, Rubens,
Vermeer, Poussin, Canaletto and sculpture by Canova, for
example. Visitors can also walk in the 42-acre garden.

The Queen's Gallery, on Buckingham Palace Road, opened
in May 2002 as a more publicly accessible display of Royal
artworks. Drawings by Leonardo da Vinci will form the focus
of this priceless collection until 9 November 2003 (examining
his obsession with the human form and its potential to be
both divine and grotesque), after which it's due to be replaced
by a Fabergé show, running from 21 November 2003 to
7 March 2004. Fabergé collecting has become a Royal tradition; Edward VII began a collection, which has been added
to by Queen Mary and our very own QEII. The well-stocked
shop retails what are supposed to be tasteful souvenirs (tea
towels, mugs, replica jewellery and so on) but has the feel of
an airport shop. School and study groups are often found in
the gallery on Mondays.

The Royal Mews stables are next door, showcase for the
royal carriages, including the Coronation Coach, the Glass
Coach and the fairy-tale golden State Coach built in 1761. The
horses, beautifully groomed by loving servicemen, have their
own exercise and dressage arena.

Buggy access (Royal Mews). Disabled access: lift, toilet
(Buckingham Palace). Nappy-changing facilities
(Buckingham Palace). Nearest picnic place:
Green Park. Shop.

LONDON LEGEND Big Ben

The most visible legend in Westminster, indeed
London, is Big Ben. And like any good legend,
no one is entirely sure how this mysterious
moniker arose. The name was originally applied
to the giant bell, but most visitors to the capital
apply the term to mean not only the clock but
St Stephen's Tower itself.

Architect Charles Barry originally applied to
Parliament to release money for a clock in 1844,
and he ordered it from his friend Benjamin
Vulliamy, clockmaker to the Queen. But a rival
clockmaker, EJ Dent, cried foul and, after a
competition lasting six years, Dent was given
the job. The clock is a triumph of Victorian
precision engineering, but the original bell was
a disappointment – the 16-ton chunk of copper
and tin developed a four-foot crack almost
immediately. There was public uproar.

It was around this time that the name Big Ben
was coined. One theory alleges that it is named
after Benjamin Hall, a large man and Chief
Commissioner of Works at the time. It is said

that during a parliamentary debate on the naming
of the bell, Hall rose to speak and one MP shouted
'Why not Big Ben?'. But, unfortunately, there's
no mention of this event in the records.

Another (more fanciful) theory has it that the
bell is named after the legendary Victorian boxer
Benjamin Caunt. Caunt was an 18-stone man
mountain, the publican of the nearby Coach &
Horses and a formidable fighter. On 23 September
1857 he went an epic 60 rounds with Nathaniel
Langham, another 19th-century boxing legend.
The match ended in a draw and Caunt retired,
an event that coincided with the destruction of
the original cracked bell.

Incidentally, the metal from the first bell was
melted down and recast into the bell we hear
today (now also cracked). The chimes imitate
those from St Mary's church in Cambridge, which
are traditionally accompanied by lines from
Handel's *Messiah*:

'All through this hour Lord be my guide
And by thy power no foot shall slide.'

Martial playthings at the **Guards' Museum**.

Cabinet War Rooms

Clive Steps, King Charles Street, SW1 (7930 6961/ www.iwm.org.uk). St James's Park or Westminster tube. **Open** *Oct-Mar* 10am-6pm daily. *Apr-Sept* 9.30am-6pm daily. Last entry 45mins before closing. Closed 24-26 Dec. **Admission** £7; £5.50 OAPs, students, concessions; free under-15s. **Credit** MC, V. **Map** p319 K9.

During World War II Winston Churchill, and even his wife Clementine, actually lived in these bunkers. The labyrinth as it currently exists includes the operations room with the maps, compasses and other paraphernalia left exactly as they were when the war ended. A suite of new rooms opened in spring 2003, bringing with them hefty ticket price hikes, adding Churchill's bedroom and dining room to the collection (complete with original furniture, including the war leader's famous chamberpot). Other rooms have become dedicated education suites equipped with internet link-ups to other Churchillian and military sites. A second phase of expansion, due for completion in 2005, will treble the space and add a permanent Churchill Museum. This remains a popular tourist and family destination, so be prepared to queue for tickets and to take your place in the crowd.

Buggy access. Disabled access: lift, toilet. Nappy-changing facilities. Nearest picnic place: St James's Park. Shop.

Guards' Museum

Wellington Barracks, Birdcage Walk, SW1 (7414 3271). St James's Park tube. **Open** 10am-4pm (last entry 3.30pm) daily. Closed 19 Dec- 5 Jan. **Tours** by arrangement; phone for details. **Admission** (LP) £2; £1 concessions; free under-16s. **Credit** Shop MC, V. **Map** p318 J9.

This quiet and little known museum is dedicated to the histories of the five Guards regiments – the three 'senior regiments' of the Scots (founded 1642), the Coldstream (1650) and the Grenadiers (1656), as well as the Irish (1900) and the Welsh (1915). Essentially, this is a static collection of uniforms, drums, paintings and weapons, but there are displays that bring you to a halt – the miniature Grenadiers uniform created for Queen Victoria's five-year-old son Arthur, for example, and gruesome surgical equipment. The medal collection is comprehensive, including one awarded by Oliver

Cromwell to officers of his New Model Army in 1651. Mementoes collected from the regiments' many actions over the centuries include a Nazi propaganda leaflet signed by the Führer and a bottle of Iraqi whisky captured in the first Gulf War. The toy soldier shop at the museum, the largest of its kind in London, sells all kinds of miniature models. The fabulous Guards' chapel nearby is also worth a look. Destroyed during a service by a flying bomb in 1944, this modernist composition is decorated with the names of all those whose memorials were destroyed in the attack.

Disabled access: lift. Nearest picnic place: St James's Park. Shop.

Houses of Parliament

Parliament Square, SW1 (Commons info 7219 4272/ Lords info 7219 3107/tours 0870 906 3773/www. parliament.uk). Westminster tube. **Open** (when in session) *House of Commons Visitors' Gallery* 2.30-10pm Mon; 11.30am-7.30pm Tue-Thur; 9.30am-3pm Fri. Closed bank hols. *House of Lords Visitors' Gallery* 2.30pm Mon-Wed; from 11.30am Thur; from 11am Fri. **Tours** summer recess only; phone for details. **Admission** *Public gallery* free. *Tours* £7; £5 concessions, 5-16s; £22 family (2+2); free under-4s. **Map** p319 L9.

The first Parliament was held here in 1275, but the Palace of Westminster did not become its permanent home until 1532, when Henry VIII made himself comfortable at Whitehall Palace. Parliament was originally housed in the choir stalls of St Stephen's Chapel, where members sat facing each other, a tradition which continues today. Today, the only remaining parts of the original palace are Westminster Hall, where the body of the Queen Mother lay in state before her funeral in April 2002, and the Jewel Tower *(see p82)*. The rest burned down in a fire in 1834 and was rebuilt in neo-Gothic style by Charles Barry and Augustus Pugin. It wasn't finished until 1860 after problems with the clock (mysteriously known as Big Ben; *see p79*) held things up.

Families can queue to visit any session of both the Commons and the Lords, but the wait may stretch into hours and it's best to book tickets via your MP (who can also arrange a tour of the Palace). There's such a demand to see

Prime Minister's questions at around midday on Wednesdays that you're likely to be disappointed – officials advise that it is easiest to get inside the Commons 6-10.30pm on Mondays, after 1.30pm on Tuesdays, Wednesdays and Thursdays and at 9am on sitting Fridays. Phone to check opening times before making a special journey.

Café. Nearest picnic place: Victoria Tower Gardens. Shop.

ICA Gallery

The Mall, SW1 (box office 7930 3647/membership enquiries 7766 1439/www.ica.org.uk). Piccadilly Circus tube/Charing Cross tube/rail. **Open** *Galleries* noon-7.30pm daily. Closed 24-26 Dec, 31 Dec, 1 Jan. **Membership** (LP) *Daily* £1.50, £1 concessions Mon-Fri; £2.50, £1.50 concessions Sat, Sun; free under-14s. *Annual* £30; £20 concessions. **Credit** AmEx, DC, MC, V. **Map** p319 K8.

This magnificent gallery specialises in cutting-edge contemporary art and runs ad hoc arts programmes for kids, plus more official activities at half-term. It's a pleasant place to be. An expensive refurbishment project was completed in summer 2003, which has further enhanced the quality of the spaces. The café/bar opens at noon and remains open until long after the gallery has closed.

Café. Nappy-changing facilities. Nearest picnic place: St James's Park. Shop.

Jewel Tower

Abingdon Street, SW1 (7222 2219/www.english-heritage. org.uk). Westminster tube. **Open** *Apr-Sept* 10am-6pm daily. *Oct* 10am-5pm daily. *Nov-Mar* 10am-4pm daily. Last entry 30mins before closing. Closed 24-26 Dec, 1 Jan. **Admission** (EH/LP) £2; £1.50 concessions; £1 5-16s; free under-5s. **Credit** MC, V. **Map** p319 L9.

This dry-moated Jewel Tower was once the south-western corner of the medieval Palace of Westminster. Built in 1365-6 to house Edward III's valuables, the tower later became the repository for Parliamentary records, but in 1869 the Board of Trade used it as a testing centre for weights and measures. This little fragment of a building, often the focus of school parties, now has an exhibition on the past and present of Parliament – although a Saxon sword, dug up during the excavation of the moat in 1948, is also on display. Tapestries, stationery, toiletries and ice-creams are sold in the shop.

Buggy access. Nearest picnic place: Victoria Tower Gardens. Shop.

National Gallery

Trafalgar Square, WC2 (info line 7747 2885/ www.nationalgallery.org.uk). Leicester Square tube/ Charing Cross tube/rail. **Open** 10am-6pm Mon, Tue, Thur-Sun; 10am-9pm Wed. *Micro Gallery* 10am-5.30pm Mon, Tue, Thur-Sun; 10am-8.30pm Wed. Closed 24-26 Dec, 1 Jan, Good Fri. **Tours** times vary; check info line. **Admission** (LP) free. *Temporary exhibitions* prices vary. *Tours* free. **Credit** *Shop* MC, V. **Map** p319 K7.

This magnificent collection of Western European painting is daunting in its scope. The institutional feel of the place, to say nothing of its sheer scale, might quickly deter a child from exploring very far. But to its credit, the gallery makes valiant efforts to present a friendly face to children and families: there are special audio guides, drop-in activities every second Saturday and Sunday of the month, and a decent range of educational workshops. It's also worth planning a visit, picking out specific artworks in advance rather than vaguely trudging around this labyrinth. Constable's *Hay Wain*, Van Gogh's *Sunflowers*, Seurat's *Bathers at Asnières* and Holbein's *The Ambassadors* are worth looking out for, as well as Rousseau's cuddly-looking *Tiger in a Tropical Storm*. Forthcoming temporary exhibitions focus on El Greco

(11 February-23 May 2004), Russian 19th-century Landscapes (23 June-12 September 2004) and Raphael (20 October 2004-16 January 2005).

Buggy access. Café. Lift. Nappy-changing facilities. Nearest picnic place: Leicester Square/Trafalgar Square. Restaurant. Shops.

National Portrait Gallery

2 St Martin's Place, WC2 (7306 0055/www.npg.org.uk). Leicester Square tube/Charing Cross tube/rail. **Open** 10am-6pm Mon-Wed, Sat, Sun; 10am-9pm Thur, Fri. Closed 25, 26 Dec, 1 Jan. **Admission** (LP) free. *Temporary exhibitions* prices vary. *Audio guide* free (suggested donation £3). **Credit** AmEx, MC, V. **Map** p319 K7.

This collection of portraits brings together images, painterly and photographic, of people who have contributed to the life of Britain – and it's a lot more interesting than it sounds. Recently extended, the NPG is now a well-equipped, modern and extensive gallery that presents its collection in a variety of imaginative settings. Look out for a young Edward VI, striking a regal pose in the manner of his father Henry VIII (picture 5511); the young man reappears in picture 1299, in a curious distorted image that makes sense only by looking at it at a very acute angle. Keep an eye out for a shady-looking William Shakespeare (picture 1), the first portrait acquired by the gallery and the only one of the Bard with any convincing claim to be painted from life. The extension, whose centrepiece is a vertiginous escalator, also has a swanky rooftop restaurant with views beyond Nelson's Column.

Buggy access. Café. Disabled access: lift, toilet. Lift. Nappy-changing facilities. Nearest picnic place: Leicester Square/Trafalgar Square. Restaurant. Shop.

St Martin-in-the-Fields

Trafalgar Square, WC2 (7766 1100/Brass Rubbing Centre 7930 9306/www.stmartin-in-the-fields.org). Leicester Square tube/Charing Cross tube/rail. **Open** *Church* 8am-6pm daily. *Brass Rubbing Centre* 10am-6pm Mon-Sat; noon-6pm Sun. **Admission** free. *Brass Rubbing* (LP) £3-£15 (special rates for groups and families). *Evening concerts* (7.30pm Thur-Sat) £6-£16. **Credit** MC, V. **Map** p319 L7.

This baroque haven of peace and tranquillity is probably best-known for the Café in the Crypt (*see p170*), a handsome eating place which threads its way around the vaulted base of the building. Don't miss the interior of the church, though, especially on Monday, Tuesday and Friday lunchtimes when free concerts enliven this 18th-century masterpiece: the combination of architectural beauty and the music is an almost surreal experience. The city's only brass rubbing centre, adjacent to the cafe, provides an opportunity to take home a copy of medieval images including knights and dragons. Rubbings, which are supervised, take about half an hour to complete. All materials are supplied.

Café. Disabled access: ramp to church. Nearest picnic place: Leicester Square/Trafalgar Square. Shop.

Tate Britain

Millbank, SW1 (7887 8008/www.tate.org.uk). Pimlico tube/C10, 77a, 88 bus. **Open** 10am-5.50pm daily. Closed 24-26 Dec. **Tours** 11am, noon, 2pm, 3pm Mon-Fri; noon, 2.30pm Sat, Sun. **Admission** (LP) free. *Temporary exhibitions* prices vary. *Tours* free. **Credit** MC, V. **Map** p319 L7.

Since the establishment of Tate Modern (see p46) downriver in Southwark, Tate Britain has dedicated its galleries to British art from the 16th century to the present, with displays of Blake, Constable, the Pre-Raphaelites and so on expanded to fit the greater space. The avant-garde Turner Prize

PARKLIFE Westminster's green scenes

Westminster is not short of wide open spaces, but few of them are parks – and few of these are designed with children or families in mind. That said, **St James's Park** is a wonderful place to picnic. As one of the Royal Parks it is well cared for and birdlife abounds: coots by the dozen, as well as eider ducks and (if you're lucky) grey herons. But rollerskating, cycling and other wheeled activities are banned, as discreet but plentiful notices keep reminding you.

Nonetheless, St James's is blessed relief in the centre of this frenetic borough. The low-key Cakehouse Café is a useful food-stop, but the food is basic. This state of affairs is set to change in spring 2004, when the neighbouring Cakehouse Restaurant is due to open. It's designed by Sir Michael Hopkins (designer of the Mound Stand at Lords cricket ground), and early images look encouraging. Clad in timber, the building buries itself into the ground and will even have a turf roof – irritatingly described by the parks authority as 'eco-chic'. The new restaurant replaces a 1960s eyesore, and will provide inside seating for 120, with a further 100 places accommodated by a terrace during fair weather.

Victoria Tower Gardens is a relatively unvisited tract of greenery, which is surprising given its location. Occupying a triangular slice of land next to Parliament, the gardens provide a fabulous close-up view of the southern end of this neo-Gothic masterpiece, as well as views across the river to Lambeth Palace. Remarkably, it even has a small, neat and scrupulously clean playground, containing just four swings and a slide. Better than nothing, though. No ball games are allowed, so the children have to learn to become art lovers instead: the gardens contain Rodin's *The Burghers of Calais*, and a statue commemorating the life of Emmeline Pankhurst, as well as a colourful 1865 monument to the abolition of slavery.

Westminster's other open spaces are more urban, like the benchless and disappointing plaza in front of Westminster Cathedral (focal point for many homeless). And there's **Trafalgar Square**, of course, newly pedestrianised on its northern side. The changes work well, and it is a delight to be able to arrive at the square without having to run the gauntlet of racing traffic. The equestrian statue of Charles I, epicentre of London, is also more accessible, and it's worth a closer look. This giant bronze artwork was made in the 1630s, but after the execution of the King the decision was taken to destroy it. One John Revett was given the job, but instead he buried it in his garden, where it stayed for 11 years. He later gave it to Charles II.

St James's Park
SW1 (Royal Parks 7930 1793). St James's Park tube. **Open** 24hrs daily. **Map** p318-19 J-K8-9.

Victoria Tower Gardens
Millbank, SW1 (no phone). Westminster tube. **Open** 8am-8pm daily. **Map** p319 M10.

LUNCH BREAK

ASK (160-2 Victoria Street, SW1, 7630 8228), for eternally child-friendly sustenance – pizzas.
Café Internet (22-4 Buckingham Palace Road, SW1, 7233 5786), for refreshments while online.
Café in the Crypt (inside St Martin-in-the-Fields, Duncannon Street, WC2, 7839 4342; *see p170*), for cheap and filling lunches – just the thing after a spot of brassrubbing.
Cakehouse Café in St James's Park (7839 7709), for simple snacks such as jacket potatoes, soup and ice-cream.
Christopher's Victoria (Thistle Victoria, Buckingham Palace Road, SW1, 7976 5522), a rather swanky American restaurant that does good steaks, seafood and perfect fries – a treat for sophisticated older children.

Crivelli's Garden (7747 2869), the smart restaurant inside the National Gallery has high chairs and a fancy menu.
easyEverything (9-13 Wilton Road, SW1, 7233 8456), for drinks, snacks and computers for online surfing.
Jenny Lo's Tea House (14 Eccleston Street, SW1, 7259 0399), for homely noodles from the other J-Lo.
Pizza Express (85 Victoria Street, SW1, 7222 5270 & 154 Victoria Street, SW1, 7828 1477), for pizzas galore (and more).
Texas Embassy Cantina (1 Cockspur Street, SW1, 7925 0077; *see p170*), for a children's menu of Tex-Mex faves, and sunny staff.
Best place for picnics: St James's Park.

exhibition is also based here. This gallery has always been good, but the massive Centenary Development, opened in 2001, has improved the building even further: there's a useful ramped entrance on Atterbury Street, cutting out the need to slog up the steps around the corner, and a suite of new galleries and public facilities. A major exhibition on Turner (planned to run 9 October 2003-11 January 2004) will concentrate on the great painter's visits to Venice: 55 oils and more than 100 watercolours will be on display, few of which have been seen in public for a good number of years.

The Tates make big efforts to help kids understand what they're looking at. For details of the Art Trolley (drawing and collaging every Sunday) and Artspace (every Sunday 1-5pm) and Tate Tales (on the first Sunday in the month; *see p210*). *Buggy access. Café. Disabled access: lift, toilet. Nappy-changing facilities. Nearest picnic place: lawns on either side of gallery/Riverside Gardens by Vauxhall Bridge. Shop.*

Westminster Abbey

20 Dean's Yard, SW1 (7222 5152/tours 7654 4834/ www.westminster-abbey.org). St James's Park or Westminster tube. **Open** *Nave & royal chapels* 9.30am-4.45pm (last entry 3.45pm) Mon, Tue, Thur, Fri; 9.30am-8pm (last entry 7pm) Wed; 9.30am-2.45pm (last entry 1.45pm) Sat. *Chapter House* times vary; call English Heritage for details (7222 5897). *Pyx Chamber & Abbey Museum* 10.30am-4pm Mon-Sat. *College Garden Apr-Sept* 10am-6pm Tue-Thur. *Oct-Mar* 10am-4pm Tue-Thur. Last entry 1hr before closing. Closed 24, 25 Dec, Good Fri. **Tours** phone for details. **Admission** *Nave & royal chapels* £6; £4 11-15s, concessions; £12 family (2+3); free under-11s with paying adult. *Chapter House, Pyx Chamber & Abbey Museum* (EH/LP) £2.50; £1.90 concessions; £1.30 5-15s; £1 with main entrance ticket; free with £2 audio guide; free under-5s. **Credit** MC, V. **Map** p319 K9.

Until a couple of years ago visitors entered the abbey through its grand western façade, which opens on to the Tomb of the Unknown Soldier and reveals the full length of the medieval interior. Now, however, you enter through a side door on the north façade, which is a frankly disappointing way to be introduced to this magnificent building. The abbey was consecrated in 1065 by Edward the Confessor, who died in the same year and is buried behind the high altar. On Christmas Day in 1066 his cousin William the Conqueror was crowned

King of England. From that time on, the abbey has been linked with royalty; with two exceptions, every English monarch since William the Conqueror has been crowned here, while many are also buried here (along with sundry high achieving commoners including Chaucer, Tennyson, Isaac Newton, engineer Thomas Telford and the explorer David Livingstone). The building itself is an architectural wonder, especially the chapel built by Henry VII. Years later, American writer Washington Irving gushed, 'Stone seems, by the winning labour of the chisel, to have been robbed of its weight and density, suspended aloft, as if by magic' – and you'll be churlish if you disagree.

In 1998 ten empty niches on the west front of the abbey, designed by Nicholas Hawksmoor in the 18th century, were filled with statues of selected 20th-century martyrs, including Archbishop of San Salvador Oscar Romero and civil rights activist Martin Luther King Jr. *Buggy access. Café. Nearest picnic place: Dean's Yard. Shop.*

Westminster Cathedral

Victoria Street, SW1 (7798 9055/tours 7798 9064/ www.westminstercathedral.org.uk). Victoria tube/rail/ 11, 24, 211, 507 bus. **Open** 7am-7pm Mon-Fri, Sun; 8am-7pm Sat. *Campanile Apr-Nov* 9.30am-12.30pm, 1-5pm daily. *Dec-Mar* 9.30am-12.30pm, 1-5pm Thur-Sun. **Tours** by arrangement; phone for details. **Admission** free (donations appreciated). *Campanile* £2; £1 concessions; £5 family (2+2). *Audio guide* £2.50; £1.50 concessions. **No credit cards. Map** p318 J10.

Worksheets available at the gift shop familiarise the young with this beautiful late Victorian Roman Catholic cathedral, whose disconcerting black ceiling is still waiting to be decorated (plans are afoot to begin work). Refreshingly, this is still a fully functioning religious centre, and most people inside appear to be engaging in prayer or (at least) contemplation – tourists are welcome but keep to the background. Climb to the viewing platform at the top of the Campanile, 273ft high and offering one of the finest panoramas of London.

The boys' choir, one of the finest choirs of its type in the world, sings daily Vespers (5pm) and Mass (5.30pm; more on Sundays) all year except August. Roman Catholic boys aged 8-10 can apply to the headmaster of the choir school for auditions, which are held regularly. *Buggy access. Café. Disabled access: ramp. Nearest picnic place: Ashley Gardens off Howick Place. Shop.*

Marylebone

Touch the stars, talk to the animals and drink in the beauty of Regent's Park.

A few years ago, nobody bothered much with the core of Marylebone. It seemed to be the filling in a sandwich of two thunderous thoroughfares: the Marylebone Road to the north and Oxford Street to the south. All that has changed, partly due to clever management of **Marylebone High Street** by local landowners, the Howard de Walden Estate. By hand-picking incoming retailers and restaurateurs to make an interesting mix, Marylebone 'Village' was set on an infectious spiral of fashionability. This naturally affected property values, which in turn attracted new enterprises. Capitalism clearly has its benefits.

Certainly shopping or just walking around with children in the area feels much more relaxed than further south in the West End proper. Shops are smaller, so it's much harder for infants to be mislaid, and **St Christopher's Place** is pedestrianised for safe café pitstops with toddlers. **Paddington Park** (entrance on Paddington Street) must hold the West End's only playground; it can be used as a bribe, a picnic place and somewhere to run around.

Most of the area's most enticing pleasures are free, including the **Wallace Collection** on Manchester Square with its art treasures and full programme of family activities. **Regent's Park** offers boating, playgrounds, cafes, gardens, the open-air theatre and **London Zoo**. The zoo never fails to please, but for a special treat, take a canalboat trip there from Camden Lock. **Madame Tussaud's** is a laugh if you have starstruck older children. It isn't cheap, but a visit to the Planetarium is included in the price, and at least you don't have to join the long queues on Marylebone Road – just book in advance.

The area north of the Marylebone Road is also designated Marylebone. It has its own, rather quaint, Victorian railway station behind the Landmark hotel, and a lively market on Church Street, which sells very cheap toys (as well as fruit and veg). These may prove a useful lure if your real reason for exploring is to visit the nearby antique shops.

London Central Mosque
146 Park Road, NW8 (7724 3363/www.iccuk.org). Baker Street tube. **Open** dawn-dusk daily.
You can see the golden dome of the mosque from all over Regent's Park, but those who venture inside the precincts will find the complex much bigger than the dome and minaret imply. The sense of grandeur inspired by historic monuments such as the Blue Mosque in Istanbul is missing here, but it could make an interesting outing for children of other faiths. Modern offices around a large courtyard accommodate London's most important Islamic Cultural Centre; inside the reception are a bookshop selling Koranic texts, noticeboards advertising spiritual and charitable events and a quaintly old-fashioned booth offering information. Men and boys enter the prayer hall via doors on the ground floor; women and girls pass through the 'toilets & *wudhu*' (washing facilities) and go upstairs to a screened-off balcony. Inside the dome is a huge chandelier encircled by Arabic tiles; otherwise the hall is devoid of decoration or furniture, since adherents pray kneeling (toward Mecca) on the carpet. Visitors must remove their shoes on entry; women should wear a headscarf.
Buggy access. Café. Disabled access: ramp, toilet. Nearest picnic place: Regent's Park.

London Planetarium
Marylebone Road, NW1 (0870 400 3000/www.london-planetarium.com). Baker Street tube. **Open** 9.30am-5.30pm daily, times vary during holiday periods. Closed 25 Dec. **Admission** (includes admission to Madame Tussaud's) from £14.95; from £10.50 5-15s; from £11.80 concessions; £49 family (2+2 or 1+3). **Credit** AmEx, MC, V. **Map** p316 G4.
It's too bad if you're starstruck yet don't care for Disney: until 2004, the Planetarium has a co-production that transforms the attraction into 'Treasure Planetarium', after the animated adventure about Jim Hawkins and John Silver. Of course, most children love it, and if you have to wait for the 20-minute show (which plays every 40 minutes), kids can spend their time posing for photographs on a skateboard beside a wax-

---

DON'T MISS London Zoo

A spotter's guide to unusual residents
Alpacas: look like curly-haired llamas and can be found in the Children's Zoo.
Assassin bugs: insects equipped with a long mouthpart used to suck the juice from their prey, to be found in B.U.G.S.
Golden lion tamarin: a tiny yellow monkey with wizened, humanoid face and lustrous mane, and found in the new Happy Families area.
Meerkats: sociable animals that can be found in the new Happy Families area.
Okapis: tall, donkey-like animals with zebra-style stripey bottom and forelegs; found in the Hoofed Mammal Area.
Paddlefish: have huge mouths to filter food from the water, and can be found in the Aquarium.
Pygmy slow loris: teensy tree dwellers you can see in the Moonlight World building.
Stinkpot terrapins: so called due to the odour emitted when the animal is threatened; the whiffy beasts can be found in the Reptile House.
Tamanduas: small anteaters; can be found in the Small Mammal House.
Tapirs: large black and white forest dwellers; found in the Hoofed Mammal Area.

Only the camels get the hump at **London Zoo**. *See p87.*

Baker Street bobby reporting for duty at The **Sherlock Holmes Museum**. *See p89*.

work figure of Jim. Inside the dome, the best seats are at the back, for you gaze upward at the twinkling heavens and watch an extract from the cartoon morphing into an exploration of the heavens as narrated by the voice of Brian Murray (Silver). The motion effects are spectacular and potentially nauseating. Educational value has been sacrificed to special effects, for though there's a brief mention of each planet and its attributes, phenomena such as black holes and super nova are mere plot points in a thrilling space journey. Most visitors come here as an adjunct to Madame Tussaud's along the road; booking combined tickets saves time and money. Note that prices can go up during school holidays.
Café. Disabled access: lift, toilet. Nappy changing facilities. Nearest picnic place: Regent's Park. Shop.

London Zoo
Regent's Park, NW1 (7722 3333/www.zsl.org). Baker Street or Camden Town tube then 274 or C2 bus. **Open** *Nov-Mar* 10am-4pm daily. *Apr-Oct* 10am-5.30pm daily. Closed 25 Dec. **Admission** £12; £9 3-15s; £10.20 concessions; £38 family ticket (2+2); free under-3s. **Credit** AmEx, MC, V. **Map** p316 G2.
Ask children what they would most like to see at the zoo and they'll probably name favourite circus or cartoon animals – lions and tigers, elephants and penguins. As it turns out, these aren't the most entertaining beasts on show. Big cats tend to loll about in the far corners of their enclosures; there are no elephants (they were moved to Whipsnade); and the penguins walk sedately around their designer pool when, as every Pingu fan knows, they should be making riotous use of slides and generally larking about. Nonetheless, the Zoo is still one of the best days out in London. The animals that really fascinate are often those you might struggle to identify (*see p85*).
Along with Whipsnade, London Zoo is owned and run by ZSL (Zoological Society of London), a worldwide conservation, scientific and educational charity that naturally tries to cover all the bases. Conservation goals are clearly stated around the zoo; new or improved enclosures are built every year; informative talks are given, often pointing out harmful practices that threaten wildlife (such as making handbags

out of snakeskins). This can seem po-faced (why *shouldn't* the camels give children rides in the summer holidays?), but on the whole the atmosphere is one of passionate interest in the animals' welfare, and everyone can learn a great deal.
The zoo is at its most relaxing when you can afford to drop in for a couple of hours any time you like – a luxury afforded by annual season tickets. In rainy weather, you can hang about in the reptile houses with the crocodiles and snakes, or wander through the brilliant biodiversity centre (formerly the Web of Life, now renamed B.U.G.S.). Sunshine makes encounters with goats, sheep, pigs and chickens in the children's touch paddock a delight. The most popular openings in 2003 include a new otter enclosure and an outdoor space for meerkats, whose tendency to rise on their hind legs to peer at visitors seems like the ultimate irony.
The café provides reasonably priced, reasonably healthy food, but beware long queues at lunchtime. The official guidebook is well worth buying, since it takes you on a methodical tour and lists animals you might otherwise pass by. The shop is never short of new animal merchandise, but if economy is an issue, regulate the extra treats on arrival, since paying for the merry-go-round, the bouncy castle, snacks, automated rides and irresistible helium balloons at the exit will make for a very expensive day.
Buggy access. Café. Disabled access: ramps, toilet. Nappy-changing facilities. Nearest picnic space: zoo grounds. Restaurant. Shop.

Madame Tussaud's
Marylebone Road, NW1 (0870 400 3000/www.madame-tussauds.com). Baker Street tube. **Open** 9.30am-5.30pm daily, times vary during holiday periods. Closed 25 Dec. **Admission** (includes admission to London Planetarium) from £14.95; from £10.50 5-15s; from £11.80 concessions; £49 family (2+2 or 1+3). **Credit** AmEx, MC, V. **Map** p316 G4.
The enduring popularity of this petrified celebrity city is fascinating to behold. If you've passed queues on Marylebone Road and wondered what all the fuss was about, then you owe it to yourself to take a look. The attraction strives hard

LUNCH BREAK

RIBA Café (66 Portland Place, W1, 7631 0467; see p169), the exhibition area indoors and the roof terrace outdoors make great playspaces for toddlers.

Fairuz, (3 Blandford Street, W1, 7486 8108; see p170), Lebanese café nominated for *Time Out*'s best family restaurant in 2002.

La Fromagerie (2-4 Moxon Street, W1, 7935 0341), supplier of exquisite little delicacies to eat in the park.

La Galette (56 Paddington Street , W1, 7935 1554; see p172), supplier of tasty Breton pancakes and cider.

Giraffe (6-8 Blandford Street, W1, 7935 2333; see p172), funky decor, friendly staff, child-friendly menu.

The Golden Hind (73 Marylebone Lane, W1, 7486 3644), a traditional fish and chip shop.

Maison Sagne (105 Marylebone High Street, W1, 7935 6240), a lovely patisserie that's ideal for breakfast or tea.

The Quiet Revolution (Aveda, 28 Marylebone High Street, W1, 7487 5683), purveyor of healthy stuff for that all-important inner beauty.

St Marylebone Church (Marylebone Road, W1, 7935 7315), church complete with vegetarian café in the crypt.

La Spighetta (43 Blandford Street, W1, 7486 7340; see p175), for pizza and pasta that are a cut above the chains.

Villandry (170 Great Portland Street, W1, 7631 3131), a rather fancy delicatessen-cum-café with top-notch ingredients.

to appeal to sophisticated modern audiences with new room sets and mannequins, some of which are interactive. Stroll into an exhibit entitled 'Fever', for example, and a raunchy Kylie Minogue on all fours pouts and whispers to a soundtrack of her greatest hits, while live assistants attempt to teach onlookers how to dance just like her. By summer 2003 David Beckham – complete with beating heart – should be installed in a recreation of his World-Cup-qualifying free kick. Perhaps the most surprising for older visitors, all the mannequins can be touched and prodded, while the spaces deliberately created next to the dummies make for one big photo opportunity. The Grand Hall is peopled with historic figures such as Napoleon and Queen Victoria, but these are far less popular than the chance to don a plastic tiara and be photographed next to HM the Queen. Oddly unrecognisable figures of Blair and Bush invite visitors to give their opinions.

Below stairs, the famous Chamber of Horrors, a miniature museum of torture with moving parts, seems justified by Mme Tussaud's own background as a maker of death masks in the French Revolution. For an extra £2, you can hear live actors portray yet more unspeakable acts of cruelty. The best part for most kids is the themed ride at the end; hop into a London taxi to be whirled past Big Ben, the Great Fire of London, Carnaby Street in the '60s and so on. The exit is naturally through the shop, where pens topped with sticky eyeballs draw much admiration. Note that prices go up at peak times (during school holidays) – and if you're at all hungry, you'll realise – since you can't leave the premises and return – you're a captive consumer for the Costa Coffee concession. *Café. Disabled access: lift, toilet. Nappy-changing facilities. Nearest picnic place: Regent's Park. Shop.*

The Sherlock Holmes Museum

221B Baker Street, NW1 (7935 8866/www.sherlock-holmes. co.uk). Baker Street tube. **Open** 9.30am-6pm (last entry 5.30pm) daily. Closed 25 Dec. **Admission** £6; £4 6-16s; free under-6s. **Credit** AmEx, DC, MC, V. **Map** p313 F4.

It's important to remember that Sherlock Holmes, ace Victorian detective, was a fictional character. So great is the sleuth's cult that many of his fans seem forgetful of this fact,

Madame Tussaud's. See p87.

PARKLIFE Regent's Park

The original impulse behind the creation of Regent's Park was hardly as philanthropic as this wonderful green space might seem today. In 1811 John Nash, Crown Architect and friend of the Prince Regent, designed a private residential estate set in parkland to raise revenue for the Crown. The stucco-fronted Regency terraces of the Outer Circle remain Crown property and are inhabited by wealthy leaseholders, but the park itself, like other Royal Parks in the capital, is a joy for Londoners and tourists.

In particular, parents will notice that the four playgrounds in Regent's Park (one is close to the **Central London Mosque** and children's boating lake, one is close to Marylebone Road north of Portland Place, one is by the Camden Town entrance, and the other is at the foot of Primrose Hill) are immaculately maintained. Even the bark used to provide a soft landing is carefully raked and examined for inappropriate objects every morning before opening. And all have large sandpits and children's toilets.

The cheerful, sporty atmosphere normally created by lots of Little Leaguers playing baseball and by office workers indulging in a spot of footie may not be so obvious in the 18 months between spring 2003 and summer 2004. This is because the park's seemingly perfect greensward in fact sits upon tons of bomb rubble from World War II. The rubble has affected drainage so badly that a programme of works to dig it up and improve the

sports pitches is underway – one consolation for the pitch-less being the chance of unearthing something interesting.

Meanwhile the rose gardens (amazingly, a pesticide-free zone) make a stunning backdrop for scooting, toddling or feeding the ducks. A descriptive board near the bridge over the north end of the lake lists many of the 80 varieties of exotic wildfowl. From American Bufflehead to Chinese Mandarin, nearly all are bred in Regent's Park by incubating the eggs well away from hungry foxes; surplus stock are sent to other royal parks such as St James's. Despite some controversy, scattering your sandwich crusts is not all that bad, according to wildlife officers here; it's just a question of discretion. Ducks, like humans, often don't know when to stop eating, and if they get overweight, they won't breed.

2003 is the first year that wildlife and education officers have collaborated on a programme of activities intended to introduce visitors to some of the park's wildlife. Owl prowls at dusk point out some of the 28 pairs living in NW1; telescopes focused on the herons' nests reveal how these fisher-birds live; a 'Hogwart's School of Wildlife Wizardry' introduces kids to associated plants and animals. Activities are free; for dates and details call 7298 2000.

If nature is less your thing than the arts, the **Open Air Theatre** provides three months of performances (June-Sept), including a children's play, which in 2003 is Unicorn's *Granny and the Gorilla* (see p220). Catering at the theatre (which was begun here in 1962 by a young Clement Freud serving up suppers in a marquee) is rather good, and picnic space on a lawn next to the auditorium is also provided, so family outings here can be a big event. But however warm the day has been, never turn up without coats and rugs for evening performances; just remember that the *Midsummer Night's Dream* fairies often smuggle a hot water bottle on stage to warm Titania as she sleeps in her bower. Chance of showers? No true Brit will let that put him or her off. The Open Air Theatre has been part of London's summer life since 1932, including during the war years, when even bombs were not enough to stop the performances.

Less formally, free live music is supplied by military bands and others at the bandstand next to the boating lake. Calm as a millpond and reassuringly shallow, **Regent's Park Lake** is one of the best rowing spots in the capital. Still, children who wish to propel their own pedalo must measure up to a height test on the children's circular boating lake (otherwise they won't be able to reach the pedals). Older children may enjoy a game of tennis at the courts on the Inner Circle or close to the St John's Wood entrance; all sorts of coaching opportunities are available here.

writing to him from around the world to express their undying admiration and seek his help with contemporary crimes. You can chuckle over these letters upstairs in this little commercial museum, which takes up the four floors of a terraced house at 239 Baker Street (confusingly labelled 221B, the 'tec's fictional address). Though things are looking a little worn, the room settings fit closely enough to descriptions in the stories. Labelling is lacking, so if you don't know what an opium pipe looks like you'll be mystified by that particular exhibit, and if you can't recognise the snapshots of Victorian criminals you'll take them for Holmes's relatives.

On the second and first floors are waxwork figures in various murderous or cadaverous poses – and these at least are labelled: 'The Blackmailer Charles Augustus Milverton and his surprise assailant' (woman shoots man with pistol) and so on. Children will find them delightfully gory, though they may be disturbed by a 'voodoo fetish' (baby-sized blackened body). The shop on the ground floor sells Holmes teddies, Holmes figurines, even Holmes matrioshka dolls; deerstalkers cost £40. On the other side of the road at 230 Baker Street, the associated Sherlock Holmes Memorabilia Company flogs yet more Sherlockiana, including videos, beermats, pipes and magnifying glasses. Upstairs is a small room full of photos and a set from Granada TV's version of the Sherlock Holmes adventures, which may be viewed in the presence of a shop assistant dressed in cape and deerstalker (£2.50 per person). *Nappy-changing facilities. Nearest picnic place: Regent's Park. Shop.*

St James's Spanish Place

22 George Street, W1 (7935 0943/www.spanishplace. hemscott.net). Baker Street or Bond Street tube. **Open** 7am-7.30pm daily. **Services** 7.15am, 12.30pm, 6pm Mon-Fri; 10am, 6pm Sat; 8.30am, 9.30am (*Old Rite*), 10.30am (*Sung Latin*), noon, 4pm, 7pm Sun. **Admission** free. **Map** p316 G5.

Locals sometimes call this Gothic edifice 'the Spanish church', even though its associations with that country officially ceased in 1827. St James's was first built in 1791, just after the repeal of laws banning Catholic worship; the present church opened in 1890 opposite the first one. A good number of continental Catholics live nearby, so it's well attended at mass, and even on a weekday morning, you'll find people sitting in quiet prayer in the side chapels or genuflecting at the altar. The sense of peace is palpable and the atmosphere is always bathed in a soft golden light, thanks to the many ornate gilt decorations and the hundreds of flickering votive candles. The basement accommodates a Montessori nursery, and family events are held here, too; check the noticeboards for details. A repository (shop) is open after mass on Sundays, selling crucifixes, cards and so on; at other times St James's is a convenient source of Catholic newspapers and books. *Nearest picnic place: Regent's Park.*

Wallace Collection

Hertford House, Manchester Square, W1 (7935 0687/www.the-wallace-collection.org.uk). Bond Street tube. **Open** 10am-5pm Mon-Sat; noon-5pm Sun. Closed 24, 25 Dec, 1 Jan, 1 May, Good Friday. **Admission** free. **Credit** *Shop* MC, V. **Map** p316 G5.

An antique-lover's dream, the Wallace Collection of precious works of art, furniture, miniatures, porcelain, sculpture and armoury was bequeathed to the nation in its mansion by the widow of Sir Richard Wallace in 1897. Wallace,

the illegitimate heir of the Marquis of Hertford, inherited furniture, paintings and Sèvres porcelain that his dad, a great Francophile, bought for safe keeping after the French Revolution. The result is room after room of fabulous Louis XIV and XV furnishings, lush paintings by the likes of Fragonard (*The Swing* and *Say Please*, for example), a host of Canalettos, Dutch masterpieces like Frans Hals' *The Laughing Cavalier*, and jaw-dropping quantities of gilded clocks and mirrors. Children look on it all as 'treasure', and they're right – but it's the armour that fascinates them most. The collection is happy to accommodate their interest in the basement conservation gallery, where armour can be tried on (*pictured*).

The Education Department (7563 9551) is second to none, offering a full programme of family events, trails and art workshops (*see p211*). The Café Bagatelle in the chic, glassed-over Sculpture Garden is a light-filled venue for snacks and excellent afternoon tea (lunch is too smart for kids), although young kiddies must not be allowed to maul the statues; they're priceless. *Buggy access. Disabled access: lift, toilet. Nappy-changing facilities. Nearest picnic place: grounds. Restaurant. Shop.*

North London

Camden Market may be famous, Islington may be trendy – but the coolest place is the heath that became Narnia.

There's little to grab the attention of children in and around grimy Camden High Street, although the older and more trend-conscious of them might hanker after the large open-air street market that runs at weekends. The market is said to be London's fourth largest tourist attraction, pulling in some ten million (sheeplike) visitors each year. On fine weekends you can hardly move from the tube station (exit only, at busy times) to **Camden Lock** for the crowds. The stalls are packed to the gills with new and second-hand clothes, crafts, bric-a-brac, gifts, jewellery, and so on, though much of the wares are overpriced and far from original. Go to experience the undeniably buzzy atmosphere by all means, but expect to be buffeted by the multitudes and to pay over the odds for the market goods. Parents with babies and small children might find the trip scarcely worth the hassle, though if you go early enough or out of season it's more bearable.

Just a few steps away from the frantic market is peaceful **Regent's Canal**, where you can escape the crowds on board a traditional narrowboat. The canal runs right through Camden and on as far as Little Venice to the west and Hackney to the east – you can also walk and cycle along the towpath. Boats plying a western course pass through **London Zoo**, and some allow you to break up the journey here. On the 45-minute one-way trip you see elegant terraces with gardens leading down to the canal, willow-fringed towpaths and converted warehouses. Elsewhere in the area civilised attractions include the fascinating **Jewish Museum**, a reflection, with many of the restaurants and bars, of the area's cultural diversity.

Jewish Museum, Camden

129-31 Albert Street, NW1 (7284 1997/www.jewish museum.org.uk). Camden Town tube. **Open** 10am-4pm Mon-Thur; 10am-5pm Sun. Closed bank hols, Jewish festivals. **Admission** (LP) £3.50; £2.50 OAPs; £1.50 5-16s, concessions; free under-5s; £8 family (2+2). **Credit** MC, V.
The history of the Jewish population of Britain, from medieval times up to the present day, is set out in an intelligent and colourful way in this renowned museum. Although it's undoubtedly of interest to students of history and world religion, it's not too dry nor too academic for the young. Children of all ages are welcome, and those aged between seven and 14 years can take part in art activities, craft workshops and storytelling sessions. Fascinating permanent exhibits pertaining to Jewish life include Hanukkah lamps and an incredible 16th-century Venetian synagogue ark. Staff are helpful and take the time to explain the exhibits to visitors.

Buggy access. Disabled access: lift. Nearest picnic place: Regent's Park. Shop.

Around Camden

You'd hardly expect to find a rural idyll next to King's Cross station, but lo – you can grab a slice of greenery at the inspirational **Camley Street Natural Park**. Across York Way from the park is the **London Canal Museum**, which brings to life the history of the local waterways.

Primrose Hill has long been a chi-chi outpost of villagey smartness, but in recent years its reputation has been further enhanced by the numerous celebs who have opted to live – and bring up their kids – here. A clutch of attractive cafés, restaurants, pubs and shops alongside the park, plus some of the prettiest houses in north London, make it worth an ogle, especially if you're already en route to nearby **Regent's Park**. Primrose Hill itself is a smallish park with quite a nice play area, crowned by a gentle slope that is ideal for flying kites. As at many parks, there's a good local firework display on the weekend closest to Bonfire Night. Again, like other parks, this is overly popular and can get horribly crowded and hard to access, which either means a long walk for little legs – or a long wait if you are able to dig in early. If you're planning to eat afterwards book well in advance, as nearby restaurants get packed out.

Just over the railway footbridge in Chalk Farm is the **Roundhouse** (7424 9991), a former train turning shed and celebrated rock concert hall that is being ambitiously reshaped as an adaptable performance space to host a wide range of arts, including music, theatre, dance, circus and digital media.

Camley Street Natural Park

12 Camley Street, NW1 (7833 2311). King's Cross tube/ rail. **Open** May-Sept 9am-5pm Mon-Thur; 11am-5pm Sat, Sun. Oct-Apr 9am-5pm Mon-Thur; 10am-4pm Sat, Sun. Closed 25 Dec-1 Jan. **Admission** free. **Map** p317 L2.
Environmentalists aged between eight and 14 can take part in a bat walk, go pond dipping or create homes for fauna when they join Wildlife Watch at this, the London Wildlife Trust's flagship reserve. They can also take part in important surveys such as Treewatch or the great stag beetle hunt. But you don't have to be a member to enjoy Frog Day in March or the festival in May at this wonderful wildlife oasis. Camley Park has marshlands and flower meadows, ponds and woodland glades, as well as a visitors' centre where you can study the park's history and reserve a place on school holiday playschemes (see p228).
Buggy access. Nappy-changing facilities.

London Canal Museum

12-13 New Wharf Road, N1 (7713 0836/
www.canalmuseum.org.uk). King's Cross tube/rail.
Open 10am-4.30pm Tue-Sun, bank hol Mons. Closed 24-26 Dec. **Admission** (LP) £2.50; £1.25 concessions, 8s-16s; free under-8s. **Credit** MC, V. **Map** p317 M2.
The warehouse containing this small museum on the Regent Canal's Battlebridge Basin was built in the 1850s by Carlo Gatti, an Italian immigrant who made his fortune importing ice from the frozen lakes of Norway, in the days before refrigeration. The blocks were carried from the docks on canal boats and stored here in huge ice wells. The museum tells the story of Gatti and the families who made their living on the canals, supplementing permanent displays with lectures and temporary exhibitions. Ring for details of any forthcoming school holiday craft and activity sessions, including boat trips, model making and painting, which the dedicated staff try to run during every school holiday.
Nappy-changing facilities. Nearest picnic place: museum terrace/canal towpath. Shop.

St John's Wood

Not really north London except by virtue of its postcode, this upmarket residential area just west of Regent's Park is pleasant to stroll around but has few specific attractions for children apart from **Lord's Cricket Ground**; most of it is dominated by pricey clothes shops and interior design studios.

Further north is **Abbey Road**, home of the recording studios and immortalised on the Beatles album cover of the same name. Tourists can often be seen risking life and limb on the zebra crossing to re-enact said cover; if you're embarrassed to be seen with them, pretend you're here to peek at Sir Lawrence Alma-Tadema's house on Grove End Road (No.44; closed to the public). Back on Abbey Road, at no.127, is **Oscar's Den**, one of the best party shops in town; it can provide everything from balloons to celebrity lookalikes (*see p245*).

Lord's & MCC Museum

St John's Wood Road, NW8 (7432 1033/www.mcc.org.uk).
St John's Wood tube. **Open** *Tours Oct-Mar* noon, 2pm daily. *Apr-Sept* 10am, noon, 2pm daily. Closed Christmas period, bank hols, all major matches; phone to check. **Admission** *Tours* £7; £5.50 concessions; £4.50 5-15s; free under-5s; £20 family (2+2). **Credit** MC, V.
The Marylebone Cricket Club Museum is the world's oldest sporting museum and includes, among the paintings, photos and battered bats, eccentricities such as a reconstruction of the shot that killed a passing sparrow in 1936, together with the stuffed bird and the ball. The guided tour takes visitors into the Mound Stand, (so called because it's built on a burial mound from the Great Plague), the pavilion, the visitors' dressing room and the historic Long Room. It's best-known as the home of the celebrated Ashes urn, but what with essential restoration and a tour round Australia, you may not get to see it. Other displays include cricket kit and memorabilia used by some of the greatest players of all time – such as Victor Trumper, Don Bradman and WG Grace. There's also a range of kit and equipment for both children and adults.
Buggy access. Lifts. Nearest picnic place: St John's churchyard playground. Shop.

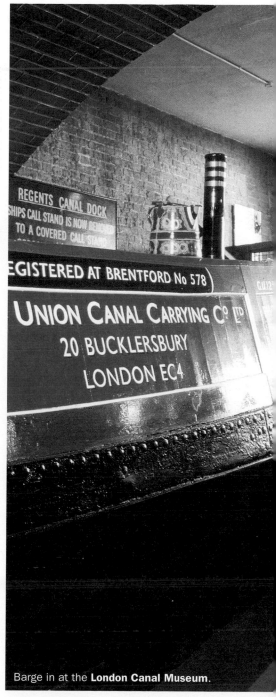

Barge in at the **London Canal Museum**.

Hampstead & around

Hampstead sits in villagey grace on top of a hill, so its air is pretty rarefied – and so is its atmosphere. This pretty urban village is one of London's most exclusive places to live, so most people have to make do with admiring its attractive old houses, quaint churches and characterful pubs on a day-trip basis. At summer weekends both the village and the Heath get horribly busy, with the High Street choked with traffic and parking all but impossible – leave the motor behind if you can. If you like snooping round old houses there are plenty here; spot the blue plaques. People of an architectural bent make for **2 Willow Road** (7435 6166), a prime example of pre-war modernism and now a National Trust property. The house was built in 1939 by Ernö Goldfinger (James Bond's creator Ian Fleming hated Goldfinger's work so much he named a villain after him) and retains its original fixtures and fittings. Those interested in the father of psychoanalysis should make a pilgrimage to the **Freud Museum** (20 Maresfield Gardens, NW3, 7435 2002), where the entry fee lets you ponder the famous couch, as well as papers, artefacts and footage about the various branches of the Freud family. There's a regular turnover of exhibitions, but they're more likely to be of interest to students. For a more general overview of Hampstead, there's **Burgh House** (New End Square, NW3, 7431 0144), a Queen Anne house containing a small museum about the area's history.

Historic houses, chic cafés and great shopping aside, the real reason to make a trip to Hampstead is, of course, glorious **Hampstead Heath**. There's a smart café on the heath, in **Kenwood House**: this English Heritage beauty full of art treasures is the picturesque setting for summer concerts.

Just south of the heath, near Gospel Oak, is a different sort of rustic retreat. **Kentish Town City Farm** is one of the capital's oldest, and it does a great job of keeping north London urbanites in touch with the nation's agricultural heritage.

Camden Arts Centre

Arkwright Road, corner of Finchley Road, NW3 (7604 4504/www.camdenartscentre.org). Finchley Road tube/ Finchley Road & Frognal rail. **Open** phone to check. **Admission** free. **Credit** Shop MC V.
This innovative venue, dedicated to contemporary visual art and art education, was closed for refurbishment at the time of going to press, but due to reopen in autumn 2003. The £4 improvement scheme will create new galleries and studios, a café and relandscape the garden. Call for details of Off-Centre, its series of off-site artistic collaborations.
Shop.

Fenton House

3 Hampstead Grove, NW3 (7435 3471/info 01494 755563/www.nationaltrust.org.uk). Hampstead tube/ Hampstead Heath rail. **Open** Mar 2-5pm Sat, Sun. Apr-Oct 2-5pm Wed-Fri; 11am-5pm Sat, Sun, bank hols. Last entry 4.30pm. *Tours* phone for times. **Admission** (NT) £4.50; £2.25 5-17s; free under-5s. *Tours* £10. **No credit cards**.
This gorgeous late 17th-century house is fêted for its award-winning garden, formally landscaped on one side and incorporating a pretty orchard and vegetable patch on the other. Spring and summer entry to this rural idyll and its wonderful, scented borders is free. The priceless collections inside the house are both quirky and appealing: the intriguing Benton Fletcher Collection of early keyboard instruments can be heard in action during the summer at fortnightly baroque concerts (call for details); other exhibits include a range of porcelain poodles in the Rockingham Room. Tours are of the instruments and porcelain only, but the views over London from the attic rooms are impressive.

Hampstead Heath

NW3 (7485 4491). Belsize Park or Hampstead tube/ Gospel Oak or Hampstead Heath rail/24, 46, 168, 214, C2, C11 bus. **Open** dawn-dusk daily.
This glorious swathe of green and wooded open space – nearly 800 acres of it – provides a wonderful retreat from the urban rush even on the hottest summer's day. Fantastic views over London (from Parliament Hill; perfect for kite flying), rolling green slopes, enchanting woodland, a couple of good cafés, an art gallery, athletics track, outdoor concerts at Kenwood, model boating, tennis, angling, boules and bowls are just a few of its attractions. Parts of the Heath have been designated a Site of Special Scientific Interest by English Nature. In addition to its 25 main ponds, the Heath has well-protected areas of ancient woodland, bog, hedgerows and grassland. Recent work by the Corporation and the Heath Hands volunteers has reinstated small but significant areas of the exceptionally rare heathland habitat, and newly-planted heather on both sides of Spaniards Road now provides a

---

LONDON LEGEND Boudicca

Could King's Cross station mark the final resting place of Queen Boudicca, as rumour would have it? Possibly – but even if her grave lies far from there, the legendary warrior queen of the Iceni, originally the widow of an East Anglian chieftain, certainly made her mark in London. She marched on the Imperial Roman forces after they had seized her land, flogged her and raped her daughters. She led the Iceni in a savage revolt, destroying the Roman colony at Colchester before marching on London.

The final Boudicca-led battle between Britons and Romans occured in AD61. According to Tacitus the Romans sustained only light casualties, but the Britons were cut down in their thousands, and the warrior queen killed herself with poison. Centuries later, the battle was commemorated by the building of the arched bridge that crossed the River Fleet at what is now King's Cross. In 1836 a statue of King George IV was put up and Battle Bridge became the King's Cross. What would the queen have thought?

Hampstead Heath, where the great outdoors is great indeed.

burst of late summer colour. Talking of which, watch out for the odd flash of brilliant blue: breeding kingfishers have returned recently, pairs have been making use of a specially constructed sand-bank as a nest site.

There's an enticing programme of family-oriented actvities throughout the summer, including bat-spotting walks, learning-to-fish sessions and children's music workshops. You can swim free of charge in three natural ponds – complete with weeds and ducks – though children must be over eight and strong swimmers to participate, as these are very deep. Otherwise you can buy a family ticket for the Parliament Hill Lido (*see p261*). On weekday mornings you might hear the mournful skirls of the lone bagpiper who practises on the bandstand, and on a snowy winter's day you might glimpse the lamp-post that is said to have inspired CS Lewis to write *The Lion, the Witch and the Wardrobe*. Sporting facilities include football, hockey, golf, cricket and bowls, but cyclists are restricted to just four routes throughout the heath. Pick up a free diary from the office at Parliament Hill to find out more about the varied summer holiday programme.
Buggy access. Cafés. Nappy-changing facilities.

Keats House

Keats Grove, NW3 (7435 2062/www.keatshouse.org.uk/ www.cityoflondon.gov.uk/keats). Hampstead tube/ Hampstead Heath rail/24, 46, 168 bus. **Open** *Easter-Oct* noon-5pm Tue-Sun. *Nov-Easter* noon-4pm Tue-Sun. Closed 25, 26, 31 Dec, 1 Jan. *Tours* 3pm Sat, Sun. **Admission** £3; £1.50 concessions; free under-16s. *Tours* (Sat, Sun only) incl in admission price.

Now that essential restoration work is complete, the house that was once home to poet John Keats is even more worth a visit. He spent two years in this beautiful white Regency cottage before, weakened by TB, he travelled to Italy and died, aged just 24, in 1821. It was in this romantic setting that he wrote some of his most popular poems, and here also that he fell in love with Fanny Brawne. A plum tree in the garden marks the site of the original tree beneath which he is thought to have penned *Ode to a Nightingale*. Cabinets contain original manuscripts, and visitors can nose round Keats' bedroom, living room and kitchen. On Saturdays and Sundays a tour of the house is included in the admission price.
Buggy access (ground floor only). Nearest picnic place: house gardens. Shop.

Kentish Town City Farm

1 Cressfield Close, off Grafton Road, NW5 (7916 5421). Chalk Farm or Kentish Town tube/Gospel Oak rail. **Open** 9.30am-5.30pm Tue-Sun. Closed 25 Dec. **Admission** free; donations appreciated.

Camden children can count themselves lucky they have their own pony club this deep in the urban jungle. Even so, they can only be put on the club's waiting list in September, and just hope a few of the members hit adolescence and swap a four-legged obsession for a two-legged one. Non-residents can pay £1 for weekend pony rides (1.30pm Sat, Sun, weather permitting), but only Camdenites can attend the summer playschemes. The others can enjoy the busy farm's charms: ducks, chickens, geese, Wiltshire Horned sheep, goats, cows and a Large Black pig. On the third Sunday in October the farm celebrates national Apple Day, with apple bobbing, tree dressing, a longest peel contest and 25 apple varieties to taste.
Buggy access. Disabled access: ramp, toilet. Nappy-changing facilities. Nearest picnic place: Hampstead Heath.

Kenwood House/Iveagh Bequest

Kenwood House, Hampstead Lane, NW3 (8348 1286). Archway tube/Golders Green tube then 210 bus. **Open** *Apr-Sept* 10am-6pm Mon, Tue, Thur, Sat, Sun; 10.30am-6pm Wed, Fri. *Oct-Mar* 10am-4pm Mon, Tue, Thur, Sat, Sun; 10.30am-4pm Wed, Fri. Closed 24-26 Dec, 1 Jan. *Tours* by appointment only. **Admission** (EH) free; donations appreciated. *Tours* £3.50; £2.50 concessions, £1.50 under-16s. **Credit** MC V.

PARKLIFE Alexandra Palace

Nowhere else in London offers such a breathtaking and panoramic view of the capital as Alexandra Palace Park: its outlook runs from the Wood Green Reservoirs at the foot of its hill right over to Canary Wharf and its new companion HSBC Towers on the Isle of Dogs, all the way across to the London Eye by the river Thames and Crystal Palace in the far south. You could happily spend an hour squinting through binoculars to pick out your favourite landmarks (kids love the long view from the fixed ones there, at 20p a shout) and use the rest of the day wandering around its 196 acres of parkland.

Ally Pally, as it's affectionately dubbed, has certainly had its ups and downs. It first opened in 1873 as a recreation centre – but burnt down after just 16 days. Two years later it was rebuilt, complete with a mighty steam-driven Willis Organ in a new Great Hall. There were displays of painting and sculpture, a museum, a lecture hall, a library, banqueting rooms, a concert room (subsequently turned into a roller skating rink) and a theatre. The Park had a popular race track, a trotting ring, a cricket ground, ornamental lakes, and a permanent funfair. In 1935, the BBC leased part of the building as studios for the first ever public television broadcasts. But the Palace caught fire (again) in 1980 and much of it was destroyed (again). More redevelopment plans were hatched and it re-opened in 1988 as a Charitable Trust administered by the London Borough of Haringey.

Alexandra Park is the biggest green space in the borough and the second largest, after Hampstead Heath, in north London. Until recently it's been an under-used resource, with some areas distinctly lacklustre if not downright shabby, but thanks to a £3.6 million five-year refurbishment project things are already looking up. There are plans to upgrade the children's playground and the lake, improvements to the nature conservation area and animal enclosure, a tree management and replanting programme and a traffic management scheme. A visitor centre for children will also be built, and security improved. The lake will be dredged, the banks made over and the lake café rebuilt. Other facilities continue to open while the work's in progress: there's an indoor ice-skating rink (*see p256*), a pitch and putt course and a rather dismal funfair throughout the summer. Ally Pally itself is used as a major exhibition hall, and on certain weekends you might find yourself sharing the facilities with the knitting'n'stitching, sailboating or motorbiking sets, but the rest of the time it's a fairly quiet and low-key park. When you've had enough of wandering the grounds you can stop off at the Phoenix Bar, which has an outdoor seating area where children are welcome – it's surely the one of the best-situated bars in London (*see p178*). An annual highlight is the wonderful firework display on the Saturday nearest to 5 November, where the whole hill is set alight with noisy and spectacular pyrotechnics, producing gasps of delight from the thousands of people of all ages who flock to the spot.

As if to confirm its loveliness, Alexandra Park has been designated an Ecologically Valuable Site, with habitats that include meadow, scrub, secondary woodland, formal parkland, pond and a lake. At the west end of the park lies the start of the Parkland Walk, which follows the route of the old railway line from Alexandra Palace to Finsbury Park. The Conservation Area is set in the southeast corner of the park next to the reservoirs, and there's a small information centre that opens during the week.

Alexandra Park & Palace

Alexandra Palace Way, N22 (park 8444 7696/ palace 8365 2121/boating 8889 9089/ www.alexandra palace.com). Wood Green tube/ Alexandra Palace rail/W3, W7, 84A, 144, 144A bus. **Open** *Park 24hrs daily. Palace times vary depending on exhibitions.* **Admission** *free. Buggy access. Café. Nappy-changing facilities. Nearest picnic place: picnic area by boating lake.*

Best foot forward at **Alexandra Park**.

Perched on top of the rolling green heath, Kenwood House is as well known for its accessible and classy Brew House Café as for its white, imposing silhouette and historic associations. Kenwood was rebuilt in the classical style for the Earl of Mansfield by Robert Adam in 1767-9 and bequeathed to the nation in 1927. Today, the building's chief attraction is the Iveagh Bequest, a collection of paintings that boasts works by Reynolds, Turner and Van Dyck, as well as a Rembrandt self-portrait tucked into a darkened corner of the Dining Room and a rare Vermeer (*The Guitar Player*). Botticelli, Guardi and a couple of classic flirtatious Bouchers round out the wonderful collection. There's also a vast library.

Kenwood has a pretty good education department, and the staff dreams up worksheets and organises treasure hunts, dressing-up sessions and family tea parties. Volunteer group Heath Hands also has its office here – it too plans family events throughout the year, mostly to do with improving the look of the heath and the estate gardens. For details of forthcoming events here and around the heath, pick up a leaflet at the visitors' centre in the Kenwood House Estate Office. *Buggy access (limited in house). Café. Nappy-changing facilities. Shop.*

Highgate & Archway

Like Hampstead, Highgate is a pretty, characterful, hilly village bursting with rummage-worthy shops, child-friendly pubs – and wealthy residents who greatly covet the sylvan backdrop. One of the main reasons to bring children here is **Highgate Wood**, one of the rare bits of surviving original woodland in the capital, which has a delightful setting, a well designed play area and a pleasant café. Waterlow Park is also gorgeous, and will be more so once its extensive refurbishment is complete. Next door, **Highgate Cemetery** (Swains Lane, N6, 8340 1834/ www.highgate-cemetery.org) is on the visiting list of many a tourist, much to the annoyance of the Friends of Highgate Cemetery, who prefer to play down the visitor pull of their historic patch. Kids are, in fact, discouraged from visiting the place unless they're coming to see the grave of a relative, but if you long to pay respects to Karl Marx, Mary Ann Evans (aka George Eliot), Max Wall or any of the other admired figures who now repose in the Eastern Cemetery, you can bring children to enjoy the peace and beauty of this delightful boneyard as long as they're well behaved.

The Western Cemetery is out of bounds to casual visitors (adults and kids aged eight and over can pay for a guided tour). A little further down the hill from the tube station is Shepherd's Close, from where you can access the **Parkland Walk** (which runs to Finsbury Park). Hornsey Lane, on the other side of Highgate Hill, leads you to the **Archway**, a Victorian viaduct spanning what is now the A1 and offering views of the City and the East End. **Jackson's Lane Community Centre** (*see p219*) off Archway Road puts on shows for children on most Saturdays, and a popular, large-scale panto at Christmas.

Highgate Wood/Queen's Wood

Muswell Hill Road, NW6 (8444 6129) . Highgate tube/ 43, 134, 263 bus. **Open** 7.30am-dusk daily.

Highgate Wood might not be as famous as its north London neighbour Hampstead Heath but it is a gem all the same, made more precious by its position just yards from the roaring traffic of the Archway Road. Originally part of the Middlesex Forest, its 70 acres are some of the last remaining ancient woodlands in London, full of gently swaying oaks and hornbeam. The wood has been lovingly tended by the Corporation of London and its trusty team of woodsmen and women since 1886, when the Lord Mayor declared the wood 'an open space for ever'. Carpeted with bluebells and wild flowers in spring and dappled with sunlight filtered by the trees, this corner of London doesn't feel like London at all.

The wood is carefully managed: trees are coppiced in the traditional way, areas are fenced off to encourage new growth, boxes are provided for owls, bats and hedgehogs to nest in, and everything that moves is chronicled. The bird population has increased dramatically in recent years, both in types and numbers – 70 different species of bird have been spotted here, including nesting sparrowhawks and visiting rare golden orioles. Alongside the usual foxes and grey squirrels are five species of bat, more than 20 of butterfly, 100 of spider and a stunning 454 of beetle: expect much rustling in the undergrowth. Those who don't know their owl from their oriole can pick up helpful leaflets in the visitors' information hut beside the café, or join one of the bird identification walks or nature trails. There's always something going on: stories around the Story-Telling Tree in summer, Christmas tree recycling in January, beetle safaris and bat watch evenings.

Families from all over north London flock to the wood at weekends for the award-winning children's playground, which has been carefully planned to allow wheelchair-users and their more mobile friends to play together. The bridge and tower structure is accessible to buggies and wheelchairs, the swings are designed to be used by children who need more support, and there are braille notice-boards. Children love the flying fox (an aerial runway up in the trees); older folk appreciate the shade and plentiful benches. The playground is supervised and there's a separate section for the under-fives. For older children and more sporty types there's a football and cricket field (in front of the café), and exercise equipment for chin-ups, sit-ups and parallel bars work has recently been installed among the trees.

The other big draw is the Oshobasho Café (8444 1505; *see p165*), a café housed in the old cricket pavilion. On summer evenings there are concerts in the garden, where parents can enjoy a glass of wine while their kids play on the grass.

Highgate Wood even has its own newspaper, the *Treetop News*, with details of new sightings of birds and animals, puzzles and crosswords. It can be downloaded from the Corporation of London's website (www.cityoflondon.gov.uk) or picked up free in the visitors' centre.

Across Muswell Hill Road is Queen's Wood, which comes under local council management and is a wilder prospect – there are no resident staff and it can be quite deserted. Walkers can join the Parkland Walk footpath from here.

Lauderdale House

Waterlow Park, Highgate Hill, N6 (8348 8716/restaurant 8341 4807/www.lauderdale.org.uk). Archway tube. **Open** 11am-4pm Tue-Fri; 1.30-5pm Sat; noon-5pm Sun; phone to check weekend openings. *Restaurant* 9am-dusk Tue-Sun. Closed 24 Dec-mid Jan. **Admission** free. **No credit cards**.

This pretty 16th-century house, once home of Nell Gwynne, is a favoured venue for wedding receptions and other bashes, so it's sometimes closed to the public. Saturdays, howev-

Horsing about at **Kentish Town City Farm**. *See p95.*

Around Town

Highbury Fields. *See p101.*

er, are sacrosanct, because that's when children come for their morning shows, usually aimed at the threes to eights. Ring for details of craft fairs, musical events, exhibitions by local artists and other events held in the busy arts centre (*see p219*). In the summer, weather permitting, the parkland surrounding the house hosts open-air shows. Whatever's on, it's lovely to sit on the terrace of the café and admire the view over a coffee and ice-cream or an Italian meal; make sure to book ahead if you fancy having your Sunday lunch here. Beautiful Waterlow Park, in which the house is set, has several lakes, a toddler's playground, an aviary and gentle grassy slopes that are great for picnicking. The Grade II-listed park has been awarded £1.2 million of Heritage Lottery money for improvement, which will include restoration of the 17th-century terrace garden and work to convert the depot building into workshops, an activities room and toilets. *Buggy access (ground floor only). Café. Nearest picnic place: Waterlow Park.*

Islington

'Merry' Islington was first famous as an idyllic village – Henry VIII owned houses for hunting in the area – but today is known as one of London's premier urban residential areas, a buzzy district characterised by its mix of graceful, listed Victorian and Georgian houses, trendy bars and shops, and numerous flourishing arts centres such as the famous **Almeida Theatre**. On a Friday night the streets are positively thronging with the after-work crowd in search of alcoholic entertainment, but there's also

plenty here for those not yet of drinking age.

Islington has 11 theatres, and it's home to the Anna Scher Theatre School where many *EastEnders* cast members learned their trade – though would-be Walfordites can expect a five-year wait to join. The **Little Angel Theatre** (*see p213*) in Dagmar Passage is a celebrated, purpose-built puppet theatre that puts on imaginative shows enjoyed for all age groups. Every June the area hosts a two-week festival of music, theatre and art, and there are regular exhibitions at the Business Design Centre.

Playground-loving kids rate **Highbury Fields**, where the equipment is challenging but extremely crowded on sunny days. Footie fans of the Gunner variety may like to tour **Arsenal Football Club** before it relocates in 2005. Due north of Arsenal, the other big park in the area is **Finsbury Park**, for which the Borough of Islington shares responsibility with the boroughs of Haringey and Hackney. It's a great sprawling green space, that until recently has become very shabby and run down. Fortunately there's help at hand in the shape of the Finsbury Park Partnership, set up to bid for a slice of the government's Single Regeneration Budget in 1999. The Finsbury Park area, which includes the huge railway and tube station, housing estates and commercial districts, has been awarded £25 million. The park's regeneration should be complete by the time the project ends in 2006, so the future looks bright. What's more, there's no shortage of sporting facilities, notably the nearby **Sobell Leisure Centre** (*see p256*), with its climbing walls, trampolining, table tennis, squash and badminton. It's star attraction for the under-threes is the Sobell Safari, an indoor adventure playground on four floors, with maze, tunnels, slides and ball ponds.

Nearby, on Green Lanes, the **Castle Climbing Centre** (*see p251*) is London's top climbing venue in a Grade II-listed Victorian folly (previously a water tower) modelled on Stirling Castle in Scotland.

Those who crave the scent of the countryside can commune with pigs at **Freightliners City Farm**, or learn about green activities at the **Islington Ecology Centre**. Rural flavours, in a form trendy urban types can stomach (think organic rocket and artistic globe artichokes) can be sampled every Sunday from 10am to 2pm at the **Islington Farmers' Market** (Essex Road, opposite Islington Green, N1). Chapel Market (on the street of the same name) is gloriously downmarket, full of fruit and vegetable, bargain linen, cut-price greetings cards, partyware, toys and not-always-durables, presided over by rowdy costers. It's still thriving, despite competition from the new **N1 Shopping Centre** that links Liverpool Road with Upper Street. The centre is home to branches of reliable childrenswear chains, plus restaurants like Wagamama and Yo Sushi!, and an eight-screen cinema.

Arsenal Football Club

Arsenal Stadium, Avenell Road, N5 (7704 4000/tickets 7413 3366/www.arsenal.com). Arsenal tube/Finsbury Park tube/rail. **Open** *Gunners shop* 9.30am-5pm Mon-Fri and before and after all first team home games. *World of Sport shop* 9.30am-6pm Mon-Sat. *Tours* 11am, 2pm Mon-Fri.* **Admission** *Museum* £2; £1 under-16s. *Tours* £4; £2 concessions, under-16s; £1 junior Gunners. **Credit** *Shop* MC, V.

The bulldozers have dug in and work has begun on Arsenal's controversial new stadium at Ashburton Grove, but until it opens in 2005, Highbury is still, as it proudly claims at its entrance, 'the home of football'. So if north London youngsters incline towards the red rather than the blue, there are still a couple of years left in which to visit this historic football ground. Check out the pitch, changing rooms and museum, which has memorabilia, info about the club's early days and a Gunner-glorifying video. The shop stocks replica kit (in all sizes) and various souvenirs.
Nearest picnic place: Gillespie Park. Shops.

Freightliners City Farm

Paradise Park, Sheringham Road, off Liverpool Road, N7 (7609 0467). Holloway Road tube/Highbury & Islington tube/rail. **Open** *Winter* 10am-4pm Tue-Sun. *Summer* 10am-5pm Tue-Sun. Closed 25-26 Dec, 1 Jan. **Admission** free; donations appreciated.

Aptly located in Paradise Park, Freightliners is a big attraction for children in the summer holidays, when the playschemes are booked weeks ahead. There's a varied bunch of animals to pet, including rabbits, chinchillas and guinea pigs, moving on up to less cuddly poultry, pigs, sheep,

goats and cows. The farm is becoming known for its rare breeds: it is currently home to Berkshire and Tamworth porkers, a small, city-friendly breed of cow called a Dexter and – its speciality – a Chilean hen that lays green eggs (a popular element in the style-conscious Islingtonian's breakfast). You can buy fresh honey, vegetables, hay, straw and animal feed from the shop, and sometimes the farm has fertile eggs for hatching or small animals looking for a good home.
Buggy access. Nappy-changing facilities. Nearest picnic place: picnic area in farm. Shop.

Highbury Fields

Highbury Crescent, N5 (7527 4971). Highbury & Islington tube/rail. **Open** *Park* 24hrs. *Playground* dawn-dusk daily.

A summertime focal point, Highbury Fields is Islington's largest open space. The unusual playground is particularly appreciated by all age groups. The outdoor tennis courts have been refurbished and are used by the excellent Islington Tennis Centre (*see p263*), an all-levels club that runs all year round. Many people make a day of it by swimming in Highbury Pool next door, lunching in the café here, then spending a lazy afternoon watching children play.
Buggy access. Café.

Islington Ecology Centre

191 Drayton Park, N5 (7354 5162/www.islington.gov.uk). Arsenal tube. **Open** *Park* 8am-dusk Mon-Fri; 9am-dusk Sat; 10am-dusk Sun. *Centre* drop-in advice sessions 10am-noon Tue; 2-4pm Thur; for other times phone to check. **Admission** free; donations appreciated.

Come here to find out about all things green and pleasant in the area. It's part of the Gillespie Park Local Nature Reserve, which is the largest reserve in the borough, with a range of wildlife habitats (woodland, meadow, wetland and ponds). The staff are welcoming and children are encouraged to join in on walks, talks and school holiday activities. The latter this year will include scavenger hunts, herbal potion making, mini beast hunts and sculpture sessions that recycle various materials. Ring for details or a leaflet covering what's on.
Buggy access.

The Islington Museum

Islington Town Hall, Upper Street, N1 (7527 2837). Highbury & Islington tube/rail. **Open** 11am-5pm, Wed-Sat, 2pm-4pm Sun. **Admission** free

Boat trips

The following outfits all run boat excursions along the Regent's Canal. Their seasons are dependent on the weather, so ring before you set out.

Jason's Trip

Blomfield Road (opposite No.60), Little Venice, W9 (7286 3428/www.jasons.co.uk).

Jenny Wren

250 Camden High Street, NW1 (7485 4433/ www.walkersquay.com).

London Waterbus Company

Blomfield Road (corner of Westbourne Terrace Road Bridge), Little Venice, W9, or Camden Lock, off Chalk Farm Road, NW1 (7482 2550/ info line 7482 2660).

The Islington Museum is housed in the former Assembly Hall, next to Islington Town Hall, and has two galleries for contemporary art exhibitions and displays on the history of Islington. There are temporary displays of local interest, information on the area and its history, facilities for research and school projects, conservation advice, workshops and school activities. During summer 2003 the museum will put on a Maps, Models, Memories exhibition inspired by after-school clubs, and events such as henna hand painting. *Shop.*

Stoke Newington

North-east of Islington, 'Stokey' first became fashionable in the 80s when property prices in N1 became prohibitive, driving 'alternative' families into the next postcode along. Now, the three-wheeled buggy brigade, long-term locals and Islington wannabes all co-exist more or less happily. It's a pleasantly bohemian, unpolished sort of area, with good independent shops and numerous places to eat and drink. The heart of the area is Stoke Newington Church Street, which hosts a street festival every June. Stoke Newington is blessed with two fine green spaces – **Clissold Park**, where local families congregate, and the rambling old boneyard of **Abney Park Cemetery & Nature Reserve**.

Abney Park Cemetery & Nature Reserve
Stoke Newington Church Street, N16 (7275 7557). Stoke Newington rail/73, 476 bus. **Open** dawn-dusk daily. Closed 25 Dec. **Admission** free.
Woodpeckers, bats and rare butterflies are known to frequent this magical old cemetery, with its crumbling statues and derelict church, but that's only when the children have cleared off. Local families love to walk and picnic here, and the warden is energetic in his efforts to keep them entertained. There are Easter egg hunts, craft workshops, guided walks (ring for dates) and treasure hunts in school holidays. The visitors' centre doubles as a shop for guides to green London and other such environmentally aware literature.
Buggy access. Shop.

Clissold Park
Stoke Newington Church Street, N16 (7923 3660/tennis courts 7923 3644/café 7923 3703). Stoke Newington rail/73, 149 bus. **Open** *Park* 7.30am-dusk daily.
The much-loved Clissold Park has any number of child-pleasing features: ponds for paddling, dipping and duck-feeding, pleasant tree-lined walks with plenty of room for ball games, a modern, well-equipped playground and a mini zoo with fallow deer, a butterfly tunnel and an aviary. This delightful green space is set around a mansion (its café serves reasonably priced vegetarian food and snacks), and during the Stoke Newington Festival (which usually takes place in June) the park becomes a hive of activity. A stage is set up for bands, there are numerous stalls, and face-painted children mill about merrily. The tennis courts here are home to the Hackney wing of the City Tennis Centre (*see p263*); ring for details of its tennis programme – family tennis evenings, junior clubs and tournaments and coaching for all. The modern, glass and steel Clissold Leisure Centre, with its popular swimming pool, is just across the road.
Buggy access in park, steps at café. Café.

Crouch End & Muswell Hill

Their plum position on some of London's highest hills give the former villages of Crouch End and Muswell Hill a wholesome aspect. The advantage of clean air and spacious Victorian and Edwardian houses is weighed against the disadvantage of no tube – residents tend to rely on buses and cars, which can make for congestion at weekends. Both areas bristle with classy independent shops and cafés catering for the exacting tastes of trendy young families. The area's main attraction has to be **Alexandra Park & Palace** (*see p96*), but there are also plenty of green spaces for locals to call their own. **Priory Park** in Middle Lane is great for cycling, rollerskating and football, and has a paddling pool, formal gardens and tennis courts; its Rainbow Café is good for snacks. Stationers Park, between Denton Road and Mayfield Road, has a good adventure playground, a pre-school children's play area and tennis courts. **Park Road Pools** (*see p261*) has both indoor and outdoor swimming pools, though the latter gets packed out at summer weekends.

Finchley

Finchley is one of those London outposts that have been waiting to 'come up' for several years now, but haven't yet managed it. Not that it isn't thoroughly affluent and well served by public transport with its three tube stations – it just hasn't got the desirable status of other smart north London villages. Its saving graces are perhaps its cosmopolitan background (it has large Jewish and Japanese communities), air of general prosperity and peaceful, treelined streets.

Around Church End, Central Finchley, the true heart of what was once a village, you catch a whiff of Middle England and will hardly believe you're still in the capital. The attraction here is **Avenue House** and its beautifully landscaped gardens, which were given to the nation in 1918.

Victoria Park, just off Ballards Lane between Finchley Central and North Finchley, has a bowling green, playground and tennis courts; in July it also provides a venue for the Finchley Carnival.

For indoor kiddy entertainment, the **Great North Leisure Park** (Leisure Way, High Road, N12) – better known among the locals as Warner Village – is an ugly but useful US-style entertainment complex. The cinema, Finchley Warner Village (0870 240 6020), has a Saturday morning kids' club. There's also an extremely popular swimming pool – a good spot for children's parties – with a lido next door, which really comes into its own on warm summer days (as the crowds testify). The **Hollywood Bowl** bowling alley (*see p264*) has a bar and burger restaurant; next door is an amusement arcade.

With you in a mo', Squadron Leader – keep her ticking over! **Royal Air Force Museum Hendon.** *Sec p104.*

A couple of rowdy games here, followed by pizza and pop next door at **ASK** (8446 0970), is a tried-and-tested children's party combination in these parts.

Across the North Circular in East Finchley, the **Phoenix Cinema** (8883 2233) has children's films on Saturdays. In East End Road the Old Manor House has been transformed by the Sternberg Centre into a cultural centre, which includes ritual baths, a school and the **Jewish Museum**, Finchley.

If you and your offspring decide to get away from it all, try the **Dollis Valley Green Walk**, which forms part of the London Loop that encircles the city and links green spaces from Moat Mount, near Mill Hill in the north, to Hampstead Garden Suburb in the south. The ten-mile stretch is split into easily manageable sections, with lovely stretches of woodland and serene picnic places along the way. You can start from several different points: a good place is at the car park at Moat Mount Open Space, accessible and clearly signposted from the southbound carriageway of the A1, just north of Mill Hill Golf Club (100 Barnet Way, NW7, 8959 2282). Dollis Brook itself rises near Arkley, not far from Totteridge, and winds its way gently southwards to join Mutton Brook and form the River Brent, which in turn flows south and west before it meets the Thames at Brentford. The walk can be easily reached at various points by public transport and is clearly signposted for much of the way. The northerly section is recommended as the most peaceful and suitable for children whose little legs might not be up to a long march. For more details ring 8359 3052 or visit www.londonwalking.com.

Avenue House

15-17 East End Road, N3 (8346 7812). Finchley Central tube. **Open** *Ink Museum* 2-4.30pm Tue-Thur. Closed 24 Dec-1 Jan. **Admission** free; donations appreciated.

The tiny Ink Museum commemorates former Avenue House owner 'Inky' Stephens and his father Henry, inventor in 1837 of the blue-black ink that is used to this day on birth and marriage certificates. Some of the beautiful rooms can be hired out and it's a popular and quite grand venue for children's parties. There's also a pleasantly situated playground and a tree trail that's accessible to buggies.

Buggy access. Café. Disabled access: toilet. Nappy-changing facilities. Nearest picnic place: Avenue House grounds.

Jewish Museum, Finchley

Sternberg Centre, 80 East End Road, N3 (8349 1143/ www.jewishmuseum.org.uk). Finchley Central tube/13, 82, 112, 143, 260 bus. **Open** 10.30am-5pm Mon-Thur; 10.30am-4.30pm Sun. Closed bank hols, Jewish hols, Sun in Aug. **Admission** (LP) £2; £1 concessions, 12-16s; free under-12s. **No credit cards**.

DON'T MISS
Royal Air Force Museum

The Bomber Hall
The Lancaster bomber; the huge Vulcan jet; the Dambusters display area.

Historic Hangars
The all-new Aeronauts interactive gallery; the simulator ride; the restored Southampton.

Battle of Britain Hall
The walk-through Sunderland flying boat; the Spitfire Mark V; the life-like talking Churchill. For full listings, *see p104.*

The more northerly branch of the affecting and informative Jewish Museum (see p92) focuses on Jewish social history. Reconstructions include a functional sewing workshop on the ground floor, which gives an idea of sweatshop life in the 19th century. Upstairs an exhibition traces the life of Leon Greenman, a British Jew who survived Auschwitz (his wife and child both perished). He's in his 90s now, but still comes in every Sunday to speak to groups of adults and children. His talks are fascinating and those who have spoken to Mr Greenman come away both better informed about the Jewish experience in the war, and full of admiration for this man.

The Holocaust Exhibition may be considered too upsetting for young children, but staff leave it to the discretion of parents as to whether they let their children venture upstairs; the images are more likely to be understood by young people of at least secondary school age. This branch also has a 12,000-strong photographic archive augmented by 2,000 oral history tapes. Forthcoming exhibitions in 2003 include Am I my Brother's Keeper? It's all about rescue in the Holocaust and will run until the end of the year. Note that the café is open only at lunchtimes, from Monday to Thursday.

Café. Nearest picnic place: museum garden/Avenue House gardens. Shop.

Further north

Jump on a bus going up the dreary A10 towards Tottenham and you eventually pass White Hart Lane, the home of **Tottenham Hotspur Football Club**, a tour of which is much easier to get into than a match. Just down from here is **Bruce Castle**, an island of stateliness in run-down surroundings.

Further west, the North Circular (an escape route or a vehicle trap depending on traffic) leads to **Brent Cross Shopping Centre** with its large range of chains and a handy crèche, and then on to Ikea, home of the affordable flatpack. Take the Edgware Road if you have a yen for Japanese goods: **Oriental City** (399 Edgware Road, NW9, 8200 0009) is a mall with several good places to eat, including a big self-service buffet. The shops are fascinating, though it's the state-of-the-art amusement arcade that children love – it's a lot less seedy than its counterparts in central London.

Set sail in a westerly direction from Brent Cross to the peace and quiet of the **Welsh Harp Reservoir** (Cool Oak Lane, NW9 8205 1240). This huge open space is not only a beauty spot but has been recognised as a site of special scientific interest. The informative environmental centre is a good starting point for nature trips, and the reservoir is used for all types of water sports (see p264). The surrounding leafy waterside areas provide space for games pitches, tennis courts, playgrounds and picnicking.

Further north, in Hendon proper, the extensively revamped **Royal Air Force Museum Hendon** is an even more lavish tribute to the history of flying machines and the magnificent men who piloted them.

Bruce Castle Museum

Lordship Lane, N17 (8808 8772/www.haringey.gov.uk). Seven Sisters tube/rail then 123 or 243 bus, Wood Green tube then 123 or 243 bus/Bruce Grove rail. **Open** 1-5pm Wed-Sun. *Summer bank hol* 1-5pm Mon. **Admission** free. Tucked away in an inconspicuous part of Tottenham, Bruce Castle is a Grade I listed 16th Century manor house in 20 acres of parkland, worth a stopover if you find yourself in these far and dusty reaches. The oldest surviving parts of the building were built by William Compton, a member of Henry VIII's court; since then the building has been modified several times by successive owners, including the Coleraine family – the ghost of one of the wives of the second Lord Coleraine is said to haunt the building. Bruce Castle opened as a Museum in 1906 and now houses the Borough of Haringey's local history collections and archives, including local paintings, photographs and prints, and an interactive exhibition devoted to local inventors. The Museum offers free workshops for schools and community groups, and lots of activities for families at weekends and during school holidays.

Buggy access. Car park (free). Disabled access: lift, toilet. Nappy-changing facilities. Shop.

Royal Air Force Museum Hendon

Grahame Park Way, NW9 (8205 2266/www.rafmuseum. org). Colindale tube/Mill Hill Broadway rail/32, 226, 292, 303 bus. **Open** 10am-6pm daily. Closed 24-26 Dec, 1 Jan. **Tours** daily; times vary, phone for details. **Admission** (LP) free. *Tours* free. **Credit** MC, V.
Thanks to a hefty £4.77 million lottery grant, the National Museum of Aviation is well on its way to becoming a world leader as it gears up to celebrate 100 years of flight in 2003. The new-look museum is three times larger, with over 200 aircraft on show, special events to show them off and interactive displays and activities to bring in even more punters. New attractions include the Aeronauts gallery, where visitors learn about anything and everything to do with flying; also of note is the spectacular sound and light show, Our Finest Hour, which tells the story of the Battle of Britain. There's also a Red Arrows flight simulator, a 'touch and try' Jet Provost cockpit and a walk-through Sunderland flying boat. The brand new Milestones of Flight building opens in late 2003, featuring planes, interactive touch screens and a mock-up 1917 Grahame White aircraft factory.

Activities for children and adults take place all year: workshops include hot-air balloon making, rocket science, and Search and Rescue role-playing. The workshops are always very popular, so do book ahead. From summer 2003 onwards you can take part in quizzes, Pulsar Battlezone interactive laser games, face painting, aircraft displays, giant garden games including snakes and ladders, and the fun-packed Summer Festival Weekend at the end of August.
Buggy access. Café. Lift. Nappy-changing facilities. Nearest picnic place: picnic ground on site. Restaurant. Shop.

Tottenham Hotspur Football Club

Bill Nicholson Way, 748 High Road, N17 (8365 5000/ www.spurs.co.uk). White Hart Lane rail. **Open** *Tours* 11am Mon-Fri; 11am, 1pm Sat. **Admission** *Tours* £7.50 adults; £4.50 under-16s, OAPs. **Credit** (only in advance) MC, V.
Tours of the pitchside, the tunnel, changing rooms, board rooms and press rooms take place regularly, but the Saturday ones tend to be booked up well in advance. Note that they cannot take place on a match day nor the day before, more's the pity. Tours last about an hour, depending on how chatty the punters are. Finish in the megastore, where you can blow £50 on a shirt or 50p on a souvenir pencil.
Buggy access. Disabled access: toilet. Shop.

LUNCH BREAK

Around Camden
Café Corfu (*7-9 Pratt Street, NW1, 7267 8088*), for cutting-edge mainland and island Greek fare.
Daphne (*83 Bayham Street, NW1, 7267 7322*), a tasteful oasis – check out the daily specials.
The Engineer (*65 Gloucester Avenue, NW1, 7722 0950; see p172*), one of London's top gastropubs.
Pizza Express (*187 Kentish Town Road, NW5, 7267 0101; see p175*), for reliable you-know-what.
Wagamama (*11 Jamestown Road, NW1, 7428 0800; see p180*), for tasty, affordable noodles.

Around Primrose Hill
Belgo Noord (*72 Chalk Farm Road, NW1, 7267 0718; see p164*), for sturdy sausages, golden chips, steaming mussels and Belgian beer.
Cachao (*140 Regent's Park Road, NW1, 7483 4422*), a friendly pâtisserie and café.
Lemonia (*89 Regents Park Road, NW1, 7586 7454; see p172*), a big Greek noise and a celebrity fave.
Manna (*4 Erskine Road, NW3, 7722 8028*), excellent, long-established vegetarian eaterie.
Marine Ices (*8 Haverstock Hill, NW3, 7482 9003; see p172*), supplier of delicious Italian ice-creams and pasta dishes – one of our favourites.
Retsina (*83 Regent's Park Road, NW1, 7722 3194*), another good Greek, and affordable with it.

Around Hampstead Village
Cucina (*45A South End Road, NW3, 7435 7814*), for superior modern European delights.
dim T Café (*3 Heath Street, NW3, 7435 0024*), for massive plates of noodles and dainty dim sum.
Giraffe (*46 Rosslyn Hill, NW3, 7435 0343; see p172*), a family favourite for good global food.
Maxwell's (*76 Heath Street, NW3, 7794 5450*), for good hamburgers, cheesy nachos and other calorie-laden US delicacies.
Pizza Express (*70 Heath Street, NW3, 7433 1600*), purveyor of predictably pleasant pizzas.
Polly's (*55 South End Road, NW3, 7794 8144*), for snacks and – she puts the kettle on – coffee.
Tootsies (*196-198 Havistock Hill, NW3 7431 3812; see p182*), famously family-friendly spot for great burgers and – healthier – inventive salads.
ZenW3 (*83 Hampstead High Street, NW3, 7794 7863*), a classy Chinese spot that pulls in families.

Around Highgate
Café Mozart (*17 Swains Lane, N6, 8348 1384; see p172*), for fabulous East European cakes.
Café Rouge (*6-7 South Grove, N6, 8342 9797*), a popular family weekend address with kids' menus.
Papa Del's pizzeria (*347 Archway Road, N19, 8347 9797*), a pleasant hilltop alternative to the ubiquitous chains – perhaps Papa knows best.
Pizza Express (*30 Highgate High Street, N6, 8341 3434*), for round, oven-cooked things with toppings.
St John's (*91 Junction Road, N19, 7272 1587*), a large-roomed pub that's a hit at Sunday lunch.

Around Islington
The new N1 Shopping Centre houses Wagamama, Yo Sushi!, Starbucks among others.
Giraffe (*29-31 Essex Road, N1, 7359 5999; see p172*), another branch of the bright and breezy chain.
Santa Fe (*75 Upper Street, N1, 7288 2288; see p174*), great Tex-Mex food and a kiddy menu.
Tiger Lil's (*270 Upper Street, N1, 7226 1118; see p181*), kids pick ingredients for the chefs to fry.

Around Stoke Newington
Il Bacio (*61 Church Street, N16, 7249 3833*), dependable for good Italian pasta and pizza.
Blue Legume café (*101 Church Street, N16, 7923 1303*), an attractive café that serves wholesome smoothies, salads and crostinis.
Cooler (*67 Church Street, N16, 7275 7266*), where you can tuck into delicious sandwiches.
Itto (*226 Stoke Newington High Street, N16, 7275 8827*), great for a cheap, tasty Thai noodle meal.
The Prince (*59 Kynaston Road, N16, 7923 4766; see p174*), a converted pub that is fast becoming a popular family address – the food's reliably yummy.
Rasa (*55 Church Street, N16, 7249 0344*), acclaimed South Indian vegetarian restaurant.
Vortex (*139-41 Church Street, N16, 7254 6516*), grown up jazz venue with fine, child-friendly food.

Around Crouch End & Muswell Hill
Restaurants are in plentiful supply in the area – Crouch End is said to have over 70 eateries alone.
Banners (*21 Park Road, N8, 8292 0001*), relaxed but crowded, with a long under-tens menu.
Caffè Uno (*348 Muswell Hill Broadway, N10, 8883 4463*), children eat free Italian at Sunday lunchtimes (in the company of a paying adult, naturally).
Pizza Bella (*16 Park Road, N8, 8342 8541*), child-friendly, and popular for birthday parties.
Pizza Express (*290 Muswell Hill Broadway, N10, 8883 5845*), a well-loved venue for – guess what.
La Porchetta (*265 Muswell Hill Broadway, N10, 8883 1500*), a popular restaurant with a nice line in giant pizzas and entertaining waiters.
Toff's (*38 Muswell Hill Broadway, N10, 8883 8656*), an award-winning spot renowned for its simply stonking portions of fish and chips.
The World Café (*130 Crouch Hill, N8, 8340 5635*), for interesting global food at reasonable prices.

Around Finchley
Chorak (*122 High Road, N2, 8365 3330; see p233*), cakes baked on the premises.
The Old Europeans (*106 High Road, N2, 8883 3964*), welcomes kids with open arms, high chairs and half portions of hearty Hungarian grub.
Rani (*7 Long Lane, N3, 8349 4386*), well-known vegetarian Indian, with under-12s menu.
Two Brothers Fish Restaurant (*297-303 Regent's Park Road, N3, 8346 0469*), always full of smart people eating fab fish and chips.

East London

From the cockle-warming East End streets, it's a fair old step to Epping.

Whitechapel & Spitalfields

Probably the easiest introduction to the East End, Whitechapel and Spitalfields give you local colour with fabulous markets and high culture at the cracking art gallery, within an easy walk of Liverpool Street or Aldgate East tubes. If you're not wrestling pushchairs, it's worth rattling in from the City on a red No.15 bus – few kids can resist a ride on the old double-deckers. Jump out near Tubby Isaacs' stall (on Goulston Street since 1919) and you can terrorise them with some genuine jellied eels or a handful of whelks in a polystyrene cup. Since 2002 a converted washhouse in next door Old Castle Street has been home to the **Women's Library** (7320 2222), which holds free exhibitions (9.30am-5.30pm Mon-Wed, Fri; 9.30am-8pm Thur) and workshops, as well as the best collection on women's history in the country. In 2003 they celebrate the centenary of the founding of the Women's Social and Political Union.

On Whitechapel Road there are two main points of interest: **Whitechapel Bell Foundry** (No.32-4, 7247 2599/www.whitechapelbellfoundry.co.uk) and **Whitechapel Art Gallery**. The foundry (tours by arrangement, 10am, 2pm Sat) was established in 1570, making it Britain's oldest manufacturing company still in operation. The buildings are a Grade II-listed idiosyncrasy on a street largely taken up with undistinguished clothing wholesalers; this are where America's Liberty Bell was cast in 1752 and Big Ben, the monster 13-ton hour bell of the Great Clock of Westminster, was made in 1858. Connoisseurs of the macabre may be drawn east to the **Royal London Hospital Museum**, tucked behind a hospital most famous for one former patient: the so-called 'Elephant Man'.

North of Whitechapel Road, you'll find **Petticoat Lane** market (Sundays, until 2pm). It's a hectic slice of the real East End: the knock-down consumer durables and cheap clothes won't keep kids happy for long, but the patter warms everyone's cockles. North again and you're in **Spitalfields** market. Open on Wednesdays and Sundays, the covered market belongs to young, ecologically aware parents buying organic food; on Sundays the friendly throng occasionally can be overwhelming. Nicholas Hawksmoor's awe-inspiring but rather crumbly **Christ Church** is just opposite the market on Commercial Street, E1 (7247 7202). Built in 1714, it's been closed for restoration since 2002. If the kids

are in a churches-are-boring phase, point out that this was also where Jack the Ripper roamed: the recently refurbished and rather handsome Ten Bells pub, where some of the unfortunate victims supped their last, is right next door to the church.

Elegant **Fournier Street** runs from here towards **Brick Lane**, its beautifully preserved early Georgian houses once inhabited by Huguenot silk barons. On parallel Princelet Street, No.19 (7247 5352) is Grade II-listed and contains a hidden synagogue – testament both to the importance of the longstanding Jewish community here and to the persecution they frequently suffered. Funding permitting, the house should open to the public by 2005. On the other side of Commercial Street, you'll find Folgate Street and **Dennis Severs' House**.

Brick Lane is now a well-established point on the tourist map, as well as nurturing a growing band of trendy clothes and furniture designers. From the 1950s to the '70s it was the focal point of a new immigrant community of Indians and Bangladeshis. Now Brick Lane is all about cheap curries, trendy bars and, on Sundays, another market. The children will want to head straight for **Spitalfields City Farm**, just to the east; if you don't want to tramp the whole Spitalfields experience (and many of the East End's joys are best appreciated on foot) the city farm is conveniently close to Shoreditch station (open peak hours and Sunday morning only).

Dennis Severs' House

18 Folgate Street, E1 (7247 4013/www.dennissevers house.co.uk). Liverpool Street tube/rail. **Open** 2-5pm 1st & 3rd Sun of mth; noon-2pm Mon (following 1st & 3rd Sun of mth); Mon eves (times vary). **Admission** £8 Sun; £5 noon-2pm Mon; £12 Mon eves. No under-12s. **No credit cards. Map** p321 5R.
There is surely no more atmospheric public attraction in London than 18 Folgate Street. Bought in the late 1970s by Dennis Severs (a Californian émigré who died in 1999), the building is what its founder called a 'still-life drama'. Each of the ten rooms stages a period in the life of the house, making it appear that any of the various occupants from 1724 to 1914 might pop back at any moment: the hearth crackles, the wine glasses stand half-drunk, the smell of cooking lingers. *Nearest picnic place: Broadgate Circus (Liverpool Street station).*

Royal London Hospital Archives & Museum

St Philip's Church, Newark Street, E1 (7377 7608/ www.brlcf.org.uk). Whitechapel tube. **Open** 10am-4.30pm Mon-Fri. Closed bank hols & adjacent days. **Admission** free.

Ways to lose the crowds at
Spitalfields Market. *See p106.*

Refurbished in 2002, this small museum has as its basic theme the hospital's history from 18th-century voluntary institution to pioneering 20th-century hospital (the 1930s X-ray machine looks like something created for a mad inventor in a B-movie), and the development of nursing and childcare, with displays on nurses like Florence Nightingale. There's a vivid display about former patient Joseph Merrick (the 'Elephant Man'), with a replica of the hat he wore to conceal his swollen head, and a video screen on which you can watch a documentary about Merrick or quaint period films about the hospital. Crime writer Patricia Cornwell has sponsored a small case on forensics, which has fascinating material on Jack the Ripper, including his foul letters to the police. It's all a bit wordy for the small children, though.
Buggy access. Café (in hospital). Nappy-changing facilities (in hospital). Shop.

Spitalfields City Farm

Weaver Street, off Pedley Street, E1 (7247 8762/ www.spitalfieldscityfarm.org). Whitechapel tube. **Open** 10.30am-5pm Tue-Sun. Closed 24 Dec-2 Jan. **Admission** free; donations appreciated.
Now able to claim more than 18,000 visitors a year, this community farm was established in 1978 after local people lost their allotments to property developers. It has chickens and geese pecking and honking about, donkeys, pigs, sheep, goats, and guinea pigs and rabbits in cuddly small animal section. Poultry, gardeners and all the livestock produce free-range eggs, vegetables in season, and manure. Staff are keen to deliver an agricultural education to city-bred young'uns (keen eight- to 13-year-olds can join the Young Farmers Club), and children can enjoy gardening and arts and crafts activities if they're booked on to school holiday playschemes. Local schools can book into the farm's egg incubation service, thus giving children to opportunity to watch hatchlings make their way into the world. There are also donkey rides, depending on staff availability (ring to check in advance).
Buggy access. Shop.

Whitechapel Art Gallery

80-82 Whitechapel High Street, E1 (7522 7888/ www.whitechapel.org). Aldgate East tube/15, 25, 253 bus. **Open** 11am-6pm Tue, Wed, Fri-Sun; 11am-9pm Wed. Closed 24-26 Dec, 1 Jan. *Tours* 2.30pm every other Sun (free). **Admission** free (one paying show a year). Map p321 S6.
The Whitechapel boasts a strong education and community programme: when the gallery was founded in 1901, Reverend Canon Barnett insisted that every exhibition have its own educational programme for children. Local schools have benefited since the 1980s from a progressive programme of artist residencies, often resulting in collaborative exhibitions. There are also exhibition-specific workshops. Particularly keen to exploit the possibilities of new media, one of the Whitechapel's projects this year is using palm pilots in co-developing internet resources with local children. Watch out for similarly stimulating events in Big Arts Week (1st week in July). The large, ground-floor gallery is augmented by an additional sky-lit upper space and a swish refurbished café (redesigned by Turner Prize nominee Liam Gillick, it's perhaps a tad grown-up for little ones).
Buggy access. Café. Lift. Nappy-changing facilities. Nearest picnic place: Altab Ali park. Shop.

Shoreditch & Hoxton

Shoreditch was once a village at the meeting point of two Roman roads. Those roads are now Kingsland Road and Old Street, and there's precious little about them that's Roman. In 1598 James Burbage founded London's first theatre here, on the corner of Great Eastern Street and New Inn Yard; its timbers were subsequently taken to build the old Globe theatre down in Southwark. **Hoxton**, the area of Shoreditch

thing, without having to worry about precious objects slipping from grubby little fingers – but there are period chairs in several anterooms that can be rigorously tested for comfort. The second half of the museum has rooms from the '30s, '60s and '90s, and temporary arts and crafts exhibitions downstairs. An imaginative and extremely popular programme of school holiday and weekend events for children reflect the changing exhibitions. Monthly Family Sundays are particularly popular, with cooking, decorative arts, model-making and other creative activities on offer. Jazz bands sometimes play on the lawn (there's a penny-whistle band booked for August 2003). The airy restaurant is a pleasure year-round, offering fine views over the gorgeous gardens, but there are plenty of other places for a sit down if you don't want to pay for a cup of tea. For Christmas every room is lovingly and evocatively decorated in period festive style, so you can trace the development of the modern Christmas and find out how indebted we are to the Victorians for so many of our yuletide traditions.

Buggy access. Lift. Nappy-changing facilities. Nearest picnic place: museum grounds. Restaurant. Shop.

Bethnal Green & Hackney

In Victorian times **Bethnal Green** held the unenviable title of 'poorest district in London'. Wholesale slum clearances notwithstanding, underfunding and badly designed council estates mean the area still has its share of social problems. It also has one of London's family must-sees: the **Museum of Childhood at Bethnal Green**. The museum's right next door to **York Hall**, famous as a boxing venue but more interesting to the children as a swimming pool with inflatable fun sessions (*see p262*). If you can get everyone up and out in time, **Columbia Road Flower Market** (held between Gosset Street and the Royal Oak Pub, 8am-1pm, on Sundays) is lovely to visit. The stalls blossom with shrubs, bulbs, bedding, pots and cut flowers.

Around here and into **Hackney** you're in the land that tubes forgot: the combination of buses and overland trains will either seem like a conspiracy to run you out of variants of I Spy to play while waiting, or convince you that you never need the underground again as long as you're in London (the feeling won't last). Mayor Ken plans to improve transport links by extending the East London line, but don't hold your breath.

Along Hackney Road, you'll find **Hackney City Farm** and **Haggerston Park** (Audrey Street, off Goldsmith Row, E2, 7739 6288), with pretty gardens, a softball pitch, a BMX track and astroturf for ball games. Try to time your visit to catch the opening times of **Clowns International Gallery**, further to the north-west. There's a little playground and benches on the common opposite the gallery.

If you have a little time and energy, take the towpath along the northern bank of Regent's Canal. About 15 minutes' walk west of Cambridge Heath rail station is **Broadway Market**, a very chi-chi

north of Old Street and west of Kingsland Road, has a more macabre claim to theatrical fame: playwright Ben Jonson fought and killed the actor Gabriel Spencer in Hoxton Fields (now **Hoxton Square**), escaping the gallows on a technicality and having his thumb branded instead. Brands round here nowadays are more likely to be the latest leisure footwear – Hoxton overflows with trendy bars.

By the 17th century the area was well known as a centre of popular entertainment, and in the 19th century it was the home to some of the most famous music halls in London, including the Britannia Theatre and Macdonald's. It was here that the famous Queen of the Music Halls, Marie Lloyd, was born in 1870 (*see p114*). The area was also infamous for slum housing, much of which was destroyed in the Blitz and subsequently replaced by 20th-century blocks of flats. But today the biggest family attractions here are the **Geffrye Museum**, an oasis of loveliness, and **Hoxton Hall** (*see p223*).

Geffrye Museum

136 Kingsland Road, E2 (7739 9893/www.geffrye-museum.org.uk). Liverpool Street tube/rail then 149, 242 bus/Old Street tube/rail then 243 bus. **Open** 10am-5pm Tue-Sat; noon-5pm Sun, bank hol Mon. Closed Good Fri, 24-26 Dec, 1 Jan. **Admission** free; donations appreciated. Under 8s must be accompanied by an adult.

It's simply a joy to walk through this beautiful place. Built in 1715 as an almshouse, the Geffrye was converted into a furniture and interior design museum in 1914, with rooms representing different periods in history from the Elizabethan era to the present day. You can't actually enter the display rooms – all are open on the third side so you can see every-

Around Town

little strip of shops and restaurants, that leads up to **London Fields** (Westside, E8). As well as sports and play facilities, the park has an intriguing sculpture of a seated couple surrounded by pretty, inset mosaic pictures – a real favourite with children (and winos). You can also play pétanque at the **Pub on the Park** (19 Martello Street, E8, 7275 9586).

In Hackney proper (actually centred on Mare Street rather than Hackney Road), the beautiful old Hackney Empire (291 Mare Street, E8, 8510 4500/www.hackneyempire.co.uk) reopens in August 2003 after extensive refurbishment, but long delays are not unfamiliar in Hackney. The theatre's seen the best in family entertainment over many years, including the essential Christmas pantos. At present, children's shows take place every couple of months in the nearby Bullion Room. The handsome new look of the Empire is just one part of Hackney's plan to create a 'cultural quarter' around the Town Hall Square, most of which came to fruition in 2002. Central to this scheme was **Hackney Museum**, housed with the Central Library in a shiny new Technology Learning Centre, and a hot local music venue, the **Ocean** (No.270; *see p228*).

There are a surprising number of places to run wild in, too – surprising, that is, until you remember that as late as the 19th century Hackney was still almost entirely rural. Hackney Downs (Downs Park Road, E8) has tennis courts, floodlit basketball, a bowling green and a playground. **Hackney Marsh**, more than 300 acres of grassland north of **Victoria Park**, is the muddy home of English Sunday League football (nearly 100 pitches) and the eastern end is a favourite for kite-flying; there are summer festivals, as well as remote-control aircraft displays, American and Gaelic football, rugby and cricket. **Springfield Park** in Clapton looks over the River Lea to Walthamstow Marshes and Springfield Marina. All these parks can be contacted on 7923 3660.

Clowns International Gallery

All Saints Centre, Haggerston Road, E8 (www.clowns-international.co.uk). Dalston Kingsland or London Fields rail, then 38, 236 or 243 bus. **Open** noon-5pm 1st Fri in mth. **Admission** free.
The world's oldest established organisation for clowns reopened their small gallery at new premises after the annual Joseph Grimaldi Memorial Service on 2 February 2003. The gallery, next to All Saints' church, and festooned with red, yellow and blue bunting, is run by volunteers (all clowns themselves) and traces the history of clowning from 16th-century *commedia dell'arte* to the present-day, and displays real props and costumes. Children like the suspended clown car and automata (one blowing bubbles, another on a trapeze). There's also the world's largest collection of painted pot eggs, carefully decorated with the faces of clowns past and present. The Clown Social is held on the first Tuesday of each month; check the website or phone Matti Faint (7608 0312, 10am-5pm only) for special events.
Free parking. Nearest picnic place: Stonebridge Common (opposite).

Hackney City Farm

1A Goldsmiths Row, E2 (7729 6381/www.hackneycityfarm.co.uk). Bus 26, 46, 55. **Open** 10am-4.30pm Tue-Sun. Closed 25-26 Dec, 1 Jan. **Admission** free; donations appreciated.
For nearly two decades this former brewery has been a cobbled farmyard, with pigs, geese, chickens, sheep and cattle. Staff run regular weekly pottery classes in the crafts workshops, and teach circus skills and music and movement. There are popular playschemes in the summer holidays too. Revive yourself in the organic café, and stock up on fresh honey and eggs from the shop; this idyllic retreat is also conveniently close to Haggerston Park.
Buggy access. Café. Nappy-changing facilities. Nearest picnic place: Haggerston Park. Shop.

Hackney Museum

Technology & Learning Centre, 1 Reading Lane, off Mare Street, E8 (8356 3500/www.hackney.gov.uk/hackney museum). Hackney Central rail. **Open** 9.30am-5.30pm Mon, Wed, Fri; 9.30am-8pm Thur; 10am-5pm Sat. Closed bank hols. **Admission** free.
Hackney Museum's resources and hands-on activities were financed to the tune of £400,000 by the Heritage Lottery Fund, with the museum designed to help visitors explore 1,000 years of cultural interchange that have made Hackney what it is today. There's a full-size model Anglo Saxon boat to clamber on board (the original is sunk into the floor beside it), a coin-operated zoetrope, and you can time yourself making matchboxes to see whether you would have survived working in a Victorian factory (in the 1860s you earned tuppence for 144 boxes). Touch screens let you trace family history or take a virtual tour of a Victorian house. There are also free Explorer Pads, full of activities, available at the entrance. Ring for details of exhibitions and drop-in events.
Buggy access. Café (in Ocean opposite). Nappy-changing facilities. Nearest picnic place: benches in square or London Fields. Shop.

Museum of Childhood at Bethnal Green

Cambridge Heath Road, E2 (8983 5200/recorded info 8980 2415/www.museumofchildhood.org.uk). Bethnal Green tube/rail. **Open** 10am-5.50pm Mon-Thur, Sat, Sun. Closed 24-26 Dec, 1 Jan. **Admission** free. Under-8s must be accompanied by an adult.
Established in 1872 as an East London branch of the V&A and eventually becoming a Museum of Childhood in 1974, this enchanting archive holds the largest collection of toys

---

DON'T MISS
The Museum of Childhood

The Marble Floor
A warm welcome and lots for £1 in the fab shop.

The Mezzanine
The Hornby train set; the oldest doll (an Egyptian from 1300BC); Molly's Super Dodgems; This is What Little Boys Are Made Of (yucky coin-op fun).

Childhood Galleries
The 1673 Nuremburg Dolls' House; clothes to try on in What We Wear; the moving teddy diorama in Teddy Bear Story (until Dec 2003).

Museum of Childhood at Bethnal Green.

and childhood paraphernalia in the UK, and one of the largest in the world. With more than 6,000 toys and games, stretching back over five centuries, the permanent displays include dolls, trains, puppets, board games… almost any toy you can remember or a youngster has ever demanded for Christmas.

The redevelopment of the Museum of Childhood's upper floor has resulted in 'Good Times', with a playable jukebox and wobbly mirror. 'The World in the East End' offers exhibits and vox pops with an appropriately multicultural slant, while the play ambulance might be the most popular part of 'Who will I be', although the hats are fun to try on as well. A temporary exhibition called Teddy Bear Story – 100 Years of the Teddy Bear runs on the upper floor until the end of 2003. Famous teds making occasional guest appearances include Rupert, Paddington and Aloysius from *Brideshead Revisited*. The range of children's activities is impressive too, and even the shop is nicely thought out, with an imaginative range of toys, stationery and gadgets for around £1 so that the kids can get some cool stuff without building up crushing pocket-money debts. Throughout, the museum does a good job of balancing the wishes of grown-ups interested in social history and design against the (usually more peremptory) demands of the younger visitor. The licensed museum café takes the weight off adult feet, only for the sticky cakes to put it back on, and if you've been organised enough to bring your own picnic, you can eat it on the many tables and benches out front. If there's too much concrete around there, the little park, called Museum Gardens (but not actually part of the museum) next door is quite lovely.
Buggy access. Café. Lift. Nappy-changing facilities. Nearest picnic place: Museum Gardens. Shop.

Sutton House
2 & 4 Homerton High Street, E9 (8986 2264/ www.nationaltrust.org.uk). Bethnal Green tube then 253, 106, D6 bus/Hackney Central rail. **Open** 1-5pm Fri, Sat; 11.30am-5pm Sun, bank hol Mon. *Gallery* 11.30am-5pm Wed-Sun. Closed *Gallery* 21 Dec-6 Jan. *Historic Rooms* 21 Dec-mid-Feb. **Admission** (NT) £2.20; 50p 5-16s; £4.90 family (2+2); free under-5s. *Tours* free after entry, phone for details. **Credit** MC, V.

This is the oldest house in east London, built around 1535 for Henry VIII's secretary of state Sir Ralph Sadleir. In the late 1980s, this essentially Tudor house was used as a community centre, until a grand National Trust restoration project saved the building's many original charms, such as the beautifully decorated oak-panel rooms. As well as Jacobean paintings and Georgian and Victorian interiors, there's some squatters' graffiti – and don't forget to look in on the 16th-century garderobe. There's the multimedia exhibition From Bryk Place to Sutton House (1535-1995) upstairs, changing artwork in the gallery, and a good roster of family Discovery Days (11.30am-5pm last Sunday of the month), including historic cookery workshops, Tudor and Victorian games, dressing-up and ghost stories. The Halloween Ghost Hunting on 27 October involves costumed characters, while Christmas Past and Presents on 15 December can't fail to get the nippers in a festive mood. Light meals, home-made cakes and drinks are served in the cosy Brick Place Café, with pretty trellises in the courtyard outside.
Café. Nappy-changing facilities. Nearest picnic place: St John's churchyard. Shop.

Mile End to West Ham

Mile End was mostly common land until the 16th century, but the Industrial Revolution saw the end of that, with workers' housing springing up everywhere. The area is still a confusing sprawl of busy roads and urban housing developments, but there are two fine parks: **Victoria Park** is the grand older statesman, **Mile End Park** (*see p113*) the shiny new upstart. The **Ragged School Museum** helps make a visit to Mile End Park even more worthwhile, and – if you cross the canal and head west past the Victorian gasometers – you'll find **Stepping Stones Farm** next door to the Norman parish church of St Dunstan's, with a surprisingly tranquil cemetery. There's a playground on Stepney Green on the other side.

Further east, industry has a much nobler heritage, dating back to the 11th century. Grain was transported by boat from Hertfordshire and unloaded at mills along the river here. **Three Mills** now attracts many visitors – and even the odd celeb, come to slave away at the day job in Three Mills Studio. Stratford used to be pretty grim, but the Jubilee Line extension has encouraged a transformation. The centre is focused around the Broadway and a soulless shopping centre, but the star turn is **Theatre Royal Stratford East** (Gerry Raffles Square, E15, 8534 0310). A delightful old theatre, it reopened in December 2001, just in time for its famously jolly family panto. The refurbishment added a café-bar and improved disabled access to the Grade II-listed auditorium. The old theatre has a new neighbour too: the state-of-the-art **Stratford Circus Arts Centre** (8279 1000; *see p208*), which runs a full programme of activities, including children's performance workshops. It also has a café, bar and crèche.

There are two good reasons to keep on heading east from Stratford. The first is the excellent **West Ham Park** and the second is **West Ham United** Football Club, whose new museum may keep fans distracted from last season's footballing woes.

Three Mills Island

Lea Rivers Trust, Three Mill Lane, E3 (8981 0040 ext 224/Lee Rivers Tidal Mill Trust 8980 4626/Pride of Lee ext 223/www.leariverstrust.co.uk). Bromley-by-Bow tube. **Open** *House Mill May-Oct* 2-4pm Sun. *Funday Sundays Apr-Dec* 11am-4pm 1st Sun of mth. **Admission** *Mill tour* £2; free under-16s. **No credit cards.**

The House Mill, built in 1776 in the Dutch style and the oldest and largest tidal mill left standing in Britain, was used to grind the grain for gin distilling. The building was taken over in 1989 as part of a big restoration project by the River Lea Tidal Mill Trust. The visitors' centre provides a history of the area and map-leaflets detailing walks in the area: Riverside Green and Three Mills Green are pleasant for picnicking and strolling (the latter gives a good view of Bazalgette's wonderfully restored pumping station). You can also wander along the network of the Bow Back rivers and enjoy the wildlife that thrives in this pocket of peace and quiet. A heron stalks behind the House Mill, and narrowboats sometimes moor along the same stretch of river. When the Mill House is closed, there are toilets in the 24-hour Tesco superstore nearby. Those with pushchairs might find the cobbles hard going – the towpaths are a much easier ride.

The first Sunday of the month is Funday Sunday, which includes a popular craft market. Children can take part in absorbing workshops (paper-making, bread-making and willow-weaving are popular) and there's a popular Christmas Fayre in the first week of December. All the activities are free and run on a first-come first-served basis. One-hour boat trips on the Pride of Lee narrowboat also run from here.

Nearest picnic place: Riverside Green/Three Mills Green.

Ragged School Museum

46-50 Copperfield Road, E3 (8980 6405/ www.raggedschoolmuseum.org.uk). Mile End tube. **Open** 10am-5pm Wed, Thur; 2-5pm 1st Sun of mth. Closed 24 Dec-1 Jan. **Tours** by arrangement; phone for details. **Admission** free.

Ragged schools were charity schools that provided a basic education for orphaned, poor or down-and-out children. Established by Dr Barnardo in 1877, these converted warehouses were until their closure in 1908 London's largest ragged school. One fascinatingly sparse Victorian classroom has been recreated and school groups come from all over London to don Victorian togs and sit in it. Their own teachers give the kids old-fashioned names such as Walter and Agatha and hand them over to a hatchet-faced 'schoolmistress' (a museum actress) for some serious learning. Downstairs is Tower Hamlets: A Journey through Time (local history) and there's also a replica front room from 1900. Free family events take place in the school holidays: in summer 2003 there'll be doing the laundry Victorian-style, a Punch and Judy show, musical instrument-making and a school lesson. Temporary exhibitions include a look at the experiences of Bangladeshi elders in Tower Hamlets. The Towpath Café is accessible from the canal.

Buggy access (ground floor only). Café. Nappy-changing facilities. Nearest picnic place: Mile End Park. Shop.

Stepping Stones Farm

Stepney Way (junction with Stepney High Street), E1 (7790 8204). Stepney Green tube. **Open** *Apr-mid Oct* 9.30am-6pm Tue-Sun; bank hol Mon. *Mid Oct-Mar* 9.30am-dusk Tue-Sun; all public hols. **Admission** free; donations appreciated.

This 4.5-acre community farm has been run by hard-working volunteers since 1979. Goats, pigs, a donkey, sheep and poultry – ducks, chickens and a surprisingly ugly turkey when we last visited – all slouch around expecting to be admired. Young ones can let rip in the play area, where a sandpit and toy tractors await their attention, keen gardeners can buy manure or stock up on jams and chutneys from the shop, while conscientious greens can bring kitchen waste to the community composting bins. Ring for details of school holiday and weekend fun for children; there's a strong educational programme too.

Buggy access. Café. Nappy-changing facilities. Shop.

Victoria Park

Old Ford Road, E3 (8533 2057). Mile End tube/ Cambridge Heath or Hackney Wick rail/8, 26, 30, 55, 253, 277, S2 bus. **Open** 6am-dusk daily. Closed 25 Dec.

The area this delightful old park sits on was the scene of riots in the 19th century. Victoria Park was opened in 1845 after demands for more public space were met by an extraordinary £100,000 in donations. With its fine, wide carriageways and smart lamp posts and wrought-iron gates, the Victoria was conceived as the Regent's Park of the East End (at 240 acres it is the largest area of formal parkland this side of town). The poverty-stricken locals may have been short of carriages to drive through the grand tree-lined drives, but they made good use of the park's two lakes instead... as baths. The Western Lake survived this ordeal and is now happily fished (you need a licence – free – to join in), and the country's oldest Model Boat Club convenes around the lake near Crown Gate East every second Sunday. There are fallow deer on the

PARKLIFE Mile End Park

Mile End Park isn't the newest of east London's many parks: that accolade now goes to the modern, manicured and marvellous **Thames Barrier Park** (see p117). **Victoria Park** (see p112) is grander, **West Ham Park** has the edge for organised activities and **Epping Forest** (see p120) will always be the first choice for nature lovers, but Mile End Park is for many the quintessential modern urban family park and – since the completion of Phase III of its development earlier this year – its credentials as a destination for children are firmly established.

Less than a decade ago Mile End Park was little more than a good idea (in germination since just after World War II) and some fragmented urban land. Now, thanks in no small part to the Green Bridge – a huge yellow-bottomed structure, 25 metres wide, that spans the dual carriageway of Mile End Road – it is a 90-acre ecological corridor that covers almost the whole distance between the Thames and Victoria Park (and thence through **Hackney Marsh**, see p110, via **Walthamstow Marshes**, and out to the northernmost reaches

of the city). Turn right out of Mile End tube station and you can see the bridge, with trees poking out of the top. Cross the unpleasant Burdett Road to enter the beautiful Terraced Gardens, with a fountain and running water. From there paths head south to **Mile End Stadium** and the **Ragged School Museum** (see p112), the go-kart track and (the other side of St Paul's Way) the brand new playground. North of the bridge lie tranquil ponds at the centre of the Arts Park and Ecological Park. Beside it all, the calming presence of Regent's Canal supports birdlife and local fishermen in apparently equal numbers.

The park has consistently stuck to educational and community development aims, bringing sculptures into the park and holding temporary exhibitions and volunteer activities. Such commitments were built into the design: the Art and Ecology Pavilions are earth-clad to reduce fuel consumption through heating; the pumps that circulate water between the park's three lakes are powered by a nine-metre wind turbine that stands in the Ecology Park. Projects for the future may include solar-powering the go-karts and installing two additional wind turbines to produce energy for the site and possibly the surrounding area.

But the park isn't just about good ideas. It's also diligent in meeting the other need for which it was set up: fun. The £2 million playground and drop-in children's centre, completed last year, has a rope slide, scrambling wall and complicated climbing frame, as well as the normal swings and see-saw, while the go-kart track provides thrills and spills for the older children. Those who get bored of placidly strolling among 850 species of plants or watching the coots putter and swans squawk on the lakes or canal, can get an adrenaline fix at the **Mile End Climbing Wall** (see p251) or go for a long, safe bike ride along the park's new cycle route.

Mile End Park

Locksley Street, E3 (8525 9416/ www.mileendpark.co.uk). Mile End tube. **Open** *24hrs daily.*

cast side of the park for nature-lovers, and tennis courts, a bowling green and football, hockey and cricket pitches for the athletically minded (though the hard-surface athletics track is still awaiting refurbishment after a fire some years ago). After a morning in the playground, stop off for refreshments at the Lakeside Pavilion Café and watch the geese and ducks play under the fountain.
Café. Nappy-changing facilities.

West Ham Park

Upton Lane, E7 (8472 3584). Stratford tube/rail/104, 238, 325 bus. **Open** *7.30am-30mins before dusk daily.*
This park is run by the Corporation of London, which means quality facilities and well-looked-after play equipment. There are nine tennis courts (in 2001 three of an original 12 courts

were replaced by an outdoor gym), two cricket squares, two football pitches, a running track and a rounders area. Children's sport is taken so seriously at West Ham Park that several schools have sports days here; there's a summer cricket clinic for under-16s and tennis coaching courses for all ages. The children's playground has a full-time attendant to look after the swings, roundabouts and climbing frames. On summer weekday afternoons it has been known for more than 300 children to turn up to see the clowns, ventriloquists and magicians who put on shows around the bandstand. There's also a paddling pool, Sunday concerts and, at times, a bouncy castle. The rose garden – recent improvements should now be complete – is a beautiful oasis, and out of season the staff run botanical tours to suit both all age groups.
Nappy-changing facilities.

West Ham United Football Club

*Boleyn Ground, Green Street, E13 (8548 2748/
www.whufc.com). Upton Park tube.* **Open** *Museum* 10am-
6pm Mon-Fri, 9am-6pm Sat. *Shop* 10am-5pm Mon-Sat.
Closed 25 Dec. **Admission** *Tours* phone for details.
Museum £6; £4 concessions, 5-16s; free under-5s; £15
family (2+2). **Credit** MC, V.
By the time you read this, the 'Happy Hammers' may
unhappily no longer be in the Premiership – a bitter blow
given the recent £35-million redevelopment of their home
ground. In summer 2002 their brand new museum, seven
years and £4 million in the making, was opened to the public. It tells the story of the club from its origins in 1895 as the
Thames Iron Works FC through to the present. Non-claret-
and-blue footie fans will make a bee-line for displays on
Bobby Moore, Geoff Hurst and Martin Peters, the West Ham
trio who helped England win the 1966 World Cup. Book in
advance if you're visiting the museum on a match day.
Bars. Café. Nappy-changing facilities. Shop.

Docklands

Docklands has mapped the major economic changes
in Britain over the last few hundred years, from its
heyday in the 18th and 19th centuries when boats
from all over the world unloaded here, through the
steady closure of the working docks, and along the
troubled road of business-led redevelopment that
gave the area its Disneyfied name. The first attempt
to regenerate derelict land by building upmarket
offices and new homes foundered with the recession
in the early 1990s, but the last decade has seen more
and more businesses move in, with the area's
fascinating history and dramatic architecture
attracting growing numbers of visitors.

Docklands is one of the most fascinating areas of
London to visit, with its stark contrasts of new and
old architecture, its rich pockets of history ad
picturesque wharves. Though the **Isle of Dogs** is
the main focus, various extensions and service
improvements to the excellent **Docklands Light
Railway** (7363 9700) have brought the whole area
into the reach of fun-seeking families – from Bank in
the City to Beckton to the east, from Lewisham on
the south bank of the Thames to Stratford in the
north. The real beauty of the DLR is that it runs on
raised tracks, making a DLR journey a sightseeing
pleasure; the fact that the trains are driverless adds
a touch of adventure. Pick quiet times of day to
travel and the kids can sit right in the front windows
of the train to 'drive' it round all by themselves. Buy
a day Travelcard and hop on and off at will, using
the Jubilee and District Line tube connections to
open up all the nooks and crannies of East London.

The DLR also joined forces with **City Cruises**
sightseeing boats to offer the Rail & River Rover
ticket, which throws in boat travel with all the fun
of the DLR. The boats offer warm seats inside or a
breezier berth upstairs, and a chirpy commentator to
name bridges and riverside buildings. Disembark at
Tower Pier and stroll the ten minutes past Tower
Bridge (*see p54*) and the Tower of London (*see p55*)
to the DLR station at Tower Gateway. Otherwise,
stay on the boat until Greenwich (*see p123*), then
take a DLR train back under the river for sightseeing
on the **Isle of Dogs**. There's a separate fast commuter
service east and west from **Canary Wharf Pier**.

LONDON LEGEND Marie Lloyd

From the 1890s until sound films appeared in the
1920s, the biggest popular entertainment was the
music halls – and their heartland was East London.
The biggest of all the music hall stars – the 'Queen
of the Halls' – was Marie Lloyd. She was born
Matilda Alice Victoria Wood in Hoxton in 1870,
the eldest of nine (some say 11) children. At the
tender age of 15 she auditioned at the Eagle
tavern where her dad worked, and was soon doing
several shows a night under the stage name Marie
Lloyd. Marrying a naughty wink to her relatively
innocuous lyrics, 'Our Marie' was soon a sensation
with hits like 'A Little of What you Fancy does you
Good'. Her suggestive stage gestures got her
hauled before the licensing committee, although
she gave them short shrift. Lloyd was also
forthright with theatre managers, helping her less
successful colleagues oppose contracts that called
for additional performances for no extra pay
through a performers' strike in 1906. When she
was subsequently 'overlooked' for the first Royal
Command Performance in 1912 (despite nearly

150 other music hall stars being invited to appear
in the grand finale), the managers found her
similarly unabashed. She simply sold out her own
show at the London Pavilion on the same night:
every poster bragged 'By order of the British
public'. Lloyd's last act was to be as legendary
as the career that preceded it. In her final
performance, she launched into one of her best
known hits. The audience roared their appreciation
as she staggered and fell as if drunk – but on this
occasion she wasn't acting. A few days later, on
7 October 1922, she died. Some 50,000 people
lined the streets for her funeral procession.

The great Hoxton Halls that made the name of
Marie Lloyd and others are long since demolished.
Nowadays the nearest thing to music hall is
Christmas panto at the **Hackney Empire** (*see p110*)
or the **Theatre Royal Stratford East** (*see p208*).
And when the male actor playing the dame leans
over the footlights to saucily banter about some
local political scandal... the hisses and boos are as
vehement as they would have been a century ago.

Goose on the loose at **Victoria Park**.
See p113.

Wapping, Limehouse & the Isle of Dogs

The westernmost point to fall under the Docklands heading is Wapping. Until well into the 19th century, convicted pirates were brought at low tide to Execution Dock (at Wapping New Stairs), hanged and left there in chains until three tides had washed over them; a rather new-looking noose dangles on the river side of the 16th-century **Prospect of Whitby** pub (57 Wapping Wall, E1). There's also a pirate ship (that you can't board, sadly) by the usually deserted Tobacco Docks shopping mall to the west. Just to the north is Cable Street, where locals defeated a police-protected march by Sir Oswald Mosley's anti-Semitic Blackshirt fascists in the 1936 Battle of Cable Street.

Between Wapping and the Isle of Dogs is **Limehouse**, so called because medieval lime kilns once stood here. A century ago this was a bustling commercial port; now it's a marina with yachts and narrow boats, surrounded by luxury flats. The enormous white church north-east of the basin, St **Anne's Limehouse**, was designed by Hawksmoor between 1712 and 1724. It has the second-highest (after Big Ben's) clock tower in Britain.

The most visitor-friendly of all Docklands areas, however, is the **Isle of Dogs**. It's only an island because the stretch of water that makes up West India Docks cuts the peninsula off from the mainland, and the origin of the name is routinely disputed: some think it's named after the royal hunting kennels that were once here, others argue 'dog' is a corruption of the word 'dykes' (built here by Flemish engineers in the 19th century). You can explore Docklands' 2,000-year history at the **Museum in Docklands**, finally due to open as

we go to press. Or you can admire its present-day splendour at the astonishing glass and steel Canary Wharf station, designed by Lord Foster, beneath Cesar Pelli's 800ft-high **One Canada Square**, the famous 'Canary Wharf Tower'. The kids might enjoy finding all the sculptures on Canary Wharf's public sculpture trail (contact 7418 2000 for a map), they include Konstantin Grcic's amusing *Six Public Clocks* in Nash Court and Pierre Vivant's *Traffic Light Tree* in the middle of the Herons Quay roundabout. There are good chain-shopping options too (Gap Kids, HMV, Maxwell & Kennedy for sweeties) with the branches smaller than their West End daddies, but blissfully low on crowds.

You can head south from here through views of the docks and grandiose commercial architecture that, on a sunny day, will even impress the children. Keep going to the southern end of the Isle of Dogs, getting out at Mudchute. The park here is a rather flat piece of grass (there are benches for picnics), but **Mudchute City Farm** is great. Island Gardens itself is, irritatingly, the other side of a main road from its namesake station, but has superb views of Greenwich over the Thames, a little caff and the spooky Victorian foot tunnel under the river. This last is free and has attendant-operated lifts (7am-7pm Mon-Sat, 10am-5.30pm Sun) large enough for a platoon of buggies – but it's a fair walk to the **Cutty Sark** (*see p123*) on the other side. The echoes keep children happily shouting and whistling.

Mudchute City Farm
Pier Street, Isle of Dogs, E14 (7515 5901). Crossharbour or Island Gardens DLR. **Open** 9am-4pm daily. Closed 25 Dec-1 Jan. **Admission** free; donations appreciated.
Ducks, chickens, goats, pigs and llamas, plus a small flock of sheep and some cattle all live here, with the Canary Wharf Tower as backdrop. Kids can learn to ride on the horses and ponies of the British Horse Society-approved riding school

(7515 0749; closed Mon). There's also a club for pony-mad children whose parents have vetoed the idea of a paddock in the back garden. Local kids can also join the Young Farmers Club, and learn all about collecting eggs, milking cows, shearing sheep and all those essential urban skills. Everyone, wherever they live, can join in with the summer arts an crafts workshops and playshemes. There's also a small aviary and petting corner for a spot of bunny-hugging. The volunteer-run café usually opens mid-morning to early afternoon (there's hot soup in winter); the shop for souvenirs and riding accessories is open in school holidays.
Buggy access. Café. Shop.

Museum in Docklands
No.1 Warehouse, West India Quay, Hertsmere Road, E14 (7001 9800/www.museumindocklands.org.uk). Canary Wharf tube/West India Quay DLR. **Open** 10am-6pm Mon-Sat; noon-6pm Sun. **Admission** (annual ticket, allows for mulit visits) £5; £3 concessions; free under-16s. **Credit** MC, V.

Housed in Grade I-listed Georgian warehouses right in the shadow of Canary Wharf, this new £15-million museum was due to finally open its doors in May 2003, thanks to the assistance of the Museum of London (*see p52*), whose collection it shares. We can't wait. It took nearly a decade to develop, and aims to tell the story of London's river, port and people over the past 2,000 years, with multimedia presentations, an interactive children's gallery and artefacts ranging from cargo hooks to quayside cranes. You can experience the walk-through Victorian sailor's town, which including atmospheric dockside sights and sounds from a rowdy alehouse, chandler's shops and other attractions. Check the website for news on the developing educational and children's activity programme or email info@museumindocklands.org.uk to request inclusion on the mailing list.
Buggy access. Café. Disabled: lift, toilet. Nappy-changing facilities. Nearest picnic place: quayside benches, refectory. Restaurant. Shop.

East of Docklands

The DLR splits after Westferry: one branch goes south through the Isle of Dogs, the other eastwards via Poplar to Beckton. (Poplar is also where passengers change for the north-south Stratford to Lewisham line.) Heading towards Beckton (again keep an eye on the windows: there's a fabulous glimpse of the Dome across the river just before East India DLR station and – if the kids are too slow the first time – just afterwards) get off at Custom House for an exciting piece of modern landscaping: **Thames Barrier Park**. Getting there is a bit tricky. The best route is a 20-minute walk from Custom House DLR station, taking the pointy footbridge high over Royal Victoria Dock (there are lifts at each end). You still have to negotiate the frankly unpleasant North Woolwich Road (there are wide pavements at least), but the quiet beauty of the park is worth the effort.

Beckton is the DLR's last stop. The 'Beckton alp' – a dry ski slope built on a huge pile of rubbish – is now closed, and plans to reopen it as a 'snow dome' seem to have a melted away, which is a tragedy among east London's skiing fraternity. Lovers of flora and fauna are still well served, however, with **Docklands Equestrian Centre** (2 Claps Gate Lane, E6, 7511 3917), the **East Ham Nature Reserve** and **Newham City Farm**.

East along North Woolwich Road, by the roundabout, the popular kart track was closed and a new location being sought, when we visited, but

the management assure us it would open in summer 2003; phone 7476 5678 for details. Over Connaught bridge on the north side of Royal Albert Docks, is the **London Regatta Centre** (Dockside Road, E16, 7511 2211; open daily). Sit and watch rowers puff and pant or follow the planes landing at London City Airport from the Regatta Centre's restaurant and bar, or if you've got the energy take the footbridge over Royal Albert Way to **Beckton District Park**.

To the south, **North Woolwich Old Station Museum** is right next to the North Woolwich Silverlink station. Just across the way, the well-kept **Royal Victoria Gardens** have a summertime café. Cross to the south bank by foot tunnel or the Woolwich ferry for Firepower! (*see p127*).

Beckton District Park
Stansfeld Road, E6 (8552 0939). Royal Albert DLR/bus 262, 300, 376. **Open** dawn-dusk daily.
There's a good-sized lake at the northern end, a wildflower meadow and woodland walk for the ecologically minded, plus play areas for the kids (along with cricket and football facilities and a trim trail for the seriously active). The snack kiosk opens in summer, and potential fishermen need a licence from Barry Julian at Newham Angling Club (4464 4612).
Buggy access. Café. Nappy-changing facilities.

East Ham Nature Reserve
Norman Road, E6 (8470 4525). East Ham tube/Beckton DLR. **Open** *Nov-Feb* 10am-5pm Tue-Fri; 1-4pm Sat, Sun. *Mar-Oct* 10am-5pm Tue-Fri; 2-4pm Sat, Sun. Closed bank hols. **Admission** free.
Pick up a nature trail round the Norman churchyard or visit the museum, which combines natural and local history. Current displays include a Victorian schoolroom to terrify the kids, a Victorian kitchen to terrify the mums, and cases of stuffed animals, stag beetles and butterflies to fascinate everyone. As with all volunteer-run attractions, it's best to ring before you set out to make sure it's open.
Buggy access. Nappy-changing facilities.

Newham City Farm
Stansfeld Road, E6 (7476 1170). Royal Albert DLR/262, 300, 376, 473 bus. **Open** *Mid Oct-mid Feb* 10am-4pm Tue-Sun. *Mid Feb-mid Oct* 10am-5pm Tue-Sun, bank hols. Closed 25 Dec, 1 Jan. **Admission** free; donations appreciated.
The farm's visitor centre welcomes families and school groups. The Berkshire and Kune Kune pigs are popular residents, but there are also a number of ducks, ferrets, geese and goats, plus guinea pigs to cuddle. There's no café as yet, so bring your own refreshments to eat in the picnic area.
Buggy access.

North Woolwich Old Station Museum
Pier Road, E16 (7474 7244). North Woolwich rail/101, 473 bus. **Open** *School holidays* 1-5pm daily. **Admission** free. *Rides* £1.
The Old Station Museum contains carefully preserved old engines, ticket machines, timetables, signs and other relics from a bygone age of steam travel. A station guard (well, a plastic model thereof) stands at his desk looking suitably busy. The pair of trains on display are Coffee Pot (a Victorian commuter train from the 1890s) and Pickett (from the 1940s), while children can climb all over Dudley the Diesel. There's a small shop and, during the school holidays, Wednesday afternoon art and crafts sessions keep small people amused.
Buggy access. Nappy-changing facilities. Shop.

Thames Barrier Park
Barrier Point Road, off North Woolwich Road, E16 (7511 4111/www.thamesbarrierpark.org.uk). Custom House DLR/Canning Town tube/DLR, then 474 bus/Stratford tube, then 69 bus. **Open** dawn-dusk daily.
This excellent new park (finished in 2001) is right on the river by the space-age Thames Barrier (though the Barrier's visitor centre is on the south side; *see p127*). From the car park you'll see fountains (switched off in winter), then a concrete and granite channel the size of a motorway that dramatically bisects the park. Called the Green Dock, it is filled with hedges and honeysuckle, and leads directly to the riverfront and a 'pavilion of remembrance' commemorating those who lost their lives in the Blitz. The flat lawns are beautifully manicured, perfect for picnics and games (though a little exposed until the young trees grow a little more foliage). There's a playground too, and plenty of ducks, geese and swans on the gleaming mud flats. Poor transport links mean you'll have the park pretty much to yourselves (at least until the new DLR station, planned for 2004, materialises). The tea pavilion isn't yet open, but you can use the toilets there (don't worry if they look shut: the doors open automatically).
Buggy access. Café. Free parking. Nappy-changing facilities.

Walthamstow

The last stop north on the Victoria Line, Walthamstow's name comes from the Old English word 'Wilcumestowe': a place where guests are welcome. We've found this rather sweet description still holds true today. Walthamstow is noticeably friendly and its streets are an intriguing mix of

North Woolwich
Old Station Museum

Around Town

quaint and urban. Around **St Mary's Church** there's a village ambience, but the famous street market bustles and fusses in best East London style. Held on Walthamstow High Street, the market is claimed to be the longest daily street market in Europe (it has a grand total of 450 stalls).

To the west at the end of Coppermill Lane are **Walthamstow Marshes** (you might prefer to cycle or drive there: it's a good 15-minute walk from St James Street rail station). There are occasional open days at the old copper mill itself, plus various rambles and boat trips from Springfield Marina. These trips are free but booking is essential (Lea Rivers Trust Waterway Discovery Team, 8981 0040). The Marshes, ideal for a picnic or leisurely stroll by the River Lea, are where the doughty Sir Edwin Alliot Verdon Roe made the first all-British powered flight in July 1909 – a plaque on the railway arches commemorates the feat.

Lloyd Park, on Forest Road, is more than your average park, containing the **William Morris** and **Changing Rooms** Galleries. There's a children's play area at the far end, a new skate park, attractive gardens and an aviary of budgies and cockatiels.

Five minutes from Walthamstow Central station lies the old village of Walthamstow, centring on St Mary's Church. Extensive guides to the village and to other historic buildings in the area are available at the **Vestry House Museum**.

Across the North Circular Road is a 20th-century landmark, the art deco façade of **Walthamstow Stadium**, where an increasing number of family groups come to watch the dogs with va-va-voom.

Changing Room Gallery

Lloyd Park, Forest Road, E17 (8496 4563/www.lbwf. gov.uk/crg). Walthamstow Central tube/rail. **Open** *late Apr-Nov 11am-6pm Wed-Sun, but varies depending on exhibitions.* **Admission** *free.*
As well as contemporary arts and crafts exhibitions, there's studio space for local artists, seminars and children's workshops (phone for details). Lloyd Park's café is next door.
Buggy access. Nearest picnic place: Lloyd Park.

Vestry House Museum

Vestry Road, E17 (8509 1917/www.lbwf.gov.uk). Walthamstow Central tube/rail. **Open** *10am-1pm, 2-5.30pm Mon-Fri; 10am-1pm, 2-5pm Sat. Closed 25, 26 Dec, 1 Jan, bank hols.* **Tours** *groups only, by prior arrangement.* **Admission** *free.*
This museum includes one of the original police cells (from 1840-70 the building was a prison), a gallery of toys and games, and a car built by local engineer Frederick Bremer in 1892-4 (it was one of the first cars built in Britain – certainly the first in London). The Vestry House museum also holds archive material on Alfred Hitchcock, who was born in Leytonstone. A lottery-funded refurbishment in 2002 created a gallery for the Bremer car, re-landscaped the garden and opened the ground floor to the public. Contact the museum for details of children's activities.
Nappy-changing facilities. Nearest picnic place: museum garden. Shop.

Walthamstow Stadium

Chingford Road, E4 (8531 4255/www.wsgreyhound. co.uk). Walthamstow Central tube/rail then 97, 357, 215 bus/Highams Park rail. **Racing** *7.30pm Tue, Thur, Sat; 1pm or 2pm Mon (call to check); 11.30am Fri; plus occasional Sun.* **Admission** *£3-£6; free under-15s if accompanied by adult.* **No credit cards**.
Apart from football, greyhound racing is Britain's most-popular spectator sport. Surprised? Head to Walthamstow Stadium and you'll find out why. This track is a lively, friendly destination for all ages. Children's entertainment is usually provided during holidays and half-term, plus occasional Sunday Fundays for the whole family. The food at the Paddock and Stowaway Grills is reasonably priced, and every table overlooks the track. Make sure you take the kids to check out the dogs as they parade up and down before a race. And try to hide your disappointment when the dog they chose for its perky tail-wag beats your scientifically-selected cur to the clockwork rabbit by five lengths.

William Morris Gallery

Lloyd Park, Forest Road, E17 (8527 3782/www.lbwf. gov.uk/wmg). Walthamstow Central tube/rail. **Open** *10am-1pm, 2-5pm Tue-Sat; 1st Sun of mth. Closed 25, 26 Dec, 1 Jan, bank hols.* **Tours** *phone for details.* **Admission** *free.*
The childhood home of the famous designer and socialist, who was born in Walthamstow in 1834, the William Morris gallery is a must-see for anyone interested in design or taking GCSE Art. Major refurbishments are due for completion in summer 2003, with a new Arts and Crafts Movement room and a better range of exhibits from Morris's followers. Furniture, stained glass, metalwork and textiles are all on display, along with pictures from the Pre-Raphaelite Brotherhood. Smaller children enjoy cheeping at the inmates of the Lloyd Park aviary, just behind the gallery.
Nearest picnic place: Lloyd Park. Shop.

Wanstead

Even more than its neighbour Walthamstow, Wanstead has a village feel – as local homeowners are proud to point out. There's a Grade I-listed church from 1790, **St Mary's**, but the attraction for visitors, especially those with kids, is Wanstead's greenery: Epping Forest, Wanstead Flats and especially Wanstead Park.

Wanstead Park

Warren Road, E11 (8508 0028). Wanstead tube. **Open** *dawn-dusk daily.* **Admission** *free.*
Formed by enclosing part of the royal hunting forest in 1545, in the early 18th century this park became the estate of Sir Josiah Child, governor of the East India Company. He planned a large formal garden and built a vast mansion in the new Palladian style. Unfortunately, the estate passed on to Catherine Tylney Long, whose husband, the Duke of Wellington's nephew, spent her fortune, then absconded. The house was demolished in 1824 and the park let for grazing. Nowadays the Grade II-listed landscape is managed by the Corporation of London as part of Epping Forest. To the left as you enter the park is the 'Long View', a vista down to the ornamental water feature and canal. At the end is a ruined grotto, built in the early 1760s with a boathouse below and domed, shell-encrusted chamber above. The main path brings you into an open plain with the classical Temple to the left

LUNCH BREAK

Around Whitechapel & Spitalfields

Brick Lane Beigel Bake (159 Brick Lane, E1, 7729 0616), for snacks with a hole lot of great fillings; try cream cheese and smoked salmon.
Café Naz (46-8 Brick Lane, E1, 7247 0234), good, cheap curries and a lunchtime buffet.
Café Spice Namaste (16 Prescot Street, E1, 7488 9242), for quite posh curry with a modern twist.
New Tayyab (83 Fieldgate Street, E1, 7247 9543), as authentic as curry gets.
Sweet & Spicy (40 Brick Lane, E1, 7247 1081), simple curries and a friendly vibe.
The stalls in **Spitalfields market** have lots of hot food, from noodles to hearty pies and cakes.

Around Bethnal Green & Hackney

Faulkner's (424-6 Kingsland Road, E8, 7254 6152; *see p176*), for quality fish 'n' chips and a kids menu.
F Cooke (9 Broadway Market, E8, 7254 6458), a proper pie-and-mash shop.
The Gallery Café (21 Old Ford Road, E2, 8983 3624), a bright, inviting Buddhist vegetarian café.
Green Papaya (191 Mare Street, E8, 8985 5486), popular Vietnamese – book at weekends.
Jones Dairy Café (23 Ezra Street, E2, 7739 5372; *see p177*), a great weekend drop-in.
Laxeiro (93 Columbia Road, E2, 7729 1147; *see p177*), a friendly, fresh fishy, tapas bar.
Little Georgia (2 Broadway Market, E8, 7249 9070), for meze dishes at £1.50 each.
Shanghai (41 Kingsland High Street, E8, 7254 2878), for lunchtime dim sum and filling noodles.
Sông Quê (134 Kingsland Road, E2, 7613 3222; *see p180*), noodles, and lots of 'em.
Thai Garden (249 Globe Road, E2, 8981 5748), for MSG-free food and high chairs; book at weekends.
Wild Cherry (241-5 Globe Road, E2, 8980 6678), excellent, women-run vegetarian café behind the London Buddhist Centre.

Around Mile End

The Crown (223 Grove Road, E3, 8981 9998), for organic pub grub, by Vicky Park.
Frocks (95 Lauriston Road, E9, 8986 3161), for solid comfort food and popular brunches.
Mojo (132 Lauriston Road, E9, 8985 5864), for ambitious but good-value fare.

Around Docklands

Bar Spice (145 Three Colt Street, E14, 7093 1111; *see p176*), for Indian grub and a warm welcome for children.
Carluccio's Caffè (Nash Court, Canary Wharf, E14, 7719 1749; *see p162*), grab one of the outside tables for views of One Canada Square.
The Gourmet Pizza Company (18 Mackenzie Walk, Canary Wharf, E14, 7345 9192), for child-sized pizza portions.
Royal China (30 Westferry Circus, E14, 7719 0888; *see p177*), for great views and fabulous dumplings and cheung fun on the dim sum menu.
Smollensky's (Hermitage Wharf, 22 Wapping High Street, E1, 7680 1818; *see p169*), not as mad about children as the Strand branch, but good for a relaxed atmosphere and popular Sunday lunches.

Around Walthamstow

L Manze (76 Walthamstow High Street, E17, 8520 2855), purveyor of fine pie and mash.
Village Kitchen (41 Orford Road, E17, 8509 2144), reasonably priced lunches (Fri-Sun) and more formal evening meals (all week).
Walthamstow Stadium (*see p118*), perfect for dogs dinners – burgers, steaks and fish 'n' chips.

Around Wanstead

Hadley House (27 High Street, E11, 8989 8855; *see p176*), a civilised setting for a family blow-out, with excellent Sunday roasts.
Nam Am (157 High Street, E11, 8532 2845), good Vietnamese; main courses for around a fiver.

(the other 'temple' you can see is a tea stall); this is the best place to throw a ball around, let the dog off its lead or fly a kite. The pretty Shoulder of Mutton Pond always has some ducks to feed. The Wren Conservation and Wildlife Group website (www.wrengroup.fsnet.co.uk) provides a comprehensive history, map and guide to the plants and birds here. *Buggy access. Café. Free parking.*

Further east

Travel further north-east and you'll find the bird sanctuaries and open spaces of **Lee Valley Regional Park** and Chingford. **Epping Forest** is a gift for walkers, riders and cyclists; 6,000 acres (2,430 hectares) is left of the originally massive ancient forest – that's still plenty to lose sight of

London in. The forest is accessible on foot from several underground stations but, to properly explore these areas and the pretty villages (and country pubs) of Essex, a car is the best option.

Lee Valley Regional Park

Covering a vast area on either side of the River Lee, Lee Valley Regional Park (which starts in Hackney and goes all the way into Hertfordshire) is a network of lakes, waterways, parks and countryside areas. There's plenty to do, though a gentle guided walk (**Lee Valley Park Information Centre** has information and leaflets) is a good way to set about it. The park's ideal for picnics, walking or fishing. It's all well signposted and is open year-round.

The park is great for birdwatchers – more than 200 species have been seen here, despite its proximity to London, and the Middlesex Filter Beds on the Hackney side of Lee Valley, are now a dedicated marshland bird reserve. Other attractions include the **Lee Valley Riding Centre** (8556 2629; *see p258*) and **Lee Valley Cycle Circuit** (Temple Mill Lane, E15, 8534 6085), next to the M11 extension. If you're feeling energetic, the **Lee Valley Boat Centre** (Old Nazeing Road, Broxbourne, 01992 462085) is the place to hire a boat or book a narrowboat holiday. **Adventuress River Cruises** set off from here too (Mar-Dec, 01992 466111).

Waltham Abbey itself is a small town with plenty of little cafés and shops. History fiends may want to visit the Augustinian abbey: founded in 1060 by King Harold, it is reputed to be where he was buried too. The abbey was once one of the largest in the country, with its own farm, fishponds and brewery; only the gateway, a few walls and a stone bridge remain, but the gardens contain a variety of public artworks and there's a 'Sensory Trail' (information available from the park information centre) highlighting the natural history of the area. A short walk away are the much-acclaimed **Royal Gunpowder Mills**. Epping Forest is only a ten-minute drive away.

Lee Valley Park Farms

Stubbins Hall Lane, Crooked Mile, Waltham Abbey, Essex (01992 892781). Broxbourne or Waltham Cross rail. **Open** 10am-4.30pm Mon-Fri; 10am-5.30pm or dusk if earlier Sat, Sun. **Admission** £3.50; £3 concessions; £2.50 3-16s; £14 family (2+3); free under-3s. **Credit** MC, V.
Hayes Hill Farm is a rare breeds centre, with a Tudor barn, a restored gypsy caravan and plenty of space in which to play. Visitors can watch the milking of cows (from 2.45pm daily). There are guided tours for school parties.
Buggy access. Café. Nappy-changing facilities. Shop.

Lee Valley Park Information Centre

Abbey Gardens, Waltham Abbey, Essex (01992 702200/www.leevalleypark.org.uk). Waltham Cross rail. **Open** *Nov-Mar* 10am-4pm Tue-Sun. *Apr-Oct* 9.30am-5pm daily. **Admission** free.
This centre has racks of literature about the various activities available to visitors to the park, including messing about on the reservoirs in boats and canoes. Fishing permits can be obtained here, and there are maps of cycle routes and information about scenic riverside pubs.
Buggy access. Nappy-changing facilities. Nearest picnic place: information centre gardens. Shop.

Royal Gunpowder Mills

Beaulieu Drive, Waltham Abbey (01992 707370/www.royalgunpowdermills.com). Waltham Cross rail. **Open** *3 May-28 Sept* 11am-5pm Sat, Sun (last entry 3pm), daily for school groups. **Admission** £5; £4 concessions; £2.50 5-16s; £15 family (2+3); free under-5s.
The story of gunpowder is a thrilling one, and the Royal Gunpowder Mills tells it well. The mills were involved in the development of explosives for more than 300 years: first gunpowder production, which relied on water supplied from

the nearby River Lee, began in the 1660s; later the site manufactured guncotton, nitro-glycerine, cordite paste and the highly explosive tetryl; after World War II the mills were a research centre for non-nuclear explosives and propellants. Few of the buildings have been renovated, in a deliberate attempt to convey their long and complex past. It's a good idea to start at the visitors' centre, which runs an excellent introductory film full of bangs and flashes, as well as a informative hands-on exhibition that concentrates on the human story behind gunpowder. Much effort has taken over the educational programme too. On a warm summer's day, rugs are set out on the central grassy area and activity packs suitable for all ages handed out. Special events include an art weekend, military re-enactments, craft fairs and sports days. It's a big site, so wear comfy shoes.
Buggy access. Nappy-changing facilities. Nearest picnic place: on-site.

Epping Forest

Epping Forest is the biggest public space in London – 12 miles long and 22 miles across – saved from development by the Corporation of London in 1878. Today, the forest contains two listed buildings – the restored **Queen Elizabeth's Hunting Lodge** in Chingford (Rangers Road, E4, 8529 6681; under-16s must be accompanied by adults) and the **Temple** in Wanstead Park, as well as two Iron Age earthworks.

An important wildlife and conservation centre, the forest is home to woodpeckers, nightingales, treecreepers and nuthatches, plus waterfowl like great crested grebes, goosanders and wigeons. There are also 650 species of flowers and more than 1,000 types of fungi. For a real back-to-nature feeling, there's a campsite at **Debden House** (Debden Green, Loughton, Essex, 8508 3008).

Riders have a huge amount of trekking space, and there are several riding schools in the vicinity (contact the Epping Forest Information Centre).

If you're coming to the forest by public transport, Chingford railway station gives access to Queen Elizabeth's Hunting Lodge and some lovely strolls. Loughton and Theydon Bois (Central Line) are the nearest tube stops, though it's a two-mile uphill walk from both – a bit of a struggle if you've got small children in tow. The best advice is to get a map and plan your route forest in advance. The Official Guide to Epping Forest (£1.50) is available from the Guildhall Library Bookshop (7332 1858).

At the High Beech car park there's a tea hut, which is good for snacks and drinks; for hot meals there's the King's Oak pub, with its children's play areas.

Epping Forest Information Centre

High Beech, Loughton, Essex (8508 0028/www.epping forest.co.uk). Loughton or Theydon Bois tube, then walk or 5min taxi/Chingford rail. **Open** *Apr-Oct* 10am-5pm Mon-Sat; 11am-5pm Sun. *Nov-Mar* 11am-3pm Mon-Fri; 10am-4pm Sat; 11am-4pm Sun.
The recently redecorated information centre is a good first stop, to pick up walking route maps and wildlife guides.
Buggy access. Disabled: toilet. Shop.

South-east London

The call of the sea, the materialist tug of malls and markets and the upward pull of urban regeneration.

Rotherhithe

Rotherhithe is best known as the spot from which the Pilgrim Fathers set sail in the Mayflower in 1620. Samuel Pepys referred to it as Redriffe, which, in Anglo-Saxon, meant mariner's haven. And that it certainly was: the neighbourhood was once the ship-building capital of the world, populated by salty sea dogs, ship-breakers, sailors and smugglers. Its maritime legacy can still be glimpsed in the atmospheric old wharves and warehouses – some of which have been converted into smart flats – and in its ancient cobbled streets. Look out for a couple of legendary pubs: the **Mayflower**, (117 Rotherhithe Street, SE16, 7237 4088) a historic seafaring inn, and the 17th-century **Angel** (101 Bermondsey Wall East, SE16, 7237 3608), which still has a smuggler's trapdoor on the premises. Just along from the Angel on Bermondsey Wall East lies a small patch of grass with the archaeological remains of King Edward III's palace. East of here is a good park and playground.

Rotherhithe Street is the quaintest, most antiquated bit of the neighbourhood. **St Mary's Rotherhithe** (St Marychurch Street, SE16, 7231 2465) was built by local sailors in 1715. The Ladychapel contains a communion table made from wood salvaged from the *Fighting Temeraire*, a ship painted by Turner. (You can admire his famous canvas in the National Gallery, *see p209*) But, apart from during services, the church interior can only be viewed from behind locked glass doors, due to the threat of vandalism. Nearby, housed in a former mortuary, is the excellent **Time & Talents Association** (7231 7845). Local women set up the group in 1887 to help the poverty-riddled families who eked out a living in the docks area. Today, the organisation's community spirit lives on through numerous arts and social programmes, including drama courses for children.

Sands Film Studios (119 Rotherhithe Street, SE16, 7231 2209/www.sandsfilms.co.uk) often shows children's films at the weekend. They're currently showing a version of *A Midsummer Night's Dream* starring the children of Southwark, which is set to run for most of the year. The **Brunel Engine House & Tunnel Exhibition** (*see p122*) celebrates the construction of the Thames Tunnel – the world's first underwater tunnel – and also provides broader historical information on the area.

More than just a maritime relic, Rotherhithe is also home to a number of green spaces, some more attractive than others. **Lavender Pond Nature Park** (Rotherhithe Street, SE16, 7237 9165) was created from an old dock inlet in 1982 and now supports newts, frogs and dragonflies. Herons and tufted ducks have also been spotted. **Russia Dock Woodland**, accessed via Watermans Walk off Redriff Road, is another ecological sanctuary. Here, ponds provide homes for fish, eels and waterbirds, and the landscape is dotted with willows, birches and ash. Sadly, the landscape is also blighted by litter, vandalism and burnt-out mopeds, but it's better than no park at all. Adjoining **Stave Hill Ecological Park** is not quite so grotty. It, too, is a haven for birds, insects and butterflies.

The most immaculate green space, however, is **Southwark Park**. Created 130 years ago, it's the city's oldest municipal park, and recently received a much-needed makeover; now its elegant planting ad picturesque boating lake seem almost too good-looking for rough old Southwark. Every summer, Rotherhithe Festival consists of a day of music, crafts, food and fun in the park (it takes place on 12 July in 2003). Just outside the park, the **Seven Islands Leisure Centre** (100 Lower Road, SE16, 7237 3296/www.fusion-lifestyle.com) has a good pool with children's swimming programmes.

Crossing Lower Road from the park brings you to Canada Water and the **Surrey Quays Shopping Centre** (Redriff Road, SE16, 7237 2388). This mega-mall is home to the Discovery Planet indoor adventure playground which is great for parties, toddler groups and after-school clubs. Next to the mall is **Decathlon** (Canada Water Retail Park, Surrey Quays Road, SE16, 7394 2000), the biggest sports store in Northern Europe. Other wonderfully mindless thrills are to be found at **Hollywood Bowl** (Redriff Road, SE16, 7237 3773), for children's parties, ten-pin bowling and video games, all conveniently next door to a Burger King.

For an escape from rampant commercialism, the **Surrey Docks Watersports Centre** (Rope Street, SE16, 7237 5555; *see also p266*) runs sailing and canoeing courses for children aged eight and over in school holidays and half-terms. And on the other side of the Rotherhithe peninsula lies **Surrey Docks Farm**, a patch of country in the city which offers activities for children during holidays.

Dedicated to seafarers. **National Maritime Museum.** *See p123.*

Brunel Engine House & Tunnel Exhibition

Brunel Engine House, Railway Avenue, SE16 (7231 3840/www.brunelenginehouse.org.uk). Rotherhithe tube. **Open** *Apr-Oct* 1-5pm Sat, Sun. *Nov-Mar* 1-5pm Sun. *Tours* 1st Sun of mth. **Admission** £2; £1 concessions; £5 family (2+2); free under-5s. *Tours* £2 donation requested. **No credit cards.**

Who'd have thought that the Eighth Wonder of the World was right here in Rotherhithe? That's what they called the Thames Tunnel, the first underwater tunnel in the world, when it was built in 1843. It was designed by Marc Isambard Brunel with the help of his more famous son, Isambard Kingdom Brunel – the only time the legendary Brunels worked together. Brunel Junior was almost drowned during its construction, but that's how risky the project was: many others lost their lives to get this engineering wonder built.

These and other hair-raising stories are told in this little museum, housed in the tunnel's boiler house. The main thrust of the exhibition is the construction of the tunnel, which is now used for the East London tube line. Truth be told, young minds might find it a bit heavy on the engineering detail. But it's also a good general Victorian history lesson, commemorating a time when the port of London was the busiest in the world. And the gentlemen who run the museum are fascinating guides – they'll happily talk your ear off about the glory days of Rotherhithe. The museum welcomes school groups, and has information packs for Key Stages 2 and 4. *Shop.*

Southwark Park

Gomm Road, SE16 (park rangers 7232 2091/art gallery 7237 1230). Canada Water tube. **Open** *Park* 8am-1hr before dusk daily. *Gallery (during exhibitions) Summer* 11am-5pm Wed-Sun. *Winter* 11am-4pm Wed-Sun; phone first to check. **Admission** free.

Southwark isn't exactly one of London's most beautiful boroughs, which is why this Victorian park comes as such a pleasant surprise. Recently restored to its original glory thanks to a £2.75 million lottery grant, the park is now one of South London's prettiest. The loveliest bit is the boating lake (fully operational in summer), where kids can feed ducks and swans, but the whole place is pleasing: there's a wildlife garden, old-fashioned bandstand, tennis courts, playing fields and an information centre. There's also a curious little gallery smack dab in the middle of the park, with a range of exhibitions, including the annual Open Exhibition (November 19-December 14), which always features children's work: it's a child-friendly gallery in other ways, too, with nappy-changing facilities on the premises. A Young Friends of the Park scheme lets kids play an active role in arts, environment and sports projects. They plant bulbs in spring, learn about flora and fauna and generally get involved. The authorities hope this will reduce incidents of crime and vandalism in the park (for more information call 7525 1538).

Surrey Docks Farm

Rotherhithe Street, SE16 (7231 1010). Canada Water or Surrey Quays tube. **Open** 10am-1pm, 2-5pm Tue-Thur, Sat, Sun. **Admission** free (except school parties and play-schemes; phone for details); donations appreciated.

If only all modern farms were like this; more to the point, if only all inner cities had one. This organic farm was opened to the public in the early 1970s in an attempt to bring a bit of nature to a depressed neighbourhood. Since then, it has thrived. Its residents include a herd of milking goats, sheep, cows, pigs, poultry, donkeys and bees. There's a classroom in the shape of an enchanted forest, a dairy and a forge where a blacksmith holds evening classes; a duck pond and a herb and vegetable garden offer further rural delights. Children enjoy clambering over the animal sculptures. Call about holiday play schemes and workshops.

Greenwich

Daniel Defoe described Greenwich as 'the most delightful spot of ground in Great Britain', and Henry VIII loved the place – his hunting grounds were Greenwich Park, and his daughters Mary and Elizabeth were born here. Even centuries later, you can understand the enthusiasm. Today, riverside Greenwich still oozes charm, from its elegant Georgian and Regency architecture to its stunning park. The area is best known, however, for its maritime history: don't miss the impressive **National Maritime Museum**. There's no danger you'll overlook the rash of nautical-themed shops and restaurants; touristy, but fun.

The best way to arrive in Greenwich is by boat. (for more information, call **Thames Cruises** 7930 3373/www.thames cruises.com, **Catamaran Cruises** 7987 1185 or **City Cruises** 7930 9033/www.citycruises.com). Viewed from the river, the ornate **Old Royal Naval College** and neoclassical **Queen's House** form a breathtaking picture, and the **Cutty Sark**, the world's last surviving tea clipper, seems even grander.

Greenwich could still pass for an elegant country town, if it weren't for its traffic-choked centre. The crowds descend at weekends for **Greenwich Market**, with its art, craft, toy and food stalls. One of the market's shops, Compendia Games, is a must-stop for children, stocking classic play items ranging from Risk to the Rubik's Cube. Other nearby shops of note include Bear Mad (3 Nelson Road, SE16, 8858 3311) and, across the road, the maritime extravaganza that is Nauticalia (25 Nelson Road, SE16, 8858 1066).

For a good overview of Greenwich delights, visit the **Tourist Information Centre** (Pepys House, 2 Cutty Sark Gardens, SE16, 0870 608 2000). But the best outlook proper can be found at the top of the hill in Greenwich Park: bella vista indeed. Up here you'll find the **Royal Observatory** and the **Planetarium**. It's a healthy ten-minute walk from the park's entrance, but for little legs that can't handle the journey, a shuttle bus runs from Greenwich Pier to the National Maritime Museum and up to the top of the hill every 15 minutes or so. Tickets last all day and cost £1.50 for adults, 50p for children and nothing for under-fives. The DLR offers a Rail & River Rover (details on 7363 9700/www.dlr. co.uk), a family pass that is also valid on some cruise boats.

Cutty Sark

King William Walk, SE10 (8858 3445/www.cuttysark. org.uk). Cutty Sark DLR/Greenwich DLR/rail. **Open** 10am-5pm (last entry 4.30pm) daily. Closed 24-26 Dec. *Tours* Mon-Fri; depending on availability. **Admission** (LP) £3.95; £2.95 concessions; £9.80 family (2+3); free under-5s. *Tours* free. **Credit** MC, V.

During her heyday, the *Cutty Sark* was the fastest ship at sea. Today, she's the last surviving tea clipper in the world, but suffering a bit with age: there's an ongoing appeal for funds to conserve the old girl and high hopes for a Heritage Lottery Fund to save her.

Launched in 1869 from Dumbarton on the Clyde, the *Cutty Sark* took tea to China and later wool to Australia. Now a museum, the lower hold is home to a large collection of merchant ship figureheads and a hands-on activities area, where young people can learn to tie bends and hitches and try out an old-fashioned hammock. The 'tween deck's history gallery, meanwhile, features children's panels below each display. The ship runs regular activities for children, including treasure hunts and storytelling sessions. In October 2003, the ship will be the scene of dramatised tours to coincide with Black History month. At Christmas, there's shanty singing and appearances by Captain Christmas. The historic ship is also the focus of many school visits.
Buggy storage. Nearest picnic place: Cutty Sark Gardens. Shop.

Fan Museum

12 Crooms Hill, SE10 (8305 1441/www.fan-museum. org). Cutty Sark DLR/Greenwich DLR/rail. **Open** 11am-5pm Tue-Sat; noon-5pm Sun. Closed 25 Dec, Easter, 1 Jan. **Admission** £3.50; £2.50 concessions; free under-7s. Free OAPs, disabled 2-5pm Tue. **Credit** MC, V.
This little museum is one of only two fan museums in the world. The other is in Paris, and this one feels very French glam too. The fans on display date from the 11th century, and are only a fraction of the museum's 3000-strong collection. Fans are retired periodically to give them a rest, so the displays are always changing. You might see Louis XIV fans and ancient fans from Spain, China, Japan, South America and Africa. Elephant tusks, tortoise shells, and pearl oysters – all materials once used to make fans – are also on display. While certainly not an obvious crowd pleaser, the place is worth a visit if the kids are interested in pretty things, fashion and design. Outside, there's an attractive Oriental-style garden, and the orangerie is open for afternoon set teas on Tuesdays and Sundays (and can be hired out for small parties). Artistic over-12s can join the fan-making workshops. The big exhibition for 2003 will focus on the lavish era of Louis XIV (3 June-21 September).
Buggy access. Shop.

National Maritime Museum

Romney Road, SE10 (8858 4422/8312 6565/tours 8312 6608/www.nmm.ac.uk). Cutty Sark DLR/Greenwich DLR/rail. **Open** 10am-5pm daily. Closed 24-26 Dec. **Tours** phone for details. **Admission** free. **Credit** *Shop* AmEx, MC, V.
One of London's must-see attractions, the National Maritime Museum charts the history of seafaring. The elegant white neoclassical building is worth a visit alone. Inside, the museum has an effective mix of traditional exhibits and interactive presentations.

The lobby stars whirlpool displays and make-your-own wave tanks which seem to intrigue the kids. The Explorers Gallery shows eerie film footage of the launch of a ship purporting to be the Titanic (in fact the Olympic) and the real wreck at the bottom of the Atlantic. It is devoted to pioneers of sea travel, covering Columbus, the Vikings and the race to the Poles. Passengers is a shrine to glamorous ocean liners of yore, Rank and Style looks at the influence of climate and class on uniform designs and Maritime London tells the capital's nautical history using old prints and model ships. Upstairs, Seapower covers naval battles from Gallipoli to the Falklands. Kids might like the Hidden Treasures gallery, with

PARKLIFE Greenwich Park

Greenwich Park is arguably London's prettiest. True, Regent's Park's gardens are more ornate, Richmond Park is more pastoral, and Hyde Park has its wonderful lakes. But Greenwich Park has elements of all three, it's as royal as any of them, and it has one spectacular feature which tops the others – the views. Looking down from the Wolfe monument, East London spreads before your eyes. There's the Millennium Dome, the Thames, the exquisite Old Royal Naval College and Maritime Museum, the razzle-dazzle skyline of Canary Wharf, the *Cutty Sark*, Tower Bridge and St Paul's.

But the view from the bottom of the hill is none too shabby either. Framed by the pristine white columns of the Queen's House, the park's verdant hills are a sight to behold. There's never a shortage of children kicking a ball around – possibly the world's most elegant football training ground, this one. Further east lies a terrific playground and boating lake. Walking south, you'll stumble across the remains of Queen Elizabeth's oak, around which Henry VIII and Anne Boleyn danced (It died in 1991, but the trunk is still here) and the Roman remains. Of more interest to the children might be the flower garden and deer enclosure, at the park's southern tip. Throughout the park are wonderfully gnarled trees, undulating hills and tame grey squirrels. And the park's beauty is matched by its brains. There are Planetarium shows twice daily, and kids can straddle the Prime Meridian Line at The Royal Observatory. If all of this doesn't impress them, the entertainment might: during the summer holidays there's a varied programme of free puppet and theatre shows for children organised by the Royal Parks Agency (call 8858 2608 for details).

Greenwich Park

Blackheath Gate, Charlton Way, SE10 (visitors centre 8293 0703/www.royalparks.co.uk). Cutty Sark DLR/Greenwich DLR/rail/Maze Hill rail/1, 53, 177, 180, 188, 286 bus/riverboat to Greenwich Pier. **Open** *6am-dusk daily.*

its giant model ships. Level 3 is devoted entirely to young people: fledgling sailors can learn how to send Morse code or navigate Viking longboats in the All Hands and Bridge exhibits. Back on the main floor, the always popular gift shop has loads of model ships, puzzles, globes, Lego submarines and stuffed toys on a vaguely marine theme.

The museum has tons of planned activities for families, such as the Crows' Nest Story Time, Shipmates (a drop-in craft session), sailor-themed singsongs, and costumed actors talking animatedly about life at sea. The big exhibition for 2003 is dedicated to Queen Elizabeth I: expect a full range of children's activities to coincide with it.
Buggy access. Café. Nappy-changing facilities. Nearest picnic place: Greenwich Park. Restaurant. Shop.

Old Royal Naval College

King William Walk, SE10 (8269 4747/tours 8269 4791/www.greenwichfoundation.org.uk). Cutty Sark DLR/Greenwich DLR/rail. **Open** 10am-5pm daily. Last entry 4.15pm. Closed 25, 26 Dec. *Tours* by arrangement. **Admission** free. **Credit** MC, V.
The majestic Old Royal Naval College was built by Sir Christopher Wren in 1696, the spectacular buildings were originally a hospital, then a naval college and are now part of the University of Greenwich. The public can still visit the rococo chapel and exquisite Painted Hall. There are free organ recitals on the first Sunday of each month, and the chapel is open every day. At weekends and during school holidays, the College runs children's events, such as storytelling, history workshops, costumed tours and knot-tying lessons.
Café. Nappy-changing facilities. Nearest picnic place: Naval College grounds. Shops.

Queen's House

Romney Road, SE10 (8312 6565/www.nmm.ac.uk). Cutty Sark DLR/Greenwich DLR/rail. **Open** 10am-5pm daily. Closed 24-26 Dec. **Admission** free; occasional charge for temporary exhibitions. **Credit** *Shop* AmEx, DC, MC, V.
One of Britain's first classical buildings, the Queen's House was designed by Inigo Jones in 1616 for James I's wife, Anne of Denmark. It was the architect's first attempt at Palladian architecture, but the building's simple design belies a more lavish exterior. The House is now home to the National Maritime Museum's impressive art collection, which includes portraits of famous maritime figures and works by Hogarth and Gainsborough. The House is also home to a ghost, which was famously captured on film by a couple of Canadian visitors in 1966, and was spotted as recently as 2002 by a gallery assistant. For the kids, the gallery occasionally holds drop-in crafts workshops, lively presentations about life aboard an old ship, the occasional baroque concert and if they're lucky, tours of the Queen's House led by costumed actors. Call the information desk to find out what's on.
Buggy access. Nappy-changing facilities. Nearest picnic place: Greenwich Park.

Ranger's House

Chesterfield Walk, SE10 (8853 0035/ www.english-heritage.org.uk). Blackheath rail or Greenwich DLR/rail/53 bus. **Open** *Apr-Sept* 10am-6pm Wed-Sun. *Oct* 10am-5pm Wed-Sun. *Nov-late Dec, Mar* 10am-4pm Wed-Sun. **Admission** (EH) £4.50; £3.50 concessions; £2.50 5-16s; free under-5s. **Credit** MC, V.
Formerly a 'grace and favour' home to the Greenwich Park ranger, this 18th-century red-brick villa now houses the

Wernher Collection. Amassed by Victorian diamond magnate Sir Julius Wernher (once the richest man in Britain), the gleaming collection includes crafts which date from 3rd century BC, Old Masters paintings, 18th-century French furniture and Britain's largest private collection of Renaissance jewellery. There are no children's activities, but the House is still a glittering spectacle which might combine nicely with a walk in the park or a visit to the nearby Planetarium. *Buggy storage. Nearest picnic place: Greenwich park. Shop.*

Royal Observatory
Greenwich Park, SE10 (8312 6565/www.rog.nmm.ac.uk). Cutty Sark DLR/Greenwich DLR/rail. **Open** 10am-5pm daily. Closed 24-26 Dec. **Tours** phone for details. **Admission** free.
The Royal Observatory was built by Wren in 1675 on the orders of Charles II, who was tired of losing ships at sea. John Flamsteed, the Royal astronomer, was assigned the task of mapping the heavens. But it was clockmaker John Harrison who, in 1763, eventually found the solution to determining longitude. The museum details Harrison's quest, has a few period rooms and a ticktastic range of clocks: the first maritime clock, 17th-century hourglasses, Chinese alarm clocks, atomic clocks and the first pocket watches. Children enjoy climbing the spiral staircase to the dome, which houses the largest refracting telescope in the world. Outside in the courtyard is the Prime Meridian Line – star of millions of pictures of happy tourists with a foot in each hemisphere. A range of spacey shows, from Legends of the Stars to Eclipse Previews to the Skies of Antarctica, can be viewed at the Planetarium. Family learning days are held on such topics as Getting Started in Astronomy or the Red Planet. The school holiday programme, meanwhile, features a range of workshops and stories (call 8312 6608 for details). *Buggy access (not in dome). Nappy-changing facilities. Nearest picnic place: Greenwich Park. Shop.*

Blackheath & Lewisham

Windswept Blackheath got its name from the darkness of its soil – contrary to myth, it was not a burial place for victims of the plague. Popular with kite-flyers, the heath is home to many of Britain's first sports clubs: the Royal Blackheath Golf Club (1745), the Blackheath Hockey Club (1861) and the Blackheath Football Club (which actually plays Rugby Union; 1862). Every year, the Blackheath Village Fair is held here on the first Saturday of June. Nearby Blackheath village rivals Dulwich in terms of prettiness, smart shops, cafés and restaurants, but is more prone to traffic pollution.

For a history of Blackheath, check out the **Age Exchange Reminiscence Centre** (11 Blackheath Village, SE3, 8318 9105/www.age-exchange.org.uk), which hosts exhibitions about the neighbourhood's past. It also has an olde-worlde shop stocking traditional sweets and wooden toys.

Blackheath Halls (23 Lee Road, SE9, 8318 9758/www.blackheathhalls.com) programmes in plenty of children's cultural activities: theatre productions, dance workshops, films, a young bands programme, a youth jazz orchestra and an all-ages community orchestra. On Sundays there's a farmer's market in Blackheath station car park.

Southwest of Blackheath lies Lewisham, a world away from its exclusive neighbour – you're in Sahf London now. Still, it enjoys excellent access to the city thanks to the DLR. The indoor shopping centre has an Early Learning Centre and an indoor playground. Lewisham also has an extensive street market (fruit and veg, fish, clothes, toys and decent, cheap household linen).

Keep walking down the amusingly named Lewisham Promenade and you'll end up in Catford, famed for its large black and white cat over the ugly shopping centre, the Catford Greyhound track and its trees lit up by blue light bulbs. Lewisham borough has a good number of parks, many of which are ripe for expensive regeneration. **Mountsfield Park** (Stainton Road, SE6) is one of these. It hosts People's Day (12 July), an annual summer festival that draws 30,000 people. Events include circus acts, live music, poetry, and sports (call 8318 3986 for details). The South London Garden Festival (9-10 August) is also a Mountsfield attraction. Other pleasant parks in the area include **Sydenham Wells Park** (Wells Park Road, SE26), which has a children's play area and a couple of rare plant gardens. The prettiest of all, however, is **Manor House & Gardens**, in a well-to-do residential area just off Lee High Road. The manor now houses a library, and the gardens are the heart of the community. A popular farmer's market is held here every second Saturday.

Manor House & Gardens
Brightfield Road, SE12 (8318 1358). Hither Green rail. **Open** Café & park 9.30am-dusk daily. **Admission** free.
Once owned by the Baring's Bank family, this 1780 Manor House is now open to the public and is a particularly child-friendly venue, with a gem of a park and a library (closed Wednesday, Friday and Sunday). The library, situated in the Manor House, has a particularly good children's collection and fine views of the park. It also has story readings for under-fives every Monday morning (call to confirm times). The park has a playground, and a pond where you can feed the ducks from a lovely boardwalk. Then there's the old ice house, where the Victorians stored their ice during the summer months, which opens on the first and third Sunday of every month. The park café is a cut above the average, offering jacket potatoes, sandwiches and hot meals. A parent-and-toddler session takes place on Tuesday mornings.

Woolwich

Woolwich may be less glamorous than Greenwich, but is just as rich in naval and military history. The Woolwich Arsenal was established in Tudor times as the country's main source of munitions. By World War I, the Arsenal was enormous: it stretched 32 miles along the river, had its own internal railway system and employed 72,000 people. Much of the

Pondlife at **Blackheath**. *See p125.*

land was sold off during the 1960s, resulting in the ghastly Thamesmead estate, but thankfully, the main section of the Arsenal, with its beautiful cluster of Georgian buildings, has been preserved. The atmospheric grounds, where Wellington drew up battle plans, are now open to the public, as is **Firepower**, a new artillery museum. South of here, the Royal Artillery Barracks has the longest Georgian façade in the country. For the best view, go to Woolwich Common or Grand Depot Road.

Woolwich high street has better shops than most in South London. It also holds the dubious distinction of being home to the first McDonald's to open in Britain. This legendary event occurred in 1974, and the current restaurant is emblazoned with fast-food factoids. There's also a bustling market across the road from Firepower, and a very elegant town hall. Kids will be more appreciative of the **Waterfront Leisure Centre** (Woolwich High Street, SE18, 8317 5000) which has flume-filled pools and an indoor adventure playground. Next door is the free Woolwich Ferry, and views downriver of the Thames Barrier, the Dome and Canary Wharf.

Firepower
Royal Arsenal, SE18 (8855 7755/www.firepower.org.uk). Woolwich Arsenal rail. **Open** *Nov-Mar* 11am-4pm (last entry 3pm) daily. *Apr-Oct* 10am-5pm daily (last entry 4pm). Closed 25 Dec. **Admission** (LP) £6.50; £5.50 concessions; £4.50 5-16s; £18 family (2+2 or 1+3); free under-5s. **Credit** MC, V.
This £15m attraction is like a boys-with-toys version of the Imperial War Museum, full of impressive-looking hardware and whooshes, bangs and booms. Exhibits trace the evolution of artillery from primitive catapults to nuclear warheads. Multimedia presentations such as Fields of Fire, which covers various 20th-century wars, are full of excitement and noise, the Gunnery Hall is full of howitzers and tanks and the Real Weapon gallery shows you how guns work.

The museum holds regular activities for children, particularly during the half-term and school holidays, when kids can have their faces painted, play paintball, dress up in military gear and learn how equipment works. The gift shop is full of military souvenirs and camouflage clothing for kids. Booming 21-Gun Salutes marks the anniversaries of the Queen's coronation and birthday (2 and 14 June); from 14 to 19 July 2003 check out the Musical Nights extravaganza in the adjoining Royal Arsenal. For a birthday with a bang, Firepower offers special children's parties (£10 per child). It includes museum admission, party food and drink, and a game of paintball. Call 8312 7134 for details.
Buggy access. Café. Lift. Nappy-changing facilities. Nearest picnic place: riverside. Shop.

Thames Barrier Information & Learning Centre
1 Unity Way, SE18 (8305 4188/www.environment-agency.gov.uk). North Greenwich tube/Charlton rail/riverboats to & from Greenwich Pier (8305 0300) & Westminster Pier (7930 3373)/177, 180 bus. **Open** *Apr-late Sept* 10.30am-4.30pm daily. *End Sept-Mar* 11am-3.30pm daily. Closed 24 Dec-2 Jan. **Admission** *Exhibition* £1; 75p concessions; 50p 5-16s; free under-5s. **Credit** MC, V.

Looking like a cross between the Sydney Opera House and a row of giant metallic shark fins, the Thames Barrier is one of London's most striking sights. The world's largest adjustable dam was built in 1982 at a cost of £535m, and since then it has saved London from flooding at least 67 times. The tiny visitors centre is nothing spectacular, but it does explain how the marvel works, sells videos and models, and has a fascinating map which shows which parts of London would be submerged if it stopped working. School groups are welcome. Time your visit to see the barrier in action: every September there's a full-scale testing of the barrier and a partial test closure once a month (ring for dates). The best way to see the barrier, however, is by boat. Campion Cruises (8305 0300) runs trips from Greenwich three times a day. Alternatively, catch an eastbound river cruise from Embankment (Thames Cruises 7930 3373).

Woolwich Ferry
New Ferry Approach, SE18 (8921 5786). **Crossings** 6.10am-8pm Mon-Sat; 11.30am-7.30pm Sun. **Admission** free.
In the absence of a bridge to connect the north and south banks of the river, the Woolwich Ferry has been shuttling people back and forth across the Thames since the 14th century. Apart from a distant view of the Thames Barrier and the Dome, there's not much to see on the crossing – the Staten Island ferry this ain't – but children will think it's fun, it's free, and you can take your car with you (vehicles up top, pedestrians sit below). Once you've reached the north shore, you should check out the North Woolwich Old Station Museum (*see p116*) and the Royal Victoria Gardens.

Shooters Hill to Eltham

It may be the epitome of suburbia these days, but this community was once a wild and scary frontier. 200 years ago, highwaymen (including the notorious Dick Turpin) lurked in the woods between Shooters Hill and Charlton. Anyone travelling the Old Dover Road took a considerable risk – but then again, so did the robbers, who, if caught were hanged on the gallows at the bottom of Shooters Hill. These days, Shooters Hill has more pleasant associations, particularly **Hornfair Park**, which during hot weather attracts sweaty Charltonians with its lido, although whether it will open for summer 2003 is unclear as we go to press. Many of the green spaces in this corner of London are connected by the **Green Chain Walk** (call 8921 5028 for maps), which takes in pastoral meadows and ancient woodlands such as Oxleas Wood (*see 134*).

Charlton House
Charlton Road, SE7 (8856 3951/www.greenwich.gov.uk). Charlton rail/53, 54, 380, 442 bus. **Open** *Library* 2-7pm Mon, Thur; 10am-12.30pm, 1.30-5.30pm Tue, Fri; 10am-12.30pm, 2-5pm Sat. **Admission** free.
From the outside, this Jacobean manor house looks like the grandest of stately homes – which, once upon a time, it was. Built in 1612, it was home to the tutor of Henry, eldest son of James I. These days, it's not quite so grandiose inside: it's now a community centre and library. But glimpses of its glorious past can be seen in the creaky oak staircase, marble fireplaces and ornate plaster ceilings. The library has a good

children's section, and is a rather delightful home to the Charlton Toy Library (8858 5579). Outside, the grounds are a bit scruffy, but a major redesign has been approved; when that happens, the venerable mulberry tree, which dates back to 1608, will get the surroundings it deserves.

Eltham Palace

Court Yard, off Court Road, SE9 (8294 2548/ www.english-heritage.org.uk). Eltham rail. **Open** *Apr-Sept* 10am-6pm Wed-Fri, Sun. *Oct* 10am-5pm Wed-Fri, Sun. *Nov-Mar* 10am-4pm Wed-Fri, Sun. Closed 24-26 Dec, Jan. **Admission** (EH) *House & grounds* (incl audio tour) £6.50; £5 concessions; £3.50 5-16s; free under-5s. *Grounds only* £4; £3 concessions; £2 5-16s; free under-5s. **Credit** MC, V.

Don't be fooled by the neoclassical exterior, the moat or the medieval remains: Eltham Palace is an art deco extravaganza. Rebuilt by Stephen Courtauld, a member of the textile family and patron of the arts, this elegant house was bought by English Heritage and restored to its 1930s glory. The interior is breathtaking: all sensuous curves, polished veneer walls and modish abstract carpets. Best of all is the retro glam entrance hall and the swish bathrooms, though kids might be tickled by the specially designed quarters for the Courtaulds' pet lemur. By contrast, the attached great hall, all that remains of the original building, is a splendid example of medieval architecture. Quiz and information sheets are available for children, who may find the greatest pleasure outside in the lush, immaculately landscaped gardens. *Café. Lifts,. Nappy-changing facilities. Nearest picnic place: palace grounds. Shop.*

Kennington & the Elephant

Kennington's attractive residential squares and proximity to central London have made it a desirable south London address. Cardigan Street, Courtenay Street and Courtenay Square are all lined with elegant Georgian houses. Across Kennington Road lies pretty Cleaver Square; another beauty, Walcot Square, is a little further north east.

A short walk from one of South London's prettiest neighbourhoods brings you to one of its ugliest: the rubicund fright known as the Elephant and Castle. It's constantly undergoing renovations of one kind or another, and there are grand plans for a spectacular Hanging Gardens of Babylon-type plaza to replace some of the grimmer concrete blocks. They say the shabby shopping centre will be gone by 2012, but don't hold your breath: the planners' grandiose schemes face endless setbacks. For some green relief from the urban jungle, head to the Geraldine Mary Harmsworth Park, with its tranquil Tibetan peace garden. But the neighbourhood's main attractions are the **Imperial War Museum** and the **AMP Oval**.

AMP Oval

Kennington Oval, SE11 (ticket office 7582 7764/ 6660/tours 7820 5750/www.surreycricket.com). Oval tube. **Open** *Ticket office* 9.30am-4pm Mon-Fri. **Tours** by arrangement; phone for details. **Admission** varies; depending on match. **Credit** MC, V.

The home of the Surrey County Cricket Club is one of London's most famous landmarks. Traditionally, the Oval hosts the final test of the summer, as well as county and league matches. All domestic games are free to under-17s accompanied by an adult. There are several educational opportunities running throughout the year. Teachers can bring their classes up to spend a whole day at the Oval, which includes a tour, free T-shirts and coaching sessions. (call 7820 5734 to enquire). An indoor cricket school offers more serious coaching programmes (7582 6660). Cricket fans can also take tours of the Oval on match days: you get a ticket which covers both match and tour. Tours take a peek at the changing rooms (not when they're in use, sadly) broadcast and media studios, and Ken Barrington training school. For tour details call 7820 5763/5780. *Shop.*

Imperial War Museum

Lambeth Road, SE1 (7416 5000/www.iwm.org.uk). Lambeth North tube/Elephant & Castle tube/rail. **Open** 10am-6pm daily. Closed 24-26 Dec. **Admission** free. **Credit** MC, V.

Housed, appropriately enough, in a former lunatic asylum, the Imperial War Museum offers a gripping history of 20th-century warfare; the hardware in the lobby – Russian tanks, German rockets, fighter planes – is awesome. But the World War I and II galleries are the main attraction: the Trench and Blitz Experiences, artefacts, film footage and maps plunge you into the thick of the battle. Another one the children might like is the Secret War gallery, which deals with intrigue and espionage and is full of James Bond-style gadgets. The 1940s House recreates a typical wartime home, and has proved so popular it's now a semi-permanent exhibition. Upstairs, there are galleries devoted to war paintings. The now permanent £17 million Holocaust exhibition is a bit grim for, say, the under-14s, but is a moving and powerful display. The dark theme of genocide is further investigated in the new Crimes Against Humanity exhibition, which screens a half-hour film about ethnic violence throughout the day.

The education department runs a full term-time programme of school visits and classes (all free; book ahead), with quiz sheets and tours for age ranges from primary to A-level. During the holidays, children aged seven to 11⁺have a wealth of activities and workshops to choose from. Activities include artefact handling, model-making, poetry trails and talks about trench life given by costumed actors. Call the education office (7416 5441) for details. Future exhibitions which children might find interesting include Women and War (Oct 2003-Apr 2004) and Submarines, an interactive exhibition about, funnily enough, submarines (until late 2003). *Buggy access. Café. Lifts. Nappy-changing facilities. Nearest picnic place: Geraldine Mary Harmsworth Park. Restaurant. Shops.*

Camberwell and Peckham

It's hard to believe that Camberwell, now one of London's most congested crossroads, was once an idyllic village. The neighbourhood's busy intersection of Camberwell Church Street and Denmark Hill still has a bit of green space – still, laughably, called Camberwell Green – with a small playground. But Camberwell, despite its urban grit, still has great appeal. Camberwell Grove is lined with elegant Georgian Houses; **St Giles Church**, on Camberwell Church Street, is a typically

LONDON LEGEND Enid Blyton

Enid Blyton might be firmly associated with a certain apple-cheeked rural wholesomeness, but the bestselling children's author was a product of South-east London. Born in 1897 above a shop in East Dulwich, Blyton went on to spend her formative years in the deepest suburbs, Beckenham, in Kent.

Her childhood began happily enough. She idolised her businessman father Thomas Carey Blyton, who took her on long nature walks, read to her, and encouraged her artistic development.

But unlike the jolly childhoods depicted in her books, Blyton's youth was soon blighted by unhappiness. When she was 13, her father left his wife for another woman. Enid was left with her mother. Theresa Blyton had no time for her daughter's literary leanings and Blyton junior turned inwards, creating her own fantasy world. When she was 14, she had her first poem published in a magazine. It soon dawned on her that children's writing was her vocation.

In 1924 she married a publisher who helped smooth her way into the book world. In 1937 she wrote her first novel, *The Adventures of the Wishing Chair*, and in 1942 – the year she divorced her first husband – the first Famous Five novel, *Five on a Treasure Island*, was published. She remarried, moved to a country house in Beaconsfield, Buckinghamshire, and gave birth to two daughters. Her output during the '40s was prolific: she wrote 15 books a year, including the Famous Five and Secret Seven series, Mallory Towers, St Clares, and her most successful project, Noddy, the little wooden chap who becomes a successful taxi driver in Toytown.

Popularity breeds contempt, however. In the late '50s Blyton faced a barrage of criticism. Librarians criticised Blyton for her limited vocabulary and, more recently, her politically incorrect stories. Noddy has been dismissed as 'the most egocentric, joyless, snivelling and pious anti-hero in the history of British fiction'. Nonetheless Blyton's adventure stories have turned millions of children around the world on to reading: her sales add up to 400 million books in 40 languages. Explaining her mass appeal, one psychologist summed it up thus, 'She was a child, she thought as a child and she wrote as a child.'

Blyton devotees can see where she was born (above a shop at 352-356 Lordship Lane, East Dulwich). To see the settings for her stories, however, they'll have to travel much further afield: the famous Kirrin Castle is based on Corfe Castle in Dorset, Mystery Moor is inspired by the heath between Stoborough and Corfe, *Five Have a Mystery to Solve* was modelled on Brownsea Island in Dorset, and the pool in Mallory Towers was inspired by the one at Dancing Ledge. For Enid Blyton family breaks, contact **Gingerpop** (01202 620660/www.gingerpop.co.uk).

grandiose Victorian building; and further along, on Peckham Road, **Camberwell College of Arts** (7514 6300) lends the neighbourhood some bohemian flair. The college is worth visiting for the shop alone, where art materials and stationery are discounted. Camberwell is also home to **Burgess Park** and, further south down Denmark Hill, **Ruskin Park**, which has a good playground and tennis courts.

If Camberwell is gritty, **Peckham** is grittier. It's had bad press of late, but good things are happening. In 2000, Will Alsop's avant-garde **Peckham Library** won the RIBA prize for Britain's best new building. Next door, the **Peckham Pulse** health centre (10 Melon Road, SE15, 7525 4999) offers further hope of renewal, with a pool, gym, all manner of sports facilities, a homeopathic drop-in-service, a baby clinic and a child-friendly (though not terribly health-foody) café.

Rye Lane, with its downmarket chains and smelly butcher's and fishmonger's, certainly isn't the prettiest high street in London. Still, there's plenty of action here, and the colours and scents are reminiscent of Brixton's lively market; the little side streets teem with interesting and exotic West Indian food shops. Walk to the end of this road and you'll reach **Peckham Rye Common**. The playground's, basic, but it's a lovely wide-open space with attractive gardens, a pond, and abundant bird life. To the east is **Nunhead Cemetery**, an overgrown Victorian cemetery which, ghoulish though this sounds, is quite a pleasant destination. Just west of here, Bellenden Road symbolises the gentrification of Peckham. It's a lovely little street, spruced up with interesting shops and a couple of good cafés. Will it become the new Clapham? Only time will tell.

Burgess Park

Albany Road, SE5 (park rangers 7525 1066). Elephant & Castle tube/rail, then 12, 42, 63, 68, 171, 343 bus. **Open** 24hrs daily. **Admission** free.

Designed as a green lung for South London, Burgess Park was created by demolishing old estates and terraced houses in the 1950s and covering over the Grand Surrey Canal. And in this somewhat depressing neighbourhood, it's literally a breath of fresh air. Although the park is not classically beautiful, it has its moments. Chumleigh Gardens is home to five different exotic garden styles:, Mediterranean, Caribbean, Islamic, oriental and English cottage. You can fish at the boating lake, rush about in the adventure playground, basketball or five-aside pitch or shelter in the indoor games room (7277 1371) with its pool table and ping pong. For some kids, the park's best bit is the kart track (7525 1110/1101) where parties cost £70 (minimum of ten drivers; ages eight to 16).

Imperial War Museum.
See p128.

On a worthier note, the park is a real boost to the community, through various creative schemes like Art in the Park (7277 4297/www.artinthepark.co.uk), which offers play and learning activities for kids throughout the year, including songs, dance and readings, as well as more park-like stuff such as tree and flower planting, picnics, and hide-and-seek.

Nunhead Cemetery

Limesford Road, SE15 (info 7732 9535). Nunhead rail. **Open** *Summer* 8.30am-7pm daily. *Winter* 8.30am-4pm daily. *Guided walks* 2pm last Sun of mth. **Admission** free; donations to FONC appreciated.

Coming here might sound like a morbid idea, but this is really one of the most tranquil and beautiful green spaces in South London. Wildly overgrown, the park resembles a lost Victorian garden. But the scruffy beauty lends itself well to the cemetery's other function as nature reserve, home to small mammals, insects, 16 species of butterfly and abundant bird life (woodpeckers and owls have been spotted here). For many people, however, the cemetery's main attraction is its elaborate 19th-century gravestones and monuments, fashioned out of limestone, granite and marble, now draped fetchingly in ivy. From the topmost paths there are fine views of London. There's a guided tour of the cemetery on the last Sunday of each month, starting from Linden Grove gates at 2pm. *Buggy access. Nappy-changing facilities.*

Peckham Library

122 Peckham Hill Street, SE15 (7525 0200). Peckham Rye or Queen's Road Peckham rail/12, 36, 63, 171 bus. **Open** 9am-8pm Mon, Tue, Thur, Fri; 10am-8pm Wed; 9am-5pm Sat; noon-4pm Sun.

Peckham Library has achieved the unthinkable: positive press for Peckham. Will Alsop's prize-winning pop-art masterpiece, opened in 2000, has brought colour and panache to a notoriously bleak high street and given the community a boost in the process. Outside, the square holds a Farmer's Market on Sundays (9.30am-1.30pm, call 7525 1073 for more info). Inside, the library's fourth floor has a good children's section with interesting coloured gass to smudge up with sticky fingers, far-reaching views over the fast-expanding estates of Lego-like houses going up all around here. There's a constant flurry of activity here: baby and toddler sessions every Tuesday, (with crafts, songs and rhymes), Bookstart sessions for under-fives, teenage and family reading groups, and a Summer Reading Challenge during school holidays. *Buggy access. Lift. Nappy-changing facilities.*

South London Gallery

65 Peckham Road, SE5 (7703 6120/ www.southlondongallery.org). Bus 12, 36, 171. **Open** 11am-6pm Tue, Wed, Fri; 11am-7pm Thur; 2-6pm Sat, Sun. Closed 25, 26 Dec, bank hols. **Admission** free.

They say Peckham is the next Hoxton, and if this cutting-edge gallery is any indication, they may be right. Although the gallery has showed classic works by artists such as John Ruskin, most of the exhibitions tend to deal with contemporary artists – Tracey Emin and Gilbert and George have been shown here in the past. To celebrate becoming independent from Southwark Council, the gallery is holding a special 'best of' show this summer, called Independents (mid-May-late July 2003), which will be a mixture of established artists and future stars. SLG director Margot Heller is keen to develop a family and schools programme at the gallery, and there are often children's quiz sheets to accompany exhibitions. *Nearest picnic place: Lucas Gardens.*

Dulwich & Herne Hill

Dulwich Village is one of south London's leafiest (and richest) neighbourhoods. If Northcote Road in Battersea is Nappy Valley, Dulwich Village is very nearly its twin, with legions of well-heeled young mums and babies roaming the high street and park. It has lovely food shops and a couple of children's clothing stores, and comes alive every May for the Dulwich Festival, a cultural jamboree with lots of activities for kids (call 8299 1011). South of the village you'll find **Dulwich Picture Gallery**, **Dulwich Park**, and **Dulwich College**, alma mater to PG Wodehouse and Raymond Chandler. East Dulwich is not quite as quaint, but is still attractive. Lordship Lane is lined with good shops and restaurants, and the area is home to the wonderful **London Wildlife Trust Centre for Wildlife Gardening**, once a derelict bus depot and now gardening nirvana for south-east Londoners.

Herne Hill is a gentler Brixton, with a nice cluster of shops, pubs and restaurants along Half Moon Lane, and some good parks – most notably **Brockwell Park**. Another visit-worthy park in the area is Sydenham Hill Wood, across the South Circular from **Dulwich Park**, which attracts all kinds of bird life. Don't miss the eccentric **Horniman Museum** in nearby Forest Hill: even if you don't go into the museum – which you surely should – the idyllic grounds and gardens preside over great views of south London.

Brockwell Park

Dulwich Road, SE24 (7926 0105). Herne Hill rail. **Open** 7am-dusk daily.

Brockwell Park is ten minutes' walk, but worlds away, from Brixton's urban grit. This hilly, verdant space is far prettier than its more famous south London counterpart, Clapham Common, and the park's highest point boasts picturesque views. There are tons of sporting facilities, too, including a bowling green, football pitch, BMX track and basketball court. Tennis courts must be booked in person.

Brockwell Park's main claim to fame, however, is one of the capital's most popular summer destinations: the Lido (*see p261*). The water's cold, but with the elegant 1930s-style architecture, sunbeds and palm trees, you feel as if you're on holiday in the tropics (if the sun shines).

Other reasons to visit include the annual Lambeth Country Show, held in July, and the First Come First Served Café. Housed in an impressive Victorian house at the top of the hill, the café is a good place for cheap Sunday roasts or weekday lunches, all-day fried breakfasts, chips, sarnies, ice cream and pop. They also do children's parties (birthday teas for around £4 per child; call 8671 5217 to enquire). *Buggy access. Café.*

Dulwich Park

College Road, SE21 (park rangers 8693 5737). North Dulwich or West Dulwich rail. **Open** 8am-dusk daily. This picturesque park is as pretty as the pastoral landscapes which hang in nearby Dulwich Gallery. It may soon be even more pleasant, as this year it came in for a vast grant for improvements courtesy of the Heritage Lottery Fund:

Around Town

improvements will include, it is hoped, the restoration of various historic features, replanting the flowerbeds, building a new car park and enhancing disabled access.

The smart playground has a brilliant 'spider web' climbing frame fashioned from taut ropes. Then there's the cycling: the London Recumbents company (8299 6636) hires and sells bikes and trailers, trikes, tandems and the eponymous horizontal bikes. Staff can also arrange cycling lessons for those who still rely heavily on their guider wheels (or have a problem with city riding). Special needs cycling and parties can also be arranged. Riders from the Dulwich Riding School (Dulwich Common, 8693 2944; lessons for children aged ten and above) can sometimes be seen on the park's sandy trails. Don't forget about the boating lake, nature trail, tennis courts, and bowling green.

If all this outdoorsy stuff makes you peckish, the well-run café with play area (independently refurbished in June 2003; the proprietors didn't get any of that grant) offers sustenance for all seasons: hot chocolate or chips on cold days, Kentish ice-cream on hot ones.
Buggy access. Café.

Dulwich Picture Gallery
Gallery Road, SE21 (8693 5254/www.dulwich picture gallery.org.uk). North Dulwich or West Dulwich rail/ P4 bus. **Open** 10am-5pm Tue-Fri; 11am-5pm Sat, Sun, bank hol Mon. Closed Good Friday, 24-26 Dec, 1 Jan. **Tours** 3pm Sat, Sun. **Admission** £4; £3 concessions; free under-16s; free to all Fri. *Tours* free. **Credit** MC, V.
The Dulwich Picture Gallery is famous for three reasons: it's England's first public gallery; the perfectly proportioned neoclassical building was designed by Sir John Soane; and, most importantly, it houses a stunning collection of Old Masters, including Rubens, Van Dyck, Cuyp, Poussin, Rembrandt, Gainsborough, Raphael and Reynolds. The gallery added a new wing in 2000, which has a smart café, where many local families meet for light lunches or a cream tea with scones after an afternoon's gazing at the Old Masters. The new wing is also where the educational department runs its activities for children. In the temporary gallery here future exhibitions

---

DON'T MISS
The Horniman Museum

African Worlds Gallery
The Egyptian mummy; the Nigerian ijele mask.

The Aquarium
The four-eyed fish from South American mangroves; clown fish from tropical reefs.

Centenary Gallery
Sri Lankan healing masks; the Spanish Inquisition torture chair.

The Gardens
Surly turkeys in the animal enclosure.

Music Gallery
Amazing listening tables in the main gallery; bashable instruments in the Hands-on room.

Natural History Gallery
The walrus, somewhat overstuffed in the 1880s. *See p132.*

---

include a Children's Art Exhibition (the work of local school kids, 20 June-6 July), Shakespeare in Art (16 July-19 October) and William Heath Robinson (November-January).

Children's activities include a Saturday arts school (ages 12 to 15), after-school art club (tens to 13s), portfolio development courses (11s to 14s) and Sunday afternoon family art or storytelling sessions. Call 8299 8731 for details. *See also p209. Buggy access. Café. Nappy-changing facilities. Nearest picnic place: gallery gardens. Shop.*

Horniman Museum
100 London Road, SE23 (8699 1872/www.horniman. ac.uk). Forest Hill rail/63, 122, 176, 185, 312, 352, P4 bus. **Open** 10.30am-5.30pm daily. Closed 24-26 Dec. **Admission** free; donations appreciated. **Credit** *Shop* MC, V.
The final stage in the improvement programme at this much-loved free museum is the grass-roofed environment room, a resource centre whose opening date was not finalised as we went to press. This, and the rest of the museum, founded by collector and tea trader Frederick Horniman more than a century ago, is accessible from gorgeous gardens. The outdoor spaces, with their views over south London, animal enclosure, a bandstand – often the focus for children's entertainments in the summer holidays – and picnic areas, are pretty all year round, and the stunning Victorian conservatory by the museum entrance is used for concerts and functions.

A stuffed walrus (actually anatomically incorrect due to enthusiastic overstuffing in the 1880s; the taxidermist clearly didn't know when to stop) presides fatly over the Natural History Gallery and specimens, and skeletons behind glass cases stare glassily. Fish, frogs and strange examples of pondlife, all alive and swimming, are displayed in the large tanks of the Aquarium. Downstairs, the music room has been revamped, so now you can look at the beautifully assembled instrument collection and hear how they sound via large table top screens. For a spot of hands-on, there's a hammered dulcimer, bongos, singing bowls and bodhrans all set up for young visitors to bash. Masks, costumes, spears and other curiosities fill the centenary gallery. The main exhibition of 2003 is Puppet Worlds, which finishes on 2 November (admission charge £3 adults, £2 children, £8 family (2+2), free under-3s). Workshops are run in conjunction with the show.

Aim to be in the vicinity of the ornate apostle clock, which adorns the balcony area of the Natural History gallery, in time for the 4pm chimes. At this time carved models of Jesus' faithful eleven come out of various crannies, but the twelfth, representing Judas, turns away. A fund has been launched to have the clock mended, since it tends to forget itself, but pop by anyway, you may strike it lucky.

The shop is full of natural history-based toys, games, puzzles and stationery. An airy café restaurant does a child-size sausage and chips, several hot dishes of the day, hot snacks, cakes, ice-creams and proper hot chocolate. Ring up to be put on the free mailing list for clubs, courses and activities. *Café. Nappy-changing facilities. Nearest picnic place: Horniman gardens. Shop.*

London Wildlife Trust Centre for Wildlife Gardening
28 Marsden Road, SE15 (7252 9186/www.wildlondon. org.uk). East Dulwich rail. **Open** 10.30am-4.30pm Tue-Thur, Sun. **Admission** free.
London is getting wilder by the minute. The London Wildlife Trust has spent the past 20 years reclaiming derelict land for wildlife reserves and campaigning to preserve existing nature spots. The LWT's flagship properties include Camley Street Natural Park in King's Cross (*see p92*) and this surprising

Avoiding the hill path in **Brockwell Park**. *See p131.*

spot. Surprising, because who knew that an old brownfield site could eventually be home to so many different types of garden? This place has a wildlife meadow, woodland, marsh and herb gardens, and a nursery for native plants and trees. In one corner there are beehives, in another large coldframes of plants you can take home in (donations to the Wildlife Trust can be given in exchange).

Every March, people descend upon the centre for Frog Day. For children, there's a play area and sandpit, and the visitors' centre – where school parties congregate – has tanks full of fish and stick insects. Children can join the Wildlife Watch, which organises environmental activities such as bat walks, pond dipping and wildlife surveys including the great stag beetle hunt. To join the Trust enquire at the centre or contact London Wildlife Trust (Harling House, 47-51 Great Suffolk Street, SE1 0BS, 7261 0447/www.wildlondon.org.uk). *Buggy access. Nappy-changing facilities.*

Crystal Palace

Crystal Palace's main claim to fame burned down many years ago. The spectacular glass and cast-iron palace, designed by Sir Joseph Paxton for the 1851 Great Exhibition in Hyde Park, was moved here in 1853 and packed in punters before being destroyed by fire in 1936. Today the park still draws the crowds, but for other reasons – mainly the sports centre, wide open spaces, and those cherished plaster dinosaurs. The outdoor stadium hosts athletic events and a number of rock concerts. There's really no Crystal Palace neighbourhood as such. The park is surrounded by Anerley, Penge, Sydenham, Gipsy Hill and Upper Norwood, and the whole area is one of hills and valleys.

Crystal Palace Museum
Anerley Hill, SE19 (8676 0700). Crystal Palace rail. **Open** 11am-5pm Sun, bank hol Mon. **Admission** free. Harking back to the glory days of Crystal Palace, this little museum tells the story of the glass structure's rise and fall.

The museum building is nothing spectacular, but it was once the old engineering school where John Logie Baird invented television, for which we are all duly grateful.

Crystal Palace Park
Crystal Palace Information Centre, Thicket Road, SE20 (8778 9496). Crystal Palace rail/2, 3, 63, 108B, 122, 157, 227 bus. **Open** *Information centre* 9am-5pm daily (later in summer). *Park* dawn-dusk daily. **Admission** free.
The much vaunted Crystal Palace park facelift goes on and on. It's about time it was restored. During its Victorian heyday, the park was home to a spectacular glass palace – built for the 1851 Great Exhibition and moved here in 1853 – and an amusement park, not to mention some of London's most exquisitely landscaped gardens. In 1950 the construction of a TV transmitter gave South London its very own Eiffel Tower (well, sort of). Visitors were also drawn to the park for its striking, life-sized model dinosaurs and London's only garden maze. But a fire in 1936 burned the ornate palace to the ground, and in recent years the park has been looking increasingly shabby. In a bid to reverse the downward trend, Bromley council has embarked on a £3.6 million restoration programme. The dinosaurs – now classified as listed buildings – have been repaired, and the gardens are being restored to their former glory: landscape gardeners are planting scores of exotic plants not seen here since Victorian times, the lakes are being streamlined and a new rhododendron dell is in the works. A city farm and woodland garden are also promised, although progress seems rather slow.

Until the work is complete, visitors must make do with a wonderfully overgrown old maze (much more romantic than the neat and tidy one at Hampton Court in Surrey), a playground, a small museum about the history of the palace (open Sundays) and a café. Italianate stone terraces nod to the park's former grandeur, and the old lion statues make a good photo opportunity for the kids.

The National Sports Centre, though shockingly ugly and in need of cosmetic attention, has a busy programme of events for all ages and abilities. It has a spectacular Olympic-sized pool, a diving pool, and a toasty-warm 25m leaning pool. There are basketball, volleyball and badminton courts, a climbing wall, trampolines, karate classes, a football pitch,

Horniman Museum.
See p132.

track and field activities, a dance studio, summer sports camps, a playroom which can be hired out for birthday parties and a crèche where adults can leave the kids while they work out in the gym. For general enquiries about sports and classes call 8778 0131. A separate building houses a mini-gym (call 8659 4561 to enquire about courses). Delicate architectural sensibilities might rue the day this eyesore went up, but the National Sports Centre has proved a popular draw, ensuring Crystal Palace Park is as vibrant a place today as it was a hundred years ago.
Buggy access. Cafe. Nappy-changing facilities.

Further south-east

Many people scoff at suburban South-east London, but the area has some natural treasures. Oxleas Wood (just across the Shooters Hill Road from Falconwood rail station, in Welling, Kent) is an 8,000-year-old piece of woodland, dating back to the Ice Age, which unbelievably, was earmarked for uprooting back in the mid-90s – until a campaign stopped the bulldozers, much to the relief of many a jogger, cyclist and day-outing family. A gallows once stood at the entrance to the woods, ready to stretch the necks of the many highwaymen that worked in the area. There are fine views of Kent all kinds of interesting fauna and, in May, spectacular bluebells; but be careful – the woods have a dense network of paths, it's easy to get lost. Some paths link up with the **Green Chain Walk**, a 40-mile network which starts near the Thames Barrier and ends at Crystal Palace (8921 5028/www.greenchain.com). The Oxleas Wood one starts at Erith and takes in the ancient ruins of the 12th-century Lesnes Abbey, a perfect place for a picnic (there are loos and an information centre), with incongruous towerblock views to the north.

Woodlands Farm, an organic farm open to the public is just off Shooter's Hill, (which is the name of an area in this part of Kent as well as the road to it that starts near Blackheath). Dick Turpin's cave is nearby (a small hole near Bostall Woods, not much to see so one doubts he spent much time in there).

Croydon and **Bromley** are both prosperous, family-friendly suburbs. Though Croydon is notorious for its office-block landscape, it has excellent environmental credentials: it's the third greenest London borough, both in terms of park space and environmentally friendly initiatives. It's also famous for its £200 million tram system, and as if that weren't enough, it has great shopping in the Whitgift Centre. In fact, as suburbs go, Croydon is a bit of a dark horse. **Croydon Clocktower** has three galleries, a library, a theatre space, a cinema and a café. The **Warehouse Theatre Company** (Dingwall Road, Croydon, Surrey CR0 2NF, 8680 4060/www.warehousetheatre.co.uk), offers a different children's production every Saturday morning and a teenage drama workshop and writing workshops, not to mention pantos at Christmas. Plane spotters will get all excited at the **Croydon Airport Visitor Centre** (Purley Way, CR0, 8669 1196) which opens to the public on the first Sunday of each month. Housed in the control tower, the centre is run by volunteers and is full of hands-on exhibits which celebrate the airport's heyday. At the other end of Purley Way lies the reason most people have been to Croydon: IKEA. Nearby is a big Toys 'R' Us, Children's World, and TGI Fridays. Bromley, meanwhile, has an excellent library on the edge of a lovely park, and a consumer magnet in the form of the Glades Shopping Centre.

But neither of the aforementioned shrines to consumerism can hold a candle to the mother of all shopping centres: **Bluewater** (08456 021021). Situated at Greenhithe, Kent, in a valley surrounded by chalk cliffs, this super-mall blends in with nature more than most behemoths of its kind. It's circled by lovely ornamental gardens, lakes and bike trails (you can rent cycles on site). Inside you'll find a crèche, cinema and other family-friendly facilities, but there's no getting around Bluewater's true purpose: parting you from your money. To this end it houses England's best collection of shops assembled under one roof.

For a change of pace, head to the pretty suburb of **Chislehurst**, which still has a nostalgic feel and is also home to one of Kent's great geographical wonders, the **Chislehurst Caves**.

Bexleyheath has South-east London's newest public attraction: **Red House** (13 Red House Lane, DA6, 0870 458 4000). Commissioned by William Morris and designed by Philip Webb, two of the founding fathers of the Arts and Crafts movement, the house was built in 1859. Morris lived here for five years and its gardens inspired many of his famous wallpaper and fabric designs. The interior was decorated by Morris and Webb with the help of Rossetti and Burne-Jones. The National Trust plans to open the house and garden to visitors in summer 2003, and promises full educational facilities, teas on the lawn and a holiday flat in the grounds.

Croydon Clocktower

Katharine Street, Croydon, Surrey (info 8760 5400/ box office 8253 1030/shop 8253 1035/ tourist info 8253 1009/www.croydon.gov.uk/clocktower). East Croydon or West Croydon rail/George Street tram. **Open** *Clocktower & library 9am-7pm Mon; 9am-6pm Tue, Wed, Fri; 9.30am-6pm Thur; 9am-5pm Sat; 2-5pm Sun. Café Opera 9am-5.30pm Mon-Wed, Fri; 9.30am-5.30pm Thur; 9am-4.30pm Sat; noon-4.30pm Sun, bank hols. Tourist Information Centre 9am-6pm Mon, Wed, Fri; 9.30am-6pm Thur; 9am-5pm Sat; 2-5pm Sun. Gallery 11am-5pm Mon-Sat; noon-5pm Sun.*

Croydon Clocktower, built in 1896, is a splendid Victorian building – a stark contrast to all the surrounding office blocks. It also has a corker of a museum, tracing the history and future of Croydon, with lots of interactive exhibits, stories about real-life Croydonites, and a dressing-up corner. Exhibitions this year include Fascinating Forces (until September) a science exhibition for children, and a big, Croydon-themed photography show (October-February). The museum offers children's workshops, ranging from sculp-

ture, poetry, calligraphy and crafts (call 8253 1023 for details) The David Lean cinema is renowned for its Tick Tock children's club, every Saturday at 11am.

The Braithwaite Hall hosts weekend and holiday theatre productions for children. There's an excellent library, with a huge children's section with regular storytelling, music and art sessions. The Clocktower also provides a Saturday crèche. *Café. Nappy-changing facilities. Nearest picnic place: Queen's Gardens. Shop.*

Woodlands Farm

331 Shooters Hill, Welling, Kent (8319 8900/ www.thewoodlandsfarmtrust.org). Falconwood rail/89, 486 bus. **Open** *9am-5pm daily.* **Admission** *free; donations appreciated.*

Spread out over 89 acres on the border of Greenwich and Bexley, Woodlands Farm is a bittersweet reminder of what Kent used to look like, pre-urban sprawl. But in 1995 it was very nearly bulldozed to make way for a proposed East London crossing. Fortunately the Woodlands Farm Trust, with the help of lottery money, came to the rescue. It bought the derelict farmhouse and surrounding field, and turned it into a thriving organic farm. And no poxy city farm, either: there are geese, hens, 170 sheep, 12 cows and a couple of Shire horses. A core staff keeps the place ticking over, but volunteers are welcome to help out. The farm hosts school tours, which include lessons on topics such as farm animal care, conservation, composting, a history of farming and, in season, making apple juice. A typical Kentish orchard is being planted, so there shoud be plenty of fruit for the juices. *Buggy access. Café (open Sun only). Nearest picnic place: farm grounds.*

Chislehurst Caves

Explore the dark and spooky caves at Chislehurst and you'll think you've stumbled into a Famous Five novel. The tour guides tell spine-tingling mystery stories about these secret hollows, but such embellishments are almost superfluous: the history of these underground chambers is fascinating in its own right.

The Druids carved the passages and chambers out of the hillside, digging for chalk and flint (they also came here to make grisly human sacrifices). In due course the Romans extracted chalk here too, and more recently the caves were used as an ammunition dump during World War I and a suitably dark mushroom farm in the 1930s. But the caves only became famous during World War II, when they formed Britain's largest bomb shelter. At one point, 15,000 people took refuge underground. Equipped with a cinema, hospital (a baby was born here) and chapel (an underground marriage is still possible), the 22-mile network became a subterranean city.

The tour covers a mile. It's not strenuous, but it's not for the claustrophobic or the faint of heart, either: at one point the lanterns are extinguished and you're engulfed by darkness. It's a tour that captures the imagination – how those plucky Kent residents could bunk down in the damp and gloom is beyond us. For an unusual birthday party, private tours are available for children

SEVEN SUBTERRANEAN FACTS

● Guitar nibbler Jimi Hendrix once performed a concert in Chislehurst Caves.

● An unfortunate baby born in the cave hospital during the war was named Cavina, which really sounds like some sort of cough medicine.

● During Victorian times, guides were accompanied by a search dog who could sniff out any visitor who had strayed from the party.

● The caves at one time had their own classroom (imagine having your lessons in a cave!), post office, bank and telephone booth.

● Resident ghosts include a Roman centurion who was speared to death in the caves, an unfortunate, whinnying horse who died when stables collapsed into the caves, and a woman who was murdered in one of the rock pools.

● In 1985, a tour guide decided to sleep in the caves overnight. He wound up in the hospital after an unknown presence knocked him out. Overnight stays in the caves have since been banned.

● A particularly spooky episode of *Doctor Who* was filmed in the Chislehurst Caves.

Chislehurst Caves

Chislehurst, Kent (8467 3264/ www.chislehurstcaves.co.uk). Chislehurst rail. **Open** 10am-4pm Wed-Sun. **Admission** £4; £2 children, OAPs.

LUNCH BREAK

Around Rotherhithe

Arbuckles (*Mast Leisure Park, Surrey Quays Road, SE16, 7232 1901*), for burgers, pizzas, chips, kids' menus and general over-excitement.
The Good Food Deli (*70 St Marychurch Street, SE16, 7394 9654*), for paninis and picnic fare.
The Mayflower (*117 Rotherhithe Street, SE16, 7237 4088*), for traditional pub grub and a welcome for kids upstairs.
Pizza Hut (*Mast Leisure Park, Surrey Quays Road, SE16, 7231 1414; see p175*), for generously proportioned pizzas and popular kids' menus.
Spice Island (*163 Rotherhithe Street, SE16, 7394 7108*), for a fairly typical kiddy menu in a former spice warehouse: kids welcome until 8pm.
Best place for picnics: Southwark Park.

Around Greenwich

Chibchas (*170 Trafalgar Road, SE10, 8293 0626*), a supper venue for pan-American food.
Goddard's Pie House (*24 Greenwich Church Street, SE10, 8293 9313*), good old seaside faves: mash, sausage, eels 'n' all.
Inside (*19A Greenwich South Street, SE10, 8265 5060*) has a decent Saturday brunch menu.
The North Pole (*131 Greenwich High Road, SE10, 8853 3020*), for good roasts and affordable nipper food on Sundays.
Park Café (*Greenwich park, main entrance, SE10, 8858 9695*), for drinks, cakes and ice-cream in prime picnic territory.
The Trafalgar Tavern (*Park Row, SE10, 8858 2437*), for kids' menus and historic atmosphere.
Best place for picnics: Greenwich Park.

Around Blackheath & Lewisham

Blackheath Fish & Chips (*1 Blackheath Village, SE3, 8852 3360*), everything it says on the tin.
Café Rouge (*16-18 Montpelier Vale, SE3, 8297 2727; see p182*), popular lunchtime spot.
Caffè Uno (*58-62 Tranquil Vale, Blackheath, SE3, 8463 9155; see p182*), a café with kids' menu.
Chapter Two (*43-5 Montpelier Vale, SE3, 8333 2666; see p177*), posh modern European cuisine.
The Clarendon Hotel (*Montpelier Row, SE3, 8318 4321*), traditional Sunday roast and kiddy portions.
Manor House Gardens Café (*Brightfield Road, SE12, 8318 1358; see p125*), a great park café.
Zero Degrees (*29-31 Montpelier Vale, SE3, 8852 5619*), for pizzas and a microbrewery.
Best place for picnics: Blackheath.

Around the Elephant

Kennington Lane Bar & Restaurant (*205-209 Kennington Lane, SE11, 7793 8313*), a trendy joint that lets in babies and kids at lunchtime.
La Luna (*380 Walworth Road, SE17, 7277 1991*), a family-run trattoria serving pizza and pasta.
Pizzeria Castello (*20 Walworth Road, SE1, 7703 2556; see p175*), for great garlic bread.

Pizza Express (*316 Kennington Road, SE11, 7820 3877*), a safe bet for pizzas.
Best place for picnics: Geraldine Mary Harmsworth park, outside the Imperial War Museum.

Around Dulwich & Herne Hill

Barcelona Tapas Bar y Restaurante (*481 Lordship Lane, SE22, 8693 5111*) is the place for an extensive tapas menu.
Blue Mountain Café (*18 North Cross Road, SE22, 8299 6953*), perfect coffee spot.
Café Noodles (*159 Lordship Lane, SE22, 8693 4016*), good for a cheap, quick carbohydrate fix.
Crown & Greyhound (*73 Dulwich Village, SE21, 8299 4976*), a much-loved pub with a children's menu and a garden to play in.
Horniman Museum (*100 London Road, SE23, 8699 1872; see p132*), a smart, light and airy café with outdoor tables and children's specials.
Olley's (*67-69 Norwood Road, SE24, 8671 8259; see p177*), fish 'n' chips that pull 'em in from afar.
Le Piaf (*75-7 Dulwich Village, SE21, 8693 9331*), another village favourite with a children's menu of soup, goujons, sausage or pasta.
3 Monkeys (*136-40 Herne Hill, SE24, 7738 5500*), posh Indian food, and children can eat free (7-7.30pm, one child per adult).
Best place for picnics: Dulwich Park

Around Camberwell & Peckham

Cohiba (*58A Camberwell Church Street, SE5, 7740 6677*), for authentic Mexican fare.
The Fox on the Hill (*149 Denmark Hill, SE5, 7738 4756*), the children's menu lists all their favourite accompaniments to chips, or spag bol.
Funky Munky (*25 Camberwell Church Street, SE5, 7277 1806*), for burgers and comfort food.
Nando's (*88 Denmark Hill, SE5, 7738 3808; see p182*), let them loose on the refillable pop! The chicken chain comes to Camberwell.
Peckham Experiment (*168 Bellenden Road, SE15, 7252 9424*), a simple venue for smart international cuisine and portions for children.
Petitou (*63 Choumert Road, SE15, 07932 508450*), a friendly café with toys, own-roasted Fairtrade coffee and sticky cakes for the kids.
The Rock 8 (*119 Grove Lane, SE5, 7733 7927*), for Spanish and South American tapas.
Seymour Bros (*2-4 Grove Lane, SE5, 7701 4944*), popular deli and sandwich bar.
Sun & Doves (*61-3 Coldharbour Lane, SE5, 7733 1525*), trendy pub-restaurant-gallery, lovely garden.
Best place for picnics: Burgess Park.

Around Crystal Palace

Domali Café (*38 Westow Street, SE19, 8768 0096*), veggie soups and pasta in kiddy portions.
Joanna's (*56 Westow Hill, SE19, 8670 4052*), friendly brasserie with a children's menu.
Best place for picnics: Crystal Palace Park.

South-west London

Where you'll find acres of greenery between the urban bits.

Vauxhall & Stockwell

What's left of the Vauxhall Pleasure Gardens? When Vauxhall was a village to the south of the city, and gentlefolk wanted to take the air, it was to this fashionable park, used for concerts, shows and displays, that they repaired. Now, there's only a small park – Spring Gardens – bounded by Tyers Street, Goding Street and Glasshouse Walk to remind you of the area's 18th-century heyday. **Vauxhall Park** (South Lambeth Road, at the junction with Fentiman Road, SW8) has some well-manicured areas for quiet contemplation, as well as tennis courts, a bowling green, a play area, a one o'clock club and a fenced ball-game area. Opposite Spring Gardens is the eminently child-friendly **Vauxhall City Farm**.

Another green space is Bonnington Square's Pleasure Garden. The garden started life as a play area during the 1970s, but subsequently lay neglected for years, until local residents pulled away the nettles to form the latest attraction – a secret garden with a restored Victorian water wheel. Look toward the river beside the trafficky Vauxhall Bridge to marvel at what many children call the 'Spies' Building', imagining James Bond flirting with Miss Moneypenny within. It's the MI6 building, once the target of a missile attack from the Real IRA.

Stockwell's green spaces are few and far between, though **Slade Gardens** on Robsart Street has an adventure playground, play areas and a one o'clock club. Over on Stockwell's west side, **Larkhall Park**, on Larkhall Rise, is a peaceful open space, with a one o'clock club, picnic areas, a café, two ball game areas, tennis courts, a walled garden, a playground and nappy-changing facilities.

The skate park at the start of Stockwell Road as you leave Brixton is a star attraction for gangs of kids, especially in summer. Graded concrete bumps let fancy-footed skaters and bladers show off their skills (*see also p259*). A bike track is popular with the BMX kids. Abundant graffiti renders the park an eyesore to older people, perhaps, but it's easy to gauge its popularity among the youth.

Vauxhall City Farm
24 St Oswald's Place, Tyers Street, SE11 (7582 4204). Vauxhall tube/rail. **Open** 10.30am-4pm Tue-Thur, Sat, Sun. **Admission** free; donations appreciated.
It's a bit of an irony that a child living in Vauxhall may know more about pigs and donkeys than one living in a rural village, but that's London for you. Bella (pig) and Jacko (donkey) and their pals (goats, chickens, rabbits, guinea pigs) have been teaching generations of city children about country life since 1977, when a couple of acres of derelict land were transformed into this miniature farm.
Buggy access. Disabled: toilet.

Brixton

The capital of liberal Lambeth still has an edgy urban vibe that is all of its own, despite pockets of genteel resistance (pop into Trinity Gardens for a glimpse of gentrified Brixton). There are artists and anarchists who've been squatting here since the 1970s, and the sizeable black population makes up almost a third of Brixton's residents. By day, the area's mixed-up craziness is best experienced by strolling through chaotic **Brixton Market**.

The lack of green spaces in the area mean that most attention in Lambeth is focused on **Brockwell Park** (*see p131*), which, by dint of its SE postcode, is included in the previous chapter. Brockwell Park in fact joins Herne Hill to Brixton, so it is as much a valued green lung here as there. People come from miles around to take a dip in the fantastic lido.

Brixton's pride is the **Ritzy** cinema (*see p212*), built in 1911 and whose Kids' Club is one of south London's best bargains: children's tickets cost only £1 (£2 for accompanying adults) on Saturdays throughout the year, and on Tuesdays and Thursdays during school holidays. Parents can partake of free tea, coffee and newspapers in the Ritzy Crush Bar. The Watch with Baby screenings let parents take their under-ones into a film.

Battersea

About 300 years ago melons, lavender, carrots and asparagus grew in Battersea fields, and the people of the area worked as market gardeners to feed the City of London. Nowadays the people of Battersea work in the City of London and have their asparagus flown in: how's that for progress? In the interim, Battersea developed as an industrial area, with factories by the river and miles of little houses in the north of the borough for the factory workers. With the coming of the railway, more substantial residences mushroomed towards the south. Today these solidly Victorian residential streets hide small treasures like the **Battersea Arts Centre** (*see p217*) and big ones like **Battersea Park**.

Vauxhall City Farm. A cheerful place to be. *See p137.*

Battersea Dogs' Home

4 Battersea Park Road, SW8 (7622 3626/www.dogshome. org). Vauxhall tube/rail then 44 bus/Battersea Park or Queenstown Road rail. **Open** *Viewings* 10.30am-4.15pm Mon-Wed, Fri; 10.30am-3.15pm Sat, Sun. **Admission** £1; 50p concessions, under-16s; free under-5s. **Credit** *Shop* MC, V.

If you're looking for a pet, there are around 300 cats and dogs in need of a new home here at any one time – though if you fall in love you'll be vetted by the rightly circumspect staff before you can take one home. Many of the dogs are unsuitable for homes with young children, but the staff do their best to match up the right animal with willing adoptive families. It's worth making a few visits before taking any serious adoption decisions, anyway. The shop is also a good source of unusual presents, with its doggy-themed stationery, souvenirs and toys, and there's a café for drinks and snacks. *Buggy access. Café. Disabled: lift, toilet. Nearest picnic place: Battersea Park. Shop.*

Latchmere Leisure Centre

Latchmere Leisure Centre, Burns Road, SW11 (7207 8004/www.kinetica.org). Clapham Junction or Battersea Park rail. Bus 319, 344, 345, 49, 44. **Open** 7am-10.30pm Mon-Thur; 7am-10pm Fri; 7am-8pm Sat; 7am-10pm Sun. *Crèche* 9.45-11.45 am Mon-Fri. **Admission** *Crèche* £3.50.

The Latchmere had a major makeover in 2002. The pool is still the same gently-shelving lagoon (with wave machine and toddler-friendly elephant slide); but the whole changing area is now unisex, with public lockers visible from poolside. The café is bright and clean, with a soft play area alongside for under-eights. *See also p261*
Buggy access. Café. Car park. Crèche. Disabled: toilet, showers. Nappy changing facilities. Nearest picnic place: Battersea Park.

Clapham

In the 18th century, the 'village on the hill' was prized for its clean air and health springs. These days the air is not quite so clean, but the area is still famously desirable. East of the common, Clapham Old Town is a precious little cluster of pubs, shops and restaurants around what might resemble a village green if it weren't for all the 88 buses (rather tweely known as the Clapham Omnibus) revving up noisily by the bus terminal.

The **Clapham Picture House** (*see p211*), a rep cinema with a busy Saturday morning Kids' Club, is a godsend on a rainy weekend; but for most local families the prime leisure destination is **Clapham Common**, whatever the weather. This flat, windy space has a chequered history. In the 18th century it had a vermin problem: hedgehogs and polecats were the main offenders, and hunters were paid to cull them. During World War I it was turned over to food cultivation; and in World War II tunnels and caverns were dug beneath it as training posts for army radio operators; these underground mazes were pressed into service as reception centres for immigrants from the Caribbean in the 1940s. Now the common is south-west London's playground. Australian rules football, a London-South American football league, camogie or softball.all take place at weekends. The Urban Games is a summer event, with motor stunts and skateboard tricks in a walled arena.

If you'd rather play than watch, book one of the seven tennis courts on the west side of the common beside the bowling green. An experienced tennis coach teaches children as young as four in drop-in sessions every summer holiday, and there are a couple of cricket nets nearby. Behind **Café Common** (8677 0514) is a rather scruffy-looking netball court, and the bandstand in the middle of the common does service as an ad hoc skateboard arena (its Oom Pah Pah Café is a popular lunch or coffee venue for parents, nannies and their charges).

The bare patch by the South Circular is the pitch for any visiting circus or fair. Recent guests have included the Moscow State Circus, the Chinese State Circus and Spirit of the Horse.

Streatham

In its heyday, Streatham was a hotbed of intellectual and artistic activity: Dr Johnson, Edmund Burke, David Garrick, Joshua Reynolds and Fanny Burney all lived here. By the late 19th century, and the coming of the railway, the area was losing its rural charm to streets of workers' houses. Inter-war development and post-war bombsite infill completed the picture in the 20th century, making Streatham the diverse residential neighbourhood it is today, popular with families who love the play spaces of **Streatham Common** and **Tooting Common**.

The big blot on the local landscape is the A23, aka Streatham High Road. Though traffic-heavy, it's also the road to Streatham's family attractions: at the top, near Streatham Hill station, is **Streatham Megabowl** (*see p264*) and further down, by the station, is **Streatham Ice Arena** (*see p256*), a fine spot for skating (including affordable six-week courses) and spectator ice hockey; it's also a good venue for birthday parties. Also on the High Road is **Playscape Pro Racing** (*see p257*), a karting track popular with speed fiends aged eight and up.

To the east, Streatham Common is an airy slope bordered on all sides by busy roads, with views south over Thornton Heath to Croydon. A top place for kite flying, you can let the kids off the leash here. The common's hidden treasure is the **Rookery** (8679 1635), a little formal garden. It's a lovely place in which to picnic and enjoy views over London, and in summer music wafts over from the seasonal open-air theatre; there's also a café. When you've restored your soul and the children are screaming for something more exciting, go exploring in the woods and commons of Norwood Grove, where – if you keep your eyes peeled – you may even see the celebrated population of ring-necked parakeets.

Tooting & Balham

Tooting Common (Tooting Bec Road, SW17) makes living here lovely. It's a wide, open space with woods, tennis courts, ponds, football pitches, playgrounds for the under-eights, Tooting Bec athletics track and **Tooting Bec Lido** (*see p261*), where up to 2,000 people a day gather in summer to enjoy the pools and the 1930s café.

As Clapham rose into the house market stratosphere during the 1990s, Tooting and Balham soaked up the overspill. Nowadays they're as sought after and almost as expensive as their prettier neighbour, although thanks to their resistance to wholesale gentrification they're more interesting.

Tooting is home to a well-established Asian community, and the annual Diwali Festival of Light (October/November) is celebrated with a street party and lights strung along Tooting High Street and Upper Tooting Road. The area has several excellent restaurants serving South Asian food, and though their proprietors stop short of kiddy menus and balloons, babies and children are welcome in most places, and smaller portions are available on request.

Tooting High Street, incidentally, has been a thoroughfare since Roman times, and was once the main road from Londinium to Regnum (Chichester).

Wandsworth

The area around Wandsworth Common toward Clapham and up to Battersea is often called Nappy Valley, because so many families with young children choose to settle here. This common is better looking than Clapham, and has a one o'clock club, various playgrounds, numerous sports clubs and facilities for young environmentalists.

Lakeside at **Battersea Park**.
See p148.

Nature Study Centre

Wandsworth Common, Dorlcote Road, SW18 (8871 3863). Wandsworth Common rail **Open** *3-5pm Wed; 4-6pm Thur; 11am-1pm Sat; 2.30-4.30pm 1st and 3rd Sun of month.* **Admission** *free.*

Wandsworth Common is cut in two by the London to Brighton railway line, but in spite of the trains rattling through up to 20 times an hour, it's a haven for a surprisingly diverse range of wildlife – stag beetles, frogs, dragonflies herons and all sorts of other birdlife. The Nature Study Centre is a timber cabin on the common, where staff teach children about wildlife through crafts, games and 'field trips' in the immediate environment. Watch, the junior branch of the Wildlife Trust, meets here on the third Sunday of the month, and there's a great little after-school nature club on Thursdays; the frequent wildlife-spotting activities are geared to Mother Nature's calendar.

Buggy access. Disabled access: toilet.

Wandle Recreation Centre, Playzone

Mapleton Road, SW18 (8871 1149/www.kinetica.com). Wandsworth Town rail. **Open** *7.30am-11pm Mon-Fri; 9am-8pm Sat; 9am-10pm Sun. Crèche 10am-noon Mon, Wed, Fri.* **Admission** *Crèche £2.70.* **Credit** *MC, V.*

Along the banks of the Wandle and just outside the gates of King George Park, the Wandle has football pitches for local teams, football and sports parties. The Kinetika fitness room allows parents a workout and there's a padded play zone with climbing frames and sliding tubes which is popular with the under-eights just outside.

Buggy access. Car park. Disabled: toilet. Nappy changing facilities. Nearest picnic space: Kin George's Park.

Wandsworth Museum

The Courthouse, Garratt Lane, Wandsworth, SW18 (8871 7074/www.wandsworth.gov.uk). Wandsworth Town BR, 28, 37, 39, 44, 77A, 156, 170, 220, 270, 337 bus. **Open** *10am-5pm Tue-Sat, 2am-5pm Sun. Closed Bank Hols.* **Admission** *free.*

Wandsworth is proud of its long history, and after a visit round the frequently changing exhibits in this friendly local museum, you will be impressed too. There are plenty of 'interactive' exhibits – you can try on the Roman helmet found in the mud at Battersea or become a Celtic chieftain for the day – and very hands-on craft and play workshops for children during holidays and half terms.

Buggy access. Disabled: toilet. Nappy changing facilities. Nearest picnic space: King George's Park or Old Burial Ground. Shop.

Wimbledon

For a fortnight in the summer the eyes of the world are on SW19; for the rest of the year it's all yours. Tennis is only the most famous sporting attraction of this leafy suburb. There's also non-league football with a new local club taking over from Wimbledon FC since its move to Milton Keynes. There's also riding from the stables on **Wimbledon Common**. For lessons try **Wimbledon Village Stables** (24A-B High Street, SW19, 8946 8579) or **Ridgway Stables** (93 Ridgway, SW19, 8946 7400).

Wimbledon Common itself is huge. You can ride on it, cycle on it, walk the dog on it or just walk on it. Whatever you choose to do, there's a rich selection of wildlife to look out for. The nature trail, which loops away from the windmill, is accessible to buggies – but if nature floods it you might not get through. If that happens, visit the **Windmill Museum** (Windmill Road, SW19, 8947 2825) instead and see where Robert Baden-Powell wrote *Scouting for Boys* in 1908. Elsewhere on the common there are ten ponds rich in water life, but the best (from a child's point of view) is **Seven Post Pond**, where a dipping platform lets you observe watery monsters might lurk in there without trampling their habitat.

Cycle up to Wimbledon Station forecourt at 10.30am on the last Sunday of each month for PPPs (Parks, Playgrounds and Pubs) family bike rides. Routes are low on, or devoid of, traffic and not too long. Kids in bike trailers are welcome, and there's no need to book – just turn up and pedal away.

Deen City Farm

39 Windsor Avenue, SW19 (8543 5300/www.deencity farm.co.uk). Colliers Wood tube/200 bus. **Open** *9am-5pm Tue-Sun.* **Admission** *free; donations welcome.*

This smartly kept farm is a comfortable suburban home to sheep, goats, pigs, fowl, two sorts of cow – Dexters and British Whites – and other animals. Deen has a friendly staff and teams of keen junior volunteers during the school holidays. The latter are young farmers (eight- to 16-year-olds) who sign up for the chance to feed, muck out and look after the animals with the farm staff. There's a riding school for able-bodied and disabled kids, and animal sponsorship schemes to support the farm. There's a party room, which can be hired for birthday bashes.

Buggy access. Café. Nappy-changing facilities. Nearest picnic place: Morden Hall Park. Shop.

Polka Theatre

240 The Broadway, SW19 (8543 4888/www.polkatheatre. com). South Wimbledon tube/rail. **Open** *Box office phoneline 9.30am-4.30pm Mon; 9am-6pmTue-Fri; 10am-4pm Sat. Personal callers 9.30am-4.30pm Tue-Fri; 10am-4.30pm Sat.* **Tickets** *£3-£10.* **Credit** MC V.

The Polka Theatre is exclusively for children. Productions run in two auditoria all year round (not just at Christmas) for two age groups. The main auditorium tends to be for older kids; the other, the Adventure Theatre, produces short works for younger children. Both stages have high production values. From 2003 the Adventure Theatre will produce new shows specifically for children as young as six months old.

LONDON LEGEND
Violette Szabó

18 Burnley Road Stockwell was the childhood home of Violette Szabó. Violette's mother was French and her father English, and the young girl grew up bilingual. She joined the Special Operations Executive in 1944 and was sent to France to make contact with a dispersed spy network. It was a dangerous mission, but Violette carried it out with flair, even finding time to do some shopping for her four-year-old daughter in Paris on the way home. Just after D-Day, in June 1944, she was parachuted into Normandy again, but this time the operation went wrong. She was ambushed by Germans, and although she tried to shoot her way out she was taken prisoner and executed in Ravensbruck concentration camp towards the end of the war. Her five-year-old daughter Tania received her brave mother's posthumous George Cross at Buckingham Palace in 1945; in 1958 she was portrayed by Virginia McKenna in the film *Carve Her Name With Pride*.

Also new for 2003 is the Polka Youth Theatre: ten-week courses in which nine- to 16-year-olds work with professional directors, writers, puppeteers, choreographers, musicians and actors to create their own shows.
Café. Disabled: toilet. Nappy changing facilities. Nearest picnic area: theatre garden or King's Road park. Shop.

Tiger's Eye

42 Station Road, SW19 (8543 1655). Colliers Wood or South Wimbledon tube. **Open** *10am-6.30m daily. Closed 25, 26 Dec, 1 Jan.* **Admission** *Mon-Fri £4.50 2-10s; £2 under-2s. Sat, Sun £4.50 2-10s; £2.25 under-2s.* **Credit** MC, V.

The Tiger's Eye is an indoor playcentre for children up to the age of ten. It's a vast barn of a place, so at least there's space to run. The soft play equipment towers high, with stuff to climb on, slide down and bounce off.
Buggy access. Café. Car park. Nappy-changing facilities. Nearest picnic place: Merton Abbey Park/Merton Park. Shop.

Wimbledon Lawn Tennis Museum

Centre Court, All England Lawn Tennis and Croquet Club, Church Road, SW19 (8946 6131/www.wimbledon. org/museum) Southfields tube/39, 93, 200 bus. **Open** *10.30am-5pm Mon-Fri. Closed 24-26 Dec, 1 Jan. Spectators only during championships.* **Admission** *£5.50; £4.50 concessions; £3.50 5-16s; free under-5s.* **Credit** MC, V.

Wimbledon Lawn Tennis Museum – London Tourist Board Small Attraction of the Year 2002 – is just great for small people. The museum has a brand new audiovisual theatre that lets you watch larger-than-life replays of some of the tournament's greatest matches. Memorabilia includes Goran Ivanisevic's match-winning racket from 2001, Venus Williams's tennis dress from the same year, and Maud Watson's voluminous skirts from 1884. Touch screen displays serve up commentary on past matches, and if all that doesn't twang your raquet strings, the mock-up Edwardian tennis party throws an unusual sidelight on the way we used to live. Tours take in the players' boards, Centre Court and Court 1: feel the thrill of standing in the place of champions. The education department is inventive, with tennis-themed activities during school holidays, and there are plenty of things to make and do for four- to 11-year-olds.
Buggy access. Café. Car park. Nappy-changing facilities. Nearest picnic place: benches outside museum/Wimbledon Park. Shop.

Putney

Riverside Putney is the jewel in the crown around these parts, familiar to millions as the starting point of the annual Varsity Boat Race. The river takes on a semi-rural aspect at Putney Bridge – looking back down the Thames you can catch glimpses of London's skyline, but upstream the Putney treeline is pretty well all that the eye can see.

Back from the river, and away from the busy high street, Putney is a peaceful, affluent spot with a number of green spaces. **Putney Heath** is the eastern edge of the huge piece of common land that eventually peters out where Wimbledon Common joins Richmond Park. It's three times the size of Hampstead Heath, but has much less glamour, and there are no areas set aside for children's play.

Infinitely tamer – but with more to entertain children – are King George's Park and Leaders Gardens at the end of Asilone Road. This dainty little riverside park is a delight for all the family, with two play areas and tennis courts. The park is also the place to come to for a tennis court (no bookings are taken by phone).

Barnes & East Sheen

These places are deep in residential south-west London. If you don't live here it might never occur to you to visit, but it would be a pity to miss some of the local attractions. Sandwiched between the river and Richmond Park there are some glorious open spaces, from the Thames Walk with its superb views of the river and boats upon it, to the famous **Wetland Centre**. Beyond these, the wooded tracks of East **Sheen Common** are rewarding to explore all year round.

East Sheen Common Nature Trail
East Sheen Common, Fife Road SW14 (Ranger 8876 2382/Borough Ecology Officer 8831 6135). Hammersmith tube then bus 33 or Mortlake rail, then 15 min walk. **Open** *dawn-dusk daily.* **Admission** *free.*
This is what happens when nature takes over. Eighty years ago, after centuries of grazing by local sheep, East Sheen Common was very nearly bald. But in the 1920s grazing was stopped and, after a brief stint as a rifle range and a ladies' golf course, the open land was allowed to run wild. Nowadays the common supports a mixture of tree species, including oak, birch, rowan and sycamore. The ponds support toads, frogs, the great diving beetle and numerous insects, and the common as a whole is a regular hunting ground for foxes and badgers. Running through it is a short nature trail marked by 13 numbered, orange-topped posts that takes in woodland, glades, ponds and streams. A few times each year Woodland Open Days invite visitors to learn about the traditional woodland activities: coppicing, bodging, spiling and weaving (and have a go yourself). Wellies are a must after wet weather.
Buggy access. Disabled access: toilet.

WWT Wetland Centre
Queen Elizabeth's Walk, SW13 (8409 4400/www.wwt. org.uk). Hammersmith tube then 33, 72, 209 (alight at Red Lion pub) or 283 (Duck bus direct to Centre)/Barnes rail/33, 72 bus. **Open** *Mar-Oct 9.30am-6pm daily. Nov-Feb 9.30am-5pm daily. Last entry 1hr before closing. Closed 25 Dec. Tours 11am, 2.30pm daily. Feeding tours noon, 3.30pm daily.* **Admission** *£6.75; £5.50 concessions; £4 4-16s; £17.50 family (2+2); free under-4s. Tours free. Feeding tours free.* **Credit** *MC, V.*
Only four miles (as the cormorant flies) from the centre of London, this extraordinary site provides 14 different wetland habitats for birds from around the world, ranging from New Zealand whitewater to African floodplains and East Asian rice paddies to Hawaiian lavaflow.
   Kit yourself out with a couple of children's trails from the visitors' centre and a pair of hired binoculars (£5) if you haven't brought your own. Then stop at the observatory for stunning views across the reserve. The viewing platform is encased in 30ft sheets of glass and splashed by light bouncing off the water below. If you look out beyond the lakes you'll recognise enough London landmarks to ground you in the capital, but otherwise it's easy to believe you've discovered a whole new world. Luckily, there are plenty of guides around to help you identify the birds. Since the Wetland Centre is a nature reserve first and a tourist attraction second, what you see will depend on what the birds show you. The attractions change with the seasons: on summer evenings bats whizz about; in winter the flocks of Arctic migrants come in.
   Visitors can take a tour with the wardens as they feed the birds. Walks last about an hour and leave from the visitors' centre at noon and 3pm. All the walks have plenty of information panels, some of them with touch screen displays. Paths around the reserve are broad, smooth and buggy-friendly, and each zone is separated from the next by a gate (which has the happy side effect that rampaging toddlers can't charge too far ahead). Special interest walks include Moth Nights, Bat Walks and Early Bird Breakfasts (with extra dawn chorus). The centre's programme of weekend and holiday events is very much geared to rural and specifically wetland crafts. Call for details or check out the website.
Buggy access. Café. Car park. Disabled: toilet. Nappy changing facilities. Nearest picnic area: grounds. Shop.

Richmond & Kew

Richmond was a seat of kings during the 12th century, when Henry I lived at Sheen Palace on the south-west corner of what is now **Richmond Green**. There are few royal connections these days (though there are lots of famous faces among the residents), but this most royal of boroughs still retains the attractions that made it a pleasure park for kings. And **Richmond Park** is king of the local pleasures. Eight miles across at its widest point, it's the biggest city park in Europe and the nearest London gets to wild countryside. Herds of red and fallow deer roam freely, much to the fascination of children, but bear in mind that these seemingly shy and gentle wild animals can be fierce in autumn during the rutting season (heed the signs warning you not to get too close to the deer).

A great way to see the park is by riding along the well-kept cycle path that rings the perimeter. If it's too much hassle to bring your own bikes, hire as many as you need from **Richmond Park Cycle Hire** (07050 209249) at Roehampton Gate. Adult bikes with tag-alongs (for the over-fives) and child-seats are available, as are children's bikes for those able to ride without stabilisers.

Tucked away in the middle of the park is **Isabella Plantation**, a secluded and tranquil woodland garden. It's primarily home to acid-loving plants such as rhododendrons, azaleas and camelias, and is best seen in all its fabulous flowering glory in early summer or in late September, when it blazes with autumn colour. It's crisscrossed with streams and ponds, whose stepping stones and wooden bridges make it a fun walking experience for children, and there are plenty of benches and grassy glades where you can sit down and enjoy your picnic.

Residents of the **WWT Wetland Centre**. *See p142.*

Adventures for all

Battersea Park

A couple of minutes walk from the Sun Gate entrance is the biggest adventure playground in London. The adventure end is for children aged eight to 15. Right beside it is a decent-sized playground with smaller equipment and soft landings for five- to eight-year-olds, and beside that again are swings and slides and climb-on trains zone for babies and the under-fives.
Albert Bridge Road, SW11 (8871 7539). Battersea park rail. **Open** *Term time* 3.30-7pm Mon-Fri; 11am-6pm Sat, Sun. *Holidays* 11am-6pm daily.

Kimber BMX Adventure Playground

Possibly the best equipped and most efficiently run adventure playground in London, Kimber has all the usual platforms, ropes and ladders, big swings, little swings, monkey bars and a basketball court. This one has a big added extra, however, in the shape of the excellent BMX bike track. Bring your own bike or, if you prefer, you can hire one at the playground. For showery days there's also an indoor section with table tennis, as well as arts-and-crafts rooms and kitchens.
Kimber Road, SW18 (8870 2168). Earlsfield rail. **Open** 3.30-7pm Tue-Fri; 11am-6pm Sat.

Lady Allen Adventure Playground

On the northwest corner of Wandsworth Common, this well-designed playground lets children with special needs and disabilities swing, slide, climb on ropes, dangle off monkey bars, and generally muck about with their mates, in a very safe, well-supervised environment. Children with disabilities are able to use this wonderful playground during all opening hours; non-disabled children are also admitted at restricted times.
Chivalry Road, SW11 (7228 0278/ www.kidsactive.org.uk). Clapham Junction rail. **Open** *Disabled access* 10am-5pm Tue-Fri; 10am-4pm Sat. *Non-disabled access* 10am-5pm Tue (under-8s); 3.30-5pm Wed, Thur; 10am-12pm Sat.

Tooting Common

Between the tennis courts and the pond is the best playground for the under-eights for miles around. It's not huge but there are swings and a good range of wooden equipment to climb on, balance on, jump on, dangle off and walk on. Bark chips make for a soft landing.
Tooting Bec Road, SW16 (8871 8688). Tooting Bec tube/Streatham rail/44, 57, 127, 133, 270 bus. **Open** dawn -dusk daily.

While here, take a moment to stroll to **King Henry VIII's Mound**. Follow the twisting path up this leafy hillock, and once at the top you'll have a spectacular view right across the city of London. On a clear day the London Eye and St Paul's Cathedral can easily be made out. Alternatively, you could walk along **Terrace Walk**, a famous Victorian promenade that stretches from the Pembroke Lodge (a great place for lunch for the picnicless, *see p165*) and beyond the park to Richmond Hill, continuing the wonderful views of West London and beyond.

Museum of Richmond
Old Town Hall, Whittaker Avenue, Richmond, Surrey (8332 1141/www.museumofrichmond.com). Richmond tube/rail. **Open** *May-Sept* 11am-5pm Tue-Sat; 1-4pm Sun. *Nov-Apr* 11am-5pm Tue-Sat. Closed 25, 26 Dec, 1 Jan. **Admission** free.
The museum celebrates the unique heritage of the surrounding area with colourful and regularly changing displays spanning prehistoric times to the present day. 2003 sees a special exhibition commemorating the 400th anniversary of the death of Queen Elizabeth I at Richmond Palace. Term-time workshops are held for the under-fives, and there's also Harry the Herald's Saturday Club for five- to 11-year-olds. Tudor Gardens, Wedding Veils and Button Holes, and Palace Decorations are all on the arts and crafts agenda.
Buggy access. Disabled: toilet. Nearest picnic space: Richmond Green and riverside. Shop.

Public Record Office
Kew (8876 3444/www.pro. gov.uk/education). Kew Gardens tube. **Open** 9am-5pm Mon, Wed, Fri; 10am-7pm Tue; 9am-7pm Thur; 9.30am-5pm Sat; **Tours** noon last Fri of mth (booking necessary). **Admission** free. *Tours* free.
The Education and Visitor Centre in the Public Record Office is an odd hoard of national treasures, ranging from the record of Guy Fawkes' confession to a copy of the last telegram sent from the Titanic. Throughout the year a variety of events and exhibitions focuses on various documents from the archive. During 2003 the museum will be dipping into the history of Britain and the Caribbean, as well as looking into World War II, the Suffrage movement and the life and times of Elizabeth I. Events can be very popular in this fascinating place, so book in advance.
Buggy access. Nearest picnic place: grounds of Public Record Office.

Royal Botanic Gardens (Kew Gardens)
Richmond, Surrey (switchboard 8332 5000/info 8332 5655/www.kew.org.uk). Kew Gardens tube/rail/Kew Bridge rail/riverboat to Kew Pier. **Open** *Feb, Mar* 9.30am-5.30pm daily. *Apr-Sept* 9.30am-6.30pm Mon-Fri; 9.30am-7.30pm Sat, Sun. *Oct-Jan* 9.30am-4.15pm daily. **Admission** (LP) £7.50; £5.50 concessions; free under-16s. **Credit** AmEx, DC, MC, V.
A walk around 300-acre Kew Gardens usually includes frequent stop-offs at the various giant, mostly Victorian, glass-houses within which botanists have been able to create conditions suitable to make any plant in the world feel at home: some of the exotic palms grow to 150 feet and press themselves against the roof panes of the sultry Palm House. The high gallery is fun if you are a six-year-old child bent on escaping your minders, as it has up and down spiral stair-

TOP FIVE Kite-flying spaces

Brockwell Park
Brixton people may share this local park with the residents of Herne Hill (*see p131*), but kite fliers from both areas congregate on its hill.

Clapham Common
Considering that it has no height to speak of, Clapham Common is surprisingly windy. Acrobat kites can be sent up most weekends. *See p138*.

Richmond Park
The best place for kite-flying in the park is probably close to the Pembroke Lodge cafeteria where it's high and grassy. *See p142*.

Streatham Common
Rising to 50m, and free of trees at the top, Streatham Common has great kite-flying conditions and fabulous views over south London. *See p139*.

Wimbledon Common
The best spots to fly are near the Windmill where it's nice and open, and on the wide green spaces of Southside Common. *See p140*.

cases. The basement is full of marine plant-life which does not attract as much attention as the fabulous tropical fish which share its tanks and give it a purpose. In the Princess Diana House the fun involves stepping straight from the orchids' rain forest through a glass wall into the cacti's desert. The permanent orchid display is a steamy experience. The star of the show is *Pendiculata Sanderina*, the Holy Grail of orchid-hunting, whose petals grow to three feet long. It has evolved a water-collecting sack in which to entice innocent insects – of which there are tens of thousands in a lower room. The ant box is especially fascinating. Endless streams of them commute from anthill to work and back, aiming only to satisfy 'er indoors – their rarely-seen queen who can grow to the size of a mouse. Meanwhile the cacti, which form fantastic shapes, enjoy a much drier heat.

Thirsty? There are half a dozen refreshment stops around the gardens. None is particularly cheap, so the best advice is to take a picnic and treat the party later to an ice cream. There are plenty of benches if you are too expensively dressed for the grass – the beautiful Japanese Garden especially looks rather forlorn if no one is sitting in it. Some visitors opt to eat their lunch on, and view the gardens from, the wooden seats in the little train which bumbles round the pathways, for an extra fee. Our advice is to sit by the cedars outside the Chinese Pagoda and enjoy the disappointment of those who arrive not knowing that it's closed until further notice.
Buggy access. Cafés. Nappy-changing facilities. Nearest picnic place: Kew Gardens grounds. Restaurant. Shop.

Further south-west

The southern reaches of the river towards **Twickenham** are lovely spots to ride a bike around, and there's the Thames Path for walkers.

In the steps of royalty. **Hampton Court Palace**.

Around Town

Marble Hill House overlooking the Thames in Marble Hill Park is a perfect Palladian villa; neighbouring **Orleans House** (Riverside, Twickenham, 8892 0221; free; call for opening times) was built in 1710 for James Johnston, William III's secretary of state for Scotland, and was later home to the exiled Duke of Orléans (hence the name); and **Ham House** is a handsome, red-brick, riverside mansion with a beautiful garden. Carrying on along the river past Twickenham, you come to the **Museum of Rugby**.

From Twickers, the river passes the busy shopping centre of Kingston-upon-Thames, then curves around to **Hampton Court Palace**. Once Cardinal Wolsey's country seat, the palace was taken over by Henry VIII, who spent much time and three honeymoons here.

Ham House

Ham Street, Ham, Richmond, Surrey (8940 1950/ www.national trust.org.uk). Richmond tube/rail, then 371 bus. **Open** *House* late Mar-Oct 1-5pm Mon-Wed, Sat, Sun. *Gardens* 11am-6pm/dusk Mon-Wed, Sat, Sun. Closed 25, 26 Dec, 1 Jan. **Tours** pre-booking essential Wed. Phone for membership details & prices. **Admission** (NT) *House & Garden* £7; £3.50 5-15s; £17.50 family (2+3); free under-5s. *Garden only* £3; £1.50 5-15s; £7.50 family (2+3); free under-5s. **Credit** AmEx, MC, V.

Built in 1610, this mansion is lavishly appointed with 17th-century furniture, paintings and decor. From the house, water meadows lead down to the Thames. The part of the grounds known as the wilderness is, in fact, a carefully planted, maze-like section divided into garden rooms. The Still House was traditionally used for fermenting rose petals to make scent. Family events take place from Easter to autumn: there are egg hunts, teddy bears' picnics, summer Sunday jazz evenings, ghost tours and creepy-crawly hunts. Ring to receive details such delights.

Café (high chairs). Lift. Nappy-changing facilities. Nearest picnic place: Orangery Gardens. Shop.

Hampton Court Palace

East Molesey, Surrey (8781 9500/www.hrp.org.uk). Hampton Court rail/riverboat from Westminster or Richmond to Hampton Court Pier (Apr-Oct). **Open** *Palace* Apr-Oct 10.15am-6pm Mon; 9.30am-6pm Tue-Sun. *Nov-Mar* 10.15am-4.30pm Mon; 9.30am-4.30pm Tue-Sun (last entry 45mins before closing). *Park* dawn-dusk daily. **Admission** *Palace, courtyard, cloister & maze* £11.30; £8.25 concessions; £7.25 5-15s; £33 family (max 5 people); free under-5s. *Maze only* £3; £2 5-15s. **Credit** AmEx, MC, V.

The royal palace beside the Thames has more than 600 acres of parkland, including 60 acres of formal gardens with fountains, ponds and the elaborate Privy Garden restored a few years ago. It takes ages to see everything; this place is like ten stately homes rolled into one. Still, the maze is what most people love here: they pay to get lost in it.

The palace's history begins in 1514, when Cardinal Wolsey started building it. Henry VIII took it over in 1529, then Oliver Cromwell fell in love with it. Finally, Christopher Wren remodelled it in the 17th-century for William and Mary. Tour highlights include Henry VIII's hammer-beam-roofed Great Hall, the Renaissance Picture Gallery and the huge kitchens, where hundreds once toiled to cater for the palace's daily consumption of six oxen, 40 sheep and 1,000-plus larks, pheasants, pigeons and swans. Today, period-clad minions make 16th-century dishes, turn meat on a spit and talk to visitors.

Every school holiday special events pull in a family crowd. Attractions for 2003 include, during August, learning swordplay and admiring gallant knights in armour in an event called The Court of Good Queen Bess (2-31 August). In the October half-term Growing Up in Elizabethan Times poses questions: what did children wear? What did they learn? How were they supposed to behave? All will be made clear during a week of roleplay, ruff-making, fun, games and stories at the palace. Christmas holiday activities (27 December 2003 -1 January 2004) hark back to 1602-3. A feast of Elizabethan food is whipped up in the Tudor kitchens. Upstairs in the Great Hall the lucky guests will learn to dance the Volta and the Galliard while speculation rages about who will be successor to the aged Queen. Ring for details of seasonal events.

Buggy access. Café. Car park. Nappy-changing facilities. Nearest picnic place: palace gardens. Shop.

Marble Hill House

Twickenham Road, Middx (8892 5115/www.english-heritage.org.uk). Richmond tube/rail/St Margaret's rail/ 33, 90, 290, H22, R70 bus. **Open** *Apr-Sept* 10am-6pm daily. *Oct* 10am-5pm daily. Closed Nov-Mar, 24-26 Dec, 1-16 Jan. *Tours* by prior arrangement. **Admission** (EH, LP) £3.50; £3 concessions; £2 5-15s; free under-5s. **Credit** MC, V.

Elegantly set in acres of parkland alongside the Thames, this Palladian villa was built in 1724-9 for Henrietta Howard, mistress of George II. It was later occupied by Mrs Fitzherbert, the secret wife of George IV. The house has been immaculately restored and filled with Georgian furnishings and paintings. The grand mahogany staircase almost led to war with Spain, after the British king ordered trees to be cut down for it in Spanish Honduras. In the grounds visitors admire the sunken grotto and England's oldest black walnut tree. There are summer concerts in the park (Sunday evenings). Send an SAE for an events brochure to find out about other family attractions planned throughout the year. From this delightful mansion you can catch a ferry across the river to admire another: Ham House (*see p146*). *Café (in park). Nearest picnic place: Marble Hill Park. Shop.*

Museum of Rugby/ Twickenham Stadium

Gate K, Twickenham Rugby Stadium, Rugby Road, Twickenham, Middx (8892 8877/www.rfu.com). Hounslow East tube then 281 bus/Twickenham rail. **Open** *Museum* 10am-5pm Tue-Sat; 11am-5pm Sun. Last entry 30mins before closing. **Tours** 10.30am, noon, 1.30pm, 3pm Tue-Sat; 1pm, 3pm Sun. **Admission** *Combined ticket* £8; £5 concessions; £25 family. **Credit** MC, V.

If your children show an interest in the game for ruffians played by gentlefolk, book a stadium tour at Twickers. Tours take place on non-match days only, and are highly entertaining. Participants see the players' tunnel, the England dressing room, the royal box, pitchside, the stadium and the museum. The museum is open whether there's a match on or not and provides an amusing insight into the history of world rugby. Interactive exhibits include a real scrum machine and have-a-go footage of some of the greatest tries of all time. Nostalgic fans can listen to early radio commentary and muse on the days when players still wore bow ties. The shop stocks the country's largest cache of England rugby merchandise: call for a catalogue or check out the website. *Buggy access. Disabled: toilet. Nappy-changing facilities. Restaurant. Shop.*

Around Town

LUNCH BREAK

Around Brixton & Stockwell

Bamboula's (*12 Acre Lane, SW2, 7737 6633*), sudden fried chicken served with sass.
Bar Estrela (*113 South Lambeth Road, SW8, 7793 1051*), the star of the local Portuguese strip, with a nice warm welcome for children.
Eco (*4 Market Row, SW9, 7738 3021; see p175*), reliable standby for perfect thin and crispy pizzas.
O Barros (*168A Old South Lambeth Road, SW8, 7582 0976*), for a wide and colourful range of dainty tapas and filling snacks.
Rebato's (*169 South Lambeth Road, SW8, 7735 6388*), for decent Spanish fare – tapas and all – amidst old-fashioned charm.
The Refectory (*6 Church Walk, SW9, 8940 6264*), a local fave which serves homely, unpretentious fare – with kiddy portions and kiddy seats.

Around Battersea

Giraffe (*27 Battersea Rise, SW11, 7223 0933; see p172*), world cuisine amid exciting zebra and leopard motifs and child-friendly staff.
Gourmet Burger Kitchen (*44 Northcote Road, SW11, 7228 3309; see p181*), for brilliant burgers, choice chips, sizeable servings.
Marzano (*53 Northcote Road, SW11, 7228 8860*), pizza and pasta in a spacious dining room.
Nightingale Patisserie (*61 Nightingale Lane, SW11, 8675 6844*), good sandwiches, tasty pastries and a kid-friendly vibe.

Around Tooting

Masaledar (*121 Upper Tooting Road, SW17, 8767 7676*), curry place with high chairs and toys.
Rick's Café (*122 Mitcham Road, SW17, 8767 5219*). Family-friendly modern European bistro.

Around Putney

Del Buongustaio (*283 Putney Bridge Road, SW15, 8780 9361*), lively Italian with high chairs and children's menu.
Loo Loo's (*Leaders Gardens, Asilone Road, SW15, 8246 6847*), ex-loo (yes) where friendly staff serve good children's' lunches with unlimited squash and ice-cream. Lav-erly.

Around Wimbledon

Est Est Est (*36 High Street, SW19, 8947 7700*) family friendly pizza and pasta.
Maison St Cassien (*71 High Street, SW19, 8944 1200*), an airy café with a Mediterranean flavour.
Nando's (*1 Russell Road, SW19, 8545 0909; see p182*). Grilled chicken with gusto; spicy peri peri chips and the pop's unlimited.
Tootsies (*48 High Street, SW19, 8946 4135; see p182*) our favourite burger place.

Around Richmond

Pavilion Café (*Richmond Park, Roehampton Gate, SW15, 8876 7933*), a great tea-and-buns favourite with mums and toddlers.
Pembroke Lodge Cafeteria (*Richmond Park, between Richmond and Ham Gates, 8940 8207, SW15*), for stunning views, ice-creams, Sunday roasts, and cream teas.
The Phoenix Bar & Grill (*162-4 Lower Richmond Road, SW15, 8780 3131*), modern European dishes and old kiddie favourites.
Sonny's (*94 Church Road, SW13, 8748 0393*), popular relaxed atmosphere and high quality food.
The Victoria (*10 West Temple Sheen, SW14 8876 4238; see p178*), a pub, but the grub is far from pub and there's a play area for the children.

PARKLIFE Battersea Park

Early 19th-century London was a pestilential place, and Battersea Fields in the south of the city was an especially heinous sinkhole of iniquity and vice, notorious for gambling, drinking and naughtiness of every sort. 'Sodom and Gomorrah' one local cleric called it, as he stumbled away ashen-faced. But in the mid 19th century the Public Parks Commission took the area by the scruff of its neck, and an Act of Parliament was passed arranging for the park to be relandscaped. The aim? To provide the local youth with a wholesome setting for healthful exercise, naturally.

The born-again Battersea Park was laid out in high Victorian style, with lakes, carriageways, subtropical gardens, wide open spaces and all. Anyone could get in, and the place overflowed on Sundays with families enjoying their day of rest. During the two world wars the park was turned over to allotments and pig farming, and barrage balloons wallowed above the trees. In 1951 the park became the site of the Festival of Britain Pleasure Gardens, a lighter alternative to the hive of high culture that was the South Bank a couple of miles further up the Thames. The end of the 20th century told a sorry tale of decline: the Festival Fun Fair became rickety and sad and eventually closed in 1974, the fountains ran dry, were patched up and ran dry again. But hope springs eternal, and in 2003 the Park is undergoing major restoration to restore its pleasure garden glory.

So what does the Park have to offer? Answer: all things to all people. Battersea Park is like south London's back garden and village green: any number of impromptu football matches take place

on its wide open fields, cricketers pound the nets and play on the square in the middle of the park. There's even a village bowling green. In 2000 the **Battersea Park Millennium Arena** (8871 7537) opened with an eight-lane running track, 19 floodlit tennis courts (8871 7542), a netball court, an all-weather sports pitch (8871 7535) and a state-of-the-art fitness centre with sauna. Tennis coaching is available to anyone over eight, and the excellent children's summer tennis camp takes place over two weeks in August every year. If watersports are more your family's thing you can at least get some practice on the picturesque Victorian boating lake from May to September. Take out a rowing boat from the elegant new Scandinavian-style boating house for £3.50 an hour.

Thirty yards away, **London Recumbents** (7498 6543; *see also p252*) offers low-down and funky pedal power (the word bicycle doesn't even begin to do these vehicles justice). Hire a bike or a tandem or a trike or a banana bike for £5 and cruise the broad pathways for an hour. London Recumbents also promises to teach you or the children to ride by their own patent methods.

And if all the activity tires you out, take a break at the Gondola al Parco café (7978 1677) – an Italian-style café with tables overlooking the boating lake. Tuesdays and Fridays have been jazz nights in recent years, and in 2002 the café owners launched a Venetian gondola to add a touch of the exotic to the rowing fleet.

Every year the park plays host to a variety of events. On Easter Monday the traditional **Harness Horse Parade** takes over, and dozens of horses and ponies haul beautiful old-fashioned carriages, shop vans, fire engines and more – all buffed to perfection – around the park. Twice a year the self-explanatory **Affordable Art Fair** sets up here, and at various times there are sponsored walks, sponsored toddles, teddy bears' picnics, fun fairs and, in November, one of the best firework displays in south London.

The southwest corner of the park is of particular interest to children, with its large one o'clock club, toddler's playground, play equipment for the under-eights and an adventure playground for over-eights.

In the centre of the northern edge the **Peace Pagoda** is a landmark meeting spot just opposite the **Children's Zoo**. We love this lovely little animal collection (8871 7540), which has occupied a spot at the edge of the Festival Gardens for donkey's years but at the time of writing it's not certain that it will still be open after 28 September 2003.

Battersea Park

Battersea, SW11 (8871 7530/7531/ www.wandsworth.gov.uk). Sloane Square tube then 19, 137 bus/Battersea Park or Queenstown Road rail. **Open** 7am-dusk daily.

West London

Where it's pretty, not too hip and even the A40 seems trendy from below.

Paddington & Bayswater

This neck of the woods is hardly London's greenest corner. There are few gardens and no parks (or woods, for that matter), while the Westway acts as a *cordon insanitaire*, cutting the area off from other, more leafy parts of suburban west London.

All that said, it's not an out-and-out no-go area. For child-friendly walks make for the **Paddington Basin**, part of the Grand Union canal which runs below the Westway to the north of Paddington Station. In the last couple of years, gleaming new office blocks and luxury apartments have turned this stretch of the canal into a mini Docklands, and from here you can walk towards Little Venice or London Zoo. Alternatively, make for the light and airy **Whiteley's** shopping centre – a big hit among local parents with children – where you and yours will find plenty of restaurants and toyshops, an eight-screen cinema and a branch of **Gymboree** (0800 092 0911), purveyor of dance, music and all-round enjoyment to the under-fives.

Alexander Fleming Laboratory Museum

St Mary's Hospital, Praed Street, W2 (7725 6528/ www.st-marys.org.uk/about/fleming_museum). Paddington tube/rail/7, 15, 27, 36 bus. **Open** 10am-1pm Mon-Thur. By appointment 2-5pm Mon-Thur; 10am-5pm by appointment Fri. Closed 24 Dec-1 Jan, bank hols. **Admission** (LP) £2; £1 concessions, children. **No credit cards Map** p313 D5.
Alexander Fleming made his momentous chance discovery of penicillin in this very room on 3 September 1928, when a Petri dish of bacteria became contaminated with a mysterious mould. His laboratory has now been recreated, and displays and a video offer insights into both his life and the role of penicillin in fighting disease. The staff run special tours for family and school groups, and other visitors get a guided tour as part of the entrance fee.
Nearest picnic place: Hyde Park. Shop.

Maida Vale, Kilburn & Queens Park

Little Venice marks the start of a nicer part of West London, as you leave the busy Edgware road behind and head north. It's a desirable residential area characterised by white stucco houses, some perched romantically along the edge of the canal. Little Venice also has a large, well-established houseboat community. If you fancy your own boating adventure, head to the **London Waterbus**

Please look after...

On Christmas Eve in 1956, a teddy bear was abandoned on the shelf of a toyshop in London. The bear was discovered by Michael Bond, who took it home as a present for his wife. Michael Bond was living near Paddington Station at the time and named him Paddington bear. Within a few days of finding him, Bond decided to write a children's story about a bear that arrives at Paddington Station as a stowaway from Peru. And thus an icon of children's literature was born. *A Bear Called Paddington* was the title of the first book; since then Bond has written over 150 books that have now been translated into 30 different languages. For his contribution to the children's literary canon, Michael Bond was awarded an OBE.

Young fans can follow in the bear's ursine pawprints at Paddington Station, where a statue of him with his suitcase stands proudly. His fictional home can be found just round the corner, at 32 Windsor Gardens; creator Michael Bond still lives just down the road in Little Venice. Don't forget the marmalade sandwiches!

ticket office (Blomfield Road, W9), where you can board a boat to London Zoo or Camden Lock. **Paddington Recreation Ground** provides a welcome bit of greenery and a good place to let off steam. There are loads of tennis courts and five-a-side football pitches and the area buzzes with activity. There's also a decent café and two excellent play enclosures for young kids, plus a playground for older children. **Queens Park** (*see p153*) is run by the ever efficient, wealthy Corporation of London; it's well kept and so a treat to visit with young children. Kilburn's claim to fame is the ever-dynamic **Tricycle Theatre** (*see p208*), an arts centre with cinema, theatre, gallery and café, all of which make bringing up children in this not-so-pretty north-western corner of town a lot easier.

Notting Hill

Notting Hill is now resolutely trendy, but it wasn't always thus. Indeed, it was yokel territory (and many of the inhabitants were pigs) until a wave of white stuccoed buildings mapped out the area in the early and mid 1800s. By the 1950s, however, the area's fortunes had dipped, and racial tension flared up between the white, working-class population and West Indian immigrants who moved in alongside them. Thanks to the race riots, the streets around Notting Hill were considered dodgy for years, until the mid 1980s when the newly coined yuppies moved in. Every August bank holiday the area explodes with revelry for the world-famous **Notting Hill Carnival** (*see below*); Europe's biggest street festival, it has its origins in attempts to defuse racial tension. At other times of the year, the streets of Notting Hill are quietly modish.

Still, when people talk about Notting Hill, they really mean **Portobello Road**. This narrow, snaking thoroughfare runs through the centre of Notting Hill and is home to one of the most popular street markets in the world. The market sells anything from antiques (up at the Notting Hill end) to fashion (under the Westway) on Fridays and Saturdays, but you need to be an early bird to catch the best bargains. Portobello Road is also home to the revamped **Electric Cinema**, which runs a Saturday kids' club. Just off Portobello Road, on Powis Square, young performers can join one of the numerous clubs run by the **Tabernacle**.

Most Portobello parents needing a bit of fresh air will make a beeline for Holland Park, but there are other, smaller parks and city gardens dotted around Notting Hill. **Avondale Park** (Walmer Road) is one of the nicest, with a country feel and a small playground and football pitch. Just off Kensal Road, is the nice little park with the unwieldy big name;

the **Emslie Horniman Pleasance Gardens**. Once you reach Ladbroke Grove, there are many other excellent resources for youngsters. If your children aspire to a life behind the camera, check out **YCTV** (77 Barlby Road, W10, 8964 4646), which provides training in camera, sound, editing and lighting for 11- to 20-year-olds. Moments away from here, younger nippers can explore science and technology in a kid friendly workshop space, the **Making Place** (3 Exmoor Street, W1; *see p228*).

Canalside Activity Centre
The Boat House, Canal Close, W10 (8968 4500). Ladbroke Grove tube or Kensal Rise rail. **Open** *Enquiries & bookings* 10am-5pm Mon-Fri; 10am-4pm Sat. Closed mid Dec-mid Jan, bank hols. *Classes & sessions* members free; non-members from £4. **Membership** £60-£120/yr. **No credit cards**.
This unusual watersports centre is open to children, families and carers and aims to promote health and education through much hilarious splashing about in the canal. Qualified instructors run courses and one-off sessions in kayaking, canoeing and water activities.
Buggy access. Nearest picnic place: canalside.

Emslie Horniman Pleasance Gardens Adventure Playground
Southern Row, W10 (8969 5740). Ladbroke Grove tube. **Open** *Term time* 3-7pm Mon-Fri; 11am-5pm Sat. *School hols* 11am-6pm Mon-Fri. Closed 24 Dec-1 Jan. **Admission** free.
The multicoloured soft-surface playground for infants keeps the tinies happy. Older siblings bundle straight over to the adventure playground and football pitch. In spring and summer, staff open a small kiosk serving local Disotto's ice-cream, so all the children crowd around that. Clean toilets and nappy-changing facilities are another bonus. The quiet garden has

LONDON LEGEND Notting Hill Carnival

In 1958, ten years after the *Windrush* docked, rioting and racist attacks took place in Nottingham. A couple of weeks later, racial tension took hold of west London. At the time, journalist Claudia Jones was working at the *West Indian Gazette*. She suggested organising carnivals as an answer to the oppression West Indian communities were experiencing. The first carnival was held in St Pancras Town Hall on 30 January 1959, timed to coincide with the annual carnival in Trinidad, and involved masquerade, calypso and fine Caribbean refreshments. For the next five years the carnivals remained indoors, but by 1964 the first carnival was held outside, on the streets of Notting Hill. Costumes were borrowed from Madame Tussaud's, floats came courtesy of the fire brigade and gas board and Portobello Market stallholders lent out horses and carts. A thousand people turned up and a new tradition was born.

As the number of people attending increased, different tensions arose between the black community and the state. What had originated

as a celebration of culture had become associated with crime. The first riots during the carnival were in 1976 and every year since then talk of banning the event or moving it to a more contained location has threatened its existence.

Now, more than one million people hit the streets of Notting Hill for what is the largest street festival in Western Europe. It's an irrefutable sign of the permanent presence and cultural contribution of many different ethnic groups in London and is well worth staying in town for during August.

Carnival takes place over Sunday and Monday of the August bank holiday weekend (24 & 25 August 2003). Sunday is children's day, but can still be a bit crazy. Local schools organise floats and everyone dresses up in incredibly ornate costumes. Monday is even more hectic and it's best to leave the buggy at home; the sheer mass of people can be pretty overwhelming. Whenever you come, don't forget to sample as much food as possible: some of the best jerk chicken in London can be found at the numerous food stalls.

Take to the water among the houseboats at **Little Venice**. *See p149.*

vine-covered walkways and water features. At the Golborne Road end, below the Trellick Tower, are Meanwhile Gardens (the subject of an online soap opera) and a wildlife garden. *Buggy access. Disabled access.*

The Tabernacle
Powis Square, W11 (7565 7890/www.tabernacle.org.uk). Ladbroke Grove or Westbourne Park tube. **Open** 8.30am-10.30pm daily; ring for details of late evening activities. **Map** p312 A6.

The buzzing community centre in this converted church has a packed programme of family events. There are parent and baby fitness sessions, Tiny Tots dance and music classes and a community education breakdancing project for young and old. Music technology and new-media classes are popular, and the 8am yoga classes attract all ages.
Buggy access. Nappy-changing facilities.

Holland Park

Holland Park is a favoured spot with the rich and famous – those who like to be near the moves and grooves of Notting Hill but seek more luxury. Grand houses line the wide, curving tree-lined avenues and the area is home to one of London's swankiest parks. There are several houses around the park that are worth a visit, although they may be a little dull for the younger generation. **Leighton House** (12 Holland Park Road, W14, 7602 3316) is worth a visit to ogle at the grandeur of its former inhabitant Lord Leighton. Nearby **Linley Sambourne House** was

the home of Edward Linley Sambourne, cartoonist for the satirical magazine *Punch*. It was due to open as we went to press (phone the curator of Leighton House for more details). **Holland House**, in the centre of the park, has a cloistered exterior painted with beautiful murals and surrounded by fountains. It is a lovely spot to sit and watch the world go by. If you fancy a longer stay, the house contains one of London's most picturesque youth hostels.

Holland Park
Ilchester Place, W8 (7471 9813). Holland Park tube. **Open** 7.30am-dusk daily. **Map** p314 A9.

This is where the offspring of the affluent congregate, with nannies in tow. The whole park can be rather tricky to negotiate at first as it has a walled entrance on one side and lots of densely wooded areas. The best bet is to approach it from Kensington High Street and wander across to the Ecology Centre (7471 9802), where you can pick up a map of the area and details of the wildlife walk. Most of the buggy brigade head straight to the rather precious One O'Clock club. If you want somewhere a little bit more down-to-earth, there are ample play areas throughout the park.

The newly designed futuristic adventure playground is a great spot for the over-fives and is challenging enough to keep energetic ten-year-olds well entertained for an afternoon. The park also has a lovely Italian café serving kids' meals, as well as ample facilities for a range of sporting activities. Furthermore, if you fancy just relaxing on the grass with a picnic, you'll find a secluded spot at the Zen Garden or Rose Garden without any difficulty. Watch out for the hungry peacocks that roam freely throughout the park.
Buggy access. Café. Nappy-changing facilities.

Earl's Court & Fulham

This is another relatively barren spot when it comes to finding ways to entertain children. Earl's Court is most associated with the huge **Exhibition Centre** dominating the whole area. The centre was built in 1887 after a period in British history when holding exhibitions had become an important part of social life in London. This began with the Great Exhibition in Hyde Park in 1851 and ended with the First World War. The centre is still one of London's largest venues for exhibitions, such as the annual Boat Show in January and the Ideal Home Exhibition in March, as well as concerts.

In the post-war years, the area surrounding Earl's Court went into decline and huge houses previously owned by wealthy Victorians were gradually converted into flats for poorer residents. In the 1960s and '70s the area became known as 'Kangaroo Valley' as it appealed to travellers from Australia and New Zealand seeking cheap accommodation. Nowadays the area is still full of small bedsit flats and hostel accommodation, so few families have made a home here. If you are in need of greenery the closest open space is the **Brompton Cemetery** although it really is a last resort with not much on offer other than a few historic tombstones.

Instead, most parents rely on the resources in Hammersmith and Fulham, where there are a few more open spaces and activities available. The most obvious spot to head for, if you're seeking an antidote to bustling London life, is the river. **Bishop's Park** is set alongside the Thames Path and has a small boating lake in the summer, two playgrounds and a basketball pitch. They also have a One O'Clock club (Bishops Rainbow Playhouse) for under-fives with a good selection of trikes and bikes. The café has some nice outside seating, but the menu could do with a bit of inspiration.

Fulham Palace on the edge of Bishop's Park is amusing to visit. It has lovely grounds and a walled kitchen garden, providing ideal spots for lazy riverside picnics. They also organise half-term workshops for six- to 14-year-olds, which allows parents to visit the palace unencumbered.

Fulham football ground is at the opposite side of the park and can be reached along the Thames Path. Unfortunately, supporters have to make do with the Queen's Park Rangers ground at Loftus Road while the Fulham stadium is being renovated. Just down the Fulham Road at **Stamford Bridge** the Premiership Chelsea football club can oblige anyone looking to clad themselves in 'the Blues' kit courtesy of the Chelsea Village megastore.

Dressing-up time at **Fulham Palace**. *See p154*.

PARKLIFE Queens Park

Queens Park is owned by the wealthy Corporation of London, and has everything a park should have in its six acres. Most little people stampede to the playground and the excellent sand play area, which has a good range of interactive toys. In the heat of the summer, the adjacent paddling pool opens its gates and becomes the centre of activity. Directly opposite the playground, across the main lawn, is a little animal enclosure, where a couple of goats, some ducks and rabbits co-exist quite happily. At the centre of the park, next to the Mediterranean garden, there's a decent café that serves a wide variety of meals for all tastes and ages, and in summer months the outside tables are packed until sunset.

After refuelling there are ample opportunities for further physical activity. A picturesque Pitch and Putt area and six tennis courts surround the café's outside area, and clubs, balls and courts can be hired by the hour from the club hut. Those looking for some peace and quiet chill out in the sensory garden, where the smell of herbs and the sound of trickling water calm most hyperactive toddlers. Failing that, in summer months there are occasionally musicians playing at the bandstand on a Sunday afternoon. The local capoeira group have been know to put on a performance too.

The most recent addition to the park's family-friendly attractions is the nature trail through a wild and overgrown section at its top, forested end. Pamphlets relating to the nature trail can be picked up at the park entrance.

Queens Park
Kingswood Avenue, NW6 (information 8969 5661). Queens Park tube/rail. **Open** *7.30am-dusk daily.* **Admission** *free.*
Buggy access. Café. Disabled access: toilet. Nappy-changing facilities.

Bishop's Park is home to Fulham Palace, former residence of the Bishops of London...

If you're near Bishop's Park, look out for the ice-cream van that is parked in Stevenage Road throughout the year and serves some of the best ice-cream in west London.

Fulham Palace

Bishop's Avenue, off Fulham Palace Road, SW6 (7736 3233). Putney Bridge tube/220, 414, 430, 74 bus. **Open** *Museum* Mar-Oct 2-5pm Wed-Sun. Nov-Feb 1-4pm Thur-Sun. Closed 24-31 Dec. **Tours** 2pm 2nd & 4th Sun of mth. **Admission** (LP) *Museum* free. *Tours* £3; free under-16s.
This was the official residence of the Bishops of London from 704 until 1973: some of the oldest buildings here date back to 1480, although the main house is 16th century. The most recent addition is William Butterfield's neo-Gothic chapel, from 1866. The museum traces the buildings' history and has some funny old exhibits, not least the mummified rat. Imaginative staff organise children's workshops (suitable for 6-14s) during the school holidays; a recent workshop series was based on wartime Britain, but most relate to Roman, Tudor and Victorian periods. Ring to check what's coming up. Leave plenty of time to admire the lovely grounds, planted with rare trees, which provide a sanctuary off the busy Fulham Palace Road. The original moat trench can still be found around the grounds. There is also a walled kitchen garden full of herbs and rare plants.
Buggy access. Disabled access: toilet. Shop.

Shepherd's Bush & Hammersmith

Most children ask an obvious question when they see the roadsign: why is it called Shepherd's Bush, when it looks like the most unlikely spot in the world to find a shepherd? You can reassure them that there would have been plenty of sheep here up until the 19th century. Shepherds on their way to Smithfield Market regularly grazed sheep on the roundabout site, which is an ancient piece of common land. Hammersmith roundabout, on the other hand, is far more of an urban creation for a bus garage, shopping centre and tube station.

The transition from rural serenity to urban sprawl was rapid and the population of the area multiplied after the introduction of the metropolitan railway in the early 1900s. In recent years, both Hammersmith and Shepherd's Bush have experienced a gradual gentrification and have become popular places for young families to set up home.

Other than sheep, Shepherd's Bush has a long association with music and theatre. The **Empire** at Shepherd's Bush roundabout has been a popular venue for concerts and many big names, including the Rolling Stones, the Who, and Eric Clapton, have graced its stage. The BBC once used it as a studio (the hugely popular children's show *Crackerjack* was broadcast from here, parents).

The area is also full of opportunities for kids to take to the stage. **Music House** at Bush Hall (310 Uxbridge Road, W12) provides tuition and workshops in music and performing arts for all ages. Closer to Hammersmith are a few more good venues for entertainment and inspiration. The **Riverside** has a kid's cinema club and runs various workshops throughout the year. The **Dramatic Dreams Theatre Company** (8740 9925) is based here for those who want to hit the stage. Another popular haunt for the energetic is the circus workshop **Albert and Friends** (Gliddon Road, W14, 8237 1170; *see also p217*), where apprentice clowns can master the traditional skills of juggling, unicycling and acrobatics. Courses are run for children from 15

... and offers plenty of outdoor fun too. *See p152.*

months to 18 years. The **Lyric Theatre** also runs acting workshops for all ages, particularly during the summer months. If you're still seeking further inspiration, go to **Wood Lane**, where the BBC studios invite groups to take backstage tours (tickets need to be booked in advance and the minimum age is ten years; call 0870 603 0304 to book a ticket).

If a life on the stage is not your cup of tea, there are other fun ways to fill your days. West of Shepherd's Bush is **Loftus Road Stadium**, home to Queen's Park Rangers, where young players are trained to fulfil their ambitions of football stardom. For a good spot to practise football skills, you can't beat **Ravenscourt Park**, off Chiswick High Road, with its huge green spaces and other attractions. **Brook Green** is the only other proper park, which has in recent years become a congregating point for parents with pushchairs. This is because the park is ideal for toddlers, especially since the new interactive play area was set up to keep them amused.

Queen's Park Rangers Football Club
Loftus Road Stadium, South Africa Road, W12 (8743 0262/www.qpr.co.uk). White City tube. **Open** *Shop* 9am-5pm Mon-Fri; 9am-1pm Sat. **Tours** by appointment only. **Admission** *Tours* £4; £2 under-16s. **Credit** MC, V.
Loftus Road, home to QPR and London Wasps rugby, and currently being shared by Fulham FC, is also a hub of community football for young people. The match-day coaching package for children aged 5-16 gives them an exhausting morning of football training, followed by a welcome sit-down to see QPR play at home. The match-day birthday party includes a tour of the ground, two hours of outdoor football training, a £5 lunch voucher to spend in the ground, a ticket to see the match and a goodie bag, all for £16 per head. For more information, phone 8740 2509.
Buggy access. Disabled access: toilet. Nappy-changing facilities. Nearest picnic place: Hammersmith Park. Shop.

Ravenscourt Park
Ravenscourt Road, W6 (www.lbhf.gov.uk). Ravenscourt Park tube. **Open** 7.30am-dusk daily. **Admission** free.
In summer the packed paddling pool is the most popular spot in this family-friendly park. It has three play areas, including a challenging wooden adventure playground and a One O'Clock club (8748 3180) for under-5s. There's also a big pond, a nature trail and an exotic scented garden for the visually impaired. Kids with spare energy can run it off in the large grass pitch area or enjoy a game of tennis. The café is a useful spot for a family lunch; the Kiddies Corner menu (£2.50) lists such dishes as penne with tomato sauce or nuggets and chips. Parents tend to go for the imaginative salads and the delicious own-made cakes, which can be eaten outside on the shady lawn. There's an annual flower show with children's fair on the weekend before the August bank holiday (12 and 13 July in 2003). Fun days with bouncy castles and face painting run throughout the summer holidays.
Buggy access. Café. Nappy-changing facilities.

Chiswick

Chiswick is a stylish riverside suburb with a relaxed village feel. In the 18th century this was an area famous for cheesemaking, and was known as Ceswican. A pre-historic hammer and chisel, found near **Syon House**, suggest that some of the earliest human habitation may have started here, long before this quaint rural life. Another historical feature is the part of Chiswick High Road running from Turnham Green towards Brentford, which is part of an original Roman road to the West Country.

Chiswick's closeness to the M4 and Heathrow airport is one of the benefits of living here. It has become increasingly popular with wealthy families attracted by the large red brick houses and acres of green spaces for fun and frolics.

LUNCH BREAK

Around Bayswater

Beirut Express (112-114 Edgware Road, W2, 7724 2700), for freshly-squeezed juices.

Edgware Road is the heart of the Middle Eastern community in London and the stretch of the city from the Westway to Marble Arch is quite often referred to as 'Little Mecca'.

Mandola (139 Westbourne Grove, W2, 7229 4734), for African dishes and a relaxed vibe.

Nando's (63 Westbourne Grove, W2; see p182), for chicken-chicken and peri-peri (chips).

Ranoush Juice Bar (43 Edgware Road, W2, 7723 5929), for juices and snacks.

Around Queens Park

Lola's Café (26 Chamberlayne Road, NW10, no phone), a pleasant spot for Spanish sandwiches, pastries and drinks.

Orange, Lemon & Lime Café (16 College Parade NW6, 7372 1404) has an ambitious international menu but a friendly attitude toward families.

The Salusbury Deli (56 Salusbury Road, NW6, 7328 3287), for incredible pizzas, paninis and deli fare, and a café at the back.

Around Maida Vale

Café Rouge (30 Clifton Road, W9, 7286 2266), an oft-used family lunch spot.

Red Pepper (8 Formosa Street, W9, 7226 2708), a much-loved Italian restaurant with queues.

Around Notting Hill

Café Rouge (31 Kensington Park Road, W11, 7221 4449), where the children's menu is fab.

Osteria Basilico (29 Kensington Park Road, W11, 7727 9372), for fine pizzas in a cosy, family-friendly farmhouse kitchen setting.

S&M Café (268 Portobello Road, W10, 8968 8898; see p174), for a toothsome choice of sturdy sausages and creamy mash.

Around Earl's Court

Basilico (690 Fulham Road, SW6, 0800 0283531), for excellent family-sized pizzas.

The Gate (51 Queen Caroline Street, W6, 8748 6932), for some of London's best vegetarian fare.

Nando's (204 Earl's Court Road, SW5, 7259 2544), for chicken tonight.

Pizza Express (35 Earl's Court Road, W8, 7937 0761; see p175), for pizzas galore.

The River Café (Thames Wharf, Rainvill Road, W6, 7386 4200), for classical but pricey Italian food.

Wok Wok (140 Fulham Road, SW10, 7370 5355), for stir-fry noodles the way little ones like it.

Around Holland Park

The Holland Park Cafeteria (inside the park), for lovely home-made Italian food and ice-cream.

IT'S (128 Holland Park Avenue, W11, 7342 1106), for reliable Italian pizzas.

Julie's Restaurant (135 Portland Road, W11, 7229 8331; see p182), for weekend lunches.

Maison Blanc (102 Holland Park Avenue, W11, 7221 2494), for a lovely drop of tea.

Around Shepherd's Bush

Bush Bar & Grill (45A Goldhawk Road, W12, 8746 2111; see p182), for inventive brasserie fare.

Café Med (320 Goldhawk Road, W6, 8741 1994), a highly popular destination for those leisurely weekend family lunches.

Patio (5 Goldhawk Road, W5, 8743 5194), a cheap, cheerful and very tasty Polish café just round the corner from Shepherd's Bush Empire.

Polanka (258 King Street, W6, 8741 8268), supplier of decent Polish deli fare and half-price portions for children.

Shepherd's Bush Market on Goldhawk Road is also a decent place to stop for a quick bite, with lots of food stalls selling all sorts of goodies.

Smollensky's Bar & Grill (Bradmore House, Queen Caroline Street, W6, 8741 8124), popular with families, especially on Sundays when they bring on a children's entertainer.

Around Chiswick

Burlington Café (grounds of Chiswick House, W4, 8987 9431), for great breakfasts, simple wholesome lunches and serene gardens.

Chiswick High Road is pavement café heaven, perfect for al fresco dining with the nippers.

Coyote Café (2 Fauconberg Road, W4, 8742 8545), a Tex-Mex joint with outside tables and a choice of children's menus.

Grove Park Deli (22 Fauconberg Road, W4, 8995 8219), excellent for takeaway options.

IT'S (404 Chiswick High Road, W4, 8995 3636), for pizza and pasta.

The Natural Café (216 Chiswick High Road, W4, 8995 6655), a café a kid's corner and a menu that offers lots of wheat-free and dairy-free options for the nutritionally aware.

Around Ealing

Café Grove (65 The Grove, W5, 8810 0364), for a child-friendly Eastern European menu, outside tables and a garden.

My Old Dutch (53 New Broadway, W5, 8567 4486), a place where you can invent your own pancake filling combinations.

Nando's (284-286 Uxbridge Road, W5, 8746 1112), for chicken and spicy peri-peri chips.

Southall is little Punjab, so for paratha, kebabs and tandooris, head to caffs like the **New Asian Tandoori Centre** (114-8 The Green, Southall, Middlesex, 8574 2597) and **Gifto's Lahore Karahi** (162-4 The Broadway, Southall, Middlesex, 8813 8669).

Tootsie's (35 Haven Green, W5, 8566 8200), for great burgers and a great, friendly vibe.

Full steam ahead at **Kew Bridge Steam Museum**. *See p158.*

Turnham Green is a little pocket of Chiswick that has a particularly villagey feel and Turnham Green High Street has a few good children's clothes shops. At the end of Turnham Green is **Acton Green Common**, just one of the many open spaces that gives the whole area such a green and pleasant aspect. The **Green**, just off Chiswick High Road, has a church at the centre and local teams play cricket on the pristine lawns during the summer months. However, both these are simply large open spaces and lack the facilities for anything other than a picnic or run around. Just opposite Turnham Green is **Art 4 Fun** (444 Chiswick High Road, 8994 4100; *see p277*) a popular and well-equipped ceramics café.

Take a stroll along the Mall, on the edge of the Thames, to appreciate the mellowness of Chiswick life. **Duke's Meadows** are one of the first green spaces you reach: it has tennis courts, boat houses, cricket pitches and a nine-hole golf course. Junior golf coaching is organised on Saturday afternoons: contact Dukes Meadow Golf Club (8995 0537). If you continue even further along the river you will soon forget that you are in London at all. **Strand-on-the-Green** is a very picturesque stretch of the river where a fishing community lived and worked during the 18th century. There are a couple of child-friendly pubs here with riverside terraces.

Further adventures can be had beyond Strand-on-the-Green on Brentford High Street. The **Kew Bridge Steam Museum** can be identified by its huge chimney and is best visited at the weekends. The **Musical Museum**, a fantastic collection of organs and self-playing keyboard instruments, used to be just down the road but is in the throes of relocation as we go to press (for more info, write to 368 High Street, Brentford, Middlesex, TW8 OB1). **Watermans** (40 High Street, 8232 1010) is a riverside arts venue with children's theatre productions and art and drama workshops.

Sporting urges can be fulfilled at the **Fountain Leisure Centre** (658 Chiswick High Road, 8994 9596), which is renowned for its huge pool complex with waterslide and wave machine. It also has a popular activity area for toddlers called Little Tikes, as well as most other leisure centre activities from basketball to yoga. One of the best places in west London for fresh air and fluttery fun is found at **Syon Park**. The house itself may not be top of many children's lists of fun days out, but the surrounding grounds are full of child-friendly activities. The Butterfly House has over 1,000 live butterflies, and there's a reptile house and Snakes and Ladders, a huge indoor adventure playground.

Further into the suburban expanses beyond Brentford you come to **Gunnersbury Park**. **Hogarth House** (8994 6757) is located in the grounds and was home to the 18th-century painter William Hogarth, whose work is on display here. The **Gunnersbury Museum** (8992 1612), depicting the heritage of the surrounding area, is also an eye-opener. They open the Victorian kitchens to the public at weekends for a real step back in time. More fun in the kitchen can be had at the **Kids Cookery School** (107 Gunnersbury Lane, 8992 8882) where young chefs aged three to 16 can learn new culinary techniques all year round.

Chiswick House

Burlington Lane, W4 (8995 0508/www.english-heritage. org.uk). Turnham Green tube then E3 bus to Edensor Road/Chiswick rail or Hammersmith tube/rail then 190 bus. **Open** *Apr-Sept* 10am-6pm daily. *Oct* 10am-5pm daily. *Nov, Dec, Mar* open only for pre-booked appointments. Last entry 30mins before closing. Closed 24-26 Dec, Jan, Feb. **Tours** by arrangement; phone for details. **Admission** (EH/LP) incl audio guide £3.50; £3 concessions; £2 5-16s; free under-5s. **Credit** MC, V.
Walking through the picturesque gardens of Chiswick House you'll come across various delights – obelisks hidden among the trees, a classical temple, a lake and a cascading waterfall. Lots of families come here on summer days and plonk down for a picnic, have lunch at the café or play a game of cricket on the well-maintained grounds. You can also take a jaunt along the river, which is only a stone's throw away. The Burlington Café, in the grounds, is a splendid place for lunch. English Heritage, which runs the site, sometimes stages family activity days and various re-enactments at Chiswick House: check its website for details.
Buggy access. Café. Disabled access. Nearest picnic place: Chiswick Park. Shop.

Go Westway

Built in the late 1960s, the Westway (aka the A40) stretches from Marylebone Road to White City and dominates the North Kensington skyline. As well as providing a useful mile-long umbrella, the Westway is shelter for various regeneration projects: it's a grisly concrete monstrosity, yes, but now also an appealing urban playground. Its underworld is one of London's funkiest places where children can let off steam.

Just off the Portobello Road is one of London's premier skate zones. **Playstation Skate Park** (Bay 65-6, Acklam Road, W10, 8969 4669; *see also p259*) has the only vert ramp in London, along with a mini ramp and a street course. The Park is only a short ride away from Latimer Road and Meanwhile Gardens, which have been popular skate haunts since the 1970s. If you're lucky, you might even catch iconic skater Tony Hawk in action as he practises here. Listen out for the pumping tunes and you'll know you've reached the right place.

The **Westway Sports Centre** (1 Crowthorne Road, W10, 8969 0992; *see also p251*) is a well-maintained multi-sports facility with the biggest climbing wall in the country, with overhangs, chimneys and mountain surfaces. The wall reaches an impressive 15 metres.

The **Westway Stables** (Stable Way, W10, 8964 2140) are simply heaven for urban cowboys. There are 36 horses here and treks take place on the nearby open spaces of Wormwood scrubs, 200 acres of common land.

Finally, there's **Bramley's Big Adventure** (136 Bramley Road, W11, 8 960 1515; *see p247*) for the little ones, a fun-filled world of ropes, ball pools and padded climbing frames all combined in a three-storey assault course.

Gunnersbury Triangle Nature Reserve

Bollo Lane, W4 (8747 3881/www.wildlondon.org.uk). Chiswick Park tube. **Open** 24hrs daily. **Admission** free.
In the late 19th century this area of land was enclosed by railway tracks and unfit for human habitation. As the woodland grew up and the wildlife took over, it became one of the most important sites for urban wildlife in this part of the city. Following the trail today, visitors can admire the pond and meadowland and try to spot the 19 species of butterfly that have been recorded fluttering by here. The warden (present full time during the summer) works hard to produce a wonderful programme of activities (craft workshops, mini beast safaris) for young visitors. They're free and run on a drop-in basis. The reserve's open day is usually in June: to find out more, call the warden and ask for a programme. There's a small information cabin (open Tuesday and Sunday afternoons), where you can ask the staff questions of urban ecology, pick up trail leaflets, find out about guided tours (summer only) or hire a net to go pond dipping.
Buggy access.

Kew Bridge Steam Museum

Green Dragon Lane, Brentford, Middx (8568 4757/ www.kbsm.org). Gunnersbury tube/Kew Bridge rail/65, 237, 267, 391 bus. **Open** 11am-5pm daily. Closed 25 Dec, Good Friday. **Tours** by arrangement; phone for details. **Admission** (LP) *Mon-Fri* £3.60; £2.70 concessions; £1.50 5-15s; £8 family (2+3); free under-5s. *Sat, Sun* £4.60; £3.70 concessions; £2.50 5-15s; £11.95 family (2+3); free under-5s. Free to all after 4pm Mon-Fri. Under-13s must be accompanied by an adult. **Credit** MC, V.
Visit this Victorian riverside pumping station on high days and holidays; it's all sound and fury when the engines are in steam, but this only happens on specific days, so ring before you set out. The Cornish beam engine is fired up at 3pm most weekends and holiday periods, and there are usually a couple of others powering away. During the school holidays and bank holidays, there's a lot of action, because the education department and friendly volunteers run all kinds of activities for family groups. The Water for Life exhibition gives the lowdown on the history of London's vast sewer system and a walk-through section of the city's water ring main, just to show how much water flows around this city all the time. Don't worry about getting wet, though – the section is only for demonstration purposes so there's no water in it. Log on to the website for up-to-date information on special events and exhibitions at the museum. Events need to be booked ahead to guarantee joining in the fun.
Buggy access. Nearest picnic place: Kew Green. Shop.

Syon House

Syon Park, Brentford, Middx (8560 0882/London Butterfly House 8560 0378/Aquatic Experience 8847 4730/Snakes and Ladders 8847 0946/www.syonpark. co.uk). Gunnersbury tube/rail then 237, 267 bus. **Open** *House Apr-early Nov* 11am-5pm Wed, Thur, Sun, bank hol Mon. Last entry 4.15pm. *Gardens* closed 25, 26 Dec. **Tours** by arrangement; phone for details. **Admission** *House & gardens* £6.95; £5.95 concessions 5-16s; £15 family (2+2); free under-5s. *Gardens only* £3.50; £2.50 concessions, 5-16s; £8 family (2+2); free under-5s. *Aquatic Experience* £4; £3.50 3-15s; free under-3s; £12.50 family (2+3). *Butterfly House* £4.95; £3.95 3-16s; £4.25 concessions; £15 family (2+3). *Snakes and Ladders* no adults without a child. *Term time* £3.15 under-5s; £4.15 over-5s; free adults. *School hols & weekends* £3.90 under-5s; £5 over-5s. **Credit** MC, V.

The Butterfly House at
Syon House. *See p158.*

While parents love Syon House for its gracious location, many children find other attractions more enjoyable. The London Butterfly House, for instance, is a memorable experience, where you wander around a tropical plant- and bird-filled conservatory, home also to thousands of multicoloured butterflies and wooden cases of their cocoons. There are also leaf-cutter ants and other insects, and pools of fish. Next door is the equally tropical Aquatic Experience, where visitors step gingerly between more fish-filled pools and tanks of big Nile and Caiman crocodiles, as well as a few harmless looking babies. Red-bellied piranha fish and a tank of really vast, evil-looking piranhas leer hungrily throught their tank glass. At the back of this house is a pond dipping and identification area with nets for scooping. Both houses have gift shops selling plastic creepy crawlies and souvenir jewellery, and both have ample outside picnic space.

The site that most children yearn for is Snakes and Ladders, an indoor adventure playground designed like a castle, with three tiers of play areas, which include slides, hanging ropes and masses of huge balls. There's also a good area for under-5s and a café where parents can chill out There's also an outside area with motorised bikes, which cost £1 a ride. In summer you should bring a picnic with you, as the nicest locations to eat are outside. In the winter, when indoor eating is the only real option, the Patio Cafeteria (8758 1175) has a selection of hot meals and a junior menu.

If you do find the time and finances to visit the house and grounds as well as all the child-pleasers above, you can easily spend half a day here. On the weekends, a wooden mini steam railway travels through the trees and around the flowerbeds. The house itself is also quite an adventure as each room seems more impressive than the last, from the grand Roman hallway to the Red Drawing Room, with its crimson silk walls and Roman statues.

Café. Nappy-changing facilities. Nearest picnic place: Syon House Gardens/Syon Park. Shop.

Further west

The comfortable suburb of **Ealing**, at the westerly end of the District and Central lines, is a prime location for family life. You're never more than a toddler's ramble from a park or open space, and many parts are distinctly rural in character. The largest open spaces are nestled around the Brent River, where you can find golf courses, fields of ponies and acres of common land. **Brent Lodge Park**, or 'Bunny Park' as locals refer to it, is a good place to start. It has a lovely playground, maze and a small zoo for the bunnies and other cuddleworthy guests. From here you can wander for hours along the river in either direction away from any signs of urban life. Other green spots to consider include **Horsenden Hill**, the highest point in Ealing borough with great views over the whole of London; **Ealing Common**, close to the busy high road; and **Osterley Park** on the outskirts of Hanwell. **Osterly House** is a gorgeous place to visit, with a brilliant café. In summer there are all sorts of events for children around the grounds.

The central green lung, where most parents congregate, is **Walpole Park**. During July and August the park hosts the majority of events at the Ealing Summer Festival, with lots of child-friendly activities. Walpole Park is in the grounds of **Pitshanger Manor**, where the programme of events includes regular shows and workshops for young people. Ealing Town Hall is the venue for parent and toddler groups through out the year, and they also organise kids discos during half-term.

Ealing has a number of sports centres, the most interesting is the **Gurnell Leisure Centre** (8998 3241), which boasts an Olympic-sized pool, three grass pitches, toddlers groups and fitness clubs.

Riders tack up at **Ealing Riding School** on Gunnersbury Avenue (17-19 Gunnersbury Avenue, Ealing, W5, 8992 3808; *see also p257*). Young golfers shouldn't have much trouble finding a place to practise their swing, and **Brent Valley Golf Course** (Church Road, Hamwell, W7, 8567 1287) is a good place for beginners.

Further west of Ealing is **Southall**, home to London's largest Asian community. This is the venue for London's only surviving agricultural market, where they auction horses on a Wednesday. It is also a great place to pick up saris, bangles, sandals and other bits and bobs at bargain prices. The largest Sikh temple outside India opened in spring 2003 in Southall. The **Sri Guru Singh Sabha Gurdwara temple** (Alice Way, Hanworth Road, Hounslow), only second in size to the Golden Temple in Amritsar, has a capacity for 3,000 people. The glorious **Shri Swaminarayan Mandir Temple**, to the north of Southall, is a breathtakingly beautiful monument to Hinduism.

Brent Lodge Park
Church Road, W7 (8825 7529). Hanwell rail. **Open** 7.30am-dusk. *Maze & animals Apr-Sept* 10.30am-5pm daily. *Sept-Mar* 10.30pm-4pm daily. **Admission** £1; 50p concessions. **No credit cards.**
The Millennium Maze, planted in 1999, continues to bulk up and provide outdoor fun at this sweet local park. Young explorers like to stand triumphantly on the central tower once they've worked their way round. Anxious parents can stand on the viewing platform outside to locate their squawking progeny. The benches around the maze area are covered in plaques bearing the millennial wishes of various people.

Walk up the hill from the maze to reach the hub of the park's activities: there's a café for ice-cream and sandwiches, a playground and an animal centre. The centre (25p children, 50p adults, 8758 5019) houses a handful of squirrel monkeys, a pair of sleepy geckos and some scary spiders, along with a few birds and the odd bunny.
Buggy access. Café. Disabled toilet. Nappy-changing facilities (in park).

Osterley House
Osterley Park, off Jersey Road, Isleworth, Middx (8232 5050/recorded info 01494 755566/www.nationaltrust. org.uk/osterley). Osterley tube. **Open** *House late Mar-early Nov* 1-4.30pm Wed-Sun. *Park* 9am-dusk daily. **Tours** by arrangement; min 15 people. **Admission** (NT) *House* £4.50; £2.25 5-15s; £11.20 family (2+3); free under-5s. *Park* free. **Credit** (kiosk only) MC, V.
Osterley House was built for Sir Thomas Gresham (founder of the Royal Exchange) in 1576, but transformed by Robert Adam in 1761. Adam's revamp is dominated by the imposing colonnade of white pillars before the courtyard of the house's red-brick body. The splendour of the state rooms alone makes the house worth the visit, but the still-used Tudor stables, the vast parkland walks and the ghost said to be lurking in the basement add to Osterley's allure. Children can pick up a house trail from the office to help them explore these delightful surroundings. In August children can get in free, and Mondays are Fundays in the same month.
Café. Car park (£3 per day, NT members free). Disabled access: lift, toilet. Nappy-changing facilities. Nearest picnic place: front lawn/picnic benches in grounds. Shop.

Pitshanger Manor & Gallery
Walpole Park, Mattock Lane, W5 (8567 1227/ www.ealing.gov.uk/pmgallery&house). Ealing Broadway tube/rail. **Open** 1-5pm Tue-Fri; 11am-5pm Sat; 1-5pm Sun (May-Sept). Closed Good Friday, 25, 26 Dec, 1 Jan, bank hols. **Tours** by arrangement; phone for details. **Admission** free.
A beautiful Regency villa in Walpole Park, most of Pitshanger was rebuilt in 1801-3 by Sir John Soane, architect of the Bank of England. His highly individual ideas in design and decoration make this a very special place. Among the exhibits is the Hull Grundy Martinware collection of pottery. There is an art gallery adjacent to the museum (8567 1227), where contemporary exhibitions are held, plus a lecture and workshop programme for all ages. Walpole Park is enlivened by loads of music festivals in summer; phone Ealing council for details (8579 2424). The Walpole Park playground is also up and running with a new range of play equipment.
Buggy access. Disabled access: lift, toilet. Lift. Nearest picnic place: Walpole Park.

Shri Swaminarayan Mandir Temple
105-15 Brentfield Road, NW10 (8965 2651/ www.swaminarayan.org). Wembley Park tube then BR2 bus. **Open** 9.30am-6pm daily. **Admission** (LP) free. *Exhibition* £2; £1.50 6-15s; free under-6s.
Built in 1995, this Hindu temple is an extraordinary structure, intricately carved by master sculptors. Much of the stone was sent to India to be carved and then brought back to Neasden at a cost of more than £10 million. It also has a permanent exhibition, with a video, called Understanding Hinduism, presented in a clear and entertaining way (it's particularly useful for those Year Sixes studying world religion). Stock up on incense sticks at the shop and try to recreate the temple's serenity at home.
Buggy access. Café. Disabled access: lift, toilet. Nappy-changing facilities. Shop.

Consumer

Eating

And mind you finish your peas.

One child's chicken nugget is another child's poison – that much we know. So our selection of family-friendly restaurants is based on more than the promise of a kiddy menu. Children's menus are a bonus, certainly when you're trying not to spend a fortune, but they can be overly reliant on convenience freezer fare. If there's one dish that irks organically-minded, vegetarian or nutritionally clued-up parents, it's chicken nuggets with chips.

So while certainly not a nugget-free zone, this chapter highlights the alternatives. Places that give children a taste of world cuisines, and our favourite vegetarian restaurants, pizza parlours, burger bars, bistros, posh restaurants, cafés, cake shops, noodle shops, chip shops. It's a wide selection, but all the places have one thing in common: they extend a warm welcome to babies and children. Most can provide a high chair, as well as spare plates and spoons for sharing, straws for drinks and a smile.

Where possible, we've included the contact details for other branches of the restaurants we list, but bear in mind that not all branches will have the same facilities. For more useful places to eat in a particular area of town, see the **Lunch Break** boxes in the **Around Town** chapters.

Southwark & Bankside

fish!

Cathedral Street, Borough Market, SE1 (7407 3803/ www.fishdiner.co.uk). London Bridge tube/rail. **Meals served** 11.30am-3pm, 5-10.45pm Mon-Fri; 11.30am-11pm Sat; noon-10pm Sun. **Main courses** £8.90-£16.95. **Credit** AmEx, DC, MC, V. **Map** p319 M8.
And chips? Yes, of course. Not the best place for fish dishes (there are fish soups, cakes and other seafood classics on the menu), but this branch in a dwindling chain has the benefit of a great location, right by Borough Market and Southwark Cathedral. The children's menu also lists either tuna bolognese or chicken and chips if the fish doesn't appeal. The price includes a drink and a pud.
Buggy access. Children's menu (£6.95). High chairs. Tables outdoors (pavement).
Branch County Hall, Belvedere Road, SE1 (7401 6734).

The People's Palace

Level 3, Royal Festival Hall, South Bank Centre, SE1 (7928 9999/www.peoplespalace.co.uk). Embankment tube/ Charing Cross or Waterloo tube/rail. **Lunch served** noon-3pm, **dinner served** 5.30-11pm daily. **Main courses** £12.50-£17. **Set lunch** £12.50 2 courses, £16.50 3 courses. **Set dinner** (5.30-7pm Mon-Sat, all day Sun) £16.50 2 courses, £20.50 3 courses (£21.50 Sun). **Credit** AmEx, DC, MC, V. **Map** p319 M8.

Lunch at the Palace should perhaps be reserved for children who enjoy their food – it would be a shame to waste this lovely grub on fussy types. While they tuck in, kids can enjoy the splendid river views. The cooking has Mediterranean influences and portions are generous; the junior menu lists excellent sausage and mash, pasta in a variety of guises, chicken and chips or pizza, with ice cream, banana and custard or other sweet treats to follow.
Buggy access. Children's menu (£10 2 courses). High chairs. No-smoking tables.

Southwark Cathedral Refectory

Southwark Cathedral, Montague Close, SE1 (7407 5740/www.digbytrout.co.uk). London Bridge tube/rail. **Open** 10am-5pm daily. **Credit** MC, V. **Map** p321 P8.
A serene place indeed, the Cathedral's pleasant, friendly café comes as a relief after the busy riverside scene. Children home in, quite rightly, on the own-made cakes – and if it's a hot meal they're after, a daily specials board lists the cooked lunches (pasta bake, for example, or braised sausages with creamy mash). Children can share the large portions.
Buggy access. High chairs. Disabled: toilet. No smoking. Tables outdoors (12, courtyard).

The City

Carluccio's Caffè

12 West Smithfield, EC1 (7329 5904/ www.carluccios.co.uk). Farringdon tube/rail. **Meals served** 8am-11pm Mon-Fri; 10am-11pm Sat; 10am-10pm Sun. **Main courses** £4.95-£8.95. **Credit** AmEx, MC, V. **Map** p320 O5.
Winner last year of the *Time Out* Award for best Family restaurant, Carluccio's always comes as a big treat after the umpteenth burger bar. For top notch pasta with interesting, fresh sauces, rice dishes with bite, salads with zing, bread with flair and the loveliest hot chocolate in town, come here for dinner, late breakfast, a long coffee break or afternoon tea.
Buggy access. High chairs. Children's menu. Tables outdoors (8, pavement).
Branches throughout town. Check the phone book for your nearest.

Smiths of Smithfield

67-77 Charterhouse Street, EC1 (7251 7950/ www.smiths ofsmithfield.co.uk). Farringdon tube/rail. **Ground floor bar/café** **Meals served** 7am-5pm Mon-Fri; 10am-5pm Sat; 9.30am-5pm Sun. **Main courses** £3.50-£8.50. **Credit** AmEx, MC, V. **Map** p320 O5.
Trendy it may look, with its exposed brick and pipework, long bar and leather sofas, but the ground floor at Smiths is a fab place to take the children for a weekend lunch, although as they take no bookings you may have to wait for a table. The all-day breakfast is a big hit with kids: team the £3 worth of egg, bacon, beans and toast with a bowl of the most perfectly golden chips and you have an inexpensive blowout. Grilled organic chicken in a salady roll makes a good lunch. Few children can resist the full cream milkshakes to finish.
Buggy access. High chairs. Tables outdoors (6, pavement).

Sweet things, **Sticky Fingers**. *See p164*.

The Place Below

St Mary le Bow Church, Cheapside, EC2 (7329 0789/ www.theplacebelow.co.uk). St Paul's tube/Bank tube/DLR. **Breakfast served** 7.30-10.30am, **lunch served** 11.30am-2.30pm, **snacks served** 2.30-3.30pm Mon-Fri. **Credit** AmEx, LV, MC, £TC, V. **Map** 320 P6.

If you like to take in a slice of history with your quiche, this excellent vegetarian café in the church crypt should be right up your alley. The staff don't go all out to encourage family diners, so there are no high-chairs or anything, but children are certainly welcome and there are lots of cosy nooks and crannies to tuck yourselves into. Choose from a hearty meatless menu of soups, casseroles, cakes and puds. The pumpkin and coriander soup is delicious, the salads good to share and the brownies are pure, squidgy chocolate heaven.

Bloomsbury & Holborn

Bank Aldwych

1 Kingsway, WC2 (7379 9797/www.bankrestaurants. com). Holborn tube. **Breakfast served** 7-10.30am Mon-Fri; 8-10.30am Sat. **Brunch served** 11.30am-3.30pm Sat, Sun. **Lunch served** noon-3pm Mon-Fri. **Dinner served** 5.30-11pm Mon-Sat; 5.30-9.30pm Sun. **Main courses** £8.95-£19.50. **Set meal** (lunch, 5.30-7pm, 10-11pm) £12.50 2 courses, £15 3 courses. **Credit** AmEx, DC, MC, V. **Map** p317 M6.

A sea of suits during the week, this vast and imposing restaurant still offers a children's menu for families unintimidated by the businesslike vibe. Come for lunch at the weekend, however, and the atmosphere is keenly child-centred, with a big central play table providing refuge from parental drones. Linguine with tomato sauce, chipolatas with chips and beans, breaded chicken or beefburger with chips can be followed by ice cream, sticky toffee pudding or a milkshake.

Booking advisable. Children's menu (£6.95 brunch, £6.95 2 course dinner). Crayons. High chairs. Nappy-changing facilities. Toys.

Navarro's

67 Charlotte Street, W1 (7637 7713/www.navarros. co.uk). Goodge Street tube. **Lunch served** noon-3pm Mon-Fri. **Dinner served** 6-10pm Mon-Sat. **Tapas** £3.05-£15. **Credit** AmEx, DC, MC, V. **Map** 316 J5.

Handy for Pollock's Toy Museum (*see p59*), this attractive Spanish restaurant is far too popular, but come for an early lunch and you'll be rewarded with fine, fresh tapas, of which there are 50 varieties, including juicy grilled prawns, meatballs, tortillas and pancakes, rice dishes, potatoes, lovely fresh bread and quality olives and much more. Pick a selection for a filling, varied family lunch.

Buggy access. High chairs.

Table Café

Basement of Habitat, 196 Tottenham Court Road, W1 (7636 8330). Goodge Street tube. **Breakfast served** 10am-noon, **lunch served** noon-4pm, **tea served** 4-5.30pm daily. **Main courses** £6.95-£7.90. **Set lunch** £7.50 2 courses. **Credit** MC, V. **Map** p316 J4.

The best shop café we know has a short but delightful menu and efficient staff who are always pleasant to children. The big colourful salads with herby focaccia are great to share, and there are pasta dishes, risottos, well filled sandwiches and cakes and puds to keep you out of the shop all afternoon.

Booking advisable (lunch). Disabled: lift. High chairs. Nappy-changing facilities. No smoking.

Kensington & Chelsea

Big Easy

332-4 King's Road, SW3 (7352 4071/ www.bigeasy.uk. com). Sloane Square tube then 11, 19, 22 bus. **Meals served** noon-11.30pm Mon-Thur, Sun; noon-12.30am Fri, Sat. **Main courses** £7.95-£19.50. **Set lunch** (noon-5pm Mon-Fri) £8.95 2 courses. **Credit** AmEx, MC, V. **Map** p315 E12.

Noisy big eaters will love it here. We do. The music might be

loud and the decor unnerving, but the welcome is warm and the food consistently good. The menu veers from seafood to steak to barbecue, so there's something for all tastes. The children's menu lists hot dogs, chicken dippers and burgers, and there are fruity children's cocktails too.
Children's menu (£4.95, dessert £2-£3.95). Balloons. Crayons. High chairs. Nappy-changing facilities. No-smoking tables. Tables outdoors (5, pavement).

Bluebird

350 King's Road, SW3 (7559 1000/www.conran.co.uk). Sloane Square tube then 11, 19, 22 bus. **Brunch served** noon-3.30pm Sat, Sun. **Lunch served** 12.30-3pm Mon-Fri. **Dinner served** 6-11pm Mon-Sat; 6-10pm Sun. **Main courses** £11.50-£19.25. **Set lunch** (Mon-Fri) £15.50 2 courses, £20 3 courses. **Credit** AmEx, DC, MC, V. **Map** p315 D12.
Bluebird is stylish and polished, like all Conran places, and like many of them encourages children to partake of brunch at weekends: little ones get linguini in tomato sauce, fish and chips or other well executed favourites. For adults, the set menu represents reasonably good value.
Buggy access. Children's menu (£4-£5.50). High chairs. Nappy-changing facilities. Tables outdoors (25, courtyard).

Sticky Fingers

1A Phillimore Gardens, W8 (7938 5338/www.sticky fingers.co.uk). High Street Kensington tube. **Meals served** noon-11pm Mon-Thur, Sun; noon-11.30pm Fri, Sat. **Main courses** £8.45-£15.95. **Credit** AmEx, DC, MC, V. **Map** p314 A9.
Come on a Sunday and you can get your face painted as well as ketchup-smeared at ex Rolling Stone Bill Wyman's like-able burger joint. This place is very child friendly and teenage rock historians will also be impressed by the Stones memorabilia strategically placed. Little children may find the

music a bit too much of a blast, but everything else is just dandy, especially on Sundays. The children's menu, available every day, gives them nuggets, burgers (they're very good here; we recommend them for all ages) and pasta. Dessert and a soft drink is included. Adults can have ribs, prawns, steaks, wings, excellent crisp chips and cocktails.
Buggy access. Children's menu (£7.25). Entertainment: face painting 1-4pm Sun. High chairs.

West End

Amato

14 Old Compton Street, W1 (7734 5733/www.amato. co.uk). Leicester Square or Tottenham Court Road tube. **Open** 8am-10pm Mon-Sat; 10am-8pm Sun. **Main courses** £5.50-£8.50. **Credit** AmEx, DC, MC, V. **Map** p317 K6.
You'll love this Soho café, whose window display of fabulously creamy and intricately decorated *pasticcini* (cakes) tempts hungry passers by inside. The menu runs from pastries to cooked breakfasts through toasted sandwiches to well executed pasta dishes.
Bookings not accepted. Buggy access.

Belgo Centraal

50 Earlham Street, WC2 (7813 2233/www.belgo-restaurants.com). Covent Garden tube. **Meals served** noon-10.30pm Mon, Sun; noon-11.30pm Tue-Sat. **Main courses** £8.95-£18.95. **Set lunch** (noon-5pm) £5.95 1 course. **Credit** AmEx, DC, MC, V. **Map** p317 L6.
On a budget? Choose the excellent value set lunch at this busy seafood, chips and beer tavern. If you choose to eat à la carte, however, two children can choose from their menu free of charge. Choice, choices. This flagship branch of Belgo feels like it's in the bowels of the city, and the noise levels can be offputting. The food is pretty good though. Children can

Nippers and nuggets at **Browns**. *See p167.*

PARKLIFE Cafés

Brew House

*Kenwood, Hampstead Lane, NW3 (8341 5384).
Bus 210, 214.* **Open** *Oct-Mar* 9am-dusk daily. *Apr-Sept* 9am-6pm (7.30pm on concert nights) daily.
Credit (over £10) MC, V.
The café that Heath walkers love so much is
situated in the former coach house of Kenswood
House. Much of the food is prepared (where
possible) with organic or free-range ingredients.
It's canteen-style service for the hot food, which
means when the place is packed you stand
salivating in a queue for a while.

Burlington's Café

*Chiswick House, off Burlington Lane, W4 (8987
9431). Turnham Green tube/Chiswick rail.* **Open**
Oct-Mar 10am-4pm Wed-Sun. Apr-Sept 10am-5pm
daily. **No credit cards**.
A delightfully homely café much loved by dog
walkers and visitors to Chiswick House,
Burlington's does a children's menu (chips,
pasta, beans on toast) but the fresh sandwiches
and exceptionally moist cakes (we love the
lemon cake here) are far more attractive.

Golders Hill Park Refreshment House

*North End Road, NW3 (8455 8010). Golders
Green or Hampstead tube.* **Open** 10am-dusk daily.
No credit cards.
A lovely spot in north London, the refreshment
House is famous for the Arte Gelato ice creams,
many made by the proprietor using fruit he grows
himself, the Refreshment House is heavenly on a
hot summer's day. The simple food, such as pasta
dishes, salads, soups and sandwiches, has been a
bit hit-and-miss in the past, but if you go with one
of the recommended dishes of the day you're
unlikely to be disappointed.

Oshobasho Café

*Highgate Wood, Muswell Hill Road, N10 (8444
1505). Highgate tube/43, 134 bus.* **Open** 11am-3pm Mon (no food served); 8.30am-30mins before
dusk Tue-Sun. **No credit cards**.

Its sylvan setting draws big crowds when the sun,
schools and north London families are out: expect
queues at weekends. If you can bag a table on the
terrace on a fine day, consider yourself blessed.
The menu is usually short and on a blackboard,
listing crowd-pleasing exotica like foccaccia
sandwiches, salads, pastas and own-made cakes.
You order your food at the counter.

Pavilion Café

*Dulwich Park, off College Road, SE21 (8299
1383). North Dulwich or West Dulwich rail.* **Open**
Summer 9am-6pm (with some late evenings) daily.
Winter 9am-dusk daily. **No credit cards**.
The pretty pavilion has been refurbished to include
a swisher patio for eating out, indoor play area, ice
cream parlour and, at long last, loos (you used to
have to use the park ones). The new owners have
plumped up the menu, too. Now the daily specials
list is eclectic and Mediterranean in flavour, but all-day fry-ups and bacon sarnies are also bestsellers.
Everything, including the cakes, is made on the
premises. The children's menu is a godsend for
the area's many tricycle riders. The ice cream is
by Beechdean; glorious stuff from a Jersey herd in
Kent. A brilliant place for a family meal.

Pembroke Lodge Cafeteria

*Richmond Park, Richmond, Surrey (8948 7371).
Richmond tube/rail.* **Open** 10am-5.30pm daily.
Credit (over £10) MC, V.
The Lodge was the childhood home of philosopher
Bertrand Russell, and stands in one of the most
stunning parts of this vast park. Its location, half
way between Richmond and Ham Gates and
perched high up on Richmond Hill, affords
spectacular views west over the Thames valley. On
mild days you can sit on the pretty terrace while
kids roam in the gardens of the Lodge (quite steep
in places). In colder weather you can enjoy the view
from the huge windows of the former drawing
rooms. The cooks here provide a children's lunch;
there are roasts at the weekends and usually four
hot dishes of the day, as well as cream teas, ice
creams and great cakes. Heaven.

choose a bowl of moules, or pork and leek sausages, rotisserie chicken or breaded fish, all served with chips. There's
ice-cream to follow, and cranberry juice to wash it all down.
*Buggy access. Children's menu (£4.95). Crayons. High
chairs. Lift.*
Branches Belgo Bierodrome 173 Upper Street, N1 (7226
5835); Belgo Noord 72 Chalk Farm Road, NW1 (7267
0718).

Benihana

*37 Sackville Street, W1 (7494 2525/www.benihana.co.uk).
Piccadilly Circus tube.* **Lunch served** noon-2.30pm daily.
Dinner served 6-10.30pm Mon-Sat; 5-10pm Sun. **Set
meals** *Lunch* £8.75-£25 4 courses. *Dinner* £17-£50 6
courses. **Credit** AmEx, DC, MC, V. **Map** p318 J7.

It's not just teppanyaki here, but the hotplate at Benihana is
where it's at. Red-hatted chefs cook the food in front of diners, juggling their pepperpots and applying soy sauce with
dramatic flourishes. Children enjoy the entertainment and
the golden chicken, prawns and steak are served fresh and
sizzling. Sushi, sashimi and tempura are also on the menu in
this international chain founded by ex-wrestler Rocky Aoki.
Set menus are good; for adults the teppan specials include
green tea, onion soup, a salad, rice, prawn roll and ice cream
to follow. At the NW3 branch, Sunday lunch-time is fun time,
with children's entertainment, included in the bill of fare.
Buggy access. High chairs. Nappy-changing facilities.
Branches 77 King's Road, SW3 (7376 7799); 100 Avenue
Road, NW3 (7586 9508).

Consumer

Browns

82-4 St Martin's Lane, WC2 (7497 5050). Leicester Square tube. **Meals served** noon-11.30pm Mon-Sat; noon-11pm Sun. **Main courses** £7.95-£16.95. **Set meals** (noon-6pm daily) £10.95 2 courses. **Credit** AmEx, DC, MC, V. **Map** p319 L7.

This busy central London branch of the successful chain endears itself to families with a reasonably priced, good quality children's menu. Pasta, pork and leek sausages, grilled chicken or burger with chips (or mash, if preferred) costs £3.95, and ice cream is thrown in. Soft drinks are just 65p. Adults can go for decent quality brasserie food: steaks, pies, sausages, salads and fish dishes. Beware, it's busy just after office hours; but at quiet times there's plenty of room in this big polished barn of a place to spread out.
Children's menu (£3.95). High chairs. Nappy-changing facilities. No-smoking tables.

Café Pacifico

5 Langley Street, WC2 (7379 7728/www.cafepacifico-laperla.com). Covent Garden or Leicester Square tube. **Meals served** noon-11.45pm Mon-Sat, noon-10.45pm Sun. **Main courses** £6-£14.95. **Credit** AmEx, MC, V. **Map** p317 L6.

This tequila-flavoured cantina is spacious, colourful and pleasingly relaxed. Children are warmly welcomed during the day; their menu *para niños* is remarkably good value. It lists the usual nuggets (pepitas de pollo), chips and fish fingers (dedos de pescado), but children who prefer a less deep-fried option can tuck into a yummy platter of cheese-filled quesadillas with rice, avocado and mayo. The price includes pop and an ice cream. The menu for adults lists all the typical Mexican specials, and the £6 lunch-time menu is excellent value. Parents in charge of buggies might have to forgo the margarita jugs in favour of the delicious alcohol-free cocktails (which children will also love). Our favourite is the cancun cooler, all crushed strawberries and citrus (£2.90). Don't miss the funny fairground mirrors outside the loos.
Buggy access. Children's menu (£2.75). Crayons. High chairs.

Café Emm

17 Frith Street, W1 (7437 0723). Piccadilly Circus tube. **Lunch served** noon-2.30pm Mon-Fri; 1-4pm Sat; 1-4pm Sun. **Dinner served** 5.30-10.30pm Mon-Thur; 5.30-11.30pm Fri; 5-11.30pm Sat; 5-10.30pm Sun. **Main courses** £5.95-£8.95. **Credit** MC, £TC, V. **Map** p317 6K.

A handy lunch spot in Soho, Café Emm is lively in the evenings (office parties are a speciality). Nevertheless, the staff are accommodating toward children, recommending starters to suit small appetites or divvying up main courses for two children to share. Expect filling favourites such as potato skins, crêpes, salads, fish dishes and glorious own-made puddings – who could resist the treacle tart with a great blob of vanilla ice-cream on top?
High chair. Tables outdoors (2, pavement).

Christopher's

18 Wellington Street, WC2 (7240 4222/www.christophers grill.com). Covent Garden, Embankment or Temple tube/ Charing Cross tube/rail. Restaurant **Brunch served** 11.30am-4pm Sat, Sun. **Lunch served** noon-3pm Mon-Fri. **Dinner served** 5pm-midnight Mon-Sat. **Main courses** £11.50-£28. **Set menu** (5-7pm; 10pm midnight Mon-Sat) £12.95 2 courses; £16.50 3 courses. **Credit** AmEx, DC, MC, £TC, V. **Map** 319 L7.

If you want to push the boat out in Theatreland, you'd do well to consider this plush, yet relaxed first-floor restaurant. Despite the fairly formal air (the staircase is magnificent), it's

friendly, especially at weekends and early evenings (lunchtimes seem more corporate). The children's menu includes little gems like mini hamburgers, chicken or fish strips and chips, drink included.
Children's menu (£6.50). No-smoking tables.

Ed's Easy Diner

12 Moor Street, W1 (7434 4439). Leicester Square or Tottenham Court Road tube. **Meals served** *Winter* 11.30am-11.30pm Mon-Thur; 11.30am-1am Fri, Sat; 11.30am-11pm Sun. *Summer* 11.30am-midnight Mon-Thur; 11.30am-1am Fri, Sat; 11.30am-midnight Sun. **Main courses** £4.40-£7.90. **Minimum** (peak hours) main course. **Credit** MC, V. **Map** p317 K6.

Teens love this famously retro burger bar, where the patties are meaty and made to order, the shakes creamy and as filling as puddings, and the fries crisp and fluffy inside. Further diversions include little counter-mounted jukeboxes and the delightful range of toppings you can order to enhance your burger (cheeses, bacon, fried egg). Toddlers and babies wouldn't manage those stools bolted to the bar, however, so forget it if your children are under four.
Buggy access. Children's menu (£4.45 incl drink). Crayons. No smoking.
Branches Mall 5, Brent Cross Shopping Centre, NW4 (8202 0999); 362 King's Road, SW3 (7352 1956); 19 Rupert Street, W1 (7287 1951); 02 Centre, 255 Finchley Road, NW3 (7431 1958).

Food for Thought

31 Neal Street, WC2 (7836 0239). Covent Garden tube. **Breakfast served** 9.30-11.30am Mon-Sat. **Lunch served** noon-5pm daily. **Dinner served** 5-8.15pm Mon-Sat. **Main courses** £3.80-£6. **Minimum** (noon-3pm, 6-7.30pm) £2.50. **No credit cards. Map** p317 L6.

Covent Garden's vegetarian legend is as popular as it was 30 years ago. Come before the lunchtime rush and you can bag a table, (but you'll still be rubbing shoulders with your neighbours) or a cushion in the little alcove in the basement. If it's full (and it nearly always is), use the takeaway counter and take your meal to eat in St Paul's Churchyard (see p77) or on the piazza. The food is hearty and highly calorific: big slabs of mushroom or leek quiche, well dressed salads, chunky stir-fries, brown rice and curries, galumphing great flapjacks filled with dried fruit and nuts, creamy scrunches and trifles – not worthy at all, just delicious.
No smoking.

Consumer

Yo! Seaweed at **Yo! Sushi**. See p170.

The Fountain

Ground floor, Fortnum & Mason, 181 Piccadilly, W1 (7734 8040). Piccadilly Circus tube. **Meals served** 8.30am-7.30pm Mon-Sat. **Main courses** £8.95-£21.50. **Credit** AmEx, DC, MC, V. **Map** p318 J7.

A famous place to break for lunch, where the service is incredibly polite and the surroundings ornate. Children get their own menu, running to classics like Welsh rarebit with beans and bacon, chicken goujons or haddock with chips or sausage and mash. The sundaes are a great big treat.
Buggy access. Children's menu (£4.25-£5.25). Crayons. High chairs. Nappy-changing facilities (in shop, until 6.30pm). No-smoking tables.

Hard Rock Café

150 Old Park Lane, W1 (7629 0382/www.hardrock.com). Hyde Park Corner tube. **Meals served** 11.30am-12.30am Mon-Thur, Sun; 11.30am-1am Fri, Sat. **Main courses** £7.95-£14.95. **Minimum** main course when busy. **Credit** AmEx, DC, MC, V. **Map** p318 H8.

They don't really need to try to bring in the younger punters here – wild horses couldn't keep them away – but the Hard Rock has rethought its provision for children a bit, introducing a rock 'n' roll character called Rocky the Guitar to get the party restarted. The children's menu still lists the ever-terrific Hard Rock burgers, there are toys and toy musical instruments to play with in the corner near the bar, and you

still need to turn up early to bag a table (no bookings accepted). Ring for details of other entertainment planned for children. The food is consistently good: all portions are massive, the ingredients fresh and of a high quality.
Buggy access. Children's menu (£4.25). Entertainment: occasional face painting Sat, Sun. High chairs. No-smoking tables. Tables outdoors (10, pavement). Toys.

Masala Zone

9 Marshall Street, W1 (7287 9966/www.realindianfood. com). Oxford Circus tube. **Lunch served** noon-2.45pm, 5.30-11pm Mon-Fri. **Meals served** 12.30-11pm Sat, Sun. **Main courses** £5-£11. **Credit** MC, V. **Map** p316 J6.

It's great here – a perfect place to introduce children to the pleasures of Indian cuisine. With space enough for buggies and child paraphernalia, safe banquette seating, unfussy decor and helpful service, it's easy to relax. The food is inexpensive for children to try out new flavours and textures. Light bites, meal-in-one curries, including meat or vegetarian thalis, noodle dishes, varieties of bread and pastries provide enough choice for adventurous eaters. A child-sized thali, with all its various little dishes of dips, crunchy bits, rice and pickles, represents the best value. Arrive early for lunch: it can get busy and they don't take bookings.
Buggy access. Children's menu (£3.50). High chairs. No smoking.

Maxwell's

8-9 James Street, WC2 (7836 0303/www.maxwells.co.uk). Covent Garden tube. **Meals served** 9.30am-midnight daily. **Main courses** £8.25-£18.95. **Minimum** main course when busy. **Credit** AmEx, DC, MC, V. **Map** p317 L6.

Flying the stars and stripes proud and loud, Maxwell's is a brash, good-humoured place at which to tuck into generous portions of chicken fajitas, nachos, fish cakes, steaks and, naturally, burgers. The latter are particularly good – full of flavour and served with plenty of relish. The mini max burger is the version on the children's menu, and there are hot dogs or chicken strips if the burger won't do.
Buggy access. Children's menu (£7.25). Crayons. High chairs. Nappy-changing facilities. No-smoking tables. Tables outdoors (6, pavement).
Branch 76 Heath Street, NW3 (7794 5450).

Mezzonine

100 Wardour Street, W1 (7314 4000/ www.conran.co.uk). Leicester Square, Piccadilly Circus or Tottenham Court Road tube. **Lunch served** noon-2.45pm Mon-Fri, Sun; noon-3.45pm Sat. **Dinner served** 5.30pm-13.30am Mon-Thur; 5.30pm-2.30am Fri, Sat; 5.30-10.30pm Sun. **Main courses** £9-£11. **Set meals** (noon-2.30pm, 5.30-7pm) £8.90 2 courses, £11.90 3 courses. **Credit** AmEx, DC, MC, V. **Map** p316 J6.

This smart, open-plan compartment of Mezzo gets busy and bustling in the evenings, but for an early lunch, or at weekends, it's understandably attractive to families. There's plenty for young children to see in the kitchens, there's a noodly menu to share, (noodles with chicken breast is a favourite). Older children appreciate the undeniably cool surroundings and trendy, upbeat waiting staff, who are are only too happy to explain the complexities of the winning oriental menu and provide extra plates and spoons for little ones angling for a sample of what's on mum's or dad's plate. And if dishes like Thai green chicken curry or rare seared tuna with shredded daikon are too exotic, you can always order chips.
Booking advisable, essential weekends. High chairs.

Neal's Yard Bakery & Tearoom
6 Neal's Yard, WC2 (7836 5199). Covent Garden tube.
Meals served 10.30am-4.30pm Mon-Sat. **Main courses**
£3.50-£5. **Minimum** (noon-2pm Mon-Fri; 10.30am-
4.30pm Sat) £2.50. **No credit cards. Map** p317 L6.
The menu changes daily at this traditional vegetarian restaurant: Thai yellow curry is a favourite of ours, and the veggie
burgers are generously proportioned and dressed. If you have
a buggy in tow, the upstairs tearoom might be a bit of a pain,
but once you're up there, the outlook's tranquil and relaxing.
If the children don't fancy a full-scale meal, treat them to
moist, hearty cakes, croissants or scones, and juice. Dairy-,
yeast- and wheat-free dishes are available from the slightly
pricier but equally pleasant (and buggy accessible) Neal's
Yard Salad Bar just nearby.
No smoking. Tables outdoors (2, courtyard; 3,
1st floor patio).

Paul
29 Bedford Street, WC2 (7836 3304). Covent Garden
tube. **Open** 7.30am-9pm Mon-Fri; 9am-9pm Sat, Sun.
Credit AmEx, JCB, MC, V. **Map** p319 L7.
The high chairs provided for babies in this delightful French
pâtisserie-boulangerie are handsome, old-fashioned articles,
and the nostalgic, dark wood decor looks almost too elegant
for jam-smeared toddlers. Yet little ones are treated with ten-
derness here and given pens and paper to play with. Bakers
working on site turn out an amazing variety of breads, cakes
and pastries to go with the light lunches on the menu:
omelettes, salads, crêpes and tarts. There's plenty of choice,
but most children make a play for the gorgeous patisserie.

Planet Hollywood
13 Coventry Street, W1 (7287 1000/
www.planet hollywood.com). Piccadilly Circus tube. **Meals**
served noon-11pm Mon-Thur, Sun; 11.30am-12.30am Fri,
Sat. **Main courses** £8.50-£17.95. **Credit** AmEx, DC,
MC, V. **Map** p319 K7.
Movie paraphernalia greets you at every turn, televisions
blare and waiting staff are always ready with a balloon and
a big smile. Sensitive adults may find it all a bit much, but
most children love it. The food is of consistently high quality, so that's at least one reason to endure the cacophony.
Organic ribeye steak and chips is a great adult choice; children, meanwhile, can choose between five dishes on their own
menu, which features the inevitable burgers alongside fish,
chicken or a vegetarian pasta dish. Fries are skinny and gorgeous, and the Snickers cheesecake shouldn't be allowed.
Balloons. Bookings advisable (weekends; no reservations
Sat). Buggy access. Children's menu (£7.95). Crayons.
High chairs. Nappy-changing facilities. No-smoking tables.

Quod Restaurant & Bar
57 Haymarket, SW1 (7925 1234/
www.quod.co.uk). Piccadilly Circus tube. **Open** noon-
midnight Mon-Sat. **Main courses** £7.95-£17.95. **Credit**
AmEx, DC, MC, V. **Map** p319 K7.
A big, bright, noisy but very friendly place, with what's
described as an Italian-style menu, Quod makes sure it gets
the full attention of passing tourists with its 'children eat free'
deal. As far as adults are concerned, the food is pretty good,
the pasta dishes are fresh and interesting, and mains like the
tender slow roasted lamb and creamy risotto go down well.
Puddings, such as tiramisu and lemon tarte, are tempting.
Kiddy freebies include cheese and tomato pizza, spaghetti
with tomato sauce and the usual burger or nuggets served
with chips. Ice cream follows, also free.
Buggy access. Children's menu (free). High chairs. No-
smoking area.

Rainforest Café
20 Shaftesbury Avenue, W1 (7434 3111/
www.therain forestcafe.co.uk). Piccadilly Circus tube.
Meals served noon-10pm Mon-Wed, Sun; noon-7.30pm
Thur, Fri; 11.30am-6pm Sat. **Credit** AmEx, DC, MC, V.
Map p319 K7.
Upstairs, rainforest-themed soft toys and T-shirts; downstairs, an authentically steamy rainforest-themed restaurant,
where animatronic animals lurk in gloomy corners. Wherever
you go, you'll spend a good deal of money. Young children
are all agog, though, and most enjoy the dishes available on
their special menu. Mojo Bones means pork ribs with fries
and carrot salad, or there's the Rainforest Rascal burger or
Hot Diggety dogs. Puddings are fruity (bananas and custard,
fruit salad in a basket, raspberry jelly), but also involve
Smarties and ice cream. The ambient sounds include thun-
derstorms and animal roars – or could that be the sound of
parents reacting to their bill?
Children's menu (£9.45). Crayons. High chairs. Nappy-
changing facilities. No smoking.

RIBA Café
66 Portland Place, W1 (7631 0467). Oxford Circus tube.
Open 8.30am-6pm Mon-Fri; 9am-4pm Sat. **Credit** AmEx,
DC, MC, V. **Map** p316 H5.
A lot more sophisticated than your average café, but the wait
ing staff at the Royal Institute of British Architecture's water-
ing hole are friendly toward young ones and the outdoor
terrace is spacious and a boon in this part of central London.
Sophisticated salads, crostini and other light lunches are
colourful and well presented and there are plenty of sandwiches, snacks and juices for children to lunch on.
High chairs. Tables outdoors.

Rock & Sole Plaice
47 Endell Street, WC2 (7836 3785). Covent Garden or
Leicester Square tube. **Meals served** 11.30am-10.30pm
Mon-Sat; noon-9.30pm Sun. **Main courses** £7-£13.
Credit MC, V. **Map** p317 L6.
London's oldest surviving chip shop attracts tourists as well
as Covent Garden workers who know a good fish supper-
when they see one. One portion easily feeds two small children. Come early on a summer evening and grab one of the
pavement tables under the flower-filled hanging baskets, and
watch London wind down after the working day.
Buggy access. High chairs. Tables outdoors (20,
pavement).

Smollensky's on the Strand
105 Strand, WC2 (7497 2101/www.smollenskys.co.uk).
Covent Garden or Embankment tube/Charing Cross
tube/rail. **Meals served** noon-midnight Mon-Wed; noon-
12.30am Thur-Sat; noon-5.30pm, 6.30-10.30pm Sun. **Main**
courses £8.85-£19.95. **Set meal** (noon-7pm, after 10pm
Mon-Fri) £10 2 courses, £12 3 courses. **Credit** AmEx,
DC, MC, V. **Map** p319 L7.
This is the most child-friendly part of the lively Smollensky's
empire, and at weekends they lay on special entertainment
for the youngsters. Lunchtimes are generally more jolly.
Smollensky's steaks are very good, and the items on the children's menu – macaroni and cheese, chicken breast, fish and
chips, spag bol, pizza, burgers – are wholesome and attractively presented. Puddings cost £2.25: favourites are the
white chocolate brownie and the endearing gingerbread man
and ice cream combo. Check the website for branches.
Booking advisable. Buggy access. Children's menu
(£4.95). Crayons. Entertainment: Punch & Judy show,
magic show, Nintendo games, face painting (Sat, Sun).
High chairs. No-smoking. Play area for under-7s. Toys.

Consumer

Spiga

84-6 Wardour Street, W1 (7734 3444). Leicester Square or Piccadilly Circus tube. **Lunch served** noon-3pm Mon-Sat; 1-4pm Sun. **Dinner served** 6-11pm Mon, Tue, Sun; 6pm-midnight Wed-Sat. **Main courses** £7.50-£14. **Credit** AmEx, MC, V. **Map** p316 J6.

Smart, friendly and efficient, Spiga has top quality pasta dishes and thin-crust pizzas that can be shared by the children. Other delights such as sautéed prawns and sophisticated antipasto dishes can be brought into the mix to create a gloriously coourful, healthy Mediterranean feast.
Booking advisable. Buggy access. High chairs.

Stanleys

6 Little Portland Street, W1 (7462 0099). Oxford Circus tube. **Meals served** noon-11pm Mon-Sat. **Main courses** £8.50-£10.95. **Credit** AmEx, MC, V. **Map** p316 J5.

Give 'em a bash of great bangers and mash (much better than mother could ever make) at this jolly sausage diner. Pared-down diner-meets-beer-hall decor, complete with handsome red banquette seating, is the setting for a sausage fest, and they come in all guises – straight, game, Thai and vegetarian (the Glamorgan), with fries, with mash – and cost around £8.50. Further comfort is provided in the form of hearty puds and, for adults, a good range of beers.
Buggy access. High chairs. Nappy-changing facilities. No-smoking tables. Reduced-price children's portions.

TGI Friday's

6 Bedford Street, WC2 (7379 0585/www.tgifridays.co.uk). Covent Garden or Embankment tube/Charing Cross tube/rail. **Meals served** noon-11.30pm Mon-Sat; noon-11pm Sun. **Main courses** £7.15-£15.45. **Credit** AmEx, MC, V. **Map** p319 L7.

The staff have all gone to Cheery school and they make a fuss of little ones. It's lovely to feel so welcome, which is probably why people in suits like to come here and let their hair down too. The main menu has loads on it to excite the interest of children, with starters such as nachos, skins and wings all big enough to share. Otherwise there's a children's menu to choose from: the £7.25 Clubhouse menu, which gets them a main course, dessert and a drink – or there's the £8.25 Superclub variant, which lets them go very large.
Balloons. Buggy access. Children's menu. Crayons. Entertainment: occasional face painting (Sat, Sun). High chairs. No-smoking tables.
Branches throughout town. Call or check the website.

World Food Café

Neal's Yard Dining Room, 1st floor, 14 Neal's Yard, WC2 (7379 0298/www.worldfoodcafe.com). Covent Garden or Leicester Square tube. **Meals served** 11.30am-4.30pm Mon-Fri; 11.30am-5pm Sat. **Main courses** £4.65-£7.95. **Minimum** (noon-2pm Mon-Fri; 11.30am-5pm Sat) £5. **Credit** MC, V. **Map** p317 L6.

A vegetarian restaurant with a reputation for adventurous food, the first-floor Café draws good-sized crowds at lunch times (and service can be rather flustered as a result). Still, its signature dishes from around the world (sweet potatoes, salsas, guacamole and nachos) are easy to share and eat.
High chairs. No smoking.

Yo! Sushi

52 Poland Street, W1 (7287 0443/www.yosushi.co.uk). Leicester Square tube. **Meals served** noon-11pm daily. **Credit** AmEx, DC, MC, V. **Map** p316 J6.

Though an acquired taste – probably best for adventurous eaters with small appetites – the famous conveyor-belt (*kaiten*) sushi bar is great entertainment for children, and certainly

encourages healthy habits. Not only do the plates (colour coded according to price, from £1.50) bear vitamin-packed salmon, tuna, seaweed-and-rice combos, but there's unlimited mineral water at the touch of a button. And the drinks robot always goes down a storm.
Balloons and stickers. Booster seats. No smoking.
Branches throughout town. Check the phone book.

Westminster

Café in the Crypt

Crypt of St-Martin-in-the-Fields, Duncannon Street, WC2 (7839 4342)/www.stmartin-in-the-fields.org). Embankment tube/Charing Cross tube/rail. **Lunch served** 11.30am-3pm daily. **Dinner served** 5-7.30pm Mon-Wed; 5-10.30pm Thur-Sat. **Main courses** £5.95-£7.50. **Set meal** £4.95 two courses. **No credit cards**. **Map** 319 7L.

A tranquil, subterranean place to repair to in a noisy part of town, especially if you happen to have been doing some brass rubbing beforehand, staff in this café are sociable and pleasant. You queue up for the food, which is of the traditional variety – stews, meat and two vegetables, salad and quiche – and that includes puddings such as fruit pie and custard.
High chairs. No smoking tables. Takeaway service (drinks only).

Texas Embassy Cantina

1 Cockspur Street, SW1 (7925 0077/ www.texasembassy. com). Embankment tube/Charing Cross tube/rail. **Meals served** noon-11pm Mon-Wed; noon-midnight Thur-Sat; noon-10.30pm Sun. **Main courses** £7.50-£16.95. **Credit** AmEx, DC, MC, V. **Map** p319 K7.

The ambassadors for Tex-Mex grub always have a big smile and a stack of colouring-in materials for small diners. With room for buggies and a benevolent attitude toward rampaging toddlers, this restaurant handily is placed for the National Gallery and scores points for offering milk to replace the pop served with the fare on the children's menu. Kiddy dishes include cheese nachos, grilled cheese quesadillas (melted cheese in tortillas served with chips), hot dogs, chicken strips and hamburgers, all at £4.50. Ice cream or apple pie for pud costs £1.75-£2. Portions for adults are vast.
Balloons. Buggy access. Children's menu (£4.50 main meals). Crayons. High chairs. Tables outdoors (8, pavement). Nappy-changing facilities.

Marylebone

Fairuz

3 Blandford Street, W1 (7486 8108/8182). Baker Street or Bond Street tube. **Meals served** noon-11.30pm Mon-Sat; noon-10.30pm Sun. **Main courses** £9.95-£12. **Set meals** £16.95 meze, £24.95 3 courses. **Cover** £1.50. **Credit** AmEx, DC, MC, V. **Map** p316 G5.

With its rustic demeanour, this branch of the Lebanese success story is more homely than the swish Westbourne Grove address. The meze selection here is a treat, and a sensible way to enjoy a family meal. You can choose from about 50 dishes – houmous, small sausages, aubergine purée, falafel, chicken and much more – all accompanied by warm, soft flatbread. The barbecued lamb is also good and the sticky baklava pastries are a sugary delight.
Booking advisable. Buggy access. High chairs.
Branch 27 Westbourne Grove, W2 (7243 8444).

Food fit for a princess at **The Engineer**.
See p172.

La Galette

56 Paddington Street, W1 (7935 1554/ www.lagalette. com). Baker Street or Bond Street tube. **Breakfast served** 8.30am-noon Mon-Fri. **Meals served** 10am-11pm Sat, Sun. **Main courses** £3.50-£8.50. **Set lunch** (noon-5pm Mon-Fri) £6.95 2 courses. **Credit** AmEx, MC, V. **Map** p316 G5

Pancakes, always a family favourite, are quite poshly presented in this bright modern crêperie. Many children may prefer a plain crêpe with sugar or chocolate and ice cream, but you can have them as a main meal, stuffed with cheese or meat sauce with salad. There's French cider to drink. *Bookings not accepted for less than 6 people. Buggy access. High chairs. Tables outdoors (2, terrace).*

Giraffe

6-8 Blandford Street, W1 (7935 2333/www.giraffe.net). Baker Street or Bond Street tube. **Open** 8am-4pm, 5-11.30pm Mon-Fri; 9am-11.30pm Sat; 9am-10.30pm Sun. **Drinks and desserts only served** 4-5pm Mon-Fri; 4-5.30pm Sat, Sun. **Main courses** £7-£10. **Set dinner** (5-7pm Mon-Fri) £6.95 2 courses; £8.95 7-10.45pm Mon-Fri. **Credit** AmEx, MC, V. **Map** p316 G5.

World music, personable and international staff, an exciting menu and all-round delightfulness toward children make family groups hang lovingly around the Giraffe's neck. Dishes such as grilled chicken, Thai green vegetable curry, big mixed salads and noodles are all attractively presented. The menu for children runs through their favourites: they can have chips and beans (£2) if they want, crunchy chicken with chips (£3.95) or saucy noodles (£2.95). Plastic cups with a Giraffe straw can be filled with a variety of juices, smoothies or brown fizz, and puddings include chocolate fudge cake or ice cream with a chocolate flake. *Buggy access. Children's menu (£2.95-£3.95). Crayons. High chairs. No smoking. Tables outdoors (5, pavement patio).* **Branches** throughout town. Call or check the website.

North London

Café Mozart

17 Swains Lane, N6 (8348 1384). Highgate tube/Gospel Oak rail/214, C2, C11, C12 bus. **Meals served** 9am-10pm daily. **Credit** (over £10) MC, V.

After a runaround on Parliament Hill, come here for a light lunch – or better still, a heavy tea, taking in some of the tarts, pastries and cakes this delightful place is famous for. Amadeus memorabilia abounds, classical music is played to soothe the soul, and the excellent sachertorte fills the stomach. Savoury dishes, such pasta with sauce or swordfish steaks, change daily, but it's not excessively posh –you can always find a decent fry-up here. The interior can be a bit cramped for buggies, but the pavement tables are popular all year round. Be prepared to queue at weekends. *Buggy access. Reduced-price children's portions. High chair. No smoking. Tables outdoors (8, courtyard).*

The Engineer

65 Gloucester Avenue, NW1 (7722 0950). Camden Town or Chalk Farm tube/C2 bus. **Open** 9am-11pm Mon-Sat; 9am-10.30pm Sun. **Food served** 9-11.30am, 12.30-3pm, 7-10.30pm Mon-Sat; 9-noon, 12.30-3.30pm, 7-10pm Sun. **Main courses** £9.50-£15. **Credit** MC, V.

A pub with a reputation for excellent food, the Engineer makes sure that people with children don't miss out, welcoming the kids with plates of comfort grub. Egg and chips,

ham and chips, fish or pasta, with ice cream to follow, cost about £4. Diners are accommodated in the warren-like rooms off the main bar and (weather permitting) in the attractive back garden. Sunday lunch is hugely popular with families: arrive early to be sure of a table.. *Buggy access. Children's menu (noon-3pm daily). Crayons. High chairs. Nappy-changing facilities. Tables outdoors (10, garden).*

Iznik

19 Highbury Park, N5 (7354 5697). Highbury & Islington tube/rail. **Meals served** 10am-4pm Mon-Fri. **Dinner served** 6.30pm-midnight daily. **Main courses** £7.50-£9.50. **Credit** MC, V.

It's a bit out of the way, but for authentic Turkish food (with loads of dishes to choose from), Iznik is the business. It's a pretty place, too, where families gather at weekends for long, lingering lunches. The meze part of the menu lends itself to small appetites, and sharing a range of dishes is always fun; there's also a choice of kebabs served with rice and salad. *Booking advisable (weekends). Buggy access.*

Lemonia

89 Regent's Park Road, NW1 (7586 7454). Chalk Farm tube/31, 168 bus. **Lunch served** noon-3pm Mon-Fri, Sun. **Dinner served** 6-11.30pm Mon-Sat. **Main courses** £8.75-£13.75. **Set lunch** £7.25 2 courses incl coffee; £8.50 3 courses. **Credit** MC, V.

Lemonia has a fine reputation that goes back many years, but more recently it has become known as the haunt of celebrities. Tabloid legend has it that Kate Moss was dining here when her waters broke. Family groups are much in evidence, particularly at weekends, and children are treated very nicely. Come to Lemonia for a weekday lunch, to fully appreciate the lovely surroundings and a changing daily special list to supplement the reliable Greek menu. Food is beautifully fresh; the meat dishes are always of a high quality. *Buggy access. Tables outdoors (4, pavement).*

Marine Ices

8 Haverstock Hill, NW3 (7482 9003). Chalk Farm tube/31 bus. **Open** 10.30am-10pm daily. **Meals served** noon-3pm, 6-11pm Mon-Fri; noon-11pm Sat; noon-10pm Sun. **Main courses** *Restaurant* £5.20-£9.60. **Credit** MC, V.

A family restaurant in every respect, this institution was founded by the Mansi family, whose ice cream know-how quickly turned the place into a north London institution. Nowadays the gelateria comes with a light, bright, spacious restaurant, whose walls are adorned by compliments and signatures from satisfied celebrity customers. Once you've struggled to get your children away from the ice cream window and bagged your table (book at weekends), the menu offers a range of Italian pasta dishes and pizzas. *Buggy access. High chairs. No-smoking area (restaurant).*

Mosaica @ The Factory

The Chocolate Factory, Wood Green Business Centre, Clarendon Road, N22 (8889 2400). Wood Green tube. **Open** 10am-10pm Tue-Fri; 7-10pm Sat; noon-4pm Sun. **Main courses** £12-£16. **Credit** AmEx, MC, V.

Don't let the kids see the address, they'll get their hopes up. This place is in a depressing location on an industrial estate, but don't let that put you off. Mosaica is a top place for a stress-free family lunch: try own-made dishes such as vegetable soups, sautéed prawns, roast pork with apple sauce, salmon and lovely puddings. The interior is homely-shabby. *Buggy access. No smoking tables. Tables outdoors (15, courtyard).*

Light lunch for the girls at **Boiled Egg & Soldiers**. *See p177.*

The Prince

59 Kynaston Road, N16 (7923 4766). Bus 73. **Open** noon-11pm Mon-Sat; noon-10.30pm Sun. **Food served** 12.30-10pm Mon-Sat; noon-9.30pm Sun. **Credit** MC, V.
Once a scruffy old pub called the Prince of Wales, this is now the haunt of Stokey's well-spoken parents. A large part of its new-found popularity has to do with the reliably delicious food, sourced from the Cooler deli nearby and served in a separate little restaurant area which looks on to a small outside yard at the back. There are plans for a dedicated family area, with childminder; in the meantime, children can enjoy the kids' menu, with chicken nuggets, fish fingers and pasta. *High chairs. Children's menu (main course £2.95, ice cream £1.95). Tables outdoors (garden, pavement).*

Santa Fe

75 Upper Street, N1 (7288 2288/www.santafe.co.uk). Angel tube. **Meals served** noon-10.30pm Mon-Thur, Sun; noon-11pm Fri, Sat. **Main courses** £6.95-£12.95. **Credit** AmEx, DC, MC, V.
A fashionable Islington crowd hang-out, this, but you don't have to be a yummy mummy (or hunky daddy) to eat here. It's perfectly friendly and the food is pretty sophisticated, in a Mexican sort of way. Enjoy tortillas, ceviche, chillis and enchiladas and cool off with sweet fruit tortillas and cinnamon ice cream. If that sounds too challenging for children, check out their kiddy menu – chicken breast, burger and chips, and pasta with either cheese or a robust tomato sauce. *Booking advisable (weekends). Buggy access. Children's menu (£3.95). Crayons. High chairs. Nappy-changing facilities. No-smoking tables. Toys.*

S&M Café

4-6 Upper Street, N1 (7359 5361). Angel tube/19, 38 bus. **Meals served** 9.30am-11.30pm Mon-Thur; 9am-midnight Fri, Sat; 9am-10.30pm Sun. **Main courses** £2.50-£5.75. **Credit** MC, V.
In the lovely old art deco cafè that old Islingtonians will always know as Alfredo's, the second Sausage & Mash Café lures in banger fans from all over. This is caff food with flavour – lots of it – in inventive sausage guises, served with creamy mash and rivers of gravy in all sorts of different flavours. Children will be amused by the way the susages stick out of the mash, just like in a comic book. There's a whole menu of other comfort food, too – steak and kidney pie grab you? – as well as salads, proper puddings like crumbles and pies, and breakfast boiled eggs and fry ups until 11.30am. *Buggy access. Children's menu (£3.50).*
Branch 268 Portobello Road, W10 (8968 8898).

Shish

2-6 Station Parade, NW2 (8208 9290). Willesden Green tube/260, 266 bus. **Meals served** 11.30am-11.45pm Mon-Sat; 10.30am-11.30pm Sun. **Main courses** £5.25-£8.45. **Credit** MC, V.
Shish is rather swish, as kebab restaurants go, and the staff are happy to recommend dishes from the Silk Road menu (covering specialities from Turkey to Indonesia) for junior diners. The extensive wooden bar winds around the kitchen area, providing ringside entertainment for the children; even the taps are a novelty, supplying as much mineral water as you want for a pound. Food to share includes chicken, beef or lamb shish, marinated in yoghurt and tender, as well as fries, bread and dips, spicy cous cous, juices, sticky, honey-drenched baklava and ice creams.
Buggy access. No smoking (downstairs).

Tartuf

88 Upper Street, N1 (7288 0954). Angel tube. **Dinner served** 5.30-11pm Mon-Thur; 5.30pm-midnight Fri. **Meals served** noon-midnight Sat; noon-10.30pm Sun. **Main courses** £4.90-£10.80. **Set lunch** (noon-6.30pm Sat, Sun) £6.90 2 courses. **Set meal** £11.90 eat as much as you like. **Credit** MC, V.

Pizza the action

Some branches of all-round family favourite **Pizza Express** are taken over by children during the weekend. The company has a reputation for reliability, cleanliness, thinness of crust and freshness of toppings; its quality pizzas (priced from £4.95), from the margarita to the meaty Americana, are easy to dole out among children.

Never really a serious rival for Express, the other national chain is the rather more square **Pizza Hut**, whose restaurants seemmore old-fashioned. Hut to Express is like Woolworth's to IKEA. That's not to say that families don't get a great deal in the Hut. With walloping big Quad pizzas to share, children's menus and pizza lunch buffets for about a fiver, it's value for money.

Ask's clean, white restaurants are easy on the eye. The staff seem to be picked for friendliness, which is a bonus when you're out with the children. The pizza list has about 20 varieties.

Strada's wood-fired pizzas are extra thin, crustwise, but come loaded with goodies. The pasta concoctions are equally impressive. Children can order half portions of the pasta and risotto dishes or share a pizza.

Eco is excessively noisy at times, and incredibly busy at weekends, but its pizzas (from about £6) are well presented and fun to share.

Of the independents, **La Spighetta** is lovely: staff are delightful to children, and the pizzas (from about £7) are fresh, light and generously topped. It's a dignified place, children must behave.

If you're not feeling flush or you're worried about Spighetta's table linen, you could do worse than choose the celebrated **Pizzeria Castello** – celebrated because it's in such an unremittingly depressing part of town. Castello annoints the air with its garlic fumes; just follow your nose. Alternatively, if you're in this neck of the woods looking for pizza, you could do worse than taking a bus from the Elephant toward Camberwell as far as **La Luna**. It's a small, plainly-decorated place, with a menu of pizza and pasta specials. The pizzas here are crisp and smothered with toppings, and the little extras, such as own-made breadsticks and bruschetta, are delicious.

ASK
56-60 Wigmore Street, W1 (7224 3484/ www.askcentral.co.uk). Bond Street tube. **Meals served** noon-11.30pm daily. **Map** p316 6H.

Eco
162 Clapham High Street, SW4 (7978 1108). Clapham Common tube. **Meals served** noon-4pm, 6.30-11pm Mon-Thur; noon-4pm, 6-11.30pm Fri; noon-11.30pm Sat; noon-11pm Sun.

Pizzeria Castello
20 Walworth Road, SE1 (7703 2556). Elephant & Castle tube/rail. Meals served noon-11pm Mon-Thur; noon-11.30pm Fri; 5-11.30pm Sat.

Pizza Express
9-12 Bow Street, WC2 (7240 3443/ www.pizzaexpress.co.uk). Covent Garden tube. Meals served 11.30am-midnight daily. Check the website for branches.

Pizza Hut
Cambridge Circus, WC2 (7379 4655/ www.pizzahut.co.uk). Leicester Square or Tottenham Court Road tube. **Meals served** 11.30am-11pm Mon-Thur; 11.30am-11.30pm Fri, Sat; noon-10.30pm Sun. **Map** p317 K6.

La Luna
380 Walworth Road, SE17 (7277 1991). Bus 12, 35, 40, 45, 68, 68A, 171. **Lunch served** noon-3pm, 6-11pm Tue-Sat; noon-10.45pm Sun.

La Spighetta
43 Blandford Street, W1 (7486 7340). Baker Street or Bond Street tube. **Lunch served** noon-2.30pm Mon-Fri; 12.30-3pm Sat. **Dinner served** 6.30-10.30pm Mon-Thur, Sun; 6.30-11pm Fri, Sat. **Map** p316 5G.

Strada
15-16 New Burlington Street, W1 (7287 5967/ www.strada.co.uk). Piccadilly Circus tube. **Meals served** noon-11pm Mon-Sat; noon-10.30pm Sun. **Map** p318 J7.

The tarte flambée (described by the staff as 'French pizza') is an Alsatian speciality. It consists of crisp, thin dough, spread with yoghurt and a variety of toppings (chicken with peppers, mushroom and spinach, emmenthal and bacon, for example) then baked and served at the double. They're great to share, and the sweet ones in particular go down well with children of all ages. Our favourite is the warm banana and chocolate sauce tarte, with creamy vanilla ice-cream. A selection of the tartes flambées makes a pleasant family supper in cheerfully rustic surroundings.
Booking advisable (Fri, Sat). Buggy access. High chairs. Reduced-price portions for children. Tables outdoors (10, pavement).
Branch 169 Clapham High Street, SW4 (7622 8169).

East London

Arkansas Café
Unit 12, Old Spitalfields Market, E1 (7377 6999). Liverpool Street tube/rail. **Lunch served** noon-2.30pm Mon-Fri; noon-4pm Sun. **Dinner served** party bookings only, by arrangement. **Main courses** £5-£14. **Credit** MC, V. **Map** p321 R5.
Crowds gather at this little place every lunchtime. The air scented with its steaks, chicken and ribs. Portions of chicken with mash and own-baked beans are huge, and the same goes for the gooey great slabs of cake and pecan pie.
No-smoking tables. Tables outdoors (terrace inside market).

Bar Spice

145 Three Colt Street, E14 (7093 1111/www.barspice. com). Westferry DLR. **Meals served** noon-2pm, 6-11pm Mon-Fri; 6-11pm Sat. **Main courses** £5.95-£8.75. **Credit** AmEx, DC, MC, V.

This is an Indian bar diner on two floors, where staff are helpful and accommodating toward children, especially if families visit outside office lunch hours. The ground floor is best for traditional Indian staples, such as tikka, dahl and biriani. *High chairs. No smoking tables.*

Faulkner's

424-6 Kingsland Road, E8 (7254 6152). Dalston Kingsland rail/67, 76, 149, 242, 243 bus. **Lunch served** noon-2pm Mon-Fri. **Dinner served** 5-10pm Mon-Thur; 4.15-10pm Fri. **Meals served** 11.30am-10pm Sat; noon-9pm Sun. **Main courses** £7.50-£13. **Minimum** £4. **Credit** MC, V.

This doughty old east Londoner has kept local costermongers in fish suppers for many a long year. The portions are large, if not exactly cheap. Children's portions of scampi or nuggets and chips keeps them happy while adults tuck in to lovely fishcakes or rock salmon, followed by fruit pie and custard, while and admiring the old pictures on the walls. *Buggy access. Children's menu (£3.95). High chairs. No-smoking tables.*

Hadley House

27 High Street, E11 (8989 8855). Snaresbrook or Wanstead tube. **Lunch served** 11.30am-2.30pm Mon-Sat. **Dinner served** 7-10.30pm Mon-Sat. **Meals served** 10.30am-9pm Sun. **Main courses** £8.95-£16.95. **Set dinner** (Mon) £16.95 3 courses. **Credit** MC, V.

It's far east, yes, but Hadley House is a lovely place to go to for lunch with the family, and this part of London is great for walks in the fantastic Wanstead Park. The menu here is international, but there are always a number of comforting, familiar dishes such as Sunday roasts or pasta, and we've found that children can share adult portions quite easily; the staff are happy to arrange this. *High chairs. Reduced-price children's portions. Tables outdoors (6, patio).*

Chinatown choices

Where better to eat Chinese? Lisle, Gerrard and Wardour Streets in the West End became Chinatown when many of London's Chinese citizens moved here from the East End (and Hong Kong) in the 1950s. The pagoda-topped phone boxes and peculiar stone lions adorning the area for the benefit of tourists are a bit on the OTT side, but kitsch garnish aside, these Chinese streets are a close-knit residential and working enclave, and the restaurants bring in punters from every nation. And what a lot of restaurants there are. If you're not hungry when you start wandering around the area, you will be when you've passed your tenth shop window hung with roast ducks.

Some of the restaurants around here are friendlier than others. We're fond of the **Royal Dragon**, because it's quiet and there's plenty of space to move around. Its dim sum menu is long and quite daunting. Go for the £8.90 dim sum deal, which gives you a tableful of the traditional breakfast and lunchtime snacks of little dumplings and other tasty morsels to try. Service is patient and child-friendly. Sunday lunchtimes see the **Hong Kong** full of families, both Chinese and foreign, enjoying slap-up meals from the ginormous dim sum list. The cooked-at-table sizzling dishes go down well, and so do the seafood specials. Another favourite is the friendly **Harbour City**, where plump prawnsand savoury dumplings make the dim sum special. **New Diamond** does proper Cantonese cuisine – lots of stir fries and hot pots – as well as listing all the favourites on its long, long menu. **New World** is famed for its popularity (and disconcerting speed of service) at Sunday dim sum lunches (and other days aren't that much quieter), and the food is good. At **Imperial China**, a through a courtyard off rowdy Lisle Stree, the menu is lengthy, and full of child-pleasers like chicken satay, pancake rolls and rice cakes.

Harbour City

46 Gerrard Street, W1 (7439 7859). Leicester Square or Piccadilly Circus tube. **Dim sum served** noon-5pm Mon-Sat; 11am-5pm Sun. **Meals served** noon-11.30pm Mon-Thur; noon-midnight Fri, Sat; 11am-1030pm Sun. **Main courses** £5.50-£20. **Map** p319 K7.

Hong Kong

6-7 Lisle Street, WC2 (7287 0352). Leicester Square or Piccadilly Circus tube. **Dim sum served** noon-5pm daily. **Meals served** noon-11.30pm Mon-Thur; noon-midnight Fri, Sat; 11am-11pm Sun. **Main courses** £5.50-£10.50. **Map** p319 K7.

Imperial China

White Bear Yard, 25A Lisle Street, WC2 (7734 3388). Leicester Square tube. **Meals served** noon-11.45pm Mon-Sat; 11.30am-10.15pm Sun. **Main courses** £6-£30. **Map** p319 K7.

New Diamond

23 Lisle Street, WC2 (7437 2517/7221). Leicester Square tube. **Meals served** noon-3am daily. **Main courses** £5.80-£12.80. **Map** p319 K7.

New World

1 Gerrard Place, W1 (7734 0396). Leicester Square or Piccadilly Circus tube. **Dim sum served** 11am-6pm daily. **Meals served** 11am-11.45pm Mon-Sat; 11am-11pm Sun. **Main courses** £5.90-£18. **Map** p319 K7.

Royal Dragon

30 Gerrard Street, W1 (7734 0935). Leicester Square or Piccadilly Circus tube. **Dim sum served** noon-5pm daily. **Meals served** noon-3am Mon-Sat; 11am-3am Sun. **Main courses** £6.30-£23. **Map** p319 K7.

Jones Dairy Café
23 Ezra Street, E2 (7739 5372). Bus 26, 48, 55. **Open** 9am-3pm Fri, Sat; 8am-2pm Sun. **No credit cards.**
For weekend lunches, particulary on Sunday morning after a stroll through the Columbia Road flower market, Jones is perfect (if crowded). The brunch-style food – omelettes, scrambled egg and smoked salmon, tomatoes on toast – is of a high standard, and the cakes are dreamy. If you can't get in, they'll do you a takeaway.
Buggy access. No smoking. Tables outdoors (3, patio).

Laxeiro
93 Columbia Road, E2 (7729 1147/www.laxeiro.com). Bus 26, 48, 55. **Lunch served** noon-3pm, **dinner served** 7-11pm Tue-Sat. **Meals served** 9am-3pm Sun. **Tapas** £2.95-£7.50. **Credit** MC, V.
Typical Spanish tapas – barbecue sardines, patatas bravas, chorizo, garlic mushrooms and tomato and mozzarella salad – can be ordered for a family lunch-time feast at this inexpensive and amiable restaurant. You'll have to book for Sunday luchtime, though, because there's no shortage of people looking for a post-flower-market feed here.
Booking advisable (dinner). Tables outdoors (pavement).

Royal China
30 Westferry Circus, E14 (7719 0888). Canary Wharf tube/DLR/Westferry DLR. **Meals served** noon-11pm Mon-Thur; noon-11.30pm Fri, Sat; 11am-10pm Sun. **Dim sum** noon-4.45pm daily. **Main courses** £6-£40. **Dim sum** £2.20-£4.50. **Set meal** £28 per person (minimum 2). **Credit** AmEx, DC, JCB, MC, V.
London's best dim sum, super views over the Thames and staff that seem pleased as punch with the excellent food they're serving – all in all, this excellent Chinese restaurant is a real treat. The grub isn't cheap, but it's such a fascinating part of London to come to for a meal, and children can choose their favourites from a selection of dishes and enjoy the atmosphere as much as the accompanying adults.
Disabled: toilet. High chairs. Tables outdoors (garden).

South-east London

Chapter Two
43-4 Montpelier Vale, SE3 (8333 2666/ www.chapters restaurants.co.uk). Blackheath rail. **Lunch served** noon-2.30pm Mon-Sat; noon-3.30pm Sun. **Dinner served** 6.30-10.30 Mon-Thur; 6.30-11pm Fri, Sat; 7-9.30pm Sun. **Set lunch** (Mon-Sat) £14.50 2 courses, £18.50 3 courses. **Set dinner** (Mon-Thur, Sun) £16.50 2 courses, £19.50 3 courses; (Fri, Sat) £22.50 3 courses. **Credit** AmEx, DC, JCB, MC, V.
It might seem a bit too posh for a family meal out, but the staff here are well used to locals bringing babies, toddlers and teens in, and can dole out extra plates and spoons for the inevitable sharing that goes on. Modern European dishes, such as sea bream with an omelette and buttery leeks, or plump chicken breast with gnocchi and broad beans, are delicious and well presented. The puddings, such as blueberry madeleines ad tarte tatin, are legendary, but children can stick with a selection of ice creams if they prefer. If the main restaurant is too posh, but you want a bash of those excellent puds, sample the sweet pleasures of the café next door. Apricot bakewell tart, chocolate tarte or a praline mousse can be downed with coffee for just a few quid. Sandwiches and pastries are also available.
Disabled: toilet. High chairs. Nappy-changing facilities. No smoking. Tables outdoors (café next door).

The High Chaparral
35 Greenwich Church Street, SE10 (8293 9143). Cutty Sark DLR. **Meals served** noon-11pm Mon-Sat; noon-10pm Sun. **Main courses** £4.95-£12.95. **Credit** AmEx, MC, V.
A funky little place which gets quite noisy in the evenings, but is nonetheless friendly towards children. It has a a menu as long as your arm, so it might be a while before you make up your mind: little snacky things such as chicken fajitas, panini, Tex Mex nachos or enchiladas? The party vibe swells the later it gets, so come for lunch or an early evening bite.
Buggy access.

Olley's
67-9 Norwood Road, SE24 (8671 8259/ www.olleys.info). Herne Hill rail/3, 68 bus. **Meals served** noon-10.30pm Tue-Sat. **Dinner served** 5-10.30pm Mon, Sun. **Main courses** £5.75-£18.25. **Credit** AmEx, MC, V.
A smart little fish and chip shop, and rather famous in a quiet little way, thanks to a series of high-profile reviews identifying it as the best chippie in London. Traditional fried fish suppers can be eaten in or taken out; you can go all sophisticated and choose breaded calamares or swordfish; or all healthy and have steamed fish and salad. Children can have a smaller portion of something and chips, with a drink, for £3.50.
Buggy access. Children's menu (£3.50). High chairs. Tables outdoors (12, pavement).

South-west London

Boiled Egg & Soldiers
63 Northcote Road, SW11 (7223 4894). Clapham Junction rail. **Open** 9am-6pm Mon-Sat; 10am-5pm Sun. **Main courses** £3.95-£4.95. **No credit cards.**
Come here on a quiet weekday for a family lunch and the atmosphere couldn't be more homely. Inexpensive luncheon and teatime favourites include beans on toast, egg and soldiers, sausages, healthy crudités and sandwiches and not so healthy cakes and buns for the little ones and their parents. The big fry-ups are popular with the bright young things of Clapham, while the very young can have their food on plastic plates and their drinks in beakers. It's a phenomenally popular café, and if you come at nursery chuck-out time you won't be able to move for buggies.
Buggy access. Children's menu (from £1.50). Crayons. High chairs. Tables outdoors (3, pavement; 8, garden). Toys.

Bread & Roses
68 Clapham Manor Street, SW4 (7498 1779/www.bread androsespub.com). Clapham Common or Clapham North tube. **Open** noon-11pm Mon-Sat; noon-10.30pm Sun. **Food served** noon-3pm, 7-9.30pm Mon-Fri; noon-4pm, 6-9.30pm Sat, Sun. **Credit** MC, V.
This is a right-on pub, whose facilities for children, and African buffet on Sundays, are the stuff of legend. The small back room with children's games and toys are a boon for grown-ups who want to linger over their pub food, which may include sausage and mash or vegetarian burritos. There's also an activities room upstairs and an outside space. Bread & Roses is is the home of music workshop Mwalimu Express (see p228). The pub is non-smoking till 6pm.
Buggy access. Children's portions at reduced prices. Family room (conservatory). High chairs. Nappy-changing facilities. No-smoking tables. Tables outdoors (patio, garden).

We're going down the pub

So many pubs have family rooms, gardens and kids' menus that it would be impossible to list them all. Instead we've chosen the best places for a family pub lunch, in good locations for sightseeing, walking and playing in the park.

Boaters Inn

Canbury Gardens, Lower Ham Road, Kingston-upon-Thames, Surrey (8541 4672). Kingston rail. **Open** 11am-11pm Mon-Sat; noon-10.30pm Sun. **Food served** noon-9pm Mon-Sat; noon-3pm Sun. **Credit** AmEx, MC, V.

The modern-looking Inn was refurbished in spring 2003, so now the river terrace is bigger – more seats outside for peaceful riverside refreshments – and so is the kitchen, which means an extended menu. The children's menu hasn't changed much so far. It's sausage, fish fingers and nuggets with chips and beans, but children can share dishes from the main menu. In any case, it's the glorious setting that makes families come here in droves. Sit by the river or spread out in the park. *Buggy access. Children's menu (£3.95). Nappy-changing facilities. No-smoking area. Restaurant. Tables outdoors (riverside patio, front balcony).*

Cutty Sark

Ballast Quay, off Lassell Street, SE10 (8858 3146). Cutty Sark DLR/Maze Hill rail. **Open** 11am-11pm Mon-Sat; noon-10.30pm Sun. **Food served** noon-9pm Mon-Fri; noon-6pm Sat, Sun. **Credit** MC, V.

Walk about ten minutes along the Thames Path east from the tea clipper of the same name, past the old and lovely Trafalgar Tavern (with children's menu but no outdoor seating), an old warehouse and a housing development in progress, and you get to this lovely old pub. It's perfect for pre- and post riverside walks, park play or riverside sightseeing. Inside, its all dark wood and maritime memorabilia, with plenty of secluded tables where families can spread out. The picnic tables outside look out over the water to the Dome and Canary Wharf. An extensive menu chalked up includes traditional warmers such as liver and bacon casserole, vegetable lasagne, chilli and some excellent fish dishes, including a cod and chips that tends to sell out. The children's menu means sausage, nuggets or fish tiddlers and chips. *Children's menu (£2.75). Tables outdoors.*

Old Ship

25 Upper Mall, W6 (8748 2593/www.oldshipw6. co.uk). Hammersmith, Ravenscourt Park or Stamford Brook tube. **Open** 9am-11pm Mon-Sat; 9am-10.30pm Sun. **Food served** 10am-10.30pm Mon-Sat; 10am-10pm Sun. **Credit** AmEx, MC, V.

There are canoes hanging from the ceiling in this bright, modern pub, and staff are quite relaxed about the children running about on the waterfront veranda (which is where everybody goes, given half a chance). Children have their own menu, which lists not especially exciting nuggets, fish fingers, pasta and so on. On Sundays things look up: children can have smaller portions of adults' lunches; home-made ice creams also go down a treat. There's a play area (with swings and roundabout) on the green right next to the pub. *Buggy access. Children's menu (£2.95). High chairs. Nappy-changing facilities. Tables outdoors (garden).*

Phoenix

Alexandra Palace Way, N22 (8365 2121). Wood Green or Turnpike Lane tube/Alexandra Palace rail/W3 bus. **Open** *Winter* 11.30am-8pm Mon-Thur; 11.30am-11pm Fri, Sat; 11.30am-10.30pm Sun. *Summer* 10.30am-11pm Mon-Sat; 10.30-10.30pm Sun. **Food served** *Winter* 11.30am-7pm daily. *Summer* 10.30am-7pm daily. **Credit** MC, V.

An inspirational place for eating sausage and chips and gazing at fabulous views, the Phoenix looks like it should be on the Bournemouth seafront, with its great lounge and sedate air. Hot drinks, fish and chips, cottage pie and ice-creams are available at the bar. Well behaved children are welcome; if they get hyper after a couple of colas, there's Ally Pally park to run riot in afterwards. *Disabled: toilet. Nappy-changing facilities. Indoor beer garden. Tables outdoors (patio, terrace).*

Royal Inn on the Park

111 Lauriston Road, E9 (8985 3321). Mile End tube then 277 bus. **Open** noon-11pm Mon-Sat; noon-10.30pm Sun. **Food served** noon-2.30pm, 6-9.30pm Mon-Fri; noon-9.30pm Sat; noon-4pm Sun. **Credit** MC, V.

A pub this close to a park has to be child-friendly. The Royal sees most family action during the weekend, when parents bring in their littl'uns for a post playground lunch. To this end, there's a dedicated dining room, plus a heated tent area out the back, but food can be eaten anywhere. Although there's no specific catering for the children, they're welcome to share dishes of steak and chips, cottage pie and vegetables or large ciabatta sandwiches; all sorts of other choices are chalked up on the menu blackboards. *High chair. Nappy-changing facilities. No-smoking area (restaurant). Tables outdoors (garden).*

Spaniards Inn

Spaniards Road, NW3 (8731 6571). Hampstead tube/210 bus. **Open** 11am-11pm Mon-Sat; noon-10.30pm Sun. **Food served** noon-9pm daily. **Credit** MC, V.

Former home of the Spanish ambassador to the court of James I, the Spaniards is also, rumour has it, the birthplace of notorious rogue Dick Turpin. Even if the highwayman come into the world

here (and others insist he was captured here), most agree he certainly spent time in the area – his equally famous horse Black Bess was stabled in the tollhouse opposite. Byron, Bram Stoker, Dickens and Keats all drank here, too. Much is made of the pub's history, and it's a creaking, atmospheric place, with a pretty summer garden (which draws huge crowds). It's also perfectly placed for post Heath refreshments. There's no children's menu, but they are welcome to share bowls of chips, or houmous and warm pitta, filled ciabattas and salads, from the menu.
Buggy access. No-smoking room. Tables outdoors (50, garden).

Victoria

West Temple Sheen, SW14 (8876 4238/ www.thevictoria.net). Richmond tube/rail/Mortlake rail. **Open** 7.30am-11pm daily. **Food served** 7.30-9.30am, noon-2.30pm, 7-10pm Mon-Fri; 8-10am, noon-3pm, 7-10pm Sat, Sun. **Credit** AmEx, MC, V.

This pub and small hotel right near the lovely expanses of Richmond Park specialises in smart family lunches, and child-friendliness is evident from the attractive, timber-built play equipment (a small climbing frame, slides and stepping stones) in the garden. Families congregate in the bright conservatory area, so progeny can be watched over with ease. There's no children's menu in evidence, but personable waiting staff gently suggest a small portion of plain grilled chicken with chips or a boar and apple sausage with mash or chips, instead of the more complicated grown-up fare. Adults make short work of Victoria tapas, beetroot risotto, the boar sausages with mash and gravy or delectable steak and chips. Puddings are fantastic: try the chocolate sponge – all molten inside– with Seville orange ice cream (or vanilla if you prefer), the mango bavarois or the totally gorgeous banana, toasted pecan and toffee sundae.
Buggy access. Nappy-changing facilities. Tables outdoors (garden and play area).

The Depot

Tideway Yard, Mortlake High Street, SW14 (8878 9462). Mortlake rail/209 bus. **Open** 10am-11pm Mon-Sat; 10am-10.30pm Sun. **Meals served** noon-3pm, 6-10.30pm Mon-Thur; noon-3pm, 6pm-midnight Fri; noon-4pm, 6-11pm Sat; noon-4pm, 6-10.30pm Sun. **Main courses** £9.95-£15. **Set meal** (Mon-Fri lunch) £10.95 2 courses. **Credit** AmEx, DC, MC, V.

A brasserie noted for the river views from the picture windows, and a firm favourite for moneyed family groups. This is mostly because the menu is a huge success, with some perfect vegetarian dishes as well as juicy rib-eye steaks, char-grilled swordfish, cod and crab cakes and rack of lamb. While adults indulge themselves in such fare, children can work their way through their own simple menu. There's penne with a napolitana or bolognese sauce, or plain with butter and cheese if they prefer, as well as fish goujons and chips, sausage and mash or grilled chicken breast with chips. Service is friendly and encouraging toward young diners. *Buggy access. Children's menu (£3.50 incl free ice cream). Crayons. High chairs. No-smoking tables. Tables outdoors (6, courtyard).*

Dexter's Grill

20 Bellevue Road, SW17 (8767 1858). Wandsworth Common rail. **Meals served** noon-11pm Mon-Fri; 10am-11pm Sat. **Credit** AmEx, MC, V.

The latest addition to the Tootsie's family has an organic section on its children's menu, listing curly wurly chicken (a pasta dish), Broccoli Bill's pasta, Ali Baba's shepherd's pie and Mr MacGregor's Pie (minced beef). The main children's menu, pudding and drink included, has families from Nappy Valley and beyond hammering on Dexter's door. Children and adults can indulge in excellent lean burgers (relishes provided separately), baby back ribs, hot dogs, fish and chips

Saucy noodles...

The acceptable face of fast food, noodles go down well with many children, especially those who enjoy a chopstick challenge. Their health-giving properties are undoubtedly overstated, but **Wagamama**, London's best known Japanese ramen chain (it celebrated its tenth anniversary last year), certainly seems wholesome. Free green tea, no smoking, no fizzy pop and large amounts of purifying garlic, ginger and green vegetables may sound worthy, but the noodles and rice dishes, particularly those served with lean, stir-fried chicken or big char-grilled king prawns are highly acceptable to children with a yen for oriental grub. Dishes are big, so grab an extra pair of chopsticks and let children share: they can pick their favourite bits out of yaki soba (ramen noodles with shrimp, chicken, egg, peppers and loads more wonderful colour), or fried ramen noodles with beef, salmon, egg or tofu. You don't often associate noodle bars with puds, but Wagamama also does some lovely coconut and fruit sweets for afters.

Not only minimalist, but mini, **Jenny Lo's Tea House** is a Chinese noodle joint in central London, where the cooking is homely and the surroundings idiosyncratic. Though it's not as cheap as the many noodle suppliers springing up all over London, at Jenny Lo's you can rely on the ingredients being fresh and the welcome warm.

For those with a family to feed on a budget, noodles are the ultimate cheap eat, especially when you move out of central London to the steamier locals, most plentiful in east and south-east London. The **Tai Won Mein** chain are more like old-style Chinese cafés. You sit on benches and eat at long tables (as at Wagamama), but cola and beer tend to be the drinks of choice with the clientele, and the vast bowlfuls of meat, veg and noodles cost from about £3. The Greenwich branch, just near the Cutty Sark, is a real boon. A landmark in Deptford is **Noodle House**, a pile-'em-high, sell-'em-cheap place. Most popular with the Hackney trendies is **Sông Quê**, a serious rival to the much-loved **Viet Hoa**, where a glass of carrot juice and a bowl of noodles to feed a family cost about a fiver. Don't consider another burger chain until you've done ramen.

Jenny Lo's Tea House

14 Eccleston Street, SW1 (7259 0399). Victoria tube/rail. **Lunch served** 11.30am-3pm Mon-Fri; noon-3pm Sat. **Dinner served** 6-10pm Mon-Sat. **Main courses** £5.50-£7.95. **Map** p318 H10.

Noodle King

36 Deptford Broadway, SE8 (8692 9633). New Cross tube/rail. **Meals served** 11.30am-11.30pm daily. **Main courses** £3.10-£3.70.

Sông Quê

134 Kingsland Road, E2 (7613 3222). Bus 26, 48, 55, 67, 149, 242, 243. **Meals served** noon-3pm, 5.30-11pm Mon-Sat; noon-11pm Sun. **Main courses** £4-£8.50.

Tai Won Mein

39 Greenwich Church Street, SE10 (8858 2688). Greenwich Cutty Sark DLR/Greenwich rail. **Meals served** 11.30am-11.30pm daily. **Main courses** £3.10- 3.80. **Branches** 90-92 Rushey Green, SE6 (8690 8238) and 14 Walworth Road, SE1 (7277 1918).

Viet Hoa

70-72 Kingsland Road, E2 (7729 8293). Bus 26, 48, 55, 67, 149, 242, 243. **Lunch served** noon-3.30pm, **dinner served** 5.30-11.30pm daily. **Main courses** £3.50-£6.99.

Wagamama

101A Wigmore Street, W1 (7409 0111/ www.wagamama.com). Bond Street or Marble Arch tube. **Meals served** noon-11pm Mon-Sat; 12.30-10pm Sun. **Map** p316 6G. **Branches** throughout town. Call or check the website.

Consumer

Noodles that cheer at **Jenny Lo's Tea House**. *See p180.*

or all-day breakfasts. Their pudding might be a knicker-bocker glory, banana split or a sundae with loads of extra topping served separately, so children can 'build their own' and create an almighty mess with the raspberry fizz sherbet, chocolate knobbles and so on. We can recommend the imaginative salads, the savoury house fish cakes or the chicken satay with rice. A magician comes in to twist up balloons and amaze the children with tricks at lunch times most weekends. Book in advance, this place is well loved.
Buggy access. Children's menu (£4.95 2 courses and drink). Crayons. High chairs. Nappy changing. No-smoking area. Tables outdoors (7, balcony terrace).

Don Fernando's
27F The Quadrant, Richmond, Surrey (8948 6447/ www.donfernando.co.uk). Richmond tube/rail.
Meals served noon 3pm, 6-11pm Mon, Tue; noon-11pm Wed-Sat; noon-10pm Sun. **Main courses** £7.25-£13.25. **Tapas** £3-£5. **Set meals** £15-£19 2 courses. **Credit** AmEx, MC, V.
Especially cosy for a winter lunch, as the spicy stews and hot savouries of the huge Spanish menu are low in price and high in flavour. The tapas menu being so long, there are loads of possibilities for picky children (even chips), and the staff are always friendly when we visit. Favourites with the young reviewers include the garlicky snails, light tortillas with cheese, pincho pollo (barbecued chicken and sausage on a stick), jumbo prawns, meatballs, ham, lamb and ribs.
Buggy access. High chairs. No-smoking tables.

Gourmet Burger Kitchen
44 Northcote Road, SW11 (7228 3309/ www.gbkinfo. co.uk). Clapham Junction rail. **Meals served** noon-11pm Mon-Fri; 11am-11pm Sat; 11am-10pm Sun. **Main courses** £4.95-£6.95. **Credit** MC, V.
Not more burgers! Well, yes, but they're no ordinary burgers and they don't count as fast food. Using top-quality meat and a great deal of nouse, the chef here makes the best burgers in town. Most children prefer the straight cheeseburger, with chunky chips, salad and fries on the side, but adventurous and hungry types might choose the Jamaican (with ginger

and mango) or a chicken satay burger. Or you can add exotic relishes from a selection available. Portions are huge, but children need not feel overwhelmed – the Junior plate scales things down a bit. Leave enough room for one of the thick, creamy shakes
Buggy access. Children's menu (£3.80). High chairs. No smoking. Tables outdoors (4, pavement).
Branch 331 West End Lane, NW6 (7794 5455).

Sonny's
94 Church Road, SW13 (8748 0393). Barnes Bridge rail/ 209 bus. Café **Open** 10.30am-6pm Mon-Sat. **Lunch served** 12.30-2.30pm Mon-Sat; 12.30-2.45pm Sun. **Dinner served** 7.30-11pm Mon-Sat. **Main courses** £10.50-£16. **Set lunch** (Mon-Fri) £13 2 courses, £19 3 courses. **Credit** AmEx, MC, V.
With its relaxed atmosphere and carefully prepared modern European dishes, this place scores a perfect ten in the neighbourhood restaurant category. Families tend to congregate here for lunch at weekends, when the atmosphere seems bubbly and relaxed. Friendly waiting staff tell the children what's available for the smaller appetite: simply grilled chicken and chips, perhaps, or bangers and mash, or a pasta portion with a meat or tomato sauce. Otherwise there are more sophisticated options, a variety of salads and a selection of seasonally fruity puddings, which are always lovely.
Children's menu and reduced portions. High chairs. No smoking tables.

Tiger Lil's
16A Clapham Common South Side, SW4 (7720 5433/ www.tigerlils.com). Clapham Common tube. **Lunch served** noon-3pm Mon-Fri. **Dinner served** 6-11.30pm Mon-Thur; 6pm-midnight Fri. **Meals served** noon-midnight Sat; noon-11pm Sun. **Unlimited stir-fry** £12.50; £5.50 5-10s; free under-5s. **Credit** AmEx, MC, V.
Choose your raw ingredients from the selection of chopped meat, seafood and vegetables just near the cooking area, then approach the wok chefs presiding over huge gas ovens to your left. They ask you which frying oil and sauce you want (they're all pretty cloying, so tell the chef to go easy), then get

cracking with woks, oils and leaping flames. The result is a bit of a muddle if children have free rein with the food combining, but they always insist they love it. Tiger Lil's will, however, provide a friendly, affordable family meal, and it proves beyond doubt that cooking can be fun. It's a reasonably healthy option, too, especially if you stick to the many varieties of chopped up vegetables and avoid the prawn crackers, spring rolls, ribs and other fatty favourites.
Buggy access. Crayons. High chairs. Toys.
Branches 270 Upper Street, N1 (7226 1118); 75 Bishop's Bridge Road, W2 (7221 2622).

Bush Bar & Grill
45A Goldhawk Road, W12 (8746 2111/ www.bushbar. co.uk). Goldhawk Road tube. **Lunch served** noon-3pm Mon-Sat; noon-4pm Sun. **Dinner served** 6.30-11.30pm Mon-Sat; 6.30-10.30pm Sun. **Main courses** £9.75-£15.50. **Set lunch** (Mon-Sat) £10.50 2 courses, £12 3 courses. **Credit** AmEx, MC, V.
Nicely placed for Shepherd's Bush Market, this is a cool place for a lunch break. The children's menu on Saturday and Sunday changes every weekend, but on a recent visit included salmon fish cakes or chicken strips with chips, or risotto. Try to head the kids off at the pass when it comes to pudding, as they aren't included in the price; but if they share a selection of ice creams from the à la carte menu (£4.50), it won't break the bank. Adult favourites include generous platefuls of Aberdeen Angus steak and chips, or excellent swordfish steaks. We always save the main-course salads with their really innovative dressings.
Buggy access. Children's menu (£5 1 course). High chairs. Tables outdoors (pavement).

Chain attractions

The following restaurants often come to the rescue with their children's menus or portions and benevolent attitude toward chip-chucking toddlers. Branches across the city tend to be conveniently placed for sightseeing and shopping and the food is generally pretty reliable. Check websites for the branch of your choice.
Café Pasta (www.pizzaexpress.co.uk)
No printed children's menu, but there are children's plates of spaghetti bolognese or carbonara, or penne pasta pomodoro with mozzarella, all costing £3.25.
Café Rouge (www.caferouge.co.uk)
The reasonably priced children's menu has been praised by many readers: for £3.95 kids get a drink, a choice of fish cake, croque monsieur, sausage or chicken, with chips, salad or green beans. Ice-cream follows.
Caffè Uno (www.caffeuno.co.uk)
The generous £3.95 Rugrats menu lists pasta with a variety of sauces, or risotto, or various items with chips, plus ice cream and a soft drink.
Spaghetti House (www.spaghettihouse.co.uk)
This chain offers a variety of £5 pasta meals with ice-cream and a soft drink.

Julie's Restaurant
135-7 Portland Road, W11 (7229 8331/www.julies restaurant.com). Holland Park tube. **Lunch served** 12.30-2.45pm Mon-Fri; 12.30-3pm Sun. **Dinner served** 7-11.30pm Mon-Sat; 7-10.30pm Sun. **Set meal** (Sun lunch) £20 2 courses, £24 3 courses. **Main courses** £11.50-£17. **Credit** AmEx, MC, V.
Julie's is quite a grown-up place during the week, but staff are always pleasant to the children. The place comes into its own on Sunday, however, for then they do a children's menu: it changes often but might run to organic pasta with tomato sauce, roast chicken with potatoes and veg or sausage and chips, all followed by ice cream. A crèche is included in the price. First come, first served– which means join the queue.
Buggy access. Children's menu (Sun, £10). Crèche (1-4pm Sun). High chairs. Tables outdoors (12, pavement).

Nando's
63 Westbourne Grove, W2 (7313 9506/www.nandos. co.uk). Bayswater tube. **Meals served** noon-11.30pm Mon-Thur, Sun; noon-midnight Fri, Sat. **Main courses** £4.75-£6.95. **Credit** DC, MC, V.
Most links in the Nando's chain are inundated with families. Chicken, lean, chargrilled and spiced according to taste, is the main ingredient. Choose chicken here – a whole bird, wings, grilled breast in pitta, in burger form – and you're laughing. Select the delectable peri-peri chips and the feast is complete.
Nandos is marketed as a Portuguese cuisine (although the empire is based in South Africa), and though its detractors scorn it as the 'chicken McDonald's', to dismiss it as just another fast food chain would do it a disservice. In fact the service is not fast at all (but always, in our experience, smiley, helpful and a bit dizzy), and the food is, where it counts, good. The chicken is tender, moist and grilled either plain, with lemon and herb seasoning, or hotly spiced. Nandinos (kids to you and me) can choose from a children's menu priced £3.75 for either wings, strips of breast or chicken burger, with a soft drink and refillable (addictive) frozen yoghurts.
Buggy access. Children's menu (£3.75-£3.95). High chairs. Nappy-changing facilities. No-smoking tables.
Branches throughout town. Check the phone book for your nearest.

Tootsies
120 Holland Park Avenue, W11 (7229 8567/ www.tootsies restaurants.co.uk). Holland Park tube. **Meals served** 11am-11pm Mon-Thur; 11am-11.30pm Fri; 9am-11.30pm Sat; 9am-11pm Sun. **Main courses** £5.95-£14.95. **Credit** AmEx, MC, V.
You can always rely on Tootsies for a blowout. This is our favourite branch of the 14-strong chain, because the decor is sunny and rather elegant. The burgers here are large but lean, perfectly dressed with cheese or a host of other toppings. Steak and chips is of the highest quality, and the salads are no hardship at all – the junk salad, in particular, is loaded with vitamin-packed avocados, sugar snap peas and crunchy greens; order one to share with the family. With a nicely presented, inexpensive children's menu (burgers, hot dogs, fishcakes or a junior rack of ribs), and a simple but delicious range of honest-to-goodness US specialities on the grown-up one (the grilled chicken sandwich is a delight), plus thick shakes we keep coming back for, Tootsie's is a hoot.
Balloons. Buggy access. Children's menu (£4.95 incl drink & dessert). Crayons. High chairs. No-smoking tables. Tables outdoors (4, pavement).
Branches throughout town. Check the phone book for your nearest.

Shopping

All the treasures pocket money – or the parental credit card – can buy.

You're in the best city in the world for specialist children's fashion, book and toy shops. There are the smart boutiques to satisfy parents seeking labels for their progeny; or the familiar high-street names for reliable mid-range gear. Then there are the department stores, which can provide everything a child could wish to own, from the pram to the PlayStation. The perfectly formed little toy and book stores in pleasant, family-friendly areas of the city such as Muswell Hill and Wandsworth are a delight to visit, with their play areas and tolerant staff. We've also checked out the best suppliers of nursery furniture, baby equipment and accessories, sportswear and shoes. And since an eye for a bargain never goes amiss in these relentlessly consumerist times, we've cast ours over the city's best second-hand outlets and bargain centres.

Not all branches of shops have the same opening hours, stock or facilities, so ring before you visit.

All-rounders

Daisy & Tom
181-3 Kings Road, SW3 (7352 5000/www.daisyandtom. com). Sloane Square tube then 11, 19, 22, 49 bus. **Open** 9.30am-6pm Mon-Wed, Fri; 10am-7pm Thur, Sat; 11am-5pm Sun. **Credit** AmEx, MC, V. **Map** p315 E12.
Children's pleasure dome Daisy and Tom has books, toys, clothes, prams, buggies and baby accessories on two floors. The wide collection of dolls goes from vapid Barbie to antique baby dolls in the Designer Collection. The first floor is for clothes; summer T-shirts, bridesmaids dresses, trousers and shirts by Kenzo, Elle, Catimini and IKKS. On the same floor the half-hourly automated Peter and the Wolf puppet show provides entertainment, and there's a merry-go-round on the ground floor and rocking horses on the balcony.
Buggy access. Delivery service. Disabled access. Mail order. Nappy-changing facilities. Play area.

Lilliput
255-9 Queenstown Road, SW8 (7720 5554/0800 783 0886/www.lilliput.com). Queenstown Road rail. **Open** 9.30am-5.30pm Mon, Tue, Thur, Fri; 9.30am-7pm Wed; 9am-6pm Sat. **Credit** MC, V.
The Lilliput kingdom of equipment and toys for babies and toddlers has prams, pushchairs, high seats and car seats, nursery furniture and massage oils. The store's own range includes a sturdy pine chest of drawers-cum-babychanger (£325), a Stokke Sleepi cot (£399) and a Tripp Trap high chair (£99). A bestseller in holiday season is the Bebe Confort Cot (£69.99), with mini mattress and carry bag. Once a month Pure Photography is on hand for children's portraits.
Buggy access. Delivery service. Mail order. Nappy-changing facilities. Play area.
Branch: 100 Haydons Road, SW19 (8542 3542).

Mothercare
461 Oxford Street, W1 (7629 6621/www.mothercare. com). Marble Arch tube. **Open** 10am-7pm Mon-Wed, Sat; 10am-8pm Thur, Fri; noon-6pm Sun. **Credit** AmEx, MC, V. **Map** p316 G6.
It used to be the first stop for women aglow with the thrill of a newly-positive pregnancy tester kit, but the last few years have been tough for Mothercare. It may be that its baby clothes and equipment seem a bit predictable and passé, or that its staid nurseryware competes in neither price nor flair with the range in places like IKEA. There's certainly no quibble with the quality of essentials such as wipes, nursing bras, terry nappies, muslins, bowls, beakers and baby vests at reliable Mothercare, though.
Buggy access. Delivery service. Disabled access; toilet. Mail order. Nappy-changing facilities. Play area.
Branches: throughout town. Check phone book or website.

Educational

Books

Bookseller Crow on the Hill
50 Westow Street, SE19 (8771 8831/www.bookseller crow.com). Gypsy Hill rail. **Open** 9am-7.30pm Mon-Fri; 9am-6.30pm Sat; 11am-5pm Sun. **Credit** AmEx, MC, V.
Colourful classics by Ralph Steadman, Jan Pienkowski and Lauren Child are just part of the bumper children's section at this excellent general bookstore, whose owners have a young family and are experts on kiddy lit. Children can browse books of their choice at the shop's tables and chairs.
Buggy access. Mail order. Play area.

Bookworm
1177 Finchley Road, NW11 (8201 9811/www.thebook worm.uk.com). Golders Green tube. **Open** 9.30am-5.30pm Mon-Sat; 10am-1.30pm Sun. **Credit** MC, V.
A lovely central rotunda full of cushions and bean bags, and a cubbyhole with tables and chairs for quiet reading and play at the back: two reasons to cherish this local bookshop. Another is the story-telling sessions (on Tuesdays and Thursdays at 2pm) for under-fives, when badges and stick ers are handed out and not-so-literary friendships forged.
Buggy access. Mail order.

Children's Book Centre
237 Kensington High Street, W8 (7937 7497/ www.childrensbookcentre.co.uk). High Street Kensington tube. **Open** 9.30am-6.30pm Mon, Wed, Fri, Sat; 9.30am-6pm Tue; 9.30am-7pm Thur; noon-6pm Sun. **Credit** AmEx, MC, V. **Map** p314 A9.
Stationery, multimedia, jewellery, books and toys are packed into this extremely useful shop. Staff are friendly and willing to help out those looking for a particular gift, or those confused by the reading matter to suit a particular age group. There's a decent choice of books for older readers – including popular teen lit, and fantasy fiction by Rowling and Tolkien. Plenty for early readers too.
Buggy access. Mail order.

They got rhythm. **Northcote Music**. *See p185*.

Children's Bookshop

29 Fortis Green Road, N10 (8444 5500). Highgate tube then 43, 134 bus. **Open** *9.15am-5.45pm Mon-Sat; 11am-4pm Sun.* **Credit** AmEx, MC, V.

The atmosphere is one of earnest and learned enthusiasm for children's books, the staff areunfailingly helpful and the depth of stock is unequalled in London. Children, from babies to teenagers, can always find something new, and teachers come from all over north London to buy the resource materials. There are occasional author events and signings, and a quarterly newsletter.

Buggy access. Mail order. Play area.

The Golden Treasury

97 Wandsworth Bridge Road, SW6 (7384 1821). Fulham Broadway tube. **Open** *9.30am-6pm Mon-Fri; 9.30am-5.30pm Sat.* **Credit** MC, V.

Books for babies and children up to the age of 16 includes colourful pop-ups with myths and fantasies, as well as young fiction and colouring books. Educational books for children and teachers are also in plentiful supply.

Buggy access. Delivery service. Nappy-changing facilities. Play area. Storytime (4pm Fri).

Branch: 29 Replingham Road, SW18 (8333 0167).

The Lion & Unicorn

19 King Street, Richmond (8940 0483/www.lionunicorn books.co.uk). Richmond Station and tube. **Open** *9.30am-5.30pm Mon-Fri; 9.30am-6pm Sat; noon-5pm Sun.* **Credit** MC, V.

A specialist children's bookshop of 25 years standing. The tiny shop is crammed with books, and the knowledgeable staff, who seem nicely attuned to the reading habits of most children, gladly recommend books for all tastes and ages – tweenie to teen. Regular events, usually on a Saturday, include visits by writers.

Buggy access. Mail order. Play area.

Owl Bookshop

209 Kentish Town Road, NW5 (7485 7793). Kentish Town tube. **Open** *9.30am-6pm Mon-Sat; noon-4.30pm Sun.* **Credit** AmEx, MC, V.

For years one of few shops worth seeking out in Kentish Town, the Owl is starting to see more illustrious neighbours, but it continues its very locally-oriented literary offerings. Adults fiction blends into psychology, women and babies' health and children's titles. The sizeable collection fills half the retail space and all sections are clearly labelled by age and interest. There's even a version of the chains' largesse: 'Owl Value' offers three picture books for the price of two.

Buggy access. Mail order.

Musical instruments

Chappell of Bond Street

50 New Bond Street, W1 (7491 2777/www.chappellof bondstreet.co.uk). Bond Street tube. **Open** *9.30am-6pm Mon-Fri; 9.30am-5pm Sat.* **Credit** AmEx, MC, V. **Map** p318 H6.

A basement location means it's possible to walk past for years without ever noticing this famous music store, but once on the stairs you'll get the flavour of it, since Chappell is especially good for sheet music and keyboards and many musicians drop in to play their stunning instruments. An upright piano weighs in at around £2,000, though light relief (for the wallet) comes in the form of electric portables, which start at £79. Certain instruments may be hired on a rent-buy scheme (typically flutes, saxes, clarinets, trumpets). Quarter- and half-size instruments must be purchased and the child has to be measured before they can be ordered in, so call first for advice. Recorders remain the most popular starting position; Yamaha does them in pink, green or blue plastic for £5.50, so they look pretty enough, at least.

Delivery service. Mail order.

Dot's

132 St Pancras Way, NW1 (7482 5424/www.dotsonline.
co.uk). Camden Town tube/Camden Road rail. **Open**
9am-5.30pm Mon-Sat. **Credit** MC, V.
Dot's is everything you could hope for in a small, independent shop. It's run and staffed by its owner, an experienced music teacher who communicates a love of her subject easily to young and old. New instruments – mostly stringed and wind – cost, say, £5 for a recorder, £40 for a guitar and £59 for a violin at the low end of the price ranges. There's also a rent-to-buy scheme, in which hire costs eventually offset the purchase price if a child shows consistent interest. But the great joy here is unpressured advice (keyboard devotees are often sent to Chappell's, for example) and a friendly setting. Dot helps match would-be pupils to teachers and those teachers may recommend an instrument; ads for tuition and second-hand instruments are complemented by Dot's own recorder club and there's sheet music of all sorts. Come here, too, for repairs when the urge to brain your child with his squeaky cello starts to become too overwhelming.
Mail order.

Dulwich Music Shop

2 Croxted Road, SE21 (8766 0202). Herne Hill rail.
Open 9.30am-5.30pm Mon, Tue, Thur-Sat; 9.30am-
7.30pm Wed. **Credit** AmEx, MC, V.
This excellent shop has been around for six years, dispensing brass, wind and string instruments for children and adults. Sheet music is particularly strong on classical, although all musical tastes are catered for. Accessories, such as reeds, strings and cleaning cloths are also sold, alongside knick-knacks, gifts, CDs and stationery. There's a repair service for damaged instruments.
Buggy access. Delivery service. Mail order.

Northcote Music

155C Northcote Road, SW11 (7228 0074). Clapham
Junction rail. **Open** 10.30am-6pm Mon, Wed, Fri; 10am-
6pm Sat. **Credit** AmEx, MC, V.
A very thorough outlet for music lovers, this shop boasts accounts with all the local schools, which is a pretty good advert for success. All instruments are sold here, from brass and string to digital keyboards, with any repairs taking place in the on-site workshop. They also stock a good selection of classical and contemporary sheet music.
Buggy access. Delivery service. Mail order.

Museum & gallery shops

National Gallery

Trafalgar Square, WC2 (7747 2549/www.nationalgallery.
co.uk). Charing Cross tube/rail.
Open 10am-6pm Mon, Tue, Thur-Sun; 10am-8.45pm.
Credit MC, V. **Map** p319 K7.
The gallery has in fact two shops. Its Orange Street outlet, primarily for parties of schoolchildren who want to get rid of their pocket money, is open 11am-3pm weekdays during term time. Kids Corner, in the Sainsbury Wing, carries a greatly expanded stock and is a useful source of unusual birthday gifts, books, craft equipment, stationery and toys. Attractive fillers for going-home bags, such as erasers, pencils, keyrings, marker pens and little notebooks are sold alongside such educational material as books about artists and a worthy Disney book entitled *Looking at Paintings with the National Gallery* (£9.95). Frivolities includes some imaginative toys; try the Battling Knights paper model kit (£9.95) or the £4 finger puppets for junior showtime.
Buggy access. Café. Mail order. Nappy-changing facilities.

Science Museum

Exhibition Road, SW7 (7942 4499/www.sciencemuseum.
org.uk). South Kensington tube. **Open** 10am-6pm daily.
Credit AmEx, MC, V. **Map** p315 D9.
Always full of children and harassed parents urging them to be realistic about what pocket money can buy, the Science Museum shop is staffed by helpful souls who can tell you how such mysteries as the fruit and potato clock (£12.99) work. Brilliant presents such as Stomp rockets (from £14.99) and kites (£3.99-£25) catch the eye, but there are loads of little stationery, puzzle and souvenir items for £1 or less.
Buggy access. Café. Mail order. Nappy-changing facilities.

Fashion

Budget

Adams

Unit 11, Surrey Quays Centre, Redriff Road, SE16
(7252 3208/www.adams.co.uk). Surrey Quays tube.
Open 9.30am-6pm Mon-Thur, Sat; 9.30am-8pm Fri;
11am-5pm Sun. **Credit** AmEx, MC, V.
The children's clothing giant can be relied upon for most everyday essentials: decent-quality underwear, T-shirts, tights, jellies in the summer and gumboots in the winter. The 'special occasion' garb (especially the Christmas stuff) strikes us as slightly on the naff side, but for playwear in cheerful colours for children aged between nought and ten (and up to 12 in the school uniform range), Adams is a godsend. Coin-operated sit-on rides and a toy table make shopping more fun for the little ones. Adams concessions can also be found in larger branches of Sainsbury's.
Buggy access. Disabled access; toilet. Mail order.
Play area.
Branches: throughout town. Check phone book or website.

H&M

103-111 Kensington High Street, W8 (7368 3920/
www.hm.com). High Street Kensington tube. **Open** 10am-
7pm Mon-Wed, Fri, Sat; 10am-8pm Thur; noon-6pm Sun.
Credit AmEx, MC, V. **Map** p314 A9.
The Swedish style merchant never fails to impress for less. A recent visit yielded an entire spring-into-summer wardrobe for a five-year-old – at a total of about 50 quid. For babies too, the look is trendy and relaxed (even though they're too young to care), with those essential little three-popper vests in a variety of colours and patterns for about £3. The labels say Chilboogi and Dubster, and the clothes say street fashion in a wide range of styles and sizes for boys and girls: combats, baggy shorts and long-sleeved Ts to wear under short-sleeved ones. Then there are the accessories: hairwear, tights, socks, belts and bags. Is it any wonder Santa shows up here so often in the run up to 25 December?
Buggy access. Disabled access; lift, toilet. Nappy-changing
facilities. Play area.
Branches: throughout town. Check phone book or website.

M&G Junior Fashions

73 Kingsland High Street, E8 (7249 9728). Dalston
Kingsland rail. **Open** 9.30am-6pm Mon-Sat.
Credit MC, V.
Close to Ridley Road market, this discount outlet has to compete with open air prices – and it does so effectively. School shirts for £1.99, tiny vests or gloves for £1 and anoraks for £7.99 are among the bargains, and not all are low quality: feel along the racks for pure cotton T-shirts (£1.99) and smart microfibre baby suits. Some items still carry labels like

Consumer

Ladybird (£1.99 sweat pants); others are more esoteric, but they might once have hung in expensive boutiques, so look out for some fancy pants and dresses.
Buggy access.
Branches: 353 Barking Road, E6 (8552 1112); 91-93 Seven Sisters Road, N7 (7263 9200).

Primark

King's Mall, King Street, W6 (8748 7119/www.primark. co.uk). Hammersmith tube. **Open** 9am-6pm Mon-Sat; 11am-5pm Sun. **Credit** MC, V.
This is the nearest the Irish bargain chain gets to central London, but there are Primarks all over outer London (one of the biggest we know is in Lewisham) and the rest of the country. It's pointless being snobbish about this sell-'em-cheap store: it has plenty of uses. If you need white tights for the Nativity play, inexpensive knickers for a child being potty trained, baby vests for a mewling puker, T-shirts for mummy and daddy, play clothes for the sandpit and bright fleece blankets for the pram and nursery, buy them at Primark. Tights, pants and vests? £2 for multipacks. T-shirts? From £3. Blankets? About a fiver. Primark is cool, in an ironic sort of way, and it saves you money.
Buggy access.
Branches: throughout town. Check phone book or website.

Designer

Barney's

6 Church Road, SW19 (8944 2915). Wimbledon tube/rail. **Open** 10am-6pm Mon-Sat; noon-5pm Sun. **Credit** MC, V.
Clothes for newborns up to 16-year-olds include European labels from France and Italy (Petit Bateau, Gasolio, Catimini and Les Robes). Quicksilver and O'Neill streetwear sells well. Gifts, toys and accessories are neatly packed into the store.
Buggy access. Play area.

Breezy Stores

142 Crouch Hill, N8 (8341 2020). Finsbury Park tube then W7, 41 bus. **Open** 10am-6pm Mon-Fri; 9.30am-6pm Sat; noon-4pm Sun. **Credit** MC, V.
This tiny but irresistible shop specialises in lovely Yorkshire handknits (two-colour cardigans at £24.95 make a distinctive and practical present for the baby in your life). Other stuff to make you go 'aah!' includes so-cute-they're-frameable bootees with pom-poms, sequins and other decorative nonsense. Umbrellas with ears, sparkly slippers, wands and fairy dresses maintain the fanciful tone.
Buggy access.

Caramel

291 Brompton Road, SW3 (7589 7001). South Kensington tube. **Open** 10am-6.30pm Mon-Sat; noon-5pm Sun. **Credit** AmEx, MC, V. **Map** p315 E10.
A dinky boutique for babies, children, adults and capacious wallets. Upmarket design, high quality clothes and funky kids are the defining characteristics here. Printed cotton or silk dungarees, leather-and-sheepskin baby carriers and wrapover tunics and kimonos are all reverently displayed. Labels include Quincy, Marni and Caramel's own.
Buggy access.

Catimini

52 South Molton Street, W1 (7629 8099/www.catimini. com). Bond Street tube. **Open** 10am-6pm Mon-Wed, Fri, Sat; 10am-7pm Thur. **Credit** AmEx, MC, V. **Map** p316 H6.
Distinctive designer clothing for 12s and unders is characterised by lots of appliqué, top stitching and double-layered dresses and tops. A new range of formal wear (for over-twos) kits out the little dears in typically sophisticated fashion for christenings and weddings. Young shoppers are given a balloon on a stick as they leave.
Buggy access. Disabled access. Mail order. Play area.

H&M is hot for tots. *See p185.*

Clementine

73 Ledbury Road, W11 (7243 6331). Notting Hill Gate tube. **Open** 10am-6pm Mon-Sat. **Credit** AmEx, MC, V. **Map** p312 A6.

Friendly and upbeat staff preside over the gorgeous clothes at this well-located corner shop. Bright selections for anyone from babies to teenagers are found on the ground floor where the Petit Bateau clothing range features strongly. The basement stocks prams, buggies and customised beds. *Buggy access. Delivery service. Mail order. Nappy-changing facilities.*

The Cross

141 Portland Road, W11 (7727 6760). Holland Park or Notting Hill Gate tube. **Open** 11am-5.30pm Mon-Sat. **Credit** AmEx, MC, V.

Fashionable babes from nought to six can deck themselves out in designer labels at this classy shop. Cookie, Quincy, Pipsi, Toby Pimlico and Alberta Creations can all be had here, along with gifts, accessories and toys. The staff are tolerant of toddlers who get stuck in with the toys. *Buggy access. Delivery service. Mail order.*

Early Clothing

79-85 Fortis Green Road, N10 (8444 9309). Highgate tube. **Open** 9.30am-5.30pm Mon-Sat. **Credit** AmEx, MC, V.

Polished floorboards and calculatedly old-fashioned shopfittings set a shabby-chic tone in this independent store dealing in women's and children's clothing and shoes. Flowery tights lie in wooden hosiery drawers; church pews are used to seat kids' while their feet are measured, and little wooden stands display adorable floppy sunhats. There's a good range of Petit Bateau, French Connection, Ali Bali, Jean Bourget, Balu and so forth, plus shoes from Start-Rite and D&G Junior. *Buggy access. Delivery service. Disabled access. Play area.*

Gotham Angels

23 Islington Green, N1 (7359 8090/www.gotham-angels. com). Angel tube. **Open** 10.30am-7pm Mon-Fri; 10am-6pm Sat; 11am-5pm Sun. **Credit** MC, V.

Primarily women's fashions, Angels has retrenched to that base of late, so fewer of the Gotham Devils (ie girls' label) are produced. Still, there are T-shirts (£22.50) for tots by Toby Pimlico (sample text: 'I love bananas' repeated three times) and Nippers with Attitude (Tike written like Nike etc). Aidan B's babygros come in tin cans or wrapped like lollipops.

Hobby Horse Riders

50-52 Crouch End Hill, N8 (8348 9782). Finsbury Park tube then W7 bus. **Open** 10.30am-5.30pm Mon-Fri; 10am-6pm Sat. **Credit** AmEx, MC, V.

This large, somewhat blank shop is a must for mini tag hags. Labels run from MiniMan and Kenzo to Chipie and Christian Dior in the nought to eight age range. The colours are gorgeous, the clothes exquisite; too bad the prices are fit for a prince. Petit Bateau underwear, christening robes, buggies by Maclaren and Bebecar are other lines. Most original is the nursery furniture featuring digital prints of jelly beans, tropical fish and so on (wardrobe £299; chest of drawers £199.) *Buggy access. Delivery service.*

Little Willie's

16 The Pavement, SW4 (7498 7899). Clapham Common tube. **Open** 11am-6pm Mon-Fri; 10am-5.30pm Sat. **Credit** MC, V.

Top-to-toe grooming for babies and children up to 15 is the business at the Little Willie's hairdressing salon for children, and a there's well-chosen clothing collection too. A range of funky clothes is the other reason for its popularity in stylish Clapham: T-shirts, fleece tops, summer dresses, mini handbags and colourful tights look good on nippers between nine months and seven years. *Nappy-changing facilities. Play area.*

Membery's

1 Church Road, SW13 (8876 2910). Barnes Bridge rail. **Open** 10am-5pm Mon-Sat. **Credit** AmEx, MC, V.

Sally Membery's own label and those of Petit Bateau, OshKosh and IKKS for boys and girls are sold at this friendly little shop. A limited selection of made-to-measure bridesmaid dresses can be bought, although selections of smart linen or summer dresses should also do the trick for that special occasion. Nought to eight is the general age range. *Buggy access. Delivery service. Play area.*

MikiHouse

107 Walton Street, SW3 (7838 0006/www.mikihouse. co.uk). Knightsbridge tube. **Open** 10am-6pm Mon-Sat. **Credit** AmEx, MC, V. **Map** p315 E10.

Owner Kim Dunn spent her childhood in Japan, where the MikiHouse brand is a big noise. The colours shout, too. Co-ordinated clothes and accessories for boys and girls from one to nine years are cartoon-like in their bright primary hues (with logos). The quality is reflected in the prices of clothes and toys (a cooking set for three-year-olds costs £43.50). *Buggy access. Delivery service. Mail order.*

Notsobig

31A Highgate High Street, N6 (8340 4455). Archway or Highgate tube. **Open** 9.30am-6pm Mon-Fri; 10am-6pm Sat; 11am-5pm Sun. **Credit** MC, V.

The harder you look in this tiny jewelbox of a shop, the more delights you see. Tiny outfits by Cacharel, Braez, Diesel and No Angel hang on the walls; Wright and Teague silver jewellery for babies (from £40 for a chain with bell), Little Chums cute T-shirts sit in organza bags in baskets alongside French hand-crocheted monkeys. Down the windy stairs are fancy dress costumes by Bandicoot Lapin (from £60). The basement features vintage ranges, including Miss Hollywood robes made from multi-coloured chenille, and adjustable dressing-up gear by Childhood Enchantment which lets you justify those luxury prices by providing several years' wear. *Buggy access. Delivery service. Play area.*

Oilily

9 Sloane Street, SW1 (7823 2505/www.oilily.nl). Knightsbridge tube. **Open** 10am-6pm Mon, Tue, Thur-Sat; 10am-7pm Wed. **Credit** AmEx, MC, V. **Map** p315 F9.

2003 is the 40th anniversary of Dutch company Oilily and their trademark colourful prints for children. Girls can go for pink Princess party dress with organza layers, or ruffle-hemmed summer dresses. Boys get bold stripes and earthy colours on T-shirts, playpants and thick zip-up hoodies. *Buggy access. Delivery service. Mail order. Play area.*

Patrizia Wigan

19 Walton Street, SW3 (7823 7080/www.patriziawigan. com). Knightsbridge or South Kensington tube. **Open** 10.30am-6.30pm Mon-Fri; 10.30am-6pm Sat. **Credit** AmEx, MC, V. **Map** p315 E10.

Gifts and childrenswear for special occasions range from baby linen, shower gifts and smock dresses or rompers all the way to christening gowns, page boy and bridesmaid outfits and tartan kilts and trousers. Things look pretty regal overall, with velvet, silk and lace featuring liberally. *Buggy access. Delivery service. Nappy-changing facilities. Play area.*

Rachel Riley

82 Marylebone High Street, W1 (7935 7007/www.rachel riley.com). Baker Street or Bond Street tube. **Open** 10am-6pm Mon-Sat. **Credit** AmEx, MC, V. **Map** p316 5G.

RR has a well-established mail order business and unmistakeable 50s retro look which can be predicted from one season to the next, so it's not hard to order from the catalogue. But a visit to the two stores allows you to wallow in antique French chic, and in Marylebone the model-like Ms Riley often steps straight out of the pages of her catalogue to serve you. For children, hand-smocked dresses (£85), Harris tweed coats with velvet collars (£95) and tiny ruched bikinis (£45) in Liberty print are staples, along with Start-Rite shoes and lovely baby clothes. Women's fashion is at the back.

Buggy access. Delivery service. Mail order.
Branch: 14 Pont Street, SW1 (7259 5969).

Semmalina

225 Ebury Street, SW1 (7730 9333). Sloane Square tube. **Open** 9.30am-5.30pm Mon-Sat. **Credit** AmEx, MC, V. **Map** p318 G11.

A sweet little place to visit, with its fantasy drawbridge and prettily presented gifts. The shop's own label is sold alongside Cookie, Kind Hearts and Gotham Angels: gypsy-style tops and printed or embroidered cotton cropped trousers and jeans are popular choices with small girls. Toys, gifts, games and party paraphernalia include £1.50 going-home bags. A range of piñatas for parties is also available.

Buggy access. Delivery service. Nappy-changing facilities. Play area.

Tartine et Chocolat

66 South Molton Street, W1 (7629 7233). Bond Street tube. **Open** 10am-6pm Mon-Sat. **Credit** AmEx, MC, V. **Map** p316 H6.

You can't imagine the classic French snack of the title being consumed by any child dressed in T et C's exquisite clothes. Though other pastels appear each season, they are famous for their pink and blue, not to mention purest snowy white, baby clothes with white embroidery. A snowsuit costs from £90; swimwear around £35-£45. Matching pyjama and dressing gown sets make wonderful gifts, as do the divine linen party dresses with organza sashes.

Mail order.

Tots

39 Turnham Green Terrace, W4 (8995 0520/www.tots chiswick.com). Turnham Green tube. **Open** 10am-6pm Mon-Sat; noon-5pm Sun. **Credit** AmEx, MC, V.

The one-time Tots in the Terrace has shortened its name, but not its stock. Oilily, Marese, Lily Gaufrette, Miniman, Timberland and Kenzo are all still on offer, and the not-for-sale toy basket at the rear of the shop is still there too.

Buggy access. Mail order. Play area.

Trendys

72 Chapel Market, N1 (7837 9070). Angel tube. **Open** 9.30am-6pm Mon-Sat; 9.30am-4pm Sun. **Credit** AmEx, MC, V.

Its curious location among the discount shops lining this market street does not seem to prevent the well-established designer kidswear shop from thriving. It stocks a small range of shoes by Moschino and BMS, but its main attraction is a collection of cute clothes by the likes of French Connection, Oilily, Elle, Cacharel, Diesel and, just lately, Bengh for little girls who like pink, bows and flowers. Burberry feeding bottles (£11) to match the label's plaid trimmed denim clothes are also available, if you really must.

Buggy access.

Aah! **Semmalina**.

Shops by area

Kensington & Chelsea
Caramel (Designer, *p186*); **Daisy & Tom** (All-rounders, *p183*); **Dragons of Walton Street** (Equipment & accessories, *p198*); **Early Learning Centre** (Fun & games, *p206*); **Gap Kids** (Mid-range, *p191*) **H&M** (Budget, *p185*); **Iana** (Mid range and high street, *p191*); **MikiHouse** (Designer, *p188*); **Nursery Window** (Equipment, *p200*); **Oilily** (Designer, *p188*); **Patrizia Wigan** (Designer, *p188*); **Science Museum** (Museum shops, *p185*); **Traditional Toys** (Traditional toys, *p205*); **Tridias** (Traditional toys, *p205*); **Trotters** (Mid-range & high street, *p192*), **What Katy Did** (Designer, *p191*).

West End
Benjamin Pollock's Toyshop (Traditional toys, *p204*; **Buckle My Shoe** (Shoes, *p193*); **Catimini** (Designer, *p186*); **Chappell of Bond Street** (Musical instruments, *p184*); **Child** (Mid-range & high street, *p191*); **Disney Store** (Fun & games, *p206*); **Gymboree** (Mid-range & high street, *p191*); **Hamleys** (Fun & games, *p206*); **Iana** (Mid-range, *p191*); **John Lewis** (Department stores, *p199*); **Lillywhite's** (Sportswear, *p196*); **Monsoon Girl** (Mid-range & high street, *p191*); **Mothercare** (All-rounders, *p183*); **O'Neill** (Street, *p197*); **Ocean Leisure** (Sportswear, *p196*); **Oriental Martial Arts Centre** (Sportswear, *p197*); **Petit Bateau** (Mid-range & high street, *p192*); **Quiksilver** (Street, *p197*); **Selfridges** (Department stores, *p199*); **Skate of Mind** (Street, *p198*); **Slam City Skates** (Street, *p198*); **Soccerscene** (Sportswear, *p197*); **Speedo** (Sportswear, *p197*); **Tartine et Chocolat** (Designer, *p189*); **Wigmore** (Sportswear, *p197*).

Westminster
National Gallery (Museum shops, *p185*); **Semmalina** (Designer, *p189*).

Marylebone
Rachel Riley (Designer, *p189*).

North London
Ace Sports & Leisure (Sportswear, *p196*); **Baby Munchkins** (Equipment, *p198*; **Bookworm** (Books, *p183*); **Breezy Stores** (Designer, *p186*); **Brent Cross** (Bargain centres, *p200*); **Brian's Shoes** (Shoes, *p193*); **Chamberlaine & Son** (Bikes, *p201*); **Children's Bookshop** (Books, *p184*); **Dot's** (Musical instruments, *p185*); **Early Clothing** (Designer, *p188*); **Fagin's Toys** (Local toyshops, *p203*); **Frederick Beck** (Local toyshops, *p203*); **Gotham Angels** (Designer, *p188*); **Green Baby** (Equipment, *p198*); **Happy Returns** (Local toyshops, *p203*); **Hills** (Bikes, *p201*); **Hobby Horse Riders** (Designer, *p188*); **Humla Children's Shop** (Equipment, *p198*); **Infantasia** (Bargain centres, *p200*); **Instep** (Shoes, *p193*); **Kristen Baybars** (Traditional toys, *p205*); **Look Who's Walking** (Shoes, *p193*); **Mini Kin** (Equipment, *p200*);

Mystical Fairies (Fun & Games, *p206*); **Never Never Land** (Traditional toys, *p205*); **Notsobig** (Designer, *p188*); **Owl Bookshop** (Books, *p184*); **Rainbow** (Second-hand, *p192*); Traditional toys, *p205*); **Route 73 Kids** (Local toyshops, *p203*); **Rub-a-Dub-Dub** (Second-hand, *p201*); **Soup Dragon** (Traditional toys, *p205*; **Toy City** (Bargain centres, *p200*); **Toy Wonderland** (Local toyshops, *p204*); **Trendys** (Designer, *p189*); **Two Wheels Good** (Bikes, *p201*); **Word Play** (Local toyshops, *p204*).

East London
Baby This 'n' Baby That (Equipment & accessories, *p198*); **Chocolate Crocodile** (Second-hand, *p192*); **Family Care** (Equipment, *p198*); **M&G Junior Fashions** (Budget, *p185*); **Merry-Go-Round** (Second-hand, *p192*).

South-east London
Adams (Budget, *p185)*; **Biff** (Mid-range & high street, *p191*); **Bookseller Crow on the Hill** (Books, *p183*); **Decathlon** (Sportswear & trainers, *p196*); **Dulwich Music Shop** (Musical instruments, *p185*; **Edwardes** (Bikes, *p201*); **London Recumbents** (Bikes, *p201*); **Toys R Us** (Fun & games, *p206*).

South-west London
Barney's (Designer, *p186*); **Bunnies** (Second-hand, *p192*); **Centre Court** (Bargain centres, *p200*); **The Farmyard** (Traditional toys, *p204*); **Fun Learning** (Fun & games, *p206*); **The Golden Treasury** (Books, *p184*; **Havana's Toy Box** (Local toyshops, *p203*); **Lilliput** (All-rounders, *p183*); **The Lion & Unicorn** (Books; *see p184*); **Little Willie's** (Designer, *p188*); **Membery's** (Designer, *p188*); **Northcote Music** (Musical instruments, *p185*); **Patrick's Toys & Models** (Local toyshops, *p209*); **QT Toys** (Local toyshops, *p203*); **The Shoe Station** (Shoes, *p193*); **Stock House** (Clothes, *p203*); **Swallows & Amazons** (Second-hand, *p193*); **Tiny Set Toys** (Local toyshops, *p204*); **Tomboy Kids** (Street, *p198*; **The Toy Station** (Local toyshops, *p204*).

West London
Boomerang (Second-hand, *p192*); **Cheeky Monkeys** (Fun & games, *p205*); **Children's Book Centre** (Books, *p183*); **Children's Book Company** (Books, *p194*); **Clementine** (Designer, *p188*); **The Cross** (Designer, *p188*); **Jigsaw Junior** (Mid-range, *p191*); **Junior Living** (Equipment, *p200*); **The Little Trading Company** (Second-hand, *p192*); Petit Bateau (Clothes, *p201*); **Pixies** (Second-hand, *p192*); **Pom d'Api** (Shoes, *p193*); **Primark** (Budget, *p186*); **Snap Dragon** (Local toyshops, *p204*); **Stepping Out** (Shoes, *p196*); **Tots** (Designer, *p188*); **Whiteley's** (Bargain centres, *p200*).

Out of Town
Bluewater (Bargain centres, *p200*), **Lakeside** (Bargain centres, *p200*).

What Katy Did

*49 Kensington Church Street, W8 (7937 6499). High
Street Kensington or Notting Hill Gate tube.* **Open**
10.30am-5.30pm Mon-Sat. **Credit** AmEx, MC, V.
Map p312 B8.

Owner Kate Malloy's turquoise-coloured boutique has a lovely collection of children's clothes, from tiny, colourful cro-
cheted hats to cashmere rompers and cardigans. Younger
ages are catered for on the first floor, while downstairs the
unique collection of older boys and girls includes light and
colourfully striped blazers, summer dresses and embroidered
cotton tops. The fact that items only come in limited numbers adds to the sense of exclusivity. Labels to look out for
include Quincy and Bunny London.
*Buggy access. Delivery service. Mail order. Nappy-
changing facilities.*

Mid-range & high street

Biff

*41-43 Dulwich Village, SE21 (8299 0911). North Dulwich
rail.* **Open** 9.30am-5.30pmMon-Fri; 10am-6pm Sat.
Credit AmEx, MC, V.

Now with an additional outlet next door for teenage and
womenswear, Biff pulls in plenty of grown-ups these days.
Excellent quality children's clothes for casual and formal
wear include a fabulous stock of striped tights and tops for
winter toddling, and an irresistible summer and swimwear
range. Christening clothes (of the tasteful kind) are also sold.
The label-obsessed can check off the following: Quicksilver,
O'Neill and French Connection.
Buggy access. Play area.

Child

*49 Shelton Street, WC2 (7240 8484) Covent Garden
tube.* **Open** Mon-Fri 10.30am-6pm, Sat 11am-6pm.
Credit MC, V.

Away from the tourist throngs of the Piazza, this independent shop strives to offer unusual kids' clothes and accessories for kids between nought and six at prices slightly
higher than Gap. Clothing labels tend to be European and
include Simple Kids, Garçon, Jules et Julie and No Added
Sugar. Shoes are a new line; for girls, there are Agatha de la
Ruiz in bright colours and funky designs, alongside Diesel
and less well known names. Downstairs, fairytale cots and
bedroom furniture by Planet Little provide a convenient
roomset for playthings by Jellycat and Manhattan, as well as
hand-made rag dolls and soft toys on wheels.
Buggy access. Mail order.

Gap Kids

*122 Kings Road, SW3 (7823 7272/www.gap.co.uk).
Sloane Square tube.* **Open** 9.30am-7pm Mon-Sat; noon-
6pm Sun. **Credit** AmEx, MC, V.

A trendy link in the fashion essentials chain. Generally considered to have the best children's sale rail, the Chelsea Gap
has provided us with countless toasty hoodies, puffas, striped
tights and cardies at knockdown prices. Frequent sales mean
that visiting any branch of the chain can be rewarding, and
the normal prices aren't bad considering the excellent quality
of the sweatshirts (from £20), which wash well and can be
passed down from sibling to sibling; similarly well made are
the jeans (from £25) and khakis (from £20). The babywear
is of a high standard and softly stylish, and toddlers look
good enough to eat in the denim dungarees and pinafores
teamed with striped jumpers.
Buggy access. Nappy-changing facilities.
Branches: throughout town. Check phone book or website.

Gymboree

*198 Regent Street, W1 (7494 1110/www.gymboree,com).
Oxford Circus tube.* **Open** 10am-7pm Mon-Wed, Fri, Sat;
10am-8pm Thur; 11.30am-5.30pm Sun. **Credit** AmEx,
MC, V. **Map** p316 J6.

This central London store has more charm than other chains,
with its spiral marble staircase and Paris-style wrought iron
lift blending well with a clothing range that sits midway
between French conservative and American casual. You'll be
able to pick up little woollen coats with velvet collars (for
about £50) here in winter, and great quantities of spotty leg-
gings and appliquéd T-shirts (for around £20) in summer. Its
main advantage, however, is a totally co-ordinated style that
teams pull-up wellies in gorgeous patterns with raincoats,
brollies, hats and scarves, or bikinis with towelling robes,
sunglasses, hats, slippers, bags and bath toys. Sales are held
bi-monthly, Gap-style, to encourage frequent visits.
*Buggy access. Delivery service. Disabled access: lift.
Play area.*
Branches: throughout town. Check phone book or website.

Iana

*186 King's Road, SW3 (7352 0060/www.iana.it).
Sloane Square tube.* **Open** 10am-6pm Mon, Tue, Thur,
Fri; 10am-7pm Wed; 10am-6.30pm Sat; noon-6pm Sun.
Credit AmEx, MC, V. **Map** p315 F11.

An impressive Italian brand, Iana clothes look as fashionable
as Gap's, but cost less and have a pretty exclusive style.
There are two ranges, a basic play selection for children aged
up to two, then three-14 years, which yields inexpensive Ts
and little shirts from £5. Slightly more dressy wear costs
from about £15 for trousers and shirts. A sweet little denim
dress for a little girl costs £21, sundresses in coll colours are
priced from £12 and there's some gorgeous babywear from
about £5.50. Great stuff. Seasonal stuff includes swimwear
and sandals. Service is helpful.
Buggy access. Mail order.

Jigsaw Junior

*190 Westbourne Grove, W11 (7229 8654/www.jigsaw-
online.com). Notting Hill Gate tube.* **Open** 10am-6.30pm
Mon-Wed, Sat; 10am-7pm Thur, Fri; noon-6pm Sun.
Credit AmEx, MC, V. **Map** p312 A6.

Trends in (classy) women's fashion are closely echoed in the
junior range, so little girls can enjoy the fluffy/suede Afghan
coat revival or rejoice in the latest assymmetric skirts (in
denim, £26.95.) An unmissable classic is the ribbed cardigan
trimmed with velvet (£42.95; this detail also available on
nicely shaped jeans and t-shirts.) Padded coats are lined with
flower prints and stripes are much in evidence; more girly
sparkle tends to be restricted to jewellery and hair accessories
(butterfly clip, £9.95). A silver slide with a cushioned landing divides the two levels at this branch.
Buggy access. Play area.
Branches: throughout town. Check phone book or website.

Monsoon Girl

*25 The Market WC2 (7497 9325/www.monsoon.co.uk).
Covent Garden tube.* **Open** 10am-8pm Mon-Sat, 11am-
6pm Sun. **Credit** AmEx, MC, V. **Map** p319 L7.

Little girls float around looking absolutely adorable in
Monsoon's winsome styles. The baby rage for tinies aged
from two months upwards includes delicate little dresses for
that all-important first outing (at about £20) and cardies in
beautiful shades of raspberry, mauve and green. T-shirts
with attractive detailing, skirts, and oh-so-enchanting lined
dresses – for anyone from toddlers of 18 months through to
hippy chicks aged about ten – all come in at around £20. Top
girly looks, but not too pink and prissy.

Petit Bateau

62 South Molton Street, W1 (7491 4498/www.petit-bateau.com). Bond Street tube. **Open** 10am-6.30 Mon-Wed & Fri-Sat; 10am-7pm Thur. **Credit** AmEx, MC, V. **Map** p316 H6.

Representing the less frou-frou end of French fashion, Petit Bateau may be best known in the UK for its fine cotton underwear, but the rest of its clothing range will find favour with those who appreciate discreet luxury and subtle colours. Prices are middling to high: £27 buys a striped jersey dress, £64 a padded anorak. The cost of their famous baby vests may still make you blanch: £9.
Buggy access. Delivery service. Play area.
Branches: 106-108 King's Road, SW3 (7838 0818); 188 Chiswick High Road, W4 (8987 0288); 56-58 Hill Street, Twickenham, TW9 (8940 6734).

Trotters

34 King's Road, SW3 (7259 9620/www.trotters.co.uk). Sloane Square tube. **Open** 9am-7pm Mon-Sat; 10.30am-6.30pm Sun. **Credit** AmEx, MC, V. **Map** p315 F11.

There's always a good deal going on at Trotters, both in terms of frequent sale items and activities in the shop. Look out for delightful summer frocks in florals for wee girls, sensible navy hoodies and long shorts for the lads and a whole range of colourful gear carrying Diesel, Chipie and Elle labels. There's also a Starship Troopers area for children's haircuts, and the Trotters Express train at the back of the shop is a good place to get fitted for sensible Start Rite shoes. A central juice bar provides the refreshments.
Buggy access. Café. Delivery service. Mail order. Nappy-changing facilities. Play area.
Branches: 127 Kensington High Street, W8 (7937 9373); Unit A6 Brent Cross Shopping Centre, NW4 (8202 1888).

Second-hand

Boomerang

69 Blythe Road, W14 (7610 5232). Olympia tube. **Open** 9.30am-6pm Tue-Sat. **No credit cards.**

New and nearly-new items to be found at this very personable shop run from maternity wear to prams, buggies, toys and nursery equipment. There's also a generous selection of well-known labels in stock, including perennial favourites like OshKosh and Petit Bateau.
Buggy access.

Bunnies

201 Replingham Road, SW18 (8875 1228). Southfields tube. **Open** 10am-5.30pm Tue-Fri; 10am-5pm Sat. **No credit cards.**

This clothing agency is a great one-stop for discounts, exchanges and sale-or-returns. New and nearly-new clothes from Next, OshKosh, Gap and Benetton come in sizes for kids up to ten, with puzzles, games and toys for all ages. Limited opening hours see loyal faithfuls flocking to bag the bargains.
Buggy access.

Chocolate Crocodile

39 Morpeth Road, E9 (8985 3330). Mile End tube then 277 bus. **Open** 11am-5pm Mon-Sat. **Credit** MC, V.

Its proximity to Victoria Park and various trendy pubs and cafés make this cute recycling centre well worth a special visit, even if you don't live locally. It is, besides, packed to the gunnels with clothes, shoes, nursery equipment and toys. Some of the latter are brand new – typically wooden toys, priced from £2.99 for jigsaw puzzles to £50 for a doll's house. A Maclaren buggy that sells for £69 in high street chains is £59 here; pretty girls' dresses sell for £4-£5, immaculate boys' trousers for £3.85 and new picture books for between 99p and £2.99. Designer gear (a small rail near the till) might have T-shirts by Young Versace, Oilily and French Connection, a great find when you consider how much these little pieces cost new. Everything is in good nick, and if you need something – a swimsuit, say (£2) or a child's vacuum cleaner (£4.50) – just ask; it will appear from under a pile.
Buggy access. Play area.

The Little Trading Company

7 Bedford Corner, The Avenue, W4 (8742 3152). Turnham Green tube. **Open** 9am-5pm Mon-Fri; 9am-4.30pm Sat. **No credit cards.**

Pick up a bargain among the toys, books, games, garden equipment, nursery furniture and cots sold here. A wide range of clothes is also available for children up to 14. A profit-share or sale-and-return policy exists for those who want to trade in their unwanted wares; pretty useful if you're looking to flog spurned judo or riding kit.
Buggy access. Delivery service. Play area.

Merry-Go-Round

12 Clarence Road, E5 (8985 6308/www.merrygr.net). Hackney Central rail. **Open** 10am-5.30pm Mon-Sat. **Credit** MC, V.

One of the largest kids' second-hand agencies still trading in London, Merry-Go-Round thrives in the absence of any local toy or kids' clothing stores. It's spacious and ordered by type, with items for nought to 23 months on ground floor, and stuff for twos to teenagers in the basement. But toys, buggies and baby walkers spill out on to the pavement, bottle sterilisers line high shelves, and strings from floor to ceiling display wellie boots (£2.50-£4), baby bootees (£2), even football and skating boots. This is not a place for designer labels (though you'll find the odd one on the racks); it deals in the likes of Next, Gap and Hennes for clothes, or Fisher Price and Chad Valley (toys). But there are videos, books, car seats and cycling helmets in impressive quantities.
Buggy access. Nappy-changing facilities. Play area.

Pixies

14 Fauconberg Road, W4 (8995 1568/www.pixiesonline. co.uk). Chiswick Park or Turnham Green tube. **Open** 10am-4.30pm Tue-Fri; 10am-3pm Sat. **Credit** MC, V.

This popular store in a well-to-do area covers new and nearly-new toys, clothes, books and equipment for noughts to 12s. Tripp Trapp high chairs, booster seats, sleepbags, baby shoes and UV-resistant swimwear are neatly arranged. You can also sell your children's outgrown or unwanted items for 45 per cent to 60 per cent of the resale price – depending on the item.
Buggy access. Mail order.

Rainbow

249 Archway Road, N6 (8340 8003). Highgate tube. **Open** 10.30am-5.30pm Mon-Sat. **Credit** MC, V.

This valuable local resource has lived under the threat of complete transformation for some time now, but still does a roaring trade in second-hand kids' clothes, helpfully arranged by type (trousers/jackets/jumpers/dresses/shorts etc) and size. Pick up some jeans for £2.95 or a sunhat for £1.50; meanwhile the intended recipients can peruse recycled toys, some of which may be slightly damaged versions from Rainbow's delightful toyshop next door. Fancy labelled clothes often hang from the ceiling and bear a slight premium, but regular hardy play wear like hoodies and combats from Gap can be in excellent condition too.
Buggy access.

Swallows & Amazons

91 Nightingale Lane, SW12 (8673 0275). Clapham South tube. **Open** 10am-5.15pm Mon-Sat. **No credit cards.**
Two floors of second-hand clothes for boys and girls aged nought to 12, all at encouragingly nifty prices. There's a rich spread of labels from high street to designer, and babies' and children's haircuts can also be done on site.
Buggy access. Play area.

Shoes

You can also try the renowned children's shoe department in **John Lewis** (*see p199*), but expect a ticketed queue at busy times.

Brian's Shoes

2 Halleswelle Parade, Finchley Road, NW11 (8455 7001/ www.briansshoes.com) Finchley Central or Golders Green tube. **Open** 9.15am-5.30pm Mon-Wed, Fri, Sat; 10.30am-1.30pm Sun. *School holidays only* 9.15am-5.30pm Thur. **Credit** MC, V.
A boon for busy parents in Temple Fortune, this dedicated children's shoe shop is close to the Bookworm (*see p183*) and offers Timberland, Start-Rite, Ricosta, Skechers, Babybotte, Nike and Kickers in a helpful, calm atmosphere. Registering on the website brings updates on sales and special offers.
Buggy access.

Buckle My Shoe

18-19 St Christopher's Place, W1 (7935 5589/ www.bucklemyshoe.com). Bond Street tube. **Open** 10am-6pm Mon-Wed, Fri, Sat; 10am-7pm Thur. **Credit** AmEx, MC, V. **Map** p316 H6.
A pleasure to visit if only because it is set in a quiet, pedestrianised enclave, the Buckle My Shoe HQ stocks largely its own, stylish brand along with a few BMS clothes. The clothes are a new venture – very sweet. The stuff for girls (aged one to 12) is all starry T-shirts, and tye-dye denim jackets to team with floral dresses. Boys aged two to eight can get down the skate ark in cropped baggy jeans and logo T-shirts. The Selfridges branch has Prada, B&G and Moschino shoes too, while the one in Harvey Nicks has a bigger clothing line. All shoes are packed in fun 'radio' boxes with carry handles and cost from around £42 for a school shoe.
Buggy access. Delivery service. Mail order.
Branches: Selfridges, 400 Oxford Street, W1 (7629 1234); Harvey Nichols, 109-25 Knightsbridge, SW1 (7235 5000); Brent Cross Shopping Centre, NW4 (8202 4423); Bentalls, Kingston-upon-Thames, Surrey (8546 1001).

Instep

45 St John's Wood High Street, NW8 (7722 7634). St John's Wood tube. **Open** 9.30am-5.30pm Mon-Sat; 11am-5pm Sun. **Credit** AmEx, MC, V.
This sizeable shoe store close to Regent's Park has a huge stock of good-looking footwear and mature, helpful staff. Expect to pay around £30 for expertly-fitted baby shoes; £40 for school shoes and from £50 for Italian made, fantasy-oriented delights in pastel-coloured leather. Stock takes in Start-Rite, Skechers, Nike, Kipling, DKNY, Babybotte and Ricosta. Ballet shoes and tights can also be picked up here.
Buggy access.
Branches: throughout town. Check the phone book.

Look Who's Walking

78 Heath Street, NW3 (7433 3855). Hampstead tube. **Open** 10am-5.30pm Mon-Sat; noon-6pm Sun. **Credit** AmEx, MC, V.

This tiny boutique is crammed full of designer gear, including clothes by Roberto Cavalli, Replay, Maharishi, Juicy and Oilily, and shoes by D&G, Mod 8, Naturino and Skechers. Staff are friendly and cope well with brat attacks; prices for shoes range from £35 to £70. A branch in Loughton carries a range of more sparkly stuff.
Buggy access.
Branch: 166a High Road, Loughton (8508 7472).

Pom d'Api

3 Blenheim Crescent, London W11 (7243 0535). Ladbroke Grove or Notting hill Gate tube. **Open** 9.30-6pm Mon-Sat. **Credit** MC, V.
We're chuffed to see a Pom d'Api shop open in London – the groovy French footwear is popular the world over. The distinctive, colourful sandals and beach shoes for summer (£25-£65), as well as sturdy special occasion shoes and warm winter boots (£25-£100) come in sizes for all ages, and there are cute pram shoes for newborns. This shop has plenty of room for the parking of push chairs, and there are chairs and a sofa for children to relax on while parents enthuse over the dinky little desert boots; toys and books are also provided. Each shoebox contains a little toy for the proud wearer, and children are coaxed out of this jolly shop with a balloon.
Buggy access. Mail order. Nappy-changing facilities. Play area.

The Shoe Station

3 Station Approach, Kew, Surrey (8940 9905/ www.theshoestation.co.uk). Kew Gardens tube. **Open** 10am-6pm Mon-Sat. **Credit** MC, V.
Smiling, approachable staff (even on the last day of the holidays) make this shoe shop a pleasure to visit. The play area helps, especially if you're accompanied by a fractious pre-schooler on the school-shoe run. Shoes are by Start-Rite, Babybotte (first shoes), Elefanten and the always good Buckle My Shoe. Bestsellers in an area that likes to be well

Cool runners at **O'Neill**. See p197.

It's magic by mail

Fancy a trip to the West End with two small children and a slim chance of finding a parking space? No, nor do most parents, which is why mail order catalogues have seen something of a boom. Ordering on the web is another way to shop comfortably at home – then you just look forward to the postman calling with a great big box...

Dormitory
at Camden Source; 7209 1105 for brochures & price lists.
The home furnishings of Sue Baker and Cathy Marriott at Camden Source proved so irresistible that parents insisted the women start a range for the nursery. The result is Dormitory: exquisite chambray pyjamas (from £25.50) for babies and kids, hooded towels, embroidered cot sheets (from £15.95) and trimmed bed linen in baby-soft cotton.

The Great Little Trading Company
PO Box 2000, Gateshead, NE85 2BT (0870 850 6000/www.gltc.co.uk). **Open** *Telephone enquiries 8am-8pm Mon-Fri; 9am-5pm Sat, Sun.* **Credit** AmEx, MC, V.
Plain, sensible clothes at OK prices – dresses for £17, as well as underwear, wellies, wetsuits and swim shoes. A separate catalogue has such kit as fire extinguishers, car seat protectors, playhouses, dressing-up clothes and party accessories – in fact everything you need for a fun family life.

Tridias
www.tridias.co.uk.
Full of fun, and still true to its founding mission: a mix of educational, general and creative toys, from puppet theatres to construction kits, with lots of dolls and table games in between.

Hawkin's Bazaar
St Margaret, Harleston, Norfolk, IP20 0HN (01986 782536/www.hawkin.com). **Open** *Telephone enquiries 8.30am-5.30pm Mon-Fri; 9am-1pm Sat.* **Credit** MC, V.
Weird and irresistible stuff. A vibrating, 'hatching' egg is a fun addition to the refrigerator; a cat soap that grows hair when wet sends kids rushing for the bath; a projector torch keeps them in bed during sleepovers. The catalogue itself makes excellent bedtime reading.

Manufactum
Ground Floor, 6-12 Triangle Road, E8 3RP (0800 096 0937/www.manufactum.co.uk). **Open** *Telephone enquiries 8am-8pm Mon-Fri; 8am-2pm Sat.* **Credit** MC,V.
A German catalogue written with breathtaking erudition and purveying stylish, traditional goods. These include toys like the folding beechwood sledge (£110) and shoot-the-chicken game with wooden rifle (£37), which may not be PC but has the neighbourhood kids queuing up for a turn.

Letterbox
www.letterbox.uk.com.
A good option for special gifts. The wide range of hand-painted wooden toys includes a Noah's Ark alphabet jigsaw (£14.99) and a rocking horse (£49.99). Personalised baby gifts are popular, with named cutlery sets from £7.99.

Science Museum
www.sciencemuseumstore.com.
There comes a time when footballs and pink sparkles no longer do the trick. That's when pace rockets, telescopes, robot kits, and other wonders of science and technology could be the answer.

The Talking Book Shop
11 Wigmore Street, W1U (7491 4117/ www.talkingbooks.co.uk). **Open** *Telephone enquiries 9.30am-5.30pm Mon-Fri; 10am-5pm Sat.* **Credit** AmEx, MC, V.
Invalids, young travellers and even treehouse dwellers like to listen to stories on tape; this shop has an unparalleled selection.

The Children's Audio Company
www.kidsmusic.co.uk.
The Children's Audio Company offers a full range of cassettes and CDs, including Postman Pat, Mr Men and Sesame Street. A three-CD slipcase set for £7.99 has 180 minutes of nursery classics.

J&M Toys
01274 599314/www.jandmtoys.co.uk.
It's school play time and you must have an angel/ fireman/animal costume by next week. Try this company, a specialist in dressing up outfits.

Dawson & Son
www.dawson-and-son.com.
Our favourite among the many traditional toys, games and puzzles from Dawson's is the playhouse (£25) with shutters and toy rooster.

Mini Boden
Elliott House, Victoria Road, NW10 6DB (8453 1535/www.boden.co.uk). **Open** *Telephone enquiries 8am-8pm Mon-Sat.* **Credit** AmEx, MC, V.
Among Johnnie Boden's delectable clothes for children aged up to 12 are girls' dresses (from £20) in patterns and florals and boys' baggy shorts (from £14) and sweats (from £22).

Natural Collection
Eco House, Monmouth Place, Bath BA1 2DQ (order line 0870 3313333/www.naturalcollection.com). **Open** *Telephone enquiries 9am-5.30pm Mon-Fri.* **Credit** JCB, MC, V.
Organic babygro or flappy sunhat for your poppet? Eco-disposable nappies? Enzyme-free baby wipes? The green way to bring up babies is embraced wholeheartedly by the natural folk.

Consumer

heeled are trendy French Pom d'Api in their jewel colours
and chunky styles and the distinctive Mod 8 (from first walkers to ten years; summer sandals cost from about £40).
Buggy access. Play area.

Stepping Out

*106 Pitshanger Lane, W5 (8810 6141). Ealing Broadway
tube.* **Open** 10am-5.30pm Mon-Fri; 9am-5.30pm Sat.
Credit AmEx, MC, V.
Shoes start from a petite size three to a limited range of
mature 42s at Stepping Out, which has branched into ladies
shoes for mothers looking for a piece of the footwear action.
It's also good to know that older children with larger-sized
feet are thought of with a selection of hardy O'Neill trainers
and distinctly un-babyish Start-Rite shoes for school, which
go up to a size eight or nine. Other children's brands are
Ricosta, Mod 8, and Naturino.
Buggy access. Delivery service. Mail order. Play area.

Sportswear

Ace Sports & Leisure

*341 Kentish Town Road, NW5 (7485 5367). Kentish
Town tube.* **Open** 9.30am-6pm Mon-Wed, Fri, Sat;
9.30am-7pm Thur. **Credit** AmEx, DC, MC, V.
This handy sports specialist opposite the tube station is an
excellent pitstop for football, cricket, swimming and raquet
sports equipment and clothing. Trainers start at 00 sizes for
newborns (leather Adi-Cribs from £15) and go up by half
sizes to 12 or 13 in brands such as Adidas, Nike, Reebok and
Puma. After the untrained nonchalance of adolescent staff in
the big-name trainer stores, where many seem to regard children as an unnecessary evil, it's a joy to receive prompt,
knowledgeable attention (including expert shoe fittings) in
this old-fashioned, family-run store.
Buggy access. Disabled access.

Decathlon

*Canada Water Retail Park, Surrey Quays Road, SE16
(7394 2000/www.decathlon.co.uk). Canada Water tube.*
Open 10am-7.30pm Mon-Thur; 10am-8pm Fri; 9am-7pm
Sat; 11am-5pm Sun. **Credit** MC, V.
A sport and leisure megastore with clothes, equipment and
accessories for more than 60 types of sport. Frequent sales
and bargain sell-offs make it a useful focus for birthday and
Christmas present-buying to suit those sporty members of
the family. Mountain bikes, footballs, tracksuits and trainers
are all reasonably priced.
Buggy access. Delivery service.

Lillywhites

*24-36 Regent Street (0870 333 9600). Oxford Circus
tube.* **Open** 10am-8pm Mon-Wed, Fri; 10am-9pm Thur,
Sat; noon-6pm Sun. **Credit** AmEx, MC, V. Map 319 K7.
Old names die hard, and this may be the first one that crosses
the mind of a busy parent with sporting requests to satisfy.
It does still supply skiwear and cricket gear in their respective seasons, as well as swimsuits, football and tennis kit all
year round. But the store's layout over several
half-levels is confusing, and our impression is of a store
noticeably understocked and understaffed. The new owners
may yet rectify these problems – watch this space.
Buggy access.

Ocean Leisure

*11-14 Northumberland Avenue, WC2 (7930 5050).
Embankment tube.* **Open** 9.30am-6pm Mon-Wed, Fri;
9.30am-7pm Thur; 9.30am-5.30pm Sat. **Credit** MC, V.
Fancy body boarding in Cornwall with the kids? They'll need
short-sleeved wetsuits (£44) in summer or a full steamer suit
(£74.99) in winter, or the experience will be nothing but teeth-
chattering misery. Boards may be purchased more cheaply
at the seaside than here, but there's a good range of Reef sandals and neoprene Aquashoes (£6) in small sizes, as well as

Rub a Dub Dub. *See p201.*

baby life jackets for sailing, fins (£11.95), masks and snorkels (set £21.95), and even scuba equipment (from age eight) if they want to join a local club for training.
Buggy access. Disabled access. Mail order.

Oriental Martial Arts Centre

69 Broadwick Street, W1 (7734 9461). Oxford Circus tube. **Open** 10am-6pm Mon-Sat, noon-5pm Sun. **Credit** MC, V. **Map** p316 J6.
Aficionados come here for gear; youngsters might come to be inspired. All you need for most martial arts is a uniform (£20-£25) and bare hands and feet. For older kids who require more elaborate kit, there are Thai boxing gloves, punch- and kickbags, strike shields, body protectors and various fearsome-looking oriental weapons, all at very reasonable prices. There are books by Bruce Lee, videos featuring master Austin Goh and a quiet, serious atmosphere.

Selfridges

400 Oxford Street, W1 (7629 1234/www.selfridges.com). Bond Street or Marble Arch tube. **Open** 10am-7pm Mon-Wed; 10am-8pm Thur, Fri; 9.30am-7pm Sat; noon-6pm Sun. **Credit** AmEx, MC, V. **Map** p316 G6.
If you are right in the centre of town, you'll find the first floor of Selfridges easier to navigate than the mediocre sportswear chains on Oxford Street. We've found that it is easier to locate a member of staff here too. Concessions include CycleSurgery (7318 2448), which has small crash helmets and bikes by Ridgeback, Specialised and Trek suitable for over-eights. Skateboards hang from the ceiling and there's even a tiny climbing wall which kids find impossible to resist. If you want a taste of the frustration you may experience beyond Selfridges, venture into the JD Sports concession, where thumping music and a very limited range for small feet characterises this self-styled 'king of trainers'. *See p199.*
Buggy access. Disabled access: lift, toilet. Nappy-changing facilities.

Soccerscene

56-7 Carnaby Street, W1 (7439 0778/www.soccerscene. co.uk). Oxford Circus tube. **Open** 9.30am-6.30pm Mon-Sat; 11.30am-5.30pm Sun. **Credit** AmEx, MC, V. **Map** p316 J6.
A sizeable store selling tiny replica football strips (for twos and up), balls, boots, shinpads, trainers, socks, cups, scarves and hats. Service is friendly and the cluster of other shops on this quiet, pedestrianised backstreet – sister shop RugbyScene, a branch of O'Neill's, a motorsports retailer and various independents offering casualwear and trainers – is interesting to sport-obsessed children.

Speedo

41-43 Neal Street, WC2 (7497 0950). **Open** 10am-7pm Mon-Wed, Fri, Sat; 10am-8pm Thur; noon-6pm Sat. **Credit** AmEx, MC, V. **Map** p317 L6.
You can get children's swimwear in any department store, but this outlet makes you feel proud to be a water baby. As a brand, Speedo has traditionally catered to lane swimmers who look for comfort and coverage, but it also sells beachwear, towelling capes, sun tops and knee-length sun suits (£20) with up to 98 per cent UV protection. The regular range lets kids look cool in their swimming lessons and clubs (the elongated 'tankini' bikinis are lovely for little girls). There are more and more kids' accessories here: come for aquanappies, armbands, snorkel sets (£17), 'find the fish' games, goggles and – crucially – caps that match your swimsuit.

Wigmore

81-83 Wigmore Street, W1 (7486 7761/www.wigmore sports.co.uk). **Open** 10am-6pm Mon-Wed, Fri, Sat; 10am-7pm Thur. **Credit** AmEx, V. **Map** p316 G6.
This racquet specialist is a boon for adult tennis, squash and badminton players, with a huge range of clothing and equipment that extends to junior players and plenty of expert advice. Tennis shoes (K-Swiss, Adidas, Nike and others, £30-40) are stocked in half sizes from 12 up, but more important for children are the shorter racquets (from 19ins, £15-£100) and softer balls which together prevent young beginners from becoming discouraged on court.
Branch: Selfridges (7318 2498).

Street

O'Neill

7 Carnaby Street, W1 (7734 3778/www.oneilleurope. com). Oxford Circus tube. **Open** 10am-7pm Mon-Wed, Fri, Sat; 10am-8pm Thur; noon-6pm Sun. **Credit** AmEx, MC, V. **Map** p318 J6.
The Californian beach-bum look for pint-sized street surfers can be acquired upstairs here. Those all-important wallets, T-shirts and droopy trousers are expensive but adored by near-teens around the world.
Buggy access.
Branch: Bluewater Shopping Centre, Greenhithe, Kent (01322 623300).

Quiksilver

Units 1 & 23, Thomas Neal Centre, Earlham Street, WC2 (7836 5371/www.quiksilver.com). Covent Garden tube. **Open** 10am-7pm Mon-Sat; noon-6pm Sun. **Credit** AmEx, MC, V. **Map** p317 L6.
For many adolescents, Quiksilver is the label to crave. This Australian surfwear shop has sporty clothes (for girls and boys aged two and all the way up to adults) that are casual looking but hardwearing. If the trousers (from about £40), all-important hoodies (from £30) and T-shirts (from around

£15) seem too expensive, check out the accessories – wallets start at less than a tenner and rucksacks can be had from about £18. Staff are pleasant and helpful in this branch.
Buggy access.
Branch: Unit 7, North Piazza, Covent Garden, WC2 (7240 5886).

Skate of Mind
Unit 26, Thomas Neal Centre, Earlham Street, WC2 (7836 9060). Covent Garden tube. **Open** 10am-7pm Mon-Sat; noon-6pm Sun. **Credit** AmEx, MC, V. **Map** p317 L6.
Young teens come here for the decks as well as the essential look to ride them with. Baggy T-shirts and low-slung trousers are all present and correct.
Bugg access. Delivery service. Disabled access.
Branch: 4 Marlborough Court, W1 (7434 0295); Unit 3, Camden Wharf, James Town Road (7485 9384).

Slam City Skates
16 Neal's Yard, WC2 (7240 0928/www.slamcity.com). Covent Garden tube. **Open** 10am-6.30pm Mon-Sat; 1-5pm Sun. **Credit** AmEx, MC, V. **Map** p317 L6.
The epitome of cool, says our 13-year-old-reviewer. Tousle-haired young things working here can drive reasonable adults mad with their laid-back air and descending trousers. Best to let your sk8er boy or girl go in alone than wait hours for staff to help them find the correct size of gear by Stüssy, Silas, Fresh Jive, Volcom, Droors et al.

Tomboy Kids
176 Northcote Road, SW11 (7223 8030/www.tomboykids. com). Clapham Junction rail. **Open** 10am-5pm Mon; 10am-5.30pm Tue-Sat. **Credit** MC, V.
Look elsewhere if it's frilly dresses you're after; most of the stuff here is practical, American-style clothing. The owner imports pint-sized camouflage fatigues for tots (aged one upwards); the simple elastic-waist play trousers in camo cost £9, though prices go up a bit the more side pockets and detailing there is. For girls and boys who like to play rough in the mud there are also Hunter gumboots, or rugged Blundstone boots from Australia. Other labels to seek out for active kids aged up to 14 include Quiksilver, IKKS, Little Badger and Cookie. Service is tolerant towards tomboys who can't wait to get out of the shop before they start playing.
Buggy access. Delivery service. Play area.

Equipment & accessories

Baby Munchkins
91 Kentish Town Road, NW1 (7424 0833/www.baby munchkins.com). **Open** 10am-5.30pm Mon-Sat.
Credit MC, V.
This enticing baby store close to Chamberlaine's bike shop has branched out from its core business of all-terrain buggies (Mountain Buggy from £255; dolly buggy at £45) to squeeze in some unusual, contemporary wooden toys, from string puppets to doll's lofts (£80, with pulley) and hobby dragons (£75). Tripp Trapp high chairs are also here.
Buggy access. Delivery service. Mail order. Nappy-changing facilities.

Baby This 'n' Baby That
359 Forest Road, E17 (8527 4002). Blackhorse Road tube/rail. **Open** 10am-5pm Mon-Wed, Fri, Sat.
Credit AmEx, MC, V.
Jane (pronounced 'hanay' by all those in the know) ranks among the most popular baby buggies at this do-it-all nursery equipment store (its recent lie-flat car seat gizmo with

three-wheeler costs £379); but there are plenty of other brands – from Maclaren to Mamas and Papas, and even baby toys. Cots, cotbeds, chests and changing stations start at £280 for a set. Bambino Mio cotton nappies are also sold.
Buggy access. Delivery service.
Branch: 26 Station Road, North Chingford, E4 (8524 0009).

Dragons of Walton Street
23 Walton Street, SW3 (7589 3795/www.dragonsof waltonstreet.com). Knightsbridge or South Kensington tube. **Open** 9.30am-5.30pm Mon-Fri; 10am-5pm Sat.
Credit AmEx, MC, V. **Map** p315 E10.
Hand-painted children's furniture from New York, London and Stockholm. Dragon's have been in the business for around 25 years, offering children's murals, interior design, classic and antique toys, and even fully-designed and installed nurseries. Prices can be sturdy for children's furniture – the likes of wardrobes, drawers and four-poster beds.
Buggy access. Delivery service. Mail order.

Family Care
90-94 Kingsland High Street, E8 (7254 8720). Dalston Kingsland rail. **Open** 10am-6pm Mon-Sat. **Credit** MC, V.
Scaffolding and a leaky ceiling marred our last visit to this vast nursery equipment store, but no doubt completion of building work will improve the environment. Baby clothes are cheap and cheerful; clothes for older kids err on the side of nylon and frills, but the nursery furniture bears names such as Mamas and Papas (cot with mattress, £215) and a good third of the retail space is devoted to toys. Come here, then, if your yen is for dancing bunnies, a furry rocking horse (£129) or a big, motorised jeep (£400). The elaborate doll buggies cast Family Care as Dalston's answer to Mothercare.
Buggy access. Café. Delivery service. Mail order. Nappy-changing facilities. Play area.

Green Baby
Leeroy House, N13 (0870 240 6894). Angel tube. **Open** 10am-5pm Mon-Fri; 10am-6pm Sat. **Credit** MC, V.
If the concept strikes you as holier-than-thou, think again: this tiny shop has a great deal more than reusable nappy systems. Organic, unbleached cotton is made into wonderfully soft vests and nightgowns for mother and baby, though clothing is more extensive for the latter, and comes in stripes and virulent red and blues (eco-friendly dyes), as well as natural tints. Coloured sheepskins, wool shampoo, cherrystone hot water bottles, natural bristle and wood toothbrushes, Green Baby's own skincare range and goat's milk formula are other reasons why this outlet is often packed.
Buggy access. Delivery service. Mail order.

Humla Children's Shop
13 Flask Walk, NW3 (7794 7877). Hampstead tube.
Open 10.30am-6pm Tue-Sat; noon-6pm Sun. **Credit** AmEx, MC, V.
Number 9 on Flask Walk is the main repository for Humla's now famous handknits and designer baby clothes; the shop in St Christopher's Place carries both clothes and a good range of wooden toys. But here at number 13 is a collection of not-too-pricey nursery furniture (toybox £215, wardrobe £425) by the likes of Heather Spencer, characterised by carved woodland animals. Amazing Scandinavian bunkbeds (£520) may be ordered from a catalogue (these double as puppet theatres or have slide accessories). More portable are the original mobiles featuring teddy bears' picnics, classic pedal cars and sit-on wooden tractors and buses.
Buggy access.
Branch: 23 St Christopher's Place (7224 1773).

London's top department stores

Harrods

*87-135 Brompton Road, SW1 (7730 1234/
www.harrods.com). Knightsbridge tube.* **Open**
10am-7pm Mon-Sat. **Credit** AmEx, DC, MC, V.
Map p315 F9.

Whatever you think of Harrods, there's no denying
its usefulness as a place of entertainment for
children. Be sure to take them up the Egyptian
escalators, with their ancient regal decor. 'Children
on four' is your destination: once there, the choice
is almost overwhelming. Fashion departments
stock leading designer brands, from Armani Junior
to Kenzo and Monnalisa in every age from newborn
to 16. Harrods' own collection is top quality – if it's
your desire to dress a two-year-old in a navy blazer
(£119); their nightwear is more relaxed and better
value. Shoes include Tod's and Start-Rite but
lean towards fancy Italian labels such as Missouri
and Mirella. Other departments please with pure
fantasy – take nursery furniture: how about a
Cinderella carriage for a bed (£2,299) or a red
London bus as a bunk (£2,999) with matching
telephone box as wardrobe?

Each room of the massive toy department aims
to appeal to a different age range. Classic soft
toys are displayed on the shelves of a static
'merry-go-round' and a small replica of the Globe
Theatre is peopled with animated Steiff bears.
Try to steer Barbie fans away from the collectors'
editions (Marilyn Monroe, £49.95), because there
are some affordable toys (jacks, hamsters in balls,
walking Westie dogs etc) in the next room. The
remote-controlled cars operated by friendly staff,
not to mention the petrol-driven miniature cars
(Range Rover £14,995) which can only be looked
at. There's usually a demonstrator for Marvin's
Magic, and clowns and balloon modellers appear
in school holidays. Despite these activities, it is
much less busy here than in Hamleys; the only
downside is the blaring pop music. The children's
book room has a fake treehouse in the middle
and is strong on elaborate pop-up publications.

Themed café Planet Harrods has a wall of
video screens for cartoons and a children's
menu (£5.50). Alternatively, if you can tolerate
the stultifying atmosphere of the main restaurant,
with its potted palms and live pianist at lunchtime,
the ice cream parlour serves omelettes, crêpes
and waffles. Walk through the food halls on your
way out for more educational eye candy.
*Buggy access. Café. Car park. Delivery service.
Disabled access: toilet. Mail order. Nappy-changing
facilities. Play area.*

John Lewis

*278-306 Oxford Street, W1 (7629 7711/
www.john lewis.co.uk). Bond Street or Oxford
Circus tube.* **Open** 9.30am-7pm Mon-Wed, Fri;
9.30am-8pm Thur; 9.30am-7pm Sat. **Credit** MC,
V. **Map** p316 H6.

'Dull but safe' is probably a fair description of John
Lewis's children's department. Covering the whole
of the fourth floor, it's practical and convenient;
while you wait for your pager to beep with your
shoe fitting appointment, you can wander through
the clothes department picking up own-label
pyjamas, swim or ski suits. The stock includes
some designer labels such as Timberland and Ben
Sherman, and the school uniform department is
second to none. Nursery equipment is carefully
chosen and advice is patient and sensible. It may
be hard to keep the kids out of the adjacent toy
department, but at least aisles are wide and
everything is logically set out with clear signs and
prices. Check out the Mischief (JL's own toy brand)
wooden games for value (pinball football £21.95,
chess and draughts set £10.50). You'll appreciate
levels of service most at busy times – even when
children have tantrums or hi-jack bikes and
diggers, good humour and efficiency prevails.
*Buggy access. Café. Delivery service. Nappy-
changing facilities. Play area.*

Selfridges

*400 Oxford Street, W1 (0870 837 7377/
www.selfridges.com). Bond Street tube.* **Open**
10am-8pm Mon-Fri; 9.30am-8pm Sat; noon-6pm
Sun. **Credit** AmEx, MC, V. **Map** p316 G6.

There are two good reasons to visit Selfridges as
a family. The first is a sort of teenage enclave on
the first floor, where aspirational beach bum-type
labels (O'Neill, Quiksilver etc) are offered in an
environment dominated by sportswear, bikes and
skateboards (*see p197*) The second is Kids'
Universe, a self-consciously funky retail 'concept'
on the third floor, where designer clothes (up to
eight years) and edited toy collections are
displayed in floating white plastic pods. The theme
is sky and clouds, but the effect is sub-James
Bond. The department is gratifyingly open as a
space, so you can sit on a padded mushroom and
see everything from one position. For cherished
infants, there are Bill Amberg sheepskin baby
carriers (£285) and Burberry edged towelling
robes; for toddlers Petit Bateau, Cacharel, Catimini
and DKNY. A small party section does glitzy hats,
sparkly fairy dresses and a few magic tricks, and
Buckle My Shoe provides footwear. Older boys
are appeased by combat colours from French
Connection or a timeless preppy look from Ralph
Lauren – but there's a lot of pink (not to mention
Hello Kitty products) here. An area entitled
Create & Play features Crayola products and an
interesting modern cubbyhole with daisy-shaped
CD player. The latter did not work on our last visit
(headphones missing, natch) and the colouring
stuff can't be tried out, proving this universe is
in the real, commercial world like any other.
*Buggy access. Café. Delivery service. Disabled
access: toilet. Mail order. Nappy-changing facilities.*

Consumer

Bargain centres

Appalled by the cost of the modern, designer baby or child? Boutique shopping and the glamour of the West End make for one sort of retail therapy, but gratifying your offspring's boundless desires for a minimal outlay is another. Markets, second-hand stores (*see p192*) and suburban malls in less chic areas can prove appealing for just this reason.

There are few places less chic than **Wood Green Shopping City**, for example. It's here, however, that you'll find the excellent nursery emporium **Infantasia** (Unit 103, 8889 1494) on the first floor, a veritable parking lot of prams, cots, car seats, Moses baskets, mobiles, baby walkers and some clothes, including christening robes (of the stiff white satin variety). Mamas and Papas is the favourite brand here and prices are very reasonable. Opposite is the small but useful toy pitstop, **Toy City** (Unit 62, 8881 0770), its entrance obscured by party balloons. All the usual suspects are here – action heroes, colouring sets, Lego, plus amazingly cheap trikes (£12.99) and beautiful wooden rocking horses for £39. Also on this floor is an outlet of the discount retailer **TK Maxx** (Unit B, First Floor, 8888 8803). It's big, messy and offers little service, but if you're willing to sort through the bulging rails and shelves yourself, you'll find half-price Nike trainers for kids, Quiksilver and Lily T-shirts for under a fiver. The ground floor of the mall is a market hall where sparkly hair accessories, mini jeans, and jolly character brollies and bags can be picked up so cheaply that you'll rejoice in the fact that children have very bad taste. If you get beyond the Shopping City, **Lollipop** (127 High Road, N22, 8889 1626) is a low price babywear store and source of inexpensive junior formalwear.

Wood Green Shopping City
Wood Green, N22 (8888 6667) Wood Green tube. **Open** 11am-5pm Mon; 9am-6.30pm Tue-Sat.

For more bargains...

Try the **street markets**. Not the touristy ones, but the workaday, local ones. **Brixton Market**, particularly in the Granville Arcade (SW9; open 8am-6pm Mon, Tue, Thur-Sat; 8am-3pm Wed) is good for inexpensive babywear and children's clothes. **Chapel Market** in Islington (N1; open 9.30am-3.30pm Tue, Wed, Fri, Sat; 9am-1pm Thur, Sun) yields play clothing, toys and party equipment. **Walthamstow Market** (Walthamstow High Street, E17; open 8am-6pm Mon-Sat) is long on clothes, toys and equipment, and **Lewisham Market** (Lewisham High Street, SE13; open 9am-4pm Mon-Sat) has stalls for party stuff, kids' bed linen, brollies, bags and sportswear, and a mini fairground on sunny weekends into the bargain.

Other **shopping centres** worth crossing (or leaving) town for include:

Bluewater
Greenhithe, Kent (08456 021021/ www.bluewater.co.uk). Greenhithe rail/A206 off M25 or M2.

Brent Cross
NW4, (8202 8095/www.brentcross-london.com). Brent Cross or Hendon Central tube/North Circular Road (A406).

Centre Court, Wimbledon
SW19 (8944 8323). Wimbledon tube/rail.

Lakeside
West Thurrock, Grays, Essex (01708 869933/ www.lakeside.uk.com). Chafford Hundred rail/Junction 30/31 off M25.

Whiteley's
(151 Queensway, W2 (7229 8844/www.whiteleys. com). Bayswater tube.

Junior Living
293 Fulham Road, SW10 (7376 5001/www.juniorliving. co.uk). Fulham Broadway tube/14, 211 bus. **Open** 10am-6.30pm Mon-Sat; noon-5pm Sun. **Credit** MC, V. **Map** p315 D12.
Give your child's room a total makeover with a Junior Living stamp on it. Work, rest and play are all catered for at this Fulham-based store that opened in 2002. Desks, beds, wardrobes, interesting storage solutions and whole bedroom suites come in traditional or contemporary styles for children and young adults, with a concern for well-being extending to a range of quality pocket sprung mattresses to keep growing backs in good shape.
Buggy access. Delivery service. Mail order. Nappy-changing facilities.

Mini Kin
22 Broadway Parade, N8 (8341 6898). Finsbury Park tube then W7 bus/41 bus. **Open** 1-5.30pm Mon; 9.30am-5.30pm Tue-Sat. **Credit** MC, V.

The popular children's hairdressing and beauty salon (baby cut from £10; mini makeovers and the 'Full Princess Treatment' for considerably more) has relocated from Mini Kin's Muswell Hill branch to Crouch End. This means a bigger space at the back of the shop, here got up as a kitsch forest with unicorn and swan seats. Kids love it. The front is devoted to mother and baby cosmetics (Miss Molly face paint for little girls, Weleda toothpaste and calendula-scented soap, Kneipp herbal bath foam) and nursery desirables. The latter include sheepskins (£39.95), retro-style dragon and cowboy bibs, organic wool layettes, Tyrell Katz dressing gowns, Baby Björn potties, Little Green Earthlets products and Moltex eco-friendly disposable nappies.
Buggy access. Disabled access: toilet. Nappy-changing facilities. Play area.

Nursery Window
83 Walton Street, SW3 (7581 3358/www.nurserywindow. co.uk). South Kensington tube. **Open** 10am-6pm Mon-Sat. **Credit** AmEx, MC, V. **Map** p315 E10.

Nursery Window does its own range of old-fashioned, pastel-coloured nursery fabrics, which come by the metre for curtains, or ready made as matching accessories. There's everything a new mother might need, from Moses sheets and soft toys to changing mats, cot quilts, cushions and sheets. *Buggy access. Mail order.*

Rub a Dub Dub

15 Park Road, N8 (8342 9898). Finsbury Park tube then W7 or 41 bus. **Open** Mon-Fri 10am-5.30pm Mon-Sat; 9.30am-5.30pm Sat. **Credit** MC, V.

This bright and trendy store has evolved from a second-hand outlet on Stroud Green Road to take over the premises previously inhabited by Gooseberry Bush. True to its humble origins, prices remain realistic and all advice given is down-to-earth. Three-wheel baby joggers can be had for £99 and Baby Bjorn baby carriers are cheaper here than anywhere else in London. Ample floorspace is devoted to vital baby accessories such as car seats, Stokke nursery furniture and high chairs, lambskins, cute Groovy Girl dolls, grobags, buggy snuggles, swim nappies and anything else the cool Crouch End sprog might need. *Buggy access. Delivery service. Nappy-changing facilities. Mail order. Play area.* **Branch**: 198 Stroud Green, N4 (7263 5577).

Toys

Bikes

Chains worth visiting for well-priced children's bikes include Daycocks and Halfords (check the phone book for branches) – both have a decent range of junior models.

Bikefix

48 Lamb's Conduit Street, WC1 (7405 1218/www.bikefix. co.uk). Russell Square tube. **Open** 8.30am-7pm Mon-Fri; 10am-5pm Sat. **Credit** MC, V. **Map** p317 M4.

Only muscular parents need apply to this shop: they sell adult bikes, plus two-wheeled trailer buggies (you can get a kit to convert them into three-wheel buggies for pushing as well) from £200 – fun for the kids, but hard work for the pedaller. Tagalongs (from £120) are another option, but only for kids old enough to ride a two-wheeled bike without stabilisers. *Buggy access. Delivery service. Mail order.*

Chamberlaine & Son

75-7 Kentish Town Road, NW1 (7485 4488/ www.chamberlainecycles.co.uk). Camden Town tube. **Open** 8.30am-6pm Mon-Sat. **Credit** MC, V.

This long-established shop has a relaxed and down-to-earth attitude, neither hyping things up nor recommending expensive items for small bikers with a limited attention span. They sell Raleigh and a Dutch brand of bike for children called Cool!Loekie – both are rather heavy, but nobody makes anything lighter. The latter rejoice in a colour scheme reminiscent of Noddy's car. Both cost around £100, but there are often second-hand bikes at £30 or so, and young children are unaware of the difference – especially once their set of wheels has been fitted with character bells, baskets, dolly carriers and streamers (accessories from about £5). Crash helmets cost £19.99. Chamberlaine are also great for bike 'add ons', such as Tagalong (from £120), which let kids get the feel of road riding behind mum or dad, and trailers with seating for two children (from £150). *Buggy access. Delivery service. Mail order.*

Edwardes

221-25 Camberwell Road, SE5 (7703 3676/5720). Elephant & Castle tube/rail then P3, 12, 68, 17, 176 bus. **Open** 8.30am-6pm Mon-Sat. **Credit** AmEx, MC, V.

It gets pretty busy in here as every cyclist within a mile's radius seems to have cottoned on to the casual but thorough service that the chaps at Edwardes offer. Bikes for children aged two to 12 include the Pro Bike, Bronx and Giant ranges. Repairs for slipped chains, punctured tyres and damaged wheels are all dextrously carried out. *Buggy access. Delivery service. Mail order.*

FW Evans

111-15 Waterloo Road, SE1 (7928 2208/www.evans cycles.com). Waterloo tube/rail. **Open** 9am-8pm Mon-Fri; 9am-6pm Sat; 10am-5pm Sun. **Credit** AmEx, MC, V. **Map** p320 N8.

Trek mountain bikes for kids are stocked at this two-wheeler emporium; other brands for boys and girls are the Badd Max, Mega Max, Kool Max, Ollie 14 and Micro Max. *Buggy access. Delivery service. Mail order.* **Branches**: 178 High Holborn, WC1 (7836 5585); 51-52 Rathbone Place, W1 (7580 4107); 77-9 The Cut, SE1 (7928 4785); 127 Wandsworth High Street, SW18 (8877 1878); 69 Grays Inn Road, WC1 (7430 1985).

Hills

58 Fortis Green Road, N10 (8883 4644). Highgate tube. **Open** 9am-5.30pm Mon-Fri; 9am-5pm Sat. **Credit** MC, V.

It's odd to find a family cycle store at the top of a very long hill, but this one thrives, thanks to friendly service and very good prices. Kids' bikes here are by Raleigh, Falcon and Concept and typically cost £69. Another speciality is roller skates (from £25) and skateboards (mini boards £9.99, junior boards £24.99). Then there are unicycles just for fun (£60), tag-alongs (£125) and giraffes (to let you attach a regular child's bike to the back of an adult's, £79) and ice skates. *Buggy access. Disabled access.*

London Recumbents

Dulwich Park, (Access from College Road) SE21 (8299 6636). **Open** 10am-5pm Mon-Fri; 10am-6pm Sat, Sun. **Credit** MC, V.

Must a kid's bike always be sit-up-and-beg? A three-year-old can learn to ride a recumbent, which requires steering by feet – terrific fun and extremely cool. This company hires out an astonishing variety of two- and three-wheel pedal machines (£5/hour), but also sells them at around £200. Stock includes superior tag-alongs, which clip into a rear carrier (rather than seat stem) and offer gears to the secondary pedaller (£250). *Buggy access. Delivery service. Mail order.* **Branch**: Battersea Park, East Carriage Drive, SW11 (7498 6543).

Two Wheels Good

143 Crouch Hill, N8 (8340 4284/www.twowheelsgood.co. uk). Finsbury Park tube. **Open** Mon-Sat 8.30am-6pm, Sun 11am-5pm. **Credit** AmEx, MC, V.

This dynamic store run by former bike couriers manages to combine cool racing and mountain biking gear with kids' stuff and workaday family touring accessories. Children's bike brands include Puky (£92-£106) and the more expensive Ridgeback and Trek brands (from £160). There are wonderfully old-fashioned Pashley tricycles (£250), Roadgear Limos (aka child seats, £100 – a notch up from Hamax), taga-longs (£120), helmets and so on. *Buggy access.* **Branch**: 165 Stoke Newington Church Street, N16 (7249 2200).

Soup Dragon. *See p205.*

Consumer

Telling tales

Author signings and storytelling sessions occur regularly in every self-respecting children's bookshop. Events and activities may be sporadic or seasonal, depending on the size of the shop in question, but with membership schemes, newsletters or mailing lists serving as noticeboards, it's easy enough to keep tabs on the popular scribes holding court in your area. The **Golden Treasury** (see p184) in Wandsworth is looking to expand on its Friday afternoon storytelling sessions, with future author events thrown in for good measure. The tiny **Bookseller Crow on the Hill** (see p183) manages to squeeze in occasional Sunday sessions in archaeological object-handling with author Caroline Lawrence. Storytelling sessions take place at **Bookworm** (see p183) on Tuesdays and Thursdays at 2pm, while north London's **Children's Bookshop** (see p184) offers signings and readings by well-known authors: celebrities Posy Simmonds, Anthony Horowitz and Jaqueline Wilson have turned up, pen in hand, to recent events. However, for bookworms who really want to be ahead of the London literary game, it's worth checking out **CALL** (Children and Literature in London) on the website www.booktrusted.com, or by calling the **Booktrust Charity** on (8516 2977) for updated listings of special children's book events and workshops throughout the city.

Local toyshops

Fagin's Toys

84 Fortis Green Road, N10 (8444 0282). East Finchley tube. **Open** 9am-5.30pm Mon-Sat; 10am-3pm Sun. **Credit** MC, V.
This is a cavernous shop, run along utilitarian lines (ie, without much thought for presentation) but much appreciated by its customers for its wide range of stock and very reasonable prices. There's a plastic playhouse at the back for restless toddlers, but why linger here when you can test a glitter hoop (£2.99), peruse the dolls from baby to Barbie, ponder the relative educational merits of Ant World or Worm World, or pick up a sword-and-armour playset (£9.99) or some garish fairy wings? You won't find much here that's high on the cute factor, but there are plenty of art and craft supplies, plus a big table of penny dreadfuls.
Play area.

Frederick Beck

22-6 Camden Passage, N1 (7226 3403). Angel tube. **Open** 9.30am-5.30pm Mon, Tue, Thur, Fri; 9am-5.30pm Wed, Sat. **Credit** AmEx, MC, V.
Tucked away on Camden Passage, Beck's blends in well with the antique shops and twice weekly markets (and provides a welcome distraction from all those delicate glasses and silver). Charmingly, it has creaking wooden floorboards, a huge Brio train layout to play with and two rooms full of tidily ordered toys and games. You can find pretty much everything here, from traditional sets of soldiers to talking Buzz Lightyear dolls, but there's not much of the sparkly variety.
Local delivery service. Play area.

Happy Returns

36 Rosslyn Hill, NW3 (7435 2431). Hampstead tube. **Open** 9.30am-5.30pm Mon-Fri; 10am-6pm Sat; noon-5.30pm Sun. **Credit** MC, V.
Too bad Happy Returns is not at the very top of the hill, for many a dawdling child has been bribed with a visit here if only they will step smartly. It's a quintessential local toyshop with a pleasant atmosphere and everything you need to fill a rainy day, from Galt and Crayola pencils and finger paints to a Plan wooden dolls house (with three furnished rooms, £115). Pocket money offerings run from toy watches and bouncy balls to bubbles and stickers. Branded dolls include the ubiquitous Barbie and Action Man, plus Groovy Girls and Madeline. Many items are conceived as gifts, like the Brio buckets and spades (£4.99 and £7.99 with garden tools) or a canalway system for wet play and a kite for windy play. Party stationery is also available here.
Buggy access. Play area.

Havana's Toy Box

Ground Floor, Putney Exchange Shopping Centre, Putney High Street, SW15 (8780 3722). Putney Bridge tube/ Putney rail. **Open** 9am-6pm Mon-Sat; 11am-5pm Sun. **Credit** AmEx, MC, V.
Traditional wooden toys for children aged nought to eight are just one part of this shop's range of gifts and accessories for little adults. Fairy dresses, snuggle sacks, cuddly toys and night lights are all cosily displayed in this bijou outlet.
Mail order.

Patrick's Toys & Models

107-11 Lillie Road, SW6 (7385 9864/www.patrickstoys. co.uk). Fulham Broadway tube. **Open** 9.15am-5.45pm Mon-Sat. **Credit** MC, V.
In business since 1948, this family-run outfit is the main service agent for Hornby and Scalextric. With a model department specialising in rocketry, planes, cars and science fiction, this place is a real toy-lover's dream. Playthings for outdoors include the Big Thunder or Lightning Go Karts, Brio and TP climbing frames, swings, slides and trampolines. The full spread of Lego includes Technic, Basic, Duplo or Primo.
Buggy access. Local delivery service.

QT Toys

90 Northcote Road, SW11 (7223 8637). Clapham Junction rail. **Open** 9.30am-5.30pm Mon-Sat. **Credit** MC, V.
Jam-packed with goodies and rightly popular, QT's collection is imaginative and wide-ranging. Reliable stalwarts Lego, Duplo, Brio and Meccano sell like billy-o, but there's dollies, dressing up, art and craft materials, models, ride on and pushalong toys too. Outdoor toys for the small London garden include paddling pools and simple swings. Pocket money-priced items change frequently to prevent boredom.
Mail order.

Route 73 Kids

92 Stoke Newington Church Street, N16 (7923 7873/ www.route73kids.com). 476, 393 or 73 bus. **Open** 10am-5.30pm Tue-Sat; noon-5pm Sun. **Credit** AmEx, MC, V.
Oddly isolated in an area teeming with young families, Route 73 tries to be all things to all ages. It succeeds admirably, and its windows make even a wait at the bus stop opposite a pleasure. Joke boxes and plastic cowboys tumble out of mini suitcases, teddies sport children's handknits, fairy dresses hang from a washing line. Inside, this Tardis-like store stocks everything from pram toys and sit-on wooden trains to kites and board games. Tin seaside buckets hold balloons and bead jewellery for pocket money, while dressing-up gear

includes trendy felt soldiers' tunics (£15) to wear with wooden swords and shields. Prices are fair, and there are plans to sell more baby clothes at less than designer prices.
Buggy access. Delivery service. Mail order. Nappy-changing facilities. Play area.

Snap Dragon
56 Turnham Green Terrace, W4 (8995 6618). Turnham Green tube. **Open** 9.30am-6pm Mon-Sat; noon-5pm Sun. **Credit** MC, V.
This tiny shop is crammed with toys and games for children, as well as a wide range of board games suitable for all the family. Contemporary and traditional toys are stocked, but classic wooden options are popular too. Play furniture includes large doll houses and accessories and TP climbing frames (£180-£200).
Buggy access. Delivery service. Mail order.

Tiny Set Toys
54 Lower Richmond Road, SW15 (8788 0392). Putney Bridge tube/22 bus. **Open** 9.30am-5.30pm Mon-Sat; 10am-2pm Sun. **Credit** MC, V.
Outdoor play equipment at this 35-year-old shop includes TP aluminium climbing frames for little monkeys, plus swings and paddling pools. Jigsaws, puzzles, dolls and teddies are some of the smaller items on offer.
Buggy access. Delivery service. Mail order. Play area.

The Toy Station
10 Eton Street, Richmond, Surrey (8940 4896/ www.thetoystation.co.uk). Richmond tube/rail. **Open** 10am-6pm Mon-Fri; 9.30am-6pm Sat; noon-5pm Sun. **Credit** *Over £8* MC, V.
A well-stocked little place on two floors where favourite names Brio, Meccano, Lego and Airfixand radio-controlled toys are sold alongside dollies, craft sets, paints and plasticine and pocket-money priced toys.

Toy Wonderland
10-11 Northways Parade, Finchley Road, NW3 (7722 9821/www.toywonderland.co.uk). Swiss Cottage tube. **Open** 10am-6pm Mon-Sat; 11am-4pm Sun. **Credit** MC, V.
This friendly store has a distinct masculine feel to it – it's great for racing cars, Airfix, Action Man, plastic guns and handcuffs. Still, to be fair, there are also lots of Tomy baby toys, board games, some dolls and sticker books and, usefully, racks of party bag fillers and wrapping paper.
Buggy access. Delivery service.

Word Play
1 Broadway Parade, N8 (8347 6700) Finsbury Park tube then W7 bus/41 bus. **Open** 9am-5pm Mon-Sat; 11am-5pm Sun. **Credit** MC, V.
Tiny rings, giant pencils, clattering teeth, tricks and novelty pens – ranging in price from 20p to 99p – litter a large table at the front of this handy store. A Beanie Baby hammock chock-full of soft toys swings above the till, and one wall lines up children's books covering the noughts to 16s age range. What with Playmobil and Brio, Tonka toys and cinema tie-ins, Word Play aims to please all ages and tastes, erring on the side of craft and games rather than dolls and sparkles.
Buggy access.

Traditional toys

Benjamin Pollock's Toyshop
44 The Market, Covent Garden, WC2 (7379 7866/ www.pollocks-coventgarden.co.uk). Covent Garden tube. **Open** 10.30am-6pm Mon-Sat; 11am-4pm Sun. **Credit** AmEx, MC, V. **Map** p319 L7.
Best known for its toy theatres, Pollock's is an educational wonderland for young thesps, and hugely enjoyed by other kids on a more superficial level. The most popular paper theatre for kids to assemble is Jackson's theatre (£5.95) with

Jolly **Traditional Toys**. See p205.

its set and characters for the ballet *Cinderella*. A Victorian Gothic version features the nativity play and an Elizabethan one (£8.95) puts on *A Midsummer Night's Dream*. Other theatrical items are marionettes, glove and finger puppets. Beautiful French musical boxes with a circus theme (£37.50) are popular christening presents; smaller, traditional ballerina boxes (£17.95) appeal to starry-eyed little girls bound for Covent Garden. And if the historic subject of paper theatres sparks an interest, there are books on the subject. Collectors pop in for antiques and hand-made English bears (from £82), but there are also quirky toys for pocket money. *Mail order.*

The Farmyard
63 Barnes High Street, SW13 (8878 7338). Barnes or Barnes Bridge rail. **Open** 10am-5.30pm Mon-Fri; 9.30am-5.30pm Sat. **Credit** MC, V.
There are indeed mini farm animals and farmyards to keep them in at this gift shop, although dairy stock isn't a particular specialism. Small and large gifts include puzzles, games, wooden toys, dolls and puppets. Dressing up for that all important party could also cue a trip here, as it stocks princess dresses and other costumes.
Buggy access. Mail order. Play area.
Branch: 54 Friar's Stile Road, Richmond, Surrey (8332 0038).

Kristen Baybars
7 Mansfield Road, NW3 (7267 0934). Kentish Town tube/Gospel Oak rail/C2, C12 bus. **Open** 11am-6pm Tue-Sat. **No credit cards**.
You need to look hard for the little red door to this tiny and utterly eccentric shop, but once you've found it you'll come back time and again. Ms Baybars is a craftswoman, miniaturist and local character who will paint you a period doll house to order. But she's also enthusiastic about her stock of classic Escor wooden toys (little painted men sitting in single file in a boat, on merry-go-rounds and so on). And if you aren't in the market for exquisite dolls' house furniture, pick up a hobby horse, push-up animal or tiny car (from 49p). Best value of all is the circus automaton – just 10p in a slot to see the tightrope walker do his stunts.
Buggy access.

Never Never Land
3 Midhurst Parade, N10 (8883 3997). East Finchley tube. **Open** 10am-5pm Tue, Wed, Fri, Sat. **Credit** MC, V.
Is it always necessary to own a dolls' house in order to enjoy the miniature furnishings? Almost every little girl would be enchanted by the tiny china tea sets (£3.50), cradles, baby dolls (25p), rocking horses, mice and musical instruments on sale here. The houses themselves are not that costly, if considered as heirlooms: £99 buys a handsome Victorian mansion in kit form (£135 assembled). Quirkier and as much fun for a young gardener is the shed (£17.95) to be filled with lawn mower, pots, rakes, forks, flowers and bags of apples.
Buggy access. Delivery service. Mail order.

Rainbow
253 Archway Road, N6 (8340 8003). Highgate tube. **Open** 10.30am-5.30pm Mon-Sat. **Credit** MC, V.
Still distinguished by its rainbow painted window, this shop has something of a hippy-dippy aura, but it's a real treasure trove of fascinating bits and bobs. Mobiles and paper lightshades got up as hot air balloons (£5.75) hang from the ceiling. Wooden toys are heaped in one corner, as are puppets. Beanie Buddies are heaped in one corner, while display counters nearest the till offer a motley assortment of glass and clay marbles, practical jokes, kids' jewellery and such doll

house furnishings as tiny plates of food, coathangers and books (from 15p, often bought on their own). The back room has a useful variety of dressing-up costumes, dolls, balloons and little plastic figures on and off horseback.
Buggy access. Delivery service. Mail order (toys only).

Soup Dragon
27 Topsfield Parade, Tottenham Lane, N8 (8348 0224/ www.soup-dragon.co.uk). Finsbury Park tube/rail then W7 or 41 bus. **Open** 9.30am-6pm Mon-Sat; 11am-5pm Sun. **Credit** MC, V.
A small shop held in great affection by locals, Soup Dragon takes in quaint metal vintage cars (£119), wooden dolls' houses (a cute, rose-sprigged cottage with furniture costs £69; a big, paint-yourself Georgian mansion £110), red gingham and wicker dolls' prams, rocking boats (£75) and other wooden delights right down to skipping ropes. There are pocket money toys, and a helpful on-site playhouse amuses youngsters while carers browse the slightly hippified clothes. The free community noticeboard is excellent and bargain hunters may leave an email address to be advised of warehouse sales.
Buggy access. Play area.
Branch: 106 Lordship Lane, SE22 (8693 5575).

Traditional Toys
53 Godfrey Street, SW3 (7352 1718). Sloane Square tube then 11, 19, 22 bus/49 bus. **Open** 10am-5.30pm Mon-Fri; 10am-6pm Sat. **Credit** AmEx, MC, V. **Map** p315 E11.
Toys for children aged up to eight are piled high and packed tight at this well-to-do shop. Classics include Steiff animals, Plan toys and Muffy Bear from the North American Bear range. Julip horses are extremely endearing, and toddlers make a beeline for the wooden trikes.
Buggy access. Mail order.

Tridias
25 Bute Street, SW7 (7584 2330/www.tridias.co.uk). South Kensington tube. **Open** 10am-6pm Mon-Sat. **Credit** MC, V. **Map** p315 D10.
Everything needed for a party or stocking filler can be found at Tridias. Brimming with gifts, toys, costumes and masks, there's something for all ages here. Six- to nine-year olds can dream of Hogwarts in a Harry Potter costume, complete with wand and trademark glasses. Space suits, fairy dresses and mermaid outfits also get a look in, while craft paper, water colours, poster paints and fuzzy felt are all on hand for those with an artistic turn of mind.
Buggy access. Delivery service. Mail order (0870 240 2103).
Branch: 6 Lichfield Terrace, TW9 (8948 3459).

Fun & games

Cheeky Monkeys
202 Kensington Park Road, W11 (7792 9022/ www.cheekymonkeys.com). Notting Hill Gate tube. **Open** 9.30am-5.30pm Mon-Fri; 10am-5.30pm Sat. **Credit** MC, V. **Map** p312 A6.
These lovely modern toyshops exemplify all that is good about independent ownership, being strong on presentation and good at stocking unusual, attractive and fun products. Its vintage cars have recently been joined by pedal aeroplanes, wooden dolls houses now feature alongside paint-your-own bird boxes, and some of London's best fancy dress costumes (from smart soldiers and tigers to frogs) have been boosted by Angelina Ballerina tutus and T-shirts. New for summer 2003, and practically flying off the shelves in this branch, is the Zamiloo range of houses (£27.99), people (a

family is £10.99) and railways (£29.99), all designed as a set of stackable cardboard bricks to be assembled by imaginative children. The Zamiloo story cubes cost £17.99. Then there's Playstack, a brilliant vertical puzzle system which comes with a book telling the story of, say, Jack in the Beanstalk. Pocket money toys and small gifts (for around £1.99) also tend to be offbeat; we like the coloured bath bombs and raggy dolls, and children could spend ages deciding what to spend their pocket money on in here.
Buggy access.
Branches: throughout town. Check phone book or website.

Disney Store
140-144 Regent Street, W1 (7287 6558/www.disneystore. co.uk). Oxford Circus or Piccadilly Circus tube. **Open** 10am-8pm Mon-Sat; noon-6pm Sun. **Credit** AmEx, MC, V. **Map** p316 J6.
This is the place to come to if you're in the market for a fancy dress costumes, should your fantasies lean towards the Little Mermaid, Buzz Lightyear, Woody or classic characters like Snow White, Cinderella and Peter Pan. Trouble is, the costumes are rather shiny – that is, made of enough nylon to stiffen every hair on your body with electricity. There are brash mounds of cuddly toys, and the famous characters have been fashioned into covetable twirly straws, beach towels, pencil cases etc (from £3.99). You'll be lucky if you escape after nothing more expensive than a few minutes spent watching cartoons on the giant screen.
Buggy access. Delivery service. Mail order.
Branches: throughout town. Check phone book or website.

Early Learning Centre
36 King's Road, SW3 (7581 5764/www.elc.co.uk). Sloane Square tube. **Open** 9am-6pm Mon, Tue, Thur-Sat, 9am-7pm Wed; 11am-5pm Sun. **Credit** AmEx, MC, V. **Map** p315 F11.
Young children learn through imaginative play and imitating their elders, and ELC helps that process along with its wide range of toys, games and art materials. Here you'll find chunky musical instruments, play food and cookware, plus plastic animals, dinosaurs, play houses, swings, sandpits, wooden train sets, science sets and arty-crafty sets. Every branch has its own play space, and this one holds play sessions for little ones on Tuesdays (9.30am-11am). The chain is really best at pleasing the under-sevens, though: as soon as children get to the Barbie/Action Man/Nintendo age, ELC tends to lose its appeal.
Buggy access. Delivery service. Play area.
Branches: throughout town. Check phone book or website.

Fun Learning
Bentall's Centre, Clarence Street, Kingston-upon-Thames, Surrey (8974 8900). Kingston rail. **Open** 9am-6pm Mon-Wed, Fri, Sat; 9am-8pm Thur; 11am-5pm Sun. **Credit** MC, V.
Fun Learning has toys for everyone from fives to 15s, including some brainteasers and puzzles that will flummox even grown-ups. Eager learners can try out the educational software at the computer table in the centre, while others head straight to the toys and books arranged around the edges, encompassing themes such as the night sky and the animal kingdom. Toys to play with outdoors include Frisbees, skipping ropes, Stomp Rockets and balls. Craft y toys are for those children keen to make lovely things with pipe-cleaners, tissue paper and Hama Beads.
Buggy access. Delivery service. Mail order. Nappy-changing facilities.
Branch: Brent Cross Shopping Centre, Hendon NW4 (8203 1473).

Hamleys
188-96 Regent Street, W1 (0870 333 2450/www.hamleys. com). Oxford Circus tube. **Open** 10am-8pm Mon-Sat; noon-6pm Sun. **Credit** AmEx, MC, V. **Map** p316 J6.
If there aren't bubbles or balloons spewing out of Hamley's entrance on Regent Street, the crowds of jostling youngsters will alert you to its location. The (allegedly) largest toyshop in the world is first and foremost a loud, frenetic, exciting experience – and you can get most of the products you're looking for here, though prices tend to build in a margin for the convenience. The ground floor is where the latest fun toys are demonstrated and a mountain of soft toys, including impressive big cats and softly appealing woodland creatures, is accommodated. The basement is the Cyberzone, full of games and consoles, hi-tech gadgets all whirring and buzzing on the play tables, and a Sega games arcade. The first floor has items of a scientific bent, plus a sweet factory and bear depot. On second is everything for pre-schoolers. Third is girlie heaven – Barbie World, where whacking great pink boxes contain Barbie's people carrier, princess carriage and fairy castle make five-year-olds' eyes pop. Once you've escaped the plastic princess' world there are departments for dressing up clothes, make-up and so on. Fourth has some jaw-droppingly large, and pricey remote controlled vehicles, plus die-cast models. Fifth, if you can make it that far, is Lego World, which has its own café and resident Darth Vader. Little princes and princesses can even have their birthday party here – typically on a Sunday morning – and they also arrange Christmas parties and other events.
Buggy access. Café. Delivery service. Nappy-changing facilities. Mail order. Play areas.
Branch: 3 The Piazza/Central Market Hall, WC2 (7240 4646).

Mystical Fairies
12 Flask Walk, NW3 (7431 1888/www.mysticalfairies. co.uk). Hampstead tube. **Open** 10am-6pm Mon-Sat; 11am-6pm Sun. **Credit** MC, V.
If you don't believe in fairies already, you'll surely be convinced once you've stepped into this shop. The little creatures hang from the ceiling on beaded swings, endure shaking inside glitter storm bubbles and lend their wings to little girls' rucksacks. Is there anything in this shop which doesn't sparkle in a magical-mystical-most-amazing way? What's more, fairy costumes are available in great profusion, some even incorporating animal faces on the bodice (£40); ballet is a sub-theme. A glittering basement area, complete with tinkling water features and fairy queen's throne, makes for a small but atmospheric party venue (*see p241*).
Buggy access.

Toys 'R' Us
760 Old Kent Road, SE15 (7732 7322/www.toysrus. co.uk). Elephant & Castle tube/rail then 21, 56, 172, P13 bus. **Open** 9am-8pm Mon-Fri; 9am-7pm Sat; 11am-5pm Sun. **Credit** AmEx, MC, V.
Geoffrey's toy warehouses are rather soulless places to hunt for playthings, but you can usually rely on them – buried in retail parks and spacious as they are – to stock the toy of the moment in industrial quantities – and equally, you can pretty much guarantee it will sell its whole stock of said item two weeks before Christmas and be unable to get more until January. Inexpensive bikes, car seats, baby accessories and buggies are another attraction. Party paraphernalia is pretty good: there's themed paperware, party bags and fillings.
Buggy access. Car park. Delivery service. Nappy-changing facilities.
Branches: throughout town. Check phone book or website.

Activities

Arts & Entertainment

There's a whole world beyond the goggle-box.

London is one vast, exciting playground, yet the majority of urbanites now spend their formative years in front of the telly or games console. Take heart: it doesn't have to be this way.

The information below will unlock the unexpected in even the most cramped and overcrowded parts of the city: from dainty dancing in Deptford to glimpsing kingfishers in King's Cross. More and more activities and events are accessible to disabled children and those with special needs; just ask about facilities before you book. Bear in mind that programmes for all the workshops and classes we mention change seasonally, so check listings by phone, and keep an eye on council websites for details of arts fairs and local festivals.

Most of all, have fun! The best days of their lives start here, and – thanks to them – so can yours.

Arts centres

Barbican Centre

Silk Street, EC2 (box office 7638 8891/cinema hotline 7382 7000/arts education programme 7382 2333/ www.barbican.org.uk). Barbican tube/Moorgate tube/rail. **Open** *Box office* 10am-8pm Mon-Sat; noon-8pm Sun, bank hols. *Gallery* 10am-6pm Mon, Tue, Thur-Sat; 10am-9pm Wed; noon-6pm Sun, bank hols. **Admission** *Library* free. *Exhibitions, films, shows, workshops* phone for details. **Membership** (BarbicanCard) £10/yr. *Film Club* £5/yr per family. **Credit** AmEx, MC, V. **Map** p320 P5.
The frankly confusing layout of the Barbican is just another arrow in the quiver of those who question its aesthetic worth, but two things are clear. The first is that kids, not yet steeped in architectural cynicism, love exploring the dense maze of carpeted halls, courtyards and castle battlements; the second is that parents, left to study the centre's education and entertainments programme, tend to be pleasantly surprised.

The Saturday morning Family Film Club has graced the Barbican's catalogue of children's events since the 1980s. The club shows a good range of major releases, popular classics and foreign language movies; it also runs themed workshops, with games based around the day's screening and a special, hour-long activity session on the last Saturday of each month. And in April 2003 the Barbican hosted a second Animate The World festival, with six animated movies from around the globe shown in parallel with a series of classes offering hands-on experience in animation.

South Bank Centre

Belvedere Road, South Bank, SE1 (7960 4242/box office 7960 4201/www.rfh.org.uk). Waterloo tube/rail. **Open** *Box office phone bookings* 9am-9pm daily. *Personal callers* 10am-9pm daily. **Credit** AmEx, MC, V. **Map** p319 M8.
It may have the architectural delicacy of corrugated iron, but the South Bank Centre is not a book to be judged by its concrete cover. Its enlightening programme is often aimed at younger audiences: highlights this year have included the First Vienna Vegetable Orchestra having its cucumberphone and eating it. Performances take place in one of three elaborate venues including the Royal Festival Hall, the grand foyer of which is host to five small Ballroom exhibitions this year, each designed for families to interact with.

Those seeking more musical interaction might like to sign up for the Gong Club, a weekly class giving over-sevens the chance to try their hand at Gamelan (traditional Indonesian percussion instruments). It was off the menu at the beginning of the year after a change in teaching staff, but we hear it's only a matter of time before the popular pursuit returns.

But perhaps most inspiring are the occasional FUNharmonics concerts given by the London Philharmonic at the Festival Hall (£7 adults, £3.50 children). These mix old classics with African tribal dance or give well-loved movie themes orchestral oomph, with face-painting, circus performance and a party atmosphere that in summer spills out of the foyer and on to the river terraces. Just don't blame us if you're shelling out for a violin next week.

Stratford Circus

Theatre Square, E15 (8279 1000/www.stratford-circus. org.uk). Stratford tube/rail/DLR. **Open** *Box office* 11am-6pm or until 15mins after show starts Mon-Sat. **Tickets** £10; £3-£5 concessions, under-16s. Go-card £24 (6 shows). **Credit** MC, V.
Stratford's purpose-built Circus opened its great glass doors in June 2001. It may look like another superclub, but kids are well catered for, with a show each Saturday afternoon bringing puppetry, panto, mime and music theatre to one of two main stages (£3 children, £4 adults). Those hoping to headline at the Rex might consider taking a DJ course in one of the Circus's studios; other available courses include dance, drama, writing and choreography, with theatrical performance classes for children over 14 starting at £1 per session.

Tricycle Theatre & Cinema

269 Kilburn High Road, NW6 7JR (7328 1000/ www.tricycle.co.uk). Kilburn tube/Brondesbury rail. **Open** *Box office* 10am-9pm Mon-Sat; 2-9pm Sun. *Children's shows* 11.30am, 2pm Sat. *Children's films* 1pm Sat. **Tickets** *Sat theatre* £4.50; £4 advance bookings. *Sat films* £4; £3 under-16s. **Credit** MC, V.
Such a comprehensive range of arts classes and events is offered here that parents may be inclined to move to Kilburn. Dance and drama workshops, which run in synch with the school term, cater for kids as young as 18 months (£20 for 10 weeks), and a series of half-term workshops offers help in developing everything from practical artistry to acrobatics.

The highly regarded Tricycle Youth Theatre, meanwhile, runs a twelve week course (£20) for 16- to 25-year-olds, at the end of which they produce and perform a play of their own, often to public acclaim. The Young Artists Group offers gifted youths the opportunity to polish their coursework under the experienced eye of an artist in residence.

A new Creative Space studio offers socially excluded kids the chance to harness their passion for hip hop in various breakdance or rap poetry classes, or take their love of grunge a step further with guitar lessons. Prices for workshops like these vary, but most are free and all are led by professionals. They also tend to be oversubscribed, so book well in advance.

The Tricycle houses a 300-seat cinema, which shows U and PG certificate movies a little after they've been on general release. Energetic theatre comes courtesy of touring companies like Purple Fish, with a different production shown twice each Saturday (11.30am, 2pm; £4.50, £4 advance).

Art galleries

Courtauld Institute Gallery

Somerset House, Strand, WC2R 1LA (7848 2526/ education 7848 2922/www.courtauld.ac.uk). Covent Garden, Holborn or Temple (closed Sun) tube. **Open** *Gallery* 10am-6pm daily (last entry 5.15pm); 31 Dec 10am-4pm; 1 Jan noon-6pm. Closed 24-26 Dec. *Tours* pre-booked groups only; phone for details. **Admission** *Gallery* £5; £4 concessions; free under-18s, students. Free to all 10am-2pm Mon (not bank hols). *Annual ticket* £10. **Credit** MC, V. **Map** p319 M7.
Children are both entertained and enlightened by the family activities offered free of charge on the first Saturday of every month (from 11.30am). Tours highlight an aspect of art history and conclude with various practical assignments: recently kids were shown how European Fauvist painters were influenced by African art, then shown tribal masks loaned by the British museum before making up their own from materials supplied by the gallery.

Holiday workshops (£10) are similarly themed, with sessions for children aged five to ten (10am-noon) and 11 to 16 (2-4pm). Activities include etching and dry-point printing with established artists, recreating Impressionist views of the Thames in favourable weather or dressing up in period costume to replicate famous portraits. Activity and materials packs are available from behind the desk all year round, and an after-school arts club is in the pipeline.

Dulwich Picture Gallery

Gallery Road, SE21 (8693 5254/www.dulwichpicture gallery.org.uk). North Dulwich or West Dulwich rail/3, 37, 176, P4 bus. **Open** *Gallery* 10am-5pm Tue-Fri; 11am-5pm Sat, Sun, bank hol Mon. Closed Good Friday, 24-26 Dec, 1 Jan. *Tours* (incl entry fee) 3pm Sat, Sun. **Admission** *Gallery* £4; £3 concessions; free under-16s. *Temporary exhibitions* £3; free under-16s. Free to all Fri. **Credit** MC, V.
This gem of a gallery in the heart of well-to-do Dulwich Village offers an arts club on Thursday afternoons (4.30-6pm), where children aged between ten and 13 can get creative making masks or drawing – and still be home in time for tea. The Saturday art school (10.30am-1pm) offers slightly more advanced workshops – such as wire sculpture – for young people aged between 12 and 15. Both classes draw inspiration from current exhibitions within the gallery, and prices start at £40 for a five-week course.

Hayward Gallery

Belvedere Road, South Bank Centre, SE1 (box office 7960 4242/www.hayward-gallery.org.uk). Embankment tube/Waterloo tube/rail. **Open** *Gallery* during exhibitions 10am-6pm Mon, Thur-Sun; 10am-8pm Tue, Wed. **Admission** *Gallery* varies; phone for details. **Credit** AmEx, DC, MC, V. **Map** p319 M8.
This February the Hayward became a building site. The gallery is closed while interior refurbishments take place and a new foyer space is built. Work is scheduled for completion in October 2003, when a new educational programme is promised for under 16s; phone for details later in the year.

Courtauld Institute Gallery.

National Gallery

Trafalgar Square, WC2 (7747 2885/2424/ www.nationalgallery.org.uk). Embankment/Leicester Square tube/ Charing Cross tube/rail. **Open** *Gallery* 10am-6pm Mon, Tue, Thur-Sun; 10am-9pm Wed. **Admission** *Gallery* free. *Temporary exhibitions* prices vary; phone for details. **Map** p319 K7.
The National Gallery operates an admirable range of activities for kids. Hour-long family talks are given each Saturday and Sunday (11.30am), except on the second weekend of every month, when contemporary artists are invited to choose a particular painting and, after a 15-minute talk, oversee a drawing workshop for children aged four to 11. Recent 'Second Weekends' have seen the likes of Ansel Krut and Matthew Burrows taking charge, and when school's out these workshops expand into practical art sessions twice daily (11am-1pm, 2-4pm), with one twilight session for 12- to 16-year-olds (5-7pm) during major holidays.

During the holidays under-fives can board the magic carpet, landing at random in front of paintings which inspire staff-led storytelling. All workshops are free, and there are audio tours and paper trails for those who prefer to go it alone.

National Portrait Gallery

2 St Martin's Place, WC2 (7306 0055/www.npg.org.uk). Leicester Square tube/Charing Cross tube/rail. **Open** *Gallery* 10am-5.50pm Mon-Wed, Sat, Sun; 10am-8.50pm Thur, Fri. **Admission** *Gallery* free. *Temporary exhibitions* £6; £4 concessions. **Map** p319 K7.
First experiences of the Portrait Gallery often come via the school trips for students aged five to 18. There are also workshops during weekends and school holidays, held in the Clore Studio, where children practise sculpture, photography and related activities while being supervised by professional artists (phone for more information).

Activities

Parp! The **South Bank Centre**. See p208.

On the last Saturday of each month, the ever-popular Tour and Draw gives families the chance to view parts of the gallery with a guide, and then use their experiences to create pieces of their own. On a more regular basis, free (returnable) rucksacks, containing the wherewithal for a range of activities, make exploring more fun for creative youngsters. There's an interactive IT studio for more technical enthusiasts. Occasionally, exhibitions are geared towards a family audience – last years display, 'From Beatrix Potter to Harry Potter: Portraits of Children's Writers', was a treat.

Orleans House Gallery

Riverside, Twickenham, Middx (8832 6000/ www.richmond.gov.uk/orleanshouse). St Margaret's or Twickenham rail/33, 90, 290, H22, R68, R70 bus. **Open** *Gallery Apr-Sept* 1-5.30pm Tue-Sat; 2-5.30pm Sun. *Oct-Mar* 1-4.30pm Tue-Sat; 2-4.30pm Sun. **Admission** *Gallery* free. **No credit cards.**
Peacefully set in six acres of garden, the dramatic 18th-century edifice of Orleans House is home to a less dusty exhibition than you might imagine. Collections include plenty of contemporary sculpture and installation art from artists such as Cornelia Parker, as well as a pictorial record of the surrounding countryside from the early 1700s to the present day. In keeping with such breadth of vision, art classes at the Gallery are informal, with after-school activity sessions (3.45pm-5pm Wed, Thur) for five- to nine-year-olds available alongside the recently established Star Club (4pm-5.30pm, Tue), which offers those aged seven to ten a place to try their hands (and feet) at dance and drama. Both are £5.50 per session, and worth booking in advance.

Half term and holiday workshops are £6 for the morning (phone for information). There are also year-round activity packs, including paper trails and treasure hunts for younger children, and on occasional Sunday Fundays the whole family is invited to use the current exhibition – and the gallery's materials, free of charge – as a launchpad for art of their own.

Royal Academy

Burlington House, Piccadilly, W1J 0BD (7300 8000/ www.royalacademy.org.uk). Green Park or Piccadilly Circus tube. **Open** *Gallery* 10am-6pm Mon-Thur, Sat, Sun; 10am-10pm Fri. **Admission** *Gallery* varies; phone for details. **Credit** AmEx, MC, V. **Map** p318 J7.
The unprecedented popularity of this year's Aztecs exhibition – the duration of which was extended by several weeks, with the gallery staying open late on some nights to meet demand – led to previously occasional children's workshops being held on a daily basis. These are always tied in with what's on show: in this case, kids were given the chance to make their own papier mâché death masks, or just listen to Aztec stories in front of the pieces themselves.

Not all collections are so appealing to young audiences, and the nature and frequency of the related activities varies accordingly. Always a big hit, however, is the annual Summer Exhibition, when the Academy selects works submitted by the general public (of an average 12,000 entries, only ten per cent make it past the judges), and the London Philharmonic Orchestra holds workshops to compose and perform music inspired by the displays (phone for information). There's also the Art Tray for kids to get creative with, family tours to introduce the exhibition and, this year, a printed Summer Snapshots guide trail to make exploring fun for eight- to 13-year-olds. Activities are free with the ticket.

Tate Britain

Millbank, SW1P 4RG (7887 8000/info 7887 8008/ family events 7887 3959/www.tate.org.uk). Pimlico tube/ 88, 77A, C10 bus. **Open** *Gallery* 10am-5.50pm daily. **Admission** *Gallery* free. *Temporary exhibitions* prices vary; phone for details. **Credit** MC, V. **Map** p319 L11.
It may have a snootier reputation than its mad, bad Mod of a brother, but the 'old' Tate is arguably a better organiser of events for kids – especially on Sundays. This is when the famous Art Trolley comes out (noon-5pm, also Thursday in school holidays), and staff supervise cutting, sticking and drawing activities related to works on display, or dispense art packs letting kids explore the rooms by themselves.

Meanwhile, parents with pushchairs might be better off in the Art Space (noon-5pm), a play area for families to unwind in while smaller children make the most of simple sculpture, jigsaw and dressing-up activities. Little ones will also love the improvised Tate Tales on the first Sunday of every month (11am-noon), when storytellers, singers and poets bring works of art to life with unpredictable results.

There are also children's audio tours, and blue felt activity bags – available all year round at no charge – filled with games, puzzles and other tactile objects to help kids enjoy interacting with the galleries. School holiday workshops give them the chance to experiment with established artists in developing their creative skills (phone for more information).

Tate Modern

Holland Street, SE1 9TG (7887 8000/booking 7887 3959/ recorded info 7887 8008/www.tate.org.uk). Blackfriars or Southwark tube/London Bridge tube/rail. **Open** *Gallery* 10am-6pm Mon-Thur, Sun; 10am-10pm Fri, Sat. **Admission** *Gallery* free. **Map** p320 O7.
The big, brooding Tate Modern might not be the first thing you'd associate with childhood innocence, but just let your little ones loose in the dream-like Turbine entrance hall and see what happens. Works like Anish Kapoor's 'Marsyas' installation may 'permeate physical and psychological space', but their sheer size also makes kids go 'wow'. The gallery also offers several imaginative events, including Tate Tales (every third Saturday of the month; free), which sees writers

and poets engaging children with displays through impro-vised storytelling. Activities are also regularly added to the Start studio – including simple looking and drawing games for toddlers – which aims to make modern art fun, each Sunday afternoon at no cost to the accompanying parent (BSI assisted on the first Sunday of each month).

More intrepid kids may prefer the audio tour, brilliantly narrated by Michael Rosen (£1), or – for the under-fives – follow one of the many Explorers adventure trails (£1.50). Before you know it, they'll be pickling sharks of their own.

Wallace Collection

Hertford House, Manchester Square, W1 (7563 9500/ education 7563 9551/www.the-wallace-collection.org.uk). Bond Street tube. **Open** *Gallery* 10am-5pm Mon-Sat; noon-5pm Sun. **Admission** *Gallery* free. **Map** p316 G5.
The Wallace Collection, in a wonderful mansion bedecked with period furnishings, is perhaps most famous for its world class display of medieval armour, which thrills kids of all ages and provides the focus of half-term and holiday work-shops. Children aged five to 11 can spend a half or a whole day (£6 or £12 respectively) drawing, painting and donning armour which, occasionally, kids make themselves from papier mâché and whatever else is to hand. Parents need not fear though – it isn't all gladiatorial death-matches, and the gallery also houses a fine restaurant tucked into the glassed-over courtyard, plus an incredible range of sculpture, porce-lain and Victorian paintings from across Europe. Which at least means you can put off the jousting until bed time.

Whitechapel Art Gallery

80-2 Whitechapel High Street, E1 (7522 7888/recorded info 7522 7878/education 7522 7855/www.whitechapel. org). Aldgate East tube. **Open** *Gallery* during exhibitions 11am-6pm Tue, Thur-Sun; 11am-8pm Wed. **Admission** *Gallery* free. **Map** p321 S6.
The romantic façade of this beautiful stone building is set roughly into the surrounding brickwork, but everything else within its grand doors stands alone. Its collection of con-temporary and installation works, throughout the ground floor and upper skylight galleries, continues to enlighten East London's children as to the elusive essence of 'modern' art.

Most of the work is done with local schools: the recent Art of Inquiry programme, for example, let GCSE students develop their own ideas of individual pieces and then pass their wisdom on, through a series of 20 minute talks, to younger students in the gallery. Term-time workshops are themed to correspond with exhibitions (there are five every year); occasional family activities coincide with events like National Children's Art Day (phone for more information).

Cinemas

Movie-wise, this city is best known for the monoliths in Leicester Square, with the **Empire** (08700 102030/ www.uci-cinemas.co.uk), **Warner Village West End** (7437 4347/www.warnervillage.co.uk) and the mighty **Odeon** (0870 505 0007/www.odeon.co.uk) bringing a whiff of Hollywood to central London. Still, bigger isn't necessarily better – and the price to pay for seats can provoke the sort of adult language that would land any flick a 15 rating. Instead, keep your cool (and more of your cash) and try one of the smaller movie houses, many of which run Saturday morning kids' clubs. Prizes for ingenuity go to the following picture palaces, which shuffle blockbusters with classics, and often combine them with themed activity workshops to prolong the movie experience.

Clapham Picture House

76 Venn Street, SW4 0AT (7498 3323/ www.picturehouse-cinemas.co.uk). Clapham Common tube. **Open** *Box office (telephone bookings)* 10am-8.30pm daily. *Film Club Activities* 11.15am Sat. *Screening* 11.45am Sat. **Tickets** £3; members £2. **Membership** £3/yr. **Credit** MC, V.

Drawing kids together

Where other organisations send food, clothing and financial aid, the London International Gallery of Children's Art sends drawing materials to schools in socially deprived and third world communities. It may seem an odd idea at first, but the pictures commissioned by this eminently creative charity – from African, Kosovan or Mexican children, for example – are exhibited in the gallery, and all of them are used to educate visitors of all ages about the forces that shaped each work.

In 2002 the gallery showcased works by underprivileged New York schoolchildren reacting to the World Trade Center attacks, and a more recent display came courtesy of young Lisbon artists. The collections are always heartfelt reflections of their geographical origins: the former included great strips of skyscraper grey, while a highlight of the latter was a collage castle made of coloured squares, looking very much like a mosaic seen through water. The exhibitions are used as reference points for educational workshops (from £8 per session, running in six-week courses from £40), which encourage kids to respond personally with their own drawings and paintings. The best of these are shown in the gallery, and all proceeds are sent to relevant charities.

Separate Saturday morning classes for the under-fives (10.30-11.30am; £10) offer simple arts activities based on storytelling sessions. After the mess has been cleared away, children aged from five can dabble in creative techniques, such as mural design, monoprinting to self-portraiture (2-3.30pm; £10). Little Artist courses and holiday workshops are also available (phone for details).

London International Gallery of Children's Art

02 Centre, 255 Finchley Road, NW3 6LU (7435 0903/www.ligca.org). Finchley Road tube. **Open** *Gallery* 4-6pm Tue-Thur; noon-6pm Fri-Sun. **Admission** *Gallery* free; donations requested. **No credit cards.**

The Clapham Kids Club offers Saturday screenings of everything from new releases to timeless classics like *Watership Down*, with activity workshops preceding the show and three questions to answer afterwards – prizes are at stake, so pay attention! Membership of the Kids Club is £3 per year; individual tickets are £3 or £2.50 for members. Babysitterless parents with babies aged up to one can bring them along on Thursdays at 10.30am to see whatever's on .

Electric Cinema
191 Portobello Road, W11 2ED (7908 9696/ www.electrichouse.com). Ladbroke Grove or Notting Hill Gate tube. **Open** *Box office* 8am-9pm Mon-Sat; 10am-9pm Sun. *Children's screenings* 11am, 1pm Sat. **Tickets** £4.50. **Credit** AmEx, MC, V. **Map** p312 A7.

Those who feel there just aren't enough arcane societies to join in this modern world will be thrilled by Electric House, for membership of which you must be proposed by a member, passed by a committee and pay up to the tune of £250 per year. It has its advantages, however: parents on the books receive two free tickets for every Kids Club screening. These show trusted classic films and previewed new releases in a truly luxurious environment, recently renovated from a historical fleapit to one of the best cinemas in the country – red leather armchairs, lovingly restored wall friezes and all. By popular demand films are now shown twice on Saturday.

Movie Magic at the NFT
NFT3, National Film Theatre, South Bank, SE1 (box office 7928 3232/www.bfi.org.uk/moviemagic). Waterloo tube/rail. **Open** *Box office phone bookings* 11.30am-9pm daily. *Personal callers* 5-9pm Mon-Thur; 11.30am-9pm Fri-Sun. *Film Club* times vary, Sat, Sun, school hols. **Tickets** £1 film, £5.50 workshop and film (children only); £4 adults. **Credit** AmEx, MC, V. **Map** p319 M8.

If you're keen on turning square eyes into widescreens, take them to Movie Magic, where the NFT runs a programme of high-quality, often eclectic film for kids under 16 at weekends and during school holidays. Movies are more Pooh Bear than Pokemon, so nostalgic parents may want to tag along. Meanwhile, children aged between six and 12 can take part in themed activity workshops that precede all screenings – perhaps making papier mâché Harry Potter masks, trying out scriptwriting and prop design, or even using a movie camera. Foreign-laguage films come with headphones for those who find subtitles a bit of a chore, and there are occasional subtitled screenings for the hearing impaired. Booking in advance is advisable; phone for a list of upcoming shows.

Rio Cinema
103-7 Kingsland High Street, E8 2PB (7241 9410/ www.riocinema.co.uk). Dalston Kingsland rail. **Open** *Box office* opening times vary depending on programme. *Film Club* 4.15pm Tue (term time only); 11am Sat. **Tickets** £3; £2 under-15s. **Credit** MC, V.

The Rio is a fun, friendly place where kids can sample something a bit different from the Hollywood blockbusters. The Saturday Morning Kids Club intersperses major new releases with popular oldies like *The Seventh Voyage of Sinbad*, with a repeat performance – the Playcentre Matinee – during term time every Tuesday afternoon at 4.15pm. Membership of the club is free, and comes with a card that's gets stamped on each visit. Ten stamps are a worth a free movie, 25 bring a movie poster to the faithful young viewer.

Ritzy Cinema
Brixton Oval, Coldharbour Lane, SW2 1JG (7733 2229/ www.ritzycinema.com). Brixton tube/rail. **Open** *Box office bookings* 11am-8pm Mon-Sat; 1-8pm Sun. *Film Club* 10.30am Sat. **Tickets** £2; £1 under-16s. **Credit** MC, V.

Truly a blessing for parents who are starting to tire of the latest in toy-related, animated tie-ins. The grand old Ritzy shows two films every Saturday – the first aimed at under-sevens and the second at over-eights – while adults get free newspapers, tea and coffee thrown in with the ticket. During the school holidays the club also runs on Tuesdays and Thursdays, with related activity sessions, competitions and special events often set up at short notice; phone for details.

Heavens above

Just because Londoners have put a thick layer of smog between themselves and the night sky doesn't mean the sky isn't still there. There are places across the city where kids can gaze at the stars, you just have to know where to go.

Hampstead Observatory (8346 1056/ www.hampsteadscience.ac.uk/hss_obs.htm) is a good place to start, open to the public on Friday and Saturday nights (8-10pm, if the sky is clear) between September and April, and home to an antique refracting telescope – usually pointed at the moon or one of the brighter planets to startling effect. Over the next couple of years, Earth will have a prime view of Saturn – a state of affairs that only occurs once every three decades, so wrap up well and go north to take a look.

The **University of London Observatory**, a delightfully down-to-earth installation surrounded by allotments on Mill Hill Park (8238 8870/ www.ulo.ucl.ac.uk), holds similar nocturnal sessions on the first and third Friday of each month between October and March (6.30-7.30pm).

The **Royal Observatory** in Greenwich (8858 4422/www.rog.nmm.ac.uk) has a more explicitly educational timetable of events, but from January 2004, its nine-week Evening With The Stars programme will give children over nine a unique insight into their local corner of space. A 45-minute display in the planetarium will elaborate on the current state of the night sky, followed by one hour in the dome, aiming the main 28in refractor lens at the moon, Saturn, and whatever else is on show at the time (£6 at 5pm, £8 at 6pm, £10 at 7pm).

All of the above are weather-sensitive: on cloudy nights the best you can hope for is a tour of the telescopes themselves – informative. of course, but somewhat frustrating. For stellar inspiration whatever the weather, you're better off taking in one of the planetarium displays at the Royal Observatory (2.30pm and 3.30pm; £2 kids, £4 adults) or at the more cinematic (and excessively dramatic) **London Planetarium** (0870 400 3000/ www.london-planetarium.com; *see p85*), which holds shows every 20 minutes.

TOP FIVE Theatres

For a breath of fresh air
Open Air Theatre. *See p220.*

For a blast from the past
Shakespeare's Globe. *See p221.*

For strings attached
Little Angel Theatre. *See below.*

For getting involved
Chicken Shed Theatre. *See p218.*

For après show activities
Polka Theatre. *See p220.*

Music venues

Coliseum
St Martin's Lane, WC2 (box office 7632 8300/fax credit card bookings 7379 1264/textphone 7836 7666/ www.eno.org). Leicester Square tube/Charing Cross tube/rail. **Open** *Box office* 10am-8pm Mon-Sat. **Credit** AmEx, DC, MC, V. **Map** p319 L7.
Home to the English National Opera, the Coliseum, as you might expect, is a largely adult-oriented venue, both in terms of its annual programme and its rather august interior. That said, the in-house educational team, Baylis – named after Lilian Baylis, founder of ENO and the National Theatre – offers a huge range of activities to make opera a less intimidating and more relevant medium for younger audiences.

Most of their work is done in classrooms – including musical drama workshops and interactive performances for children from primary school and upwards – but some activities take place in the Coliseum itself, and in 2004, when restoration work on the building is due to reach its conclusion, staff
and, of course, visitors – will have a brand new educational studio to play with. Check the website for information on upcoming activities, or phone Baylis (7739 5808).

Royal Albert Hall
Kensington Gore, SW7 2AP (7589 8212/ www.royalalberthall.com). South Kensington tube. **Open** *Box office* 9am-9pm daily. **Credit** AmEx, MC, V. **Map** p315 D9.
The major refurbishment continues, so the Albert Hall's education department is pretty much inoperative until the scaffolding comes down in 2004, when a new director of children's events will swing into action. Until then it's up to occasional family-oriented events – like the annual Blue Peter concert given as part of the BBC Proms – to fill the gap.

Royal College of Music
Prince Consort Road, SW7 2BS (7589 3643/ www.rcm.ac.uk). South Kensington tube. **Map** p315 D9.
It's not the place for air guitar lessons, but the highly respected RCM has shaped the musical career of many a national jewel (although usually in the classical category). Jazz piano and sax lessons also turn up in a programme otherwise based on orchestral and choral performances, staged (usually free) by pupils throughout the year. Lessons are for over eights, and run in step with school term (on Saturdays, 8am-5pm). Applications are by audition only.

Royal Opera House
Bow Street, WC2E 9DD (7304 4000/www.royalopera house.org). Covent Garden tube. **Open** *Box office* 10am-8pm Mon-Sat. *Backstage tours* 10.30am, 12.30pm, 2.30pm Mon-Sat; phone to check. **Credit** AmEx, DC, MC, V. **Map** p319 L6.
Opera, like caviar, is one of those things that seldom appeals to youngsters unless they've been brought up on it: as much a reaction to the way it's dished up as to the overpowering taste of fish. And yet, despite a dramatic recent overhaul to make the ROH more inviting to all ages, there's little beyond the clockwork novelty of the Nutcracker Suite to persuade cynical kids that these fancy halls aren't just for grown ups.

The ROH works in collaboration with other creative organisations and charities to promote opera and ballet at schools across the country, but only the occasional family matinee or guided tour takes place in the Opera House itself. That said, last December's inspired production of *The Wind In The Willows* made for a perfect family night out, and a similarly light-hearted show is planned for this Christmas.

Wigmore Hall
36 Wigmore Street, W1 (7935 2141/education 7258 8240/ www.wigmore-hall.org.uk). Bond Street tube. **Open** *Box office* 10am-7pm Mon-Sat; 10.30am-6.30pm Sun. **Credit** AmEx, DC, MC, V. **Map** p316 H5.
Visually, the intimate and aesthetically stunning auditorium at Wigmore Hall is a cut above most other venues in the capital. Staff also run an excellent programme for families, starting with the oversubscribed Chamber Tots classes, which encourage two- to five-year-olds to create music after listening to a mini-concert (£5 children, adults free).

From there the only way is up – blossoming Beethovens can either take in one of the many family concerts (£3 children, £6 adults), or partake of the Young People's Day workshops, which normally occur in half terms and major school holidays (£8 children, £10 adults). These cover everything from song and story writing (five- to six-year-olds) to more challenging jazz classes, and can be held in any number of rooms, even the stunning main hall itself.

Classes and concerts are organised on an ad hoc basis, so contact the education department for current information.

Theatre

Puppet theatre

Little Angel Theatre
14 Dagmar Passage, off Cross Street, N1 (7226 1787/ www.littleangeltheatre.com). Angel tube/Highbury & Islington tube/rail. **Open** *Box office* 11am-5pm Mon-Fri; 9.30am-5pm Sat, Sun. Closed 24-25 Dec, 1 Jan. **Tickets** £7.50; £5 children. **Credit** AmEx, MC, V.
Children whose only experience of puppetry can be summed up in the words 'Punch and Judy' learn here just how inspiring a medium it can be. The Little Angel – established in 1961 and now this city's only permanent puppet theatre – has been rescued from financial straits by generous donors. This means it can continue presenting its deservedly popular weekend shows (Sat 2pm and 5pm, Sun 11am and 2pm), put on by touring companies who relish the pleasure of using so rare a proscenium stage, and which change weekly. The in-house society performs four shows annually – the recent *Frog Prince* was a leaping success, while Time Out voted *Jonah And The Whale* one of its top ten children's shows of 2002. A Puppet Club is held on Saturday mornings during term time, when children can learn to make and manipulate types

Activities

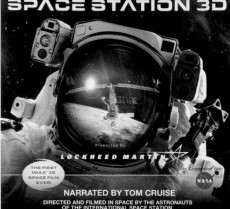
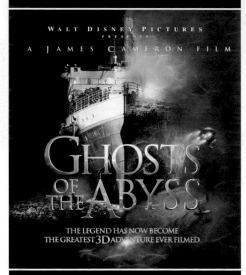

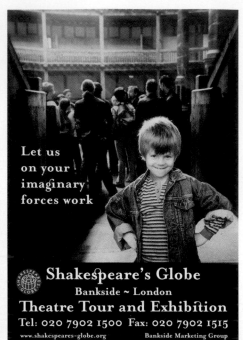

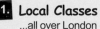
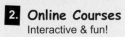

of puppet including glove, rod, shadow and marionette. Family days are held on Sundays after certain shows (1-5pm) and cost £9.50, and the Angel is always touring schools, sometimes taking up residencies in their art departments.

Puppet Theatre Barge
opposite 35 Blomfield Road, Little Venice, W9 (7249 6876/www.puppetbarge.com). Warwick Avenue tube. **Open** *Box office* 10am-8pm daily. Closed 25 Dec, 1 Jan. *Children's shows* term time Sat, Sun; school hols daily. **Tickets** £7; £6.50 under-16s, concessions. **Credit** MC, V.
As genuinely enchanting experiences go, the Puppet Theatre Barge is in a lake of its own: where else can you combine the genius of puppetry with the aesthetic pleasure of bobbing merrily afloat? From November to June this unique little boat, with just 60 seats and a suitably cosy stage, is moored on the towpath in Little Venice, with a variety of shows taking place on Saturday and Sunday afternoons (3pm) during term times, and occasional weekday and evening slots over holidays.

From July until the end of October, the Barge chugs away on a summer tour of the Thames, dropping in on pretty riverside towns Henley, Clifton, Marlow and Richmond along the way. During this time shows take place at 2.30pm and 4.30pm, and there's a special Saturday evening performance (7.30pm) aimed at adults. Most shows are based around marionette and shadow puppetry, and all mix atmospheric lighting with strong narratives and often specially-commissioned music to make for an unforgettable event.

Touring companies

Some people see children's theatre as a valuable educational resource; others condemn it for 'dumbing down' more traditional theatrical values. To the second lot, we say 'cobblers'. For a generation used to high-speed, high-quality images and sound, traditional theatre can seem a little static at first. The best children's groups work towards developing the emotional maturity of younger audiences and opening their minds to the creative possibilities that a bare stage can offer. Below London's best: ladies and gentlemen, take a bow.

Oily Cart
8672 6329/www.oilycart.org.uk.
Oily Cart continues to engage and enlighten two theatrically excluded groups – very young children and children with special needs – with bold, innovative productions. Touring since 1981 to great critical acclaim, the company's work has in the last few years taken a turn for the truly interactive, with shows based in creative spaces or 'Wonderlands', where groups of children can not only watch, but also take part in performances. Even more commendable is the fun they inject into each show – *Boing!*, for disabled kids, was based around trampolines. The concept was so successful they're using it for 2003's Moving Pictures show, with an enormous screen to magnify the delight on visitors' faces by 20 times.

Pop-Up Theatre
7609 3339/www.pop-up.net.
After the success of last year's *Nightwatch*, Pop-Up will this autumn be touring another play by much-lauded writer Michael Punter. This one, *Dummy*, is a light-hearted but intriguing tale about twins aimed at seven- to 11-year-olds. November will see the company begin touring their

seasonal Christmas show, which combines magical environments, musical effects and plenty of puppetry, poetry and visual trickery to keep the under-eights engaged.

Generally, Pop-Up's work is informative and enriching, with Dramatic Links workshops (held at the Robert Blair school in North London) letting young people work with professional writers, inspiring and then helping them produce scripts that are relevant to children's experiences. The Equal Voice sessions, toured around local schools, use the concept of of performance to encourage empathy, develop emotional range and help kids achieve new levels of self-confidence.

Quicksilver Theatre
7241 2942/www.quicksilvertheatre.org.
At Quicksilver the emphasis is on presenting original theatre that develops children creatively by engaging, rather than preaching to or 'educating' them. This summer sees the revival of the highly acclaimed *Sea Of Silence* (for ages seven and up), about a runaway fisherman whose magical adventures in an underwater kingdom give him a new perspective on his former life. New for this spring is *Upstairs In The Sky*, a warm, reassuring piece for three- to five-year-olds.

Theatre Centre
7377 0379/www.theatre-centre.co.uk.
The readiness of many companies simply to rehash the same old stories and characters only exacerbates the feeling among many that plays for children just aren't 'proper' theatre. The Theatre Centre, meanwhile, is actively fighting such lazy and ill-informed logic by bringing new writing to young people in ways that are challenging and respectful. The Centre touring two shows in 2003/4 with two shows: the first, *Glow*, follows a teenage Asian girl as she dreams of becoming a professional boxer. The second is *Precious*, a play by Angela Turvey for young people aged from 14.

Theatre-rites
8946 2236/www.theatre-rites.co.uk.
Dazzling and endlessly innovative, Theatre-rites is probably best known for site-specific projects like *Houseworks*, which in 1996 turned a disused Brixton residence into a beautiful and mysteriously interactive theatre space, and follow ups *Millworks* and *Cellarworks*. Guided by a puppet, children were led from room to magical room.

Theatre-rites have been commissioned to set up two similar projects in 2003, so keep an eye on their website. Otherwise, the company continues to tour work that is more conventionally stage based, if no less ingenious: the haunting *Sleep Tight* (2000) was part lullaby, part laudable examination of death, while last year's *Catch Your Breath* was a whirlwind of imaginative madness.

Unicorn Theatre for Children
7700 0702/www.unicorntheatre.com.
Wandering minstrels of the children's stage, Unicorn are still looking forward to 2004, when their purpose-built youth theatre in Southwark is due to be completed.

Till then it's business as usual, with the gang touring several productions over the coming months. Works range from adaptations (a version of *Great Expectations*, earned critical acclaim) to new writing (the recent, excellent *Diary Of An Action Man*), with all of it aimed at challenging and entertaining four- to 12-year-olds. This summer, *Granny And The Gorilla* will be performed at the Open Air Theatre, Regent's Park, between the 30th July and the 23rd August (*see p87*), with an autumn production in collaboration with Theatre-rites to be held in Southwark's Livesey Museum from October, and the ever-popular Christmas show later in the year. Check the website for updates.

What's the story?
The **National Gallery**.
See p209.

See p209.

Activities

Send in the clowns

You'd think that nothing about kid's entertainment is the same as it was 30 years ago – with the possible exception of a trip to the circus. Old-style circuses like **Zippo's** (www.zippo.dial.pipex.com) are reliably popular, pitching up in summer at venues including Blackheath, Peckham Rye and Alexandra Park. Here you'll get the clowns, the acrobats, the taste of candy floss, the smell of sawdust. Some things never change – or do they?

In recent years more diverse acts; the **Moscow** (www.moscowstatecircus.co.uk) and **Chinese State Circus** (www.chinesestatecircus.co.uk) have performed widely in the capital, bringing a fresh, exotic perspective. The amazing **Cirque Du Soleil** (www.cirquedusoleil.com) launches its new show, *Dralion*, early in 2004 – though some of its acts are more suitable for children than others. The **Shaolin Wheel Of Life** (www.wheeloflife.co.uk) is undeniably breathtaking, but has a high 'don't try this at home' factor: you might not want your children hoisting each other on the points of spears in your sitting room (or anywhere else).

That said, should your offspring show an urge to acquire circus expertise, there are places that are only too happy to oblige. The **Circus Space**, in a renovated generating station in Hoxton, runs ten-week foundation courses that give youngsters aged eight to 16 the chance to learn skills on tightrope,

trapeze stilts and more (Sunday mornings during term times; £60 for ten weeks), with the cream of each crop invited to take part in the prestigious ongoing Young Persons Programme, which runs at the same time (£6 per session). At **Albert and Friends' Instant Circus**, Albert the Clown (aka Ian Owen) draws on 20 years of teaching and performance experience to pass on skills such as daredevil stilt-, ball- or wire-walking to classes of 200 children each week – many of whom join the Albert and Friends' troupe, the UK's largest children's circus theatre. A&FIC also runs occasional master classes in disciplines such as drumming, mime or movement. Finally, at the **Jacksons Lane Community Circus** there are kid's classes in trapeze, rope climbing and acrobatics.

Albert and Friends' Instant Circus
8237 1170/www.albertandfriendsinstantcircus. co.uk.

The Circus Space
Coronet Street, N1 (7613 4141/www.thecircus space.co.uk). Old Street tube.

Jacksons Lane Community Circus
Jacksons Lane Community Centre, Archway Road, N6 (8340 5226). Highgate tube. See p219.

Venues

Although several of the places listed below are specifically childrens' theatres, most are just adult venues that offer good family programmes. Always phone to check the suitability of any show before you book tickets, and remember that most venues put on extra performances during school holidays.

BAC (Battersea Arts Centre)
Lavender Hill, SW11 (7223 2223/www.bac.org.uk). Clapham Junction rail/77, 77A, 345 bus. **Open** *Box office* 10.30am-6pm Mon-Sat; 4-6pm Sun. *Puppet Centre* 2-6pm Mon, Wed, Sat. **Tickets** £5.75; £4.50 under-16s, concessions; £3.50 young BAC club members; £16 family (2+2). *Membership* £10.75/yr; £16.50 family (2+2). **Credit** AmEx, MC, V.

The BAC is a bastion of creativity in South London. The ever-popular Christmas productions shun more conventional panto routines, and the emphasis is often placed upon new and experimental writing. But that doesn't mean kids are forced to endure puppet renditions of *Mulholland Drive*: far from it. The Saturday children's theatre for four- to seven-year olds (2.30pm) is just that, with charming tales from all the most accomplished touring companies. What it does mean is that occasionally productions take the road less travelled: the increasing number of so called 'Scratch' performances lets writers air work in progress, and – through improvisation and participation from the young audience.

During the academic term, Arts Factory workshops are held on Wednesday, Thursday and Saturday afternoons, giv-

ing kids aged six to 15 an opportunity to engage in everything from practical craft classes to role play, with the more advanced groups working towards a show at the end of course (£45.75 per term). There's also an in-house Puppet Workshop (7228 5335) that organises occasional post-production activities – phone for more information. BAC membership offers useful discounts on all events.

Broadway Theatre
Catford Broadway, SE6 (8690 0002/www.broadway theatre.org.uk). Catford or Catford Bridge rail. **Open** *Box office* 10am-6pm Mon-Sat. **Tickets** £3.50-£20. **Credit** MC, V.

After a protracted period of inactivity while the former Lewisham Theatre was restored to former glories, the Broadway's varied kids programme is slowly finding its feet. Regular performances by chart idol tribute bands like S Club Heaven and Robbie impersonators keep the teenage masses screaming, while adaptations of classic tales (*Tarzan* and *Treasure Island* were big hits in 2002/3) please the younger audiences. More educational projects like the Shakespeare 4 Kids events combine loud and energetic performances with fun seminars in a commendable effort to make the Bard more appealing to audiences of modern youth.

The Bull
68 High Street, Barnet, Herts (8449 0048/tours 8275 5375/www.thebull.org.uk). High Barnet tube. **Open** *Box office* 10am-5.30pm Tue-Sun. **Tickets** £4.50. **Credit** MC, V.

With The Bull's comprehensive Learning Ladder programme, kids can start work here while still in nappies and leave as the next De Niro. Classes – from the Tiny Bull to

Bull Act groups and Youth Theatres – cover all ages from under-threes to 19 years and upwards, with courses (£40 for several weeks) running throughout term time and ending with the kids putting on a play of their own. Touring companies perform throughout the year, with shows catering for all age groups. Half term and holiday workshops vary from voice coaching to spatial awareness and more conventional performance activities – phone for more information.

Chicken Shed Theatre

Chase Side, N14 (8292 9222/www.chickenshed.org.uk). Cockfosters or Oakwood tube. **Open** *Box office* 10am-7pm Mon-Fri; Sat varies. **Tickets** *Workshops* £2.50/hr. *Shows* £4.40-£10.80. **Credit** MC, V.

Chicken Shed is a truly inclusive theatre company: from a waiting list of 3,000, its 800 members will always include men, women and children drawn from more usually excluded groups, with no auditions to get through and the only essential requirement being a desire to perform.

Workshops for younger members take place after school during term time, and are divided into Tales From The Shed (for under-fives), the Children's Theatre Group (five- to 12-year-olds) and the Youth Theatre (12- to 19-year-olds). At the same time, a full programme of in-house productions is played out across the Theatre's four creative spaces – the main auditorium (280 seats), the studio (100 seats), the bar and – in summer months – the outdoor amphitheatre.

Any member can take part in one of these plays – which tackle new and classic material alongside Chicken Shed's own take on traditional faves like *A Midsummer Night's Dream* or *Romeo And Juliet*. Most enjoyably, there's a great deal of cross-pollination between groups: children can act alongside adults, and all 800 members have a part – however small – in the annual Christmas show. Watch out this summer for the Book Shed and Groovy Garden Shed kids activity days on 21 and 27 July respectively.

Colour House Theatre

Merton Abbey Mills, Watermill Way, SW19 (box office 8640 5111/theatre school 8648 4180/www.wheelhouse. org.uk). Colliers Wood tube. **Open** *Box office* 10am-5pm Mon-Fri; 1hr before the start of show. **Tickets** £6; £5 for parties of 4 or more. **No credit cards**.

This pretty little theatre, tucked into a picturesque corner of Wimbledon, has been winning hearts of all ages with more than 40 productions since its doors first opened in 1995. The plays – which bring old faves like Goldilocks and Dick Whittington to life in original and amusing ways – are the offspring of Wheelhouse Productions, and performances are held each weekend throughout the year with tickets costing £6 for all ages. Their most recent production, *Rumplestiltskin* (19 April to 22 June), combined the company's bright humour with occasional (mild) frights.

The building is also home to the Colour House Theatre School, which takes four- to 16-year-olds and develops their singing, dancing and acting techniques, culminating in twice-yearly shows which let the kids perform an audience – indispensable experience. Classes are held on Saturday mornings and Monday or Tuesday evenings, and the course costs £100.

Edward Alleyn Theatre

Dulwich College, Dulwich Common, SE21 (8299 9232/ www.dulwich.org.uk). West Dulwich rail/Brixton tube then 3 P4, P13, 115 bus. **Tickets** £5; £3.50 under-16s, concessions. **No credit cards**.

In the noble shadow of Dulwich College stands the Edward Alleyn, a 180-seat theatre that gives children the chance to act up both in and out of term time. This summer, week-long youth theatre activity workshops will be held with both

junior (seven- to 11-year-olds) and senior (12- to 16-year-olds) classes from the 14th July till the end of the month. Junior workshops are less formal (although children are encouraged to attend daily in preparation for a performance to beaming parents at the end of the week), while the senior course, without auditions, caters for kids with a serious interest in theatre and requires two weeks commitment. Both cost £13 per session or £60 for a week, and need booking well in advance.

Meanwhile, the theatre is regularly let out to touring companies, who perform family shows roughly once a month (with one for each major holiday and half term), and the Christmas break brings a typically seasonal production.

Half Moon Young People's Theatre

43 White Horse Road, E1 (7709 8900/www.halfmoon. org.uk). Stepney Green tube/Limehouse DLR/rail. **Open** *Box office* 10am-6pm Mon-Fri; 11am-4pm Sat. **Tickets** £5; £3.50 under-18s, concessions. **Credit** MC, V.

The Half Moon continues to offer an invaluable creative outlet in a borough not generally known for its artistic adventurousness. The Youth Theatre, for kids aged from five to 17, runs after-school groups without audition: the emphasis here is very much on developing talent. Kids are encouraged to turn up on the same day each week to help cultivate a sense of community in the build up to a show at the end of term. Sessions are £1.50 each and are oversubscribed, so be pre-

Polka Theatre. *See p221.*

pared to wait. The in-house production team also puts on two pieces every year before taking them on tour nationally, and each Saturday afternoon (2pm) sees different touring companies perform for the under-tens: puppetry, physical theatre, storytelling – you name it.

Jackson's Lane Community Centre

269A Archway Road, N6 (box office 8341 4421/admin 8340 5226/www.jacksonslane.org.uk). Highgate tube. **Tickets** £4.50; £3.50 members. *Annual Membership* £15, £5 children. **Credit** AmEx, MC, V.

This theatre's renovated church space may have the scruffy, comfortable feel of an old pair of shoes, but they're shoes well used to treading the boards. Saturday children's shows (11am, 2pm) are put on by various touring companies, and these range from abridged Shakespeare to nursery rhymes and myths dramatised through the medium of puppetry. There's also one show on the Wednesday of every half term and, in addition, a vibrant and well-established programme of activity workshops (from ballet to breakdance) for various ages. These range from the After School Club for five- to 11 year-olds (Mon-Fri, 3.30-6pm) to off-the-cuff sessions with visiting groups like Kaos! Organisation. Prices vary; an 11-week course might cost £77, while a drop-in afternoon class with dance impresario Debbie Cambell can be £5, but all are oversubscribed, so phone in advance.

Lauderdale House

Highgate Hill, Waterlow Park, N6 (8348 8716/ www.lauderdale.org.uk). Archway tube. **Open** *Box office* 30mins before performance; bookings not accepted. **Tickets** £3.50; £2.50 concessions. **No credit cards**.

Lauderdale House, a beautiful 16th-century manor backing on to the appropriately tranquil Waterlow Park, is a hotbed of creative activity aimed at younger children. Every Saturday at 10am and 11.30am, touring companies bring a different production to the stage, with an eclectic mix of traditional theatre, puppetry, music and magic to enthral three- to eight-year-olds all year round.

Classes are aimed at younger kids too. Jumping Jacks is a popular parent and toddler group that uses the principles of dramatic dance to nurture creative movement to music, while a group for three- to five-year-olds introduces theatrical and storytelling elements. Classes run on Thursday mornings for toddlers (9.45am, 10.30am) and Thursday afternoons for the older group (1.20pm, 2pm), and cost £40 or £45 (£20 to £25 concessions) for about ten weeks. There's also a painting and drawing workshop for six- to eight-year-olds on Tuesdays (4.30pm) and nine- to 15-year-olds on Thursdays (5pm).

The house takes advantage of the proximity of Waterlow Park during holidays, with several ad hoc activity days, including the annual Halloween ghost walk and a family-friendly summer Jazz In The Park festival.

Activities

All the world's a stage

It may be sniffed at by narrow-minded culture vultures and broadsheet critics alike, but the West End is still the best place in this country to impress on kids the timeless power of performance. The lights go down, the curtain comes up, and the stage is set for a lifelong relationship with the theatre.

Who better placed, then, than the **Society of London Theatres (SOLT)** to help children not only see the magic from the auditorium, but experience it first hand? During their annual Kids Week (22-29 August), one five- to 11-year-old attending a variety of West End shows – from *Les Mis* to *The Lion King* – gets in free with every accompanying adult (up to two additional children's tickets are available for half price). On top of that, participating restaurants, hotels and transport companies will let kids eat, sleep and even travel between shows for reduced rates, often free (phone for more information).

Most impressive is SOLT's programme of pre-performance workshops, which aim to immerse children in the very fabric of theatre. Details of this year's activities were unavailable when going to press, but highlights from the last Kids Week included Bollywood dance lessons from the *Bombay Dreams* choreographers, Stage Fighting The Shakespeare Way with top director Terry King, and a singalong with the cast of *Chicago*.

SOLT also runs a year-round Kids Theatre Club for eight- to 12-year-olds on Saturday mornings (10am-noon) at the **Theatre Museum** (*see p74*), when children perform with professional cast and crew from a favourite West End production; sessions are informal and free, but only 15 places are available per class, so phone in advance.

Society Of London Theatres
32 Rose Street, WC2E 9ET (7557 6700/ www.solt.co.uk).

Lyric Theatre Hammersmith
King Street, W6 (08700 500511/www.lyric.co.uk). Hammersmith tube. **Open** *Box office* 10am-6pm Mon-Sat (until 8pm during showtimes). **Tickets** £5-£7. **Credit** AmEx, MC, V.
Appearances can be deceptive: the Lyric may look fresh-faced from the outside, but the seating plan is decidedly Victorian, and as such doesn't really cater for the visual fields of younger audiences. Not that it's a problem, as most children's projects take place in the foyer, the stalls or – most commonly – in the purpose-built, 120-seat studio. It's here that the annual Catch festival (23rd Feb-26th April) comes into its own, with performance art and related activities from touring companies around the world. The material varies dramatically – from Bollywood dance classes and computer projection to percussion workshops and madcap culinary mayhem – with something different almost every day.

There's plenty on the main theatre's programme to attract the youth: recent plays like *After Mrs Rochester* and *The Hanging Man* – performed by Shared Experience and the alway ingenious Improbable Theatre respectively – sat very well with teenage audiences, and there's always the annual Christmas show for those seeking less in the way of emotional range and more raucous fun.

Nettlefold Theatre
West Norwood Library, 1 Norwood High Street, SE27 (7926 8070/www.lambeth.gov.uk). West Norwood rail. **Open** *Box office* 9am-4pm Mon-Fri. **Tickets** £3. **Credit** (advance only) MC, V.
A small but perfectly formed 200-seater built on to West Norwood Library, the Nettlefold offers regular concessions to creative and artistically curious minors. Various ages are catered for: two- to five-year-olds recently enjoyed a Saturday-afternoon production of *Twinkle Twinkle Little Star*, and a similar age group lapped up *Kazzum's Nocturne*, a mesmerising work inspired by the music of Miles Davis and using slideshows, puppetry and physical theatre. The Nettlefold is also used by the Bigfoot Theatre Company (8761 5447/www.bigfoot-theatre.co.uk) to stage drama, dance and singing workshops for sevens to 12s.

Open Air Theatre
Inner Circle, Regent's Park, NW1 (box office 7486 2431/www.open-air-theatre.org.uk). Baker Street tube. **Tickets** £9. **Credit** AmEx, MC, V. **Map** p316 G3.
Watching a play in the sunshine is in itself an appealing prospect for youngsters. Having the open sky for a canopy has traditionally made *A Midsummer Night's Dream* the best way for kids to discover Shakespeare, and this year Puck will weave his gentle magic from 2 June alongside *Two Gentlemen of Verona* (less family oriented, but featuring a real dog), with *High Society* – a musical made famous by the Sinatra movie – joining them on 22 June. August is the time of the annual children's play (in collaboration with Unicorn Theatre; *see p215*): this year it's a romp called *Granny and the Gorilla*, aimed at the over-sevens. Tickets for this charming 1,200-seat venue – the only truly open-air auditorium in the city – are £9; book well in advance.

Polka Theatre
240 The Broadway, SW19 (8543 4888/www.polka theatre.com). South Wimbledon tube/Wimbledon tube/rail. **Open** *Phone bookings* 9.30am-4.30pm Mon; 9am-6pm Tue-Fri; 10am-5pm Sat. *Personal callers* 9.30am-4.30pm Tue-Fri; 10am-5pm Sat. **Tickets** £5-£10. **Credit** AmEx, MC, V.
As dedicated and comprehensive a children's theatre as you'll find anywhere in the land: in 23 years the Polka has earned a fine reputation for performance-related work. Daily children's shows are staged in the main auditorium by touring companies (10.30am, 2pm), with weekly performances – rarely featuring more than two actors, and often puppet-based – taking place in the designated Adventure Theatre for those younger than four (who aren't allowed in the main room). The in-house team also produces five major productions each year – phone or check the website for details.

Entertainment isn't just limited to walking the boards, however, and after taking in a play and enjoying the puzzles and quizzes on the programmes, children can view costumes and props from previous shows in the exhibition centre, let off steam at the adventure playground, peruse the small toy store or take a break in the café. There's also a great little Reading Corner with storytelling on the first Saturday of every month. Even more popular are the clubs and activity sessions that run during term time (three- to 16-year-olds are catered to by an after-school Drama Club) and in half terms and holidays, when workshops expand to cover the whole dramatic spectrum: from voice coaching and puppet making to magic and origami. Prices start at £55 for entire courses and £15 for one-off drop-ins. Also, look out for occasional Polka Days, which combine performances with themed workshops for all the family to enjoy.

Royal National Theatre
South Bank, SE1 (box office 7452 3000/info 7452 3400/ children's events 7452 3327/www.nationaltheatre.org.uk). Waterloo tube/rail. **Open** *Box office* 10am-8pm Mon-Sat. **Credit** AmEx, DC, MC, V. **Map** p319 M8.
The Olivier – the late Larry's playhouse and one of three main stages at the National – certainly does its bit for children. As soon as school is out, makeshift theatres are put up in areas cordoned off from the grand foyer, and performances (child-friendly takes on classic tales, juggling, comedy magic and loveable chaos) are played out in front of kiddies over six. During holidays the NT also puts on free daily concerts at the indoor Djanogly Concert Pitch, lining up anything from Celtic jigs to North African drumming and Russian Gypsy dance. Also, come 20 June, the fifth Watch This Space outdoor festival kicks off: a free summer spectacle showcasing musicians, acrobats and actors from around the world and drawing huge family crowds to this riverside setting.

Shakespeare's Globe
21 New Globe Walk, Bankside, SE1 (7401 9919/ tours 7902 1500/www.shakespeares-globe.org). Mansion House tube/London Bridge tube/rail. **Open** *Box office* (theatre bookings, Feb-Sept 2002) 10am-6pm Mon-Sat; 10am-5pm Sun. **Tickets** £5-£27. *Tours* Oct-Apr 10.30am-5pm daily. **Tickets** £8; £6.50 concessions; £5.50 5-15s; free under-5s; £24 family (2+3). **Credit** AmEx, MC, V. **Map** p320 O7.
The fresh-faced DiCaprio may have sparked many a precocious interest in Montagues and Capulets, but there's nowhere better to impress on young minds the legacy of Shakespeare's plays than the Globe. Beautifully situated by the river, this replica of Bard's playhouse theatre stands only 100 yards from the site of the original. There's no roof, so Theatre Season runs from May to September (and even then, the British climate being what it is – rain still occasionally stops play), during which children can take part in pre-performance activities (phone 7902 1433 for details).
Come rain or shine, however, the Globe's merry band of educators enlightens and delights with year-round workshops – both half and full days are available – for children aged between seven and 11 (exploring performance conditions at the playhouse, for instance), for 11s to 14s (learning to engage with Shakespearian language) and for 14s to 16s (examining the social and historical context of theatre). Although the workshops are aimed at large parties and school groups (and tailored to Key Stage coursework), an exhibition in the vast UnderGlobe brings Shakespeare to life on a daily basis, and culminates in a guided tour of the stage itself.

Warehouse Theatre
Dingwall Road, Croydon, Surrey (8680 4060/ www.warehousetheatre.co.uk). East Croydon rail. **Open** *Box office* 10am-5pm Mon-Fri; 10am-1pm Sat; extended opening hours during shows. **Tickets** £4.50; £3.50 2-16s. **Credit** AmEx, MC, V.
Housed in a delightful Victorian warehouse, this small theatre has taken a daring approach to new writing since 1977, earning a reputation for quality that *Time Out* said

'outshines the West End's big cheeses'. But adults aren't the only ones getting a whiff of greatness – the Croydon Young People's Theatre workshops (CRYPT) offer childen aged between 13 and 16 the chance to develop their creative sides through the writing, production and – ultimately – performance of a play of their own. CRYPT convenes every Saturday during school terms (2-5pm), with fees for the entire course set at only £10 per person; there are no auditions to pass, but a good level of commitment is expected. Younger sprogs get their kicks at the Theatre4Kids shows on Saturdays at 11am, when touring companies bring puppetry, poetry, music, magic and theatrical madness to the stage.

Wimbledon Theatre
The Broadway, SW19 (8540 0362/www.wimbledon theatre.com). Wimbledon tube/rail. **Open** *Box office* 10am-8pm Mon-Sat; also Sun during shows. **Credit** MC, V.
This is not so much a great children's theatre as a great stage that occasionally offers theatre for children. The 1,650-seat Wimbledon often uses its size to capitalise on touring teenyboppers and tribute bands, but this year's programme also lines up plenty of shows that cater to kids in more interesting ways. Many of these are held in the studio, and run from emotionally challenging, thought-provoking pieces like Alan Ayckbourn's *The Boy Who Fell Into A Book* to Pop-Up Theatre's *The Snow Children*, for kids between three and eight. Check the website for up-to-date listings.

Young Vic
66 The Cut, SE1 (box office 7928 6363/www.youngvic. org). Waterloo tube/rail. **Open** *Box office* 10am-7pm Mon-Sat. **Tickets** prices vary; phone for details. **Credit** MC, V. **Map** p320 N8.
Function eclipses fashion at the Young Vic, and everything is informed by a principle of simple, theatrical democracy: art is for everyone. Nothing illustrates this better than the stage itself – built of steel and breeze blocks, with only five rows of (unreserved) seating – which emphasises the importance of an engaged imagination. It might all sound a bit academic, but imagination is something kids have in spades. That said, the Vic is clearly in the older half of being young, as only the Christmas season serves up a production aimed specifically at smaller sprogs (last year's *Sleeping Beauty* was for ages six and over, although there was a related show, *Beauty Sleeps*, for the under-fives). Every play in the annual programme, however, is subject to Teaching, Participation and Research workshops (TPR), inviting local schools and colleges to come in and work with actors and technicians, learning in the process about the theatre and how they can get involved. Check the website for more information.

West End shows

All the plays and musicals listed below are suitable for under-16s. The majority of them clock in at well over two hours, however – which younger children may find a little exhausting.

Blood Brothers
Phoenix Theatre, Charing Cross Road, WC2 (7369 1733). Leicester Square or Tottenham Court Road tube. **Times** 7.45pm Mon-Sat. *Matinée* 3pm Thur; 4pm Sat. **Tickets** £15-£40. **Credit** AmEx, MC, V. **Map** p317 K6.
A powerful folk-opera, *Blood Brothers* is first and foremost a rousing show with ultimately tragic lead characters – and some great tunes. It tells the story of separated twins reunited in later life and deals with issues of family ties and class divisions. The ending may upset very young children.

Chitty Chitty Bang Bang

Palladium, Argyll Street, W1 (0870 890 1108/
www.chittythemusical.co.uk). Oxford Circus tube. **Times**
7.30pm Mon-Sat. *Matinée* 2.30pm Wed, Sat. Tickets
£15.50-£40. **Credit** AmEx, MC, V. **Map** 316 J6.
A flying car, a sweet factory and a nice, clean fight between
good and evil: there's really very little about this lavish production of Ian Fleming's classic novel that doesn't go down
well with children. The whole thing is ingeniously designed,
and rumoured to be the most expensive West End musical
ever, but it's also well acted and utterly engaging.

The Complete Works of William Shakespeare (Abridged)

Criterion Theatre, Piccadilly Circus, WC2 (7413 1437/
www.ticketmaster.co.uk). Piccadilly Circus tube. **Times**
8pm Mon-Sat. *Matinée* 3pm Thur; 5pm Sat; 4pm Sun.
Tickets £14.50-£32.50. **Credit** AmEx, MC, V.
Map p319 K7.
Culturally aligned parents can huff and puff all they like: this
is a joy for all kids (and adults) who find the Bard a bit of a
bore. All 37 plays are hilariously edited, spliced together and
spat out in under two hours – and if the irreverent approach
appeals, you can follow on with the *Complete History of
America (Abridged)* on Tuesdays at 8pm, or *The Bible –
Complete Word of God (Abridged)* on Thursdays at 8pm.

Fame: The Musical

Aldwych Theatre, Aldwych, WC2 (70870 400 0805/
www.famethemusical.co.uk). Charing Cross tube/rail.
Times 7.30pm Mon-Thur; 8.30pm Fri; 7.30pm Sat.
Matinée 5.30pm Fri; 3pm Sat. **Tickets** £17.50-£35.
Credit AmEx, MC, V. **Map** p319 M6.
Fame may not live forever, but it certainly seems to have
learned how to fly: which is just another reason to catch this
unfeasibly energetic show before it dances itself into an early
grave. The story – revolving around a bunch of leotard-clad,
tantrum-throwing wannabes at New York's High School of
the Performing Arts – will appeal to drama queens of all ages.

Joseph And The Amazing Technicolour Dreamcoat

*New London Theatre, Drury Lane, WC2 (0870 890
1110). Holborn tube.* **Times** 7.30pm Mon-Fri. *Matinée*
2.30pm Wed; 2pm, 5pm Sat. **Tickets** £20-£40 (£5
reduction for children). **Credit** MC, V. **Map** p317 L6.
Andrew Lloyd Webber's *Joseph* took to the same stage that
Cats vacated. Whether it will have quite the same staying
power is perhaps up to Stephen Gately, who plays Joseph.

The Lion King

*Lyceum Theatre, Wellington Street, WC2 (0870 243
9000). Covent Garden tube.* **Times** 7.30pm Tue-Sat.
Matinée 2pm Wed, Sat; 3pm Sun. **Tickets** £17.50-£40.
Credit AmEx, DC, MC, V. **Map** p319 L7.
Few children will be unfamiliar with this charming tale – it's
a Disney classic, after all. This elaborate adaptation lived up
to the unprecedented hype surrounding its opening night
more than three years ago. Lush set designs, a combination
of puppetry and live actors and a cocktail of West End cho-
ruses and African rhythms: *The Lion King* is a delight.

Les Misérables

Palace Theatre, Shaftesbury Avenue, W1 (7434 0909/
www.lesmis.com/kids/club.htm). Leicester Square tube.
Times 7.30pm Mon-Sat. *Matinée* 2.30pm Thur, Sat.
Tickets £7.50-£40. **Credit** AmEx, DC, MC, V.
Map p317 K6.

An enduring and consistently powerful adaptation of Victor
Hugo's tale of revolution in 19th-century France: almost 20
years since its London premiere, *Les Mis* still manages to
impress. Some of the plotlines may be lost on a younger audience, but older children will enjoy the emotional tension,
lavish battle scenes and moving, memorable score. The *Les
Mis* kids' club lays on a backstage tour, drama and singing
workshop, the chance to meet a cast member, a
commemorative certificate – and, of course, a matinee ticket
for the show. There are several permutations of the kids club
package available: call 7439 3062 for details.

Mamma Mia!

*Prince Edward Theatre, Old Compton Street, W1
(7447 5400). Piccadilly Circus or Leicester Square tube.*
Times 7.30pm Mon-Thur, Sat; 8.30pm Fri. *Matinée* 5pm
Fri; 3pm Sat. **Tickets** £18.50-£40. **Credit** AmEx, DC,
MC, V. **Map** p317 K6.
It may be thin on storyline, but what *Mamma Mia!* lacks in
dramatic development it more than makes up for with feel-
good musical numbers – based on ABBA's greatest hits –
that kids will be singing for days afterwards. There's a reason
why they're still so popular, you know.

My Fair Lady

*Drury Lane Theatre Royal, Catherine Street, WC2
(7494 5000). Covent Garden tube.* **Times** 7.30pm Mon-
Sat. *Matinée* 2.30pm Wed, Sat. **Tickets** £7.50-£40.
Credit AmEx, MC, V. **Map** p317 L6.
The essential tale of high jinks in a London society built on
little more than manners. Recently revived to great critical
acclaim, *My Fair Lady* is a rich and rewarding experience.

Performance workshops

See also **Theatre Museum** *(p77)*.

Centrestage

Office: 33 Margaret Street, W1 (7328 0788/
www.centrestageschool.co.uk). **Classes** Sat mornings,
afternoons. **Fees** £200 + VAT 12wk term.
Credit AmEx, MC, V.
With another one opened in Camden earlier this year,
Centrestage venues now stand at a total of five. The others
– in Chelsea, Hampstead, Harley Street and Holland Park –
offer classes on Saturdays during term time, when the whole
spectrum of dance, drama and song is covered in a way that's
both fun and eminently successful at turning kids on to the
performing arts. Holiday workshops let kids take on well-
known scripts (from gentle tales like *The Elves And The
Shoemaker* for younger kids to full-blown musical extravaganzas for advanced classes) and in just six days turn them
into shows fit for public consumption.

Club Dramatika!

*King Alfred's School, North End Road, NW11 (8883
1554). Golders Green tube.* **Classes** 10-11am Sat. **Fees**
£7 session. **No credit cards.**
Quintessential drama group Dramatika! offers kids the
chance to relieve stress while releasing creative energy and
building on the basic skills of dramatic performance. Run by
Vicky Levy, former head of drama at King Alfred's, classes
are aimed at children aged four to ten. Vicky's company also
offers theatrical parties, by arrangement *(see p230)*.

Dance Attic

*368 North End Road, SW6 (7610 2055). Fulham
Broadway tube.* **Fees** from £48 11wk term; phone for
individual class prices. **No credit cards.**

Activities

Ballet is for boys

Lynne Page – choreographer to the stars and, more recently, founder of the perkily named **Nifty Feet!** dance school in Wimbledon – takes the credit for turning young actor Jamie Bell into a twinkle-toed Billy Elliot in the blockbuster of the same name. In doing so, a stigma that had for too long separated ballet from the modern boy took a serious blow to the head, and in the run-up to the opening of the school in March 2003, she was contacted by a huge number of hopeful young males longing to follow in Billy's airy footsteps.

Reacting to evidence that, around the age of nine, children's interest in ballet begins to wane, Page lays on urban dance classes with chart-topping teenybopper beats. As boyband attitude and Nike-clad feet meet the polish of the studio floor, and without kids even realising it, Page niftily slips in the ballet without the slippers. Exercise can be mental too, and rather than battle the boys she engages their preferences wholeheartedly to challenge their prejudices. About as far from the traditional image of the prim ballet academy as it's possible to get, the vibrant classes – always mixed – cater for two- to 16-year-olds, and leave the whims of convention by the wayside.

Lynne Page's lively classes run on Tuesdays for fives to eights (4-6pm) and Thursdays for twos to fives (11am-noon) at the Southfields Baptist Church. They also take place on Saturdays for ages nine to 12 (2-4pm) and 12 to 16 (4-6pm) at the Wimbledon Theatre. For more information, contact Nifty Feet! on 8879 1618.

One thing's for sure: Dance Attic is a professional studio, regularly hired by big shots to rehearse for big shows. It also offers a huge range of classes from salsa to street and tango to capoeira (an ancient and athletic Brazilian martial arts and dance amalgam that makes tai chi look clumsy). The centre opens 9am-10pm daily, and lessons are on a drop-in basis all year round, but to increase levels of progression the above examples are for teenagers only (phone for more information). Children under ten are encouraged to take part in Saturday morning workshops on tap (for over-fives) and ballet (for over-threes), the second of which work towards the prestigious RADA exams, with both costing £5 per hour-long session between 9am and 3pm.

Dramarama

Holiday courses at *South Hampstead High School, Maresfield Gardens, NW3;* Sat morning classes (term time) at *South Hampstead Junior School, Netherhall Gardens, NW3 (8446 0891). Finchley Road tube.* **Fees** prices available on request from Jessica Grant.
Jessica Grant's drama courses, established in 1987, run during school holidays and on Saturday mornings during term time. Various age groups covering three to 14 years, are catered for: small children can have fun improvising; older ones can work toward their prestigious Guildhall speech and drama exams. Half-term and holiday activities are designed to challenge, build confidence and entertain. The summer school has kids devising and producing a show for performance in just five days. Past productions include *Oliver!*, *The Borrowers* and *Grease.* A popular sideline is themed parties, which can be organised at the venue of your choice: phone for more information. Dramarama is registered with Ofsted.

Helen O'Grady's Children's Drama Academy

Headquarters: Garenne House, Rue de la Cache, St Sampsons, Guernsey GY2 4AF (01481 200250/ www.helenogrady.co.uk). **Classes** times vary; phone for details. **Fees** £60 12wk term. **No credit cards.**
About as far from the fantasy world of luvvies and daahlings as it's possible to get (though presumably not immune to the occasional tantrum), Helen O'Grady is more interested in building self-confidence in a wide range of children – including those hyperactive, disabled and socially disadvantaged – than she is in developing their knowledge of Chekhov. Of

37 O'Grady branches across the country, eight are in London, using school halls to carry out hour-long workshops after lessons have finished, with separate groups for five to eight, nine- to 12- and 13- to 17-year-olds. Classes run concurrently with term time and cost £5 per session or £60 for a 12-week term. Parents are invited to watch three open lessons a year, as well as the annual summer performance, open to the public. See the website or phone for your nearest branch.

Hoxton Hall

130 Hoxton Street, N1 (7739 5431/www.hoxtonhall. co.uk). Old Street tube/rail. **Classes** times vary; phone for details. **Fees** £1.50 session. **Credit** MC, V.
Set in a refurbished music venue, Hoxton Hall's programme for promotion of the arts is refreshing to say the least – and entirely in keeping with its trendy locale. No fumbling with the unwieldy bassoon here: at Junior Arts Class (Tuesday, 4.30-6.30pm), eight- to 11-year-olds make imaginative musical instruments of their own from the centre's resources and materials. Those with less flair for cutting and pasting can opt for the parallel Junior Music Class, which gives the same age group a chance to try out musical instruments, devise a piece of their own and then not only perform it for an audience, but record it onto CD. Both the Junior Drama (Mondays, 4-5.30pm) and Youth Theatre (Wednesdays, 7.15-9pm) groups – for eight to 11 and 11 to 18 years olds respectively – are equally democratic, allowing kids to write and produce a piece for performance in the main hall. All classes run in term time, and cost £15 for the whole course.

Laban Centre

Creekside, SE8 (8691 8600/www.laban.co.uk). Deptford rail. **Classes** Sat. **Fees** from £28 11wk term. **No credit cards.**
Recently relocated to an accessible, state-of-the-art complex in Deptford, classes now take place in one of 13 new studios, with most using the principles of contemporary dance to enlighten all ages from tots to teens. Carer And Toddler groups (£43 per term) take place on Wednesday mornings at 10.30am, and more advanced courses for older children (£38-£50 per term) are held on Saturday mornings. There are also Dance-Ability classes on Wednesday afternoons for five- to 11-year-olds (4.40pm-5.30pm) and nine- to 11-year-olds (5.45pm to 6.45pm), which promote the creative union of both disabled and non-disabled children. Youth Dance Classes, meanwhile, offer £1 dance workshops for 13- to 18-year-olds

(Mondays at 6.15pm) and classical ballet classes for 13- to 16-year-olds (Thursdays at 6.30pm), the stars of which can then audition for Laban's own Youth Dance Company, soon to be performing regularly in the brand new, 300-seat auditorium.

Lewisham Youth Theatre

Broadway Theatre, Catford Broadway, SE6 (8690 3428/ www.broadwaytheatre.org.uk). Catford or Catford Bridge rail. **Classes** *1hr lessons* 10.30am Sat (8-11yr olds); 11.45am Sat (11-14-yr olds). *Youth theatre* 6-8pm Mon, Thur (14-21yr olds). *Childrens Theatre Performances* 11.30am Sat. **Fees** free.

Things have been going rather well at the Lewisham Youth Theatre: not only are they consolidating their resources after relocating from the Deptford Albany to the Broadway Theatre in Catford, they're also reaping the rewards of a third nomination at the prestigious International Connections festival (for last year's production of Christian Martin's *Starstone*). As a result, waiting lists for their free, no-auditions theatre group have been getting so long that after school workshops have now been added to a previously weekends-only programme. Two groups cater to the eight to 11 and 11 to 13 groups respectively, with tuition centred around classes rewriting a well-known text – *Twelfth Night*, for example – and then producing, rehearsing and finally performing it in the 100-seat studio theatre. A Senior Youth Theatre (for young people aged between 14 and 21) runs in parallel, with a similar no-fee, no-auditions policy and plenty of cross-pollination with the younger groups.

London Bubble Theatre Company

5 Elephant Lane, SE16 (7237 4434/www.londonbubble. org.uk). Bermondsey tube. **Open** *Box office* 10am-6pm Mon-Fri. **Credit** MC, V.

This year rings in another of the Bubble Company's tri-annual community projects, which engage the abilities of local would-be, wannabe and will-be actors of all ages. The play in question – a modern twist on the Indian myth of Punchkin – is taken up by a group of 70 people working around a core of professional dramatists, with the finished production setting off on a sort of theatrical Reclaim The Streets tour of performances in parks and other urban spaces not usually associated with the arts. rehearsals begin in earnest in June (there are usually some fun, informal auditions to attend). The project's great charm lies in its unusual mingling of young and old, experienced and green actors. Parents who would like to involve their offspring in a less intensive theatrical adventure may prefer a more traditional route into the company. Enrolling at the Bubble's Youth Theatre, which runs after school every Monday during term, gears up young people for one performance per season. Two separate groups between them cover a wide age range: nines to 11s and 12s to 16s, and full drama courses are £30 per term (£15 for financially disadvantaged parents).

National Youth Music Theatre

www.nymt.org.uk.

This is the UK's leading music theatre company for young people. The NYMT tours music theatre productions nationally and internationally; their big London hit in 2003 was an exuberant production of Oklahoma!, which played to packed houses in the Peacock Theatre. Young people aged ten to 19 who would like to get involved in The Lab courses (drama courses held all over the country) should check the informative website. Every autumn, the website posts details of how hopeful performers can audition for the following year's big shows. The spring auditions always attract a great deal of interest, but the rewards, if you're lucky enough to get involved in a professional NYMT show, are great.

New Peckham Varieties

New Peckham Varieties at Magic Eye Theatre, Havil Street, SE5 (venue 7703 5838/office 7708 5401). Peckham Rye rail/Oval or Elephant & Castle tube/12, 36, 171, 345, 45A, P3 bus. **Classes** times vary; phone for details. **Fees** £1.50-£3. **No credit cards.**

The programme at New Peckham Varieties grows apace, and this year the group has been forced to divide itself between the Magic Eye Theatre and the Sojourner Truth centre on Sumner Road to make space. Peckham is an area that benefits greatly from having a local artistic focus like this, and the company has started attracting usually reluctant males by introducing the Boys Project on Sunday afternoons, which gives seven- to 14-year-olds a chance to try breakdance, steel bands or – a fine stress reliever – stage fighting. More inclusive drama groups for four- to 18-year-olds run on Mondays (4-9pm), and there are tap lessons on Tuesdays from 4.30pm. Wednesdays bring Musical Theatre For Beginners, Thursdays are for jazz lessons and each Saturday there's the chance to find harmony in a town centre not known for peace and quiet. Classes cost £1-£3 after an initial membership fee (£15 per year, £6 per term), and there are always huge waiting lists. Alongside occasional one-off concerts, the in-house drama team organises four annual productions to be performed on the Magic Eye's main stage, for which members from any class or age group can audition; the Christmas show, in particular, is always a lot of fun.

Millfield Theatre School

Silver Street, N18 (box office 8807 6680/www.millfield theatre.co.uk). Silver Street rail/34, 102, 144, 217, 231, 444 bus. **Classes/fees** £85 11wk term (4-5s) 10.30am-noon Sun. £165 11wk term (8-16s) 11am-2pm Sun. £75 11wk term (14-21s) 6.30-9pm Fri. **Credit** MC, V.

The Place to dance. *See p226.*

Millfield runs classes throughout term time that centre on performance-oriented drama, with the Theatre School itself, for 14s to 21s, putting on one show for family and friends each season after rehearsing dutifully through Friday nights and half terms, bless 'em. Younger children will slot neatly into either the Youth Theatre (eights to 16s) or the Junior Classes (fours to fives, sixes to sevens), which run on Sundays in the Arts Centre. Courses cost from £75 to £185 per term. The Theatre school also plays host to a number of touring theatre companies, whose travelling players occasionally organise more unusual day-long courses and workshops in performance, theatre skills and crafts.

Perform

66 Churchway, NW1 (7209 3805/www.perform.org.uk). **Classes** times vary; phone for details. **Fees** £107 weekday 10wk term; £160 weekend 10wk term. **Credit** MC, V.

Perform is the place where conscientious parents can send creative offspring: with more than 36 centres across London offering themed workshops every week, developing dramatic flair can be as convenient as it is fun.

Perform uses movement games, speaking and singing exercises and improvised storytelling to engage the imagination and develop what they call the four Cs: confidence, concentration, co-ordination and communication. Classes are for one hour after school and an hour and a half on weekends, and the organic fruit and Evian water used to break up longer sessions should give some idea of the physical as well as emotional wellbeing that Perform takes so seriously.

Classes are neither preachy nor pretentious, however, and kids are encouraged to learn through laughter alone. Week-long courses take place in summer, with three-day projects in the shorter holidays, and all follow a set theme, often based on a popular children's story (*Alice In Wonderland*, for example, or *The Magician's Workshop*). Ten weekday sessions cost £107, with ten weekend sessions at £160, although a child's first class is free, so you can test for keenness beofre making a financial commitment.

Pineapple Performing Arts School

7 Langley Street, WC2 (8351 8839/www.pineapplearts. com). Covent Garden tube. **Classes** *7s-12s* 1-2pm Sat. *13s-16s* 2-3pm Sat. *Over-17s* 3-4pm Sat. *3s-4s* 11am-noon Sun. *5s-12s* 11am-2pm Sun. *13s-14s* 1-4pm Sun. *15s-18s* 2-5pm Sun. **Fees** £226 12wk term; trial class £19. **Registration fee** £30. **Map** p317 L6.

This Pineapple isn't cheap: membership for each term costs £226 after a £30 enrolment fee, with a charge for most classes. That said, its central location (the school benefits greatly from having so many big-name shows within walking distance) and the ardent enthusiasm of its young, professional staff make it a fantastic resource for anyone who can afford it – and some who can't. The Community Outreach courses, for example, give a week of drama coaching to children and young people who wouldn't normally get the opportunity. Many such courses culminate in a trip to a popular in a West End show as one of the benefits.

Such projects take place in holidays and half terms, when members can engage in week-long performance courses of their own. There are no after-school classes: activities are reserved for weekends, when kids can give their full attention to street jazz classes on Saturdays afternoons (open to non-members for £5, £4 for members), or the intensive Sunday workshops, which offer one hour of dance and one of drama in several groups for five- to 18-year-olds. Sundays also sees the Pineapple Chunks classes: theatrical activities for three- to four-year-olds (£6, members only).

The Place

16 Flaxman Terrace, WC1 (box office 7387 0031/classes 7387 7669/www.theplace.org.uk). Euston tube/rail. **Fees** from £62 term for 1 weekly class; £10 family discount. **Credit** MC, V.

Fully redeveloped, bristling with energy and verve, The Place is considered by many to stand at the cutting edge of contemporary dance in the UK. For younger children, however, the emphasis lies firmly on learning through having fun, and creative expression is nurtured in a relaxed and unpretentious environment. To this end, The Place takes children as young as five in a series of popular Saturday dance classes, honing their dance skills for a performance in front of family and friends at one of many regular open days (phone 7388 8430 for more information).

Offspring, meanwhile, is the centre's programme of rolling dance workshops for young people, commissioning work for various age groups and then complementing rehearsals with educational activities, talks and family events. These tend to be more challenging projects, from Virgilio Sieni's fairytale *Cappux Red* to a performance of Protein Dance's *Banquet* that may just be The Place's most ambitious show to date.

Stagecoach

Head office: The Courthouse, Elm Grove, Walton-on-Thames, Surrey KT12 1LZ (01932 254333/ www.stagecoach.co.uk). **Fees** £260 (£130 for 4-7-yr-olds) for classes during school term. **No credit cards**.

With schools from Germany to Gibraltar sending their pupils here for tuition, Stagecoach can comfortably claim to be leader of the international pack – but don't think that makes them the Starbucks of the children's stage. There are more than 60 venues in London alone, yet each one maintains a close, intimate atmosphere, with classes never larger than 15 pupils, and total attendance figures no higher than 45 students per school. The three hours of tuition each week break down into one hour of modern dance, one of drama and one of singing, all led by highly qualified staff drawn from various creative fields, and an in-house agency to represent the brightest of each year's rising stars.

Holiday workshops tend to last for five days, and are open to members as well as non-members of the school, with casting, script-reading and both technical and dress rehearsals preceding a final performance at the end of the week. Places are limited and granted on a first come, first served basis: check the website for more details and a list of prices.

Sylvia Young Theatre School

Rossmore Road, NW1 (7402 0673/Saturday classes 7724 1693/www.sylviayoung.freeuk.com). Marylebone tube. **Fees** from £4.50/class. *Summer school* (10-18s) £250/1 wk. **No credit cards**.

Sylvia Young's teaching remains well respected among the theatrical community, and many of her pupils go on to scale the dizzy heights of the Royal Shakespeare Company. Billie Piper and the Appleton sisters were also students, but don't let such populist alumni put you off: Sylvia Young's is a professional outfit through and through. The school for kids aged between nine and 16 offers a full-time vocational course to those who show more than just a passing interest in the stage. Students' weeks are divided into three days of academic study (like most independent schools, the staff use the National Curriculum as their guide) and two days vocational work. Waiting lists for the school are appropriately dramatic, and would-be pupils are required to take a vocational assessment as well as an academic test. Saturday workshops include tutorials on disciplines such as tap dancing, contemporary dance, speech and diction and various acting skills.

Monster fun at **Art 4 Fun**. *See p227.*

There are excellent holiday courses available – including three one-week-long summer schools for hardworking performance-mad young people aged ten to 18.

Workshops
Art
Art 4 Fun
Various venues (head office 8994 4800/www.art4fun. com). **Fees** *Weekend workshops £15. Half-day course* £25.85. *Full-day course* £38.80. **Credit** AmEx, DC, MC, V.
If the highlight of creative arts in the home is getting poster paint out of the Persian rug, take your little Jackson Pollocks to one of the Art 4 Fun venues across London. Here artistic children can flick paint all over the shop with impunity; the only thing parents need worry about is what kind of muffin to have with their cappuccino.

Regular two-hour Painting With The Masters workshops teach children more unusual skills like making stamps, kites and frames (£12.75 per session, minimum of four sessions). Meanwhile, a twice-daily Little Artists Club (10.30-11.30am, 2.30-3.30pm) offers under-fours the chance to get really messy and creative with clay, dough, plaster and papier mâché (£7.60 per session, minimum of four sessions). School holidays bring excellent seasonal courses from the Winter Wonderland to the Summer Art Camp, which this year will offer a different creative experience on each day of the week (£155 for a five day week), at either the West Hampstead (7794 0800) or Chiswick (8994 4100) branches. There are two other branches in smart parts of London: Notting Hill (7792 4567) and Muswell Hill (8444 4333).

Ceramics Café
215 King Street, W6 (8741 4140/www.ceramicscafe.com). Ravenscourt Park tube. **Open** 10am-6pm Tue, Wed, Fri, Sat; 10am-10pm Thur; 10am 6pm Sun. **Fees** £2. **Credit** MC, V.
Thanks to mass production, the only affordable handmade objects in this city tend to be resigned to the corners of small antique shops. Not so at Ceramics Café, where for £9.90 and a £2 studio fee, kids can choose their own piece of crockery – from mugs, bowls and plates to less functional and more decorative bisque shapes – and paint away in comfortable surroundings with snacks and drinks to fuel the artistic fires. This is a large branch, so it's one of the best for good for organised parties, where a minimum of ten over-fives can have a lovely time getting creative for a reduced price of £10 a head, and take home the best party bag ever.
Branches: 1A Mortlake Terrace, Kew Green, Richmond, Surrey (8332 6661); 6 Argyle Road, W5 (8810 4422).

Colour Me Mine
168-70 Randolph Avenue, W9 (7328 5577/www.colour memine.com). Maida Vale tube. **Open** 9am-9pm Mon-Thur; 9am-7pm Fri, Sat; 10am-7pm Sun. **Fees** *Studio fee* £6.60; £5.50 concessions; £4.40 under-12s. *After-school club* £20 child (incl materials). **Credit** AmEx, MC, V.
More practical than your average creative café, Colour Me Mine has its ceramics divided into sections with titles like 'Bathroom', 'Kitchen' and 'Garden', so creative home-improvers can choose between decorating their own ceramic tiles for the shower unit, bowls and plates for the dresser or even funky plant pots. While all this practical stuff isn't that appealing to children, there's plenty here to get their creative juices flowing. A good start are the kids club workshops, irregular during term time but a safe bet when school's out:

children can spend three hours a day at the café, at £25 for lunch and the costs of glazing and firing whatever they paint. Otherwise, young ones pay a £4.40 studio fee and then for individual items (from £1.50), although there are good party rates for 12 or more (*see p229*). Parents can take home casts of their babies' hands and feet (£39 each or £55 for a pair), while fashion-conscious kids can create their own jewellery with Silver Alchemy, a clay that turns silver in the kiln (£35 per three hour session, individual materials from £3).

Cooking
The Kids' Cookery School
107 Gunnersbury Lane, W3 (8992 8882/www.thekids cookeryschool.co.uk). Acton Town tube. **Open** *Office* 9am-5.30pm Mon-Fri. **Fees** £15 75mins. **No credit cards**.
Kids these days think that choosing Nando's over KFC is the height of haute cuisine – and why not? After all, in a city where so many people don't have time to eat lunch, let alone make their own, who is there to tell them otherwise?

The answer lies in Acton, where the KCS promotes an enjoyably hands-on education in nutritional values and physical wellbeing through what they call 'food therapy'. After school classes (£15 for 75 minutes) and holiday workshops (from £24, minimum two hours) give children from all walks of life the opportunity to make healthy dishes, (favourite recipes include sweetcorn fritters and funny-face pizzas, but older children can learn to make quite complicated meals). The price you pay covers all the ingredients, tuition and a recipe card to take home. Classes never number more than 12: safety and hygiene are taken very seriously indeed, and no small children are allowed to handle sharp utensils.

The cookery school is a registered charity and can offer a number of assisted places to children from low-income families (parents pay whatever they can on a sliding scale of £1.50 to £10), and one of three new training kitchens is designed to accommodate disabled children and wheelchair users. Staff also encourage visits from children and young people with eating disorders, who have been known to benefit greatly from food therapy in the past.

French
Le Club Tricolore
10 Ballingdon Road, SW11 (7924 4649/www.le-club-tricolore.co.uk). **Fees** vary; £100 10wk term, with reductions for siblings. **No credit cards**.
Most children wouldn't list French lessons under Entertainment, but then Le Club Tricolore offers something a bit different. No verb tables, no grammar and definitely no tests: everything here is learnt orally, from role-play sessions and good old fashioned singalongs. After-school classes are complemented by Saturday morning ones; holiday workshops dish up cookery, craft making and treasure hunting. The club is aimed at children aged three to 11, and operates in venues across London – phone for details of your nearest.

1.2.3 Soleil
Head office 0845 085 0048/www.123-soleil.co.uk.
A fast expanding organisation which gives under-fives (from as young as nine months old, incredibly) a jolly introduction to French language, using songs, stories, games and craft workshops. Classes take place six days a week and last 45 minutes. The teaching takes place in appropriately chic parts of London comme Notting Hill, Hampstead and Harrow. O là là! For details of times and prices of the baby classes, and these, and new venues opening up, check the website.

Music

London Suzuki Group
Various venues (7386 8006/www.suzukimusic.net).
Fees vary; phone for details. **No credit cards.**
There are currently 17 teachers all over London who practise the Suzuki Method, first used in 1948 by Dr Shinichi Suzuki at his own revolutionary music school in Japan. Working with children as young as three, they expound the idea that all are musically gifted at birth, and can become great musicians with the right tuition: the key is to learn by listening, and then to pursue music for pleasure. Children do weekly group work as well as individual lessons, with high levels of parental participation. Classes (for violin, viola, cello and piano) are held after school and at weekends and are for members only, although occasional holiday workshops encourage non-members to come and have a go. Phone for a price list and details of your nearest branch.

Music House for Children
Bush Hall, 310 Uxbridge Road, W12 (8932 2652/ www.musichouseforchildren.co.uk). Shepherd's Bush tube.
Fees vary; phone for details. **Credit** MC, V.
When it first opened its doors in 1994, the Music House was primarily concerned with introducing kids to classical instruments. Much has changed since then, and these days the school also offers drum tuition, electric guitar classes and a whole range of resources for jazz lovers. The Music House has over 150 qualified tutors on its books, so parents can phone in and find a suitable teacher locally who will then give lessons in kids' homes. Those seeking a more sociable environment in which to practise should get along to Bush Hall, where group workshops are held every day after school. Half term and holiday activities give children a chance to familiarise themselves with more obscure instruments, and the Hall also hosts cracking children's parties.

Mwalimu Express
Bread & Roses pub, 68 Clapham Manor Street, SW4 (7498 1779/www.breadandrosespub.com). Clapham Common tube. **Fees** free.
This is an unusual, family-oriented take on the tradition of Sunday pub jazz. Percussionists, singers and storytellers come from as far afield as Poland and Cuba to entertain the children. There's plenty of interaction all afternoon (noon-5pm), with performers often inviting younger members of the audience to join them onstage. The pub (*see p177*) also screens monthly activities – from African board games to world cinema – that are occasionally aimed at children.

Ocean
270 Mare Street, E8 (box office 7314 2800/info 8533 0111/www.ocean.org.uk). Hackney Central or Hackney Downs rail. **Open** 11am-7pm Mon-Fri; noon-4pm Sun.
Fees vary; phone for details. **Credit** MC, V.
The fruit of an ingenious £2.3 million music hall project in the heart of Hackney, Ocean leans strongly towards the urban segment of the musical spectrum. The Rising Tide project caters to youngsters aged between 15 and 18, with practical DJing, drum programming and songwriting courses. Meanwhile creative but unemployed 16- to 25-year-olds can take advantage of Under Currents, a resource seeking to develop skills needed to work in the UK music industry – it even occasionally funds the careers of young artists.
Inclusion is the key: Ocean offers assisted places to financially disadvantaged local school children, and children with disabilities can make music with electronic interfaces, housed in the specially designed and wheelchair-friendly RTC studio. Phone for a list of current events.

Whippersnappers
The Whippersnapper workshop room, Brockwell Lido, Dulwich Road, SE24 (7738 6633/www.thelido.co.uk). Herne Hill rail/Brixton tube/rail/3, 37, 196 bus.
Fees from £3.50. **No credit cards.**
Whippersnappers holds morning workshops at the fabulous Brockwell Lido, livening up life for under-fives with virtuoso song-and-dance routines. Although puppet shows, nursery rhymes and dressing-up activities are included, the musical side of the shows – based around African djembe drums – is a great way to introduce babies and toddlers to an enjoyably easy-going brand of music-making. Workshops are held daily at the Lido, and on Tuesdays and Wednesdays at the Ecology Centre in Holland Park (*see p151*).

Science & environment

Camley Street Natural Park
12 Camley Street, NW1 (7833 2311/www.wildlondon. org.uk). King's Cross tube/rail. **Open** *Summer* 9am-5pm Mon-Thur; 11am-5pm Sat, Sun. *Winter* 9am-5pm Mon-Thur; 10am-4pm Sat, Sun. **Admission** free. **Map** p317 K2.
Much of the wildlife around Kings Cross isn't the kind you'd expose your children to, but in the case of Camley Street's incredible nature reserve you'll no doubt make an exception. The large pond is teeming with life, and enthusiastic kids can borrow a net from the office any time they want to get a closer look. Delightful creatures of the air, like kingfishers or bats, make their presence known from time to time, much to the amazement of school parties and nature-loving families. There's also a good range of free activity days all year round, running from barbecues to boat trips, and a birthday festival is held every May. A play scheme through the summer hols lets parents drop their kids off for funtastic clay modeling, trail-blazing and teepee-making.

The Making Place
3 Exmoor Street, W10 (8964 2684/www.the-making-place.co.uk). Ladbroke Grove tube. **Open** 10am-3pm daily.
No credit cards.
As any child will tell you, the greatest fun to be had in science comes from putting those boring theoretical equations into practice and watching the sparks fly. During term time the centre deals with school groups, but workshops are organised for kids up to 14 years old during half term breaks. The duration (from two to four hours) and cost (£5-£10 per child) of these workshops varies depending on how in-depth the activities are, but each session offers the same hands-on approach to the snap, crackle and pop side of physics and chemistry, and always lay on experiments with practical rewards: from honeycomb candles to jumping beans.

Roots & Shoots
The Vauxhall Centre, Walnut Tree Walk, SE11 (7582 1800). Lambeth North tube. **Open** *July-Apr* 9.30am-5.30pm Mon-Fri. *May, June* 9.30am-4pm Mon-Fri; 10am-2pm Sat, Sun. Phone before visiting. **Admission** free; donations welcome.
Roots & Shoots is perhaps best known for training young people with physical and learning disabilities to derive great pleasure from tending a simple garden. The one-acre site is also a popular destination for school groups, where David, the wildlife outreach worker, takes kids pond dipping, bug hunting and honey collecting (the centre is home to the London Beekeepers' Association), while informing them about surrounding flora and fauna. Seasonal family days are held on an ad hoc basis: phone for details of the next one or sign up to the activities mailing list.

Parties

This way to the birthday bash with panache.

Some parents dread their children's birthday parties for 364 days of the year. Understandable perhaps, unnecessary for sure: help is at hand.

There are people who relish the thought of entertaining hordes of screaming, sugar-crazed horrors, whereas others might run a mile. Those who aren't up to the task generally phone those who are, and while there are enough hired hands in London to fill up this book – from clowns and kid-o-grams to make-up artists, musicians and comedy magicians – we've stuck with the best we know to include here. There's also a list of great venues (most of which have facilities for disabled visitors), caterers and party shops around the capital. Who knows? Next time round you may even have more fun than your children do – or at the very least start dreading their birthdays less than your own.

Activities

Arts & crafts

Art 4 Fun
172 West End Lane, NW6 (8959 7373/www.art4fun.com). West Hampstead tube/rail. **Open** 11am-7pm Mon-Fri, 10am-7pm Sat, Sun; by appointment until 10pm. **Credit** AmEx, DC, MC, V.
Dropping the kids off at one of the four Art 4 Fun venues in London lets you disappear for a coffee and lets them make as much mess as they want. After a £3.95 studio fee (which covers firing and glazing costs for ceramics, ready for collection a few days later), items start at £1 each, although most (mugs, plates, money boxes) cost around £5. Kids tend to make their own gifts to take home, although close friends might like to chip in and make a personalised canvas for the birthday boy or girl. All paints are lead-free and ceramics are food safe. And speaking of food, staff are perfectly happy to clear the tables and let little Michaelangelos tuck into cakes, takeaway pizzas and whatever else you care to bring along.
Branches: 444 Chiswick High Road, W4 (8994 4100); 212 Fortis Green Road, N10 (8444 4333); 196 Kensington Park Road, W11 (7792 4567).
Buggy access. Café (snacks only). Disabled access. Nappy-changing facilities. Shop.

The Art Yard
318 Upper Richmond Road West, SW14 (8878 1336). Mortlake rail. **Open** *Classes* term time 9am-6pm Mon-Fri, school holidays 9.30am-3.30pm Mon-Fri. **No credit cards.**
Parties at the Art Yard are more method than mess. Kids choose from a list an item they'd like to make, then each participant creates his or her example of that item in an informal, step-by-step tutorial led by staff. It might be less spontaneous than hurling oil paint at an unglazed vase, but at least kids come away with well-rendered, recognisable

objects that range from papier mâché mirrors to decorative treasure chests. Parties cost £15 per child; all parents have to provide is the food. Phone for details of term-time classes (from £90 for several weeks) and occasional drop-in holiday workshops (from £27.50 per day).

Colour Me Mine
168-70 Randolph Avenue, W9 (7328 5577/www.colourme mine.com). Maida Vale tube. **Open** 10am-6pm Mon-Wed, Fri-Sun; 10am-9pm Thur. **Credit** AmEx, MC, V.
For £12 per head, kids paint unglazed ceramics, while for an extra £4 they get to decorate plain T-shirts as well. Costlier options include decorating small mirrors with mosaic and making bead necklaces and bangles (both £15 per child). Coffee and cake are supplied, though most parents opt to order takeaways at no extra cost. CMM provides invitations and party bags, and for £50 a professional face painter will bring out the animal in even the most timid artist.
Branch: 452 Muswell Hill Broadway, N10 (8444 6886).
Buggy access. Café. Disabled access: toilet. Nappy-changing facilities.

Nellie's Art Parties
01298 872752.
Fenella Shepherd's famous art parties are evolving: from this year Nellie will take the whole package on tour to living rooms, gardens and hired halls across the capital – at no extra cost. Kids spend an hour painting and decorating a giant collage, followed by a craft session (so each partygoer has something to take home), games and refreshments (courtesy of Nellie's mum). All parties follow a theme chosen by the birthday child. The price is £390 for 22 children (smaller parties can be arranged), with £12 for each extra head. Book ahead.

Pottery Café
735 Fulham Road, SW6 (7736 2157/www.pottery-cafe. com). Parsons Green tube. **Open** 11am-6pm Mon; 10am-6pm Tue-Sat; 11am-5pm Sun. **Credit** MC, V.
While not letting kids take the potter's wheel just yet, the Café does put over-sixes in the driver's seat when it comes to painting unfired crockery: from mugs to jugs to little teapots short and stout. A £17 fee per child covers invitations, paints, materials and clay items up to £10.50 each, plus sandwiches, crisps and a drink to keep artists' block at bay (Mon-Sat only).
Buggy access. Café. Nappy-changing facilities. Shop.

Cookery

Cookie Crumbles
8876 9912/0845 601 4173/www.cookiecrumbles.net.
If your heart lurches at the thought of making lunch for a group of hell-raising birthday-goers, why not let them cook their own? Carola Weymouth is a Cordon Bleu chef who'll come to your home and help kids aged between five and 15 prepare a three-course meal: pizza faces for younger kids and chicken in breadcrumbs for the over-tens. What could have been a food fight becomes a sophisticated dinner party, with all dishes made from wholesome ingredients. The two-hour parties start at £145 for six children and cater for a maximum of 30; prices cover everything from shopping to mopping up.

Gill's Cookery Workshop

7 North Square NW11 (8458 2608). Golders Green tube.
No credit cards.
Teaching 12 kids to cook raisin crispy cakes is the sort of stress-defying stunt best left to the pros – people such as food technology teacher and event caterer Gill Roberts. Gill's Workshop took off when she moved her after-school club for young children to her Hampstead home, and when her two-day holiday classes for six- to 13-year-olds (£80) and Saturday morning sessions for three- to six-year-olds (£25) were supplemented by Saturday cookery parties (10am-1pm or 2-5pm; £225 for 12 children, £10 per extra child up to a maximum of 20). Parents leave kids in Gill's capable hands, and tend to be surprised at the results when they return to pick them up: animal bread rolls, home-made ice cream, funny face pizzas and, best of all, smiling eyes the size of birthday cakes.

Drama

Club Dramatika!

8883 1554.
Vicky Levy's theatrical activities aren't limited to enlivening after-school activities or holiday performance groups: she also offers drama parties for birthday kids with thespian sides, bringing classic tales of magic and mystery to life. Parties follow the format of her popular workshops, starting with voice exercises and ending in a full-blown production. Parties are £80 for one hour, £130 for two.

Fairy Tale Theatre

01727 759661. **No credit cards**.
There's no shortage of drama teachers looking to turn parties of chocolate-caked toddlers into stars of the small stage. Less common are touring actors willing to bring their trade to people's homes and perform exclusively for kids. Fairy Tale Theatre's charming shows, which change regularly and cover classics like Rapunzel and Little Red Riding Hood, are sized to be enacted in living rooms across the land. All props are provided, as is the only required 'stage': screens behind which the actors change costume. The two-hour parties also include theatrical takes on traditional party games (Pass The Parcel becomes Pass The Prickly Hedgehog), and cost £180.

Lydie Children's Parties

7622 2540. **No credit cards**.
Some people seem born to make life fun for children, and French impresario and all-round charmer Lydie is one of those blessed with an imagination – and an accent – every-

---

TOP FIVE Activities

For painted faces
Mini Makeovers. *See p231.*

For learning the ropes
Mile End Climbing Wall. *See p233.*

For driving ambition
Playscape Pro Racing. *See p233.*

For creating a scene
Perform. *See p230.*

For drawing conclusions
Nellie's Art Parties. *See p229.*

---

one falls for. Her lively themed parties, for children aged four to nine, turn living rooms into delightful fantasy lands filled with fabulous decorations, as up to 26 kids take on roles from popular tales like Peter Pan. There are also plenty of ingenious games, funny songs and special goody bags: prices start at £350 for a two-hour party.

Marvellous Productions

8679 0917/www.marvellous-productions.com.
No credit cards.
Rosy-cheeked, silver-wigged and sporting her trademark red apron, drama therapist Roya Hamid not only looks the part as old mother Marvel, but plays it to perfection. She whisks children away on her magic carpet to other worlds and time periods – Hogwarts, Narnia or ancient Egypt – with interactive storytelling sessions that have her audiences enthralled. A professional face painter is on hand to get kids in character (or can be hired independently), while Make and Take workshops offer the chance to make puppets, masks or toys based on the story (all materials provided, any mess removed). Prices vary, ranging from £145 for up to 20 children.

Miss Sparkle

07939 358854.
Former drama tutor Rain Harris channels her extensive theatrical experience into parties that kids talk about for ages afterwards, using anything from low-key magic to handmade puppets to capture the hearts and attention of her audience of under-fives. Older kids (under 14) can play parts of their own in one of her popular performance parties (murder mysteries go down a storm), which are loosely plotted and have the kids producing their own video or acting for parents. Prices are £90 for one hour or £130 for two; phone for details.

Perform

7209 3805/www.perform.org.uk. **Credit** MC, V.
Staff at Perform – the respected drama workshop specialists – bring a unique element of interaction to their largely improvised parties. Parents liaise with performers in advance to pick a theme that most suits the kids in question, but the possibilities are endless: discos for aspiring divas or dramatic escape scenes for young action heroes. The show is set in a pre-arranged venue – usually a living room – and costs £115 per high-octane hour. Specially commissioned songs can also be written if the staff are given enough notice.

Tiddleywinks

8964 5490/www.tiddleywinks.co.uk. **No credit cards**.
All the living room's a stage at Kate Gielgud's parties. The fun starts when she turns up at a house in character (and in costume) to narrate and direct traditional tales (Sleeping Beauty is a favourite with girls, boys prefer Peter Pan), with kids aged three to seven acting out various roles. Later, traditional party games offer themed prizes, while older kids (eights and over) are treated to three hours of rehearsals for a 15-minute murder mystery – starring the children – that slowly turns into a comedy. Prices start at £200 for two hours; all costume and props are provided.

Face paints & make-up

Magical Makeovers

01932 244347/07957 681824/www.magicalmakeovers.com. **No credit cards**.
The Magical Makeovers team of beauty specialists comes to your house to offer light-hearted but sound advice on everything from skin care to general grooming, with hair accessories for girls to keep when the party's over. The service

Mamma mia! Kids take over the kitchen at **Gill's Cookery Workshop**. *See p230.*

caters to girls aged six to 18. Small kids have makeup applied for them (which keeps lipstick off the sheepskin rug), and older girls get a practical, hands-on tutorial. Prices start at £150 for eight kids; all materials are provided.

Mini Makeovers

8398 0107/www.minimakeovers.com. **No credit cards**.
Diamonds may still be a girl's best friend, but a load of glitter, makeup and hair accessories never hurt anyone. Mini Makeovers bring a vast supply of hypoallergenic, age-appropriate cosmetics to your home for five- to 12-year-olds to raid. They'll get anything from nail treatments to temporary tattoos, either as part of a sleepover or before the girls head elsewhere; if it's the latter, Mini Makeovers also offers a limo service. Other options include dance tuition, goody bags and mounted photographs of the young stars themselves.

Sport

Alexandra Palace Ice Rink

Wood Green, N22 (8365 2121/www.alexandrapalace. com). Wood Green tube/Alexandra Palace rail/W3 bus. **Open** 11am-5.30pm Mon-Fri; 10.30am-12.30pm, 2-4.30pm Sat, Sun. **Admission** *during week* £4.20, £3.50 concessions £17.50 family (2+2); *weekends* £5.50, £4.50 concessions £17.50 family (2+2) **Credit** MC, V.
The Palace is a wonderful place for kids who like to get their skates on: elaborate in design and beautifully located atop a grand hill, it's a million miles away from the out-of-town warehouses that rinks usually inhabit. Parties are equally special, with between ten and 20 kids given 15 minutes of light-hearted tuition before taking off for an hour on the ice. Prices are £7.95 per head including a cold snack, or £8.95 including a hot meal, and parties take place at weekends only at 10.30am, 11am and 2pm. Booking is essential.

The Elms Soccer School Parties

The Elms, Pinnacles Close, Stanmore, Middx HA7 4AF (8954 8787/www.theelms.co.uk). **Open** *Enquiries* 9am-6pm Mon-Fri. **Credit** AmEx, MC, V.
It's a game of two halves at the Elms. They'll send an FA-qualified football coach to your garden, local park or other pre-arranged venue, where kids get professional tuition (without the abusive shouting), followed by a mini-game with the birthday boy or girl as captain. The whole shebang costs £120 for up to 20 kids and lasts 90 minutes, the length of a premiership game (which is exactly where your little ones might end up if the Elms has anything to do with it).

Mallinson Sports Centre

Bishopswood Road, N6 (8342 7272). Highgate tube. **Credit** MC, V.
Facilities at Mallinson are first rate, something to do with it being attached to the highly sporty Highgate school for boys. Kids wanting a piece of the action can opt for one of two party packages. The first, on Saturday mornings, gives kids aged five to six an hour on a bouncy castle (£145), while the second, held throughout each weekend, offers seven- to 15-year-olds a more comprehensive sporting experience (£155). From the many options available – basketball, hockey and football, for example – kids choose one for an hour of supervised team sport, followed by half an hour in the pool and then 45 minutes in the social room, reflecting on the day's highlights and wolfing down whatever party food parents care to supply. Party packages are only available at weekends and half term.

Michael Sobell Leisure Centre

Hornsey Road, N7 (7609 2166/www.aquaterra.org). Finsbury Park tube/rail. **Open** 7.15am-10.30pm Mon-Fri; 8.45am-5.30pm Sat; 8.45am-8.30pm Sun. **Credit** MC, V.
A concrete monster it may be, but the Michael Sobell complex has a range of events that prove eminently popular with

Please join us: Dora the Explorer

Where: Nick Jr.

When: Everyday at 8am, 11am, 1pm and 5pm

Join in TV

www.nickjr.co.uk

sky   ntl:home   Telewest Broadband

young partygoers. Most children opt for the Sobell Safari, where four- to eight-year-olds can take over the centre's Jungle Jim facilities (£65 Mon-Wed; £130 Thur-Sun). Trampoline and ice skating parties are available for the over-eights, with equipment and tuition provided (£85 or £111 respectively): all three last for an hour and a half, and parents bring their own refreshments.

Mile End Climbing Wall
Haverfield Road, E3 (8980 0289/www.mileendwall.org.uk). Mile End tube. **Open** noon-9.30pm Mon-Thur; noon-9pm Fri; 10am-6pm Sat, Sun. **Credit** AmEx, MC, V.
Mile End's extensive indoor facilities may not be as swanky as those in the more recently developed Westway climbing centre (*see below*), but they're designed with greater freedom and flexibility for those still learning the ropes. They also do nice parties for over-eights, putting beginners under the wing of an experienced instructor (one to eight children, £50; each additional instructor £40) and laying on climbing and abseiling for an adrenalin-filled 90 minutes. Parties end in the Monkey Room – imagine a fully padded squash court with a sloping ceiling and holds everywhere – after which the little monkeys will probably sleep all the way home. Refreshments aren't included, and the café only serves basic snacks, but there's a small park outside for picnics.

Pro-Active 4 Parties & Entertainment
8440 2682/www.magicalparties.net. **No credit cards**.
Alongside less strenuous theme parties (the Big Brother Bash, for example, which requires kids to sit around eating biscuits while nominating less popular classmates for eviction), Pro-Active also organises high-energy activities. The Premier Football theme is in a league of its own, putting small teams through a series of tournaments and shootouts, while the Sports Combo parties and Mini-Olympics cover everything from basketball to ultimate Frisbee. Older kids tend to go for Junior Gladiators (over-sixes) or a popular take on *Crystal Maze*-style challenges. Pro-Active can set up events in your garden if it's big enough, but recommends you hire a hall (and will find one near you).

Playscape Pro Racing
Streatham Kart Raceway, 390 Streatham High Road, SW16 (8677 8677/www.playscape.co.uk). Streatham rail. **Open** 10am-10pm daily. **Credit** MC, V.
The capital's favourite karting circuit really burns rubber. Parties are held for eight- to 16-year-olds from Monday to Friday from 10am-5pm, and 10am-1pm at weekends, with an hour on the track for up to ten kids (£195), 90 minutes for 15 (£292.50) and two hours for 20 kids (£390). Full training and safety gear is provided, and there's a trophy presented to every 'driver of the day' – usually the birthday boy or girl, however shaky his or her three-point turns may be.

Westway Sports Centre
1 Crowthorne Road, W10 (8969 0992/www.nkat.org.uk). Latimer Road tube. **Open** 10.30am-10pm Mon-Fri; 10am-8pm Sat, Sun. **Credit** AmEx, MC, V.
The Westway is a cut above most sports centres in the city: expansive, relatively inexpensive and, most rewardingly, still new-smelling. Activities available to party animals include tennis, football and the capital's largest (if least well heated) indoor rock-climbing wall. Invitations and decorations are provided, as well as equipment and any relevant training (how not to look down, for example), with catering available as an optional extra. Prices start at £80 for ten children, with a maximum of 25 kids (phone for more information).

Cakes

There are still many who prefer to make their own cakes for special occasions, and they needn't suffer in silence: *No-time Party Cakes* by Carol Deacon, and *New Children's Party Cakes* by Joanna Farrow, are invaluable resources for all things cake – simple or more elaborate. Both are available in paperback at £9.99 from bookstores or www.amazon.co.uk.

Still, most people take the easier, pre-packaged supermarket cake route (at around £8): no cardinal sin, though the quality of the cake will depend on whose shelf it came from, and it's a safe bet that the joy in eating it will be much smaller than the joy in looking at it. As a rule of thumb: the more convincing the cartoon character or the colour of the football pitch on top, the less effort has gone into the filling underneath. Never judge a cake by its cover.

But there is a third option. Parents who aren't already spending their life savings on entertainers and decorations might like to try a more luxurious creation from one of the many professional cake makers listed below. Some are progressive European patisseries, some are traditional English bakers, but all combine ingenuity (fancy a cake shaped like a ski boot?) with years of experience in making cakes that not only look good, but taste even better.

Amato Caffè/Pasticceria
14 Old Compton Street, W1 (7734 5733). Leicester Square/Tottenham Court Road tube. **Open** 8am-10pm Mon-Sat; 10am-8pm Sun. **Credit** AmEx, DC, MC, V. **Map** p317 K6.
Gone are the days of barely recognisable Basil Brushes and misshapen or frightening Superteds. Amato, one of the more technically advanced bakers in the capital, can feed designs into a computer, manipulate them on screen and then print, say, an image of your little angel at the wheel of a tractor onto sugar sheet paper for a truly personalised design (from £45). And if you're after something more elaborate, Amato can shape cakes that stagger the imagination, from freestanding Star Wars droids to a five-month Starship *Enterprise* project (prices vary). Eat me up, Scotty.

Choccywoccydoodah
47 Harrowby Street, W1 (7724 5465/www.choccywoccy doodah.com). Edgware Road or Marble Arch tube. **Open** 11am-6pm Fri, Sat; or contact Brighton branch daily on 01273 329462. **No credit cards. Map** p313 F5.
At Choccywoccydoodah, the most indulgent dreams become reality. Layered with fresh Belgian truffles, their delightful creations can be coated in white, plain, milk chocolate or even in chocolate dyed to match your party's colour scheme. Eight to ten portions cost from £18, with £80 for up to 70 portions; hand-moulded figures can be added for an additional cost, and cakes can be tailored to the most demanding imaginations. Prices vary (phone for details).

Chorak
122 High Road, East Finchley (8365 3330). East Finchley tube. **Open** 8.30am-6pm daily. **No credit cards**.
Alongside the usual range of gateaux, cream pies and cheesecakes in all shapes and sizes, Chorak specialises in hand-

Activities

Not just a pretty face.
Escapade. *See p236.*

making party cakes with iced designs, from well known TV characters to tractors, toys and nursery rhyme characters. Cakes come in two sizes, with set prices for small (£38) and large (£46) creations – which means you may even have money left over for presents.

Dunn's

6 The Broadway, N8 (8340 1614/www.dunns-bakery. co.uk). Finsbury Park tube/rail, then W7 bus/Crouch Hill rail. **Open** *7am-6pm Mon-Sat.* **Credit** MC, V.
In an ocean of progressive European artistry, traditional English bakers are becoming ever harder to find. Dunn's is one highly respected example, and for five generations has been turning out cakes of the highest quality, available in a huge number of prepared designs, including 3D football pitches and snooker tables (£39.60). Bespoke designs can be

iced on to order – a popular cartoon character, perhaps – and the new line in impressive photo-quality images is selling like, er, hot pastries (£34.30). Basic cakes start at £20 (8in).

Jane Asher Party Cakes

22-4 Cale Street, SW3 (7584 6177/www.jane-asher.co.uk). South Kensington tube. **Open** *9.30am-5.30pm Mon-Sat.* **Credit** AmEx, MC, V. **Map** p315 E11.
Jane Asher's seasonal collection of off-the-peg, mail order cakes is quite something. For kids, designs include 3D books, Gameboy machines and an all-too-realistic hamburger, with a choice of fruit or sponge bases and a variety of fillings (£35-£55). A bespoke service is available: recent work has included ladybirds, sleeping lions and, for the Mafia child, a lovely horse's head (prices vary). Cake mixes and Jane Asher sugar-craft materials are available if you'd rather bake your own.

Maison Blanc

102 Holland Park Avenue, W11 (7221 2494/www.maison blanc.co.uk). Holland Park tube. **Open** 8am-7pm Mon-Thur, Sat; 8am-7.30pm Fri; 8.30am-6pm Sun. **Credit** MC, V.
French from the base to the peaks of the icing, Maison Blanc cakes may be more refined than the sort most children are used to getting, but that's no reason not to cultivate their sweet tastes at an early age. Any of the delicious gateaux from this chain of charming patisseries can be personalised with a handwritten message for an extra £2.10 (cakes start at around £14), while marzipan animal figures can be popped on for £1.20 each. If that doesn't sound elaborate enough, more deluxe creations can also be whipped up – perhaps featuring child-pleasing cartoon characters such as Winnie the Pooh (for the younger ones) or bearing distinguished designs like Persian rug motifs or the musical notation of a favourite song (for older children). Phone for more details.
Branches throughout town. Check phone book or website.

Pierre Péchon

127 Queensway, W2 (7229 0746). Bayswater or Queensway tube. **Open** 7am-7pm Mon-Wed; 7am-8pm Thur-Sat; 8am-7pm Sun. **Credit** MC, V. **Map** p312 C6.
The creations on offer from this high class French patisserie are picture-perfect slices of cake heaven. With enough warning, the imaginative staff will shape your child's dream cake – plane? Shetland pony? Easy-peasy – from vanilla or choco-late sponge with fresh or butter cream, with the option of iced messages, characters or printed designs. If you're low on ideas, a catalogue of past work is available – though the sweet smelling interior is usually enough to spark inspiration. Prices start at £9.85 for a 6in cake, while a 12in cake (which will provide 30 portions) costs from £53.60.
Branch: 4 Chepstow Road, W2 (7229 5289).

Costumes

Mail order

Hill Toy Company

Unit 1 The Tavern, Lower Green, Higham, Bury-St-Edmonds, Suffolk, IP12 6NL (0870 607 1248/www.hilltoy. co.uk). **Open** *Phone orders* 9am-5.30pm Mon-Fri.
Credit MC, V.
The greatness of the Hill Toy Company isn't limited to dressing up, but as well as an excellent range of toys and games, it stocks a selection of outfits that are simply impossible to ignore. Forget realism: most of the costumes – from the Indian brave's get-up (£24.95) to the unbelievably huggable, all-in-one lamb suit (£19.95) – are designed to make kids look cute, and they do it with style. The accessories list runs from impressive-looking medical kits (£12.95) to wigwams (£44.95), and the online ordering system is top notch.

Get splattered

There's no denying the sheer thrill of hiding behind an abandoned double-decker bus before making a run for the cover of nearby trees, dodging fire and letting off a few speculative paintballs on the way. The bus is just one obstacle among many at the various branches of the **Paintball Centre** around south-east England, from Effingham in Surrey to Shoreham in Kent (with new venues at Upminster and Hemel Hempstead – check the website for a full list). For £17.50 per head, children (11s to 17s, minimum of 20 kids on weekdays) gets 150 paintballs to fire off during a morning and early afternoon, with a barbecue lunch while the young guns debrief. The day runs from 9.15am-4pm, with helmets and overalls provided.

Campaign Paintball in Surrey, meanwhile, is a 180-acre playground for the gung-ho, whose owners insist that warlike combat is just a cover for the centre's primary objective: team building. They may well be right – in any case, Campaign is a regular venue for corporate events (and hen nights), though kids will be far more interested in becoming lone heroes and infiltrating enemy camps than relying on their dozy schoolmates for covering fire in a group attack. By planning a Sunday attack they get the centre when it's free from City types, and a party package (£27.50 per head) offers kids 300 paintballs to fire at will between 9.30am and 4pm, with lunch provided and an awards ceremony afterwards.

Children with a warrior instinct but who don't fancy the mild sting of paintballs will be thrilled by the claustrophobic, panic-inducing but painless tension of laser-based games. Kids love ducking and diving through futuristic stage sets, with dramatic lighting, smoke and sound effects, and the more of them there are, the more involving and cinematic the atmosphere. Party packages at **Quasar** let up to 20 kids over seven years old go laser crazy for 40 minutes – and then brag about their cosmic skills over a complimentary burger and a drink – for £10.95 per head. At **Laserquest**, two 20-minute games for up to 20 kids (over six years old) cost from £7.30-£8.30 per child depending on when they play (weekends are more expensive). Bringing birthday grub is up to you: just make sure the cake isn't of a style that would embarrass a highly decorated space marine.

Campaign Paintball

Old Lane, Cobham, Surrey (01483 285151/ www.campaignpaintball.com). Effingham Junction rail. **Credit** MC, V.

Laserquest

155 Clarence Street, Kingston-upon-Thames, Surrey (8974 8484/www.laserquest.co.uk). Kingston rail. **No credit cards**.

The Paintball Centre

0800 917 0821/www.paintballgames.co.uk. **Credit** MC, V.

Quasar

13 Junction Road, N19 (7281 5001). Archway tube. **Credit** AmEx, MC, V.

Activities

Is it a bird? Is it a plane? Neither – it's **Laurie Temple & the Party Wizard Company**. *See p241.*

Hopscotch

108 Rangefield Court, Farnham Trading Estate, Farnham, Surrey, GU9 9NP (01252 717768/ www.hopscotchmail order.co.uk). **Open** *Phone orders 9.30am-5.30pm Mon-Fri.* **Credit** MC, V.

There's something charming about the way Hopscotch outfits fit kids so well: maybe it's because each one is assessed for comfort and ease of use by a rigorous group of young testers. Costumes here are first rate, with plenty of unusual takes on traditional faves: cowboy suits, for example, come with sheepskin chaps and cowhide waistcoats (£32.95), and there are plenty of extras for those looking to accessorise.

J&M Toys

46 Finsbury Drive, Wrose, Bradford, W Yorks BD2 1QA (01274 599314/fax 01274 591887/www.jandmtoys.co.uk). **Open** *Phone enquiries 9am-5.30pm Mon-Fri.* **Credit** MC, V.

When it comes to fancy dress J&M Toys takes the biscuit, offering a costume catalogue organised by profession: truly striking firemen, traffic wardens with lollipops, and enough medical outfits and paraphernalia to kit out a hospital. Owners Jim and Melanie are also medieval enthusiasts, with regal robes, Robin Hoods and a comprehensive range of knights' armour – helms and tabards, anyone? It's all surprisingly cheap: most outfits cost little more than £17, with discounts on group purchases. Orders are taken by post or fax only.

Make Believe

PO Box 343, Guildford, Surrey GU5 9YW (01483 203437/ www.make-believe.co.uk). **Open** *Enquiries & orders 9am-3pm Mon-Fri.* **Credit** MC, V.

The majority of costumes for sale at Make Believe hover around the £45 mark, which may seem excessive, but most accessories are included. Pirates come with stripey socks and silver-buckled shoes, and Star Wars anti-hero Darth Maul gets a double-bladed light sabre to play with. The costumes are made from high quality materials embellished with extra features – the Gorilla, for instance, has flashing red eyes. Check online for details, or phone for the catalogue.

Shops

Escapade

150 Camden High Street, NW1 (7485 7384/www.escapade. co.uk). Camden Town tube. **Open** *10am-7pm Mon-Fri; 10am-6pm Sat; noon-5pm Sun.* **Credit** AmEx, MC, V.

Most of the costumes here are lovingly crafted in the store – and while that makes them all utterly unique, it also means that for copyright reasons they can't supply popular Disney characters. Instead, Escapade is home to animals (kittens are popular with girls, bears with boys), alongside well-rendered Cinderellas, Prince Charmings and more accessories, hats and wigs than you could shake a pirate sword at. Three-day hire costs between £15-£20 after a £50 deposit.

Harlequin

254 Lee High Road, SE13 (8852 0193). Hither Green rail/Lewisham rail/DLR. **Open** *10am-5.30pm Mon, Tue, Thur-Sat; 10am-1pm Wed.* **Credit** MC, V.

A great little shop with a good range of kid's costumes for sale, with plenty of characters from well-loved fables – Snow White, Peter Pan, Cinderella and friends. Prices start at £8.95 for a wizard's robe (it's not Harry Potter, but gadzooks if you can tell the difference) and go up to £28 for more elaborate animal suits or suits made of finer materials. For parents on a budget, there are costume kits for £3.95: the pirate kit, for example, contains a patch, bandanna, moustache and earring.

Deals on wheels

The Party Bus

07836 605032/www.childrenspartybus.co.uk.

The bus in question, a colourful converted single-decker that holds up to 24 children and runs on fun, is a great way to get any party moving. Events are tailored to the age group in question (from fours to nines), with traditional games and comedy magic for the younger ones, and London's most mobile disco venue for older kids. For £300/£350 the bus will come to your house, and provides all catering except the cake. When the music stops, the mess just drives off into the sunset.

The Wonderbus
8968 3798/www.wonderbus.co.uk.
The double-decker Wonderbus is a gleaming silver joy machine, complete with mini ball pool and slide for party animals, and a quiet corner where shy types can read or draw. A padded dance floor lets kids get on down to the latest chart hits, while less energetic activities include face painting, passing the parcel or simply munching on party food. The bus takes passengers between two and seven years old, and a stop at your house costs from £250 for up to 15 children.

The Wonder Years
07000 123455/www.limousinehireheathrow.com.
Kids with stars in their eyes will never forget their first ride in a stretch limo. The Wonder Years gives kids just that, with leather seats, fairy lights, mirrored ceilings and chauffeur as standard. Soft drinks are thrown in free (parents can supply non-alcoholic champagne if they see fit). Cars seat up to eight kids, and hire starts at £175 for three hours.

Entertainers

Billy the Disco DJ
8471 8616/07949 936 864.
Billy's disco for party people aged four to 11 includes dance contests, disco lights, pop quizzes and karaoke. He also has a bubble machine, and will entertain with Pass the Parcel and hand painting. Billy charges £125 for a 90-minute do.

Blueberry Playsongs Parties
8677 6871/www.blueberry.clara.co.uk.
An established parent-and-toddler music group with branches across the capital, Blueberry also sends its entertainers to kids' parties (one to six years old) for 45 minutes of guitar-led singing, dancing and fun. Prices start at £75 for 20 children, and include Blueberry balloons as well as a special present for the birthday boy or girl. Phone for more details.

Boo Boo
7727 3817/www.mr-booboo.co.uk.
Boo Boo is a charmer: part clown, part magician, part comic. His popular shows for three- to eight-year-olds incorporate music, balloon modelling, dancing and general buffoonery,

---

TOP FIVE Party suppliers

For sound systems
Young's Disco Centre. *See p239.*

For going-home bags
Baker Ross. *See p243.*

For the icing on the cake
Amato Caffè/Pasticceria. *See p233.*

For crisis management
Action Station. *See p239.*

For something different
Mexicolore. *See p244.*

---

while older kids get to shake their tail feathers to more contemporary tunes in a Boo Boo disco party; most shows last for two hours. Prices vary: phone for details.

Chris Howell
7376 1083.
Chris is a member of the fast-moving, smooth-talking school of American conjuring (and the Magic Circle), but that doesn't mean that his shows go over the heads of younger audiences – far from it. Sometimes he's the one who appears slightly out of his depth, letting the audience think he's faffed a trick before pulling it off with spectacular flair. Hour-long parties for four- to eight-year-olds weave through a story in which the kids play an active part, and there's balloon modelling to round things off. Prices start at £85 – phone for details.

Foxy the Funky Magic Genie
8769 3370/www.foxythefunkygenie.com.
Foxy, funkmaster extraordinaire and all-round fun geezer, goes down a storm with kids who like celebrations to have a little soul. Foxy offers four separate party packages for children aged two and up: conjuring and balloon shows or games, puppetry and full-blown discos – all tied together with the main man's brand of comedy magic and irrepressible '70s cool. Prices start at £95 for a 45 minute show and go up to around £250: phone or check the website for details.

Jenty the Gentle Clown
8207 0437/07957 121764.
As featured on John Peel's *Home Truths* programme, and as beloved of the children in Great Ormond Street Hospital, Jenty's parties for children aged two to 11 include singing to banjo music, puppet shows, storytelling, balloon-modelling, face-painting and limbo dancing. Choose the activities to suit your child, and know that Jenty charges £135 for two hours.

Jugglers Etc
0870 777 2425/www.jugglingjohn.com.
John Haynes has been a rock musician, street magician and professional children's worker, but it was as Juggling John – master of slapstick and mime at kids' parties and corporate events – that he found his niche. Success led to his launch of the Jugglers Etc agency, which supplies unicyclists, stiltwalkers, storytellers and fire eaters. Not that John has stopped doing the rounds himself, of course: he's still available for children's parties in several guises, including Reggie the Raccoon, Ronnie the Robot and good old JJ. Shows cater to kids aged three and up, and prices start at around £100.

Lee Warren
8670 2729/www.sorcery.org.uk.
Lee moves in exalted circles: he has performed for Lawrence, Lord of Llewellyn Bowen and Edward, Earl of Wessex. More importantly, his brilliant kids' shows combine deft sorcery with audience participation that goes beyond the usual disappearing acts. Boys and girls dress up, often as pirates and princesses, and take part in stories as they unfold, with plenty of conjuring, illusion and amusing calamity along the way. Lee's hour-long shows – for four- to eight-year-olds – cost £100 for a home performance and £110 in a hired hall, and he'll deal with nearly any size of audience (eight minimum).

Lisa the Disco Diva
8908 0705/07778 122277.
Lisa's collection of mobile DJ and disco equipment includes bubble and smoke machines, fancy lights and mirrorballs. She'll speak with the birthday boy or girl beforehand (or liaise with parents if the whole thing's a surprise) and choreograph a whole dance routine to a favourite tune; kids can then do

their new grooves for grown-ups, or just party the rest of the afternoon away in peace. Events cater to boys and girls aged four and upwards, with games and competitions, magic and more in the high-energy, two-hour package.

Little Blisters
8948 3874.
Actress Ava Desouza uses her dramatic skills to make parties sparkle for three- to seven-year-olds. As one of three characters – Flossie the Fairy, Sea Lily the Mermaid or Kitty Willow the Cat – she brings her own brand of musical magic to kids' homes and tells a story with plenty of visual trickery, singing and dancing. One- and two-hour shows are available (£100 or £220), with games, prizes and face-painting.

Merlin Entertainments
8866 6327.
At least a quarter of the hundred-odd entertainers on Merlin's books specialise in children's events. Choose from a long list of performers, from caricaturists and comedy waiters to fortune tellers and fire eaters. Prices start at £110 for a one-hour performance, or £140 for a more interactive, two-hour show.

Pekko's Puppets
8575 2311/www.pekkospuppets.co.uk.
Veteran of the touring circuit and regular at both Jackson's Lane and the Lyric Hammersmith, Stephen Novy is also an old hand at birthday parties, with puppet plays aimed at kids aged three to 11. Shows for under-fives pack in two shorter tales with lots of singing and audience participation, while older children get a full performance from a repertoire which runs to Celtic folk tales, popular classics and the puppeteer's take on legends like Dracula. All are enacted from one of two mobile booths (from £120 for one hour).

Peter McKenna
7703 2254/07956 200572/www.childrensentertainer.net.
Magic Circle member McKenna brings welcome relief from the usual top-hat-and-floppy-wand routine, appearing in a variety of guises suitable for various age groups – and conjuring with a degree of competence rarely seen at kids' parties. Illusions include levitating, sawing in half and even decapitating audience members, but there are plenty of less overwhelming tricks for smaller children, with discos, party games and goody bags all available by arrangement. Prices start at £90 for one hour, £145 for two.

Professor Fumble
01395 579523.
Professor Fumble is a right old butterfingers, and utterly endearing as he repeatedly bungles his tricks, juggles like a seasoned amateur and sits down in his own custard pies. Shows can last one or two hours (£95 or £135 respectively); the former include balloon animals for the kids and – where space permits – a chance for partygoers to have a crack at spinning plates themselves or even walking on small stilts. Longer performances do amusing takes on old party games, with the mad Professor providing the prizes.

Equipment hire

Disco

Jukebox Junction
12 Toneborough, Abbey Road, NW8 (7328 6206). St John's Wood tube. **Open** by appointment only 9am-5pm Mon-Fri. **No credit cards.**

Their pick of tunes may not boast the current number one: as staff point out, if they bought the chart each week, where would they keep the jukeboxes? Instead, they have the best in rock and pop from the '50s to the '80s, and even the most jaded teenyboppers will love having a 1970s Seeburg jukebox to play with. Up to 50 tunes can be chosen from 3,500 in the archives, all for a £50 deposit and £275 rental per night (free delivery within five miles).

Young's Disco Centre
20 Malden Road, NW5 (7485 1115/www.youngsdisco. com). Chalk Farm tube. **Open** 11am-6pm Mon-Sat. **Credit** AmEx, MC, V.
Dancing kings and queens will find everything they need to get their groove on at Young's. A state-of-the-art sound system comes with a DJ, from £150 for a two-hour weekday party (£200 at weekends), and karaoke setups are available from £80; further refinements include a smoke machine (from £20) or industrial bubble blower (from £15), popcorn and candy-floss makers (from £50 each), and even fake snow machines (£30).
Branch: 2 Malden Road, NW5 (8585 8885).

Fairground

PK Entertainments
07771 546676/www.fairandfate.co.uk. **No credit cards.**
What do you get for the kid who has everything? Well, an indoor fairground might be a start. If your house is large enough, PK can set up a basic package (from £200) in your living room, with mini bouncy castle, bucking bronco and stalls of the pop gun variety; more capacious lounges can even include a toboggan run. Outdoor events start at around £250 for 20 children, though a fully-blown fair can be built for roughly £400: roundabouts, swingboats and all.

Marquees

Sunset Marquees
20 Bradmore Park Road, W6 (8741 2777/www.sunset marquees.com). Hammersmith tube. **Open** enquiries 24hrs daily. **Credit** AmEx, MC, V.
If the thought of washing blackcurrant cordial out of the sheepskin rug is too much to bear, why not put up an outdoor marquee, and localise the next round of birthday madness to a clearly defined and disposable space? Basic 10ft by 10ft packages start from £100 and go up (literally) from there, and with the advent of double and triple-decker marquees (prices vary), the sky is the limit. Even circus big tops are available (from £900), although you'll have to find up to 250 little friends to fill it. Lighting, heating and underfoot carpeting cost extra. Phone for more information.

Organisers

Action Station
7263 8468/www.theactionstation.co.uk.
The Action Station agency is a fine resource for any parent on the verge of a last-minute planning meltdown. Their books are positively bursting with entertainers: jugglers, acrobats, clowns who take kids for a spin in madcap cars or fire engines, you name it. There are storytellers who give children acting parts as the tale unfolds (making bad guys to walk the plank in the pirate yarn, for example). Two-hour drama parties are available (kids pick a theme and perform for parents), while face-painters and film make-up parties

Activities

Who's the fairiest of them all?
Ask **Mystical Fairies**. *See p241.*

between them create everything from tiger faces to (more gruesome) fake scars, warts and boils. Most activities cost £125 for one hour or £175 for two, and staff also organise discos and karting events (phone for details).

Adam Ant's

8959 1045/www.adamantsparties.com.
Adam Ant stands and delivers the nuts and bolts of memorable parties: music and dancing, magic, balloon sculpture and general japery, all courtesy of a range of entertainers. Depending on the length of the party (from £75 for one hour), activities can be stopped for a birthday lunch: Adam also caters (phone for details), though parents tend to provide the cake. Increasingly popular are the kid-o-gram characters who turn up to wow the party for half an hour (from £85): Cinderella, for example, tells a gentle story, and Batman chases bad guys around your garden. Party accessories are available for hire, including ball ponds and bouncy castles (from £45).

Crechendo

8772 8140/www.crechendo.co.uk.
The events arm of this well-respected childcare company offers an astonishing selection of 'off the peg' theme parties, from Pooh Bear picnics for under-fives to Hollywood Showbiz spectaculars for ten- to 16-year-olds, with stretch limos and celebrity lookalikes as optional. The company can tailor occasions to fit the most demanding bill: recent highlights have included a winter wonderland with an indoor ice rink, and a medieval banquet held in a real castle with fairground rides, jousting and fireworks – though don't expect extravagance to come with a fairytale receipt. Prices start at £190 for a two-hour event (phone for more details).

popKidz

07929 218987.
There's only one way to handle mini celebrities: pamper them, pander to their every petulant demand and let them hog the camera. And that's something staff at popKidz know how to do very well: their recording equipment can be set up in any living room, as the wannabe stars get made up and spend three hours preparing for the five-minute final take – which comes back a week later, professionally edited on VHS or DVD with special effects and a five-minute 'bloopers' reel. There's a long list of contemporary tunes and ditties to suit boys and girls aged between seven and 11, and the whole package costs £500, including two VHS or DVD copies of the performance (extra copies cost £7 per VHS and £15 per DVD).

Laurie Temple & the Party Wizard Company

8840 5293/ www.thepartywizard.co.uk.
He may never have studied at Hogwarts, but Laurie's brand of comedy magic is a big hit with kids of all ages. His Party Wizard Company is expanding, too, with personnel ranging from face painters to funky DJs, all able to supply fun and games to parties. Event planning is also a speciality: Laurie can take care of the whole thing or simply lend you all the essentials from a huge range of inflatable toys, tableware and decorations (phone for more details). Basic entertainment costs £100-£150 for one hour, £150-£250 for two.

Mystical Fairies

12 Flask Walk, NW3 (7431 1888/www.mysticalfairies. co.uk). Hampstead tube.
Fairytale parties are organised and directed by Riea Elliot-Jones from this twinkly Hampstead shop. Birthday girls and boys choose between characters ranging from Hogwarts stalwarts to fairytale heroines. The parties are all asparkle with fairy dust, disco lights and glittering entertainers. Children can borrow gauzy outfits from the shop as part of the package. Prices depend on whether you have your mystical fairy party at home or in the Enchanted Garden (a grotto with toadstools and a fairy throne in the basement here). A home party (two hours with a fairytale character face painter) costs £180 plus VAT; a glitter disco and karaoke package in the Enchanted Garden with a makeover, party suppies and invitations costs £395 plus VAT. If you'd like the good fairies to tailor a party to your child's needs, ask for a quotation.

Animal antics

For that challenging mix of children and animals, you're best calling in the professionals. **Nick Spellman** is the guy to arrange close encounters of the zoological kind. As if kids' birthdays didn't call for enough animal management, Nick can bring barn owls, bird-eating spiders or snakes to the party. Alternatively, **Westway Stables** offers pony lovers the perfect birthday package. With the stables closed to other visitors, children get roughly an hour of gymkhana games in a safe, well-supervised environment, followed by an hour spent petting and grooming the ponies. Food is available, and the whole event costs £35 per child (maximum 20 children) for roughly three-years).

The **London Aquarium** lets children celebrate in the company of manta rays, remoras and moray eels. For £6.25 per child over seven (£9.75 for accompanying adults; free for under-threes), a group of ten to 20 partygoers gets an hour-long, up-close-and-personal tour of the aquarium's most interesting tanks, with a rare opportunity to feed certain fish at the end. A 45-minute version

operates for children aged between five and seven (£6.25 each), though health and safety restrictions rule out feeding any of the fishy friends.

London Aquarium

County Hall, Riverside Building, Westminster Bridge Road, SE1 (7967 8000/children's tour enquiries 7967 8007/www.londonaquarium. co.uk). Westminster tube/Waterloo tube/rail. **Open** 10am-6pm (last entry 5pm) daily. Phone for opening times during hols. **Credit** MC, V. **Map** p319 M9.

The Nick Spellman Show

Impeyan Productions (01992 446211/ www.impeyan.co.uk). **Prices** £150-£280; phone for details. **No credit cards**.

Westway Stables

20 Stable Way, W10 (8964 2140). Ladbroke Grove or Latimer Road tube. **Open** 9am-9pm Tue-Fri; 9am-5pm Sat, Sun. **No credit cards**.

Puddleduck Parties

8893 8998/www.puddleduckparties.co.uk.
Ordinarily stressful party preparations flow like water off Puddleduck's back, so why not pass on the burden of booking entertainment, baking the cake and sorting out the goody bags? PP's list of quacking good party themes can satisfy children of all ages – Teddy Bears' Picnics for the youngest, perhaps, or Batman birthdays for the more heroically inclined – and provides the option of drama parties, sports parties and discos for older kids. Phone for more details.

Splodge

7350 1477/www.planetsplodge.com.
If your kids are balking at the prospect of a birthday down the local burger joint, fly them to Splodge. Trained actors – or 'Splodgas' – immerse groups of up to 20 kids in a choice of themed environments at either Battersea Park or Holland Park. Parties range from Bombay Dreams to girl band rehearsals, with optional extras like Stegosaurus Sandwiches, face-painting and video footage of the big day (from £295). Parties last two hours, with craft activities included. Prices are from £295 for ten kids, and lunch boxes can be provided (£7.85 per child). Events at a second venue, the Nature Study Centre on Wandsworth Common (8871 3863), follow a similar format: imaginative adventures are followed by tea, traditional games and a treasure trail, with gifts that mini safari hunters haul in with nets. Prices start at £295 for 20 children.

Twizzle Parties

8789 3232/www.twizzle.co.uk.
Twizzle has been turning kids' parties into magical occasions for more than 20 years, establishing a reputation as one of London's finest organisers. They put on different events for different age groups: imaginative, toddlers will enjoy a visit by the double-decker fun bus (£350) or a giant bubble-blowing party (£125); and there are circus, pirate and beach themes for small children and a highly popular creepy-crawly party for their older siblings (£280). Wannabe pop stars can cut their own CD and music video in a real London recording studio (£350 for two hours, with up to 16 kids) and take away a copy to play repeatedly at home.

Paraphernalia

Mail order

Baker Ross

Unit 53, Millmead Industrial Estate, Millmead Road, N17 9QU (enquiries 8808 6948/orders 0870 241 1867/ www.bakerross.co.uk). **Open** *Shop* Jan-Sept: 9am-5pm Mon-Fri. Oct-Dec: 9am-5pm Mon-Fri; 9am-1pm Sat. *Phone orders* 24hrs daily. **Credit** MC, V.
Aiming to put more than a balloon, a pencil and a piece of birthday cake in the party bags this year? Visit Baker Ross, wholesaler of educational materials and novelty gifts for schools, and now also supplier to the general public. One way to make a favourable impression on young party guests would be to give each boy and girl a teddy bear bearing his or her name on a printed sash (£1.85 for 12). The vast range of toys is equally appealing, and runs from stretchy aliens (£1.32 for six) to glitter-filled water bracelets (£2.40 for 12). Phone or visit the website for the catalogue.

Party Directory

14 Woodbourne, Farnham, Surrey GU9 9EF (01252 336100/www.partydirectory4kids.co.uk). **Open** *Phone orders* 9.30am-6pm Mon-Fri; 9am-noon Sat. **Credit** MC, V.

This mail order catalogue contains everything you could need to make even the most last-minute celebration look like it was planned months in advance. Themed tableware will convert living rooms into party palaces, with paper plates, cups and tablecloths, matching balloons and invitations in styles such as Pirate's Treasure, Prehistoric or Party Girl (items sold separately). Accessories like conical hats (eight for £1.55), animal masks (50p) and Happy Birthday banners (£1.25) can also be supplied. Phone for the catalogue.

Party Pieces

Child's Court Farm, Ashampstead Common, Berks RG8 8QT (01635 201844/www.partypieces.co.uk). **Credit** MC, V.
With 15 years of mail order experience under its belt and more than 500,000 parties catered for, Party Pieces is possibly the best supplier of activities and accessories you'll find. Their huge range of themed tableware includes famous faces like the Tweenies and the unstoppable Harry Potter (items sold separately), while themes for older kids offer ingenious spins on ever-popular themes: the Action Man jeep-shaped cup holder, for example, or a girly version in the shape of a stagecoach (both 55p each). There are loads of party bag fillers, traditional games (the Pin the Tail on the Donkey stalwart costs a very reasonable £1.95), and a whopping range of banners, balloons and assorted decorations.

Partyworks

The Buffer Depot, Badminton Road, Acton Turville, Glos GL9 1HE (0870 240 2103/www.partybypost.co.uk). **Open** *Enquiries & orders* 9am-5.30pm Mon-Fri. **Credit** MC, V.
As well as the practical necessities and decorative accessories, Partyworks offers a lifesaving selection of last-minute presents: most are stocking fillers, but some – like the Kick And Go practice football (£7.99), or the his 'n' hers Teach The Time watches (£9.99) – are spot on. There's themed tableware (with luminaries like Harry Potter and Pooh Bear alongside generic pirate and princess types), plus plenty of costumes, invitation cards and a good range of cake tins and novelty candles to spice up the culinary side of proceedings.

Purple Planet

Unit 36, The Wenta Business Centre, Watford WD24 7ND (8969 4119/www.purpleplanet.co.uk). **Open** by appointment only 10am-5pm Mon-Fri; 10am-2pm Sat. **Credit** AmEx, MC, V.
Purple Planet's original Portobello party shop is sadly no more, but the beat goes on to the tune of an online mail order service. Many items are still available: helium balloons from 85p, a good selection of themed partyware and, most importantly, the fine selection of sugarcraft accessories and cookie cutters (from 90p to £19.99) for which the Planet is best known. And when it comes to the birthday centrepiece, there's everything you could think of to put on a truly magnificent cake, from opulent fountain candles (£2.50 each) to edible paint: check the new website or phone for a catalogue.

Shops

Balloon and Kite Company

613 Garratt Lane, SW18 (8946 5962/www.balloonand kite.com). Tooting Broadway tube/Earlsfield rail. **Open** 9am-5.30pm Mon-Sat. **Credit** AmEx, MC, V.
With all that helium in store, it's a wonder London's premier supplier of party balloons has never accidentally relocated. Floating balloons are available in rubber or foil (£1 or £2.99 apiece), bearing images of bright-eyed characters like Barney, while personalised names can be added to Happy Birthday

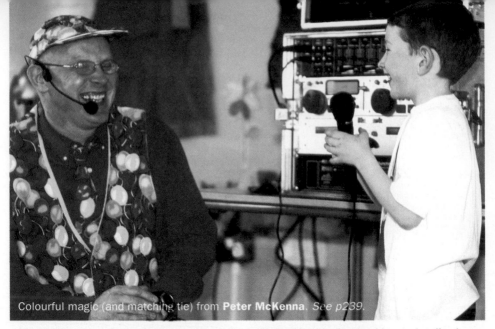

Colourful magic (and matching tie) from **Peter McKenna**. *See p239.*

variants while you wait (£3.24 each). There's also a nice line in paper tableware for many of the more popular party themes, while kites (from £10) make for good last-minute gift ideas. Delivery in London is available for orders over £10 – but alas they don't float them in by balloon.

Balloonland
12 Hale Lane, NW7 (8906 3302/www.balloonland.co.uk). Edgware tube/Mill Hill Broadway rail. **Open** 9.30am-5.30pm Mon-Fri; 10am-5.30pm Sat. **Credit** MC, V.
Probably best known as professional decorator for large-scale celebrations and corporate events, Balloonland also offers a range of products to lend children's parties a touch of the spectacular. Foil balloons come at £3.25 each (or less if bought in bulk) and are available in a staggering variety of shapes and sizes. The choice is inflated further by various designer creations (balloon clusters, jumbo balloon trees and balloons attached to soft toys or chocolate boxes), as well as themed tableware and decorations such as birthday banners (from £2.99). If none of that fits the bill, they can print personalised latex balloons in batches of 25 for £30.

Circus Circus
176 Wandsworth Bridge Road, SW6 (7731 4128/www.partysource.co.uk). Fulham Broadway tube. **Open** 10am-6pm Mon-Sat. **Credit** AmEx, MC, V.
If you have a particular kids' party them in mind – one with a police twist, for example, or one featuring pirates of the high seas – Circus Circus will supply everything that's needed to bring the whole thing to life, from the style of background music to the decorations; they'll even bake the right sort of cake, blow up the right balloons and bring the right entertainer to your home. Individual items are available for those who trust their own event co-ordination skills, including children's costumes from £10.99, invitation cards, bouncy castles and a useful supply of kiddie sized chairs and tables for hire (£1.49 and £4.99 each respectively).

Just Balloons
127 Wilton Road, SW1 (7434 3039/www.justballoons. com). Victoria tube/rail. **Open** 9am-6pm Mon-Fri; 10am-5pm Sat. **Credit** AmEx, MC, V. **Map** p318 J10.

A thoroughly misleading name for a store that offers the complete party package – bunting, bubble blowers, face paints, party poppers et al – but one which gives a good indication of the inflatable empire lying behind these tiny doors. Foil balloons come in a range of styles from £2.95 each, and novelty balloons like animal-shaped foils or floating pieces of fruit can be had from £4.99 a pop. Balloons can also be printed with personalised messages, although more extravagant types may want to relive some memorable moment with a printed photograph balloon (£67.78 for 25).

Mexicolore
28 Warriner Gardens, SW11 (7622 9577/www.pinata. co.uk). Battersea Park or Queenstown Road rail. **Open** by appointment only. **No credit cards**.
Children bored with pinning a tail on the donkey might prefer to smash the thing to pieces. Such gratifyingly violent antics are a traditional feature of a Mexican Christmas, and are becoming increasingly popular at children's parties in this country. The animal target, known as a piñata, is made of papier mâché and can be filled with fruit, sweets or small toys (staff at this friendly store are happy to take care of this side of things for an extra fee), and lovingly decorated and designed. Piñatas are available here in various animal forms, from a small fish (£24.50) to a large elephant (£58). When you see the finished item you may well feel a pang to think that, come party time, blindfolded guests will be queuing up to take turns at whacking it with a stick, as the host raises and lowers it to the amusement of those watching. When will the piñata break? Who will reap the most copious rewards?

The Non-Stop Party Shop
214-16 Kensington High Street, W8 (7937 7200/www.nonstopparty.co.uk). High Street Kensington tube. **Open** 9.30am-6pm Mon-Sat; 11am-5pm Sun. **Credit** AmEx, MC, V. **Map** p314 A9.
As its name implies, this is a fully operational fun factory. The Non-Stop Party Shop has a wealth of accessories to make memorable occasions of even the smallest kids' events, which means themed tableware, plenty of dressing-up materials, with hats from around the world (from the starchy would-be aristo top hat to the battered Australian bushwhacker's head-

piece, starting at £3), a range of plastic *Thunderbirds* masks (£2.50) and – to complete the look – a range of decorative face paints for clowns and proper little princesses alike (£3.99).

Oscar's Den
127-9 Abbey Road, NW6 (7328 6683/www.oscarsden.com). Swiss Cottage tube/West Hampstead tube/rail. **Open** 9.30am-5.30pm Mon-Sat; 10am-2pm Sun. **Credit** MC, V.
Looking nothing like the rubbish bin occupied by the loveable grouch from *Sesame Street*, Oscar's Den is instead an Aladdin's cave of party-related paraphernalia, and has a sturdy reputation for excellence. Its staff have organised kids' parties, on more than one occasion, for none other than the Prime Minister. They don't only co-ordinate grand affairs for famous personages, however: celebrations cater for individual budgets, and their range of services runs from face paints to year-round firework displays. Ball ponds, bouncy castles (from £40) and big toys (seesaws, slides, pedal-cars and more, from £10) are permanently for hire, and individual items are always on sale in the store: drop in some time for inspiration, or phone for a list of prices.

Party Party
11 Southampton Road, NW5 (7267 9084/ www.party partyuk.com). Chalk Farm tube/Gospel Oak rail. **Open** 9.30am-5.30pm Mon-Sat. **Credit** MC, V.
Family run for more than a decade, David and Lou's incredibly well stocked little store has over the years brought the personal touch to thousands of kids' parties across London. These days their range is hard to beat, with a bespoke piñata service offering any character, animal or object you desire, and a whole catalogue of party bag fillers, from 5p stickers to £5 soft toys and beyond. Fireworks are sold all year round, decorations cover everything from balloons to mirror balls, and there's a good range of dressing up costumes (from around £10) and accessories, including all the usual pirate swords, devil forks and angel wings.

Party Superstore
268 Lavender Hill, SW11 (7924 3210/www.partysuper store.co.uk). **Open** 9am-6pm Mon-Wed, Fri, Sat; 9am-7pm Thur; 10.30am-4.30pm Sun. **Credit** AmEx, MC, V.

Psycho therapist

With more than 30 years in the business, **Ali Do Lali** (*01494 774300*) can rightly claim to have pioneered many tricks and illusions that are now par for the course at children's parties. He discovered magic at the age of six, and started winning competitions at 16, but his dad insisted (as dads do) that conjuring remain a hobby, and the young Ali stuck to his studies.

Ali's skills were honed and his routines were perfected during any spare time he had after qualifying as a pathologist (specialising in haematology) and, appropriately enough, working as resident hypnotherapist at his local psychology department. 'Back in those days, if you didn't pull a rabbit out of a hat at some point, you weren't a real magician', says Ali. So he trained rabbits not only to sit in hats, but also to leap on to his back, then walk from shoulder to shoulder in an 'it's behind you' routine that had young audiences in stitches. 'These days', he adds, 'kids want more elaborate illusions, because of what they see on TV.'

Again, Ali obliges, swallowing razor blades, levitating kids, decapitating dads and appearing to saw volunteers in half (usually exhausted mums looking for any excuse to lie down). The shows are age appropriate: under-fives are treated to more gentle trickery and balloon modelling, with the explosive stuff saved for over-12s.

But all the pyrotechnics in the world can't cover up discomfort around kids. 'To be a successful entertainer, you have to enjoy working with kids', says Ali. 'If

you're enjoying yourself, they start enjoying themselves.' Much has changed since he started out, and not just in terms of the tricks: despite the huge number of party magicians available for hire these days, Ali remains one of the most likeable and professional there is, no longer tied to routines and able to milk hilarity from the strangest, most unpredictable places.

The late Roald Dahl, a patient at Ali's hospital in the '80s, was so impressed with the entertainer's way with kids that he asked him to perform for his own grandchildren: and you don't get greater praise than that.

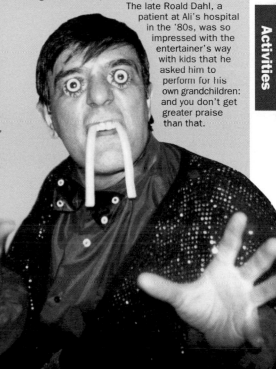

Activities

For 12 years the Superstore has been supplying London's fun lovers with all the tools of their trade. The first floor is dedicated to children's party accessories, from quality fancy dress costumes (from £7.99) to novelty hats (from £1.99) and wigs (from £2.99), with most items are available for hire on the ground floor. There are also more than 50 themed tableware collections, many of which are suitable for children, as well as practical jokes, mock jewellery and a lovely collection of cake decorations and candles. Plus this year the city's biggest party shop is opening an adjoining branch and getting even bigger –in itself a cause for a celebration.

Venues

All aboard

Golden Hinde
St Mary Overie Dock, Cathedral Street, SE1 (0870 011 8700/www.goldenhinde.co.uk). London Bridge tube/rail. **Credit** MC, V. **Map** p321 P8.
Even the saltiest of sea dogs couldn't fail to be impressed by a pirate party aboard the mighty Golden Hinde. Moored between Shakespeare's Globe and London Bridge, the ship is a full-size, meticulously reconstructed version of the vessel used by Sir Francis Drake to circumnavigate the world in the late 1500s. Don't worry, though – your little sailors won't be going any further than the galley, where two costumed crew members greet and lead them on a series of shipshape activities: from a broadside and treasure hunt to hoisting the anchor and stories of adventure on the high seas.
After all that the bloodthirsty pirates will be ravenous, and luckily enough a sailor's meal of crisps, sandwiches and sausage rolls is on hand – all you provide is a cake. The minimum charge is £175 for 15 children (extra kids board for £10 each), and party bags can be provided. Children are encouraged to come in costume – preferably as pirates (cowboys will be made to walk the plank). Regular sleepovers are also organised for more dedicated ocean-goers looking to rough it in the ship's hold: phone for more information. *Shop.*

HMS Belfast
Morgan's Lane, Tooley Street, SE1 (7940 6328/ www.iwm.org.uk/belfast/). London Bridge tube/rail. **Credit** MC, V. **Map** p321 R8.
Soldiers taking part in the Normandy Landings never thought their beloved *Belfast* would one day be boarded by armies of under-16s armed with cakes and crumbly biscuits, but that's exactly what happens on a regular basis. For £75, one family per day (up to 26 kids) can hire a party room within the ship's hull: parents can provide their own refreshments or, for £5 per head, the onboard caters will supply basic food and drink (though you bring your own cake). A private tour of the *Belfast*, led by the charming Captain Corky, can also be arranged for an extra £100: in the various nautical activities involved, children get the chance to man the bridge, marvel at the gun turrets and even dress up in costume. *Buggy access. Café. Disabled access: toilet. Nappy-changing facilities. Nearest picnic area: quarterdeck. Shop.*

London Waterbus Company
58 Camden Lock Place, NW1 (7482 2550). Camden Town tube. **No credit cards.**
Bobbing along the Thames on your own private 70ft canal boat can make for a truly memorable birthday experience – but make sure you wait for good weather before you give it a try, or it may be a birthday you'll never be able to forget.

TOP FIVE Venues

For movie magic
Screen West. *See p246.*

For bobbing merrily along
London Waterbus Company. *See p246.*

For walking the plank
Golden Hinde. *See p246.*

For video games
Namco Station. *See p248.*

For horsing about
Westway Stables. *See p241.*

Up to 20 children can take to the water for two or three hours (£190 or £255 respectively), with parents allowed to bring their own food, decorations and whatever entertainment they see fit (even a clown, providing he's seaworthy). The route runs return between Camden Lock and Little Venice: which end you start from is entirely up to you.
It's a luxury that many parents won't be able to afford, although that's no reason for them to resign themselves to dry land. If the party's small enough, why not just buy standard return fares (£4 kids, £6.20 adults), and break up the trip with a picnic at one end? Even better, special reduced rate tickets are available that combine a boat ride with entry to London Zoo (at the Camden End), and a trip back down the river (£9.40 kids, £12.90 adults).

Cinemas

BFI London IMAX Cinema
1 Charlie Chaplin Walk, South Bank, Waterloo, SE1 (7902 1234/group bookings 7960 3120/www.bfi.org.uk). Waterloo tube/rail. **Credit** AmEx, MC, V. **Map** p319 M8.
The dimensions of the IMAX cinema make most other big screens in the West End look like wind-up radios. The sheer scale of the place also makes it a dramatic party venue, and any group of ten or more gets a discounted ticket rate (kids £4.20, adults £6.20). There are usually four or five films to choose from at any given time (most tend to last about an hour), and all are suitable for children. After the movie, you can choose to have birthday tea in the Film Café. For £5.95 per child (between five and ten years old), staff can organise a suitably lightweight selection of party food, from mini pizzas and sausage rolls to sandwiches and a drink: phone 7960 3118 (after 1pm) for more information. *Buggy access. Café. Concessions stand. Disabled access: lift, toilet. Nappy-changing. Nearest pinic place: Jubilee Gardens.*

Screen West
The New Boat House, 136-42 Bramley Road, W10 (7565 3030/bookings 7565 3102/www.screenwest.co.uk). Latimer Road tube. **Credit** MC, V.
Children who'd rather not spend their big screen birthday experience craning to see over a selection of oversized heads can banish adults altogether (or at least boss them around in the seating arrangements) at Screen West. A special 74-seat screening room is hired out for parties, with children able to bring along their favourite video or DVD to watch. A separate function room with sofas, tables, chairs and a CD player is also on hand, and seats up to 30 children: parents can

Activities

provide whatever food, drink and additional entertainment they wish, but are expected to clean up after themselves. Prices start at £200 for up to two hours; phone for details.

Museums

Museum of Childhood at Bethnal Green

Cambridge Heath Road, E2 (8983 5200/recorded info 8980 2415/www.museumofchildhood.org.uk). Bethnal Green tube/rail. **No credit cards**.

The mostly static displays at the Museum of Childhood may be better suited to nostalgic adults than their Pokemon generation offspring, but parties here are informal, enjoyable affairs. The facilities include a specially decorated party room, complete with kitchen facilities for parents bringing food and tableware (there's no catering, although staff will take care of the clean-up operation), and exclusive use of the soft play area as an optional extra (from 2.55pm). Parents also provide their own music and entertainment, although galleries and exhibits are free to the group until closing (5.50pm), which means dinner may be best left till later. Hire of the party room is £50 for a maximum of 12 kids, with 40 minutes in the soft play area for an extra £30.

Buggy access. Café. Disabled access: toilet. Nappy-changing facilities. Shop. Nearest picnic place: museum grounds.

Science Museum

Exhibition Road, SW7 (7942 4747/www.sciencemuseum. org.uk). South Kensington tube. **Credit** AmEx, MC, V. **Map** p315 D9.

There may be no designated party set-up during the day, but the Science Museum offers something even more special at night. For £27 per child, a minimum of five children (and one adult, £20) can indulge in the most exciting sleepover of all time. As of 7pm, the empty halls are theirs alone, with a fantastic series of displays, shows and demonstrations to both entertain and enlighten the little Einsteins. The next morning (kids pitch up with sleeping bags and kip in one of the main rooms) an early breakfast is provided, with the option of staying on for more fun in the day. A brilliant party idea, blighted only by the need to book months in advance.

Playgrounds & games

Bramley's Big Adventure

136 Bramley Road, W10 (8960 1515/www.bramleysbig. co.uk). Latimer Road tube. **Open** 10am-6pm Mon-Fri; 10am-6.30pm Sat, Sun. Closed 25 Dec, 1 Jan, Aug bank hol. **Credit** AmEx, MC, V.

Bramley's isn't vast, which means that the quantities of attractions crammed into it (slides, ball parks, monkey swings) provoke almost deafening chaos when wild packs of delighted kids are let loose. Parties cost from £7 per head on weekdays and £10 at weekends, and offer 75 minutes in the playground followed by 45 minutes in the party room (divided by a curtain to separate smaller parties, which isn't ideal). Food is provided (hot dogs, chicken nuggets and the like), as are party bags. Silver and gold packages are available (£12 and £14 per child respectively), with extra large party bags, helium balloons and other treats, and for £12.50 Barney the Brontosaur spends 20 minutes amusing the kids.

Buggy storage. Café. Disabled access: toilet. Nappy-changing facilities. Shop.

Clown Town

222 Green Lanes, N13 (8886 7520). Southgate tube. **Open** 10am-7pm daily. **No credit cards**.

Clown Town is a typically rowdy playground, equipped with all the climbing nets, treehouses and Tarzan ropes needed to

Clown Town

help parties go with a swing. For £7.50 each, up to 35 kids (minimum of ten in the week, 12 at weekends) spend one hour clambering about, and then a second hour in the party room upstairs, where food, drink and ice cream are provided alongside a small party bag to take home. There's no top age limit, but there is a 4ft 9in height restriction on entry to the park. *Buggy access. Café. Disabled access: toilet. Nappy-changing facilities. Nearest picnic place: Broomfield Park.*

Coram's Fields
93 Guilford Street, WC1 (7837 6138). Russell Square tube. **Open** 9am-dusk daily. Admission free (adults admitted only if accompanied by a child under 16). **No credit cards. Map** p317 L4.
Set up in the 18th century as a Foundling Hospital by Thomas Coram (a children's charity still operates in his name), the Fields are now a brilliant spot for a party, with plenty of play areas to keep children amused: a sand pit, several climbing frames, a helter-skelter, swings, and – in summer – a paddling pool. Perhaps the greatest attraction is the small animal pen, with sheep, goats and rabbits adding a furry and lovable element to an already pleasant day. At weekends rooms at the Fields can be rented – complete with kitchen facilities – from £30, with parents providing food and entertainment.

Discovery Planet
Surrey Quays Shopping Centre, Redriff Road, SE16 (7237 2388/www.discovery-planet.co.uk). Surrey Quays tube. **Open** 10am-6pm Mon-Sat; 11am-5pm Sun. **Credit** (over £10) MC, V.
Parties at Discovery Planet come in gold, silver or bronze packages (£10.99, £8.99 or £6.99 per child respectively, with reduced rates Mon-Thur). Some things they have in common: kids always get 75 minutes on the extensive indoor playground followed by 45 minutes in a private party room (with their own party host to provide fun and games). But while the bronze party includes ice cream, balloons and a goody bag for each child, the silver one throws in food from Burger King and bigger party bags all round, and the gold deal rounds it all off with a birthday cake. Still, kids are there primarily to act up in the playground: the rest is just icing. *Buggy access. Disabled access: lift. Nappy-changing facilities. Nearest picnic place: Southwark Park.*

Kidzmania
28 Powell Road, E5 (8533 5556). Clapton rail. **Open** 10am-6.30pm daily. **No credit cards.**
Kidzmania parties combine 90 minutes of tearaway heaven on the usual slides, chutes and ropes with 40 minutes of food and fun in a designated party room. The price is £8 per child aged one to 12, with a minimum of 12 children and a maximum of 40 – as if anyone under 12 could possibly have more than 40 friends. Or anyone over 12, for that matter. *Buggy access. Café. Car park. Nappy-changing facilities.*

Namco Station
County Hall (riverfront entrance), Westminster Bridge Road, SE1 (7967 1066/www.namcostation.co.uk). Westminster tube/Waterloo tube/rail. **Open** 10am-midnight daily. Closed 25 Dec. **Admission** free. **Credit** MC, V. **Map** p319 M9.
Namco Station means aural and visual overload, with more than 200 video game arcades, state-of-the-art dodgems and a bowling alley to leave kids in ways that musical chairs can't match. Most games cost 50p or £1 a go; dodgems are £2 per car and bowling costs £2 per person per game. Party groups can buy tokens in bulk with a £2 discount on every £10 spent, though even then you may end up spending far more than planned. Inconveniently, there's nowhere to eat or drink on

site (the bar is for adults only), though there's an enormous McDonald's with a good view of the river next door. *Buggy access. Disabled access: toilet. Nearest picnic place: Jubilee Gardens.*

Snakes and Ladders
Syon Park, Brentford, Middx (8847 0946/www.syonpark. co.uk). Gunnersbury tube then 237, 267 bus. **Open** 10am-6pm (last entry 5.15pm) daily. **Credit** MC, V.
All three tiers of indoor adventure here are available to children for birthday packages. Kids get 90 minutes of madness in the playground, then half an hour of food and fun in the party room, with a private host to oversee proceedings. Party bags and invitations are provided, and the price is £7.95 per head with cold food (sausage rolls, crisps, sandwiches), or £8.95 with hot food (nuggets, pizza or burger and chips). *Buggy access. Café. Car park. Disabled access: toilet. Nappy-changing facilities. Picnic area on site.*

Take in a show

Jackson's Lane
269A Archway Road, N6 (8340 5226/www.jacksonslane. org.uk). Highgate tube. **Credit** MC, V.
Saturday kids' shows at Jackson's Lane (11am and 2pm, for three- to eight-year-olds) are justifiably popular, and party rooms can be rented out for after-show dos. Three rooms are available at £50 for one or £75 for two, and catering of the nuggets and chips variety (£3.50 per child) can be provided by Chef Kwaks at the Veggie House theatre café (8348 7666), though you may prefer to bring your own. Tickets for the performance (normally £4 each) are £3 each for party bookings. *Buggy access. Café. Nappy-changing facilities. Nearest picnic place: Highgate Wood.*

Lyric Hammersmith
King Street, W6 (08700 500 511/www.lyric.co.uk). Hammersmith tube. **Open** Enquiries 10am-7pm Mon-Sat. **Tickets** from £7 adults; £5 under-16s, concessions. **Credit** AmEx, DC, MC, V.
The Lyric supplies great birthday entertainment, and while there are no reduced rates for group bookings (kids £5.50, adults £7), parties can be held in the foyer at Café Brera (8741 9291). Two menus are available, both of which venture beyond the usual sausage rolls and crisps routine: a cold menu includes sandwiches, fruit and biscuits (£3.50 per child); hot food is pizza or pasta (£4.50 per child), and parents are welcome to bring their own cake. Parties are for a minimum of five and a maximum of 30 kids, and food is served at noon or 2pm to coincide with the 11am or 1pm performance. *Buggy access. Café. Disabled access: lift, toilet. Nappy-changing facilities. Nearest picnic place: Riverside. Shop.*

Puppet Theatre Barge
opposite 35 Blomfield Road, Little Venice, W9 (7249 6876/www.puppetbarge.com). Warwick Avenue tube. **Credit** MC, V. **Map** p312 C4.
The puppet barge is a brilliant place for a truly magical birthday party. Tickets for the children's performances (weekends and daily in school holidays, usually at 3pm) are £6.50 for kids and £7 for adults, and for £50 extra the boat can be rented out for an hour of fun, games and feasting once the rest of the audience has left (parents bring their own food). Better still, kids can be treated to a private performance for £295, which includes an hour on the barge afterwards. The boat is moored at Little Venice between November and June: for the rest of the year it's off on a tour of the Thames (*see p216*). *Drinks kiosk. Nearest picnic place: Rembrandt Gardens.*

Sport & Leisure

Don't vegetate: we have ways to turn couch potatoes into runner beings.

With school now dominated by league tables, SATs and academic pressure, sport can seem like an also-ran. Yet alarming statistics about the unhealthy state of British children show how vital physical education still is. The skills it develops are essential if kids are to enjoy life to the full.

The capital plays every kind of sport, from classic team games like cricket, rugby and football to fashionable individual pursuits such as yoga and martial arts. There are hundreds of venues and options to suit all budgets, and London is also well provided with child-friendly facilities and qualified instructors. And as if that weren't enough, there are major sports clubs like Arsenal, London Towers, and Harlequins, plus hounds that race and bangers that crash with aplomb – great for spectating too.

Note that class details and opening times change frequently, so you'll also need to check this information first; for many classes and most courses you'll need to book in advance. For many more athletic ideas and contacts, see the *Time Out Sport Health and Fitness Guide* (£8.99).

PARTICIPATION SPORTS

American football

Wildly popular across the pond, American football has no such following in the UK. Still, the **London Capitals Youth American Football Club** (Finsbury Park Sports Arena, N4, 8265 1156/www.capitals.scsuk.net) accepts members between 14 and 20, and those outside that range can come and train on Sunday mornings. Standards and success rates are high.

Athletics

Track and field is a vibrant sport, and most clubs run a junior section for children aged nine and over. There are 18 disciplines in athletics, from sprinting to shot putt, triple jump to javelin: most children, whatever their size, will find one they're good at.

If your kids want to try athletics, contact senior UK Athletics coach **Maureen Jones** (8224 7579/ 07956 807689), who organises 'Run, Jump, Throw' courses during the school holidays at several tracks around London for eights to 13s. Courses run from 10am until 3pm and cost £12 per day.

South of England Athletics Association

Suite 1, 23 Mitcham Lane, SW16 (8664 7244/ www.seaa.org.uk).
The SEAA has details of clubs around London; there's also a national directory at www.british-athletics.co.uk. The following clubs have sections for young athletes.
Belgrave Harriers *Carl Lawton (8669 0971/ www.belgraveharriers.com).*
Blackheath Harriers *John Baldwin (01825 768193/ www.blackheath-harriers.org.uk).*
Enfield & Haringey AC *Ray Gibbins (8805 6543/ www.enfield-haringeyac.co.uk).*
Havering Mayesbrook AC *Doug Tierney (01708 341547/www.havering-mayesbrook.org).*
Newham & Essex Beagles AC *Gaye Strevens (01708 349597).*
Shaftesbury Barnet Harriers *Joyce Smith (01923 672945/www.shaftesburybarnetharriers.co.uk).*
Thames Valley Harriers *Kathy Davidson (01895 676513/www.thamesvalleyharriers.com).*
Windsor, Slough, Eton & Hounslow AC *Contact Dennis Daly (01753 686169).*
Woodford Green AC with Essex Ladies *Keith Hopson (8524 1959/www.woodfordgac-essexl.org.uk).*

Badminton & squash

Both sports have junior development programmes. The **Badminton Association of England** (01908 268400/www.baofe.co.uk) or **England Squash** (0161 231 4499/www.englandsquash.co.uk) to locate a club near you. The following all have junior programmes; phone for prices and times.

Dulwich Sports Club
Burbage Road, SE21 (7274 1242). Herne Hill rail.

New Grampian Squash Club
Shepherd's Bush Road, W6 (7603 4255). Hammersmith tube.

Southgate Squash Club
Walker Cricket Ground, Waterfall Road, N14 (8886 8381/www.thewalkerground.org.uk). Southgate tube.

Wimbledon Racquets & Fitness Club
Cranbrook Road, SW19 (8947 5806). Wimbledon tube/rail.

Baseball & softball

These two sports have joined forces to create a single agency, **BaseballSoftballUK** (7453 7000/ www.baseballsoftball.com), which aims to boost the number of young players. The organisation has put

Howzat!

Just over a decade ago, only 24 primary schools out of more than 800 in the Inner London boroughs taught even the most basic form of cricket and the sport seemed in terminal decline. Now, thanks to pioneering organisations like Capital Kids Cricket and initiatives developed by the counties and local clubs around London, England's traditional summer game can look forward to a bright future.

Cricket can seem complicated, but variations on the game have been developed to make learning the basics fun. Kwik Cricket is a soft-ball game using plastic equipment and is ideal for kids up to 11. Inter-Cricket also uses a soft ball, is aimed at 12- to 14-year-olds and can be played on tarmac, grass or a roll-up plastic pitch. These act as a feeder to hard-ball Terrier Cricket, in which kids bat in pairs and lose runs whenever they're 'out'.

There's a strong emphasis on safety in hard-ball cricket, with all under-16s required to wear a helmet when batting, wicket-keeping or fielding close to the wicket. Most clubs will provide this, along with the other essential protective equipment, until a youngster opts to play regularly.

The four County Cricket Boards around London (and the Hertfordshire Cricket Association) are also involved in coaching and matchplay projects with clubs and schools, and both Middlesex and Surrey organise courses during school holidays. Middlesex have even appointed a development officer specifically for girls' and women's cricket. To find out what's happening, or for details of suitable clubs running junior sections, contact the following county representatives: Essex (Rob Hayne, 01245 254035); Hertfordshire (Derek Dredge, 01707 658377); Kent (David Sear, 01227 456886); Middlesex (*Girls* Lorraine Poole, 07890 806711; *Boys* David Holland, 7266 1650). Surrey (*Under-10s* Brian Ruby, 01483 453531; 11s-16s Karen Meaney 7820 5734).

When it comes to spectating, Lord's (*see p93*) and the AMP Oval (*see p128*) stage at least one Test match and limited-overs international each summer, as well as county matches. Tickets for England matches must be booked in advance (for county matches you can pay on the gate) and information is usually released the preceding winter. Call or check the websites for details. The season runs from mid-April to mid-September.

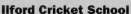

Capital Kids Cricket

Lord's Cricket Ground, St John's Wood Rd, NW8 (7226 2705).
Set up by volunteers in 1990, this charity helped reintroduce the game to more than 700 primary schools and now works with secondary schools. Adults can support the scheme by joining the London Heavy Rollers Club for £10. Website: www.capitalkidscricket.co.uk.

Ilford Cricket School

Sussex Close, Beehive Lane, Ilford, Essex (8550 0041).
Run by Joe Hussain (Nasser's dad), this useful local centre offers nets, bowling machine, video analysis and coaching. The England Test captain has been known to pop in!

Ken Barrington Cricket Centre

AMP Oval, SE11 (7820 5739/ www.surreycricket.com).
This centre has six nets, bowling machines, video analysis and a shop. It's used for some of Surrey's excellent coaching courses.

MCC Indoor School

Lord's Cricket Ground, St John's Wood Rd, NW8 (7432 1014/www.mcc.org.uk).
Regular users include Middlesex players and international stars. Individuals can also use the superb facilities, and the regular sessions can be booked with or without cricket coaches.

Middlesex County Cricket Centre

East End Road, N3 (8346 8020/www.middlesexccc.com).
This is the home of Middlesex's 'academy', and it organises a host of holiday courses for players of all ages and standards. Fine facilities and coaching.

Peter May Centre

135 Wadham Road, E17 (8531 9358/ www.solutionsfitness.com).
This purpose-built centre has six nets for hire.

together impressive packages, entitled 'Pitch, Hit and Run' and 'Play Ball', to teach the basics in schools and clubs to children aged six upwards.

Windsor is an established centre for junior baseball. Based at Windsor Boys School, the 12-year-old Little League run by the Windsor Bears club attracts some 500 players, in age groups spanning the sixes to under-16s.

To find a club with junior teams, contact Geoff Ellingham (*08702 382134*) or one of the following.
Essex Darts *Phil Chesterton (01376 551254).*
London Baseball Association
(www.londonsports.com).
South London Ravens *Dave Ward (8656 5234).*
Thames Valley Softball Club *John Middlemist (0118 962 8469/www.tvsoftball.com).*
Windsor Baseball & Softball Club *John Boyd (07769 655496).*

Basketball

Hoops certainly has a cool image, and there are clubs all over the capital playing in local leagues. The sport is extremely well organised at junior level. For more details, contact regional development manager Steven Alexander (7641 5876) or the **English Basketball Association** (0113 236 1166/www.basketballengland.org.uk), who can put you in touch with a local club. The following clubs have established junior programmes.
Brixton Topcats *Brixton Recreation Centre, Station Road, SW9* (7737 3354).
Jimmy Rodgers runs mixed sessions from schools and the recreation centre, with players as young as six.
Croydon Flyers *Lewis Sports Centre, Maberley Road, SE19* (www.croydonflyers.com).
A girls' club for nines to 16s that plays against the best in the country. Weekend training sessions and matches.
Hackney Academy *SPACE, Hackney Community College, Falkirk Street, N1* (01702 298613).
The Academy incorporates 11 teams with facilities and coaching among the best in the capital. Boys and girls from 12 years old are welcome.
London United *Harrow High School, Gayton Road, Harrow* (07710 578346).
A merger between Ealing Tornados and North London Lords created this club, which has an academy for kids from 11-yearsolds upwards. There are plans to establish basketball scholarships at Brunel University for outstanding players.

Boxing

The rights or wrongs of boxing are for you to assess, but it would be unfair to deny kids the chance to try the sport if they show an interest. Boxing at amateur level has an impressive safety record, and children are simply not powerful enough to inflict the sort of damage that has disfigured the professional game. The **Amateur Boxing Association of England** (8778 0251/www.abae.org.uk) lists local clubs.

Climbing

Climbing demands a unique blend of physical and mental agility, which explains why reaching the top brings such enormous satisfaction. London's indoor centres all cater for kids over eight, with safe, structured sessions run by qualified instructors.
For information on climbing, contact the **British Mountaineering Council** (0870 010 4878).

Castle Climbing Centre
Green Lanes, N4 (8211 7000/www.castle-climbing.co.uk). Manor House tube. **Open** 2-10pm Mon-Fri; 10am-7pm Sat, Sun. **Admission** Registration £4 (adults only). Visits £7.50; £3.50 children (accompanied by a climbing adult/ instructor).
This atmospheric Grade II-listed Victorian pumping station was designed to look like Scotland's Stirling Castle. But it's as if the folly was built with its current use in mind, since it has a 120ft drop ideal for aspiring spiderboys and girls. It runs the Geckos children's club on Friday evenings and weekend mornings, and on midweek afternoons during school holidays. A two-hour session costs £16. The minimum age is eight for unaccompanied children; with a climbing adult, children can be any age.

Mile End Climbing Wall
Haverfield Road, E3 (8980 0289/www.mileendwall.org.uk). Mile End tube. **Open** noon-9.30pm Mon-Thur; noon-9pm Fri; 10am-6pm Sat, Sun. **Admission** Registration £4, then £6/session. Children's introduction £6 Fri; £5 Sat, Sun.
Located in a converted pipe-bending factory, this centre runs children's sessions every Friday evening and Saturday morning, as well as birthday parties and a summer holiday programme. You can't miss this place at peak times: banging jungle tunes and general commotion alert you to its presence long before you reach the building.

Westway Climbing Complex
Westway Sports Centre, 1 Crowthorne Road, W10 (8969 0992/www.westway.org). Latimer Road tube. **Open** 10.30-10pm Mon-Fri; 10am-8pm Sat, Sun. **Admission** *Off peak* £5, £3 children. *Peak* after 5pm £6, £4 children.
This recently upgraded indoor centre beneath the rumbling Westway will inspire the novice and challenge the best of climbers. Active local children enjoy holding their birthday parties here (for more details, *see p158*).

Court sports

For those who enjoy netball's combination of speed, skill and sleight of hand, London has plenty of clubs running junior sections for girls aged 11 and up. The **All-England Netball Association** (01462 442344/ www.england-netball.co.uk) has addresses.

Volleyball, though a minor sport in this country, is great fun to play for children aged nine upwards. Many clubs around the capital run junior teams, with nine to fourteen-year-old beginners playing three-a-side 'mini volley' on a badminton-sized court with a lower net. To find your nearest set-up, contact the **London Volleyball Association** (07951 727595/www.whiteeaglesvc.org.uk).

Perfectly balanced at **Herne Hill Stadium**.

Cycling

Only two per cent of children cycle to school in the UK, but **Safe Routes to Schools** (0117 929 0888/ www.saferoutestoschools.org.uk) exists to change this state of affairs: for more information, see the *Official Guide to the National Cycle Network* by Nick Cotton and John Grimshaw (Sustrans, £9.99).

The **London Cycling Campaign** (Unit 228, 30 Great Guildford Street, SE1; 7928 7220/ www.lcc.org.uk) produces 19 free maps showing cycling routes across Greater London: you can get them at some tube stations, sports centres and bike shops, or from the 24-Hour Travel Information Line (7222 1234). The best guide to family rides around the capital is the *London Cycle Guide* (Haynes, £8.99), published in association with the LCC.

Cycle training

Cycle Training UK (7582 3535/ www.cycletraining.co.uk)
Male and female instructors offer individual tuition anywhere in Greater London, from complete beginners upwards with the emphasis on safe, confident road cycling. Accompanied journeys to school are also available.
London Recumbents (8299 6636)
Specialists in off-road training in Battersea and Dulwich Parks. Special bikes are available so that people of all abilities can enjoy learning to cycle.
London School of Cycling (7249 3779)
Private tuition for adults, teenagers accompanied by adults, and special needs.

Cycle sport

There are three main venues in London, all offering a range of activities for cyclists of every age – but Herne Hill Stadium is the capital's only purpose-built velodrome for racing. All have kids' clubs; phone the venues for details of times and prices.

Herne Hill Stadium
Burbage Road, SE24 (7737 4647). Herne Hill rail.
First opened in 1892 and used for the 1948 Olympics, the 450-metre banked concrete track is one of the fastest in the UK; there's also a new mountain bike track for dramatic bunny-hopping. Pedal Posse mountain bike camps run in the school holidays, along with cycling proficiency and skills courses.

Hillingdon Cycle Circuit
Springfield Road, Hayes, Middlesex (8570 3230). Hayes & Harlington rail.
This is a tarmac track for racing and tuition.

Lee Valley Cycle Circuit
Quarter Mile Lane, E15 (8534 6085/ www.leevalleypark.com). Leyton tube.
This 45-acre site has a tarmac track, a mountain bike/BMX circuit and Saturday morning sessions for fours to 16s.

Dance

If you're looking for a chance to dance, a useful resource is the **London Dance Network** (www.londondance.com), which has an extensive directory of dance venues and organisations. The following centres offer classes for children.

Chisenhale Dance Space
64-84 Chisenhale Road, E3 (8981 6617/ www.chisenhaledancespace.co.uk). Mile End tube.

Danceworks
16 Balderton Street, W1 (7629 6183/ www.danceworks.co.uk). Bond Street tube.

Drill Hall
16 Chenies Street, WC1 (7307 5060/www.drillhall.co.uk). Goodge Street tube.

Greenwich Dance Agency
Borough Hall, Royal Hill, SE10 (8293 9741/ www.greenwichdance.org.uk). Greenwich rail.

The Place
17 Duke's Road, WC1 (7387 7669/www.theplace.org.uk). Euston tube/rail.

Ravenscourt Theatre School
30-40 Dalling Road, W6 (8741 0707/ www.dramaschoollondon.com). Hammersmith/ Ravenscourt Park tube.

Rona Hart School of Dance
Rosslyn Hall, Willoughby Road, NW3 (7435 7073). Hampstead tube.

Tricycle Theatre
269 Kilburn High Road, NW6 (7328 1000/ www.tricycle.co.uk). Kilburn tube.

Disability sport

A number of organisations have responsibilities in this area, which – as the success of the Paralympic movement has shown – is finally being given the recognition and funding it deserves.

The Wimbledon Football Club, the Limbless Association and the One2One Ability Counts programme operated by the English Federation of Disability Sport have formed a partnership to provide regular training sessions with qualified coaches and opportunities to play in tournaments, plus free kit and match tickets. The junior squad welcomes players aged seven to 14. More details from 8788 1777/football@limbless-association.org.

Another development of note is TOP Sportsability, a package developed by the **Youth Sport Trust** (7278 7208/www.youthsporttrust.org) to encourage children to get involved in activities such as boccia.

Programmes are run by the following organisations: **British Blind Sport** (01926 424247/www.britishblindsport.org.uk); **British Deaf Sports Council** (www.britishdeafsportscouncil.org.uk); **English Sports Association for People with Learning Disability** (01924 267555/www.esapld.co.uk); **Limbless Association** (8788 1777/www.limbless-association.org).

British Wheelchair Sports Foundation

01296 395995/www.britishwheelchairsports.org.
This is the umbrella body for 17 wheelchair sports, from archery to rugby. It organises a number of major events each year at the National Wheelchair Sports Centre in Stoke Mandeville, Buckinghamshire, provides a comprehensive information service and is currently developing regional sports camps for children aged from six with disabilities.

English Federation of Disability Sport

0161 247 5294/www.efds.co.uk.
This is the umbrella organisation for disability sport. Its local office is the London Sports Forum for Disabled People (7354 8666/Minicom 7354 9554/www.londonsportsforum.org.uk).

Family fitness

The message is clear: one of the most effective ways parents can encourage their children into an active lifestyle is to exercise together – not necessarily in the same class, but by making a trip to the gym a family occasion. This helps children recognise that fitness is fun and for everyone, which means that they are (hopefully) more likely to keep up the regular exercise habit as they grow older.

A key advantage of choosing a chain over an independent operator is that membership often includes use of other UK, and even international, clubs. However, not all chains welcome kids, and some offer little beyond a crèche. Every centre has a different strategy, but the broad approach of each major chain is listed below.

Cannons

08707 808182/www.cannons.co.uk.
The upper-middle class of chains, with crèche facilities at most clubs, Easter and summer camps for kids and family holidays included in the Cannons Adventure brochure.

David Lloyd

08708 883015/www.davidlloydleisure.co.uk.
Far more than just a chain of tennis clubs. Kids are welcome here with crèche and nursery facilities, baby massage, soft play areas, specific kids' exercise classes and racket sports.

Esporta

0118912 3500/www.esporta.com.
Esporta has the best provision for kids and most family-friendly outlook of all the chains. Two levels of crèche, nurseries, outdoor playgrounds, sports activities for three-year-olds upwards, separate changing facilities, restaurants with times set aside for families as well as adults-only hours.

Get lost!

The sport of orienteering has been likened to tackling the *Times* crossword while out on a run. The aim of this 'cunning running' is to navigate around a course (which can vary in length from just over one mile to eight miles) from one control point to the next with the aid of a special map. For children, though, orienteering is all about hidden targets and an adventure in the woods. Few sports are more sociable and family-friendly – you can actually go round a course together – and it's a great way to add interest to a day out in the fresh air.

There are 14 clubs in the south-east, most organising regular competitions. These vary in standard, so the best way to find a suitable event or 'come and try it' day is to contact the **South-Eastern Orienteering Association** (8948 6056). Some club events include a special route for very young children (to be tackled with or without parents), with a line of string to take them round a set of controls marked by cartoon characters. Children who are keen to take up the sport competitively may be invited to join the regional junior squad run by the Association.

For a low-key introduction, try a 'permanent course'. There are nine in the capital, at places like **Barnes Common** or **Hampstead Heath** – and more than 40 in the surrounding countryside at locations like **Lee Valley Park** and **Harlow Park** in Essex, **Horton Country Park** near Epsom, **Redhill Common** in Surrey, and **Whippendell Woods** near Watford. These let you proceed at your own pace, and most are buggy-friendly. A leaflet listing permanent courses and sales points for maps is available free of charge from the **British Orienteering Federation** (01629 734042/www.britishorienteering.org.uk).

Holmes Place

7795 4100/www.holmesplace.com.
The princess of the chains, with a slightly haughty attitude to match. All clubs have childcare facilities for under-fives, while child access to the pool, restaurant and club room is available at certain times.

Park Club

East Acton Lane, W3 (8743 4321/www.mytpc.co.uk).
There are plenty of facilities for kids at what feels like a posh country club in an urban setting, including the Ark in the Park, tennis courts, two indoor pools and one outdoor.

Topnotch

8232 6800/www.topnotchhealthclubs.com.
Centres with pools offer kids' swimming during quiet times.

Fencing

If you're seeking a sport with real cut and thrust, fencing is for you. It's physically demanding, very skilful and a cool alternative for kids who don't like team games. You can begin fencing young: at the Finchley Foil Fencing Club, youngsters aged eight to 16 turn up every Saturday afternoon for two hours of enthusiastic swishing.

Most junior classes involve warm-up activities to develop co-ordination, flexibility and balance, formal work towards the nine fencing grades and finally the best bit: free fighting. The sport has a strong safety ethic, and no one is ever allowed to participate without protective clothing and the supervision of a qualified instructor.

Contact the **British Fencing Association** (8742 3032/www.britishfencing.com) for details of fencing clubs. Ring the ones listed below before turning up.

Egham Fencing Club

Egham Sports Centre, Vicarage Road, Egham, Surrey (Terry Albano, 01784 243518). Egham rail.

Finchley Foil Fencing Club

Copthall School, NW7 (Clare Halsted, 7485 1498). Mill Hill tube.

Haverstock Fencing Club

Haverstock School, Haverstock Hill, NW1 (7267 0975). Belsize Park tube.

Kingston Fencing Club

Beverley School, Blakes Lane, New Malden, Surrey (Karen Vinson, 8943 2157). Motspur Park rail.

King's College & Wimbledon High School Joint Fencing Club

Southside Common, SW19 (8255 5300). Wimbledon tube/rail.

Salle Paul Fencing Club

Highgate School, The Old Gym, Hampstead Road, N6 (Tony Coton, 8640 4702). Highgate tube.

Saxon Fencing Club

Twyford Sports Hall, Twyford Crescent, W3 (Gordon Collett, 8567 6819). Ealing Common tube.

Streatham Fencing Club

Dunraven Lower School, Mount Nod Road, SW16 (Roger Barnes, 8677 6207). Streatham Hill rail.

Football crazy...

... football mad.

Football

Professional football's financial bubble may have burst, but the game has lost none of its popularity. It's by far the best-attended spectator sport, and, lower down the pyramid, more than 45,000 clubs cater for all standards and ages, and both sexes.

Finding a club

Most local newspapers have a column of classified ads placed by clubs looking for players; noticeboards at public libraries and sports centres are also a good source. When helping your child to find a team to play for, make sure that he or she is of the appropriate standard. Also ask about the number of children in each age group (in some large clubs only the best get to play regularly), whether the club coaches hold FA qualifications, and the atmosphere and ethos – is it a club where winning is all that matters, or is 'sport for all' the goal?

To find a girls' team, contact the **Football Association** (7745 4545/www.TheFA.com/women) or Ann Mason, secretary of the **Greater London Women's League** (8977 3658). Clubs with extensive girls' programmes include Arsenal (contact Clare Wheatley on 7704 4520) and Fulham (contact Natalia Lodge on 8336 7481).

Coaching

All professional clubs in London run 'Football in the Community' coaching courses, fun days and skills clinics. These are suitable for boys and girls of all standards aged from about six upwards. They usually take place within the club's immediate locality and are staffed by FA-qualified coaches. Phone or see the club websites (*see p267*) for details and dates: **Arsenal** (7704 4140); **Brentford** (8758 9430); **Charlton Athletic** (8850 2866); **Chelsea** (7385 5545); **Crystal Palace** (8768 6000); **Fulham** (7384 4759); **Leyton Orient** (8556 5973); **Millwall** (7740 0503); **Queens Park Rangers** (8740 2509); **Tottenham Hotspur** (8365 5000); **Watford** (01923 440449); **West Ham United** (8548 2707).

Similar schemes operate through the **County FAs**. Call the following offices for details: **Essex** (01245 357727); **Hertfordshire** (01462 677622); **Kent** (01634 843824); **London** (8690 9626); **Middlesex** (8424 8524); **Surrey** (01372 373543).

A highly rated scheme is run by former Queens Park Rangers goalkeeper **Peter Hucker**. This is based in Newham, Barking and Wanstead and offers weekly coaching sessions, matchplay and football parties for children of all abilities between ages five and 16. Hucker also founded the **East London & Essex Small-Sided Soccer League**. Details from www.peterhucker-soccer.com.

Finally, there are plenty of commercial football clinics to choose from, some of which dangle the promise of visits from Premiership stars. An **Ian St John Soccer Camp**, (0151 207 3334/www.soccercamps.co.uk) for example, costs £70 for five days (10am-3.45pm) and caters for children aged eight to 15. Other local organisations for tuition include **League One Sports Academy** (8446 0891), which trains in Hampstead, is Ofsted inspected and runs holiday and Saturday morning courses. **Powerleague** (www.powerleague.co.uk) is a great organisation for Saturday-morning footie.

Golf

Too many golfers still want their clubhouses to be a refuge from children (and in some cases from women) for the sport to offer a widespread welcome to juvenile thwackers. That said, the **English Golf Union** (01526 354500/ www.englishgolfunion.org) has developed 'Tri-Golf' for sixes to 12s and is working to introduce the game in primary schools.

Beckenham Place Park
The Mansion, Beckenham Place Park, Beckenham, Kent (8650 2292).
Juniors can use this course at any time. Lessons are available on Saturdays at 11am and cost £2 (booking essential). It costs £6.50 to play a round or £4.50 for nine holes.

Regent's Park Golf & Tennis School
North Gate, Outer Circle, Regent's Park, NW1 (7724 0643/www.rpgts.co.uk). **Open** 8am-8pm daily.
Children who are 'old enough to take instruction' are welcome here (to give you an idea what that means, the coaches have taught kids as young as five). Junior membership costs £30; the Saturday afternoon young golfers' clinic costs £5 per hour (book in advance) Club hire is £1.

Gymnastics & trampolining

The **British Amateur Gymnastics Association** (01952 820330/www.baga.co.uk), has around 100,000 members, proof that many kids want to pursue the sport after learning the basic rolls and vaults. Sessions for four-year-olds and under in its clubs and schools are based around soft play equipment and simple games. After that, young gymnasts can work their way through a series of proficiency awards. As well as a general scheme for boys and girls, there are separate awards for rhythmic gymnastics and sports acrobatics. **The British Trampoline Federation** (contact details as above) offers a similar structure.

With small children in mind, Bill Cosgrove, a former national gymnastics coach, launched **TumbleTots** and, later, **Gymbabes** and **Gymbobs**. Gymbabes is for babies from six months to the crawling stage, TumbleTots is for walkers,

Activities

and Gymbobs from school age up to seven. For details of centres around the country, call 0121 585 7003 or see www.tumbletots.com.

These clubs offer a range of age-appropriate activities. Be sure that any club you choose displays a current certificate of inspection by BAGA or the London Gymnastics Federation (8529 1142).

Hillingdon School of Gymnastics
Victoria Road, South Ruislip, Middx (8841 6666/ www.hsg-swallows.co.uk). South Ruislip tube.

Islington Gym Club, Arts & Media School
Turle Road, N4 (8983 6799). Finsbury Park tube/rail.

Plumstead Leisure Centre
Speranza Street, SE18 (8855 8289). Plumstead rail.

Redbridge School of Gymnastics
Pulteney Road, E18 (8530 3810). South Woodford tube.

Richmond Gymnastics Centre
Townmead Road, Kew, Surrey (8878 8682). Kew Gardens rail.

Ice skating

London's ice rinks offer an ideal combination of free skating, formal instruction and discos. Session times vary from day to day as the ice needs regular sweeping and refreezing, but venues usually open from 10am until 10pm. Prices below include skate hire. For more information about the sport, contact the **National Ice Skating Association** (0115 853 3100/www.nisa.uk.org).

Alexandra Palace Ice Rink
Alexandra Palace Way, N22 (8365 4386/ www.alexandrapalace.com/ice). Wood Green tube/Alexandra Palace rail/W3 bus. **Open** 11am-5.30pm Mon-Fri; 10.30am-4.30pm, 8.30-11pm Sat, Sun. **Admission** during the week £4.20, 3.50 concession; weekends £5.50, £4.50 concession.
A six-week course of lessons at this international-size rink costs from £44. Parties are also available.

Broadgate Ice Arena
Broadgate Circle, Eldon Street, EC2 (7505 4068/www.broadgateestates.co.uk). Liverpool Street tube/rail. **Open** noon-2.30pm, 3.30-6pm Mon-Thur; noon-2.30pm, 3.30-6pm, 7-10pm Fri; 11am-1pm, 2-4pm, 5-8.30pm Sat; 11am-1pm, 2-4pm, 5-7pm Sun. **Admission** £7; £4 under-16s.
This tiny outdoor rink is a wonderful spot amid the high-tech offices of the City. It opens from late October to April and is the best value of all the outdoor rinks.

Lee Valley Ice Centre
Lea Bridge Road, E10 (8533 3154/ www.leevalleypark.co.uk). Clapton rail. **Open** noon-4pm Mon; noon-4pm, 6.30-9pm Tue, Wed; noon-4pm, 8.30-10.30pm Thur; noon-4pm, 8.30-11pm Fri, Sat; noon4pm, 7-9.30pm Sun. **Admission** *Mon-Thur* £5.70 adult, £4.70 under-15s; *Fri-Sun* £5.90 adult, £4.90 under-15s.

The disco nights are popular at this large, well-maintained rink, but it's never too busy because it's hard to get here by public transport. Rink management says Lee Valley has high-quality ice (it certainly feels hard enough when you fall over) and the warmest skating environment in the UK.

Leisurebox
First Bowl, 17 Queensway, W2 (7229 0172). Bayswater or Queensway tube. **Open** 10am-7pm daily (additional disco evening sessions call for details) **Admission** £6.50.
Once known as Queens, this is the most famous rink in London: countless top skaters learned their moves here. The loud and crowded disco nights with DJs on Fridays and Saturdays are legendary, but beginners and families are also well looked after at quieter times.

Michael Sobell Leisure Centre
Hornsey Road, N7 (7609 2166/www.aquaterra.org). Finsbury Park tube/rail. **Admission** £3/person; £2.70 parent & toddler session.
Children from four upwards are welcome at this small rink, which runs popular after-school sessions. A six-week course of lessons costs £29. You can also hold parties here.

Somerset House
Strand, WC2 (7845 4600/www.somerset-house.org.uk). Holborn or Temple tube (closed Sun). **Admission** free to courtyard and terrace, phone for skating prices.
Every December (ring for the exact date), the beautiful courtyard here is iced over, and becomes the most attractive rink in London. It's a limited season, however, as the ice has usually melted by mid January. It's also hugely popular with children, so be prepared to queue.

Streatham Ice Arena
386 Streatham High Road, SW16 (8769 7771/www.streathamicearena.co.uk). Streatham rail. **Open** 10am-4pm Mon, Sun; 10.30am-4pm, 8pm-10.30pm Tue, Thur; 10.30am-4pm, 4.30-6.30pm, 8-10.30pm Wed; 10.30am-4pm, 6-8pm, 8.30-11.30pm Fri, Sat. **Admission** £6.40, £20 Family (2+2).
This is another of London's famous old rinks, where a six-week course of lessons costs £39 for adults, £30 for children and £23 for 'toddlers' aged up to four.

Karting & motor sports

Many of the world's top Formula One drivers got an early taste for speed on a kart circuit. It's thrilling stuff for eight-year-olds upwards as the little buggies zip around at speeds exceeding 30mph. All drivers receive a full briefing before they begin and anyone disobeying the marshals is removed from the track. Modern karts are very easy to drive (accelerator on the right and brake on the left). There is no gearbox involved, so all your child needs to do is concentrate on steering, braking and accelerating.

The karting venues listed below welcome children and can be booked for exciting parties.

Brands Hatch
Fawkham, Longfield, Kent (01474 872331/ www.octagonmotorsports.com). Swanley rail. **Open** 8.30am-6pm Mon-Fri, times vary Sat, Sun. **Admission** varies depending on racing schools, rally schools or race meetings.

Tae kwondo for littl'uns and large'uns at **Hwarang Academy**.

Activities

Since being taken over by Octagon Motorsports, Brands Hatch has become the country's most impressive on-track activity venue. There are loads of things to do here (on two and four wheels), including 'Early Drive', which puts your youngster in control of an Audi A2 – a brilliant educational concept that should be adopted everywhere.

Playscape Pro Racing
390 Streatham High Road, SW16 (8677 8677/ www.playscape.co.uk). Streatham rail. **Open** 10am-10pm daily.
This centre can be booked for children's parties (*see p233*) or for half-hour taster sessions. Those bitten by the bug can join the Playscape Cadet School, a founder member of the RAC's Association of Racing Kart Schools. The school operates on the first and third Saturday of each month (9.30am-12.30pm; cost £30) and students are put through their paces before gaining an RAC racing licence.

Martial arts

You need only consider how often they feature in computer games to grasp their appeal. Martial arts are exotic, offering a glimpse of cultures which children may have studied at school; they require interesting clothes (often supplied by a club as part of the membership fee); and many have grading systems with belts and badges. Most importantly, martial arts impart self-confidence, body awareness and resilience – valuable assets for children.

Most local sports centres will be home to at least one martial arts club; many more are based in church halls and community centres. Look for evidence of a lively but disciplined atmosphere, with well-organised and age-appropriate teaching. Ask the instructor about his or her qualifications – the grading systems used in judo and karate, for example, help to ensure that teachers are of a suitable standard. Ask for proof of insurance cover: martial arts involve physical contact and accidents can happen (few community facilities extend their insurance to the instructors). For more information, contact the **Amateur Martial Arts Association** (01332 663086/www.amauk.co.uk). **The National College of Martial Arts** (7278 5608) offers various classes for children, with the emphasis on self-discipline rather than combat.

Academy Health & Fitness Centre
16 Hoxton Square, N1 (7729 5789/www.bobbreen.co.uk). Old Street tube/rail.
Kung fu is an ancient art that the Chinese regard as part of the historical tapestry of their lives. This centre offers Saturday morning classes for children aged from seven.

The Budokwai
4 Gilston Road, SW10 (7370 1000/www.budokwai.org). Gloucester Road tube.
This is one of Britain's premier martial arts clubs, offering judo tuition for children aged six to 12.

Hwarang Academy
The Armoury, 25 Pond Street, NW3 (7348 3963/07941 081009/www.hwarangacademy.com). Belsize Park tube.
The Korean martial art of tae kwondo is now an Olympic sport, and youngsters aged between five and 18 can learn to master its spectacular kicks here.

Hacking out in **Hyde Park**.

School of Japanese Karate (Shotokan International)
Various venues (8368 6249).
Karate is the most popular Japanese martial art in the UK. There are no holds or grappling, just strikes and kicks. David and Lilian Alleyn run this well-established school and teach children aged five and up at various north London venues.

Riding

London has a large number of riding schools. The following are by no means all of them, just our favourites (and all British Horse Society approved).

Some schools run 'Own a Pony' days and weeks, which involve some lucky rider's parents paying about £40 (for a day) or over £100 (for a week) for the privilege of looking after their favourite pony in the school: mucking out, grooming, feeding, exercising and schooling. Many places offer birthday party packages, while most also have facilities for disabled riders.

Riding lessons and hacks must always be booked in advance: ask whether there are 'taster' sessions for newcomers. Riders, whatever their age, should always wear a hard hat (establishments can usually lend one if you don't have your own, sometimes for a small fee) and boots with a low heel; sturdy trousers or jodhpurs are also recommended. Rates given here are for children and per hour.

Aldersbrook Riding School
Empress Avenue, E12 (8530 4648). Manor Park rail. **Lessons** from £14.
This is a small, friendly school with a countryside feel to it. There are eight ponies and four horses working here. Lessons take place in an outdoor manège, hacking on Wanstead Flats.

Ealing Riding School
Gunnersbury Avenue, W5 (8992 3808/ www.ealingridingschool.biz). Ealing Common tube. **Lessons** £17.
Riders aged from five can take part in many activities at this benevolent school, even the occasional gymkhana. Lessons are held in an outdoor manège.

Hyde Park & Kensington Stables
Hyde Park Stables, 63 Bathurst Mews, W2 (7723 2813/ www.hydeparkstables.com). Lancaster Gate tube. **Lessons** *Individual* £49 Mon-Fri; £59 Sat, Sun. *Course of 10* from £300. **Map** p313 D6.
Children aged five upwards can enjoy an hour-long instruction with patient, streetwise ponies in the glamorous surroundings of Hyde Park.

Lee Valley Riding Centre
Lea Bridge Road, Leyton, E10 (8556 2629/ www.leevalleypark.com). Clapton rail/48, 55, 56 bus. **Lessons** £16.
Local children love to help at this well-appointed school, where 28 extremely placid horses and ponies enjoy the breezy open spaces of Walthamstow Marshes.

London Equestrian Centre
Lullington Garth, N12 (8349 1345). Mill Hill East tube. **Lessons** from £18.
This busy yard in North Finchley has 30 assorted horses and ponies; some are delightfully placid and deservedly popular with local children (minimum age four). There's a junior members club for regulars, who may be able to take part in occasional informal gymkhanas. There's a restaurant on site.

Mudchute Equestrian Centre
Pier Street, E14 (7515 0749). Crossharbour & London Arena or Mudchute DLR. **Lessons** £16/hr; £1.50 under-7.
Regular clients aged seven and over should find out about joining the Mudchute arm of the Pony Club. All new clients join the waiting list, then are given a half-hour assessment lesson. As part of a city farm, Mudchute's birthday package involves both fun on the farm and a pony ride.

Newham Riding School & Association
The Docklands Equestrian Centre, 2 Claps Gate Lane, E6 (7511 3917/www.linda@docklandsequestriancentre.com). Beckton DLR. **Lessons** £13/hr.
There is a long waiting list at this stables, where 22 horses and poniesgive riding lessons to children (aged from five).

Ross Nye's Riding Stables
8 Bathurst Mews, W2 (7262 3791). Lancaster Gate tube. **Lessons** £35; £25 Pony Club members. *Pony Club Membership* £20yr. **Map** p313 D6.
Membership of the Hyde Park branch of the Pony Club brings reduced prices, newsletters, and the chance to complete Pony Club achievement tests. Children aged six and up can learn to ride in the park, and Club members can take part in Pony Club Days in the Christmas holidays (£30/day) and in week-long pony camps at the stables' Surrey farm.

Activities

Suzanne's Riding School
Brookshill Drive, Harrow Weald, Middx (8954 3618/www.suzannesridingschool.co.uk).Stanmore tube/Harrow & Wealdstone rail. **Lessons** from £15.
Suzanne's has 200 acres of rolling Harrow Weald for its 70 horses to canter over. The school is an important social centre, with a weekend café and a separate junior riding school.

Trent Park Equestrian Centre
Bramley Road, N14 (8363 9005/www.trentpark.com). Oakwood tube. **Lessons** £17/hr.
Excellent hacking out in Trent Park (£23 per hour) and a benevolent attitude towards young riders aged four and over make this a fab place to ride.

Willowtree Riding Establishment
The Stables, Ronver Road, SE12 (8857 6438). Grove Park or Lee rail. **Lessons** from £7.70/30mins.
There are plenty of game Shetlands for the tiny tots here; experienced children enjoy the spirited Arab ponies. Lessons take place in an indoor school.

Wimbledon Village Stables
24A/B High Street, SW19 (8946 8579/ www.wvstables.com). Wimbledon tube/rail. **Lessons** from £30.
Wimbledon's riding club gives children with a pony habit all sorts of perks, including gymkhanas, newsletters and special events. Riding takes place on Wimbledon Common.

Rugby league

The 13-a-side game is finally building a profile in the capital. The London Skolars have been granted a place in the new National League and are working alongside the Broncos to introduce the sport in schools around London. The other two clubs listed below play in the Rugby League Conference and have thriving junior sections. To find out more about the sport, contact the **Rugby Football League** on 0113 232 9111/www.rfl.uk.com.

Greenwich Admirals
Old Brockleians Rugby Club, Eltham Palace Road, SE9. Eltham rail. Contact Alan Bacon on 07734 082754/ *www.greenwichrl.com.*

London Skolars
New River Stadium, White Hart Lane, N22. Contact Andrew Jackson on 07775 854377/www.skolars.com.

South London Storm
Streatham-Croydon Rugby Club, 159 Brigstock Road, Thornton Heath. Contact Dave Bold on 8650 0691/www.southlondonstorm.co.uk.

Rugby union

Most rugby union clubs have a junior section, playing 'mini rugby' on weekend mornings in front of hordes of screaming parents. In the younger age groups – some clubs take children as young as six – the aim is to encourage handling, passing and running, with tackling outlawed. Women's and girls'

rugby has made rapid progress in recent years, with the traditionally staid hierarchy of the men's game coming to recognise the benefits of working together. Contact the **Rugby Football Union** (8892 2000/www.rfu.com) for advice on finding a club offering junior rugby for boys or girls, although you may only need turn to the sports pages of a local newspaper to see what's available.

Skateboarding

Hot-dogging, double deckers and hanging tens may not mean much to most parents, but there's no denying skateboarding's popularity with the kids. On the one hand, the sport has retained its cool and radical edge with children still skating free on the smooth concrete of the South Bank, Shell Centre and beneath the Westway. On the other, the centres listed below offer a more structured environment.

Meanwhile
Meanwhile Gardens, off Great Western Road, W9 (no phone). Westbourne Park tube.
Three concrete bowls of varying size and steepness, surrounded by grass, and with no flatland for practising the basics: huge potential for more accomplished riders, but beginners may be better off at the PlayStation Skate Park just round the corner. The bowls are linked from high ground to low, offering the possibility of long, technical lines as well as suicidal transfers: just beware of the sizeable ollie bumps inconveniently located in the middle of the two main bowls.

PlayStation Skate Park
Bay 65-6, Acklam Road, W10 (8969 4669/ www.pssp.co.uk). Ladbroke Grove tube. **Open** 11am-4pm, 5-9pm Mon-Fri; 10am-9pm Sat, Sun. **Admission** £6-£7.
PS:SP has revolutionised the London scene. Sheltered beneath the A40, and lent an apocalyptic air by the artics thundering overhead, this enormous park includes two half-pipes, a long mini-ramp and more funboxes, grind boxes, ledges and rails than you can shake a deck at. The enormous variation within the course makes it as suitable for beginners as it is addictive for old soldiers; there's also an on-site shop.

Stockwell Park
Stockwell Road (next to Brixton Cycles), SW9 (no phone). Brixton tube/rail.
Stockwell is a concrete wonderland unlike any other in the city, made up of an unbroken series of bumps, hips, waves, bowls and lips: perfect for tricks or just good old-fashioned carve-ups. The park offers grand scope for riders of varying ability, and while the lack of rails and ledges might put off more technical skaters, those seeking pure fun will have to try pretty hard not to fall for this place. Brixton Cycles is just yards away, so the park is predictably popular with BMXers.

Skiing & snowboarding

There's nothing like the feel of proper snow, but a few practice turns on a dry slope make excellent preparation for the real thing. Gloves, long sleeves and trousers are compulsory, as the surface can deliver a nasty burn should you fall. Also note that

Activities

Ready to hit the decks. *See p259*.

if you're thinking of taking a mixed-ability group out for a recreational session, perhaps as a birthday activity, each participant must be able to perform a controlled snowplough turn and use the ski lift.

The feel of real snow in east London, once promised for summer 2003, might never happen, now funding for the project has been withdrawn. There are plans afoot to apply for money elsewhere, but it really looks as if the old Beckton Alp will not become the London Snow World we were all so excited about. For more information about Beckton, and snow sport in general, contact the **Ski Club of Great Britain** (8410 2000/www.skiclub.co.uk).

Bromley Ski Centre
Sandy Lane, St Paul's Cray, Orpington, Kent (01689 876812). St Mary Cray rail. **Open** *Oct-Easter* noon-10pm Mon-Thur; 10am-10pm Fri; 9am-6pm Sat; 9am-8pm Sun. *Easter-Oct* noon-10pm Tue-Thur; 10am-10pm Fri; 9am-6pm Sat; Sun. **Admission** call for details.
Three lifts serve the 120m main slope; there's also a mogul field and nursery slope. Skiing and snowboarding taster sessions cost £13 respectively. Booking is essential.

Sandown Sports Club
More Lane, Esher, Surrey (01372 467132/www.sandown-sports.co.uk). Esher rail. **Open** call for details. **Admission** half hour Ski lesson £20 per child.
The 120m main slope, 80m nursery area and 90m snowboarding slope are closed during horse racing meetings. This is a lessons-only venue: tuition is available for seven-year-olds upwards, although special half-hour classes can be arranged for children as young as four.

Swimming

Swimming is more than a mere sport. It can be a matter of life and death, yet one in five children leave primary school unable to swim, (in an ideal world learning to swim would be a core subject). Most local authority pools run lessons for children aged from around three upwards, plus parent and baby sessions to develop water confidence from as young as three months. However, these can be over-subscribed and have long waiting lists. Ask at your local pool for a timetable and booking details.

For children past the lesson stage, joining a club is the best way to improve, make like-minded friends and swim competitively. Enquire at your local pool or contact the **Amateur Swimming Association** (01509 618700/www.britishswimming.org), which also provides information on 'Aquagoal', a junior version of water polo.

Dolphin Swimming Club
University of London Pool, Malet Street, WC1 (8349 1844). Goodge Street tube. **Classes** 9.15am-2.45pm Sat. **Admission** £214.50/11 individual 30min lessons; £71.50/11 30min small-group sessions (max 5/group).
There are some children whose fear of the water needs more specialised treatment than even a caring parent can provide. The Dolphin Swimming Club teaches aquaphobic children (and adults) to overcome their fear, and takes children from about three years old all the way to gold standard. The club also teaches diving and life-saving.

Activities

Leander Swimming Club
Balham Leisure Centre, Elmfield Road, SW17 (7733 2029/www.leanderswimmingclub.org). Balham tube/rail. **Classes** times call for details. **Membership** £21 £33/mth; £4.50/lessons.
This competitive swimming club takes its name from the Greek mythological character Leander who swam huge distances to visit his lover. His determination and strength is echoed in the club's dedication to the sport. Leander offers a programme for children over seven who are already swimmers and keen to develop competitively; it hosts sessions in Balham, Tooting, Crystal Palace and Dulwich.

Outdoor pools

Outdoor swimming pools, or lidos, always seem to be under threat of closure. London is blessed with a number of quite beautiful lidos, many dating from the 1930s when public baths meant goosepimples and blue lips. People were tougher then. Nowadays, the pools only attract a crowd during a heatwave. Note that Hampstead Ponds, where you really can enjoy a dip at one with nature, are pretty deep, so are suitable for strong swimmers only.

Brockwell Lido
Brockwell park, Dulwich Road, SE24 (7274 3088/ www.thelido.co.uk). Herne Hill rail. **Open** *May-Sept* 6.45am-7pm Mon-Fri; noon-6pm Sat, Sun. **Admission** *6.45-10am* £2.50; £1.50 under-16s. *Noon-7pm* £5; £3 under-16s.
The future of this wonderful 1930s outdoor pool continues to hang in the balance, now Evian is no longer a sponsor, but as we went to press the lido was due to open for another season. Hurrah! There are paddling pools and sunbathing terraces though these suffer from a lack of shade.

Finchley Lido
Great North Leisure Park, High Road, N12 (8343 9830/ www.gll.org). East Finchley tube. **Open** *May-Sept* 9am-7pm Mon-Fri; 9am-4.30pm Sat, Sun. **Admission** £2.90; £1.70 concessions.
There are two indoor pools here, but it's the outdoor pool and terrace that everyone flocks to in summer.

Hampstead Heath Swimming Ponds
Men's and women's ponds: Millfield Lane, N6. Gospel Oak rail. Mixed pond: East Heath Road, NW3 (7485 4491). Hampstead Heath rail. **Open** 7am-dusk daily. **Admission** free.
Children need to be eight or over, able to swim at least 25 metres and accompanied by an adult in the water. The authorities close the ponds if ice or algal bloom appear, so call first.

Oasis Sports Centre
32 Endell Street, WC2 (7831 1804/www.camden.gov.uk). Covent Garden tube. **Open** 7.30am-8.30pm Mon-Wed; 7.30am-8pm Thur; 9.30am-5pm Sat, Sun. **Admission** £3; £1.10 concessions.
The 27m outdoor pool is open all year round and is popular with local office workers (so it gets packed at lunchtime in hot weather). But if it's cold, plunge into the indoor pool.

Park Road Pools
Park Road, N8 (8341 3567/www.haringeyleisure.com). Hornsey rail/Alexandra Palace rail then W7 bus. **Open**

Lido (May-Sept) 11am-6pm daily. *Indoor pools* 7.15am-6pm Mon; 7.15am-9.30pm Tue-Thur; 7.15am-7.30pm Fri, Sat; 7.15am-6.30pm Sun. **Admission** *Lido* £4.20, £2.10 concessions. *Indoor pools* £3; £1.25 concessions.
Outdoors, on sunny days, it's difficult to find a patch of grass to put your towel on here, but the water in the outdoor pool is heated – which means swimming in the rain is an option.

Parliament Hill Lido
Parliament Hill Fields, Gordon House Road, NW3 (7485 3873). Gospel Oak rail. **Open** *Sept-Feb* 7am-10.30am daily. *May-Sept* 7-9am, 10am-6pm daily. Closed for maintenance early spring (ring for details). **Admission** £3.60; £1.80 children.
This lovely 1930s lido gets very busy on hot days, though the 60m pool is always alluring.

Pools on the Park
Old Deer Park, Twickenham Road, Richmond, Surrey (8940 0561/www.springhealthleisure.co.uk). Richmond tube/rail. **Open** Apr-Sept 6.30am-7.45pm Mon; 6.30am-9pm Tue, Thur, Fri; 6.30am-9.30pm Wed; 8am-6pm Sat, Sun. **Admission** £3.25; £2.50 children.
A 33m indoor pool and another one the same size outside; there's a delightful sunbathing area, too.

Tooting Bec Lido
Tooting Bec Road, SW16 (8871 7198). Tooting Bec tube/Streatham Hill rail. **Open** *May 24-Sept* 7am-8.30 daily. *Oct-May* closed except for club members. **Admission** £2.60-£3.10; £2.10-£2.25 children. **Membership** £16/mth; £80 season ticket for members.
At 94m by 25m, this is the second largest open-air pool in Europe. The South London Swimming Club has access to the popular pool all year round.

Indoor pools

Most swimming pools are 25m rectangles, and there isn't space to list every facility in London here. These are a little bit special. Opening times and prices change seasonally.

Barnet Copthall Pools
Great North Way, NW4 (8457 9900/www.gll.org). Mill Hill East tube. **Open** 6.45-8am, 9am-9.30pm Mon-Fri; 9am-4.30pm Sat; 8am-4.30pm Sun. **Admission** £2.90; £1.70 children; free under-5s.
Two 25m pools, a smaller activity pool and diving area, plus coaching and a swimming club.

Crystal Palace National Sports Centre
Ledrington Road, SE19 (8778 0131/diving courses 8659 4561/www.crystalpalacensc.co.uk). Crystal Palace rail. **Open** 8am-5pm Mon-Wed, Fri; noon-7pm Thur; 10am-7.45pm Sat; 10am-1pm, 2-5.45pm Sun. **Admission** £2.35; £1.30 children; free under-3s.
One of only two 50m Olympic-size pools in London, with fabulous diving facilities.

Gurnell Leisure Centre
Ruislip Road East, W13 (8998 3241/www.leisureconnections.co.uk). Perivale tube. **Open** 7am-7pm Mon, Fri; 7am-9pm Tue-Thur; 8am-4.45pm Sat, Sun. **Admission** £2.75; £1.55 children; free under-5s.
The capital's other 50m Olympic-size pool with floor to ceiling windows and heavy usage.

Ironmonger Row Baths

Ironmonger Row, EC1 (7253 4011/www.aquaterrra.com).
Old Street tube/rail. **Open** 6.30am-9pm Mon; 6.30am-8pm
Tue-Thur; 6.30am-7pm Fri; noon-6pm Sat; noon-5pm Sun.
Admission £2.90; £1.30 children; £7.90 family (2+2);
free under-3s.
Take a trip back in time at this handsome 1930s 30m pool
and Turkish baths (one of only three remaining in London).

Latchmere Leisure Centre

Burns Road, SW11 (7207 8004/www.kinetika.org).
Clapham Junction rail. **Open** 7am-9.30pm Mon-Wed, Sun;
7am-6.30pm Tue, Thur ; 7am-6pm Fri; 7am-7pm Sat.
Admission £3.17; £2.12 children; free under-5s.
Lane swimming, a teaching pool and a beach area with palm
trees. A wave machine springs into action on the hour.

Queen Mother Sports Centre

*223 Vauxhall Bridge Road, SW1 (7630 5522). Victoria
tube/rail.* **Open** 6.30am-8pm Mon; 9.30am-8pm Tue;
7.30am-8pm Wed, Fri; 8am-5.30pm Sat, Sun. **Admission**
£2.45; £1 children; free under-5s.
Main pool, teaching pool and separate diving area in a centre that's always packed with schoolchildren.

York Hall Leisure Centre

Old Ford Road, E2 (8980 2243). Bethnal Green tube/rail.
Open 7.15am-8.30pm Mon; 7.15am-9.30pm Tue, Thur;
7.15am-5.30pm Wed, Fri; 8am-8,30pm Sat 8am-3.45pm
Sun. **Admission** £2.55; £1.05 children; free under-3s.
Built as a bath house in the 1920s and still housing Turkish
and Russian baths, the future of this 33m main pool and separate children's pool is uncertain.
*Café. Disabled access: lift, toilet (male only). Nappy-
changing facilities.*

Water games

London's a fluming great place if you want to splash
as well as swim. These centres have flumes, wave
machines and various child-friendly bits of kit.

Leyton Leisure Lagoon

*763 High Road, E10 (8558 4860/www.gll.org). Leyton
tube.* **Open** 7am-10pm Mon-Fri; 8am-4.15pm Sat, 8am-
6pm Sun. **Admission** *Peak* £3.65; £1.60 children. *Off-
peak* £2.35; 75p children.
The Lagoon has exotic appeal: a flume, slides, fountains,
rapids and cascades in a tropical island setting.

Tottenham Green Leisure Centre

*1 Philip Lane, N15 (8489 5322/
www.haringeyleisure.com). Seven Sisters tube/rail.*
Open 7am-10.30pm Mon-Fri; 7am-5.30pm Sat, Sun.
Admission £3; £1.40 children.
Splash amid the waves and slides in the 'beach pool'.

Waterfront Leisure Centre

*High Street, SE18 (8317 5000/www.gll.org). Woolwich/
Arsenal rail.* **Open** 3-8pm Mon-Thur; 3-6pm Fri; 9am-5pm
Sat, Sun. **Admission** peak £4.50; £3.25 children; off peak
£3.35, £2.40 children.
Three pools, a 65m 'anaconda' slide, five-lane multi-slide,
waves, jets and water 'volcano' in Greenwich's super centre.

Wavelengths Leisure Centre

Griffin Street, SE8 (8694 1134). Deptford rail.
Open session times change regularly, ring for details.
Admission £2.90; £1.50 children.
Expect to find flumes, waves, wild water and cannons in the
flashiest building on the edges of Deptford Market.

Brockwell Lido. Cool, blue and inviting. *See p261.*

Stick sports

The British men's hockey team won gold at the 1988 Seoul Olympics and the women took bronze four years later, but the years since have seen this exciting and accessible sport lurch from crisis to crisis. Still, the game has a strong club network around the capital and most clubs run a junior section. The governing body, **England Hockey** (01908 544644/www.hockeyonline.co.uk), has a London office which can give local contacts.

Then there's Pop Lacrosse, a non-contact version of a sport which in any case doesn't really deserve its St Trinian's image. Many of the London clubs offer Pop Lacrosse to boys and girls; contact the **English Lacrosse Association** (0161 834 4582/ www.englishlacrosse.co.uk) for details.

Table tennis

There's a mini renaissance going on in kids' table tennis. Some 20 weekend junior leagues are now running in the capital, a new purpose-built centre in Southall is about to open, and links with sports colleges such as Langdon School in Newham and the Ealing duo of Compton and Featherstone are producing high-quality players. There are several clubs around the capital that offer coaching for kids, and a competitive system to feed into. What's more, most sports centres will have at least one table and many will host a club. For more information contact the **English Table Tennis Association** (01424 722525/www.etta.co.uk).

Tennis

Despite the best efforts of Tim Henman, tennis remains Britain's biggest sporting embarrassment. This country invented the game and hosts the greatest of the four Grand Slam tournaments, yet our status in the game is low. Only when the sport sheds its cosy image and reaches out beyond the middle-classes might things change. Facilities are an issue: public courts offer easy access at cheap prices, but may be of poor quality or lack a coaching programme. Private clubs, on the other hand, require the commitment of an annual fee (anything from £10 to £500-plus per person). But if families plan to play together or want qualified coaching for a young beginner, they're often worth it.

Look for a club that values children rather than sees them as an inconvenience: are there coaching courses for all standards? Are times set aside for kids to play casually? Is equipment available for first-timers? If not, look elsewhere. Alternatively, most London boroughs run holiday courses at Easter and in the summer: contact your local sports

development team or public library for details. The **Lawn Tennis Association** (7381 7000/www.lta. org.uk) publishes free, comprehensive guides giving contacts for hundreds of private clubs and public courts listed by borough or county, along with contact details for local development officers. Details of tennis holidays are also available.

Clissold Park Junior Tennis Club
Clissold Park Mansion House, c/o Rangers' Office, Stoke Newington Church Street, N16 (Court bookings 7923 3660/Tennis Club 8318 4856/www.clissoldparkjtc.co.uk). Stoke Newington rail/73 bus. **Open** 5-8pm daily. **Court hire** £3.50/hr.
The LTA paid for resurfacing of the four hard courts and four mini-tennis courts at this, Britain's first City Tennis Centre. Rackets of all sizes and balls are free to borrow. The club is active with squads, coaching and competitions. There's another City Tennis Centre in Highbury Fields.

David Lloyd Leisure
08708 883015/www.davidlloydleisure.co.uk.
There are eight David Lloyd clubs in the London area combining tennis with upmarket fitness facilities. They're not cheap, but all are very family-friendly – check out the website or phone for your nearest venue and membership details.

Islington Tennis Centre
Market Road, N7 (7700 1370/www.aquaterra.org). Caledonian Road tube. **Open** 7am-11pm Mon-Thur; 7am-10pm Fri; 8am 10pm Sat, Sun. **Admission** *Indoor* £16.50, £7.40 children per court per hour. *Outdoor* £7.40, £3.70 per court per hour.
Developed under the LTA's Indoor Tennis Initiative, this centre offers excellent subsidised coaching on a membership or 'pay as you play' basis. Short tennis and transitional tennis for youngsters learning the basics are also available.

Redbridge Sports & Leisure Centre
Forest Road, Barkingside (8498 1000/ www.rslonline.co.uk). Fairlop tube. **Open** 9am-10pm Mon-Fri, Sun; 9am 9pm Sat. **Admission** £14 per hour, £6.50 5s-16s.
Developed over 30 years and nine phases by an independent charitable trust, this outstanding multi-sports centre has eight indoor and 18 outdoor courts which you can use as a member or 'pay as you play'. Excellent holiday activities for six- to 14-year-olds include one-day and week-long courses for beginners and improvers, together with two-hour fun play sessions. There's also a short tennis club for eights and unders and an excellent development programme.

Sutton Junior Tennis Centre
Rose Hill Recreation Ground, Rose Hill, Sutton, Surrey (8641 6611/www.sjtc.org). Morden tube. **Court hire** £5/hr. **Open** 7am-11pm Mon-Thur; 7am-10pm Fri; 7.30am-8pm Sat; 7.30am-10pm Sun. **Membership** £75/yr, £50/yr child.
Set up 11 years ago, this is now the top tennis school in Britain. Its performance coaches include Wimbledon semi-finalist and Davis Cup captain, Roger Taylor. There are residential courses for full-time players seeking professional status and a scholarship scheme linked with Cheam High School. Children can start at three with Tiny Tots classes, move on to short tennis, join in holiday programmes and book tennis birthday parties. There are six clay, ten acrylic and 11 indoor courts, so the centre is accessible all year round. Membership enables you to book cheaper courts in advance.

Westway Tennis Centre

1 Crowthorne Road, W10 (8969 0992/www.westway.org). Latimer Road tube. **Open** 8am-10pm Mon-Fri; 8am-8pm Sat; 9am-10pm Sun. **Court hire** *Peak* £18.50, £8 children per court per hour. *Off peak* £12, £6 children per court per hour. **Registration** £1.50, £1 children

Also the product of the LTA's Indoor Tennis Initiative, Westway follows a similar model to Islington – excellent subsidised coaching, short tennis and transitional tennis.

Tenpin bowling

Few sports are more accessible to all ages, which makes tenpin ideal for a fun (and relatively cheap) birthday party or family day out. Side bumpers and ball rollers help the very young to get involved while computerised scoring has simplified play. For youngsters keen to progress towards the 'perfect score' of 300, there's a network of regional and national youth tournaments and leagues. For details, contact the **British Tenpin Bowling Association** (8478 1745/www.btba.org.uk).

All of the centres listed here are open seven days a week, typically from 10am to 11pm. Phone for information about parties.

AMF Bowling

Lewisham 11-29 Belmont Hill, SE13 (8318 9691/ www.amfbowling.co.uk). Lewisham rail/DLR. **Open** 10am-midnight daily. **Admission** free. **Cost** £2.65-£3.50 per person per game; £2.10-£3.40 under-16s. **Shoe hire** £1; 70p under-16s. **Lanes** 24. **Credit** MC, V.
Branch: AMF Bowling Purley 112 Brighton Road, Purley, Surrey (8668 2200).

Dagenham Bowling

Dagenham Leisure Park, Cook Road, Dagenham, Essex (8593 2888/www.dagenhambowling.co.uk). Becontree or Dagenham Heathway tube. **Open** 10am-11pm Mon-Thur, Sun; 10am-1am Fri, Sat. **Admission** free. **Cost** (includes shoe hire) £3.60-£4.25 per person per game; £2.65-£3.50 under-16s. **Lanes** 20. **Credit** MC, V.

Elephant & Castle Superbowl

Top Floor, Elephant & Castle Shopping Centre, SE1 (7252 6677/www.leisuregate.co.uk). Elephant & Castle tube/rail. **Open** 10am-midnight Mon-Thur, Sun; 10am-1am Fri; 9.30am-1am Sat. **Admission** free. **Price** (includes shoe hire) £3-£4.50 per person per game; £2.50-£3.40 under-16s. **Lanes** 26. **Credit** (minimum £5) AmEx, MC, V.

Funland

Trocadero, 1 Piccadilly Circus, W1 (7439 1914/ www.funland.co.uk). Piccadilly Circus tube. **Open** 10am-midnight Mon-Thur, Sun; 10am-1am Fri, Sat. **Admission** free. Cost (includes shoe hire) £3-£5 per person per game. **Lanes** 10. **Credit** AmEx, MC, V.

Harrow Bowl

Pinner Road, North Harrow, Middx (8863 3491). North Harrow tube. **Open** noon-11pm Mon; 10am-11pm Tue-Sat; 10am-10.30pm Sun. **Admission** free. **Cost** (includes shoe hire) £4.95 per person per game; £3.95 under-16s. **Lanes** 28. **Credit** AmEx, MC, V.

Hollywood Bowl

Finchley Great Northern Leisure Park, Finchley High Road, N12 (8446 6667/www.hollywoodbowl.co.uk). Finchley Central tube. **Open** 10am-midnight Mon-Thur, Sun; 10am-1am Fri; 9am-1am Sat. **Admission** free. Cost (includes shoe hire) £3-£4 per person per game; £2.25-£3 under-16s. **Lanes** 26. **Credit** AmEx, MC, V.
Branches: see website.

Leisurebox

17 Queensway, W2 (7229 0172). Bayswater tube. **Open** 10am-10.45pm daily. **Admission** free. **Cost** £5.50 per person per game; £4.50 under-14s. **Shoe hire** £1. **Lanes** 12. **Credit** AmEx, MC, V.

Rowans Bowl

10 Stroud Green Road, N4 (8800 1950/ www.rowans.co.uk). Finsbury Park tube/rail. **Open** 10.30am-1am Mon-Thur, Sun; 10.30am-2.30am Fri, Sat. **Admission** £1-£3. **Cost** £2-£3.25 per person per game. **Shoe hire** £1. **Lanes** 24. **Credit** AmEx, MC, V.

Streatham MegaBowl

142 Streatham Hill, SW2 (8678 6007/ www.megabowl.co.uk). Streatham Hill rail. **Open** noon-midnight Mon; noon-1am Tue-Fri; 10am-1am Sat; 10am-midnight Sun. **Admission** free. **Cost** *including shoe hire* £4.75 per person per game; £3.75 under-16s (must be accompanied by over-18s); £17.95/hr family (up to 6 people incl at least one child, last game 6pm Mon-Fri, noon Sat, Sun). **Lanes** 36. **Credit** AmEx, MC, V.
Branches: see website.

XS Superbowl

15-17 Alpine Way, E6 (7511 4440). Beckton DLR. **Open** noon-midnight Mon-Thur, Sun; noon-2am Fri, Sat. **Admission** free. **Cost** £2.75-£3.55 per person per game; £2.25-£2.75 under-16s. **Lanes** 22. **Credit** MC, V.

Water sports

Despite being a landlocked city, London has more than 430 acres of water in Docklands, plus numerous reservoirs and the vast natural resource of the Thames. Indeed, some of the best watersports venues in Europe are accessible by tube. Most cater for ages eight and above, and are ideal for parents and children to join together. What's more, the activities are very affordable.

The **Welsh Harp** (or Brent) Reservoir, is one of London's busiest venues for sailing, windsurfing and canoeing. A number of London clubs run courses on this 70-acre expanse of water, which is also a nature reserve: these include the **Welsh Harp Sailing Association** (8205 1240). The only licensed activity centre to use the reservoir is the **Youth Sailing Base** (8202 6672), which runs courses for school groups and child-friendly weekend activities. The **Royal Yachting Association** (08453 450400) operates a Young Sailors' scheme, and its website (www.rya.org.uk) lists numerous training courses. **Capital Sailing** (07050 223817) has details of RYA courses and

Activities

Afloat in the heart of the city with **Westminster Boating Base**. *See p266.*

marine activities around London. There's also a vast resource at www.uksail.com. Most sailors learn the basics in one-person dinghies such as Toppers or Lasers. Once you've got to grips with turning (tacking and gybing), you can progress to bigger boats. Clubs usually supply all the kit while you're deciding if this is for you.

Amateur Rowing Association
6 Lower Mall, W6 (8748 3632/www.ara-rowing.org).
The governing body of rowing has over 600 clubs affiliated to it. It also endorses a scheme called Go-Row, run by the National Junior Rowing Programme, which aims to encourage more junior members into its ranks. Clubs that have the Go-Row seal of approval have been deemed friendly, safe and suitable for junior activities. To find out about a Go Row scheme in your area, check the website.

Broadwater Sailing Club
Moorhall Road, Harefield, Middx (01494 436314). Denham rail.
A very family-friendly club based at Broadwater Lake, close to the Grand Union Canal. Casual sailing is available every day, and there's an annual 'junior fun week'.

BTYC Sailsports
Birchen Grove, NW9 (8731 8083/ www.btycsailsports.org.uk). Neasden or Wembley Park tube/83, 182, 245, 297, 302, N98 bus.
Among its members, the initials stand for Better Than Your Club, although they really date from the 1950s, when private companies had their own sailing interests. This one started life as the British Transport Yacht Club before becoming a public club years ago. The initials stuck, however. Dinghy-racing, windsurfing, basic training and RYA courses are offered. Family membership is available.

Docklands Sailing & Watersports Centre
Millwall Dock, 235A Westferry Road, E14 (7537 2626/ www.dswc.org). Crossharbour DLR.
Kids (aged eight upwards) and adults can choose from canoeing to dragonboat racing, windsurfing to dinghy sailing. All levels are catered for, although youngsters must be confident in the water: give the centre a call prior to visiting if you have concerns. The Dock has a restaurant and bar, plus facilities and sailing courses for people with disabilities.

Lea Rowing Club
Spring Hill, E5 (8806 3097). Stamford Hill or South Tottenham rail.
Rowing and sculling for over-tens who can swim at least 50m. The Lea also runs intensive school holiday courses.

Lee Valley Watersports Centre
Banbury Reservoir, Harbet Road, E4 (8531 1129). Angel Road rail.
Sailing courses, plus canoeing and waterskiing, on 94 acres of water for eight-year-olds upwards.

London Corinthian Sailing Club
Linden House, Upper Mall, W6 (8748 3280/ www.lcsc.org.uk). Hammersmith tube.
Dinghy sailing courses for beginners.

Princes Club
Clockhouse Lane, Bedfont, Middx (01784 256153/ www.princesclub.com). Hatton Cross tube.
Come here to learn waterskiing or wakeboarding, (which involves having both your feet strapped to a single board and you're pulled behind a speedboat generating a 'fat wake'). The latter is easier than it might sound, though the tricks performed by the pros take years to master.

Activities

Royal Victoria Dock Watersports Centre
Tidal Basin Road, off Silvertown Way, E16 (7511 2326). Royal Victoria DLR.
Low-cost summer sailing, canoeing and rowing for children aged from eight upwards.

Shadwell Basin Project
Glamis Road, E1 (7481 4210/www.shadwell-basin.org.uk). Shadwell DLR.
Downriver from Tower Bridge and run on a voluntary basis, this multi-activity centre offers affordable summer sailing, canoeing and dragonboat racing. The Shadwell Basin Project takes children aged nine and over.

Surrey Docks Watersports Centre
Greenland Dock, Rope Street, SE16 (7237 4009). Surrey Quays tube.
Sailing, windsurfing and canoeing for eight-year-olds upwards takes place in the sheltered dock throughout school holidays and half-terms. Children take part in the RYA's structured sailing courses, which require three days to complete. Once the juniors have their certificates, they can join in Thursday and Friday 'Splashday' activities.

Westminster Boating Base
136 Grosvenor Road, SW1 (7821 7389). Pimlico tube.
Right in the heart of London, this charitable training centre offers low-cost sailing and canoeing on the tidal Thames for children aged ten and over.

Keep it safe

After some high-profile cases of abuse, sport is taking the subjects of child protection and good coaching practice seriously indeed. This means that parents can now make an informed choice about sports clubs, activity centres and the people running them. Coaches are being encouraged to advertise their skills, and should have certificates to back up their claims. Don't be afraid to ask for proof.

All coaches should hold a qualification from the governing body of their particular sport, and they should also hold public liability insurance. Many sports, including football and cricket, now require coaches to hold a basic first-aid qualification, while coaches in direct contact with children should have completed the Criminal Records Bureau's 'disclosure' process.

Ask about the availability of first-aid equipment, and ask how children with specific medical needs are identified. Clubs and centres should hold this information, along with contact numbers for parents. Some governing bodies, including cricket, rugby union, hockey, tennis and football, operate a system called 'Clubmark', by which clubs can show that they are safe and child-friendly and that they operate to high ethical standards. A club holding – or working towards – this seal of approval is almost certain to offer structured coaching and matchplay with suitably qualified staff and a supportive ethos.

Far from being the contemplative and inward-looking pursuit of popular myth, yoga is actually an expressive art that uses the whole body. Many of its postures are drawn from the movements, or take the names, of animals – a child-friendly feature if ever there was one. The cobra pose, for example, expands the chest and strengthens the back, but add a few hisses and a slither through the jungle, and the basic pose soon becomes an adventure – and each posture has an underlying physical or mental benefit.

This approach began at the **Art of Health and Yoga Centre**, where Fenella Lindsell and Jade Anderson created Yoga Bugs® for three- to seven-year-olds. There are now more than 120 trained Yoga Bugs® teachers working in nursery, prep and primary schools. The therapeutic aspect of yoga is being developed at the **Yoga Therapy Centre**, which runs weekly sessions for children with asthma – the stretches of some yoga positions assist breathing and relaxation. The following centres offer classes for kids of different ages.

Art of Health and Yoga Centre
PO Box 46701, SW17 8WY (8682 1800/ www.artofhealth.co.uk).

Holistic Health
64 Broadway Market, E8 (7275 8434/www.holistic-health-hackney.co.uk). Cambridge Heath rail.

Iyengar Institute
223a Randolph Avenue, W9 (7624 3080/www.iyi.org.uk). Maida Vale tube.

Sivananda Yoga Vedanta Centre
51 Felsham Road, SW15 (8780 0160/ www.sivananda.org/london). Putney rail/Putney Bridge tube.

Triyoga
6 Erskine Road, NW3 (7483 3344/www.triyoga.co.uk). Chalk Farm tube.

Yoga Therapy Centre
90-92 Pentonville Road, N1 (7689 3040/ www.yogatherapy.org). Angel tube.

SPECTATOR SPORTS

A trip to a top football match is a real thrill for children. Sadly, the majority of Premiership games are sell-outs, with attendance limited to club members and season-ticket holders, so children rarely get a look-in. However, London has plenty of clubs in the Nationwide League where it's far easier to gain admission, while other sports, such as basketball and rugby, in and around the capital are accessible, exciting and family-friendly. Going to the dogs (greyhound stadium) is a lot of fun too.

Basketball

It may be a minority sport here, but the atmosphere is great. The London Towers compete in the BBL Championship, where many players are imports from America. Home-grown talent like Hackney's competes in the NBL Conference. There's a game most weeks from October to April.

Hackney White Heat

SPACE Centre, Hackney Community College, Falkirk Street, N1 (7613 9535). Old Street tube. **Admission** £3; £2 under-16s.

London Towers

Crystal Palace National Sports Centre, Ledrington Road, SE19 (8776 7755/www.london-towers.co.uk). Crystal Palace rail. **Admission** £8; £6 under-16s.

Football

Any keen young football fan will enjoy being given 'junior membership' of the team they support. But if that team plays in the Premiership, it doesn't mean they'll also get easy access to match tickets. Some top clubs have three or four times as many members as the capacity of their ground, while the likes of Arsenal even have a waiting list for season tickets. In the event that you do manage to strike it lucky, you may find yourself having to pay the full adult price for children's seats. West Ham run occasional 'kids a quid' deals – but parents will still have to fork out at least £26 to come along.

The Nationwide League is a much better option. Indeed, clubs at this level positively encourage youngsters and families with cheap tickets and special deals: at Leyton Orient, a child's season ticket costs just £40, or less than £2 a match.

Ticket prices and membership packages are too numerous to list for each club: call for details or check out the website. As a rule, a seat at a Premiership match will cost £25-£30 for an adult, half that for children, with a discount for club members. Nationwide League prices are around £15-£25, again with reductions for children and club members. The season runs from August to May.

FA Barclaycard Premiership

Arsenal
Arsenal Stadium, Avenell Road, N5 (7704 4040/ www.arsenal.com). Arsenal tube.

Charlton Athletic
The Valley, Floyd Road, SE7 (8333 4010/ www.cafc.co.uk). Charlton rail.

Chelsea
Stamford Bridge, Fulham Road, SW6 (7385 5545/ticket info 0891 121011/www.chelseafc.co.uk). Fulham Broadway tube.

Fulham
(0870 442 1234/www.fulhamfc.com). Playing at Queens Park Rangers' ground next season.

Tottenham Hotspur
White Hart Lane, 748 High Road, N17 (08700 112222/ www.spurs.co.uk). White Hart Lane rail.

West Ham United
Boleyn Ground, Green Street, E13 (8548 2700/ www.whufc.com). Upton Park tube.

Nationwide League

Brentford
Griffin Park, Braemar Road, Brentford, Middx (8847 2511/www.brentfordfc.co.uk). Brentford rail. Division 2.

Crystal Palace
Selhurst Park, Park Road, SE25 (8771 8841/ www.cpfc.co.uk). Selhurst rail. Division 1.

Leyton Orient
Matchroom Stadium, Brisbane Road, E10 (8926 1010/ www.leytonorient.co.uk). Leyton tube. Division 3.

Millwall
The Den, Zampa Road, SE16 (7231 9999/ www.millwallfc.co.uk). South Bermondsey rail. Division 1.

Queens Park Rangers
Rangers Stadium, South Africa Road, W12 (8740 2575/ www.qpr.co.uk). White City tube. Division 2.

Watford
Vicarage Road, Watford, Herts (01923 496010/ www.watfordfc.co.uk). Watford High Street rail. Division 1.

Greyhound racing

Despite its rough-and-ready image, greyhound racing has worked hard to promote itself as a friendly, lively and characterful activity for all ages. The evening meetings might attract the geezers (diamond and dodgy), but Bank Holiday events and 'Sunday Fundays' pull in the families with such attractions as cheap admission, grandstand restaurants and all kinds of free entertainment. What's more, each race is over more quickly than, say, a horse race, so the thrills of the chase come round again faster. Half the fun of taking kids to the dogs is checking out the hounds as they parade up and down before a race, letting the nippers pick a favourite, then placing a small bet on their behalf. A couple of winners might even pay for lunch!

Catford Stadium
Adenmore Road, SE6 (8690 8000/ www.catfordstadium.co.uk). Catford Bridge rail. **Admission** £1.50.

Romford Stadium
London Road, Romford (01708 762345/ www.trap6.com/romford). Romford rail. **Admission** £1.50-£5.50.

Activities

Walthamstow Stadium

Chingford Road, E4 (8531 4255/
www.wsgreyhound.co.uk). Highams Park rail.
Admission £3-£6.

Wimbledon Stadium

Plough Lane, SW17 (8946 8000/
www.wimbledondogs.co.uk). Wimbledon Park tube.
Admission £5.50.

Horse racing

Most meetings at the 59 racecourses around the UK
offer excellent entertainment for all ages. Admission
to the gee-gees for under-16s is usually free, while
the majority of courses host 'family days' during
the school holidays or on Sundays.

The **Racecourse Association** website
(www.comeracing.co.uk) has details of, and links
to, all the British courses, plus a full calendar of
meetings and plenty of information for first-timers.
Admission prices stated below are for adults
attending regular meetings; children go free.

Ascot

High Street, Ascot, Berks (01344 622211/
www.ascot.co.uk). Ascot rail. **Admission** £7-£33.

Epsom Downs

Racecourse Paddock, Epsoms Downs, Surrey (01372
726311/www.epsomderby.co.uk). Epsom Downs rail.
Admission £5-£17.

Kempton Park

Staines Road East, Sunbury-on-Thames, Surrey (01932
782292/www.kempton.co.uk). Kempton Park rail.
Admission £7-£16.

Lingfield Park

Racecourse Road, Lingfield, Surrey (01342 834800/
www.lingfield-racecourse.co.uk). Lingfield rail.
Admission £12-£16.

Sandown Park

Portsmouth Road, Esher, Surrey (01372 463072/
www.sandown.co.uk). Esher rail. **Admission** £5-£22.

Windsor

Maidenhead Road, Windsor, Berks (0870 220 0024/
www.windsor-racecourse.co.uk). Windsor & Eton
Riverside rail. **Admission** £5-£17.

Motor racing

Bangers and Stock Car Racing

Wimbledon Stadium, Plough Lane, SW17 (8946 8000/
www.spedeworth.co.uk). Wimbledon Park tube.
Admission £10; £5 under-15s.
The racing is of secondary interest here; it's the crashes people come to see. Contact between cars is not only legal – it's
positively encouraged. After two hours of shunts, scrapes
and acts of premeditated mechanical violence, the race degen-
erates into a full-on demolition derby. The season runs from
August to May, with meetings held roughly every fortnight,
and it's fabulous fun for kids (and grown-ups) of all ages.

Brands Hatch

Fawkham, Kent (0870 6060 611/
www.brandshatch.co.uk). Swanley rail.
The two circuits here host racing of every description, from
the hugely popular Superbikes and Touring Cars to small
club meetings. Adult tickets start from £10, but children
always get in free or pay just a nominal £1 charge.

Rugby league

Attendances at the Broncos' Super League matches
– usually on Sundays – are steadily rising. The
London Skolars play in the National League; the
Skolars and the Broncos work jointly. The season
runs March to October.

London Broncos

Griffin Park, Braemar Road, Brentford (0871 222 1132/
www.londonbroncos.co.uk). Brentford rail. **Admission**
£10-£15 (£4-£6 under-16s), or £8-£13 (£2-£4) in advance.

London Skolars

New River Stadium, White Hart Lane, N22 (8881
2323/www.skolars.com). Wood Green tube, then W3/W4
bus. **Admission** £8, £2 concessions.

Rugby union

Victories over the Southern Hemisphere giants have
hoisted England to the top of the world league, and
they've given a boost to the club scene back home,
too. London Welsh are in the First Division of the
National League, while London's Harlequins and
Saracens sides in the Zurich Premiership boast a
slew of internationals in their line-ups. A trip to a
rugby match is a bargain compared to football: the
season runs from September to May with matches
on Saturdays and Sundays.

Harlequins

Stoop Memorial Ground, Langhorn Drive, Twickenham
(0871 871 8877/www.quins.co.uk). Twickenham rail.
Admission £12-£25; £2-£5 under-16s.

London Welsh

Old Deer Park, Kew Road, Richmond (8940
2368/www.london-welsh.co.uk). Richmond tube/rail.
Admission £10-£13; £5 under-16s.

Saracens

Watford Football Club, Vicarage Road, Watford (01923
475222/www.saracens.com). Watford High St rail.
Admission £10-£35; £7 under-16s.

Twickenham Stadium

Rugby Road, Twickenham (8892 2000/www.rfu.com).
Twickenham rail.
This superb ground plays host to England international
matches and a full programme of club games. Although tickets for the famous Six Nations Championship (held from
February to April) are almost impossible to obtain unless
you're a member of a rugby club, the others are much more
accessible and reasonably priced with enjoyable family packages usually available.

Days Out

Days Out

Castle crazy? Do like to be beside the seaside? Step this way.

London is both the best place place to arrive at and depart from. The transport links in and out of the capital cover more or less every county. Those immediately surrounding London can provide sandy beaches, wild safari parks, ancient castles and steam trains chuffing through valleys and hills. Most of the destinations we list here are within 90 minutes journey time of central London, so are easy to visit on a day trip. If the idea of staying away awhile grabs you, pick up a copy of *Time Out Weekend Breaks from London* (£12.99), which covers the getaways in more depth.

For the main entries listed in this chapter we've included full details of opening times, admission and transport details, but be aware that these can change without notice. If you're planning a trip around one particular sight, always phone first to check that it's open. Most places have informative websites for events and special dates.

To find out about more attractions, visit the offices or website of the **Britain Visitor Centre** (1 Regent Street, SW1, www.visitbritain.com). For opening hours for personal callers to the offices, *see p299*.

Travel from London

By train

When they're running to schedule, and leaves, snow, high winds and other natural disasters aren't playing havoc with the line, trains are a relaxing, family-friendly way to travel, particularly after 10am on a weekday morning.

For information on train times and ticket prices, call National Rail Enquiries on 08457 484950, or visit www.nationalrail.co.uk. The website has a journey-planning facility that is particularly helpful. Contact NRE for the lowdown on the **Family Railcard**. This costs £20, and lasts one year. It gives travellers with children one year of discounts off standard rail fares (a third off adult fares, 60 per cent off child fares, £1 minimum fare). Under-fives travel free. The railcard is valid across the whole of Britain. Up to two adults can be named as cardholders and can use the card – they do not have to be related. The minimum group size is one cardholder and one child aged five to 15; maximum group size, two cardholders, two other adults and four children aged five to 15. To pick up a form for the Family Railcard, visit your local staffed station.

London's mainline stations

Charing Cross
Strand, WC2. **Map** p319 7L.
For trains to and from south-east England (including Dover, Folkestone and Ramsgate).

Euston
Euston Road, NW1. **Map** p317 3K.
For trains to and from north and north-west England and Scotland, and a suburban line north to Watford.

King's Cross
Euston Road, N1. **Map** p317 2L.
For trains to and from north and north-east England and Scotland, and suburban lines to north London and Hertfordshire.

Liverpool Street
Liverpool Street, EC2. **Map** p321 R5.
For trains to and from the east coast (including Harwich) and Stansted airport; also for trains to East Anglia and suburban services to east and north-east London.

London Bridge
London Bridge Street, SE1. **Map** p321 Q8.
For trains to Kent, Sussex, Surrey and south London suburbs.

Paddington
Praed Street, W2. **Map** p313 D5.
For trains to and from west and south-west England, south Wales and the Midlands.

Victoria
Terminus Place, SW1. **Map** 318 H10.
For fast trains to and from the channel ports (Folkestone, Dover, Newhaven); for trains to and from Gatwick Airport, and suburban services to south and south-east London.

Waterloo
York Road, SE1. **Map** p319 M9.
For fast trains to and from the south and south-west of England (Portsmouth, Southampton, Dorset, Devon), and suburban services to south London.

By coach

Coach and bus travel is cheaper than than rail travel, and quite comfortable, but it's slower. **National Express** (0870 580 8080) runs routes to most parts of the country; its coaches depart from **Victoria Coach Station**, a five-minute walk from Victoria rail and tube station. **Green Line** (0870 608 7261) operates within an approximate 40-mile (64-kilometre) radius of London. Most buses depart from **Eccleston Bridge** (Colonnades Coach Station, SW1, behind Victoria Coach Station).

Victoria Coach Station

164 Buckingham Palace Road, SW1 (7730 3466). Victoria tube/rail. **Map** p318 H1.
Britain's most comprehensive coach company National Express and Eurolines (01582 404511), which travels to the continent, are based at Victoria Coach Station. There are many other companies operating to and from London, some of which depart from Marble Arch.

Seaside delights.

By car

Probably the most convenient and inexpensive means of getting out of town as far as families are concerned. You can stop off where you like, carry as many toys, accessories and picnic items as you need... but you need to check out your route for possible roadworks and delays, and avoid the morning rush hour (roughly 7-10am on a weekday). Travelling into London after about 4pm on a Sunday evening is often ghastly too.

Though we've given basic directions for sights (nearest rail station, which motorway and junction you should take if coming by car; most sights are signposted from there on), it's always best to check on a detailed map first. Drivers may want to check out the route with the Automobile Association (AA), whose free routeplanner service is available on www.theaa.co.uk. The Royal Automobile Association (RAC) also has one, available on www.rac.co.uk.

City awaydays

Cambridge

Getting there *By train* from King's Cross (50 mins) or Liverpool Street (1hr 15mins). *By coach* National Express (1hr 50mins). *By car* J11 or 12 off M1. Park & Ride scheme operates.

Tourist information *Old Library, Wheeler Street, Cambridge, CB2 3QB (01223 322640/www.tourism cambridge.com).*

You won't find soft play centres round every corner in Cambridge, but if you prefer more sophisticated entertainment for your offspring, there's plenty here, as befits a city with an academic heritage stretching back to the 13th century. Around the historic town centre, try the **University Museum of Archaeology and Anthropology** on Downing Street (01223 333516, restricted opening times), with an Indian totem pole and ceremonial masks in the Gallery (suitable for over-fives). Adventurers aged from nine are intrigued by the **Scott Polar Research Institute** in Lensfield Road (01223 336540, www.spri.cam.ac.uk, restricted opening times), with relics of Captain Scott's ill-fated 1912 trip to the South Pole, while the **University Museum of**

Zoology in Downing Street (01223 336650) appeals to animal lovers. The usually excellent Fitzwilliam Museum in Trumpington Street is open but undergoing renovation until 2005; then there's the cute **Folk Museum** (2-3 Castle Street, 01223 355159), which has children's workshops in the school holidays (bookable only in advance). The **University of Cambridge Science Festival** (01223 766766) held every March, has a wide, free programme of children's lectures and exhibitions. **Heffers Children's Bookshop** (01223 568573), in the modern Grafton shopping centre, is one of the largest in the country, with 17,000 kids' titles. Storytime is at 3pm on Sundays and there are regular events in-store. Some central streets are semi-pedestrianised but pavements are too crowded to be buggy-friendly and watch for bikes on the road. Visitors are allowed into the beautiful college grounds (entry £1.20-£4 per person, depending on the college) except during exams in June, but you can't picnic, walk on the grass or make too much noise. It's less restrictive – and free – to stroll along the **Backs**, scenic meadows behind the main colleges bordering the River Cam. Or take to a punt (Easter to October and some off-season weekends), for hire from Mill Lane, Magdalene Street Bridge, Garret Hostel Lane and the Granta Pub. The largest operator is **Scudamore's Boatyard** (01223 359750). Cambridge has great green spaces: Lammas Land (Newnham Road) has a play area and outdoor paddling pool, while **Christ's Pieces** hosts a children's festival 10-14 June 2003 (01223 457521) with music, storytelling and workshops. At Jesus Green, there's a seasonal café and large open-air swimming pool open from May, daily 10am-8pm, or 10am-6pm at weekends (01223 457 505).

As well as famous-name pizza, pasta and burger chains, **Browns** (25 Trumpington Street, 01223 461655) is spacious and geared up for families, with child-friendly waiters and a kids menu. For a pleasant riverside lunch, try the **Anchor Pub** (15 Silver Street, 01223 353554).
In the area: Duxford Imperial War Museum; the Orchard Tea Gardens.

Canterbury
Getting there *By train* from Charing Cross or Victoria (1hr 20min). *By coach* National Express (1hr 50min). *By car* A2, then M2, then A2 again.
Tourist information *34 St Margaret's Street (01227 378100/www.canterbury.co.uk).*
The home of the Church of England since St Augustine was based here in 597, the ancient city of Canterbury oozes atmosphere. Its compact centre, attractiveness to tourists and large student population provide a colourful counterweight to the brooding mass of history hanging around its old buildings and, of course, its cathedral. It's annoying that you have to pay even to get into the cathedral close. You can see more of St Paul's free than you can of **Canterbury Cathedral** (01227 762862), but its beauty is worth the admission fee. A plaque near the altar marks where Archbishop Thomas à Becket was murdered. His tomb has been pilgrimage destination ever since, and the pilgrimage was the focus of the book which kicks off virtually every English degree – Chaucer's *Canterbury Tales*. The exhibition based around Chaucer's book, **Canterbury Tales** (St Margaret's Street, 01227 479227), is an absolute scream. Visitors are given a walkie-talkie to point at tableaux inspired by Chaucer's Prologue and the tales of his Knight, Miller and company. As you enjoy the spectacle and listen to the stories, characters pop up to join in the fun. During half terms and weekends special events are organised for kids. The **Roman Museum** on Butchery Lane (01227 785575) is a more conventional attraction; remains of a Roman townhouse and mosaic floor count among its treasures.

The city centre nestling up to the cathedral is a pleasure to explore, with quirky, independent shops and restaurants holding their own beside the big-name chains. Every child should be given a few quid to spend in the lovely **Hawkin's Bazaar** (34 Burgate, 01227 785809), a revelatory toy shop whose treasures cost as little as 10p; AA Milne fans love the **Winnie the Pooh** shop (19 Orange Street, 01227 781909). Just around the corner on the High Street there's a brightly inviting ice-cream parlour called **Morelli's**. Just as importantly, there are two excellent sweetie shops (buy your old favourites in quarter-pound portions) and a fudge shop. For a decent meal before all that lovely sugar, try various pizza parlours overlooking the river, the Nandos on the high street, Tex-Mex in the **Café des Amis du Mexique** (95 St Dunstan's Street, 01227 464390) or cheerful service, juicy burgers, skins, ribs, cocktails and thick shakes in **Fat Freddie's Diner** (45 St Peter's Street, 01227 784770).
In the area: Wild Wood; Howletts Zoo.

Oxford
Getting there *By train* from Paddington (1hr), then use your rail ticket for a free ride into the centre on one of the electric buses (every 10mins). *By coach* frequent, cheap, fast services (1hr 40mins) from several London departure points; details from National Express, Stagecoach (01865 727000) and Oxford Bus Company (01865 785410). *By car* J8 off M40 then A40; use the Park & Ride buses.
Tourist information *The Old School, Gloucester Green (01865 726871/www.visitoxford.org).*
Oxford, one of the loftiest peaks in the scholarship Himalayas, famous for spires, gowns and a rather stuffy atmosphere – that's the common perception. True, it's short on latter-day razzmatazz, but to children with a nose for architecture and historical atmosphere, Oxford delivers a lot in a compact area. Good views of the city can be had from the tops of **Carfax Tower** (01865 792653) and **St Mary's Church** (01865 279111), or – for the classic dreaming whatnots view – out of town on Boar's Hill. The colleges themselves are usually open to the public, but access in term time is more restricted than in the hols: visit the tourist office for details of opening times and guided tours. **Christ Church** and **Magdalen** score highly for grandeur (the latter even has its own deer park), but the smaller colleges also conceal plenty of gems.

On a sunny day there are few picnic destinations as lovely as **Christ Church Meadow**, stretching from the workplace of erstwhile maths don Charles Dodgson (aka Lewis Carroll) to the river. From March to October, you can take your picnic afloat: punting is the classic Oxford summer activity. Hire a boat from **Cherwell Boathouse** (01865 515978) or **Magdalen Bridge Boathouse** (01865 202643). It's fairly hard work, but if you master the art your passengers will love you; wear comfortable togs (and, in high summer, insect repellent). Lifejackets are available for kids, though the flat-bottomed punt is virtually impossible to capsize – the person most likely to end up in the drink is the one wielding the pole.

Indoor attractions include the **Oxford Story** (6 Broad Street, 01865 728822), a sedate rollercoaster trip, with commentary, through a succession of waxwork tableaux illustrating the city's history. The University's **Pitt Rivers Museum** (Parks Road, 01865 270927) is a glorious jumble of shrunken heads, voodoo dolls and other ethnological exhibits. And the **Ashmolean Museum** (Beaumont Street, 01865 278000; closed Mon) is packed with priceless art treasures, as old as Ancient Egyptian jewellery and as recent as Pre-Raphaelite and Impressionist masterworks.

Away from the cultural trail, there's a good choice of appealing boutiques, and the **Covered Market** is good for knick-knacks and café food. At meal times **Brown's** (5-11

Willing punters at **Cambridge**. *See p271.*

Woodstock Road, 01865 319600) is a good family bet, and a short way out of town the famous **Trout** pub (195 Godstow Road, Wolvercote) does decent food in a riverside setting.

Parking in the centre is scarce (and the one-way system is for initiates only), so if you're coming by car you're best off leaving it in one of the four Park & Ride parks just inside the ring road and hopping aboard one of the frequent buses.

Winchester

Getting there *By train* from Waterloo (1hr). *By coach* National Express. *By car* J9 off M3, then Park & Ride (no buses Sun).

Tourist information *The Guildhall, The Broadway (01962 840500/www.visitwinchester.co.uk).*

The ancient fomer capital of England, Winchester has also been cited as the most likely location for Camelot, King Arthur's castle. A round table has hung up in the Great Hall (the only surviving bit of Winchester Castle) for 600 years. **The Hall** (Castle Avenue, 01962 846476) is often the first port of call for children captivated by Arthurian legend. It's free to enter and has an exhibition all about the history of the old castle. Outside, Queen Eleanor's Garden has a lovely herbal plot for dreaming in. Winchester's heart, however, is its ancient **Cathedral** (The Close, 01962 857202). It may not be as beautiful from the outside as rivals such as Wells, but inside (suggested donation for adults £3.50) the architectural features adorning the longest medieval nave in Europe are breathtaking. The cathedral has its origins in the 7th century. Its world famous Bible dates from the 12th century and its illustrations, created by illuminators in in pure gold and lapis lazuli, are exquisite. The cathedral crypt floods in the winter, but when it's dry you can go down to see Anthony Gormley's statue, Sound II. Jane Austen is buried in the Cathedral, and the house where she lived the last six weeks of her life is nearby, on **College Street**. Near the cathedral, Winchester College is the oldest continuously running school in England (founded 1382).

A short walk away from the city centre, the **Hospital of St Cross** (St Cross Road, 01962 851375) is a serene place to visit. It was founded in 1132, and is home to 25 Brothers. During the summer there's a café for paying vistors, but the Brothers have a tradition going back centuries of providing sustenance – Wayfarers' Dole – for weary travellers.

A whole series of Military museums provide further history lessons in the city. There's the **King's Royal Hussars Museum**, the **Gurkha Museum** and the **Light Infantry Museum** to name just three; more details can be had from the tourist information centre.

Shoppers have plenty of independent shops to potter – St George's and Parchment Streets are particularly pleasant for browsers. Serious spenders may prefer the bright modern Brooks Centre, where a display called the **Brooks Experience** (there's a Hawkin's Bazaar here for those keen to part with their pocket-money) harks back to Winchester's Roman and medieval roots. If they don't want to eat in chains (Pizza Express, ASK, Pizza Hut, McDonald's), families are hard pressed to find a restaurant that's really suited to children's needs. We've found the staff at the **Cathedral Refectory** to be sympathetic, and there's usally space to stow a buggy. Otherwise, there's the Italian **Giorgios** on

George Street (01962 863515) or **Alcatraz** (Jewry Street, 01962 860047), which does good half-portion pastas and pizzas that can be shared among the family.
In the area: Marwell Zoological Park; Watercress Line.

Castles

Bodiam Castle
nr Robertsbridge, East Sussex (01580 830436/ www.nationaltrust.org.uk). **Getting there** *By train* Robertsbridge rail then taxi or local rider bus (Sat only). *By car* J5 off M25. **Open** *Mid Feb-Oct* 10am-6pm/dusk daily. *Nov-mid Feb* 10am-4pm/dusk Sat, Sun. Last entry 1hr before closing. Closed 25 Dec. **Tours** groups of 15 or more only, by arrangement; phone for details. **Admission** (NT) £4; £2 5s-16s; £10 family (2+3); free under-5s. **Credit** AmEx, MC, V.
This castle, built in 1385 to defend the area from French attack, affords a fantastic day out in fine weather. Surviving original features include the moat, portcullis, arrowslits, gun-loops and murder holes. Now owned by the National Trust, it's a favourite venue for picnicking families, school groups on Medieval Castles projects and thousands of children, who love to tear around the grounds playing knights.

A £10 refundable deposit buys you a Bat Pack, which provides children with a tabard to wear, a trail to follow and various interesting activities to get stuck into while they're here. Half terms and holidays see a hugely inventive range of activities, workshops, Family Fun Days, special exhibitions and concerts for all to enjoy. Special celebrations call for castle staff to dress up in medieval dress and entertain visitors. Check the website to find out what's in store, but if you turn up at the weekend during the summer holidays there's bound to be something going on. Being a bit of a ruin, Bodiam can be a bit miserable in steady rain, although the tearoom in the car park and various intact rooms give some shelter in a downpour. Be aware that the only loos round here are in the car park too, so make sure all noses have been powdered before you explore the castle.
Car park. Disabled access: lift, toilet. Nappy-changing facilities. Nearest picnic place: castle grounds. Restaurant. Shop.

Hever Castle
nr Edenbridge, Kent (01732 865224/www.hevercastle. co.uk). **Getting there** *By train* Edenbridge Town rail then taxi, or Hever rail then 1-mile walk. *By car* J5 or 6 off M25. **Open** *Gardens Mar-Oct* 11am-6pm (last entry 5pm) daily. *Nov* 11am-4pm daily. *Castle Mar-Oct* noon-6pm (last entry 5pm daily). *Nov* noon-4pm daily. **Tours** groups (min 20 people) by prior arrangement. **Admission** *Castle & gardens* £8.40; £7.10 concessions; £4.60 5-14s; £21.40 family (2+2); free under-5s. *Gardens only* £6.70; £5.70 concessions; £4.40 5-14s; £17.80 family (2+2); free under-5s. **Credit** MC, V.
This is the 13th-century castle and 15th-century manor house where Anne Boleyn lived as a child, and where Henry VIII courted her. Hever Castle, its gardens and lake, were restored in the early 20th century by American millionaire Waldorf Astor. The castle now contains precious paintings and furniture, and two rare Books of Hours, beautifully illuminated manuscripts inscribed by Anne herself. Exploring the gardens takes all day in fine weather. There's an elaborate yew maze, an adventure playground and a water maze set on Sixteen Acre Island; the secret grottoes, formal gardens and statuary also merit investigation. The water maze is lovely in hot weather – bring a change of clothes for the children!

Special events come with the school holidays. Easter brings an egg hunt, May's celebrations and dance involve plenty of minstrels and maids in winsome period costumes. There's a Merrie England festival at Whitsun, rose extravaganzas in June but best of all, brave knights and sturdy chargers display their jousing prowess all through the summer holidays. For more dates for your diary, check the website.
Buggy access (grounds only). Car park. Nappy-changing facilities. Restaurants. Shops.

Leeds Castle
Maidstone, Kent (01622 765400/www.leeds-castle.com). **Getting there** *By train* Bearsted rail then coach service. *By car* J8 off M20. **Open** *Castle Apr-Oct* 11am-5.30pm daily. *Nov-Mar* 10am-3.30pm daily. Last entry 1hr before closing. *Gardens Nov-Mar* 10am-3pm daily. *Apr-Oct* 10am-5pm daily. Closed 25 Dec, open-air concert days in June, July (28 June, 5 July, 8 Nov 2003). **Tours** pre-booked groups only. **Admission** *Castle, gardens & Dog Collar Museum Mar-June, Aug-Oct* £11; £6-£9.50 concessions; £7.50 4s-15s; £32 family (2+3); free under-4s. *July, Aug* £12; £8.50 4s-15s; £10.50 concessions; £35 family. *Nov-Feb* £9.50; £5.50-£8 concessions; £6 4s-15s; £29 family (2+3); free under-4s. **Credit** MC, V.
The castle of queens (so named because many a king gave it to his wife), this most beautiful of country seats is also known as the queen of castles. It was built just after the Norman Conquest in 1066. Over the centuries, it was fortified and enhanced by various royal householders, including Henrys V and VIII. The castle on the lake was last used as a private home by the elegant Lady Baillie, who bequeathed it to the private Leeds Castle Foundation in 1974. She wanted it to be used as a living castle, not just a museum, and to this end the building and grounds host a number of events: conferences, receptions, arts extravaganzas and, naturally, a huge variety of family attractions during school holidays.

Inside the castle, the beautifully maintained rooms, banqueting halls and cellars tell their own tale. The Heraldry Room is lined with portraits of the royal owners of the castle. You admire coats of arms while listening to a simplified explanation of heraldry. As you're leaving the main island, just before going through the gate tower, you come to the quirky Dog Collar Museum, with its collection of exhibits spanning four centuries.

The grounds are far more likely to take up the children's time and energy: there's the delightful Culpeper cottage garden and the Mediterranean formality of the Lady Baillie garden, as well as a vineyard and greenhouses. Regal black swans swim in the moat and lake, but rare and endangered bird species live a sedate life in the aviary. The yew maze has at its centre a leafy secret grotto, decorated with mythical beasts fashioned with stone and shell mosaics.

Ring for an events leaflet to find out about children's classical concerts and open-air summer theatre. The castle hosts other events all year, including annual Easter, Whitsun and summer playtimes. There's a children promenade concert to complement those put on for adults, as well as firework spectaculars and banquets; the Great Leeds Castle Balloon & Vintage Car Weekend takes place on 13 and 14 September 2003. Check the website for the packed events programme.

About five miles up the road on the M20 is the **Museum of Kent Life** (Lock Lane, Sandling, Maidstone, 01622 763936, www.museum-kentlife.co.uk). Here, children can interact with farm animals and exotic birds and learn about various aspects of farming life through the month-on exhibits.
Buggy access. Cafés. Car park. Disabled access: lift, toilet. Nappy-changing facilities. Nearest picnic place: grounds. Restaurants. Shop.

Family RAILCARD

You pay less with a Family Railcard

(So you can get away more)

60% off children's fares* and ⅓ off for adults

Taking the train makes it a real day out. And with a Family Railcard the whole family can get cheaper train travel. It costs just £20 pounds for a whole year - and up to 4 adults and 4 children can travel on one card. So you can get away more, for less. Just don't leave the bikes where the plants can get them.

Pick up a Family Railcard leaflet at any staffed station or call 08457 48 49 50 for the telesales number of your nearest Train Company

National Rail   *Children's tickets subject to £1 minimum fare   www.family-railcard.co.uk

Little wonder

Children love miniature worlds, and Bekonscot is a real tiddler. Created as a hobby by Roland Callingham in 1929, and now a charitable organisation, there are 4,000 tiny wooden residents of six mini villages in a one-and-a-half-acre landscape of farms, fields, woodland, churches, castles and lakes. A busy gauge-one model railway stops at seven stations (listen for the station announcer). Check out Chessnade Zoo, with its chimps' tea party, aviary and elephant rides and marvel at the intricate detail of the fairground, where working mini-rides include a carousel, helter-skelter, big wheel and flying boats. It's a tranquil scene, with manicured alpine plants, lawns and dwarf conifers providing a green backdrop to the towers and spires. Children can get up close to all the models to feel part of this dolly world. For full-sized action, there's a playground and a ride-on steam railway (50p per person, runs at weekends, bank holidays and local school holidays).

Bekonscot Model Village

Warwick Road, Beaconsfield, Bucks HP9 2PL (01494 672919/www.bekonscot.com). **Getting there** *By train* Chiltern Railways from Marylebone to Beaconsfield. *By car* J2 off M40 or J16 off M25. **Open** *15 Feb-2 Nov* 10am–5pm daily. **Admission** £4.80; £4 concessions; £3 3s-16s; £13.50 family (2+2). **Credit** MC, V. *Buggy access. Car park. Nappy-changing facilities. Refreshment kiosk. Shop.*

Mountfitchet Castle & Norman Village

Stansted Mountfitchet, Essex (01279 813237/24hr info line 0906 470 0898/www.gold.enta.net). **Getting there** *By train* Stansted Mountfichet rail. *By car* J8 off M11. **Open** *2nd Sun Mar-2nd Sun Nov* 10am-5pm daily. **Admission** £5; £4.50 concessions; free under-2s. **Credit** MC, V. **The House on the Hill Toy Museum** *(address, phone & website as above).* **Open** 10am-5pm daily. Closed 24-26 Dec. **Admission** £3.80; £3.50 concessions; £3 2s-14s; free under-2s. Ten per cent discount on prices if visiting both sites on same day. **Credit** MC, V.

This motte and bailey castle and Norman village reconstructed on an original site whisks you back 900 years to give an evocative picture of life in medieval times. The approach to the castle compound is pastoral (nearby Stansted airport doesn't intrude). Once inside, there's no shying away from the fact that life in Norman times was nasty, brutish and short (the severed head of an invader is stuck on a spike at the entrance). Lifelike figures in the castle dungeon demonstrate the grisly punishments meted out for the mildest misdemeanours. But it's not all gore: you can witness a banquet in the Grand Hall (here are the remains of the original 12th-century castle); peer into a timber and thatch peasant home, where a family huddles around the cooking pot on a real fire; or admire the everyday artistry of the potter, basket maker and weaver, beautifully reconstructed with the tools of their trades. The smell of drifting wood smoke adds to the ambience, while snippets of recorded information set the scene. The layout is a manageable size for toddlers, but for older children there are twisting paths to be explored, open grassy areas, and lookout posts to climb. Tame fallow deer, goats, guinea fowl, sheep, chickens and peacocks, breeds that the Normans kept for food and fur, wander everywhere and you can buy food for them at the ticket office. Picnic in the outdoor area, eat at the on-site café, or fuel up at the chippie across the road. After lunch, drop into the House on the Hill Toy Museum next door, which has 70,000 exhibits, from end-of-the-pier games to play, and a working Meccano fairground. *Buggy access. Café. Car park. Nappy-changing facilities. Nearest picnic place: Grounds. Shops.*

Windsor Castle

Windsor, Berks (7321 2233/bookings & info 7321 2233/ www.royal.gov.uk). **Getting there** *By train* Windsor & Eton Riverside rail. *By car* J6 off M4. **Open** *Mar-Oct* 9.45am-5.15pm (last entry 4pm) daily. *Nov-Feb* 9.45am-4.15pm (last entry 3pm) daily. Closed 25, 26 Dec. **Admission** (LP) £11.50; £9.50 concessions; £6 5s-16s; £29 family (2+3); free under-5s. *Audio guide £2.95.* **Credit** AmEx, MC, V.

As it's one of the Queen's official residences, it's hardly surprising that this, the largest and oldest occupied castle in the world seems a sight more formal than our other favourites. St George's Chapel here is the final resting place of Queen Elizabeth the Queen Mother, who died on 30 March 2002.

Windsor probably wouldn't be the first choice of rampaging toddlers, as its many treasures demand reverent viewing, and the numbers of tourists it attracts can mean incessant queuing. The whole site covers 13 acres, however, so if you encounter queues in one place you can nip off to another and be rewarded. The biggest queue is for the most intriguing (certainly to children) exhibit, Queen Mary's Dolls' House, given to her in 1924. It is an amazing piece of craftsmanship, perfect in every tiny detail, right down to the vintage wine in the miniature casks.

The fabulous Windsor collection of medieval weaponry is contained in the Grand Vestibule, the Queen's Guard Chamber and the restored St George's Hall. Trophy swords, pairs of pistols, Napoleon's scarlet cloak (captured at Waterloo) and the bullet that killed Lord Nelson at Trafalgar in 1805 are sights to see. The sequel to the Grand Vestibule is the Queen's Guard Chamber: floor to ceiling weapons again. Carved eagles and lions adorn the ivory Indian throne.

The Changing of the Guard takes place from April to July outside the Guardroom in the Lower Ward, at 11am Monday to Saturday, and on alternate days the remainder of the year. (The sentries are changed throughout the day.)

If you want to spend the entire day here keep the proximity of Legoland (*see p290*) a secret, or your children will be boarding the shuttle service connecting the two attractions. *Disabled access: lift, toilet. Nappy-changing facilities. Nearest picnic place: Mote Garden (£1 charge). Shop.*

Country parks

Bewl Water

Lamberhurst, nr Tunbridge Wells, Kent (01892 890661/ www.bewl.co.uk). **Getting there** *By train* Wadhurst rail then taxi, or Tunbridge Wells rail. *By car* J5 off M25. **Open** 9am-dusk daily. Closed 25 Dec, Concert Day (Sat 12 July). **Admission** *per vehicle Apr-Oct* £4 Mon-Fri; £5 Sat, Sun. *Nov-Mar* £2.50 daily. *Concert tickets* phone for details. **Credit** MC, V.

An area of serene beauty, Bewl Water – the largest lake in the south-east, with more than 15 miles of shoreline – is the perfect place to unwind on long summer afternoons, with 450 acres of surrounding woodland in which to ramble, ride bikes or simply repose at one of many picnic spots and shelters. Ferryboats leave every hour between 11am and 4pm (April to October, weather permitting), giving families a chance to cruise the whole circumference or get off halfway and walk the rest (£3.50-£4 adults, £2.50 children), while a prescribed route of roughly 12.5 miles is recommended for hikers who are made of sterner stuff.

Bewl is perhaps most famously a fisherman's paradise: boat hire costs from £17 per person per day, while daily fishing permits cost £17 for eight fish or £10.60 for two (an Environment Agency licence is also required, available at Bewl), and an afternoon permit (four fish after 3pm) costs £12.80. Casting lines for trout is tough work for tiny hands, but experienced parents wishing to teach their kids are welcome to do so here (fishing permits for under-15s are available; £4 for two fish). Smaller fry can enjoy exploring an extensive wooden playground.

Windsurfing tuition is given by qualified RYA (Royal Yachting Association) instructors: all equipment is provided, and kids with a taste for water sports can then graduate on to rowing and powerboat lessons, also given on the premises (phone the Outdoor Centre on 01892 890716). *Car park. Cafe. Disabled access: toilet. Nappy-changing facilities. Nearest picnic place: Grounds. Restaurant. Shop.*

The Hop Farm Country Park

Paddock Wood, Kent, TN12 6PY (01622 872068/ www.thehopfarm.co.uk). **Getting there** *By train* Paddock Wood rail. *By car* J5 off M25, then A21 south. **Open** 10am-5pm daily. Closed 25, 26 Dec, 6 Sept. **Admission** £6.50; £5.50 concessions; £22 family (2+2); free under 4s. Prices vary on event days. **Credit** MC, V.

Kent's rural past comes into focus at the former Whitbread Hop Farm, still home to the largest collection of

oast houses in the world, but under private ownership since 1997 and more family-friendly than ever. At the Decades Experience, children get a walk-through guide to life during the last 100 years, with 1900s shops, a school and blitzed out streets leading to a 1960s diner, all populated by an intriguing collection of characters.

Animal encounters come courtesy of the shire horse stables, where these noble beasts also give rides in dray carts (low carriages used to haul beer) for a small fee. There's also an animal farm, and a petting zoo where kids can make friends with the guinea pigs and rabbits.

Smaller children will literally be bouncing off the walls in the Happy Hoppers soft play barn, and there's a free, nine-hole crazy golf course based around local landmarks for putters. Art and craft activities take place in the pottery workshop, and on the third week of every July, a military War and Peace exhibition gives kids a ride in a real tank. September 2003 sees Invicta FM's Party In The Park on the 6th, and a two-day country fair (with bird of prey demonstrations and sheepdog trials) starting on the 13th. Phone for a list of events.

Buggy access. Car park (free). Cafés. Disabled access: toilet. Nappy-changing facilities. Nearest picnic place: grounds. Shop.

Painshill Landscape Garden

Painshill Park Trust, Portsmouth Road, Cobham, Surrey (01932 868113/www.painshill.co.uk). **Getting there** *By train* Cobham or Weybridge rail. *By car* J10 off M25. **Open** *Apr-Oct* 10.30am-6pm (last entry 4.30pm) Tue-Sun, bank hols. *Nov-Mar* 11am-4pm (last entry 3pm) Wed-Sun, bank hols. Closed 25 Dec. **Tours** groups of ten or more only, by arrangement. **Admission** £6; £5.25 concessions; £18 family (2+2); £3.50 5-16s; free under 5s. *Season ticket* £30; £60 family (2+2). **Credit** MC, V.

The gardens at Painshill were originally intended as a Romantic retreat for culturally enlightened, high society Londoners. These days, visitors can marvel at the views regardless of

Leeds Castle. *See p274.*

their social status, taking in lakes, exotic foliage and a series of refurbished follies (including a Gothic temple, a grotto and a water wheel) along the way. Children are especially well catered for in school holidays, when Camp Hamilton days for seven- to 11-year-olds offer outdoor trails, indoor activities and creative workshops. Best of all, little explorers get to pitch a camp from scratch in their own piece of wilderness, before being treated to a proper woodland barbecue by staff (£20 per day). A range of family events takes place every Sunday throughout the summer (£6 adults, £3.50 children age five to 16), from puppet shows to teddy bears' picnics (check the website for updated information).

Lectures for adults, covering everything from botany to obscure arts and crafts, start at £15 (accompanying tours are included for a small charge), and – with a little planning ahead – can be booked to coincide with kids' activities. *Buggy access. Café. Car park. Disabled access: toilet. Nappy-changing facilities. Shop.*

Queen Elizabeth Country Park

Gravel Hill, Horndean, Waterlooville, Hampshire PO8 0QE (023 9259 5040/www.hants.gov.uk/countryside/qecp). **Getting there** *By train* Petersfield rail. *By car* off the A3, follow signs. **Open** *Apr-Oct* 10am-5.30pm daily. *Oct-Dec* 10am-dusk daily. *Jan-Mar* 10am-4.30pm Sat, Sun. **Admission** free. *Car park* £1 Mon-Sat; £1.50 Sun, bank hols. **Credit** *Shop* MC, V.

Queen Elizabeth Park, a designated Area of Natural Beauty covering 1,400 acres of the South Downs, is one of those rare places that manages to not only slow life down to a snail's pace, but also evaporate stress in the blink of an eye.

Conservation is an ongoing issue here, with 38 species of butterfly and ten endangered orchids all resident, and there are Roman and Iron Age ruins inside the grounds for those seeking more historical rarities. To this extent, walking (in the appropriate footwear, naturally) is the most popular means of transportation, and a complex network of routes and woodland trails caters to both enthusiastic (five miles)

and amateur ramblers (1.7 miles). There are also cycle routes, and riding is available through the stables on site, where the management runs riding holidays (up to three days with accommodation provided) as well as lessons for over-12s.

There's an excellent adventure playground (made all the more adventurous thanks to its imposing natural surroundings), and plenty of barbecue sites for hire alongside numerous brilliant picnic spots. Butser Hill – the highest point on the Downs – is perfect for kite flying, and becomes the focus of many special events throughout the year (Easter egg rolls, uphill races): phone or check the website for a full list. *Buggy access. Café. Car park. Disabled access: toilet. Nappy-changing facilities. Shop.*

Weald & Downland Open Air Museum

Singleton, Chichester, West Sussex, PO18 OEU (01243 811348/01243 811363/www.wealddown.co.uk). **Getting there** *By train* Chichester rail then 60 bus. *By car* A3 turn off at Millford, A286 to Midhurst and follow signs. **Open** *Mar-Oct* 10.30am-6pm daily. *Nov-Feb* 10.30am-4pm Sat, Sun. **Admission** £7; £6.50 concessions; £4 5s-16s; free under-5s; £19 family (2+3). **Credit** MC, V.

An open-air museum with a difference: here you'll find almost 50 historical buildings and installations dating from the 13th to the 19th centuries, all carefully relocated in over 50 acres of fine Sussex countryside and restored to their former glories. They include a 19th-century smithy, a rare example of a once-common windpump and a 17th-century watermill that still produces its own stoneground flour (used by the café and sold in the gift store). The museum's centrepiece is a 15th-century farmstead, the recreation of which is an ongoing (and painstaking) project. Work has moved beyond the interior furnishings – open fire included – and on to accurately plotted herb gardens and grazing for pigs, sheep and cattle.

The farmstead is not the only place where function plays a central role at Weald & Downland. Here hildren can also test out antiquated building techniques at hands-on holiday workshops, and even drive their own carthorses and brick-

---

Pet rescue

The largest of the three sites of the **Wood Green Animal Shelter**, the King's Bush animal rehoming centre is set in 50 acres. Here rescued ponies, goats, sheep and even llamas safely graze, and around 100 dogs and 100 cats look hopeful. All are well looked after here, but they're always pleased to see kindly visitors. Take a handful of dog biscuits from the reception area and spread a little sunshine among the remarkably chipper-looking canine residents of the newly built Coco Markus kennels. If any look particularly appealing, bear in mind that a dog (cat, llama) is for life, not just for Christmas (birthdays, the summer hols) and that staff are obliged to check out possible adoptive owners for their charges very carefully. There are plenty of picnic tables, grassy hills for children to run down, a small play area and several garden areas. Various events, such as dog shows and craft fairs take place in the adjacent Britten Arena (ring to check what's on). You could eat at the unremarkable Kingsbush Restaurant, but it's better to take a short detour to nearby **Houghton Mill** (01480 301 494), a beautiful National Trust-owned watermill on the River Ouse, with a riverside tearoom (open April, May and October at weekends only, and in June, July, August and September from Sat to Wed, 2-5.30pm). The nearby village of **Hemingford Grey** is a hidden gem worth visiting for its tranquil riverside views and child-friendly walks, and has the **Manor** (01480 463134, open by appointment only), a 12th-century house where children's author Lucy Boston was inspired to write her magical *Green Knowe* books. The pretty garden is open daily, the house by pre-booked tour.

Wood Green Animal Shelter

King's Bush Farm, London Road, Godmanchester, Cambs (01480 830014/www.woodgreen.org.uk). **Getting there** *By train* Huntingdon rail then taxi. *By car* J24 off M11 then A14. **Open** 10-4pm daily. Closed 25, 26 Dec. **Admission** free (except for some events in the Britten Arena). **Credit** *Shop* MC, V. *Buggy access, Café. Free parking. Nappy-changing facilities. Nearest picnic area: grounds. Restaurant. Shop.*

Animal magic at **Fishers Farm**. *See p280.*

laying, while other traditional crafts are kept alive by costumed staff offering regular period-specific demonstrations. It's informative stuff, but never dull, and there are plenty of domestic animals standing about in pens and paddocks to keep younger children amused.

Buggy access. Café. Free parking. Shop.

Wildwood Wildlife Park

Herne Common, Herne Bay, Kent (01227 712111/ www.wildwoodtrust.org). **Getting there** *By train* Herne Bay rail then bus. *By car* J7 off M2. **Open** 10am-5pm daily. Last admission 4pm. **Admission** £6.75; £5.75 concessions; £5.25 disabled, 3s-15s; £20 family (2+2); free under-3s. **Credit** MC, V.

At Wildwood, animal lovers of all ages come face to face with a growing community of furred and feathered friends in an environmentally commendable, 30-acre habitat where enclosures blend seamlessly into the surrounding woodland.

From a network of overgrown walks and pathways, visitors can observe at first hand the behaviour of a wonderful range of creatures, from wild cats and beavers to badgers, wolves and wild boars. Regular Feed and Talk activities offer kids the chance to get up close and observe animals having their lunch, learning a bit more about them in the process (check the boards for times), while designated areas both inside and out of the park make perfect picnic spots for feeding times of a (slightly) different nature. There's a small restaurant which serves snacks and hot meals, and there's an impressive adventure playground for aspiring monkeys of all ages and sizes. Check the website for a list of upcoming events, and remember that the proximity of Wildwood to Herne Bay means that visits can be easily supplemented with a short trip to the beach.

Buggy access. Car park. Disabled access: toilet. Nappy-changing facilities. Restaurant. Shop.

Barleylands Farm

Barleylands Road, Billericay, Essex (01268 532253/ 290029/www.barleylands.co.uk). **Getting there** *By train* Billericay or Basildon rail. *By car* J29 off M25. **Open** *end Mar-Oct* 10am-5pm daily. **Admission** £2.50; prices vary for special events. **Credit** MC, V.

Tractors, like handwritten letters, will never go out of style. However sleek and efficient the new variants of these agricultural workhorses become, there's something charming about the vintage tractor, whose driver had to wear a hat in the rain, never mind listening to Mozart on the in-cab CD player, like he apparently does these days (if Radio Four's *The Archers* is to be believed). There are several vintage tractors on show at this enormous farm museum, alongside a pair of original Fowler plough engines and a huge range of agricultural machinery and memorabilia from a bygone era. Martin, the resident blacksmith, links chains and shapes horseshoes while kids watch entranced, and there are also resident glass blowers who create various objects that can be picked up later in the craft shop next door.

Animal lovers will be tickled pink by the small enclosure of chickens, rabbits and turkeys near the picnic area, and there are larger animals including ponies, cows and pigs further out toward the pond. There's also an activity playground, working stables and, for sustenance, the Magic Mushroom restaurant, which serves up high-quality cuisine (at appropriately mind-blowing prices).

The 17th annual Essex Steam and Country Show takes place at Barleylands on 13 and 14 September 2003, with classic cars and bikes doing the rounds alongside work horses, model engines and a huge selection of craft stands, trade stalls and kids amusements. Children's parties are also organised: for £7 each, children are given a tractor ride, a chance

Days Out

to feed the animals and a small feast of their own. Goody bags are provided, and – for £10 extra – a group of 20 partygoers gets a ride in the miniature steam train.
Buggy access. Café. Car park. Disabled access: toilet. Nappy-changing facilities. Nearest picnic place: grounds.

Bocketts Farm Park
Young Street, Fetcham, nr Leatherhead, Surrey (01372 363764/www.bockettsfarm.co.uk). **Getting there** *By train* Leatherhead rail then taxi. *By car* J9 off M25/26. **Open** 10am-5.30pm daily. Closed 25, 26 Dec, 1 Jan. **Admission** £4.35; £3.95 3-17s; £3.25 2s; free under-2s. **Credit** MC, V.
In a world where most farming is of the conveyor belt variety, a family-run, mixed enterprise like Bocketts – with picturesque red-brick farmhouse and bounded by rolling fields of crops and pasture – is an increasingly rare scene. Also, being open to the public, it gives rural enthusiasts of all ages an insight into the history of British agricultural methods, and (more importantly) provides an ideal spot to 'ooh' and 'aah' at a range of adorable of baby animals.

Those who miss the lambs' birth can always enjoy watching their first tottering steps, and there's a reliable collection of old-timers; from Lily the llama to Ernie the ever-professional barn owl. A small track is host to regular pig races, which pit the athletic prowess of porkers sweating it out for edible treats: pick a piglet and cheer him all the way to the finish line. These absurd and thoroughly amusing events take place at 12.45pm and 3.45pm daily, weather permitting.

There's a covered barn for wet weather, with an indoor kids playground – new for 2003 – incorporating chutes, tumble towers and aerial walkways alongside the already infamous 70ft Astroslide, while a pedal tractor circuit gives aspiring farmhands room to practise their three point turns. Pony, tractor and trailer rides are also available, and kids parties are organised (phone for more information).
Buggy access. Café. Car park (free). Disabled access: toilet. Nappy-changing facilities. Nearest picnic area: grounds. Shop.

Fishers Farm
New Pound Lane, Wisborough Green, West Sussex (01403 700063/www.fishersfarmpark.co.uk). **Getting there** *By train* Billingshurst rail then taxi. *By car* J10 off M25. **Open** 10am-5pm daily; ring for details of opening times of special events. **Admission** *Oct half-term-Feb half-term; Easter hols* £7; £6.50 3s-16s; £5.50 OAPs; £3.25 2s; free under-2s. *Summer hols* £8; £7.50 3s-16s; £6.50 OAPs; £4.25 2s; free under-2s. **Credit** MC, V.
With well-orchestrated touches of drama, Fishers confounds the expectations of kids who might associate farm trips with potato peeling demonstrations and milk churn collections: the Fishers Farm Players regularly perform children's productions in the Farm Theatre (phone for details of upcoming performances), and during school holidays there are magic shows from a range of touring entertainers. Not that rabbits are in short supply, should one fail to appear from the top hat first time round: in fact, the theatre is most usually used for 'meet the animal' sessions, with feeding and veterinary demonstrations given on a daily basis.

Children seeking more active enjoyment can complement petting and pony riding with physically exhausting pursuits, from clambering around the indoor playzone to scaling a more challenging 25ft climbing wall (kids aged six and over), or just pogo-ing themselves silly on trampolines and bouncy castles. There are also slides in all shapes and sizes, miniaturised pedal tractors and a giant paddling pool with sandy shores in summer months. Check the website for information on the range of agriculturally themed birthday celebrations.

Buggy access. Cafés. Car park. Disabled access: toilet. Nappy-changing facilities. Nearest picnic place: grounds. Restaurants. Shops.

Godstone Farm
Tilburstow Hill Road, Godstone, Surrey (01883 742546/www.godstonefarm.co.uk). **Getting there** *By train* Caterham rail then 409, 410, 411 bus. *By car* J6 off M25. **Open** Mar-Oct 10am-6pm daily. Nov-Feb 10am-5pm daily. Closed 25, 26 Dec. **Admission** £4.30 2s-16s, incl one adult; free under-2s. **Credit** AmEx.
Godstone Farm is especially well suited to smaller children. It's filled with various activities to keep their wandering imaginations engaged (without being so big they walk themselves to sleep), and teeming with enough cute and cuddly animal characters to leave even the school bully doting and Bambi-eyed. The various enclosures can be as enlightening as they are heart-warming: eggs from the farm's large range of fowl are held in an incubator, for example, where hatching takes place before an audience, and gives plenty of pre-schoolers their first peek at the miracle of life.

Children with their hearts set on something altogether less profound can chase each other across the adventure playground, the under-nines can lose themselves in the ball pools and walkways that make up the play barn (90p for 30 minutes). The proximity of Godstone to London, like its sister farm, Horton Park (*see below*), makes it an ideal spot for washing some of the city out of grimy urban youngsters, and giving them not only some fresh air, but a fresh perspective.
Buggy access. Café. Car park (free). Disabled access: toilet. Nappy-changing facilities. Nearest picnic place: grounds. Shop.

Horton Park Children's Farm
Horton Lane, Epsom, Surrey (01372 743984/www.hortonpark.co.uk). **Getting there** *By train* Epsom rail then bus. *By car* J9 off M25. **Open** Apr-Oct 10am-6pm daily. Nov-Mar 10am-5pm daily. Last entry 1hr before closing. **Admission** £4.30 over-2s (accompanying adult free). **Credit** MC, V.
Like Godstone Farm, Horton Park is very much designed with kids in mind, although here the emphasis is shifted even further towards simple entertainment for smaller children. As a result, most of the enclosures are designed for close encounters of the furred kind: kids are encouraged to pet gentle animals like rabbits, chicks and hamsters, with non-venomous lizards and snakes for more intrepid handlers.

Related activities are similarly unthreatening, including a maze, soft toy barn and a climbing structure (Fort Horton) to help kids work up an appetite. Food-wise, the café offers both lunch boxes and hot meals, although if the weather's nice, you might want to take something of your own to enjoy in the designated picnic area. Great for younger kids, but probably a little too playful for the over-eights.
Buggy access. Café. Disabled access: toilet. Free parking. Nappy-changing facilities. Nearest picnic place: grounds. Shop.

Odds Farm Park
Wooburn Common, nr High Wycombe, Bucks (01628 520188/www.oddsfarm.co.uk). **Getting there** *By train* Beaconsfield rail. *By car* J2 off M40 or J7 off M4. **Open** early Feb-May, early Sept-late Oct 10am-5.30pm daily. June-early Sept 10am-6.30pm daily. Late Oct-mid Feb 10am-4.30pm daily. **Admission** £5.60; £4.50 2s-16s; free under-2s. **Credit** MC, V.
Odds is another farm that offers younger children a peaceful and uncomplicated environment in which to get up close to a huge range of adorable creatures, including lambs, pigs,

Sand plus sea plus child equals fun at **Littlehampton**. *See p285*.

goats and baby chicks. There are regular feeding demonstrations, nature trails and tractor rides to keep little ones amused. Some activities are dependent on the time of year (sheep shearing, for example, tends to occur between May and July), while more seasonal events (including Easter Egg hunts and Halloween pumpkin carving) take place over one or two weekends annually; keep an eye on the website.

Several well-maintained outdoor play areas (including a sand pit and plenty of log walkways, swings and slides) form a focal point of the many birthday parties held at Odds all year round (phone for more information), or just make a nice spot for kids to amuse themselves while parents linger over a picnic. Those who neglected to bring one will be pleased to learn that there's a café for hot food, snacks and drinks, complemented on sunny days by a mobile ice-cream kiosk.
Buggy access. Car park. Nappy-changing facilities. Shop.

South of England Rare Breeds Centre
Highlands Farm, Woodchurch, nr Ashford, Kent (01233 861493/www.rarebreeds.org.uk). **Getting there** *By train* Ashford rail. *By car* J10 off M20. **Open** *Apr-Sept* 10.30am-5.30pm daily. *Oct-Mar* 10.30am-4.30pm Tue-Sun. Closed 24, 25 Dec. **Admission** £4; £3 3s-15s; free under-3s. **Credit** MC, V.

Playfully scratching rabbits behind the ear is all well and good, but those looking for something a little more unusual are advised to make a trip to the Rare Breeds Centre, where animals once common to the British Isles, but now sadly endangered, are bred and left to roam a wonderful woodland acreage in peace. From gold goats and ginger pigs to tall ducks and cows with handlebar horns, there's nothing run of the mill about these characters, and their tranquil habitat is an ideal place to while away long afternoons with a simple picnic, especially in the summer months, when the forest floor becomes a carpet of bluebells.

Most commendably, the site is a development centre for disabled people and those with special needs (they are trained in everything from botany and veterinary science to working in the on-site restaurant). The farm is therefore accessible to wheelchair users, and there are excellent birthday packages incorporating the animals, party food and a spell in the multi-storey, soft-play barn. A special events timetable runs throughout the year, including themed picnics, classic car rallies and an annual carol service in the barn (check the website for more information).
Buggy access. Café. Disabled access: toilet. Free parking. Nappy-changing facilities. Nearest picnic area: grounds. Shop.

Wimpole Hall Home Farm & Garden
Arrington, Royston, Cambs (01223 207257/ www.wimpole.org). **Getting there** *By train* Royston rail. *By car* J12 off M11. **Open** *Farm* 10.30am-5pm Tue-Thur, Sat, Sun. *Hall* 1-5pm Tue-Thur, Sat, Sun. Extended opening times during holiday periods; call for details. **Admission** *Farm & gardens* £4.90; £3.10 3s-17s; free under-3s. *NT members Hall & garden* free. *Farm* £2.60; £1.60 3-17s; free under-3s. **Credit** AmEx, MC, V.

This small working farm (with baffling opening times) near Cambridge is a small part of the Wimpole Estate, which includes 350 acres of landscaped and wooded parkland and an impressive country house, now owned by the National Trust. It's a concentrate of character in the largely arable Cambridgeshire countryside, so the place can get overcrowded – go off-peak if possible. The farm, which was designed in the late 18th century by Sir John Soane, is the largest rare breeds centre in East Anglia. Residents include a majestic Suffolk Punch shire horse and some enormous White Park cattle, thought to be the most ancient breed in

the UK. Collections of pigs, sheep, donkeys, ponies and poultry in various sizes and colours wander paddocks and pens, and a suitably rustic playground with wooden toys and a large fleet of pedal tractors keeps little ones busy all afternoon. Older children, on the other hand, enjoy the more challenging adventure playground, which is hidden among the trees. If the heavens open, repair to the Farm Kitchen restaurant, which has indoor play facilities.

A wide programme of family activities operates throughout the year, including lambing weekends in spring, a Tractor day in June, and visits from Father Christmas in December. The gravel paths make for tough going with a lightweight buggy, and if you do venture out of this kiddie ghetto into the gardens, make sure your children obey the intermittent 'keep off the grass' signs – or they'll find themselves incurring the wrath of a gardener.
Buggy access. Café. Free parking. Nappy-changing facilities. Nearest picnic place: grounds. Shop.

Gardens

Bedgebury, the National Pinetum
nr Cranbrook, Kent (01580 211044/www.bedgebury pinetum.org.uk). **Getting there** *By train* Etchingham or Tunbridge Wells rail then taxi. *By car* J5 off M25. **Open** *Apr-end Oct* 10am-6pm daily. *End Oct-end Jan* 10am-4pm

Time for tea

When the poet Rupert Brooke wrote 'Stands the clock at ten to three/And is there honey still for tea?' he was recalling these charmingly bohemian tea gardens and their idyllic setting in the picturesque village of Grantchester. Brooke lodged here as a young Cambridge graduate and nearly a century later, the Orchard is thriving, almost unchanged. It's a great place for a slap-up tea followed by a bracing riverside walk. Collect your morning coffee and squidgy home-made cakes, light lunch (quiche a speciality) or afternoon tea with home-made scones and sandwiches from the Pavilion and adjourn to the deck chairs and tables scattered among the apple trees. Children can explore the wooded areas abutting the orchard, and afterwards race through the meadows by the river Granta, accessible from the gardens.

To travel from nearby Cambridge to the Orchard by boat, hire a punt from **Scudamore's Boatyard** (01223 359750) for around £12 an hour (deposit required). The small **Rupert Brooke Museum**, in the car park, is free of charge.

The Orchard Tea Gardens
Mill Way, Grantchester, Cambridge CB3 9ND (01223 845 788/www.orchard-grantchester. com). **Getting there** *By train* Cambridge rail, then taxi. *By car* J12 off M11. **Open** 10am-7pm daily. Closed 25, 26 Dec & for special events; phone for details. No booking.
Limited car parking. Nappy-changing facilities.

daily. *End Jan-late Mar* 10am-5pm daily. Last entry 1hr before closing. **Admission** £3.50; £3 concessions; £1.50 5s-16s; £9 family (2+2); free under-5s. **Credit** MC, V.
Bedgebury is a glorious place for a woodland walk. Bring a picnic to make a day of it (note the café is closed on Mondays). The Pinetum comprises one of the finest collections of conifers in the world. It was founded as a joint venture between the Forestry Commission and the Royal Botanic Gardens at Kew, with the first plants (having been raised at Kew) planted here in 1925. It's a year-round attraction, with spring blossoms, summer full of birds and butterflies, autumn colour and conifers for Christmas. The Pinetum has an education officer, who organises all the school field trips and team building exercises. During the holidays she runs twice-weekly events for children (£5 per child; accompanying adult free), when they go bug hunting, for example, or learn all about fungi (there are more than 900 species of them here). Ring the shop (01580 211781) to book your place, or check the website for details.
Buggy access. Car park. Shop.

Capel Manor

Bullsmoor Lane, Enfield (8366 4442/www.capel.ac.uk). **Getting there** *By train* Turkey Street rail. *By car* J25 off M25. **Open** *Mar-Oct* 10am-6pm (last entry 4.30pm) daily. *Nov-Feb* 10am-5pm (last entry 4pm) Mon-Fri. **Admission** £5; £4 concessions; £2 3s-16s; free under-3s; £12 family (2+2). **Credit** MC, V.
Just off the M25, Capel Manor is one of outer London's undiscovered secrets. It's a college specialising in horticulture, landscape and garden design, floristry and animal care, but it's also home to dozens of demonstration, themed and historic mini gardens, a lovely collection of animals, a Victorian stableyard and numerous special events held throughout the summer.

Children usually hate being dragged around nurseries, in which plants are often set out in boring old rows with little sensory appeal. But if there's any place that will help kids to develop an interest in the colour, smell and feel of plants, this is it. There are few ropes or 'keep off the grass' signs, and many of the gardens have little gates to open and sheds to hide behind. Disability access is excellent, and there are special areas for those with physical handicaps or visual impairment. When the children are tired of sniffing roses, they can meet the college's Galloway cattle, Kune Kune pigs, Soay sheep, ponies, goats, rabbits, chickens, guinea pigs and magnificent Clydesdale horses.
Buggy access. Café. Disabled access: toilet. Free parking. Nappy-changing facilities. Nearest picnic place: grounds. Shop.

Groombridge Place Gardens

Groombridge Place, Groombridge, nr Tunbridge Wells, Kent (01892 861444/recorded info 01892 863999/ www.groombridge.co.uk). **Getting there** *By train* Tunbridge Wells then taxi. *By car* A264 off A21.
Open *Easter-early Nov* 9am-6pm (dusk if earlier) daily. **Admission** £8.30; £7 concessions; £6.80 3s-12s; free under-3s; £27.50 family (2+2). **Credit** MC, V.
This land used to be pig pasture in medieval times, but was sold off to Norman barons who built a moated castle here. The present manor house (a private residence) was built here in the 17th century, after the castle was destroyed. The beautifully tended formal gardens (but not the private manor house) were opened to the public in 1994. The formal gardens feature strutting peacocks and floral bowers, a delightful secret garden, giant chessboards, a knot garden and rose gardens. The Enchanted Forest, a favourite with children, has giant swings, rainforest planting, Indian camps with

Fishy goings-on at **Groombridge Place Gardens**.

teepees, Dinosaur Valley, Romany camps and a spooky place called the Serpent's Lair. Equally fascinating in this woodland is the Valley of the Groms, with its Dark Walk Adventure Trail. Family events change with the seasons, but there's always something egg-themed for Easter, and special summer holiday entertainments such as open-air shows; then there are big event such as sheepdog trials, vintage car rallies and balloon shows. The informative website has a frequently updated calendar of events so you can plan your visit to coincide with the event of greatest interest.

Eddie's Raptor Centre is a sanctuary for all kinds of birds of prey and certain birds are prepared to give swooping demonstrations daily (three times a day). Check the website (www.raptorcentre.co.uk) for details. British Giant rabbits wander about in Grom Village (near the Enchanted Wood) and hungry trout lie in wait for feeding time in the pond. For something completely different, Groombridge also has a Conan Doyle museum.
Buggy access. Café. Car park. Nappy-changing facilities. Nearest picnic place: grounds. Shop.

RHS Gardens, Wisley

nr Woking, Surrey (01483 224234/www.rhs.org.uk). **Getting there** *By train* West Byfleet or Woking rail then taxi or bus. Wisley Bus runs from Woking to Wisley May-Sept (call 01483 224234 for times). *By car* J10 M25. **Open** *Mar-Oct* 9am-6pm Mon-Sat. *Nov-Feb* 9am-4.30pm Mon-Sat. Last entry 1hr before closing. Closed 25 Dec. **Tours** by arrangement; phone for details. **Admission** £6; £2 6s-16s; free under-6s. **Credit** MC, V.
This is the flagship garden of the Royal Horticultural Society, where horticultural techniques are investigated, gardening courses are run and new cultivars are field tested. However, for all this grown-up horticultural detail, Wisley is a delightful place to take all members of the family. The formal central pond and its koi carp and ducks attract young children, who also love the bigger duck pond across the lawn from the

restaurant and smaller froggy pools throughout the garden. Others love to run around the huge apple orchards, explore the woodland gardens, gallop down the grassy slopes and marvel at the orchid house and cactus collection. Bring a picnic – there are tables to eat them at. Special events, and occasional children's trails, are organised on a regular basis. Children's and families events crop up in the school holidays; for 2003 there's a Children's Weekend planned for the plant centre (9-10 August). For more details, check the website or send an SAE to Nicky Pickett, Education Department, RHS Garden Wisley, Woking, Surrey, GU23 6QB.
Buggy access. Cafés. Disabled access: toilet. Free parking. Nappy-changing facilities. Nearest picnic place: grounds. Restaurant. Shop.

Sir Harold Hillier Gardens

The Visitor & Education Pavillion, Jermyn's Lane, Ampfield, nr Romsey (01794 368787/www.hillier.hants. gov.uk). **Getting there** *By train* Romsey rail then taxi to the centre. *By car* J3 off M3, Romsey exit. **Open** 10.30am-6pm (dusk if earlier) daily. **Admission** £5; £4.50 concessions; free under-16s. **Credit** MC, V.
The greatest collection of hardy trees and shrubs wave their branches in the gentle Hampshire breezes in these 180 acres. The collection was started by the late Sir Harold Hillier in 1953, then given in trust to Hants County Counci 24 years later. In 2003 the gardens are all geared up for their 50th anniversary celebrations, which include plenty of interest for families. This is a beautiful place to spend the day in at any time of year, but spring magnolia time is all pink and white, and the autumn colours among the giant deciduous trees are out of this world. A bright, spacious new Education and Visitor pavilion was completed in spring 2003, where the restaurant and resources rooms are a useful stopping-off point in the garden tours. School holidays bring various forms of fun for children: the Easter egg trail is always popular. Summer picnics, shows and workshops need booking ahead (easily done via the website). Family trails give purpose to the woodland wanderings.
Buggy access. Disabled access: toilet. Free parking. Nappy-changing facilities. Nearest picnic area: grounds. Restaurants. Shop.

Seaside

Brighton

Getting there *By train* Brighton rail. *By car* M23/A23, follow A23/A27 into Brighton.
Tourist information *10 Bartholomew Square, Brighton, East Sussex, BN1 1JS (0906 711 2255/ www.visitbrighton.com).*
There's a lot more than Brighton rock and pebble beaches to this self-proclaimed London-on-Sea, but its waterside setting remains the predominant family attraction. The piers have had a bad year, what with the West Pier collapsing into the sea at Christmas 2003 and the Palace Pier being briefly illuminated by flames a month later. That said, the latter is still in business and still a big draw for kids, with plenty of side stalls, arcades and entertainers lining the long walk to funfair land, where the Crazy Mouse spins adults and children alike into giggling oblivion (01273 609361).
More tranquil entertainment can be found along the recently refurbished promenade, where bizarre sculptures make great obstacles for clambering kids, or just frames through which to view the pounding surf. A whole range of eclectic street artists doff their hats when the sun is wearing his, livening up a wooden walkway that boasts the Ellipse

performance area (host to free summer concerts) alongside beach basketball and volleyball courts, and which is also a popular haunt for local skateboarders. A free children's play area operates near the derelict West Pier, while Britain's oldest electric train carriages run the one-and-a-quarter mile Volks Railway (01273 292718) between the Palace Pier and the Marina, and constitutes possibly the brightest and breeziest way of soaking up the atmosphere in summer months.
In inclement weather, the Sea Life Centre (01273 604234/ www.sealife.co.uk) offers rock pools and underwater tunnels, while the palatial Royal Pavilion (01273 290900) has guided tours – although these may be of less interest to younger children. That said, even the shortest attention span will be tickled pink by Brighton's arterial maze of shops around the Lanes and North Lane, and there are plenty of child-friendly eateries, including Food For Friends (01273 202310) and the slightly less exotic (if no less popular) Harry Ramsden's (01273 690691).

Broadstairs

Getting there *By train* Broadstairs rail. *By car* J5 off M2.
Tourist information *6B High Street, Broadstairs, Kent CT10 1LH (01843 583334/www.tourism.thanet.gov.uk).*
Broadstairs is probably the only place (other than Rochester) where you'll see Ebenezer Scrooge access his account through a hole in the wall. Dickens spent several years writing here, and the town enjoys an annual summer Dickens Festival which – just like Rochester's – brings costumes enthusiasts from miles around for eight days of literary larking about each June (phone 01843 861827 for more information). The Dickens House Museum, meanwhile, is open throughout the year (01843 861232).
Elsewhere, the popularity of Broadstairs derives from its seven largely unspoilt beaches, the largest of which, Viking Bay, combines a crescent shoreline with a picturesque little harbour and plenty of shops, amusements and ice-cream stalls. Several beaches are more secluded – hence their popularity with 18th-century smugglers, who also made use of the network of contraband tunnels that to this day runs through the coves and cliff faces. There's also a tidal paddling pool formed between Viking and Louisa Bay, fully patrolled in the tourist season and great for smaller tots to splash about in when the tide does a runner.
The sea also permeates the town's many small and winding streets, mostly fisherman's cottages now converted into pubs, cafés and gift shops, but still retaining their essential charm. Equally appealing is the annual Water Gala, one of a list of festivals around August, including a musical Folk Week (8-15 August), and culminating each year in a rousing fireworks display over the sea (check the website for details). The oldest working lighthouse in England overlooks the North Foreland, and is best seen from Joss Bay. Joss is also a good spot for learner surfers, while those on wheels should check out Revolution Skatepark in nearby St Peter's (01843 866707), which also has a small climbing wall.

Camber Sands

Getting there *By train* Rye rail then 711 bus. *By car* A21 then A268 to Rye then follow signs.
Tourist information *The Heritage Centre, Strand Quay, Rye, East Sussex, TN31 7AY (01797 226696/ www.visitrye.co.uk).*
Camber isn't the most developed of beaches: other than small cafés and a run-down amusement arcade, its single claim to domestication is an obligatory Pontin's holiday park. But then luxury isn't Camber's strong point: those who lose their heart to it return, time and again, just to wander its enormous stretch of sandy coastline, unsurpassed in the south-east and perfect for cricket, Frisbee and kicking a ball around, or

simply flying a kite on windier days. The beach is so flat and exposed (at low tide the sea recedes by half a mile) that keeping an eye on little ones isn't a problem, so long as they don't stray too far off. Less predictable, however, is the expanse of high dunes backing on to the bay, fantastic for clambering about and jumping off (we even saw one group of kids 'snowboarding' down them), but easy to get lost in. Unsupervised play here, for small children at least, is not recommended.

Swimming is also a matter of personal choice: currents are unpredictable, and the proximity of Dungeness power station has led to many questioning the water quality. There's plenty of inexpensive car parking, however, and the possibility of driving to nearby Rye, one of the UK's smallest, most antiquated seaside towns, for dinner in one of the many restaurants on its delightful High Street.

Eastbourne
Getting there By train Eastbourne rail. By car J7 off M25. **Tourist information** Cornfield Road, Eastbourne, East Sussex BN21 4QL (01323 411400/www.eastbourne.org). Eastbourne isn't without its dramatic moments – the sheer, 575ft cliff drop at Beachy Head, for example, a popular suicide spot – but for the most part it's a laid-back, peaceful place with huge amounts of varied entertainment for families seeking more than just restorative sea air.

The pier (01323 410466) is a good starting point. It was built in the 1870s, and these days boasts cutting-edge video games, a late bar and even the resort's biggest nightclub, Atlantis. Elsewhere on the pier, more traditional seaside pleasures can be pursued in either the Waterfront restaurant or Tea Pot café, which supplies great views and hires out deckchairs from which to admire them. Which brings us back to the beaches, the most family-oriented of which is Holywell, perfect for lazing about on while more enthusiastic outdoor types wander the spectacular coastal walks – they stretch all the way to Seaford – or perhaps take a high-energy speedboat ride around the bay (from Whitsun to the end of September; ring 01323 765559 for details).

Back on dry land, the two-acre Fort Fun amusement park (01323 642833) has enough rides and rollercoasters to keep even the most hardened daredevils happy (and picnic areas for their long-suffering parents). Alternatively, if you're looking for a change from beachside fun, take the children up Lottbridge Drove to the Railway Adventure Park (01323 520229), where visitors travel behind one-eighth scale miniature locomotives as they bowl along for about a mile around a country park; young children may be impressed by the treasures inside the cunningly-named Thomas the Tank Engine gift shop. There's also a little village for the young trainspotters to play in, an adventure playground for their older siblings and a maze in which to lose the lot of them. Closer to the water, full-size electric Dotto Trains (01323 641984) go up and down the entire seafront whatever the weather.

Littlehampton
Getting there By train Littlehampton rail. By car J6 off M25. **Tourist information** Windmill Complex, Coastguard Road, Littlehampton, East Sussex BN17 5LH (01903 721866/www.sussexbythesea.com).
It may be only a short drive from Brighton, but Littlehampton is a million miles away from its busier, infinitely trendier sister when it comes to keeping the peace. As yet it's unburdened by the same excess of bars and clubs, so noise pollution isn't something you need to worry about. The same goes for the more common sort of pollution: Littlehampton's coastline wins the highest marks for cleanliness and water safety year after year, making it an ideal spot at which to throw in the towel and splash out for an afternoon. There

are two main beaches. The East Beach, a sandy paradise gently sloping into the water, is by far the busier – so much so, in fact, that areas of the bay have been colour-coded to match wristbands dished out to kids, thus enabling them to find their nearest coastguard should they get lost. And while the more rugged and undeveloped West Beach lacks the same number of cafés and shops, it more than makes up for it with a vast expanse of rolling dunes, forming a haven for rare plants and wildlife and marking the area out as a Site of Specific Scientific Interest (SSSI).

Entertainment is limited: after the fairground rides and between ice-cream breaks, the most active fun is to be had dangling a crab line off the river wall (sold in most small shops), or taking the leisurely land train on a slow tour of the promenade. But this is Littlehampton: it may be low on death-defying stunts (and isn't necessarily the best place to take a group of thrill-seeking teenagers), but as sedative breaks from the big smoke go, it's a genuine breath of fresh air.

The Sussex by-the-Sea website is worth checking if you fancy a really raucous seaside day out, at lovely Bognor Regis and its ever-ready Butlins (call Bognor tourist office on 01243 823140 for more information).

Margate
Getting there By train Margate rail. By car M2 then A2. **Tourist information** 12-13 The Parade, Margate, Kent CT9 1EY (01813 220241/583334/www.tourism. thanet.gov.uk).
The beaches at Margate are so closely associated with those now classic cartoon postcards of red-faced, kerchief-topped old men lusting after busty bathing-suited ladies, that it's not hard to see why it's enjoyed a certain cult revival in recent years. Irony aside, however, Margate remains the quintessential family beach resort for at least one very good reason: the appropriately titled Main Sands bay, a long, golden strip of the soft grainy stuff, is liberally peppered with kids' amenities, from donkey rides to swings and slides. Video arcades are ten a penny (if only the games were too), and there's a mini-funfair for tiny-tots, as well as the full-size Dreamland Fun Park (01843 227011) for older kids.

And it's not all thrills, spills and bellyaches: provided you can drag them away from more high-tech adventures, Margate is a historical town that merits exploration on its own. There are plenty of decent pubs and restaurants to fuel expeditions, and several spots of genuine interest, including the Margate Caves (01843 220139), once an infamous hangout for smugglers and other unsavoury types.

Whatever you do in Margate, don't miss the subterranean Shell Grotto (01843 220008) a really mysterious place, dug into the chalk and covered with strange markings of unknown age or origin. HG Wells thought it was a pagan dwelling – tell your little ones that it could also be linked to extraterrestrials, and they'll love every minute of it. Saucy Margate enjoyed a brief period in the limelight in 2001, thanks to positive publicity from old Margatian Tracey Emin and various 'bad taste is good' articles in the Observer and the like. But whatever the style monitors say, this historic old town, with its uncouth attractions and sandy beach, is a lovely day out – when the sun shines, that is.

Southend
Getting there By train Southend Central or Southend Victoria rail. By car J30 off M25. **Tourist information** 19 High Street, Southend-on-Sea, Essex SS1 1JE (01702 215120/www.southend.gov.uk).
As the closest seaside resort to London, it's hardly surprising that a) there's no sand at Southend, and b) Cockney ingenuity has nevertheless prevailed, with tons of the stuff regularly shipped in to soften up the otherwise inappropriate

Can you dig it?

Bob the Builder isn't the only one with access to heavy plant machinery; now anyone can get behind the wheel of a JCB, if they trundle down to Diggerland, in Kent. This rather specialist form of theme park was dreamed up by the good people of plant hire firm HE Services, which, when organising promotional Open Days, were inspired by the queues forming for the digger rides. Children and adults can now drive diggers, fork-lifts, dumpers and other machines, closely watched by instructors. There's no age limit, though very young children have to be accompanied by an adult before they can drive off in a large JCB. Height restrictions apply on some of the really big pieces of kit. Diggerland, which has branches in Durham and Devon, also organises dumper and Land Rover racing for adults, and themed birthday party packages for children. Other activities on site include a bouncy castle, ride-on toys, a vast sand pit and a land train, but it's the diggers that make it special.

Diggerland

Whitewall Road, Strood, Kent ME2 (08700 344437/www.diggerland.com). **Getting there** *By train* Strood rail. *By car* J1 off A2, then follow A289 into Medway City Estate for Whitewall Road. **Open** 10am-5pm weekends, bank hols, school hols, half-terms; check website for details. *Buggy access. Café. Car park. Disabled access: toilet. Nappy-changing facilities. Nearest picnic place: grounds. Shop.*

estuary mud banks. Bar that little gem, Southend is picture perfect: home not only to the largest rock factory but the longest pier in the world: a full 1.33 miles of wind-chaffed walking. On less fair days, a unique pleasure train runs the entire length (return fares from £2 adults, £1 children), with the usual rides and arcades at the far end, and a **Pier Museum** (01702 614553; entry is 60p, free for under-12s) offering a potted history of the construction itself.

Adventure Island (01702 468023) is Southend's token theme park, with pay-as-you-go rollercoaster fun (and wristbands for the initiated), while less intimidating soft play experiences at the **Kids Kingdom** (01702 462747) cater to smaller appetites. If the weather turns bad, check out the **Sealife Centre** (01702 601834) or just go bowling (01702 322322).

Whitstable

Getting there *By train* Whitstable rail. *By car* J7 off M2. **Tourist information** *7 Oxford Street, Whitstable, Kent CT5 1DB (01227 275482/www.canterbury.co.uk/www.visitwhitstable.co.uk).*

It's not exactly *Baywatch* (even sandcastles are out of the question), but the shingle beaches of Whitstable, an antiquated sea port on one of the quieter corners of the Thames Estuary, have an undeniable charm of their own. While away the hours clambering on the old groynes, flying a kite on the grassy Tankerton Slopes or – for more enthusiastic roamers – following the coast all the way to Margate. The harbour itself is a delight, and the numerous eateries along **Beach Walk** (many in renovated sailor's cottages) are the ideal spot to sample Whitstable's nationally renowned oysters. The most popular spot to knock a few back is the **Whitstable Oyster Fishery Company** (01227 276856), although you'll need to book in advance. More on the history of this most slipper of customers can be learned at the **Whitstable Museum & Gallery** (01227 276998; admission free), with special exhibitions (honouring devoted local luminary Peter Cushing, for example) alongside an elaborate history of the town's seafaring traditions.

Ships

Chatham Historic Dockyard

The Historic Dockyard, Chatham, Kent (01634 823800/www.chdt.org.uk). **Getting there** *By train* Chatham rail. *By car* J1-4 off M2. **Open** *15 Feb-2 Nov* 10am-6pm daily. *8-30 Nov* 10am-4pm Sat, Sun. Closed Dec, Jan. **Admission** £9.50; £7 concessions; £6 5s-15s; £25 family (2+2; £3 per additional child). **Credit** MC, V.

HMS *Victory* was built at Chatham, along with many vessels from the 16th century until its shipbuilding activities came to an end in 1984. Since then, Chatham Historic Dockyard Trust has been running the 80-acre site anchorage as a tourist attraction. Children enjoy the enthusiastic guided tours around both a 40-year-old submarine, HMS *Ocelot*, and a World War II destroyer, HMS *Cavalier*. Wooden Walls is a walk-through exhibit for a full-on experience of the sights,

winning the Battle of Trafalgar. You go aboard the ship as part of a 40-minute guided tour. It's fascinating to see the crew's quarters. The lowly crew ate, slept and fired their cannons all in the same tiny space. Nelson, of course, had spacious rooms. You take a harbour tour on by catamaran. The helmsman gives a running commentary on the passing frigates, destroyers and minesweepers as the vessel trawls the perimeter of this beautiful natural harbour.

Back at the dockyard, children press ahead for Action Stations, which has a simulated helicopter ride, ski machine, kayak machine, shooting, rock climbing and computer games in which those who do well are invited to sign up. There's also a screening of the Royal Navy film *Command Approved*, which depicts Brits of both genders tackling a band of murderous hostage-takers of swarthy complexion but non-specific nationality.

There are two other ships to visit. The *Mary Rose* was the finest galleon in Henry VIII's navy until it sank to the bottom of Portsmouth Harbour in 1530. Her rotting hull was hauled to the surface in 1980 and is now housed in the humid conditions of **Mary Rose Ship Hall**. More interesting still are the dining plates, bowls, leather shoes and bags, weapons, books and musical instruments that were salvaged at the same time and now kept in the **Mary Rose Museum**. HMS *Warrior* was a fighting ship in Queen Victoria's navy and now lies moored just outside the entrance to the dockyard. She was built for speed and was in her day one of the fastest military ships afloat. She could reach the USA in four days with a following wind.

Buggy access (not on ships). Cafés. Nappy-changing facilities. Restaurant. Shop.

sounds and smells of the 18th-century dockyard. At the ropery visitors can learn about making rope, Lifeboat! is the RNLI's national collection of boats, and the Museum of the Royal Dockyard charts the 400-year history of Chatham. The interactive displays include a radio-controlled boat and ship-docking exercise, cannon-aiming fun in a mock ship fight and a new improved history trail. Play areas include a soft play area and 'walk the plank' fun.

Check the website for all the latest on this year's festivals and events, and children's holiday activities taking place at Easter, half-term and during the summer holidays.

Buggy access. Café. Car park. Nappy-changing facilities. Shop.

Portsmouth Historic Dockyard
Building 1/7, College Road, HM Naval Base Portsmouth, Hants (0239 286 1533/www.historicdockyard.co.uk). **Getting there** *By train* Portsmouth rail. *By car* J11 off M27. **Open** *Apr-Oct* 10am-5.30pm daily. *Nov-Mar* 10am-5pm daily. Last entry half hr before closing. Closed 24-26 Dec (phone to check). **Admission** £14.85; £11.90 concessions; £11.90 5s-16s; £47.55 (2+3) family, free under-5s. **Credit** MC, V.

Nine dockyard attractions are available at this, the home of the Royal Navy. These can be paid for individually but it's more economical to purchase a Passport ticket, which gives access to everything. The main purpose of most people's visit is to see HMS *Victory*, the ship in which Admiral Nelson died

Specialist museums

Beaulieu
Brockenhurst, Hampshire, SO42 7ZN (01590 612345/ www.beaulieu.co.uk). **Getting there** *By train* Beaulieu Road rail then taxi. *By car* M3 then M27 then A326 and follow signs. **Open** *May-Sept* 10am-6pm daily. *Oct-Apr* 10am-5pm daily. **Admission** £13; £12 concessions; £7 13s-17s; £6 5s-12s; £35 family (2+2); free under-5s. **Credit** AmEx, MC, V.

Those who lust after the shimmer of exhaust fumes, the smell of burning rubber and the thrill of the race will love the National Motor Museum at Beaulieu. It's arguably one of the best in the world, home to an incredible collection of classic cars and motorbikes from commercial vehicles to racers, and even sporting some eccentric record breakers like Golden Arrow and the legendary Bluebird.

It's not all pedal to the metal, however, and families looking for a less pyrotechnic day out can wander the picturesque acreage of Beaulieu Abbey (the original 800-year-old remains of which still can still be seen in the gardens), or brave the chambers themselves, supposedly haunted by a gaggle of ghosts from the Grey Lady to an eerie Gregorian chant. Alternatively, take a journey back in time at the imposing Palace House, where a range of appropriately dressed actors give guided tours around the upstairs, downstairs existence of life in a Victorian manor.

There are well laid out gardens to explore and all sorts of wildlife to observe along the rugged pathways around the Mill Pond, and children can feast their eyes on panoramic views of the whole scene (including a recently installed adventure playtrail) from the lofty monorail.

Buggy access. Café. Disabled access: toilet. Free parking. Nappy-changing facilities. Nearest picnic place: grounds. Shops.

Bentley Wildfowl & Motor Museum

Halland, near Lewes, East Sussex, BN8 5AF (01825 840573/www.bentley.org.uk). **By train** Uckfield or Lewes rail then taxi. *By car* A22 then follow signss. **Open** *Mid Mar-Oct* 10.30am-4.30pm daily. *Nov, Feb, early Mar* 10.30am-4pm Sat, Sun. Closed Dec, Jan. **Admission** £5.50, £4.50 concessions; £3.80 4-15s; £17.50 family (2+4); free under 4s. **Credit** MC, V.

You may be hard pressed to think of two things further removed than fluffy ducklings and Lamborghini Diabolo sportscars, but both have a home in the lush and sprawling gardens of Bentley House. Simultaneously a wildfowl reserve and motor museum, this unique place appeals to both ends of the spectrum – grease monkeys as well as green-fingered botanists – with plenty to keep their offspring amused, including art workshops, a miniature steam railway and an extensive adventure playground.

The animal collection was started in the 1960s by the late Gerald Askew, and these days breeds and safeguards around 125 species of swans, geese and ducks (alongside various flamingos and cranes), many of them endangered. A tour of the reserve can incorporate a walk through the formal gardens, as well as a picnic in the less sculpted glades of neighbouring Glyndebourne Wood. Vehicle enthusiasts, meanwhile, will be in four-wheel heaven: the Motor Museum houses Veteran, Edwardian and Vintage cars, with regular rallys and owners' conventions taking place throughout the year (check the website for a list of upcoming events).

Buggy access. Café. Car park (free). Disabled access: toilet. Nappy-changing facilities. Nearest picnic place: grounds. Shop.

Duxford Imperial War Museum

Duxford, Cambs (01223 835000/www.iwm.org.uk). **Getting there** *By train* Cambridge rail then free bus. *By car* J10 off M11. **Open** *Mid Mar-late Oct* 10am-6pm daily. *Late Oct-mid Mar* 10am-4pm daily. Last admission 1hr before closing. Closed 24-26 Dec. **Admission** £8.50; free under-16s. **Credit** MC, V.

Duxford is certainly a Big Day Out, with five vast themed hangars of exhibits, as well as the futuristic glass-fronted American Air Museum, designed by Lord Foster, and the Land Warfare Hall, filled up with tanks and military vehicles. The complex is so huge that a convenient, free 'road train' operates all day, dropping off at the major attractions. The air shows are superb (there are about four each year), but you'll still see plenty of thrilling flying action if you opt for a less crowded weekend or midweek visit.

There are plenty of hands-on activities too. Take a walk through Concorde's cabin in Hangar 1 or experience the sounds and smells of the Blitz in the Land Warfare Hall. Here, tanks, military vehicles and artillery pieces are on show in dramatic battlefield scenes, and if you're lucky you may even see them rolling over the turf, as dedicated enthusiasts work to restore them. Children play happily in two excellent play areas, including an adventure playground. When meal time comes round there are cafés on site; alternatively, eat your own picnic while watching the action. And if all the aeroplanes leave you feeling flighty, you too can take to the skies in an elegant 1930s DeHavilland biplane (call Classic Wings on 0870 902 6146/www.classic-wings.uk.com).

Buggy access. Cafés. Car park. Nappy-changing facilities. Restaurant. Shops.

Roald Dahl Children's Gallery

Church Street, Aylesbury, Buckinghamshire (01296 331441/www.buckscc.gov.uk/museum). **Getting there** *By train* Aylesbury rail. *By car* J8 off M25. **Open** 10am-5pm Sat; 2-5pm Sun. *Term time* 3-5pm Mon-Fri. *School hols* 10am-5pm Mon-Sat. **Admission** £3.50; £2.75 3s-16s; free under-3s. **Credit** MC, V.

Roald Dahl may have penned his imaginative stories in an old hut at the bottom of his Buckinghamshire garden, but his legions of devoted fans can expect a more well-appointed tribute to his literature inside this converted coach house, an extension of the child-friendly Bucks County Museum. Five areas, decorated with colourful frescoes by Quentin Blake, introduce different themes based on Dahl's stories.

Visitors encounter James and his mini beast friends inside the Giant Peach and examine the insect world with the aid of a video microscope. The BFG playing on his giant pipe organ is a jolly introduction to the mysteries of sound, and there's a crawl-through tunnel inpired by *Fantastic Mr Fox*, along which children can spot buried treasure as they go. The Imagination Gallery upstairs is a chance to experience Roald Dahl's anarchic world through the lens of various fun experiments: freeze your own shadow in the dark room and watch it fade before your eyes, or see the Twits' upside-down room and touch the things hidden in their wall. Younger children will enjoy meeting Tim Burr the wooden man and loading his train for market, or riding in the Great Glass Elevator from *Charlie and the Chocolate Factory*. Oh yes, and there are even some books, in Matilda's Library, where you can discover more about Dahl's life and work.

The Dahl Gallery is a popular place for families, with prime appeal for the under-tens, but it only holds 85 people, so it's worth pre-booking in the school holidays. Picnic in the walled garden or snack in the reasonably priced museum café.

Buggy access. Café. Disabled access: lift, toilet. Nappy-changing facilities. Nearest picnic place: grounds. Shop.

Steam trains

Steam trains combine sources of sensory interest (chuff chuff!) in the young, and score high in the nostalgia stakes with parents. Note that steam train timetables change from month to month, but most lines run special trains to accommodate the half-term hordes. Ticket prices given are for round trips only; most prices are due to rise in January 2004.

Bluebell Railway

Sheffield Park Station, on A275 between Lewes & East Grinstead, Sussex (01825 723777/talking timetable 01825 722370/www.bluebell-railway.co.uk). **Getting there** *By train* East Grinstead rail then 473 bus. *By car* J10 off M23. **Open** *Easter-Sept* 11am-4pm daily. *Oct-Apr Sat, Sun, school hols, bank hols* call for details. **Admission** £8; £6.40 OAPs; £4 3s-15s; £21.50 family (2+3); free under-3s. **Credit** MC, V.

Come Spring, it seems most families with small children are minded to take a trip on the Bluebell railway. The line was the UK's first preserved standard gauge passenger railway; it reopened part of the Lewes to East Grinstead line of the old London Brighton & South Coast Railway in 1960. Each station the line passes through is restored according to a different era: Victorian, the 1930s and the 1950s. Apart from the occasional Thomas the Tank Engine extravaganzas (check the website), there are all kinds of specials in steam for children. Their favourite train is Stepney, a lovely old engine that pulls his special train between Sheffield Park and Kingscote. The Stepney Specials run during the school holidays. Fans aged three to eight can join the Stepney Club (from £4.50 per year) through which they receive a newsletter, birthday cards, reduced-price train tickets and other perks. Other delights include a bedtime story service on summer evenings, and teatime specials on Saturday afternoons, when you can scoff tea and cake while steaming through the verdant Sussex landscape. Ring for details of such fun, and the Sheffield Park special tickets, which combine a train ride with free entry to the National Trust's lovely 120 acres.

From October until Christmas Eve, there are a series of Santa Specials, which run from Sheffield Park to Kingscote, a nine-mile journey, which takes you through the atmospheric Sharpthorne tunnel, on the way to Kingscote. The ticket price includes a meeting with Santa as you board the train, a gift for your child, mince pies for the adults (a glass of wine is extra), a children's entertainer and a free ride on the children's roundabout. The Santa Special tickets start at £3 for children (rising to £9 in the observation car) and £10 for adults; all children under one go free. If all of this brings out the trainspotter in you, why not sign up for a one-day course (8am-4.30pm) on driving a steam engine (there are eight people on each course and after one hour's briefing you can use the controls, driving under instruction).
Buggy access. Café. Car park. Nappy-changing facilities. Shop.

Didcot Railway Centre
Didcot, Oxon (01235 817200/www.didcotrailwaycentre. org.uk). **Getting there** *By train* Didcot Parkway rail. *By car* J13 off M4. **Open** 10am-5pm (last entry 4.30pm) daily. **Tours** bank hols (times depend on events; phone for details). **Admission** *Steam days, incl tour* £6.50; £5.50 concessions; £4.50 3s-16s; £19 family (2+2); free under-3s. *Non-steam days* £4; £3.50 concessions; £3 3s-16s; £12 family; free under-3s. **Credit** MC, V.
Isambard Kingdom Brunel – recently voted second greatest Brit in a major poll – was the engineer behind the Great Western Railway, originally designed to link London with Bristol (Didcot is situated somewhere in the middle), and still chugging along nicely today. The centre serves on the one hand as a collection of antique carriages and engines, but there are plenty of less static attractions on the other.

Regular Steamdays, for example, give punters up close and personal encounters with traditional steam-age activities like 'turning' locomotives, as well as the chance to ride in an original 1930s carriage. Younger children are given their own printed tour guides featuring Archie the Engine Driver, who leads kids around the exhibits, and Thomas the Tank Engine makes occasional holiday stopovers on his famously hectic schedule. For a full calendar of events, check the website.
Buggy access. Café. Car park. Nappy-changing facilities. Shop.

Kent & East Sussex Railway
Tenterden, Northiam & Bodiam stations (01580 765155/www.kesr.org.uk). **Getting there** *By train* Headcorn rail then link bus to Tenterden. *By car* J9 off M20. **Open** *Apr-July, Sept-Nov* 10.40am-3.30pm Sat, Sun. *Aug* 10.40am-3.30pm daily. *Dec-Mar* times vary, call for details. **Admission** £9; £8 concessions; £4.50 3s-15s; £25 family (2+3); free under-3s. **Credit** MC, V.
A nostalgic trip down memory line if ever there was one. The antique carriages and engines servicing this railway line were scavenged and restored by the most enthusiastic enthusiasts, and on certain occasions staff will still ham it up in period costumes for the afternoon.

Usually, however, the Kent and East Sussex track is just an aesthetically pleasing method of getting from A to B. There are stops along the way (Northiam, Rolvenden and Wittersham Road), but they're small and secluded, with little to keep kids amused. You're better off getting a return

between Bodium and Tenterden – respective ends of the line – being sure to conquer the looming castle at the former and, in fair weather, wander the picturesque, tree-lined High Street of the latter. Check the website for details of cameos from the chubby-cheeked Thomas the Tank Engine (he makes around three appearances a year) and other special events including the seasonal Santa Express.
Buggy access. Café (Tenterden & Northiam stations). Car park. Nappy-changing facilities. Nearby attractions: Bodiam Castle. Shop.

Romney, Hythe & Dymchurch Railway
New Romney Station, Kent (01797 362353/www.rhdr. demon.co.uk). **Getting there** *By train* Folkestone Central rail then 711 bus to Hythe. *By car* J11 off M20. **Open** *Mar-Oct* Sat, Sun. *Easter-Sept* daily. Ring for train timetable info as times change monthly. **Admission** £9.60; £4.80 children. **Credit** MC, V.
Somewhere between dinky model trains and full-size, working engines are these wonderful and utterly unique locomotives, one-third of the scale of the real thing and able to puff cheerfully along a similarly downsized track (although still one that covers 13.5 miles) between the Cinque Port of Hythe and the picturesque lighthouses and fishermen's cottages in Dungeness. Built in 1927 by millionaire racing driver Captain Howley as the 'Worlds Smallest Public Railway', the line remains fast and efficient nonetheless, and although trains run to an eccentric timetable that varies from month to month (download a copy from the website), trips can be made all year round that take in the sandy beaches of Dymchurch and the hauntingly lovely RSPB Nature Reserve in Dungeness.
Buggy access. Cafés. Car park. Nappy-changing facilities. Shops.

Watercress Line
The Station, Alresford, Hants (01962 733810/talking timetable 01962 734866/www.watercressline.co.uk). **Getting there** *By train* Alton rail. *By car* A3 then A31. **Open** changes monthly; ring for details. Closed Jan. **Admission** £9; £8 concessions; £4 3-16s; £22 family (2+2); free under-3s; ring for prices during special events. **Credit** MC, V.
The restored steam and diesel engines of the Watercress Line remain one of the most evocative means for taking in the rolling Home Counties countryside. More a visual feast than anything else, the ten-mile round trip, which lasts roughly two hours, operates out of Alresford, along the way stopping at Alton (direct from Waterloo, and the best bet for Londoners wishing to hop on board), Ropley and Medstead & Four Marks. While the latter two offer plenty of top-notch picnic spots, Alresford itself – quieter and a bit more upmarket – has an abundance of pleasant walks, pubs and picturesque shops. Child-pleaser Thomas the Tank Engine is scheduled to visit between 9 and 17 August 2003, and there's a spooky Halloween special – Wizards' Week – starting on 25 October; phone for a full calendar of events.
Buggy access (footbridge at Alton). Shop.

Theme parks

Chessington World of Adventures
Leatherhead Road, Chessington, Surrey (0870 444 7777/ www.chessington.com). **Getting there** *By train* Chessington South rail. *By car* J9 off M25/M26. **Open** *Apr-Nov* 10am-5/6pm daily. *Late July-early Sept* 10am-7pm daily; times may vary according to special events.

Spot some of nature's monsters (and some rhinos) at **Marwell Zoological Park**. *See p292.*

Height restrictions vary on rides. **Admission** *on the day* £18-£24; £14.50-£18 4s-12s; £14.50-£18 under-12s; £12-£16 concessions; £52-£65 family (2+2); check the website for online advance bookings that give fast-track entry. **Credit** MC, V.

Chessington may not have the psychotic thousand-yard stare of its thrill-seeking sister Thorpe Park (*see p291*), but it more than makes up for it with colourful characters and family fun, and is by far the better choice for parents looking to amuse younger children. The extensive Animal Land – home to gorillas, lions and tigers – makes an ideal break from the slings and arrows of seemingly endless queues, and the Safari Skyride monorail lifts visitors above the chaos and gives then a relaxing overview of the park.

More intrepid stomachs will find thrills aplenty on the infamous Samurai, Vampire and Rameses' Revenge rides (don't brave the last one in water-based make-up), but most of the attractions are interactive adventures. The new Hocus Pocus Hall is an animated mansion (explorers don 3D glasses before entering) teeming with goblins, while the laser-based shooter Tomb Blaster continues to pull in more gung-ho punters. Smaller children will be over the moon: there are carousels and crazy cars in Toytown alongside pink elephants, fantastic playgrounds and longer, more involving trips like Professor Burp's ever-popular Bubble Works – and best of all, they all have the smallest queues. Picnic spots are everywhere, while the likes of Pizza Hut, KFC and a number of noisy theme restaurants satisfy more demanding appetites.

Buggy access. Café. Car park. Nappy-changing facilities. Shops.

Legoland

Winkfield Road, Windsor, Berkshire (08705 040404/ www.legoland.co.uk). **Getting there** *By train* Windsor & Eton Riverside or Windsor Central rail. *By car* J3 off M3 or J6 off M4. **Open** *Mid Mar-early Nov* 10am-5pm/6pm daily (until 7pm during school summer hols). **Admission** *Peak season* (school hols) £22.95; £19.95 3s-15s; £16.95 concessions. *Off-peak season* £18.95; £15.95 3s-15s; £12.95 concessions. **Credit** AmEx, MC, V.

Those with reservations about crossing the M25 needn't fear: with scaled-down Lego versions of the Millennium Eye and Buckingham Palace recently installed in Miniland London, it'll be like you never left. Alternatively – for those who can't get far enough away – take a wild trip on the Lego safari, or chase Chinese dragons along the Orient Exhibition.

The beauty of this park is the creativity that its designers have put into the use of the vastly adaptable plastic bricks. Any child who has every played with the things will be amazed by the Madame Tussaud's-style celebrities in the Hall of Fame and the elaborate fish that hang from the ceilings of the recently refurbished Big Restaurant. It's an inspiring place for adults and kids alike (they'll almost certainly want to build something of their own when they get home): literally anything is possible, from fantasy castles to space exploration, and although very few of the attractions will leave you white-knuckled, they're as much of a joy to look at as to ride. The only drawback is that the international appeal of Lego means queues tend to be enormous: if at all possible, plan a trip outside school holidays.

Buggy access. Cafés. Car park. Nappy-changing facilities. Restaurants. Shops.

Time Out
London for Children Guide
Please let us know what you think

Your feedback is invaluable to us! Please take a few minutes to tell us about yourself and let us know what you think of this guide – **you could win £100 worth of Time Out products**. Just return this card to us by December 31 2003, and if yours is the first out of the hat in our prize draw, you'll get the goodies.

1. How often, on average, do you take your children on special days out?
More than three times a week ❏
Two to three times per week ❏
Once a week ❏
Once/twice a month ❏
Less than once/twice monthly ❏

2. Which of the following activities are popular with your children (please tick the boxes which apply).
Parks ❏
Museums ❏
Galleries ❏
Party venues ❏
Organised after-school activities ❏
Sport & leisure centres ❏
School holiday courses/classes ❏
Theatre/cinemas/music ❏

3. What age are the children in your care? (tick all that apply)
0-3 ❏ 4-7 ❏ 8-10 ❏ 11-13 ❏ 13+ ❏

4. Have your children used this guide?
Yes ❏   No ❏

5. Have you found this guide useful when organising activities?
Indispensible ❏   Very useful ❏   Occasionally useful ❏
Not useful ❏
Please briefly explain your reasons
....
....
....

6. Is there anything you'd like us to cover in greater depth, or any ways in which you think we could improve the guide?
....
....

7. In your opinion, are there any places that should or should not be included in the guide?
Name of venue/event that **should** be Included
....
Address...
Comments...
....
....
Name of venue/event that **should not** be included
....
Address...
Comments...
....
....

8. Have you ever bought/used other Time Out publications?
Yes ❏   No ❏
If yes, which ones?
....
....

9. Where did you first hear of/see this guide?
Advertising in Time Out magazines ❏
Review in the press ❏
Bookshop/newsagent ❏
timeout.com ❏
Other (please specify) ❏
....

10. Where did you buy this guide?
Bookshop/newsagent ❏
Via timeout.com/shopping ❏
Via promotional leaflet/offer ❏
Mail order ❏

11. Are you? (tick all that apply)
A single parent ❏
Living with a partner ❏
Married ❏
A children's carer ❏
A teacher ❏
A youth worker ❏
Buying this guide for a friend ❏

12. Are you?
Employed full-time ❏
Employed part-time ❏
Self-employed ❏
Unemployed ❏
Student ❏
Home-maker ❏

13. At the moment, do you earn?
Under £10,000 ❏
£10,000 to £14,999 ❏
£15,000 to £19,999 ❏
£20,000 to £24,999 ❏
£25,000 to £39,999 ❏
£40,000 to £49,999 ❏
£50,000 to £59,999 ❏
£60,000 plus ❏

14. What is your occupation?
....

(BLOCK CAPITALS PLEASE)
15. Title (Mr, Mrs, Ms etc)...
First name...
Surname...
Address..
....
....
Postcode..
Email address..
Daytime telephone...

16. Year of birth...

17. Sex...

Please tick here if you do not wish to receive information about other Time Out products. ❏

Please tick here if you do not wish to receive information from third parties. ❏

Now fold your completed report and questionnaire in half, tape together (no staples please) and return to us FREEPOST. Thank you.

2

**Time Out Guides
Freepost 20 (WC3187)
LONDON
W1E 0DQ**

Fold here and tape together

Thorpe Park

Staines Road, Chertsey, Surrey (0870 444 4466/ www.thorpepark.com). **Getting there** *By train* Staines rail then bus. *By car* M25 J11 or J13. **Open** *April-early Nov* 9/10am-5/6pm daily. *Late July-early Sept* 9/10am-7.30pm daily. Height restrictions vary, depending on rides. **Admission** *on the day* £19-£25; £15.50-£18.50 4s-12s, concessions; £54-£67 family (2+2 or 1+3); free under-4s. Check the website or phone for details of online & phone advance bookings; allow min 2 days to process advance ticket purchases. **Credit** AmEx, MC, V.

Let's make one thing perfectly clear: most of the main attractions at Thorpe Park will leave you dazed, confused and quite possibly vowing never to set foot on a rollercoaster again. A park for pre-schoolers this ain't, although less stomach-churning experiences await younger brothers and sisters at Thorpe Farm, complete with petting zoo and accessed either by railroad or highly restorative waterbus, while the new Eclipse wheel is as tranquil a means to view surroundings as the London Eye. There are also plenty of carousels, swingboats and adventure playgrounds, but with the tortured screams of teens being turned inside out on all sides, smaller children may be better off at Chessington (*see p289*).

Where Thorpe Park really excels itself is with g-force (that's 'God get me off this thing-force' to you and me). The mighty Colossus covers 2,789ft of twisting, looping rollercoaster track at 40mph, while the merciless Detonator drops hapless victims a full 100ft at no less than 75mph. Recent acquisitions include Nemesis Inferno, a legs dangling, fully suspended rail ride with 360° loops taken at 4.5gs. If your bladder gives way, at least it means you're still alive.

Buggy access. Cafés. Car park. Nappy-changing facilities. Restaurants. Shops.

Wildlife reserves

Birdworld

Holt Pound, Farnham, Surrey (01420 22140/ www.birdworld.co.uk). **Getting there** *By train* Aldershot, Bentley or Farnham rail then taxi or 18 bus. *By car* M3 then A325 and follow signs. **Open** *Mid Feb-Oct* 10am-6pm daily. *Nov-mid Feb* 10am-4.30pm daily. Closed 25, 26 Dec. **Admission** £9.75; £7.50 concessions; £6.95 3-14s; £29.95 family (2+2); free under-3s. **Credit** MC, V.

The birdsongs that illuminate this lush, beautifully sculpted parkland are so pervasive that it's hard to believe you're still in Surrey. Attractions are designed to appeal to both dedicated birdwatchers and less devoted followers of our feathered friends, although the place is clearly best suited to charming the socks off children.

Penguin feeding displays (11.30am, 3.30pm daily), a must for visitors of all ages, become something extra special when young ones get to feed the waddling stars themselves (over-fives only). This level of involvement must be booked in advance (01420 22992). The Heron Theatre, meanwhile, takes birds from their enclosures to perform natural tricks for a seated audience. More hawkish kids can watch with eagle eyes as handlers feed the resident birds of prey – provided they can stomach the diet of dead baby chicks – while the best way to get an overview of the extensive 26-acre site is on a guided Safari train, complete with running commentary for those still struggling to learn their ostriches from their emus (one's a puppet, apparently).

Finally, all the best afternoons at Birdworld are rounded off with a trip to the Jenny Wren farm, where children get to see and possibly even handle new arrivals, including baby rabbits and lambs. All activities are included in the cover charge, and there's a good café, several snack kiosks and plenty of idyllic spots for a picnic. Special events from egg hunts to cowboy parties take place throughout the year: check the website for more information.

Buggy access. Café. Disabled access: toilet. Free parking. Nappy-changing facilities. Nearest picnic area: grounds. Restaurant. Shop.

Drusillas Park

Alfriston, East Sussex (01323 874100/www.drusillas. co.uk). **Getting there** *By train* Polegate or Berwick rail. *By car* M23 then A23 then A27. **Open** *Apr-Oct* 10am-6pm daily. *Oct-Mar* 10am-5pm daily. Last entry 1hr before closing. Closed 24-26 Dec. **Admission** £9.49; £8.49 concessions; free under-3s. **Credit** MC, V.

Drusilas is a strange creature indeed: equal parts fun park and zoological garden, with a highly educational centre covered in a thick layer of fun. All of the huge range of animals here – from squirrel monkeys and flamingos to fruit bats and the ever-eccentric, ever-popular meerkats – are visible from low-level viewing booths that let even the smallest kids enjoy the show, while scheduled feeding times let children see the sundry beasts doing what they enjoy most, and learn a little more about them in the process.

Children, however hyperactive you may think they are, will be hard pressed to exhaust Drusillas' many features in one day alone. Attractions range from simple fun and games (the selection of slides, swings and things to climb is second to none), to more informative activities at the Discovery Centre, the Maasai workshops or, new for this year, Mokomo's animatronic Jungle Rock exhibit, which explains the process of natural selection to children who previously took 'food chains' to mean necklaces made from spaghetti hoops. Check the website for details of party packages, animal adoptions schemes and the unbeatable experience of letting your little one be a junior keeper for the day.

Buggy access. Cafés. Disabled access: toilet. Free parking. Nappy-changing facilities. Nearest picnic area: grounds. Restaurant. Shops.

Howletts

Bekesbourne, nr Canterbury, Kent (01227 721286/ www.howletts.net). **Getting there** *By train* Bekesbourne rail. *By car* M2 then A2. **Open** *Nov-Mar* 10am-dusk (last entry 3pm) daily. *Apr-Oct* 10am-6pm (last entry 4.30pm) daily. Closed 25 Dec. **Admission** £11.95; £8.95 concessions, 4s-14s; £34 family (2+2), £39 (2+3); free under-4s. **Credit** MC, V.

For much of his controversial life, the late John Aspinall was as famous for gambling as for his dedication to wild creatures, and when he opened his Howlett's estate to the public in 1975 – originally bought to house his animals (already including elephants, tigers and rhinos) after a big win at the races nearly 20 years earlier – it was simply to fund the well-being of his living, breathing collection.

Almost 30 years later, Howlett's still operates an unorthodox policy of non-containment, ensuring that contact between animals and their handlers is close (so close that, over the years, fatal mishaps have been 'unavoidable'), and that enclosures replicate specific environments as far as is humanly possible. Almost 50 gorillas are housed here (the largest group in care), along with African elephants, Siberian tigers and many more. Children love seeing them interact with their own kind with so little of the slow, ungainly depression that affects more conventionally caged animals.

Many of the species are endangered, however, and Howletts is one of the only zoos in the world to run a genuinely commendable programme for re-introduction into the wild. If the park is low on waterslides and seesaws, then that's because the animals come first. Port Lympne (*see below*) is the sister zoo of Howletts.

Buggy access. Café. Car park. Disabled access: toilet Nappy-changing facilities. Nearest picnic place: grounds. Restaurant. Shop.

Marwell Zoological Park

Colden Common, Winchester, Hants (01962 777407/ www.marwell.org.uk). **Getting there** *By train* Eastleigh rail then X49, 48 bus. *By car* J11 off M3. **Open** *Apr-Oct* 10am-6pm (last entry 4.30pm) daily. *Nov-Mar* 10am-4pm (last entry 2.30pm) daily. **Admission** £11; £9 concessions; £7.50 3-14s; £35.50 family (2+2); free under-3s. **Credit** MC, V.

Planet Earth too often seems to be home to just one group of animals (read the papers to find out which one, mystery fans), so it's easy to forget just how diverse a natural world we inhabit. Marwell is the sort of place that can instil in children a genuine sense of awe (no bad thing), whether it's watching Humboldt penguins through six large underwater viewing windows, marvelling at multicoloured frogs in the tropical hothouse, or coming face to face with domesticated animals – from camels to guinea pigs – in the recently refurbished Encounter Village.

There's also an enchanting Bat House, where kids can see these fascinating creatures unsullied by eerie music and vampire mumbo jumbo, and an inspiring display of gazelles and black cats in the Arid Land exhibition. Special events are organised throughout the year (check the regularly updated website), but kids are consistently well looked after, especially on weekends and school holidays, with touch tables, face painting (£2 per child) and up-close animal encounters. There are guided tour trains and adventure playgrounds all year round.

Buggy access. Café. Disabled access: toilet. Free parking. Nappy-changing facilities. Nearest picnic place: grounds. Restaurant. Shop.

Port Lympne Wild Animal Park

Lympne, nr Hythe, Kent (01303 264647/www.howletts. net). **Getting there** *By train* Ashford rail then link bus. *By car* J11 off M20. **Open** *Oct-Mar* 10am-dusk (last entry 3pm) daily. *Apr-Sept* 10am-6pm (last entry 4.30pm) daily. Closed 25 Dec. **Admission** £11.95; £8.95 3-14s, disabled adult; £6.95 disabled child; £34 family (2+2), £39 (2+3). **Credit** AmEx, MC, V.

An even larger site than its sister site, Howletts (*see p291*), Port Lympne comprises a spectacular mansion overlooking 350 acres of wilderness (the word 'enclosure' has no place here), where animals are allowed to coexist in the closest thing this country has to an uninterrupted nature reserve. To which extent, the easiest way to see everything is on a safari trailer tour (£2 adults, £1 children), although on-foot expeditions (a round trip of the amphitheatre-shaped park covers roughly three miles) can be far more rewarding – just make sure you have all day. Don't miss Palace of the Apes, the largest family gorilla house in the world.

The manor itself is also worth a visit: although less than a century old, it radiates grandeur from every ornate corner, with murals, fountains and plenty of fine art along the way, and the 125 Trojan Steps lead to one of the most breathtaking views in the South-east. The combination of such high culture with the 'back to basics' attitude towards the animals (all of whom are treated with the same close affection as at Howletts, and with the same staggering record of conservational achievement), is what makes the atmosphere at Port Lympne so utterly unique, and well worth the trip.

Buggy access. Café. Car park. Nappy-changing facilities. Shop.

Whipsnade Wild Animal Park

Whipsnade, Dunstable, Beds (01582 872171/ www.whipsnade.co.uk). **Getting there** *By train* Luton or Hemel Hempstead rail then taxi or bus. *By car* J21 off M25 or J10 off M1. **Open** *9 Mar-4 Oct* 10am-6pm Mon-Sat; 10am-7pm Sun. *5 Oct-8 Mar* 10am-4pm daily. Last entry 1hr before closing. Times subject to change, so phone to check. **Tours** free tour bus around the park; phone for times. **Admission** £12.50; £10.50 concessions; £9.50 3s-15s; £39.50 family (2+2); free under-3s. *Cars* £9 (£4.50 for members) or use £3 car park opposite main gate. **Credit** AmEx, MC, V.

Just 70 miles from London, this is the site that ZSL (the Zoological Society of London) bought for the study of large animals in 1926. Nowadays it's the permanent home for the elephants that used to live in the Regent's Park site, among other beasts. The animals here are kept in more natural enclosures which take up its 600 acres. There are giraffes, bears, tigers, rhinos and hippos able to stretch their legs here. The Great Whipsnade Railway runs through the park, so passengers can view the wildlife in comfort. The Safari Bus is also available for a hop-on, hop-off tour of the park. A daily programme of activities keep family groups busy all day. You can watch long-tailed lemurs leap and learn all about them in the 'acrobat in action' session, then there are birds-of-prey flying displays, bear talks, sea lion splashes in the new Splashzone area, feeding time for the penguins (a perennially popular activity in zoos), chimp chats and giraffe encounters. Arrive early during the summer holidays to find out what's going on and to make the most of the place.

Buggy access. Café. Car park. Nappy-changing facilities. Restaurant. Shop.

Woburn Safari Park

Woburn Park, Beds (01525 290407/www.woburnsafari. co.uk). **Getting there** *By car* J13 off M1 or J13 off M11. **Open** *Late Mar-2 Nov* 10am-5pm daily. *2 Nov-early Mar* 11am-3pm Sat, Sun. Closed 25 Dec. **Admission** £14, £11 concessions; £10.50 3s-15s. Prices vary during peak season; phone for details. **Credit** MC, V. No soft-top cars or convertibles.

If cramped zoos leave you cold, visit Woburn Safari Park, where the animals range across acres and acres of the Duke of Bedford's parkland. Start with the Safari Drive, which winds past elephants, giraffes, camels, a splendid hippo with his own muddy pool, black bears, monkeys, lions, tigers and a pack of lively wolves. Expect some close encounters too – perhaps a huge rhino skimming your wing mirror. For restless tots, the full hour-long drive may be too long, but you can peel off at various points and head for the Wild World Leisure Area, which has many free attractions, picnic areas (one covered) and a packed programme of animal demonstrations, including birds of prey, and keeper talks on penguins, lemurs and sea lions. The free steam train, with open carriages, takes you past some of Woburn's more benign residents: grazing zebras and impressively horned oryx. The Australian Walkabout (open noon-6pm) gives you friendly wallabies, haughty ostriches, and paths ideal for buggies. At Rainbow Landing, an indoor aviary, buy some nectar (60p) and colourful lorikeets will land on your hand to drink (opens four times throughout the day). The new sea lion pool, with views above and below the water line, is another must-see. Let the children loose on the Tree Tops Action Trail with aerial runway; the Tiny Tots Safari Trail and Badger Valley are geared to under-fives. An indoor soft play centre, with amazing slides, is ideal for wet days.

Buggy access. Café and snack bars. Car park. Disabled access: toilet. Nappy-changing facilities. Restaurant. Shop.

Directory

Features

Directory

Help, advice, information.

Councils

Barnet *8359 2000/www.barnet.gov.uk*
Brent *8937 1234/www.brent.gov.uk*
Camden *7278 4444/www.camden.gov.uk*
Corporation of London *7606 3030/
www.cityoflondon.gov.uk*
Ealing *8579 2424/www.ealing.gov.uk*
Greenwich *8854 8888/
www.greenwich.gov.uk*
Hackney *8356 5000/www.hackney.gov.uk*
Hammersmith & Fulham *8748 3020/
www.lbhf.gov.uk*
Haringey *8489 0000/
www.haringey.gov.uk*
Hounslow *8583 2000/
www.hounslow.gov.uk*
Islington *7527 2000/www.islington.gov.uk*
Kensington & Chelsea *7937 5464/
www.rbkc.gov.uk*
Lambeth *7926 1000/www.lambeth.gov.uk*
Lewisham *8314 6000/
www.lewisham.gov.uk*
Merton *8543 2222/www.merton.gov.uk*
Newham *8430 2000/www.newham.gov.uk*
Richmond-upon-Thames *8891 1411/
www.richmond.gov.uk*
Southwark *7525 5000/
www.southwark.gov.uk*
Tower Hamlets *7364 5000/
www.towerhamlets.gov.uk*
Waltham Forest *8527 5544/
www.walthamforest.gov.uk*
Wandsworth *8871 6000/
www.wandsworth.gov.uk*
Westminster *7641 6000/
www.westminster.gov.uk*

Education

To find out more about the state schools and nurseries in your area, contact the education department of your local council. Independent school advisory services are listed below.

Advisory Centre on Education (ACE)

7704 9822/exclusion advice line 0808 800 0327/www.ace-ed.org.uk. **Open** *Exclusion advice line 2-5pm Mon-Fri.*
Ring the Advisory Centre on Education for advice pertaining to your child's schooling. The advice line is for worried parents whose children have been excluded from their school.

Anti-Bullying Campaign

7378 1446. **Open** *10am-4pm Mon-Fri.*
If school bullies are making your child's life a misery, contact the Anti-Bullying Campaign for practical advice.

British Association for Early Childhood Education

136 Cavell Street, E1 2JA (7539 5400/www.early-education.org.uk). **Open** 9am-5pm Mon-Fri.
Information on education from birth to eight years. Send an SAE for extra information.

Gabbitas Educational Consultants

Carrington House, 126-130 Regent Street, W1B 5EE (7734 0161/www.gabbitas.co.uk). **Open** 9am-5pm Mon-Fri.
The independent schools consultants, gives advice on choosing an independent school.

Home Education Advisory Service

PO Box 98, Welwyn Garden City, Herts AL8 6AN (01707 371854/www.heas.org.uk). **Open** 9am-5pm Mon-Fri.
Call the service for information if you want to educate your child at home. An introductory pack costs £2.50, and a year's subscription to the Home Education Advisory Service £11.

ISC Information Service

London & South-east 7798 1560/www.iscis.net.
The Independent Schools Council information service works to help parents find out about independent schools.

National Association for Gifted Children

Suite 14, Challenge House, Sherwood Drive, Bletchley, Milton Keynes, Bucks MK3 6DP (0870 770 3217/www.nagcbritain.org). Support and advice on education for the parents of gifted children.

Parenting Education & Support Forum

Unit 431, Highgate Studios, 53-79 Highgate Road, NW5 1TL (7284 8389/www.parenting-forum.org.uk). **Open** 10.30am-5.30pm Mon-Thur.
Information about parenting classes and support for parents.

Pre-School Learning Alliance

2nd Floor, Tabard House, 116 Southwark Street, SE1 0TA (7620 0550/www.pre-school.org.uk). **Open** 9am-5pm Mon-Fri.
The PSLA runs courses and workshops for parents of children under the age of five in pre-schools around the country.

Fun & games

Indoor play

Crechendo

1 George Mills Weir Road, SW12 (8772 8120/www.crechendo.com). **Open** *Phoneline* 9am-5pm daily.

Crechendo runs active play classes throughout London. Children aged from three months to four years can take part in the programme. Ring the above number for your nearest class.

Gymboree Play & Music

0800 092 0911/www.gymboree PlayUK.com.
A parent-and-child play organisation, based on music and movement, for children aged 16 months to four and a half years. New recruits receive a free trial session.

National Association of Toy & Leisure Libraries (NATLL)

7387 9592/www.natll.org.uk. **Open** *phoneline* 9.30am-5.30pm Mon-Fri.
Provides information on the more than 1,000 toy libraries across Britain. It's also a good source of useful publications on related subjects.

Tumble Tots

0121 585 7003/www.tumbletots.com.
Tumble Tots is a parent-and-baby play class for children from six months up to school age. The children play on a range of equipment to help build co-ordination and social skills. They also take part in music and singing sessions. Ring this central number to find out about Tumble Tot play centres in your area.

One o'clock clubs

These weekday clubs within parks, with indoor and outdoor play facilities, open around lunchtime (12.30-1.30pm) and go on till school's out. They're a useful meeting place for parents and carers of pre-school children.

North London

Alexandra Park *Islands Club at the Grove, Muswell Hill, N22 (8883 7173). Bus 134, 144, 144A, W3, W7.*
Barnard Park *Copenhagen Street, N1 (7278 9494). Angel tube.*
Clissold Park *Stoke Newington Church Street, N16 (8809 6700). Bus 73.*
Finsbury Park *Young Children & Family Drop-in Community Centre, Jamboree Playhuts, Seven Sisters Road, N4 (8802 1301). Finsbury Park tube/rail.*
Highbury Fields *The Bandstand, Highbury Fields, N5 (7704 9337). Highbury & Islington tube/rail.*
Parliament Hill Fields *Peggy Jay Centre, NW5 (7485 6907). Gospel Oak rail.*

East London

Haggerston Park *Queensbridge Road, E2 (7729 6662). Bus 26, 48, 55.*
Millwall Park *Stebondale Street, E14 (7515 6807). Mudchute DLR.*

Springfield Park *Springfield Lane, E5 (no phone). Clapton rail/253 bus.* The club is just outside the park.
Victoria Park *Cadogan Terrace, E9 (8986 6150). Bus 277, S2.*
Wapping Park *opposite St Patrick's Church, off High Street, E1 (7481 9321). Wapping tube.*

South-east London

Crystal Palace Park *Crystal Palace Park Road, SE20 (8659 6554). Crystal Palace, Penge East or Penge West rail.*
Geraldine Mary Harmsworth Park *St George's Road, SE1 (7820 9724). Lambeth North tube.*
Kennington Park *Bolton Crescent, SE5 (7735 7186). Oval tube/36, 45, 131, 159 bus.*
Leyton Square *Peckham Park Road, SE15 (7639 1812). Bus 53, 78, 172, 381.*
Myatts Fields *Cormont Road, SE5 (7733 3609). Bus P5.*
Norwood Park *Salters Hill, SE19 (8761 1752). Gipsy Hill rail.*
Peckham Rye *Peckham Rye Road, SE15 (8693 0481). Bus 12, 63, 312.*
Ruskin Park *Denmark Hill, SE5 (7733 6659). Denmark Hill rail.*
Southwark Park *Hawkstone Road, SE16 (7231 3755). Canada Water tube/Surrey Quays DLR.*

South-west London

Agnes Riley Gardens *corner of Clarence Avenue & Poynders Road, SW4 (8673 1277). Clapham South tube.*
Bishops Park *Rainbow Playroom, Stevenage Road, SW6 (7731 4572). Putney tube/14, 74, 220 bus.*
Brockwell Park *Arlingford Road, SW9 (8671 4883). Herne Hill rail.*
Clapham Common *Windmill Drive, SW4 (8673 5736). Clapham Common or Clapham South tube.*
Streatham Vale Park *Abercairn Road, SW16 (8764 3688). Streatham Common rail/60, 118 bus.*
Vauxhall Park *Fentiman Road, SW8 (7582 3209). Vauxhall tube/rail.*
Windmill Gardens *Blenheim Gardens, SW2 (8671 5587). Brixton tube/rail/3, 45, 109, 159 bus.*

West London

Acton Park *East Acton Lane, W3 (8743 6133). East Acton tube.*
Lammas Park *Playcentre, Elers Road, W13 (8810 0240). South Ealing/Northfields tube.*
Meanwhile Gardens *Elkstone Road, W10 (8960 7894). Westbourne Park tube.*
Ravenscourt Park *Under-5s centre, Ravenscourt Park, W6 (8748 3180). Ravenscourt Park tube.*

Health

Support

Contact-A-Family

7608 8700/helpline 0808 808 3555/ www.cafamily.org.uk. **Open** 10am-4pm Mon-Fri.
Contact-A-Family offers support for parents of children with disabilities.

National Asthma Campaign

Helpline 0845 701 0203/www.asthma. org.uk. **Open** 9am-5pm Mon-Fri.
Contact the campaign for advice and help if you or your child has asthma.

NHS Direct

Helpline 0845 4647/www.nhsdrect.nhs.uk. **Open** 24hrs daily.
Staffed by nurses and health information advisors, NHS Direct is a useful service, providing confidential health advice and information. Calls are charged at the local rate and all are recorded.

Safe & Sound

Unit 25 Peall Road, Croydon, CR0 3EX (8288 0181/www.safensound.biz).
First aid courses specifically designed for parents and carers of babies and young children. Courses are run all over London and the south east. Contact the office or check the website for dates and prices.

Serene

7404 5011/www.our-space.co.uk/ serene.htm. **Open** 8am-11pm daily.
If a constantly crying baby has you at the end of your tether, get in touch with Serene for advice and support.

Help for parents

Childcare

Bestbear

8675 3131/www.bestbear.co.uk.
Open 24hr answerphone.
Log on to the website for information about tried, tested and recommended childcare agencies and everything you need to know about hiring, or becoming, a child carer. Bestbear also has links to companies such as Boots and Waitrose for online shopping, as well as information about choosing schools, financial products and travelling with children.

Childcare Link

0800 096 0296/www.childcarelink.gov.uk.
Open 9am-9pm Mon-Fri; 9am-noon Sat.
Parents can ring up, or log on to the website, for information on childcare options open to them, and request leaflets on same. If possible, callers will be given a list of childcare organisations in their area.

Childminders

6 Nottingham Street, W1 (7935 3000/ www.childminders.co.uk). **Open** 8.45am-5.30pm Mon-Thur; 8.45am-5pm Fri; 9am-4.30pm Sat.
Childminders is a long-established London-based babysitting agency. Sitters on its books are locally based nurses, teachers and nannies with impeccable references. Most areas around the capital can be covered.

Daycare Trust

21 St George's Road, SE1 6ES (7840 3350/www.daycaretrust.org.uk). **Open** 10am-5pm Mon-Fri.
This is a national childcare charity promoting high-quality and affordable childcare. It publishes useful booklets,

including *No More Nine to Five: Childcare in a changing world* (£5).

Kids' Club Network

7512 2100/7512 2112/www.kidsclubs. org.uk. **Open** 9.30am-5.30pm Mon-Fri.
Information on after-school clubs.

Nannytax

PO Box 988, Brighton, East Sussex BN2 1BY (01273 626256/www.nannytax.co.uk). **Open** 9am-5pm Mon-Fri.
For £164.50 a year Nannytax will register your nanny with the Inland Revenue, issue his or her payslips and organise National Insurance payments. There's employment advice on the website for nannies too.

National Family & Parenting Institute

430 Highgate Studios, 53-79 Highgate Road, NW5 1TL (7424 3460/www.nfpi.org/ www.e-parents.org). Kentish Town tube/ rail. **Open** 9.30am-5.30pm Mon-Fri/ 24hr answerphone.
A resource centre for all families, with factsheets on all aspects of parenting.

Night Nannies

7731 6168/www.night-nannies.com.
A useful service for parents whose children are denying them sleep, Night Nannies can be contacted for professional, reliable, night-time childcare. After the initial phone call, when the parent's needs are discussed (how many nights the nanny will be needed, for example, and from what time), Night Nannies provides a list of qualified carers, with whom the parent can then get in touch.

The Parent Company

6 Jacob's Well Mews, W1 (7935 9635/ www.theparentcompany.co.uk). **Open** 9am-5pm Mon-Fri.
Information and seminars on employing nannies. *See also below.*

Simply Childcare

16 Bushey Hill Road, SE5 (7701 6111/ www.simplychildcare.com). **Open** 9am-5.30pm Mon-Fri.
Formerly known as the Register, SC is a valuable resource for working parents. If you are seeking a nanny to work in or near London, you can pay £22 for inclusion in three issues of this 32-page printed list, or £30 for five issues. Entry on the list is free for prospective nannies looking for either full- or part-time work.

Parent courses

Holy Trinity Brompton

Brompton Road, SW7 (7581 8255/ www.htb.org.uk). South Kensington tube.
Open *Office* 9.30am-5.30pm Mon, Wed-Fri; 10.30am-5.30pm Tue.
Runs 'The Parenting Course' for parents with kids under the age of 12. The price of admission is £15 'Parenting Teenagers', for parents of children aged 13-18, costs £20. Both courses are four two-hour sessions; prices include supper and materials.

The Parent Company

Runs seminars on weekday evenings on diverse subjects, from time management

to discipline issues. Seminars cost £45 per session per person, or £60 for two people. *See p295 for further details.*

Parent Network
Parentline Plus 0808 800 2222/ www.parentlineplus.org.uk. **Open** 8am-10pm Mon-Fri; 9.30am-5pm Sat; 10am-3pm Sun.
Organises nationwide courses on how to cope with being a parent. For more details phone the free helpline, Parentline Plus.

Parent Support Group
helpline 8469 0205/www.psg.org.uk. **Open** 24hrs.
As well as the helpline, staff run one-to-one support sessions and courses on parenting skills to parents and carers of adolescents who are acting in an antisocial or even criminal manner.

Parents for Inclusion
7735 7735/helpline 7582 5008/ www.parentsforinclusion.org. **Open** 10am-noon, 1-3pm Tue-Thur.
Organises a series of workshops for parents of disabled children. A helpline (7582 5008) operates 10am-noon, 1-3pm Tue-Thur.

Information

Literature

Families magazine
Families North *PO Box 14965, NW3 5WA (7794 5690);* **Families East** *Enterprise House, 113-115 George Lane, E18 1AB (8694 8694);* **Families South East** *PO Box 11591, SE26 6WB (8699 7240);* **Families South West** *PO Box 4302, SW16 1ZS (8696 9680);* **Families West** *PO Box 32231, W5 1JR (8930 4707);* **Families North West** *PO Box 32358, HA1 1GF (8810 5388);* **Families Upon Thames** *PO Box 425, Walton-on-Thames, KT12 5AG (01932 254584).* **All** *www.familiesmagazine.co.uk.*
All areas of London are covered by this informative freesheet, available in libraries, nurseries and selected children's shops, which lists places to visit, things to do, independent health practitioners and a wealth of information for anyone bringing up a child in London.

Time Out magazine
7813 3000/www.timeout.com.
For up-to-the-minute information about where to go and what to see in London, check out the Around Town and Children sections. Available from most London newsagents.

Libraries

London borough councils have lists of local libraries. Our pick of the best central London ones, with big children's libraries within, are listed below. Staff often arrange special events for families.

Barbican Library
Barbican Centre, Silk Street, EC2 (7638 0569/www.cityoflondon.gov.uk/libraries). Barbican tube/Moorgate tube/rail. **Open** 9.30am-5.30pm Mon, Wed-Fri; 9.30am-7.30pm Tue; 9.30am-12.30pm Sat. **Map** p320 P5.
Occasional events for under-fives; admission is on a first come, first served basis at this popular children's library.

Kensington & Chelsea Central Library
Phillimore Walk, W8 (7937 2542). High Street Kensington tube. **Open** 9.30am-8pm Mon, Tue, Thur; 9.30am-5pm Wed, Fri, Sat. **Map** p314 A9.
Story sessions for under-fives are arranged 10.30-11am every Tuesday. Home work clubs are held on Mondays, Tuesdays and Thursdays 3.30-6.30pm.

Marylebone Library
109-17 Marylebone Road, NW1 (7641 1041/www.westminster.gov.uk/libraries). Baker Street tube/Marylebone tube/rail. **Open** Children's Library 9.30am-5.30pm Mon, Tue, Thur, Fri; 10am-5.30pm Wed; 9.30am-1pm, 2-5pm Sat. **Map** p313 F4.
Sessions for under-fives, 10.30-11.30am Tuesdays, are for stories and crafts, on Thursdays, 2.15-3.15pm, the play for pre-schoolers is more toy-based.

Victoria Library
160 Buckingham Palace Road, SW1 (7641 4289/www.westminster.gov.uk/libraries). Victoria tube/rail. **Open** 9.30am-7pm Mon, Tue, Thur, Fri; 10am-7pm Wed; 9.30am-5pm Sat. **Map** p318 H10.
Under-fives sessions are held every Wednesday at 10-11.30am, plus a special event every month. Activities and events are arranged for children aged up to eight years throughout the year.

Travel

The prices listed for transport and services were correct at the time of going to press, but bear in mind that some prices (especially those of tube tickets) are subject to a price hike each January. A massive increase in the number of buses, and lanes for them, a cut in bus fare prices and a cap on the average increase in tube and DLR fares are a few of the many changes Ken Livingstone has introduced since becoming mayor, and chair of Transport for London (TfL). Another of his initiative has been the **Congestion Charge** (*see p299*) for people driving their cars in central London. To find out more about Mayor Ken Livingstone's Transport Strategy for London,

log on to the Greater London Authority website, www.london.gov.uk.

Public transport information

All the information below can be accessed online at www.tfl.gov.uk and www.thetube.com, or by phoning 7222 1234. Transport for London (TfL) also runs Travel Information Centres, which provide maps and information about the tube, buses, Tramlink, riverboat, Docklands Light Railway (DLR) and national rail services within the London area. You can find them in the following stations: Brent Cross bus station, Euston station, Liverpool Street station and Piccadilly Circus station.

London Transport Users' Committee
6 Middle Street, EC1A 7JA (7505 9000/ www.ltuc.org.uk). **Open** *Phone enquiries* 9am-5pm Mon-Fri.
This is the official, campaigning watchdog monitoring customer satisfaction with transport in London.

Fares & tickets

Adult fares
The single underground fare for adults within Zone 1 is £1.60, and £2 for Zones 1 and 2, rising to £3.60 for an all-zones (1-6) single fare. Single bus fares are 70p for a journey outside Zone 1 and £1 for a journey within Zone 1 or one that crosses the Zone 1 boundary.
If you are staying in London for more than a day, buy a **Travelcard**. If you're planning on making a lot of short-hop tube journeys within Zone 1 over a period of several days, it makes sense to buy a carnet of ten tickets for £11.50 (£5 for children). This brings down the cost of each journey to £1.15 rather than the standard £1.60. Note that if you exit a station outside of Zone 1 and are caught with only a carnet ticket, you are liable to a £10 penalty fare.

Child fares
On all buses, tubes and local trains, under-16s are classified as children; under-fives travel free. Under-16s pay a child fare until 10pm; after 10pm (buses only) they pay an adult fare. Fourteen- and 15-year-olds carry Child photocards, available from any post office – take a passport-size photo and proof of age (passport or birth certificate) with you. The single Underground fare for children in Zone 1 is 60p, and 80p covering Zones 1 and 2, rising to £1.50 for an all-zone (1-6) ticket. Single child bus fares cost 40p to anywhere in London.

Access all areas

Since Ken Livingstone became mayor of London, bus numbers have increased dramatically. Many of the shiny new vehicles now on the road are fully accessible for the disabled and those laden with buggies, toddlers or luggage. These low-floored buses are easy to board, have space enough for wheelchairs and low-level bell buttons for when you want to get off. Two-thirds of London's bus fleet are now low-floor and Mayor Ken has promised many more.

The London Underground can be a nightmare for people in wheelchairs or with young children. Some parts of it date back to 1863, when the world's first underground railway opened. The depth of the tunnels and stations, and the sheer numbers of people travelling by tube, make it difficult for disabled travellers to use. A programme of improvements to the stations is ongoing, and newer sections, like the Jubilee Line extension, are easier to use.

To find out which bus routes and tube stations are accessible to buggy-pushers and wheelchair users, contact **Public Transport's information line** (7222 1234). Ask an advisor for a guide to the tube system, called *Access to the Underground*, which lists all the tube stations in London and notes whether there are lifts, ramps and loos and how many steps have to be negotiated when buying a ticket or catching a train. The *Central Area London Bus Guide* lists the routes served by accessible buses.

Travelcards

These can be used on the tube system, buses, rail services within London, the Docklands Light Railway and some Green Line buses, and can be bought at all tube and rail stations as well as appointed newsagents. Travelcards also entitle you to one-third of the cost of travel on scheduled riverboat services. The most convenient cards for short-term visitors are the day or one-week Travelcards, while monthly and yearly tickets are also available.

Day Travelcards are valid in the selected zones on bus, tube, Tramlink, DLR and national rail services. The **Peak Day Travelcard** can be used from 00.01am Monday to Friday on the day of validity and for any journey that starts from 4.30am the following day. Prices are as follows: Zones 1 and 2 £5.10/£2.50 children; Zones 1-3 £6.20/£3.10 children; Zones 1-4 £7/£3.50 children; Zones 1-5 £8.80/£4.40 children; Zones 1-6 £10.70/£5.30 children.

Off-Peak Day Travelcards can be used from 9.30am Monday to Friday (12.01am Saturday, Sunday and bank holidays) on the day of validity and for any journey that starts 4.30am on the following day. Prices are as follows: Zones 1 and 2 £4.10; Zones 1-4 £4.50; Zones 1-6 £5.10; child £2.

Family Travelcards are available for families and groups of one or two adults travelling with between one and four children (aged from five). Like regular Day Travelcards, they are valid after 9.30am Monday to Friday and all day on weekends and bank holidays, and can be used until 4.30am; they cost £2.70 for Zones 1 and 2, £3 Zones 1-4 or £3.40 Zones 1-6 (set child price 80p Zones 1-6).

If you'll be travelling on consecutive weekend days, you can save time, and a couple of quid at least, by investing in a

Weekend Travelcard. They are also valid on bank holidays and on N-prefixed night buses. Prices are: £6.10 for Zones 1 and 2, £6.70 Zones 1-4 and £7.60 Zones 1-6 (child £3 Zones 1-6).

One-Week Travelcards offer unlimited trips throughout selected zones for seven days, including use of N-prefixed night buses, and are valid around the clock. Prices for adults are: £16.50 for Zone 1; £19.60 for Zones 1 and 2; £23.10 for Zones 1-3; £28.40 for Zones 1-4; £34.10 for Zones 1-5; £37.20 all zones. Prices for children are: £6.80 Zone 1; £8 Zones 1 and 2; £10.70 Zones 1-3; £13.20 Zones 1-4; £14.60 Zones 1-5; £15.90 Zones 1-6.

One-Day LT Cards

One-Day LT Cards will only be of interest if you intend to travel during peak times (ie before 9.30am on weekdays) and make several journeys during the day. They are valid on all buses (including night buses), Underground services (except those running to and from Bakerloo Line stations north of Queen's Park; this section of track is not run by London Underground) and Docklands Light Railway services, but not on overland rail services or airbuses. The cards are only available as an All Zones (1-6) ticket, and cost £8 (£3.50 child). If you are travelling around within Zones 1-4 only, a Peak Day Travelcard would be cheaper.

Bus tickets & passes

If you make a number of single journeys by bus, buy a book of six single bus tickets from Travel Information Centres or selected newsagents in advance of travel. These can be used on all bus services, including night buses. A book of adult tickets costs £3.90, while the children's rate is £2.10. One-day bus passes are great value at £2 for adults and £1 for children.

Photocards

Photocards are required for all bus passes and Travelcards except the Day and Weekend versions. Child photocards are required for five- to 15-year-olds using child Travelcards and bus passes. Fourteen- and 15-year-olds need a Child photocard in order to buy tickets at the discounted rate.

London Underground

Timetable

Tube trains run daily, starting at around 5.30am every day except Sunday, when they start one to two hours later depending on the line. The only exception is Christmas Day, when there is no service. Generally, you won't have to wait more than ten minutes for a train, and during peak times the service should (in theory) run every two or three minutes. Times of last trains vary, though they're usually around 11.30pm-1am every day except Sunday, when they finish 30 minutes to an hour earlier.

The only all-night public transport is by night bus (*see below*).

Docklands Light Railway (DLR)

Customer Services 7363 9700/ www.dlr.co.uk.
The DLR is administered as part of the London Underground network, so Travelcards and tube tickets are valid. DLR's driverless trains run on a raised track from Bank (Central, Northern or Waterloo & City Lines) or Tower Gateway, close to Tower Hill tube (Circle and District Lines), to Stratford, Beckton and down the Isle of Dogs to Island Gardens, under the Thames to Greenwich and Lewisham. Trains run from 5.30am to around 12.30am Monday to Saturday and 7am-11.30pm Sunday.

The DLR's **Rail & River Rover** tickets give unlimited travel on the DLR with a riverboat trip between Greenwich, Tower and Westminster Piers (boats from 10.30am to 6.30pm; *see also p114*). Tickets cost £8.80 adults, £4.50 children, £22.50 family ticket (two adults and up to three children). Family tickets can be bought in advance from the DLR Customer Services Department.

Buses

Despite all the new buses and lanes, it's slow progress by bus through the city, although it's a great, and cheap, way of getting to know the capital. Try the new RV1 riverside bus, which takes in many Bankside attractions. Avoid morning and evening rush hours.

Night buses

Night buses are the only form of public transport in London that runs through the night. They operate from around 11pm to 6am, about once an hour on most routes (more frequently on Fridays and Saturdays). All pass through central London and the majority stop at Trafalgar

Square, so head there if you're not sure which bus to get. All types of Travelcard are accepted on night buses. Pick up a free map and timetable from one of the LT Travel Information Centres.

Night bus fares from central London are the same as daytime fares, but there are no child fares.

For information, call the London Buses helpline on 7918 4300.

Rail services

National rail enquiries

0845 748 4950/www.nationalrail.co.uk.
Ring this number to find out how the trains are running on your route, and for timetable information.

Independently owned commuter services run out of all the city's mainline rail stations. Travelcards are valid on these services within the relevant zones.
Silverlink (0845 601 4868/www.silverlink trains.co.uk) is a handy overground service that carves a huge arc through the north of the city, running from Richmond (in the south-west) to North Woolwich (in the east), via London City Airport. The line connects with the tube network at several stations.

Tramlink

Croydon's tram service links the tube network at Wimbledon and national rail services at Mitcham Junction, East and West Croydon, Beckenham Junction, Elmers End and Birkbeck stations, and the south London bus network. The single adult fare is 90p in one zone (Zones 3 or 4) and £1.30 for travel in both; 40p for children. A one-day bus and tram pass costs £2.80 for an adult, or £1.20 for children. Weekly tram passes cost from £8 (£4 for children).

Water transport

The times of services vary, but, as a rule, most operate every 20 minutes to an hour between about 10.30am and 5pm. Services may be more frequent and run later in summer. Call the individual operators below for details of schedules and fares. The names in bold below are the names of piers; the central ones are shown on the maps at the back of this guide.
Westminster – Greenwich (1hr)
Westminster Passenger Services (7930 4097/www.westminsterpier.co.uk).
Westminster – Tower (30mins)
City Cruises (7740 0400/ www.citycruises.com).

Westminster – Festival (5mins) –
London Bridge City (20mins) –
St Katharine's (5mins)
Crown River Cruises (7936 2033/ www.crownriver.com).
Westminster – Kew (1hr 30mins) –
Richmond (30mins) – **Hampton Court** (1hr 30mins)
Westminster Passenger Service Association (7930 2062/www.wpsa.co.uk).
Embankment – Tower (30mins) –
St Katharine's (5mins) – **Greenwich** (25mins)
Catamaran Cruises (7987 1185/ www.bateauxlondon.com).
Greenland Dock – Canary Wharf (8mins) – **St Katharine's** (7mins) –
London Bridge City (4mins) –
Blackfriars (3mins) – **Savoy** (3mins)
Collins River Enterprises (7977 6892/ www.thamesclippers.com).
Savoy – Cadogan (18mins) – **Chelsea** (2mins)
Riverside Launches (7376 3344/ www.connoisseur.co.uk).
Waterloo/Westminster – Tower (30mins)
City Cruises (7740 0400/ www.citycruises.com).
Greenwich – (Thames) Barrier Gardens (25mins)
Thames River Services (7930 4097/ www.westminsterpier.co.uk).

Taxis

Black cabs

Two useful numbers are those for **Radio Taxis** (7272 0272) and **Dial-a-Cab** (7253 5000), which both run 24hr services for black cabs (with a pick-up charge). Any enquiries or complaints about black cabs should be made to the **Public Carriage Office** (7941 7800; open 9am-4pm Mon-Fri).

Minicabs

Minicabs (saloon cars) are generally cheaper than black cabs, especially at night and weekends. **Addison Lee** (7387 8888/ www.addisonlee.com) is one of the bigger companies, and claims to do pick-ups from all areas. Women and children travelling alone may prefer to use **Lady Cabs** (7254 3501), which employs only women drivers. **London Taxis International** (www.london-taxis.co.uk) is notable in that it has child seats available for younger passengers. Whoever you use, ask the price when you book and confirm it with the driver when the car arrives.

Congestion charge

Driving in London used to be wholly horrendous, and parking expensive. Now it's slightly less horrendous – and expensive before you even try to park. Mayor Ken introduced the congestion charge on 17 February 2003 and it has been generally hailed as a success. It costs £5 to drive within central London between 7am and 6.30pm

Monday to Friday. Central London is defined as within a boundary marked from King's Cross (N); Old Street roundabout (NE); Aldgate (E); Old Kent Road, (SE); Elephant & Castle (S); Vauxhall (SW); Hyde Park Corner (W) and Edgware Road tube (NW). You pay the charge either in advance, or on the day of travel, during or after your journey.

The system is enforced by countless CCTV cameras; at midnight computers check camera images of cars travelling into the zone against payment records. Anyone who hasn't paid is fined £80 (£40 if you pay within 14 days). The charge zone is clearly marked by big Cs painted on the road, and drivers are given fair warning (by roadsign) when they are about to enter the zone. For information on where to pay, call 0845 900 1234.

Tourist information

London Tourist Board & Convention Bureau

Admin line 7932 2000/London Line 0906 866 3344/www.londontown.com.
Call the LTB for information about where to stay and sights to see in the capital Its London line (60p per minute) has information for families planning a trip to London. The website has a 'fun for kids' section on the home page. You can ring or write to LTBCB at 1 Warwick Row, SW1E 5ER to ask for a special London Information Pack before your visit.

Tourist information centres, listed below, have free maps of central London and advice on attractions around the city.
Greenwich TIC *Pepys House, 2 Cutty Sark Gardens, SE10 (0870 608 2000/ 8858 6376).* **Open** 10am-5pm daily.
Richmond TIC *Old Town Hall, Whittaker Avenue, Richmond, Surrey TW9 1TP (8940 9125).* **Open** 10am-5pm Mon-Sat. *Easter-Sept* 10am-5pm Mon-Sat; 10.30am-1.30pm Sun.
Waterloo International Terminal *kiosk at Arrivals Hall, South Bank, SE1.* **Open** 8.30am-10.30pm daily.
For information on travel in the rest of Britain, try the **Britain Visitor Centre**.

Britain Visitor Centre

1 Regent Street (south of Piccadilly Circus), SW1 (no phone/www.visitbritain.com). Piccadilly Circus tube. **Open** *Jan-July, Oct-Dec* 9am-6.30pm Mon-Fri; 10am-4pm Sat, Sun. *Aug, Sept* 9am-6.30pm Mon-Fri; 9am-5pm Sat; 10am-4pm Sun. **Map** *p319 K7.* This centre is open to personal callers only, but the website has lots of useful info.

Advertisers' Index

Please refer to relevant sections for addresses and telephone numbers

Index

Index

Index

Index

Index

Index

Place of interest and/or entertainment	
Railway station	
Park	
Hospital	
Neighbourhood	SOHO
Pedestrian street	
Tube station	⊖
Church	✚
Synagogue	✡
Casualty unit	✚
Toilet	WC

Maps

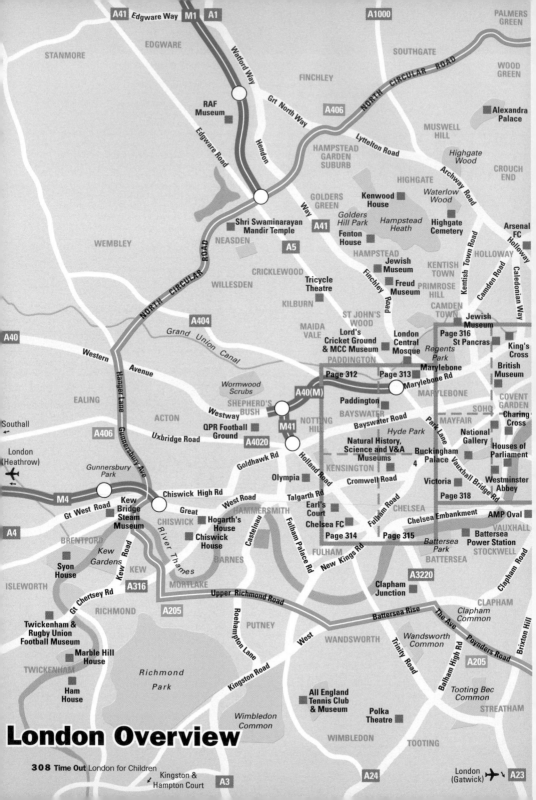

London Overview

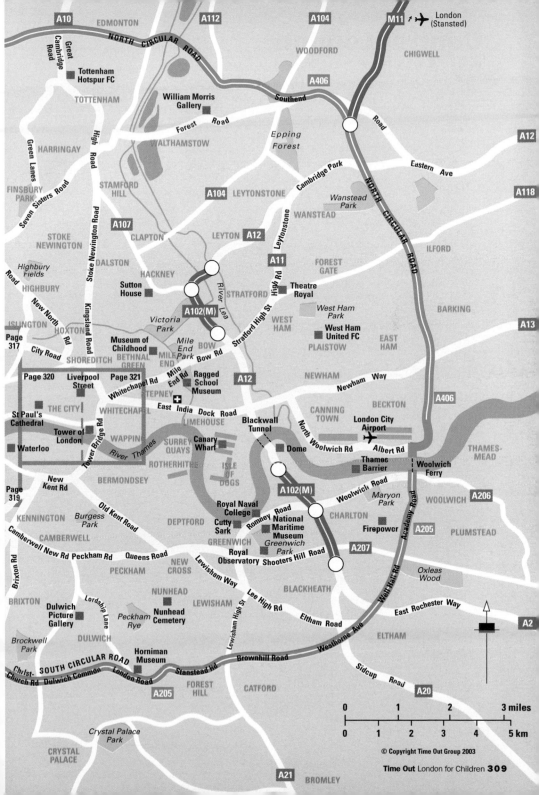

A10
EDMONTON
A112
A104
M11
London
(Stansted)
NORTH CIRCULAR ROAD
WOODFORD
CHIGWELL
Great
Cambridge
Road
Tottenham
Hotspur FC
A406
Southend
Road
TOTTENHAM
William Morris
Gallery
Forest
Road
Epping
Forest
A12
HARRINGAY
WALTHAMSTOW
Eastern Ave
Green Lanes
Cambridge Park
A118
FINSBURY
PARK
High Road
STAMFORD
HILL
A104
LEYTONSTONE
Wanstead
Park
NORTH CIRCULAR ROAD
ILFORD
Seven Sisters Road
WANSTEAD
STOKE
NEWINGTON
CLAPTON
LEYTON
A12
FOREST
GATE
BARKING
Kingsland Road
DALSTON
Leytonstone
A11
Highbury
Fields
HACKNEY
River Lea
STRATFORD
High Rd
Theatre
Royal
HIGHBURY
Sutton
House
Stratford High St
West Ham
Park
A13
New North
Road
A107
A102(M)
WEST
HAM
West Ham
United FC
EAST
HAM
ISLINGTON
HOXTON
Victoria
Park
Mile
End
Park
BOW
PLAISTOW
Page
317
City Road
SHOREDITCH
Museum of
Childhood
BETHNAL
GREEN
MILE
END
Bow Rd
A12
NEWHAM
Newham Way
A406
Page 320
Liverpool
Street
Page 321
Mile End Rd
Ragged
School
Museum
CANNING
TOWN
BECKTON
St Paul's
Cathedral
THE CITY
Whitechapel Rd
STEPNEY
East India Dock Road
LIMEHOUSE
Blackwall
Tunnel
North Woolwich Rd
London City
Airport
Albert Rd
Waterloo
Tower of
London
WHITECHAPEL
WAPPING
Tower Bridge Rd
SURREY
QUAYS
Canary
Wharf
Dome
Thames
Barrier
Woolwich
Ferry
THAMES-
MEAD
River Thames
ROTHERHITHE
ISLE
OF
DOGS
A102(M)
Woolwich Road
Page
319
New
Kent Rd
BERMONDSEY
Royal Naval
College
Romney Road
National
Maritime
Museum
CHARLTON
Maryon
Park
WOOLWICH
A206
KENNINGTON
Burgess
Park
Old Kent Road
DEPTFORD
Cutty
Sark
GREENWICH
Greenwich
Park
Firepower
A205
PLUMSTEAD
Camberwell New Rd
Peckham Rd
Queens Road
Royal
Observatory
Shooters Hill Road
A207
Brixton Rd
CAMBERWELL
NEW
CROSS
Academy Road
BRIXTON
PECKHAM
Lewisham Way
Lee High Rd
BLACKHEATH
Oxleas
Wood
Dulwich
Picture
Gallery
Lordship Lane
NUNHEAD
LEWISHAM
Eltham Road
East Rochester Way
A2
Brockwell
Park
DULWICH
Peckham
Rye
Nunhead
Cemetery
Lewisham High St
Westhorne Ave
ELTHAM
Horniman
Museum
SOUTH CIRCULAR ROAD
Brownhill Road
Sidcup Road
A20
Christ-
Church Rd
Dulwich Common
London Road
Stanstead Rd
FOREST
HILL
CATFORD
A205
Crystal Palace
Park
CRYSTAL
PALACE
A21
BROMLEY

0   1   2   3 miles
0   1   2   3   4   5 km

© Copyright Time Out Group 2003

Time Out London for Children **309**

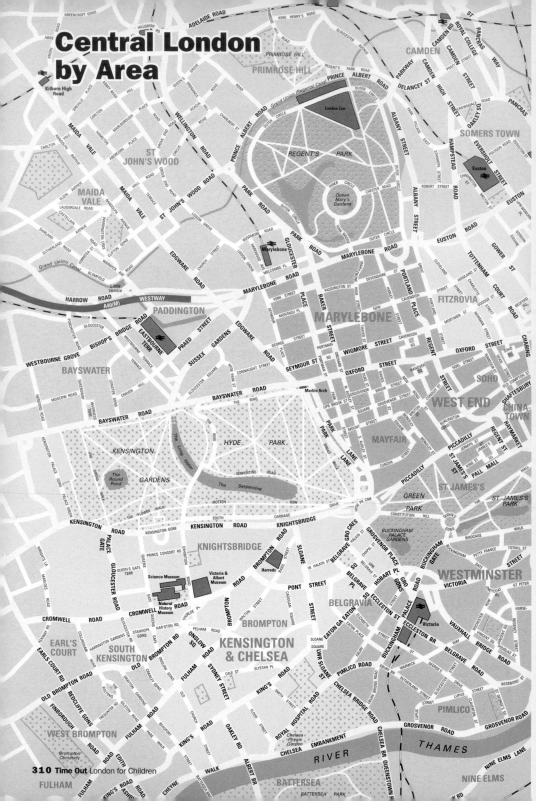

Central London by Area

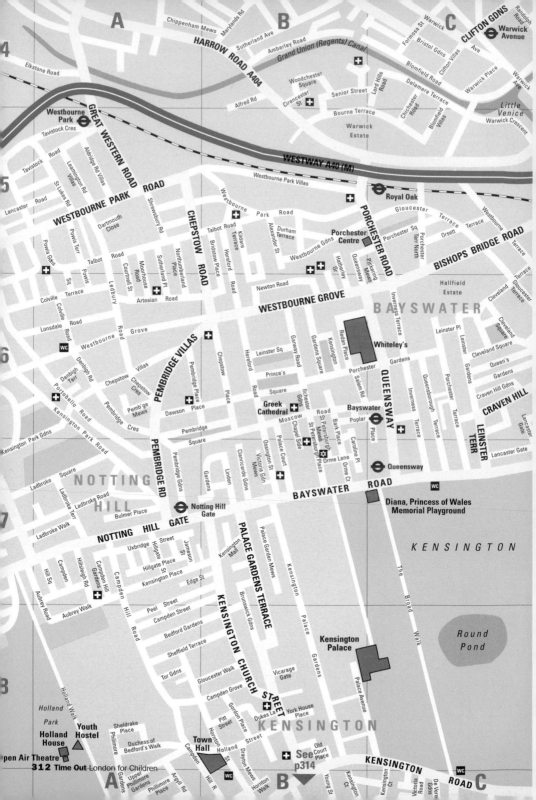

A

B

C

4

Chippenham Mews
Maryland's Rd
Sutherland Ave
Amberley Road
HARROW ROAD A404
Grand Union (Regents) Canal
Formosa St
Warwick
CLIFTON GDNS
Randolph Road
Bristol Gdns
Bristol Villas
Clifton Villas
Warwick Ave
Warwick Avenue
Ave
Warwick Place
Elkstone Road
Woodchester Square
Cirencester St.
Alfred Rd
Senior Street
Lord Hills Road
Chichester Road
Blomfield Road
Delamere Terrace
Blomfield Villas
Warwick Ave
Warwick Place
Little Venice
Warwick Crescent
Bourne Terrace

Westbourne Park
Tavistock Cres
GREAT WESTERN ROAD
Warwick Estate

WESTWAY A40 (M)

5
Tavistock
Road
St Lukes Rd
Aldridge Rd Villas
Leamington Rd Villas
WESTBOURNE PARK ROAD
Westbourne Park Villas
Royal Oak
Gloucester Terrace
Westbourne Terrace
BISHOPS BRIDGE ROAD
Lancaster Road
Powis Gdns
Dartmouth Close
Shrewsbury Rd
CHEPSTOW ROAD
Talbot Road
Westbourne Park Road
Porchester Sq
Porchester Sq Terr North
Orsett Terrace
Terrace
Powis Terr
Powis Sq
Talbot Road
Bridstow Place
Kildare Terrace
Hereford Road
Durham Terrace
PORCHESTER ROAD
Porchester Centre
Porchester
Gloucester Terrace

Colville Terrace
Colville Road
Lonsdale Road
Denbigh Terr
Portobello Road
Kensington Park Road
Westbourne
Road
Moorhouse Rd
Courtnell St.
Northumberland Place
Sutherland Pl
Artesian Road
Westbourne
Grove
Villas
Chepstow Cres
Chepstow Villas
PEMBRIDGE VILLAS
Pembridge Place
Chepstow Place
Hereford Road
Newton Road
WESTBOURNE GROVE
Hatherley Gr
Pickering Mews
Hallfield Estate
BAYSWATER
Cleveland Terrace
Cleveland Square
Queen's Gardens

WC
Ledbury Road
Dawson Place
Pembridge Place
Leinster Sq
Garway Road
Gardens Square
Redan Place
Kensington
Porchester
Gardens
Whiteley's
Leinster Pl
Cleveland Square
Cleveland Gardens
Porchester Terrace
Craven Hill Gdns
6
Denbigh Rd
Pemb'ge Mews
Pembridge Cres
PEMBRIDGE RD
Pembridge Square
Prince's Square
Ilchester Gr
Moscow Road
St Petersburgh Mews
Greek Cathedral
Bark Place
Poplar
Salem Rd
Bayswater
QUEENSWAY
Inverness Terrace
Queensborough Terrace
Porchester Terrace
Inverness Terrace
Queen's Gardens
Craven Hill
Lancaster Gate
CRAVEN HILL
LEINSTER TERR

7
NOTTING HILL
Ladbroke Square
Ladbroke Terr
Ladbroke Road
Ladbroke Walk
Bulmer Place
Notting Hill Gate
NOTTING HILL GATE
Pembridge Gdns
Pembridge Gardens
Linden Gardens
Clanricarde Gdns
Ossington St
St Petersburgh Place
Palace Court
Victoria Gdn Mews
Caroline Pl
Orme La
Orme Ct
Palace Side
Chapel Side
Orme Lane
Queensway
BAYSWATER ROAD
WC
Diana, Princess of Wales Memorial Playground

Campden Hill
Hill Sq
Aubrey Road
Aubrey Walk
Uxbridge Street
Hillgate Street
Jameson St
Hillgate Pl
Kensington Place
Edge St
Peel Street
Campden Street
Campden Hill Road
Campden Hill Gardens
Hillsleigh Rd
KENSINGTON MALL
Palace Gardens Mews
PALACE GARDENS TERRACE
Brunswick Gdns
Kensington
Palace
Gardens
KENSINGTON

8
Holland Park
Holland House
Holland Walk
Youth Hostel
Upper
Phillimore Gardens
Sheldrake Pl
Duchess of Bedford's Walk
Bedford Gardens
Sheffield Terrace
Tor Gdns
Gloucester Walk
Campden Grove
Pitt Street
Gordon Place
KENSINGTON CHURCH STREET
Vicarage Gate
York House Place
Dukes La
Kensington Palace
Palace Avenue
Palace Gardens
Round Pond

Open Air Theatre
Phillimore Gardens
Phillimore Place
Argyll Rd
Stafford Terrace
Phillimore Walk
Town Hall
Hornton Mews
Holland St
Campden Hill R
See p314
Old Court Place
York House Place
KENSINGTON
KENSINGTON ROAD
Kensington Ct
De Vere Gdns
Victoria Road
Young St
Kensington Ct
WC

A

B

C

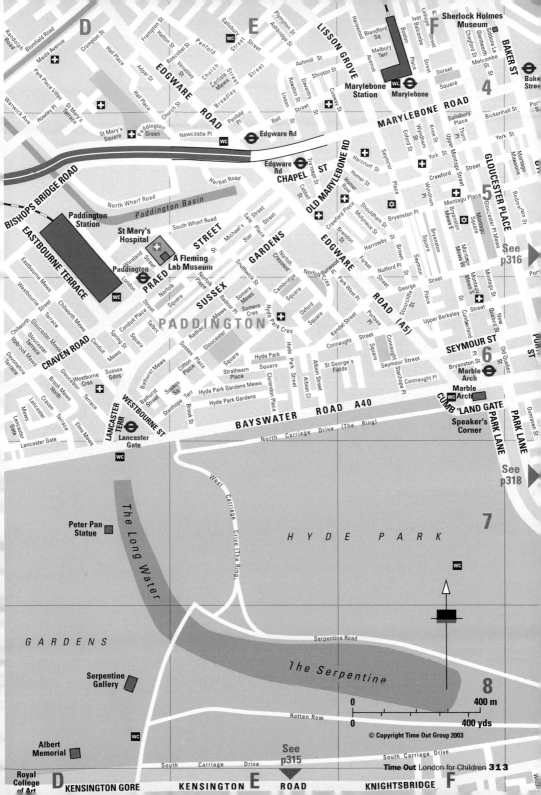

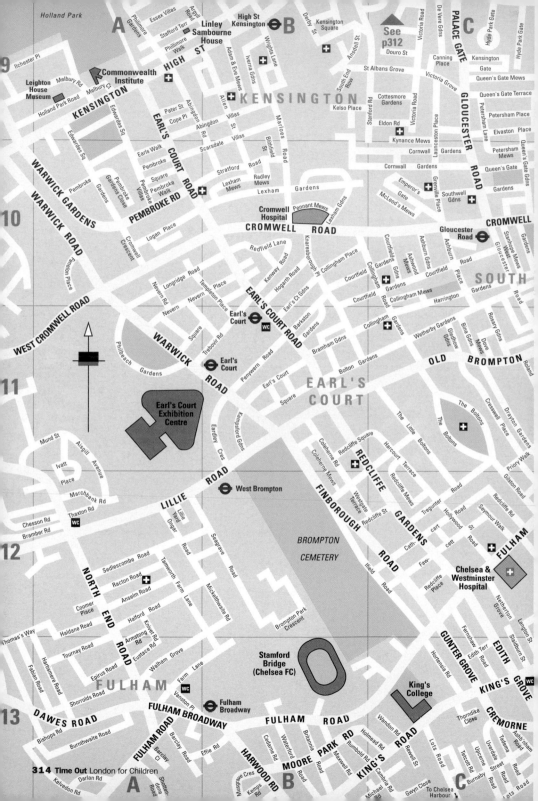

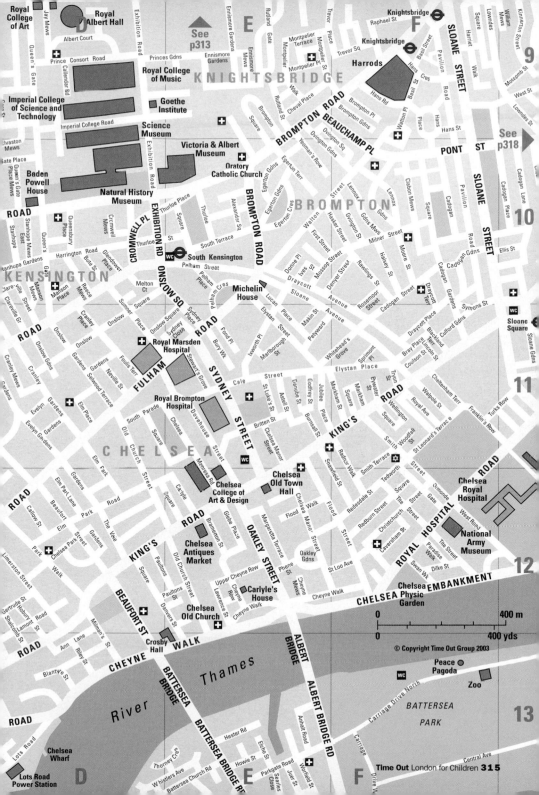

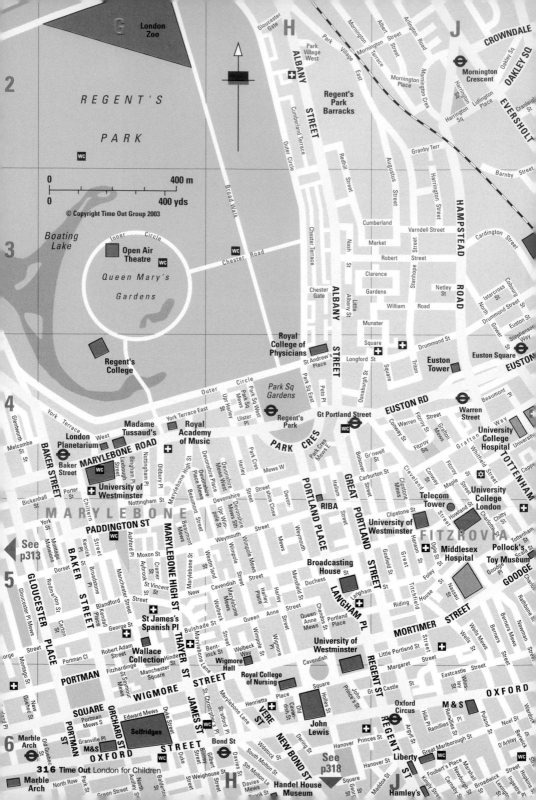

G London Zoo

REGENT'S PARK

Boating Lake

wc

0   400 m
0   400 yds
© Copyright Time Out Group 2003

Inner   Circle
Open Air Theatre
wc
Queen Mary's Gardens

Regent's College

Broad Walk

Chester Road

wc

ALBANY STREET

Gloucester Gate
Park Village West
Park Village East
Albert Street
Arlington Road
Mornington Terrace
Mornington Street
Mornington Place
Mornington Cres
Harrington Place
Lidlington Place
Harrington Sq
Harrington Street
Granby Terr
Barnby Street
Cardington Street

H

J CROWNDALE
OAKLEY SQ
EVERSHOLT

Mornington Crescent

HAMPSTEAD ROAD

Regent's Park Barracks

Cumberland Terrace
Outer Circle

Chester Terrace

Chester Gate

Nash
Redhill Street
Augustus Street

Cumberland Market
Varndell Street
Robert Street
Clarence Gardens
Stanhope Street
William Road
Munster Square
Longford St
Triton
Drummond St

Istarcross St
Colburg St
North
Drummond Street
Euston Gower
Stephenson Way
Euston Square EUSTON

Clipstone St

Little Albany St
St Andrew's Place
Peto Pl

Euston Tower

ALBANY STREET

Royal College of Physicians

St Andrew's Place

Outer   Circle
Park Sq Gardens
Regent's Park
wc

EUSTON RD
Warren Street

Beaumont

University College Hospital

York Terrace West
Melcombe St
Glenworth St

Madame Tussaud's
London Planetarium
wc

Royal Academy of Music

York Terrace East

MARYLEBONE ROAD
Luxbrough Street
Nottingham Pl
Oldbury Pl

University of Westminster

BAKER STREET
Baker Street

Park Sq West
Upr Harley St
Ulster Pl

Nottingham St
Devonshire St
Harley Street

PARK CRES
Park Cres Mews W
Park Cres Mews E
Bolsover St
Carburton St
Grnwell St
Warren St
Conway St
Fitzroy St
Fitzroy Mews
Grafton Way
Whitfield St
Howland St

University College London
University
TOTTENHAM

Gt Portland Street

Portland Place
RIBA

Cleveland St
Cleveland St
Clipstone St
Maple St
Ogle St

Telecom Tower

FITZROVIA
Middlesex Hospital
Pollock's Toy Museum

Bickenhall St
York St
Chiltern Street
Dorset St
Montagu Mansions
Crawford St

PADDINGTON ST
wc

MARYLEBONE HIGH ST

Devonshire Mews Wst
Devonshire Place
Devonshire Place Mews
Beaumont St
Upr Wimpole St
Weymouth Street

GREAT PORTLAND STREET

University of Westminster
Hanson St

Goodge St
GOODGE

See p313

BAKER STREET

Kenrick Pl
Ashford Pl
Moxon St
Aybrook St
St Vincent St
Cramer St
Paddington St

Beaumont Mews
Marylebone Mews

Weymouth Mews
Devonshire Mews Sth

Wimpole Mews
Wimpole St
Harley Place
Mansfield St
Duchess St

Broadcasting House

LANGHAM PL
Langham St

Riding House St

Foley St
Candover St
Gosfield St
Great Titchfield St
Nassau St

GOODGE STREET

Pollock's Toy Museum
Tottenham Court Road
Rathbone Pl
Newman St
Berners Mews
Wells St
Wells Mews

Blandford St
Chiltern St
George St
St James's Spanish Pl
Kendall Place

Marylebone Lane
Marylebone St
Bentinck St
Welbeck Way
Queen Anne St
Wigmore
Cavendish

Queen Anne Mews
Chandos St
Portland Place

University of Westminster

MORTIMER STREET
Little Portland St
Margaret Street
Eastcastle St

M A R Y L E B O N E

GLOUCESTER PLACE

Rodmarton St
Carlton St
Blandford Street
George Street

Robert Adam Street
Fitzhardinge St
Manchester Square
Seymour Mews

Wallace Collection

Wigmore Hall

Bulshade St

THAYER STREET
JAMES STREET

Welbeck St
Wimpole Street
Henrietta Place

VERE ST

Cavendish Square

Holles St
Oxford Circus

Argyll St
Princes St

REGENT ST

Oxford Circus

OXFORD

M & S
Poland St
Noel St
D'Arblay St

PORTMAN

Portman Cl

WIGMORE
James St
St Christopher's Pl

Royal College of Nursing

John Lewis

NEW BOND ST

Liberty
wc
wc

PORTMAN SQUARE

ORCHARD ST

Selfridges
wc

Edward Mews
Granville Pl
Duke St
Barrett St

Bond St

Dering St
Conduit St

Hanover St
Hanover Square

Great Marlborough St
Foubert's Place
Kingly St
Marshall St
Broadwick St
Lexington St

OXFORD

Marble Arch
M & S

OXFORD   STREET

wc

North Row

Duke St
Gilbert St
Davies Mews
South Molton La
Sth Molton St

Brook St

Weighouse St

Binney St

Wsbeck St

Woodstock St

Maddox St

See p318

Handel House Museum

St George St

J

Hamley's

316 Time Out London for Children

Marble Arch

Green Street
North Row
New Quebec St

H

New Bond St
Gilbert St

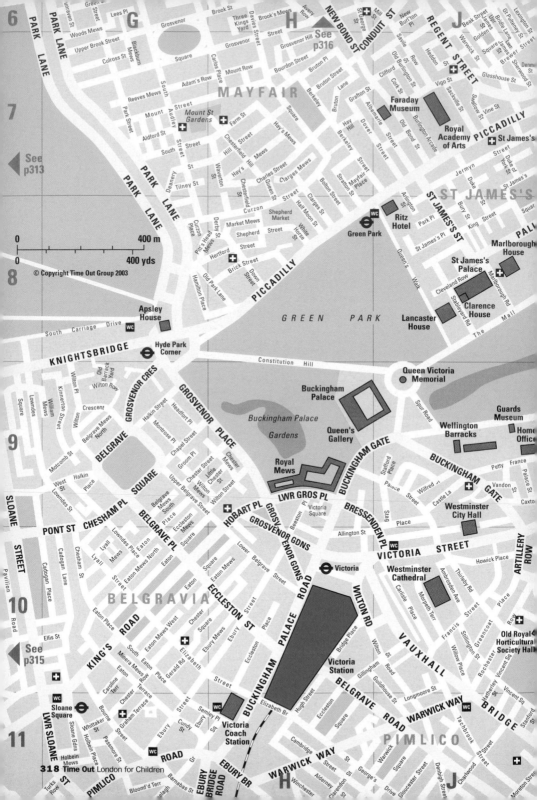

See p316

See p313

See p315

6 **G** **H** **J**

PARK LANE

Lees Pl

Woods Mews

Upper Brook Street

Grosvenor Street

Brook's Mews

Avery Row

NEW BOND ST

CONDUIT ST

Mill St

New Burl'ton Pl

St George St

Maddox St

REGENT STREET

Beak Street

Gt Pulteney St

Brewer Street

Bridle Lane

James St

Warwick Street

Golden Square

Lexington St

Denman St

Blackburn Mews

Culross St

Three Kings Yard

Davies Street

Grosvenor Hill

Savile Row

Old Burlington St

Clifford St

Cork St

Vigo St

Sackville St

Heddon St

Glasshouse St

Swallow St

Vine St

Shaftesbury Av

7

MAYFAIR

Reeves Mews

Mount Street

Carlos Place

Mount Row

Bourdon Street

Bruton Pl

Grafton St

Burlington Gdns

Faraday Museum

Royal Academy of Arts

PICCADILLY

St James's

Park Street

Adam's Row

Grosvenor Square

Mount St Gardens

Farm St

Berkeley Square

Bruton Street

Berkeley St

Dover Street

Albemarle St

Old Bond St

Burlington Arcade

Mount Street

Aldford St

South Audley

Chesterfield Hill

Hay's Mews

Hill St

Charles Street

Hay Hill

Stratton St

Dover St

Bolton St

Jermyn Street

Duke St

St James's St

York St

Duke of York St

ST JAMES'S

South St

Tilney St

Deanery St

St

Waverton St

Charles St

Chesterfield Hill

Curzon Street

Chesterfield Gdns

Bolton Street

Mayfair Place

Arlington Street

Park Pl

Bury St

King St

PALL

Curzon St

Derby St

Market Mews

Shepherd Market

Shepherd St

Half Moon St

White Horse St

Clarges St

Queen's Walk

St James's Pl

Cleveland Row

WC

Ritz Hotel

Green Park

Marlborough House

Marlborough Rd

Stableyard Rd

St James's Palace

Pitt Head Mews

Hertford St

Brick Street

Down Street

Curzon Place

Shepherd Street

Clarges Mews

8

PICCADILLY

Old Park Lane

Hamilton Place

Clarence House

Lancaster House

The Mall

Apsley House

WC

South Carriage Drive

G R E E N   P A R K

Queen's Walk

KNIGHTSBRIDGE

Hyde Park Corner

Constitution Hill

Queen Victoria Memorial

Spur Road

Lowndes Square

William Street

Kinnerton Street

Wilton Pl

Wilton Row

Wilton Cres

Grosvenor Cres

GROSVENOR PLACE

Halkin Street

Headfort Pl

Buckingham Palace

Buckingham Palace Gardens

Queen's Gallery

Wellington Barracks

Guards Museum

Home Office

BUCKINGHAM GATE

9

BELGRAVE SQUARE

CHESHAM PL

PONT ST

Lowndes St

Chapel Street

Groom St

Chester Street

Belgrave Mews North

Chester Mews

Little Chester

Wilton Mews

Wilton Street

Royal Mews

LWR GROS PL

BUCKINGHAM GATE

Stafford Place

Palace Street

Stag Place

Wilfred St

Castle La

Petty France

Vandon St

Palace St

Caxton St

Westminster City Hall

Belgrave Mews South

Upper Belgrave Street

Eccleston St

HOBART PL

GROSVENOR GDNS

Boston St

Victoria Square

Allington St

BRESSENDEN PL

Wilton Rd

Bressenden Place

VICTORIA STREET

WC

Howick Place

Ambrosden Av

SLOANE STREET

Matcomb St

West Halkin St

Place

Lowndes Place

Eaton Place

Lyall St

Lyall Mews

Eaton Mews

BELGRAVE PL

Eaton Mews

Chester Square

GROSVENOR GDNS

Lower Belgrave Street

Victoria

Victoria Cathedral

Westminster Cathedral

Carlisle Place

Morpeth Terr

Thirleby Rd

ARTILLERY ROW

10

BELGRAVIA

Cadogan Lane

Chesham St

Lyall Mews

Eaton Mews North

Eaton Place

Eaton Terrace

Eaton Mews West

Chester Square

Ebury Mews

ECCLESTON ST

Eccleston

Lower Belgrave Street

KING'S ROAD

Cadogan Place

Chesham Place

Pavilion Road

Ellis St

Minera Mews

South Eaton Place

Gerald Rd

Elizabeth Street

Ebury Street

BUCKINGHAM PALACE ROAD

WILTON RD

Victoria Station

Gillingham St

Wilton Road

Guildhouse St

VAUXHALL

BELGRAVE ROAD

Francis St

Stillington St

Greencoat Place

Rochester Row

Vincent Sq

WARWICK WAY

Hatherley

Vincent St

Old Royal Horticultural Society Hall

BRIDGE

11

Caroline Terr

Chester Row

Graham Terrace

Bourne St

Holbein Pl

WC

Sloane Square

LWR SLOANE

Turks Row

PIMLICO

Ranelagh

Bloomf'd Terr

ST

Passmore St

Whittaker Street

Holbein Mews

Cundy

Semley Pl

Ebury Bridge

Ebury

WC

Victoria Coach Station

EBURY BRIDGE ROAD

Elizabeth Br

Cambridge Street

WARWICK WAY

Winchester St

Clarendon St

Gloucester St

Alderney St

Hugh Street

Eccleston

George's Square

Warwick Square

PIMLICO

Denbigh Street

Charlwood

Moreton St

Sutherland Row

Longmoore St

Warwick Way

Tachbrook St

WC

318 Time Out London for Children

© Copyright Time Out Group 2003

0 ——— 400 m

0 ——— 400 yds

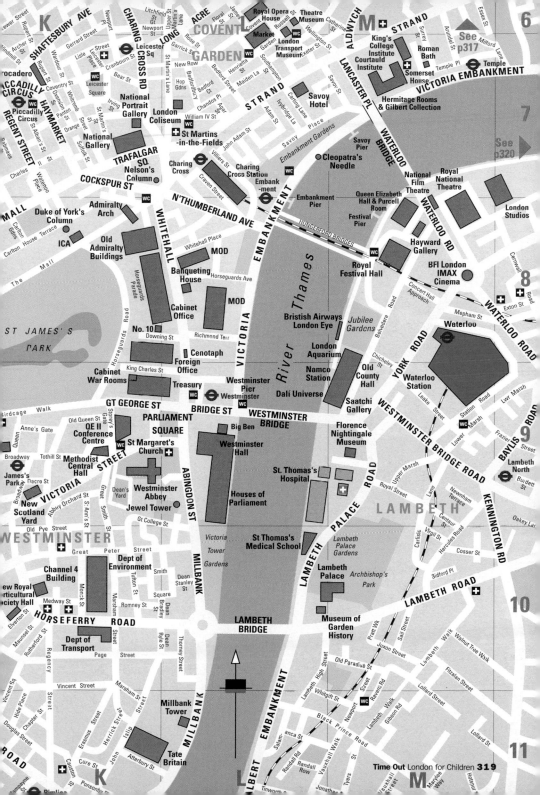

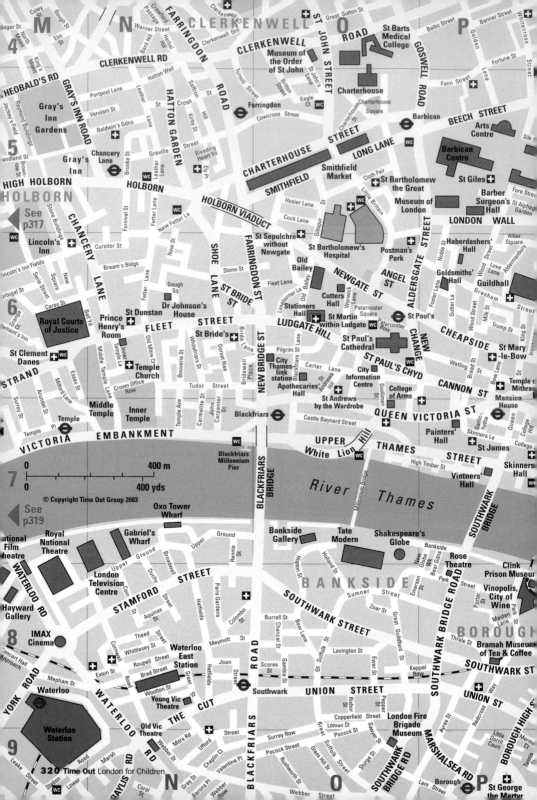